Meredith Justin Sprunger

The Abridged URANTIA Papers

Square Circles Publishing
www.SquareCircles.com

THE ABRIDGED URANTIA PAPERS
by Meredith Justin Sprunger

Copyright © 2012 Square Circles Publishing
All rights reserved.

Cover: Syrp & Co.

Profits from the sale of this work are donated to
FreeSchools World Literacy
www.FreeSchools.org

SQUARE CIRCLES PUBLISHING
P. O. Box 9682, Pahrump, NV 89060
www.squarecircles.com

ISBN: 978-0-9768896-6-3
Library of Congress Control Number: 2008904453

INTRODUCTION

MANY people are intimidated by the Urantia Book's size. Others find some of its concepts difficult to understand and would prefer a simplified presentation.

Michelle Klimesh's fine condensation of the Urantia Papers—*The Story of Everything*—addresses these concerns, but *The Abridged Urantia Papers* follows the Urantia Book's format and wording more closely. In writing this abridgment, I had in mind ministers and others who are interested in the Urantia Book but will not take the time to read the entire book.

I wish to thank Saskia Raevouri, who did the technical work of preparing *The Abridged Urantia Papers* for publication and who, along with Matthew Block and Merlyn Cox, made extensive editorial suggestions.

MEREDITH JUSTIN SPRUNGER
May 2008

TABLE OF CONTENTS

INTRODUCTION	iii
A SUMMARY OF UNIVERSE REALITY	
A Simplification of the Foreword	1
PART I—THE CENTRAL AND SUPERUNIVERSES	
Paper 1: The Universal Father	5
Paper 2: The Nature of God	8
Paper 3: The Attributes of God	10
Paper 4: God's Relation to the Universe	13
Paper 5: God's Relation to the Individual	15
Paper 6: The Eternal Son	17
Paper 7: Relation of the Eternal Son to the Universe	20
Paper 8: The Infinite Spirit	23
Paper9: Relation of the Infinite Spirit to the Universe	25
Paper 10: The Paradise Trinity	28
Paper 11: The Eternal Isle of Paradise	30
Paper 12: The Universe of Universes	34
Paper 13: The Sacred Spheres of Paradise	37
Paper 14: The Central and Divine Universe	39
Paper 15: The Seven Superuniverses	41
Paper 16: The Seven Master Spirits	47
Paper 17: The Seven Supreme Spirit Groups	50
Paper 18: The Supreme Trinity Personalities	53
Paper 19: The Co-Ordinate Trinity Origin Beings	56
Paper 20: The Paradise Sons of God	58
Paper 21: The Paradise Creator Sons	60
Paper 22: The Trinitized Sons of God	62
Paper 23: The Solitary Messengers	65
Paper 24: Higher Personalities of the Infinite Spirit	67
Paper 25: The Messenger Hosts of Space	69
Paper 26: Ministering Spirits of the Central Universe	72
Paper 27: Ministry of the Primary Supernaphim	75
Paper 28: Ministering Spirits of the Superuniverses	77
Paper 29: The Universe Power Directors	80
Paper 30: Personalities of the Grand Universe	82
Paper 31: The Corps of the Finality	85

Part II—THE LOCAL UNIVERSE — 89

- Paper 32: The Evolution of the Local Universes — 89
- Paper 33: Administration of the Local Universe — 91
- Paper 34: The Local Universe Mother Spirit — 94
- Paper 35: The Local Universe Sons of God — 97
- Paper 36: The Life Carriers — 101
- Paper 37: Personalities of the Local Universe — 104
- Paper 38: Ministering Spirits of the Local Universe — 107
- Paper 39: The Seraphic Hosts — 109
- Paper 40: The Ascending Sons of God — 112
- Paper 41: Physical Aspects of the Local Universe — 115
- Paper 42: Energy—Mind and Matter — 117
- Paper 43: The Constellations — 121
- Paper 44: The Celestial Artisans — 124
- Paper 45: The Local System Administration — 126
- Paper 46: The Local System Headquarters — 128
- Paper 47: The Seven Mansion Worlds — 131
- Paper 48: The Morontia Life — 133
- Paper 49: The Inhabited Worlds — 136
- Paper 50: The Planetary Princes — 138
- Paper 51: The Planetary Adams — 140
- Paper 52: Planetary Mortal Epochs — 143
- Paper 53: The Lucifer Rebellion — 146
- Paper 54: Problems of the Lucifer Rebellion — 149
- Paper 55: The Spheres of Light and Life — 152
- Paper 56: Universal Unity — 156

PART III—THE HISTORY OF URANTIA

- Paper 57: The Origin of Urantia — 160
- Paper 58: Life Establishment on Urantia — 163
- Paper 59: The Marine-Life Era on Urantia — 165
- Paper 60: Urantia During the Early Land-Life Era — 168
- Paper 61: The Mammalian Era on Urantia — 169
- Paper 62: The Dawn Races of Early Man — 172
- Paper 63: The First Human Family — 175
- Paper 64: The Evolutionary Races of Color — 177
- Paper 65: The Overcontrol of Evolution — 181
- Paper 66: The Planetary Prince of Urantia — 185
- Paper 67: The Planetary Rebellion — 189
- Paper 68: The Dawn of Civilization — 192
- Paper 69: Primitive Human Institutions — 194
- Paper 70: The Evolution of Human Government — 197

Paper 71: Development of the State	202
Paper 72: Government on a Neighboring Planet	205
Paper 73: The Garden of Eden	209
Paper 74: Adam and Eve	211
Paper 75: The Default of Adam and Eve	214
Paper 76: The Second Garden	217
Paper 77: The Midway Creatures	220
Paper 78: The Violet Race After the Days of Adam	223
Paper 79: Andite Expansion in the Orient	227
Paper 80: Andite Expansion in the Occident	230
Paper 81: Development of Modern Civilization	234
Paper 82: The Evolution of Marriage	237
Paper 83: The Marriage Institution	239
Paper 84: Marriage and Family Life	242
Paper 85: The Origins of Worship	245
Paper 86: Early Evolution of Religion	248
Paper 87: The Ghost Cults	250
Paper 88: Fetishes, Charms, and Magic	253
Paper 89: Sin, Sacrifice, and Atonement	255
Paper 90: Shamanism—Medicine Men and Priests	258
Paper 91: The Evolution of Prayer	260
Paper 92: The Later Evolution of Religion	263
Paper 93: Machiventa Melchizedek	266
Paper 94: The Melchizedek Teachings in the Orient	271
Paper 95: The Melchizedek Teachings in the Levant	276
Paper 96: Yahweh—God of the Hebrews	278
Paper 97: Evolution of the God Concept Among the Hebrews	281
Paper 98: The Melchizedek Teachings in the Occcident	285
Paper 99: The Social Problems of Religion	288
Paper 100: Religion in Human Experience	290
Paper 101: The Real Nature of Religion	293
Paper 102: The Foundations of Religious Faith	297
Paper 103: The Reality of Religious Experience	300
Paper 104: Growth of the Trinity Concept	304
Paper 105: Deity and Reality	307
Paper 106: Universe Levels of Reality	309
Paper 107: Origin and Nature of Thought Adjusters	313
Paper 108: Mission and Ministry of Thought Adjusters	315
Paper 109: Relation of Adjusters to Universe Creatures	318
Paper 110: Relation of Adjusters to Individual Mortals	321
Paper 111: The Adjuster and the Soul	324

Paper 112: Personality Survival ... 327
Paper 113: Seraphic Guardians of Destiny ... 331
Paper 114: Seraphic Planetary Government ... 333
Paper 115: The Supreme Being ... 336
Paper 116: The Almighty Supreme ... 339
Paper 117: God the Supreme ... 341
Paper 118: Supreme and Ultimate—Time and Space ... 344
Paper 119: The Bestowals of Christ Michael ... 348

PART IV—THE LIFE AND TEACHINGS OF JESUS

Paper 120: The Bestowal of Michael on Urantia ... 352
Paper 121: The Times of the Bestowal ... 354
Paper 122: Birth and Infancy of Jesus ... 358
Paper 123: The Early Childhood of Jesus ... 363
Paper 124: The Later Childhood of Jesus ... 367
Paper 125: Jesus at Jerusalem ... 370
Paper 126: The Two Crucial Years ... 374
Paper 127: The Adolescent Years ... 377
Paper 128: Jesus' Early Manhood ... 381
Paper 129: The Later Adult Life of Jesus ... 385
Paper 130: On the Way to Rome ... 387
Paper 131: The World's Religions ... 391
Paper 132: The Sojourn at Rome ... 395
Paper 133: The Return from Rome ... 399
Paper 134: The Transition Years ... 404
Paper 135: John the Baptist ... 409
Paper 136: Baptism and the Forty Days ... 415
Paper 137: Tarrying Time in Galilee ... 418
Paper 138: Training the Kingdom's Messengers ... 422
Paper 139: The Twelve Apostles ... 426
Paper 140: The Ordination of the Twelve ... 432
Paper 141: Beginning the Public Work ... 436
Paper 142: The Passover at Jerusalem ... 440
Paper 143: Going Through Samaria ... 443
Paper 144: At Gilboa and the Decapolis ... 445
Paper 145: Four Eventful Days at Capernaum ... 449
Paper 146: First Preaching Tour of Galilee ... 451
Paper 147: The Interlude Visit to Jerusalem ... 454
Paper 148: Training Evangelists at Bethsaida ... 457
Paper 149: The Second Preaching Tour ... 461
Paper 150: The Third Preaching Tour ... 463
Paper 151: Tarrying and Teaching by the Seaside ... 467

Paper 152: Events Leading up to the Capernaum Crisis	470
Paper 153: The Crisis at Capernaum	473
Paper 154: Last Days at Capernaum	475
Paper 155: Fleeing Through Northern Galilee	478
Paper 156: The Sojourn at Tyre and Sidon	480
Paper 157: At Caesarea-Philippi	483
Paper 158: The Mount of Transfiguration	486
Paper 159: The Decapolis Tour	489
Paper 160: Rodan of Alexandria	492
Paper 161: Further Discussions with Rodan	494
Paper 162: At the Feast of Tabernacles	496
Paper 163: Ordination of the Seventy at Magadan	499
Paper 164: At the Feast of Dedication	502
Paper 165: The Perean Mission Begins	504
Paper 166: Last Visit to Perea	507
Paper 167: The Visit to Philadelphia	509
Paper 168: The Resurrection of Lazarus	512
Paper 169: Last Teaching at Pella	514
Paper 170: The Kingdom of Heaven	516
Paper 171: On the Way to Jerusalem	519
Paper 172: Going into Jerusalem	523
Paper 173: Monday at Jerusalem	525
Paper 174: Tuesday Morning in the Temple	528
Paper 175: The Last Temple Discourse	530
Paper 176: Tuesday Evening on Mount Olivet	532
Paper 177: Wednesday, the Rest Day	534
Paper 178: Last Day at the Camp	536
Paper 179: The Last Supper	538
Paper 180: The Farewell Discourse	540
Paper 181: Final Admonitions and Warnings	543
Paper 182: In Gethsemane	544
Paper 183: The Betrayal and Arrest of Jesus	546
Paper 184: Before the Sanhedrin Court	548
Paper 185: The Trial Before Pilate	551
Paper 186: Just Before the Crucifixion	554
Paper 187: The Crucifixion	556
Paper 188: The Time of the Tomb	559
Paper 189: The Resurrection	562
Paper 190: Morontia Appearances of Jesus	564
Paper 191: Appearances to the Apostles and Other Leaders	567
Paper 192: Appearances in Galilee	570

Paper 193: Final Appearances and Ascension	572
Paper 194: Bestowal of the Spirit of Truth	575
Paper 195: After Pentecost	578
Paper 196: The Faith of Jesus	583

A SUMMARY OF UNIVERSE REALITY

A Simplification of the Foreword
Divine Counselor

THE people of Urantia have been confused about the concepts of God, divinity, and deity. It is exceedingly difficult to present enlarged concepts and advanced truth when limited by the circumscribed concepts of the English language. We are therefore defining our terms as they will be used in this presentation.

Your world, Urantia, is one of many similar inhabited planets which comprise the local universe of *Nebadon*. This universe, together with similar creations, makes up the superuniverse of *Orvonton*, from whose capital, Uversa, our commission hails. Orvonton is one of the seven evolutionary superuniverses of time and space which circle the never-beginning, never-ending creation of divine perfection—the central universe of *Havona*. At the heart of this eternal and central universe is the stationary Isle of Paradise, the geographic center of infinity and the dwelling place of the eternal God.

The seven evolving superuniverses in association with the central and divine universe, we commonly refer to as the grand universe; these are the now organized and inhabited creations. They are all a part of the master universe, which also embraces the uninhabited but mobilizing universes of outer space.

I. Deity and Divinity

Deity may exist as a personality (God) or in prepersonal (Thought Adjusters) and superpersonal forms. Divinity is the characteristic, unifying, and coordinating quality of Deity. Mortals comprehend divinity as truth, beauty, and goodness.

II. God

God is a word symbol denoting personal aspects of Deity. It may refer to *God the Father, God the Son, God the Spirit, God the Supreme, God the Sevenfold, God the Ultimate,* and *God the Absolute.*

III. The First Source and Center

God (the Universal Father), as the first source and center, is primal in relation to total reality—unqualifiedly. Total, infinite reality is existential in the seven coordinate Absolutes: The First Source and Center, The Second Source and Center, The Third Source and Center, The Isle of Paradise, The Deity Absolute, The Universal Absolute, and The Unqualified Absolute.

The maximum Deity reality fully comprehensible by evolutionary finite beings is embraced within the Supreme Being. Therefore, in order to portray the origin and nature of universal reality, many of the simultaneous events of eternity must be presented as sequential transactions. In actuality, the Universal Father, the Eternal Son, the Infinite Spirit, the Isle of Paradise, and Havona have always existed.

IV. Universe Reality

The Universal Father originates all aspects of reality. There are three phases of reality: (1) *Undeified reality*, (2) *Deified reality*, (3) *Interassociated reality*. Paradise is a term inclusive of the personal and the nonpersonal aspects of all forms of reality.

V. Personality Realities

Personality is a level of deified reality and ranges from the human plane up through morontia and spiritual levels of being to the finality of personality status. Personality is the gift of the Paradise Father. The qualities of universal reality associated with human experience are: (1) *Body*, (2) *Mind*, (3) *Spirit*, (4) *Soul*. (The soul is a morontia reality—the warp is spiritual; the woof is physical.)

VI. Energy and Pattern

Energy and *force* are inclusive terms referring to spiritual, mindal, and material realms. *Power* usually denotes linear-gravity-responsive matter. *Physical energy* is a term denoting all forms of physical motion or action. *Mind* is a phenomenon connoting the presence-activity of living ministry in addition to varied energy systems. In personality, mind intervenes between spirit and matter. Pattern can be projected as material, spiritual, or mindal energies. *Pattern* is the master design from which copies are made. Paradise is the absolute of patterns. The Eternal Son is the pattern personality.

VII. The Supreme Being

God the Supreme, God the Ultimate, and God the Absolute are actualizing, experiential Deity personalities. The Supreme is actualizing in the Grand Universe through the events of God the Sevenfold and is engaged in the ascending mobilization and perfecting unification of all finite reality to the end of embarking on the attempt to reach absonite levels of supercreature attainment.

VIII. God the Sevenfold

Because of human limitations, the Universal Father has established an evolutionary approach to Deity. This sevenfold spiritual ladder consists of the Paradise Creator Sons, the Ancients of Days, the Seven Master Spirits, the Supreme Being, God the Spirit, God the Son, and God the Father. God the Sevenfold provides the mechanism whereby mortals become immortal; it enables the finite to attain the absonite and to attempt the attainment of the Ultimate.

IX. God the Ultimate

God the Ultimate eventuates from the potentials of divinity residing in the spheres of supertime and transcended space of the Master Universe. The actualization of Ultimate Deity signalizes absonite unification of the first experiential Trinity—God the Sevenfold, the Supreme Being, and the Architects of the Master Universe. The Paradise Trinity in the eternal future will be personality-complemented by the experiential actualization of associate evolutionary Deities—God the Supreme, God the Ultimate, and possibly God the Absolute.

X. God the Absolute

The actualization of *God the Absolute* would be the consequence of the unification of the second experiential Trinity, the Absolute Trinity—God the Supreme, God the Ultimate, and the Consummator of Universe Destiny. But we are not certain regarding the total inclusion of all absolute values because we have not been informed that the Deity Absolute is the equivalent of the Infinite.

XI. The Three Absolutes

In the Paradise Trinity the Universal Father has differentiated his Havona presence from the potentials of infinity. These infinity potentials are encompassed in the three Absolutes: *the Deity Absolute*, the all-powerful activator of divine and personal events in the welfare of the total universe; *the Unqualified Absolute*, the nonpersonal, extradivine, and undeified overcontrol in infinity; and *the Universal Absolute* who so perfectly equalizes the tensions between time and eternity, finity and infinity, reality potential and reality actuality, Paradise and space, man and God. In the final analysis all three are One Absolute.

XII. The Trinities

The Paradise Trinity, composed of the eternal and infinite Deity union of the Universal Father, the Eternal Son, and the Infinite Spirit, is existential. The potentials of the Paradise Trinity are experiential, therefore God the Supreme, God the Ultimate, and God the Absolute are in the process of actualizing.

[*Acknowledgment*: In formulating Part One of the Urantia Papers we are to give preference to the highest human concepts pertaining the portrayal of the Universal Father and the nature of his Paradise associates and the encircling seven superuniverses, we are to be guided by the mandate of the superuniverse rulers which directs that we shall, in all our efforts to reveal truth and co-ordinate essential knowledge, give preference to the highest existing human concepts. We may resort to pure revelation only when the concept of presentation has had no adequate previous expression by the human mind.]

PART I
THE CENTRAL AND SUPERUNIVERSES

Paper 1: The Universal Father
Divine Counselor

THE Universal Father is the God of all creation, the First Source and Center of all things and beings. First think of God as a creator, then as a controller, and lastly as an infinite upholder. God the Father, in association with the Eternal Son and the Infinite Spirit, is the creator of all other personal universe Creators and the universe of universes. The myriads of planetary systems are populated by many different types of intelligent beings who can know God, receive divine affection, and love him in return. These children of time are embarked on the long, long Paradise journey to comprehend the divine nature and recognize the Universal Father whose supreme mandate is, "Be you perfect, even as I am perfect." This perfection pertains to self-realization and mind attainment in all finite aspects of divinity of will, perfection of personality motivation, and God-consciousness. This search for God is the supreme adventure of the inhabitants of all the worlds of time and space.

1:1. The Father's Name

Of all the names by which God the Father is known throughout the universes, those which designate him as the First Source and the Universe Center are most often encountered. The Universal Father never requires any arbitrary form of recognition, but since we believe we are his universe children, it is only natural that we call him Father. The Creator refuses to coerce his mortal children; they must of themselves recognize, love, and voluntarily worship him. The affectionate dedication of the human will to doing the Father's will is the only possible gift of true value to the Paradise Father.

The First Father is known by various names in different universes, such as: the First Creative Source and Divine Center, the Father of Universes, the Infinite Upholder, the Divine Controller, the Father of Lights, the Gift of

Life, and the All-powerful One. On worlds where a Paradise Son has lived a bestowal life, God is generally known by some name indicative of personal relationship, tender affection, and fatherly devotion. The name he is given is of little importance; the significant thing is that you should know him and aspire to be like him.

1:2. The Reality of God

God is primal reality, universal spirit, and father personality. God is not manlike nor a psychological focalization of spiritual meanings; he is a transcendent reality. The indwelling spirit Monitor in the human mind sponsors God-consciousness and assists in evolving the immortal soul. Although the existence of God cannot be proved by scientific experiment, the reality of God is reasonable to logic, plausible to philosophy, essential to religion, and indispensable to any hope of personality survival. God's indwelling presence is revealed by God-consciousness, God seeking, and the desire to do God's will.

As controller of the material universe of universes, the First Source and Center functions in the patterns of the eternal Isle of Paradise, and through this absolute gravity center exercises cosmic overcontrol throughout the universe of universes. As mind, God functions in the Deity of the Infinite Spirit; as spirit, God is manifest in the person of the Eternal Son and in the persons of the divine children of the Eternal Son. This interrelation of the First Source and Center with the co-ordinate Persons and Absolutes of Paradise does not in the least preclude the *direct* personal action of the Universal Father throughout all creation. Through the presence of his fragmentized spirit the Creator Father maintains immediate contact with his creature children and his created universes.

1:3. God the Universal Spirit

The Universal Father is an infinite spiritual reality. Spirit beings are real, notwithstanding they are invisible to human eyes. The Universal Father is not invisible because he is hiding himself away from the lowly creatures of materialistic handicaps and limited spiritual endowments. The glory and the spiritual brilliance of the divine personality presence is impossible of approach by the lower groups of spirit beings or by any order of material personalities. But it is not necessary to see God with the eyes of the flesh in order to discern him by the faith-vision of the spiritualized mind. Through his far-flung personality circuit God deals directly with the personalities of his vast creation of will creatures; and he is contactable in the presence of his fragmented entities, the Thought Adjusters. This Paradise spirit that indwells mortal minds fosters the evolution of the immortal soul. Mortal mind yielded to spirit is destined to become increasingly spiritual and ultimately achieve oneness with the divine spirit.

1:4. The Mystery of God

The infinity of the perfection of God is such that it eternally constitutes him mystery. And the greatest of all the unfathomable mysteries of God is the phenomenon of the divine indwelling of mortal minds. The physical bodies of mortals are "the temples of God." We are constantly confronted with this mystery of God; we are nonplused by the increasing unfolding of the endless panorama of the truth of his infinite goodness, endless mercy, matchless wisdom, and superb character. The Universal Father reveals all of his gracious and divine self that can be discerned or comprehended by his universe children. Only the faith-grasp of the God-knowing mortal can achieve the philosophic miracle of the recognition of the Infinite.

1:5. Personality of the Universal Father

The Universal Father is an infinite personality; he is the origin and destiny of personality throughout all creation. The Father is truly a personality, but much more than the human conception of personality. The immensity and grandeur of the divine personality is beyond the grasp of the unperfected mind of evolutionary mortals. God is lacking in none of those superhuman and divine attributes which constitute a perfect, eternal, loving, and infinite Creator personality. The truth and maturity of any religion is directly proportional to its concept of the infinite personality of God and to its grasp of the absolute unity of Deity.

1:6. Personality in the Universe

God is to science a cause, to philosophy an idea, to religion a person, even the loving heavenly Father. God is to the scientist a primal force, to the philosopher a hypothesis of unity, to the religionist a living spiritual experience. Better concepts of both human and divine personality are revealed in the bestowal life of Michael, incarnating as Jesus of Nazareth, who attained the full realization of the potential of spirit personality in human experience; therefore his life of achieving the Father's will becomes man's most real and ideal revelation of the personality of God. The more completely man understands himself and appreciates the personality values of his fellows, the more he will crave to know and become like the Original Personality. To know such a divine personality all of man's personality endowments must be wholly consecrated to the effort; halfhearted, partial devotion will be unavailing.

1:7. Spiritual Value of the Personality Concept

When Jesus talked about "the living God," he referred to a personal Deity—the Father in heaven. The concept of the personality of Deity facilitates fellowship; this personal communion is greatly facilitated by the presence of the prepersonal Thought Adjuster. Man does not achieve union with God as a drop of water might find unity with the ocean. Man attains divine union by progressive reciprocal spiritual communion, by increasingly attaining the divine nature through wholehearted and intelligent conformity to the divine will. Ultimate universe reality can be grasped only by personal experience. The fact of the Paradise Trinity in no manner violates the truth of the divine unity. The three personalities of Paradise Deity are, in all universe reactions and relations, as one. Ever bear in mind that these profound truths pertaining to Deity will increasingly clarify as your minds become progressively spiritualized during the successive epochs of the long mortal ascent to Paradise.

Paper 2: The Nature of God
Divine Counselor

IN all our efforts to enlarge and spiritualize the human concept of God, we are tremendously handicapped by the limited capacity of the mortal mind. The nature of God can best be understood by the revelation of the Father which Michael of Nebadon unfolded in his manifold teachings and in his superb mortal life in the flesh.

2:1. The Infinity of God

Notwithstanding the infinity of the stupendous manifestations of the Father's eternal and universal personality, he is unqualifiedly self-conscious of both his infinity and eternity. The Universal Father is absolutely and without qualification infinite in all his attributes. No thing is new to God; there is no past, present, or future; all time is present at any given moment. He is the great and only I AM. In the Paradise Sons, the personalities of the Infinite Spirit, the Thought Adjusters, and in many other ways does the Paradise Father lovingly and willingly downstep and otherwise modify, dilute, and attenuate his infinity in order that he may be able to draw nearer the finite minds of his creature children. Because the First Father is infinite in his plans, mortal man can glimpse the Father's purposes only now and then, here and there.

2:2. The Father's Eternal Perfection

There is finality of completeness and perfection of repleteness in the mandates of the Father. The Universal Father does not repent of his original purposes of wisdom and perfection. He is final, complete, and perfect. The perfection of divinity and the magnitude of eternity are forever beyond the full grasp of the circumscribed mind of mortal man. The personal and liberating touch of the God of perfection overshadows the hearts and encircuits the natures of all those mortal creatures who have ascended to the universe level of moral discernment. The Universal Father actually participates in the experience with immaturity and imperfection in the evolving career of every moral being of the entire universe.

2:3. Justice and Righteousness

The justice of the Universal Father cannot be influenced by the acts and performances of his creatures. How futile to make puerile appeals to such a God to modify his changeless decrees so that we can avoid the just consequences of the operation of his wise natural laws and righteous spiritual mandates! Infinite wisdom is the eternal arbiter which determines the proportions of justice and mercy which shall be meted out in any given circumstance. The final result of wholehearted sin is annihilation. Undiluted evil, complete error, willful sin, and unmitigated iniquity are inherently and automatically suicidal. The factual disappearance of such a creature is, however, delayed until the ordained order of justice current in that universe has been fully complied with. When this sentence is finally confirmed, the sin-identified being instantly becomes as though he had not been.

2:4. The Divine Mercy

Mercy is simply justice tempered by that wisdom which grows out of perfection of knowledge and the full recognition of the natural weaknesses and environmental handicaps of finite creatures. God is inherently kind, naturally compassionate, and everlastingly merciful. Never is it necessary that any influence be brought to bear upon the Father to call forth his loving-kindness. Mercy is the natural and inevitable offspring of goodness and love. Mercy is not a contravention of justice but rather an understanding interpretation of the demands of supreme justice as it is fairly applied to the subordinate spiritual beings and to the material creatures of the evolving universes.

2:5. The Love of God

"God is love"; therefore his only personal attitude towards the affairs of the universe is always a reaction of divine affection. It is wrong to think of God as being coaxed into loving his children because of the sacrifices of his Sons or the intercession of his subordinate creatures. The greatest evidence of the goodness of God and the supreme reason for loving him is the indwelling gift of the Father—the Adjuster who so patiently awaits the hour when you both shall be eternally made one. If you will submit to the leading of the indwelling spirit, you will be unerringly guided, step by step, life by life, through universe upon universe, and age by age, until you finally stand in the presence of the Paradise personality of the Universal Father. The love of God is an intelligent and farseeing parental affection. God is love, but love is not God. How unfortunate that I cannot make use of some supernal and exclusive term which would convey to the mind of man the true nature and exquisitely beautiful significance of the divine affection of the Paradise Father. Love is the dominant characteristic of all God's personal dealings with his creatures.

2:6. The Goodness of God

The goodness of God is a part of the personality of God, and its full revelation appears only in the personal religious experience of the believing sons of God. God loves not like a father, but *as* a father. He is the Paradise Father of every universe personality. God as a father transcends God as a judge. God is never wrathful, vengeful, or angry. The goodness of God rests at the bottom of the divine free-willness—the universal tendency to love, show mercy, manifest patience, and minister forgiveness.

2:7. Divine Truth and Beauty

Divine truth, final truth, is uniform and universal. All finite knowledge and creature understanding are relative. Physical facts are fairly uniform, but truth is a living and flexible factor in the philosophy of the universe. Truth is beautiful because it is both replete and symmetrical. Happiness ensues from the recognition of truth because it can be acted out; it can be lived. Divine truth is best known by its spiritual flavor. The discernment of supreme beauty is the discovery and integration of reality: The discernment of the divine goodness in the eternal truth is ultimate beauty. The religious challenge of this age is to those farseeing and forward-looking men and women of spiritual insight who will dare to construct a new and appealing philosophy of living out of the enlarged and exquisitely integrated modern concepts of cosmic truth, universe beauty, and divine goodness. Truth, beauty, and goodness are divine realities. Health, sanity, and happiness are integrations of truth, beauty, and goodness as they are blended in human experience. Such levels of efficient living come about through the unification of energy systems, idea systems, and spirit systems. The real purpose of all universe education is to effect the better co-ordination of the isolated child of the worlds with the larger realities of his expanding experience.

Paper 3: The Attributes of God

Divine Counselor

GOD is everywhere present; the Universal Father rules the circle of eternity. But he rules in the local universes in the persons of his Paradise Creator Sons. Creatorship is hardly an attribute of God; it is rather the aggregate of his acting nature. The creatorship of Deity culminates in the universal truth of the Fatherhood of God.

3:1. God's Everywhereness

The Universal Father is all the time present in all parts and in all hearts of his far-flung creation. It is literally true that God is all and in all. But the Infinite can be finally revealed only in infinity. The Father's presence unceasingly patrols the master universe. The creature not only exists in God, but a fragment of God—the Thought Adjuster—lives in the creature. This gift from the Paradise Father is man's inseparable companion. In the personality circuit and in the Adjusters God acts uniquely, directly, and exclusively. Concerning God's presence in a planet, system, constellation, or a universe, the degree of such presence in any creational unit is a measure of the degree of the evolving presence of the Supreme Being.

3:2. God's Infinite Power

It is eternally true, "there is no power but of God." Within the bounds of that which is consistent with the divine nature, it is literally true that "with God all things are possible." The power and wisdom of the Father are wholly adequate to cope with any and all universe exigencies. Regardless of appearances, the power of God is not functioning in the universe as a blind force. Such concepts of God have their origin in the limited range of your viewpoint and the profound ignorance you enjoy regarding the existence of the higher laws of the realm. God's doings are all purposeful, intelligent, wise, kind, and eternally considerate of the best good of all concerned, from the lowest to the highest. God is unlimited in power, divine in nature, final in will, infinite in attributes, eternal in wisdom, and absolute in reality.

3:3. God's Universal Knowledge

The divine mind is conscious of, and conversant with, the thought of all creation. His knowledge of events is universal and perfect. All the worlds of every universe are constantly within the consciousness of God. God is possessed of unlimited power to know all things; his consciousness is universal. We are not wholly certain as to whether or not God chooses to foreknow events of sin. But even if God should foreknow the freewill acts of his children, such foreknowledge does not in the least abrogate their freedom. One thing is certain: God is never subjected to surprise.

3:4. God's Limitlessness

In potential of force, wisdom, and love, the Father has never lessened aught of his possession nor become divested of any attribute of his glorious personality as the result of the unstinted bestowal of himself upon his manifold creatures. This giving of himself to his creatures creates a boundless, almost inconceivable future possibility of progressive and successive existences for these divinely endowed mortals.

Finite appreciation of infinite qualities far transcends the logically limited capacities of the creature because of the fact that mortal man is made in the image of God—there lives within him a fragment of infinity. Therefore man's nearest and dearest approach to God is by and through love, for God is love.

3:5. The Father's Supreme Rule

The Father rules through his Sons; on down through the universe organization there is an unbroken chain of rulers ending with the Planetary Princes, who direct the destinies of the evolutionary spheres of the Father's vast domains. In the affairs of men's hearts the Universal Father may not always have his way; but in the conduct and destiny of a planet the divine plan prevails; the eternal purpose of wisdom and love triumphs.

The uncertainties of life and the vicissitudes of existence do not in any manner contradict the concept of the universal sovereignty of God. All evolutionary creature life is beset by certain inevitabilities. Consider the following: Are courage, altruism, hope, faith, love, idealism, loyalty, unselfishness, and happiness desirable? Then must man live in a world where the opposite experiences challenge him. Man could not dynamically choose the divine life if there were no self-life to forsake. The only evolutionary world without error (the possibility of unwise judgment) would be a world without free intelligence. Mortal man earns even his status as an ascension candidate by his own faith and hope. Everything divine which the human mind grasps and the human soul acquires is an experiential attainment and is therefore a unique possession.

3:6. The Father's Primacy

The sovereignty of God is unlimited; it is the fundamental fact of all creation. All religious philosophy, sooner or later, arrives at the concept of the unified universe rule of one God. It is a great blunder to humanize God, except in the concept of the indwelling Thought Adjuster, but even that is not so stupid as completely to *mechanize* the idea of the First Great Source and Center.

The infinite and eternal Ruler of the universe of universes is power, form, energy, process, pattern, principle, presence, and idealized reality. But he is more; he is personal; he exercises a sovereign will, experiences self-consciousness of divinity, executes the mandates of a creative mind, pursues the satisfaction of the realization of an eternal purpose, and manifests a Father's love and affection for his universe children. God the Father loves men; God the Son serves men; God the Spirit inspires the children of the universe to the ever-ascending adventure of finding God the Father by the ways ordained by God the Sons through the ministry of the grace of God the Spirit.

Paper 4: God's Relation to the Universe

Divine Counselor

THE Universal Father has an eternal purpose pertaining to the material, intellectual, and spiritual phenomena of the universe of universes, which he is executing throughout all time. Havona serves as the pattern creation for all other universes and as the finishing school for the pilgrims of time on their way to Paradise. After attaining Paradise, mortals are given further training for some undisclosed future work.

4:1. The Universe Attitude of the Father

The watchword of the universe is *progress*. Divine providence is never arrayed in opposition to true human progress, either temporal or spiritual. There is no limitation of the forces and personalities which the Father may use to uphold his purpose and sustain his creatures.

There is stability in the midst of apparent instability. The Father unceasingly pours forth energy, light, and life. There is an organic unity in the universes of time and space which seems to underlie the whole fabric of cosmic events. I am inclined to believe that there is a far-flung and generally unrecognizable control of the co-ordination and interassociation of all phases and forms of universe activity that causes such a variegated and apparently hopelessly confused medley of physical, mental, moral, and spiritual phenomena so unerringly to work out to the glory of God and for the good of men and angels.

4:2. God and Nature

Nature is in a limited sense the physical habit of God. Nature is the perfection of Paradise divided by the incompletion, evil, and sin of the unfinished universes. God is not personally present in nature or in any of the forces of nature. On Urantia nature is marred, her beautiful face is scarred, her features are seared by the rebellion, the misconduct, the misthinking of the myriads of creatures. No, nature is not God. Nature is not an object of worship.

4:3. God's Unchanging Character

All too long has man thought of God as one like himself. God is not, never was, and never will be jealous of man or any other being in the universe of universes. The eternal God is incapable of wrath and anger as man understands such reactions. Much, very much, of the difficulty which Urantia mortals have in understanding God is due to the far-reaching consequences of the Lucifer rebellion and the Caligastia betrayal. God repents of nothing he has ever done, now does, or ever will do. He is all-wise as well as all-powerful. The Father's affection is undoubtedly grieved when his children fail to attain the spiritual levels they are capable of reaching with the assistance which has been so freely provided by the spiritual-attainment plans and the mortal-ascension policies of the universes. The infinite goodness of the Father is beyond the comprehension of the finite mind of time.

4:4. The Realization of God

God is the only stationary, self-contained, and changeless being in the whole universe of universes. God is purposive energy (creative spirit) and absolute will, and these are self-existent and universal. The very identity of God is inimical to change. Not until you achieve Paradise status can you even begin to understand how God can pass from simplicity to complexity, from identity to variation, from quiescence to motion, from infinity to finitude, from the divine to the human, and from unity to duality and triunity. First and last—eternally—the infinite God is a Father. In all his personal relations with the creature personalities of the universes, the First Source and Center is always and consistently a loving Father, and that tender nature finds its strongest expression and greatest satisfaction in loving and being loved. When confronted with the awful spectacle of human limitations, victorious human faith declares: Even if I cannot do this, there lives in me one who can and will do it, a part of the Father-Absolute of the universe of universes. And that is "the victory which overcomes the world, even your faith."

4:5. Erroneous Ideas of God

Religious tradition is the imperfectly preserved record of the experiences of the God-knowing men of past ages, but such records are untrustworthy. One of the greatest sources of confusion on Urantia concerning the nature of God grows out of the failure of your sacred books clearly to distinguish between the personalities of the Paradise Trinity and between Paradise Deity and the local universe creators and administrators. Many of the messages of subordinate personalities in your records are presented as coming from God himself. The people of Urantia continue to suffer from the influence of primitive concepts of God. The barbarous idea of appeasing an angry God, of propitiating an offended Lord, of winning the favor of Deity through sacrifices and penance and even by the shedding of blood, represents a religion wholly puerile and primitive, a philosophy unworthy of an enlightened age of science and truth. What a travesty upon the infinite character of God to believe that his tender mercies were not forthcoming until he saw his blameless Son bleeding and dying upon the cross of Calvary! But the inhabitants of Urantia are to find deliverance from these ancient errors and pagan superstitions respecting the nature of the Universal Father.

Paper 5: God's Relation to the Individual
Divine Counselor

AN actual fragment of the living God resides within the intellect of every normal-minded and morally conscious Urantia mortal. The indwelling Thought Adjusters are a part of the eternal Deity of the Paradise Father. Man does not have to go farther than his own inner experience of the soul's contemplation of this spiritual-reality presence to find God and attempt communion with him. The eternal God has also reserved to himself the prerogative of bestowing personality upon the divine Creators and the living creatures of the universe of universes and maintaining direct and parental contact with all these personal beings through the personality circuit.

5:1. The Approach to God

The magnitude of the spiritual difference between the highest personality of universe existence and the lower groups of created intelligences is inconceivable. Were it possible for the lower orders of intelligence to be transported instantly into the presence of the Father himself, they would not know they were there. There is a long, long road ahead of mortal man before he can consistently and within the realms of possibility ask for safe conduct into the Paradise presence of the Universal Father. However Urantia mortals may differ in their intellectual, social, economic, and even moral opportunities and endowments, forget not that their spiritual endowment is uniform and unique. They are all equally privileged to seek intimate personal communion with this indwelling spirit of divine origin. The Father desires all his creatures to be in personal communion with him. To each of you and to all of us, God is approachable, the Father is attainable, the way is open; the forces of divine love and the ways and means of divine administration are all interlocked in an effort to facilitate the advancement of every worthy intelligence of every universe to the Paradise presence of the Universal Father.

5:2. The Presence of God

God lives in every one of his spirit-born sons. What a mistake to dream of God far off in the skies when the spirit of the Universal Father lives within your own mind! The fact that you are not intellectually conscious of close and intimate contact with the indwelling Adjuster does not in the least disprove such an exalted experience. It is exceedingly difficult for the meagerly spiritualized, material mind of mortal man to experience marked consciousness of the spirit activities of such divine entities as the Paradise Adjusters. The self-realization of such an achievement is mainly, though not exclusively, limited to the realms of soul consciousness, but the proofs are forthcoming and abundant in the manifestation of the fruits of the spirit in such lives.

5:3. True Worship

In the highest sense, we worship the Universal Father and him only. Supplications of all kinds belong to the realm of the Eternal Son. Prayers, everything except adoration and worship of the Universal Father, are matters that concern a local universe. Worship is for its own sake; prayer embodies a self- or creature-interest element. But in practical religious experience there exists no reason why prayer should not be addressed to God the Father as a part of true worship. When you deal with the practical affairs of your daily life, you are in the hands of the spirit personalities having origin in the agencies of the Conjoint Actor. And so it is: You worship God; pray to, and commune with, the Son; and work out the details of your earthly sojourn in connection with the intelligences of the Infinite Spirit. True worship, in the last analysis, becomes an experience realized on four cosmic levels: the intellectual, the morontial, the spiritual, and the personal—the consciousness of mind, soul, and spirit, and their unification in personality

5:4. God in Religion

The religions of revelation allure men to seek for a God of love because they crave to become like him. Revealed religion is a living and dynamic experience of divinity attainment predicated on humanity service, an enduring unity in human experience, a lasting peace and a profound assurance. God is not only the determiner of destiny; he is man's eternal destination. The domains of philosophy and art intervene between the nonreligious and the religious activities of the human self. The religion of Jesus is salvation from self, deliverance from the evils of creature isolation in time and in eternity. Jesus revealed a God of love, and love is all-embracing of truth, beauty, and goodness. All religions are of value in that they are valid approaches to the religion of Jesus. The spiritual status of any religion may be determined by the nature of its prayers.

5:5. The Consciousness of God

Morality is superanimal but wholly evolutionary. Religion is an independent realm of human response to life situations and is unfailingly exhibited at all stages of human development which are postmoral. Moral conduct is always an antecedent of evolved religion and a part of even revealed religion, but never the whole of religious experience. Religious experience, being essentially spiritual, can never be fully understood by the material mind.

It is well-nigh impossible for human logic and finite reason to harmonize the concept of divine immanence with the idea of God's transcendence. The experience of God-consciousness remains the same from generation to generation, but with each advancing epoch in human knowledge the philosophic concept and the theologic definitions of God must change. Limitations of intellect, curtailment of education, deprivation of culture, impoverishment of social status, even inferiority of the human standards of morality resulting from the unfortunate lack of educational, cultural, and social advantages, cannot prevent the divine spirit from initiating an immortal soul in such humanly handicapped but believing individuals.

5:6. The God of Personality

The Universal Father is the bestower and the conservator of every personality. Personality is one of the unsolved mysteries of the universes. The mortal material self has personality and identity, temporal identity; the prepersonal spirit Adjuster also has identity, eternal identity. Having provided for the growth of the immortal soul and having liberated man's inner self from the fetters of absolute dependence on antecedent causation, the Father stands aside. It remains for man himself to will the creation or to inhibit the creation of this surviving and eternal self which is his for the choosing. No other being, force, creator, or agency in all the wide universe of universes can interfere to any degree with the absolute sovereignty of the mortal free will. There is a kinship of divine spontaneity in all personality. The personality circuit of the universe of universes is centered in the person of the Universal Father, and the Paradise Father is personally conscious of, and in personal touch with, all personalities of all levels of self-conscious existence. When all is said and done, I can do nothing more helpful than to reiterate that God is your universe Father, and that you are all his planetary children.

Paper 6: The Eternal Son
Divine Counselor

THE Eternal Son is the perfect and final expression of the "first" personal and absolute concept of the Universal Father. We speak of God's "first" thought and allude to an impossible time origin of the Eternal Son to relate with the time-bound minds of mortals. Members of the existential Trinity are from eternity. The Eternal Son is the spiritual personalization of the

Paradise Father's universal and infinite concept of divine reality, unqualified spirit, and absolute personality.

6:1. Identity of the Eternal Son

The Eternal Son is the Second Person of Deity and the associate creator of all things. The Eternal Son is the spiritual center and the divine administrator of the spiritual government of the universe of universes. On your world this Original Son has been confused with a co-ordinate Creator Son, Michael of Nebadon, who bestowed himself upon the mortal races of Urantia as Jesus. This Original Son is cocreator with the Universal Father of the central universe of power and perfection and of all other divine Sons who spring from the infinite Deities.

6:2. Nature of the Eternal Son

The Eternal Son is just as changeless and infinitely dependable as the Universal Father. He is also just as spiritual as the Father, just as truly an unlimited spirit. To you of lowly origin the Son would appear to be more personal since he is one step nearer you in approachability than is the Universal Father. The Eternal Son is the eternal Word of God. He is wholly like the Father; thus it is true of the Eternal Son and all of the co-ordinate Creator Sons: "He who has seen the Son has seen the Father." In divine goodness I discern no difference between the Father and the Son. The Father loves his universe children as a father; the Eternal Son looks upon all creatures both as father and as brother.

6:3. Ministry of the Father's Love

The ministry of the Eternal Son is devoted to the revelation of the God of love to the universe of universes. The Eternal Son is the great mercy minister to all creation. Mercy is applied love, the Father's love in action in the person of his Eternal Son. The love of this universal Son is likewise universal. As love is comprehended on a sex planet, the love of God is more comparable to the love of a father, while the love of the Eternal Son is more like the affection of a mother.

6:4. Attributes of the Eternal Son

The Eternal Son motivates the spirit level of cosmic reality. He exercises perfect control over all actualized spirit reality through his absolute grasp of spirit gravity. The Son is omnipotent only in the spiritual realm. The omnipresence of the Original Son constitutes the spiritual unity of the universe of universes. In the realms of knowledge, omniscience, we cannot distinguish between the First and Second Sources; like the Father, the Son knows all. The Eternal Son, as a loving, merciful, and ministering spiritual personality, is wholly and infinitely equal with the Universal Father.

6:5. Limitations of the Eternal Son

The Eternal Son does not personally function in the physical domains, nor does he function, except through the Conjoint Actor, in the levels of mind ministry. But these qualifications do not in any manner otherwise limit the Eternal Son in the full and free exercise of all the divine attributes of spiritual omniscience, omnipresence, and omnipotence. The Son gives origin to a vast spirit host, but such derivations are not personalities. When the Son creates personality, he does so in conjunction with the Father or with the Conjoint Creator. The Eternal Son is limited in transmittal of creator prerogatives. But the Son can and does bestow himself as an unlimited spirit to bathe all creation and unceasingly draw all spirit personalities and spiritual realities to himself.

6:6. The Spirit Mind

The Eternal Son is spirit and has mind, but not a mind or a spirit which mortal mind can comprehend. Spirit is ever conscious, minded, and possessed of varied phases of identity. The equivalent of mind, the ability to know and be known, is indigenous to Deity. The mind of the Eternal Son is like that of the Father but unlike any other mind in the universe, and with the mind of the Father it is ancestor to the diverse and far-flung minds of the Conjoint Creator. As you pass through the superuniverse and on to Havona many of these spirit-concealed mysteries will clarify as you begin to be endowed with the "mind of the spirit"—spiritual insight.

6:7. Personality of the Eternal Son

The Eternal Son is that infinite personality from whose unqualified personality fetters the Universal Father escaped by the technique of trinitization. The personality of the Paradise Son is absolute and purely spiritual, and this absolute personality is also the divine and eternal pattern, first, of the Father's bestowal of personality upon the Conjoint Actor and, subsequently, of his bestowal of personality upon the myriads of his creatures throughout a far-flung universe. It is impossible to convey to the human mind a word picture of the beauty and grandeur of the supernal personality of the Eternal Son. You must await your attainment of Paradise, and then you will understand why I was unable to portray the character of this absolute personality to the understanding of the finite mind.

6:8. Realization of the Eternal Son

The Eternal Son is a grand and glorious personality. Concerning identity, nature, and other attributes of personality, the Eternal Son is the full equal, the perfect complement, and the eternal counterpart of the Universal Father.

In the same sense that God is the Universal Father, the Son is the Universal Mother. And all of us, high and low, constitute their universal family. God is the initiating thought and the Son is the expressionful word. In each local universe this inseparability is personalized in the divinity of the Creator Son. Not until you spiritize and commence your spirit ascension will the comprehension of the personality of the Eternal Son begin to equal the vividness of your concept of the personality of the Creator Son.

Paper 7:
Relation of the Eternal Son to the Universe
Divine Counselor

THE Original Son is ever concerned with the execution of the spiritual aspects of the Father's eternal purpose. The Son is like the Father in that he seeks to bestow everything possible of himself upon his co-ordinate Sons and upon their subordinate Sons. The Eternal Son is the actual upholder of the vast creation of spirit realities and spiritual beings. The Son is not, however, personally responsible for the conduct of all spirit personalities. The will of the personal creature is relatively free and hence determines the actions of such volitional beings.

7:1. The Spirit-Gravity Circuit

Everything taught concerning the immanence of God, his omnipresence, omnipotence, and omniscience, is equally true of the Son in the spiritual domains. The pure and universal spirit gravity of all creation, this exclusively spiritual circuit, leads directly back to the person of the Second Source and Center on Paradise. The control of universal spiritual gravity is universal spiritual sovereignty. This gravity control of spiritual things operates independently of time and space. Spirit realities respond to the drawing power of the center of spiritual gravity in accordance with their qualitative value. Spirit is the soul of creation; matter is the shadowy physical body. There is a spiritual cohesiveness among the spiritual and spiritized personalities of any world, race, nation, or believing group of individuals. The spiritual gravity of the Eternal Son is absolute; nothing can suspend the spirit gravity of the Eternal Son.

7:2. The Administration of the Eternal Son

On Paradise the presence and personal activity of the Original Son is profound, absolute in the spiritual sense. As we pass outward from Paradise, we detect less and less of the personal activity of the Eternal Son. The administration of the Eternal Son in the superuniverses, being exclusively spiritual and superpersonal, is not discernible by creature personalities. In the local universes we observe the Eternal Son personally present in the persons of the Paradise Sons.

7:3. Relation of the Eternal Son to the Individual

In the local universe ascent the mortals of time look to the Creator Son as the personal representative of the Eternal Son. But when they begin the ascent of the superuniverse training regime, the pilgrims of time increasingly detect the supernal presence of the inspiring spirit of the Eternal Son. In Havona the ascenders become still more conscious of the loving embrace of the all-pervading spirit of the Original Son. The spiritual-gravity pull of the Eternal Son constitutes the inherent secret of the Paradise ascension of surviving human souls. The spirit-gravity circuit is the basic channel for transmitting the genuine prayers of the believing human heart from the level of human consciousness to the actual consciousness of Deity. If anything originates in your consciousness that is fraught with supreme spiritual value, when once you give it expression, no power in the universe can prevent its flashing directly to the Absolute Spirit Personality of all creation. Conversely, if your supplications are purely material and wholly self-centered, there exists no plan whereby such unworthy prayers can find lodgment in the spirit circuit of the Eternal Son. Such purely selfish and material requests fall dead. It is the motivating thought, the spiritual content, that validates the mortal supplication. Words are valueless.

7:4. The Divine Perfection Plans

The Eternal Son is in everlasting liaison with the Father in the successful prosecution of the divine plan of progress: the universal plan for the creation, evolution, ascension, and perfection of will creatures. This divine plan of perfection attainment embraces three unique, though marvelously correlated, enterprises of universal adventure: 1. The Plan of Progressive Attainment—the bestowal of the Thought Adjusters and personality. 2. The Bestowal Plan—the incarnation of Creator Sons as guides and rehabilitators. 3. The Plan of Mercy Ministry—the Infinite Spirit's enterprise of mercy ministry. Having promulgated the universal mandate, "Be you perfect, even as I am perfect," the Father entrusted the execution of this tremendous undertaking to the Eternal Son; and the Eternal Son shares the fostering of this supernal enterprise with his divine co-ordinate, the Infinite Spirit.

7:5. The Spirit of Bestowal

The Eternal Son draws near to created personalities by a series of down-stepping gradations of divine sonship until he is enabled to stand in man's presence and, at times, as man himself. The Eternal Son did come to mortal man on Urantia when the divine personality of his Son, Michael of Nebadon, incarnated in the human nature of Jesus of Nazareth. The Creator bestowal Sons have become to all evolutionary creatures "the way, the truth, and the life." Long, long ago the Eternal Son bestowed himself upon each of the circuits of the central creation for the enlightenment and advancement of all the inhabitants and pilgrims of Havona. The original Michael, the first-born Creator Son, also passed through the circuits of the central universe and made the Eternal Son real to the creatures of Havona. The Eternal Son is the exemplary inspiration for all the Sons of God in their ministrations of bestowal throughout the universes of time and space.

7:6. The Paradise Sons of God

The lack of a knowledge of the multiple Sons of God is a source of great confusion on Urantia. Every time the Universal Father and the Eternal Son jointly project a new, original, identical, unique, and absolute personal thought, that very instant this creative idea is perfectly and finally personalized in the being and personality of a new and original Creator Son. The Creator Sons go out from Paradise into the universes of time and, with the cooperation of the controlling and creative agencies of the Third Source and Center, complete the organization of the local universes of progressive evolution. Much as the Creator Sons are personalized by the Father and the Son, so are the Magisterial Sons personalized by the Son and the Spirit. These are the Sons who, in the experiences of creature incarnation, earn the right to serve as the judges of survival in the creations of time and space. The Father, Son, and Spirit also unite to personalize the versatile Trinity Teacher Sons, who range the grand universe as the supernal teachers of all personalities. All Sons of God who take origin in the persons of the Paradise Deities are in direct and constant communication with the Eternal Mother Son. And such communication is instantaneous.

7:7. The Supreme Revelation of the Father

The Eternal Son is a complete, exclusive, universal, and final revelation of the spirit and the personality of the Universal Father. The character of God is amplified by the Son and his Sons by divestment of the nonpersonal and nonspiritual for revelation to creature beings. The Eternal Son and his Sons reveal the avenue of creature approach to the Universal Father. More of the character and merciful nature of the Eternal Son you should comprehend as you meditate on the revelation of these divine attributes which was made in loving service by your own Creator Son, onetime Son of Man on earth, now the exalted sovereign of your local universe.

Paper 8: The Infinite Spirit
Divine Counselor

THE very instant that God the Father and God the Son conjointly conceive an identical and infinite action—the execution of an absolute thought-plan—that very moment, the Infinite Spirit springs full-fledgedly into existence. In reality they are all three existent from eternity; they are co-ordinate, supreme, ultimate, absolute, and infinite.

8:1. The God of Action

The God of Action functions and the dead vaults of space are astir. One billion perfect spheres flash into existence. The Infinite Spirit eternalizes concurrently with the birth of the Havona worlds. The Third Person deitizes by this very act of conjoint creation, and he thus forever becomes the Conjoint Creator. These are the grand and awful times of creative expansion. There exists no record of these stirring times. We have only the meager disclosures of the Infinite Spirit to substantiate these mighty transactions; this is the traditional starting point of the history of the universe of universes. Beyond this event lie the unsearchable transactions of eternity and the depths of infinity—absolute mystery.

8:2. Nature of the Infinite Spirit

The Conjoint Creator is from eternity and is wholly and without qualification one with the Universal Father and the Eternal Son. The Third Source and Center is known by numerous titles but would be better comprehended if he were called the Infinite Reality, the Universal Organizer, or the Personality Co-ordinator. Of all aspects of the Father's nature, the Conjoint Creator most strikingly discloses his infinity. The spirit presence, energy control, and mind potential of the Conjoint Actor is limitless. The Spirit is a mercy minister. We can the better comprehend the Father's goodness in the actions of the Spirit. The Father's faithfulness and the Son's constancy are made very real to the spirit beings and the material creatures of the spheres by the loving ministry and ceaseless service of the personalities of the Infinite Spirit.

8:3. Relation of the Spirit to the Father and the Son

The Eternal Son and the Conjoint Creator have, as partners and through their co-ordinate personalities, planned and fashioned every post-Havona universe which has been brought into existence. The Infinite Spirit is the effective agent of the all-loving Father and the all-merciful Son for the execution of their conjoint project of drawing to themselves all truth-loving souls on all the worlds of time and space. The Eternal Son is the only avenue of approach to the Universal Father, and the Infinite Spirit is the only means of attaining the Eternal Son. At the center of all things the Infinite Spirit is the first of the Paradise Deities to be attained by the ascending pilgrims. And in many other ways does the Spirit equally represent and similarly serve the Father and the Son.

8:4. The Spirit of Divine Ministry

Everlasting ministry to mind is the essence of the Spirit's divine character. God is love, the Son is mercy, the Spirit is ministry—the ministry of divine love and endless mercy to all intelligent creation. The Spirit is love applied to the creature creation, the combined love of the Father and the Son. When a Creator Son of God accepts the creatorship charge of responsibility for a projected local universe, the Creative Daughter accompanying him is devoted to the task of fostering the ascension of mortals to higher levels of spiritual attainment. The Infinite Spirit and his co-ordinate Spirits do joyfully undergo an amazing series of divinity attenuations, until they appear as angels to stand by your side and guide you through the lowly paths of earthly existence.

8:5. The Presence of God

The outstanding attribute of the Infinite Spirit is omnipresence. This Spirit pervades the universe of universes.

The Holy Spirit is the spiritual circuit of the Creative Daughter of the Paradise Infinite Spirit. There are many spiritual influences, and they are all as one, notwithstanding their diverse origins. Ever remember that the Infinite Spirit is the Conjoint Actor; both the Father and the Son are functioning in and through him. It would be consistent to refer to the liaison of all spiritual ministry as the spirit of God, for such a liaison is truly the union of the spirits of God the Father, God the Son, God the Spirit, and God the Sevenfold, even the spirit of God the Supreme.

8:6. Personality of the Infinite Spirit

The Infinite Spirit is a complete and perfect personality, the divine equal and co-ordinate of the Universal Father and the Eternal Son. The Spirit is endowed with absolute mind. Even though we behold the phenomenon of the ministry of the Infinite Spirit to the remote worlds of the universe of universes, even though we envisage this same co-ordinating Deity acting in and through the untold legions of the manifold beings who take origin in the Third Source and Center, even though we recognize the omnipresence of the Spirit, nonetheless, we still affirm that this same Third Source and Center is a person, the Conjoint Creator of all things and all beings and all universes.

Paper 9:
Relation of the Infinite Spirit to the Universe
Divine Counselor

NOTHING in the personalization of the Conjoint Actor foreshadows his identity as an unlimited spirituality co-ordinated with absolute mind and endowed with unique prerogatives of energy manipulation. His coming into being completes the Father's liberation from the bonds of centralized perfection and from the fetters of personality absolutism. The Conjoint Actor possesses unique prerogatives of synthesis, infinite capacity to co-ordinate all existing universe energies, all actual universe spirits, and all real universe intellects; the Third Source and Center is the universal unifier of the manifold energies and diverse creations which have appeared in consequence of the divine plan and the eternal purpose of the Universal Father. The Infinite Spirit is a universal and divine minister. The Conjoint Actor is the revelation of the unity of God, in whom all things consist—things, meanings, and values; energies, minds, and spirits.

9:1. Attributes of the Third Source and Center

The Third Source and Center is known by many names. As the Absolute Mind, he is the source of the endowment of intellect throughout the universes. As the God of Action, he is the apparent ancestor of motion, change, and relationship. As Conjoint Creator he embodies the fullness of the combined and infinite concepts of the First and Second Persons of Deity. The Conjoint Actor is the correlator of all actual reality. The absolute mind of the Conjoint Creator wields great power in the spiritual world, and exerts a mighty influence over energy and matter. The Infinite Spirit is a being provisionally subordinate in sovereignty but in many ways apparently the most versatile in action. He is superbly endowed with those attributes of patience, mercy, and love which are so exquisitely revealed in his spiritual ministry.

The universe of your origin is being forged out between the anvil of justice and the hammer of suffering; but those who wield the hammer are the children of mercy, the spirit offspring of the Infinite Spirit.

9:2. The Omnipresent Spirit

The Infinite Spirit is a personalized spiritualization of the Eternal Son and the Universal Father. The Third Person in his spiritual ministry may function as mind plus spirit or as spirit alone. The divine influence and beneficence of the Infinite Spirit functions as the Holy Spirit of the local universe. The divine spirits which work for man's uplifting and spiritualization all act in unison and in perfect co-operation. They are as one in the spiritual operation of the plans of mortal ascension and perfection attainment.

9:3. The Universal Manipulator

The Isle of Paradise is the source and substance of physical gravity. Gravity cannot be modified or annulled except by the forces and energies functionally associated with the Conjoint Actor. The Infinite Spirit possesses a unique and amazing power—antigravity. The Conjoint Creator is the manipulator of energy. The universe of universes is permeated by the power-control creatures who have to do with the regulation and stabilization of physical energies. Paradise is the pattern of infinity; the God of Action is the activator of that pattern and injects spontaneity into the mechanism of the physical creation.

9:4. The Absolute Mind

The absolute mind is the mind of the Third Person. The mind endowment of the seven superuniverses is derived from the Seven Master Spirits, the primary personalities of the Conjoint Creator. Cosmic force responds to mind even as cosmic mind responds to spirit. Energy is thing, mind is meaning, spirit is value. Mind transmutes the values of spirit into the meanings of intellect; volition has power to bring the meanings of mind to fruit in both the material and spiritual domains. The absolute mind of the Infinite Spirit in the Paradise ascent involves a relative and differential growth in spirit, mind, and energy.

9:5. The Ministry of Mind

The Third Source and Center is infinite in mind. The realms of creature mind are of exclusive origin in the Third Source and Center. The unique feature of mind is that it can be bestowed upon such a wide range of life. The Infinite Spirit ministers to human and subhuman intellect through the adjutants of the local universes. Human intellect is rooted in the material origin of the animal races. Too often, all too often, you mar your minds by insincerity and sear them with unrighteousness; you subject them to animal fear and distort them by useless anxiety. The contemplation of the immature and inactive human intellect should lead only to reactions of humility.

9:6. The Mind-Gravity Circuit

The Third Source and Center, is personally conscious of every mind, every intellect, in all creation, and he maintains a personal and perfect contact with all these physical, morontial, and spiritual creatures of mind endowment in the far-flung universes. The Conjoint Actor exercises a drawing power on all minds. Mind gravity can operate independently of material and spiritual gravity. The greater the spirit-energy divergence, the greater the observable function of mind. Here mind seems to function in a mid-zone between energy and spirit. Not all the observable function of mind is predictable. We believe that this unpredictability is partly attributable to the function of the Universal Absolute or the incompleteness of the Supreme Being.

9:7. Universe Reflectivity

The Conjoint Actor is able to co-ordinate all levels of universe actuality. This is the phenomenon of universe reflectivity, that unique and inexplicable power to see, hear, sense, and know all things as they transpire throughout a superuniverse and within the boundaries of the local universes. Reflectivity finally focalizes on Paradise. This enables the universe rulers to know about remote conditions instantaneously, simultaneously with their occurrence. We conjecture that certain features of the phenomenon of reflectivity can be accounted for only by postulating the activity of the Supreme Mind.

9:8. Personalities of the Infinite Spirit

The Infinite Spirit possesses full power to transmit many of his powers and prerogatives to his co-ordinate and subordinate personalities and agencies. The first Deity-creating act of the Infinite Spirit resulted in the existence of the Seven Master Spirits of Paradise, the distributors of the Infinite Spirit to the universes. The next and continuing creative act of the Infinite Spirit is disclosed, from time to time, in the production of the Creative Spirits, the local universe co-ordinates of the Creator Sons. The Third Source and Center is represented in the grand universe by a vast array of ministering spirits, messengers, teachers, adjudicators, helpers, and advisers, together with supervisors of certain circuits of physical, morontial, and spiritual nature. There are personalities of the Third Source and Center, beings who are personal to the Infinite Spirit, but who are not unqualifiedly personal to creature beings. There are numerous types of Third Source personalities. The Infinite Spirit can also act for the Father in the bestowal of First Source personality.

Infinite Spirit family summary: I. *Supreme Spirits*—Seven Master Spirits, Reflective Spirits, and Creative Spirits. II. *The Power Directors*. III. *Personalities*—Higher Personalities, Messenger Hosts, Ministering Spirits. The spirit personalities of the vast family of the Infinite Spirit are forever dedicated to the service of the ministry of the love of God and the mercy of the Son. These spirit beings constitute the living ladder whereby mortal man climbs from chaos to glory.

Paper 10: The Paradise Trinity

Universal Censor

THE Paradise Trinity of eternal Deities facilitates the Father's escape from personality absolutism. The Paradise Trinity effectively provides for the full expression and perfect revelation of the eternal nature of Deity. The Trinity is Deity unity. I deem the Trinity to have been inevitable.

10:1. Self-Distribution of the First Source and Center

There is inherent in the selfless, loving, and lovable nature of the Universal Father something which causes him to reserve to himself the exercise of only those powers and that authority which he apparently finds it impossible to delegate or to bestow. In the affairs of a local universe, he has made each Sovereign Creator Son just as perfect, competent, and authoritative as is the Eternal Son. Creators are moved to share divinity with their universe children. Mortal man must look to the Paradise Sons for reliable and trustworthy information regarding the Father, the Son, and the Spirit.

10:2. Deity Personalization

By the technique of trinitization the Father divests himself of that unqualified spirit personality which is the Son and thereby possesses himself of unlimited capacity to become the divine Father of all subsequently created, eventuated, or other personalized types of intelligent will creatures. He forever maintains personal relations of loving association with this vast family of universe children. In the Father-Son union, the eternal partners conjointly bestow those qualities and attributes which constitute another being like themselves; and this conjoint personality, the Infinite Spirit, completes the existential personalization of Deity.

10:3. The Three Persons of Deity

Notwithstanding there is only one Deity, there are three positive and divine personalizations of Deity. God speaks through the Son and, with the Son, acts through the Infinite Spirit. We observe that the Father has divested himself of all direct manifestations of absoluteness except absolute fatherhood and absolute volition.

The First Source and Center functions outside of Havona in the phenomenal universes as follows: 1. As creator, through the Creator Sons, his grandsons. 2. As controller, through the gravity center of Paradise. 3. As spirit, through the Eternal Son. 4. As mind, through the Conjoint Creator. 5. As a Father, maintaining parental contact with all creatures through his personality circuit. 6. As a person, acting *directly* throughout creation by his exclusive fragments—in mortal man by the Thought Adjusters. 7. As total Deity, functioning only in the Paradise Trinity.

The Eternal Son functions as an absolute person in the domain of the spiritual universe.

The Infinite Spirit is amazingly universal and unbelievably versatile in all his operations. He performs in the spheres of mind, matter, and spirit.

10:4. The Trinity Union of Deity

The Trinity is an association of infinite persons functioning in a nonpersonal capacity but not in contravention of personality. The Father, Son, and Spirit can collaborate in a non-Trinity manner, but not as three Deities. As persons they can collaborate as they choose, but that is not the Trinity. The Trinity is so related to total universe affairs that it must be reckoned with in our attempts to explain the totality of any isolated cosmic event or personality relationship. As a mortal in the flesh you should view the Trinity in accordance with your individual enlightenment. You can know very little of the absoluteness of the Trinity, but as you ascend Paradiseward, you will many times experience astonishment at successive revelations and unexpected discoveries of Trinity supremacy and ultimacy, if not of absoluteness.

10:5. Functions of the Trinity

The personal Deities have attributes, but it is hardly consistent to speak of the Trinity as having attributes. This association of divine beings may more properly be regarded as having functions, such as justice administration, totality attitudes, co-ordinate action, and cosmic overcontrol. The Trinity association of the three Paradise Deities results in the evolution, eventuation, and deitization of new meanings, values, powers, and capacities for universal revelation, action, and administration. The maximum self-limitation of the Trinity is its attitude toward the finite. The Paradise Trinity has regard for absonite levels of existence, levels which are more than finite but less than absolute. The *Absolute Attitude* of the Paradise Trinity is in relation to absolute existences and culminates in the action of total Deity. I do not command language which would enable me to convey to the limited human mind the full truth and the eternal significance of the Paradise Trinity.

10:6. The Stationary Sons of the Trinity

The application of law, justice, falls within the province of the Paradise Trinity and is carried out by certain Sons of the Trinity. Justice is not the attitude of the Father, the Son, or the Spirit. Justice is the Trinity attitude of these personalities of love, mercy, and ministry. Justice is never a personal attitude; it is always a plural function. Judgment is the work of the Stationary Sons of the Trinity: 1. Trinitized Secrets of Supremacy; 2. Eternals of Days;

3. Ancients of Days; 4. Perfections of Days; 5. Recents of Days; 6. Unions of Days; 7. Faithfuls of Days; 8. Perfectors of Wisdom; 9. Divine Counselors; 10. Universal Censors. The Ancients of Days and their Trinity-origin associates mete out the just judgment of supreme fairness to the seven superuniverses. Divine judgment is the soul of fairness, ever fulfilling the divine love of God.

10:7. The Overcontrol of Supremacy

As things appear to the mortal on the finite level, the Paradise Trinity, like the Supreme Being, is concerned only with the total—total planet, total universe, total superuniverse, total grand universe. This totality attitude exists because the Trinity is the total of Deity. We do not find the overcontrol of Supremacy to be wholly predictable. The mortal mind can immediately think of a thousand and one things—catastrophic physical events, appalling accidents, horrific disasters, painful illnesses, and world-wide scourges—and ask whether such visitations are correlated in the unknown maneuvering of this probable functioning of the Supreme Being. Frankly, we do not know; we are not really sure. But we do observe that, as time passes, all these difficult and more or less mysterious situations always work out for the welfare and progress of the universes. In the progress of eternity the acts of the Trinity will be revealed as altogether meaningful and considerate, but they do not always so appear to the creatures of time.

10:8. The Trinity Beyond the Finite

Many truths and facts pertaining to the Paradise Trinity can only be even partially comprehended by recognizing a function that transcends the finite. The Corps of the Finality embrace, among others, those mortals of time and space who have attained perfection in all that pertains to the will of God. Having thus found God as the Father of all creatures, these finaliters must sometime begin the quest for the superfinite Father. But this quest involves a grasp of the absonite nature of the ultimate attributes and character of the Paradise Father. Eternity will disclose whether such an attainment is possible, but we are convinced, even if the finaliters do grasp this ultimate of divinity, they will probably be unable to attain the superultimate levels of absolute Deity. It may be possible that the finaliters will partially attain the Deity Absolute. Only infinity can disclose the Father-Infinite.

Paper 11: The Eternal Isle of Paradise

Perfector of Wisdom

PARADISE is the eternal center of the universe of universes and the abiding place of the Universal Father, the Eternal Son, the Infinite Spirit, and their divine co-ordinates and associates. This central Isle is the most gigantic organized body of cosmic reality in all the master universe. The depths of the spiritual beauty and the wonders of this magnificent ensemble are utterly beyond the comprehension of the finite mind. Paradise is from eternity; there are neither records nor traditions respecting the origin of this nuclear Isle of Light and Life.

11:1. The Divine Residence

God dwells, has dwelt, and everlastingly will dwell in this same central and eternal abode. Provided with all the necessities for the journey, it is just as possible to find the personal presence of God at the center of all things as to find distant cities on your own planet.

11:2. Nature of the Eternal Isle

In form Paradise is ellipsoid, being one-sixth longer in the north-south diameter than in the east-west diameter. The central Isle is geographically divided into three domains of activity: Upper Paradise, Peripheral Paradise, and Nether Paradise. The Trinity seems to dominate the personal or upper plane, the Unqualified Absolute the nether or impersonal plane. The eternal Isle is composed of a single form of materialization not to be found elsewhere in all the wide universe of universes. The Melchizedeks of Nebadon long since named it *absolutum*. This Paradise source material is neither dead nor alive. Paradise exists without time and has no location in space. Roughly: space seemingly originates just below nether Paradise; time just above upper Paradise. The citizens of the central Isle are fully conscious of nontime sequence of events. Paradise is nonspatial; hence its areas are absolute and therefore serviceable in many ways beyond the concept of mortal mind.

11:3. Upper Paradise

On upper Paradise there are three grand spheres of activity: the Deity presence, the Most Holy Sphere, and the Holy Area. The Most Holy Sphere is reserved for the functions of worship, trinitization, and high spiritual attainment. The Holy Area, the outlying or residential region, is divided into seven concentric zones. The inner or first zone is occupied by Paradise Citizens and the natives of Havona who may chance to be dwelling on Paradise. The next or second zone is the residential area of the natives of the seven superuniverses of time and space. Each of the seven sectors of Paradise is subdivided into residential units suitable for the lodgment headquarters of one billion glorified individual working groups. The number of these units is beyond mortal comprehension. This staggering number of residential designations occupies considerably less than one per cent of the assigned area of the Holy Land. There is still plenty of room for those who are on their way inward, even for those who shall not start the Paradise climb until the times of the eternal future.

11:4. Peripheral Paradise

The peripheral surface of Paradise is occupied, in part, by the landing and dispatching fields for various groups of spirit personalities. Neither upper nor nether Paradise is approachable by transport supernaphim or other types of space traversers.

The Seven Master Spirits have their personal seats of power and authority on the seven spheres of the Spirit, which circle about Paradise in the space between the shining orbs of the Son and the inner circuit of the Havona worlds, but they maintain force-focal headquarters on the Paradise periphery. Here the slowly circulating presences of the Seven Supreme Power Directors indicate the location of the seven flash stations for certain Paradise energies going forth to the seven superuniverses. Here on peripheral Paradise are also the enormous historic and prophetic exhibit areas assigned to the Creator Sons, dedicated to the local universes of time and space. There are just seven trillion of these historic reservations now set up or in reserve, but these arrangements altogether occupy only about four per cent of that portion of the peripheral area thus assigned. Paradise is large enough to accommodate the activities of an almost infinite creation.

11:5. Nether Paradise

Concerning nether Paradise, we know only that which is revealed; personalities do not sojourn there. We are informed that all physical-energy and cosmic-force circuits have their origin on nether Paradise. The inner zone of the force center seems to act as a gigantic heart whose pulsations direct currents to the outermost borders of physical space. All forms of force and all phases of energy seem to be encircuited; they circulate throughout the universes and return by definite routes. The outer zone pulsates in agelong cycles of gigantic proportions. For a little more than one billion Urantia years the space-force of this center is outgoing; then for a similar length of time it will be incoming. All physical force, energy, and matter are one.

11:6. Space Respiration

We do not know the actual mechanism of space respiration; we merely observe that all space alternately contracts and expands. This respiration affects both the horizontal extension of pervaded space and the vertical extensions of unpervaded space which exist in the vast space reservoirs above and below Paradise. We do not know whether there is a creative intent concerning unpervaded space; we really know very little about the space reservoirs. Pervaded space is now approaching the mid-point of the expanding phase, while unpervaded space nears the mid-point of the contracting phase. It requires a little over two billion Urantia years to complete the entire expansion-contraction cycle.

11:7. Space Functions of Paradise

Space does not exist on any of the surfaces of Paradise. Paradise is the actually motionless nucleus of the relatively quiescent zones existing between pervaded and unpervaded space.

The vertical cross section of total space would slightly resemble a maltese cross, with the horizontal arms representing pervaded (universe) space and the vertical arms representing unpervaded (reservoir) space. If you imagine a finite, but inconceivably large, V-shaped plane situated at right angles to both the upper and lower surfaces of Paradise, with its point nearly tangent to peripheral Paradise, and then visualize this plane in elliptical revolution about Paradise, its revolution would roughly outline the volume of pervaded space. The relatively quiet zone between the space levels, such as that separating the seven superuniverses from the first outer space level, are enormous elliptical regions. You may visualize the first outer space level, where untold universes are now in process of formation, as a vast procession of galaxies swinging around Paradise, bounded above and below by the midspace zones of quiescence and bounded on the inner and outer margins by relatively quiet space zones. The alternate zoning of the master universe, in association with the alternate clockwise and counterclockwise flow of the galaxies, is a factor in the stabilization of physical gravity designed to prevent the accentuation of gravity pressure to the point of disruptive and dispersive activities.

11:8. Paradise Gravity

Gravity is the all-powerful grasp of the physical presence of Paradise. Space is nonresponsive to gravity, but it acts as an equilibrant on gravity. Local or linear gravity pertains to the electrical stage of energy or matter; it operates within the central, super-, and outer universes, wherever suitable materialization has taken place. Paradise is the absolute source and the eternal focal point of all energy-matter in the universe of universes.

11:9. The Uniqueness of Paradise

Paradise is unique in that it is the realm of primal origin and the final goal of destiny for all spirit personalities. In the eternity of the past, when the Universal Father gave infinite personality expression of his spirit self in the being of the Eternal Son, simultaneously he revealed the infinity potential of his nonpersonal self as Paradise. The tension between the spiritual and nonspiritual (personal and nonpersonal), in the face of will to action by the Father and the Son, gave existence to the Conjoint Actor and the central universe of material worlds and spiritual beings. Paradise is the absolute of patterns; Havona is an exhibit of these potentials in actuality. Paradise is the universal headquarters of all personality activities and the source-center of all force-space and energy manifestations. Every God-knowing mortal who has espoused the career of doing the Father's will has already embarked upon the long, long Paradise trail of divinity pursuit and perfection attainment. Such an achievement represents the reality of a spiritual transformation bordering on the limits of supremacy.

Paper 12: The Universe of Universes
Perfector of Wisdom

THE immensity of the far-flung creation of the Universal Father is utterly beyond the grasp of finite imagination. To created beings the master universe might appear to be almost infinite, but it is far from finished and the experiential revelation of the eternal purpose is still in progress.

12:1. Space Levels of the Master Universe

The successive space levels of the master universe constitute the major divisions of pervaded space which are partially inhabited or yet to be organized and inhabited. Proceeding outward from Paradise through the horizontal extension of pervaded space, the master universe is existent in six concentric ellipses: the Central Universe—Havona, the Seven Superuniverses, and four outer space levels. Havona consists of one billion spheres of sublime perfection and is surrounded by enormous dark gravity bodies. At the center of Havona is the stationary and absolutely stabilized Isle of Paradise, surrounded by its twenty-one satellites. The seven superuniverses are geographic space clusterings of approximately one seventh of the organized and partially inhabited post-Havona creation. Nebadon, your local universe, is one of the newer creations in Orvonton, the seventh superuniverse. The grand universe is the present organized and inhabited creation. The outer space levels are assembling vast and unbelievably stupendous circuits of force and materializing energies. The four outer space levels are undoubtedly destined to eventuate-evolve the ultimacy of creation. There are those who postulate an ever-expanding, never-ending universe of infinity.

12:2. The Domains of the Unqualified Absolute

The space regions extending beyond the outer borders of the seven superuniverses are generally recognized as constituting the domains of the Unqualified Absolute. The physicists of Uversa calculate that the energy and matter of these outer and uncharted regions already equal many times the total material mass and energy charge embraced in all seven superuniverses. We know very little of the significance of these tremendous phenomena of outer space. Throughout Orvonton it is believed that a new type of creation is in process, an order of universes destined to become the scene of the future activities of the assembling Corps of the Finality.

12:3. Universal Gravity

All forms of force-energy—material, mindal, spiritual and personality—are subject to those grasps which we call gravity. *Physical Gravity*: At the present moment about ninety-five per cent of the active cosmic-gravity action of the Isle of Paradise is engaged in controlling material systems beyond the borders of the present organized universes. *Spiritual Gravity*: At the present time, practically the entire spirit gravity of the Eternal Son is observable as functioning in the grand universe. *Mind Gravity*: About eighty-five per cent of the mind-gravity response to the intellectual drawing of the Conjoint Actor takes origin in the existing grand universe. This would suggest the possibility that mind activities are involved in connection with the observable physical activities now in progress throughout the realms of outer space. Personality Gravity is noncomputable. We recognize the circuit, but we cannot measure either qualitative or quantitative realities responsive thereto.

12:4. Space and Motion

The universes of space and their component systems and worlds are all revolving spheres, moving along the endless circuits of the master universe space levels. We think the Conjoint Actor initiates motion in space. In outer space the force organizers are apparently responsible for the production of the gigantic universe wheels which are now in process of stellar evolution. Space contains and conditions motion. The vast universes of the first outer space level are at the present time revolving clockwise about the central creation. The seven superuniverses revolve about Paradise in a counterclockwise direction. It is probable that these alternate directions of successive space processions of the universes have something to do with the intramaster universe gravity technique of the Universal Absolute.

12:5. Space and Time

Like space, time is a bestowal of Paradise. Time comes by virtue of motion and because mind is inherently aware of sequentiality. Time and space are inseparable only in the time-space creations, the seven superuniverses. Man's mind is less time-bound than space-bound. Unspiritual animals know only the past and live in the present. Spirit-indwelt man has powers of prevision (insight); he may visualize the future. Ethics and morals become truly human when they are dynamic and progressive, alive with universe reality.

The relatively motionless midspace zones impinging on Paradise and separating pervaded from unpervaded space are the transition zones from time to eternity, hence the necessity of Paradise pilgrims becoming unconscious during this transit when it is to culminate in Paradise citizenship. Time-conscious visitors can go to Paradise without thus sleeping, but they remain creatures of time.

12:6. Universal Overcontrol

Stability is the product of balanced energies, co-operative minds, co-ordinated morontias, spirit overcontrol, and personality unification. Stability is wholly and always proportional to divinity. The universe is highly predictable only in the quantitative or gravity-measurement sense. When matter, mind, and spirit are unified by creature personality, we are unable fully to predict the decisions of such a freewill being. Individuals have their guardians of destiny; planets, systems, constellations, universes, and superuniverses each have their respective rulers who labor for the good of their domains. The fundamental needs and overcare of the master universe is probably the result of the action of the Paradise Trinity. The Ultimate is progressively integrating the creative organization of the potentials of the three Absolutes.

12:7. The Part and the Whole

The will of God does not necessarily prevail in the part—the heart of any one personality—but his will does actually rule the whole, the universe of universes. Law is the unchanging reaction of an infinite, perfect, and divine mind. The love of the Father absolutely individualizes each personality as a unique child of the Universal Father, a child without duplicate in infinity, a will creature irreplaceable in all eternity. This very love of God for the individual brings into being the divine family of all individuals, the universal brotherhood. No person can escape the benefits or the penalties that may come as a result of relationship to other persons. As the progress of the whole, so the progress of the part. The relative velocities of part and whole determine whether the part is retarded by the inertia of the whole or is carried forward by the momentum of the cosmic brotherhood. The Father is not very far from any one of you; he dwells within you, and in him do we all literally move, actually live, and veritably have our being.

12:8. Matter, Mind, and Spirit

Physical energy is the one reality which is true and steadfast in its obedience to universal law. As the mind of any personality in the universe becomes more spiritual—Godlike—it becomes less responsive to material gravity. Mind is the technique whereby spirit realities become experiential to creature personalities. True spirit is not subject to physical gravity but eventually becomes the motivating influence of all evolving energy systems of personality dignity. The goal of existence of all personalities is spirit. On Paradise the three energies, physical, mindal, and spiritual, are co-ordinate. In the evolutionary cosmos energy-matter is dominant except in personality, where spirit, through the mediation of mind, is striving for the mastery. Spirit is unchanging, and therefore, in all personality relations, it transcends both mind and matter. Consciousness of divinity is a progressive spiritual experience.

12:9. Personal Realities

Spirit is the basic personal reality in the universes, and personality is basic to all progressing experience with spiritual reality. Man's true destiny consists in the creation of new and spirit goals and then in responding to the cosmic allurements of such supernal goals. Love is the secret of beneficial association between personalities. Not only in the realms of life but even in the world of physical energy, the sum of two or more things is very often something more than, or something different from, the predictable additive consequences of such unions. The entire fields of science and philosophy could not predict or know that the union of two gaseous hydrogen atoms with one gaseous oxygen atom would result in a new and qualitatively superadditive substance—liquid water. The understanding knowledge of this one physiochemical phenomenon should have prevented the development of materialistic philosophy and mechanistic cosmology. Technical analysis does not reveal what a person or a thing can do. Your religion is becoming real because it is emerging from the slavery of fear and the bondage of superstition. Your philosophy struggles for emancipation from dogma and tradition. Your science is engaged in the deliverance from the bondage of abstraction, the slavery of mathematics, and the relative blindness of mechanistic materialism. Mortal man has a spirit nucleus. Real trouble, lasting disappointment, or serious defeat can come only after self-concepts presume fully to displace the governing power of the central spirit nucleus.

Paper 13: The Sacred Spheres of Paradise
Perfector of Wisdom

BETWEEN the central Isle of Paradise and the innermost of the Havona planetary circuits there are situated in space three lesser circuits of special spheres. The innermost circuit consists of the seven secret spheres of the Universal Father; the second group is composed of the seven luminous worlds of the Eternal Son; in the outermost are the seven immense spheres of the Infinite Spirit, the executive-headquarters worlds of the Seven Master Spirits.

13:1. The Seven Sacred Worlds of the Father

The Father's circuit of sacred life spheres contains the only inherent personality secrets in the universe of universes. One of the reasons for the secrecy of these worlds is that each of these sacred spheres enjoys a specialized representation of the Deities composing the Paradise Trinity.

Divinington is the Paradise rendezvous of the Thought Adjusters. *Sonarington* is the Paradise home for all Sons of the Eternal Son and of his co-ordinate and associate Sons, including the secrets of the incarnation of the divine Sons.

Spiritington is the Paradise home of the high beings that exclusively represent the Infinite Spirit and the mysteries of reflectivity.

Vicegerington is the Paradise home of many glorified beings of complex ancestry and the secrets of trinitization.

Solitarington is the rendezvous of a magnificent host of unrevealed beings of origin in the conjoint acts of the Universal Father and the Infinite Spirit.

Seraphington is the home world of the vast hosts of unrevealed beings created by the Son and the Spirit, the angelic hosts, and the mystery of seraphic transport.

Ascendington is the rendezvous of the ascendant creatures of space. The secrets of Ascendington include one of the most perplexing mysteries of the universes—the evolution of an immortal soul within the mind of a mortal and material creature.

13:2. Father-World Relationships

As finaliters you will be domiciled on Paradise, but Ascendington will be your home address at all times, even when you enter service in outer space. Ascendington is the only sacred sphere that will be unreservedly open to your inspection as a Paradise arrival. When you mortals attain Havona, you are granted clearance for Ascendington. After you attain Paradise, you will know and ardently love the ten Secrets of Supremacy who direct Ascendington. After your admission to the Corps of the Finality, you are granted clearance for Sonarington since you are sons of God as well as ascenders. But there will always remain one seventh of Sonarington, the sector of the incarnation secrets of the divine Sons, which will not be open to your scrutiny.

13:3. The Sacred Worlds of the Eternal Son

The seven luminous spheres of the Eternal Son are the worlds of the seven phases of pure-spirit existence. These shining orbs are the source of the threefold light of Paradise and Havona. Personality is not present on these Paradise satellites. We infer that impersonal spirits are being assembled here for ministry in the projected new universes of outer space.

13:4. The Worlds of the Infinite Spirit

The seven worlds of the Infinite Spirit are inhabited by the offspring of the Infinite Spirit, by the trinitized sons of glorified created personalities, and by other types of unrevealed beings. The Seven Master Spirits are the supreme and ultimate representatives of the Infinite Spirit. From these seven special spheres the Master Spirits operate to equalize and stabilize the cosmic-mind circuits of the grand universe. To me, these executive worlds are the most interesting and intriguing spots outside of Paradise. In no other place in the wide universe can one observe such varied activities, involving so many different orders of living beings, having to do with operations on so many diverse levels, occupations at once material, intellectual, and spiritual.

Paper 14: The Central and Divine Universe
Perfector of Wisdom

THE perfect and divine universe occupies the center of all creation. It is of enormous dimensions and almost unbelievable mass and consists of one billion spheres of unimagined beauty and superb grandeur. This is the one and only settled, perfect, and established aggregation of worlds.

14:1. The Paradise-Havona System

The billion worlds of Havona are arranged in seven concentric circuits immediately surrounding the three circuits of Paradise satellites. Time is not reckoned on Paradise; but time is germane to the Havona circuits. Each Havona world has its own local time, and all worlds in a given circuit have the same length of year. Besides Havona-circuit time, there is the Paradise-Havona standard day. One Paradise-Havona day is just seven minutes, three and one-eighth seconds less than one thousand years of the present Urantia leap-year calendar. This Paradise-Havona day is the standard time measurement for the seven superuniverses, although each maintains its own internal time standards.

14:2. Constitution of Havona

Havona energies are threefold. The material of Havona consists of the organization of exactly one thousand basic chemical elements and the balanced function of the seven forms of Havona energy. Havona natives respond to forty-nine differing specialized forms of sensation. The morontia senses are seventy, and the higher spiritual orders of reaction response vary in different types of beings from seventy to two hundred and ten. The universal spiritual gravity of the Eternal Son is amazingly active throughout the central universe.

Likewise does the Infinite Spirit draw all intellectual values Paradiseward. Havona is a spiritually perfect and physically stable universe. So perfect are the methods and means of selection in the universes of time that no ascendant soul has ever been prematurely admitted to the central universe.

14:3. The Havona Worlds

Concerning the government of the central universe, there is none. Here may be observed the height of the ideals of true self-government. Havona requires only administrative direction. It is vested in the resident Eternal of Days. They teach with supreme skill and direct their planetary children with a perfection of wisdom bordering on absoluteness. The architecture, lighting, and heating, as well as the biologic and artistic embellishment, of the Havona spheres, are quite beyond the greatest possible stretch of human imagination. Manifold activities take place on these beautiful worlds which are far beyond human comprehension.

14:4. Creatures of the Central Universe

There are seven basic forms of living things and beings on the Havona worlds: material, morontial, spiritual, absonite, ultimate, coabsolute, and absolute. The Havona natives are all the offspring of the Paradise Trinity. Havoners minister in many ways to Paradise descenders and to superuniverse ascenders, but they also live lives that are unique in the central universe. Havoners have both optional present and future unrevealed destinies. Havona teems with the life of all phases of intelligent beings, who there seek to advance from lower to higher circuits in their efforts to attain higher levels of divinity realization and enlarged appreciation of supreme meanings, ultimate values, and absolute reality.

14:5. Life in Havona

On the seven circuits of Havona your attainment is intellectual, spiritual, and experiential. And there is a definite task to be achieved on each of the worlds of each of these circuits. The social and economic activities of this eternal creation are entirely dissimilar to the occupations of material creatures living on evolutionary worlds like Urantia. Even the technique of Havona thought is unlike the process of thinking on Urantia. There is a refreshing originality about this vast central creation. Every one of these planets is an original, unique, and exclusive creation. Each of these billion study worlds is a veritable university of surprises. Not until you traverse the last of the Havona circuits and visit the last of the Havona worlds, will the tonic of adventure and the stimulus of curiosity disappear from your career. And then will the urge, the forward impulse of eternity, replace its forerunner, the adventure lure of time.

14:6. The Purpose of the Central Universe

The Universal Father derives supreme parental satisfaction from the perfection of the central creation. Our Father beholds the central universe with perfect pleasure because it is a worthy revelation of spirit reality to all personalities of the universe of universes. To the Eternal Son the superb central creation affords eternal proof of the partnership effectiveness of the divine family—Father, Son, and Spirit. Havona affords the Eternal Son an almost unlimited base for the ever-expanding realization of spirit power. The Havona universe affords the Infinite Spirit proof of being the Conjoint Actor, compensation for his widespread and unselfish work in the universes of space. The Havona creation is the eternal and perfect proof of the spiritual reality of the Supreme Being, and a perfect pattern of the universality potential of the Supreme.

Havona is the educational training ground where the Paradise Michaels (Creator Sons) are prepared for their subsequent adventures in universe creation. The Paradise Sons regard the central creation as their home. The Universe Mother Spirits secure their prepersonal training on the worlds of Havona in close association with the Spirits of the Circuits. On the worlds of Havona the Spirit and the Daughters of the Spirit find the mind patterns for all their groups of spiritual and material intelligences. Havona is the pre-Paradise training goal of every ascending mortal, the portal to Paradise and God attainment. Paradise is the home, and Havona the workshop and playground, of the finaliters.

Havona will unquestionably continue to function with absonite significance even in future universe ages which may witness space pilgrims attempting to find God on superfinite levels. It will probably be the finishing school when the seven superuniverses are functioning as the intermediate school for the graduates of the primary schools of outer space. We incline to the opinion that the potentials of eternal Havona are really unlimited.

Paper 15: The Seven Superuniverses
Universal Censor

EARLY in the materialization of the universal creation the sevenfold scheme of the superuniverse organization and government was formulated. The rulers of these seven superuniverses are rightly called Ancients of Days. Their marvelous organization provides for spiritual governments and for the intellectual advancement of the will creatures who dwell on the myriads of inhabited planets scattered throughout.

15:1. The Superuniverse Space Level

The seven superuniverses traverse a great ellipse, pursuing a definite and well-understood counterclockwise course around the central universe. Urantia is situated in a local universe and a superuniverse not fully organized. Your local universe of Nebadon belongs to Orvonton, the seventh super-universe, which swings on between superuniverses one and six, having not long since (as we reckon time) turned the southeastern bend of the superuniverse space level. Urantia belongs to a system which is well out towards the borderland of your local universe.

15:2. Organization of the Superuniverses

The *system* is the basic unit of the supergovernment and consists of about one thousand inhabited or inhabitable worlds. Each inhabited planet is presided over by a Planetary Prince, and each local system has an architectural sphere as its headquarters and is ruled by a System Sovereign. The *constellation* has one hundred systems (about 100,000 inhabitable planets). Each constellation has an architectural headquarters sphere and is presided over by three Vorondadek Sons, the Most Highs. Each constellation also has a Faithful of Days in observation, an ambassador of the Paradise Trinity. The *local universe* has one hundred constellations (about 10,000,000 inhabitable planets). Each local universe has a magnificent architectural headquarters world and is ruled by one of the coordinate Creator Sons of God, of the order of Michael. Each universe is blessed by the presence of a Union of Days, a representative of the Paradise Trinity.

The minor sector has one hundred local universes (about 1,000,000,000 inhabitable planets). It has a wonderful headquarters world, wherefrom its rulers, the Recents of Days, administer the affairs of the minor sector. There are three Recents of Days on each minor sector headquarters. The major sector has one hundred minor sectors (about 100,000,000,000 inhabitable worlds). Each major sector is provided with a superb headquarters and is presided over by three Perfections of Days. The superuniverse has ten major sectors (about 1,000,000,000,000 inhabitable planets). Each superuniverse is provided with an enormous and glorious headquarters world and is ruled by three Ancients of Days.

The grand universe has seven superuniverses, consisting of approximately seven trillion inhabitable worlds, plus the architectural spheres and the one billion inhabited spheres of Havona. The superuniverses are ruled and administered indirectly and reflectively from Paradise by the Seven Master Spirits. The billion worlds of Havona are directly administered by the Eternals of Days, one such Supreme Trinity Personality presiding over each of these perfect spheres.

15:3. The Superuniverse of Orvonton

The vast Milky Way starry system represents the central nucleus of Orvonton. The rotational center of your minor sector is situated far away in the enormous and dense star cloud of Sagittarius. The nucleus of the physical system to which your sun and its associated planets belong is the center of the onetime Andronover nebula. Some of the confusion of Urantian star observers arises out of the illusions and relative distortions produced by multiple astronomical revolutionary movements.

15:4. Nebulae—The Ancestors of Universes

Paradise force organizers are nebulae originators which are the source of suns and their varied systems. Nebulae vary greatly in size and in the resulting number and aggregate mass of their stellar and planetary offspring. There are not many sun-forming nebulae active in Orvonton at the present time, though Andromeda, which is outside the inhabited superuniverse, is very active. This far-distant nebula is visible to the naked eye, and when you view it, pause to consider that the light you behold left those distant suns almost one million years ago.

15:5. The Origin of Space Bodies

The bulk of the mass contained in the suns and planets of a superuniverse originates in the nebular wheels. There are numerous techniques for evolving suns and segregating planets. As your star students scan the heavens, they will observe phenomena indicative of the many modes of stellar evolution, but they will seldom detect evidence of the formation of those small, nonluminous collections of matter which serve as inhabited planets, the most important of the vast material creations.

15:6. The Spheres of Space

The various spheres of space are classifiable into the following major divisions: suns, dark islands, comets, meteors, planets, and architectural spheres. The stars of space exist in no fewer than a thousand different states and stages. Some suns shine without heat. The actual energy stored in the invisible particles of physical matter is well-nigh unimaginable. The suns serve as local accelerators of energy circulation, acting as automatic power-control stations.

The dark islands of space are dead suns and other large aggregations of matter devoid of light and heat. The density of some of these large masses is well-nigh unbelievable. These dark islands function as powerful balance wheels. The meteors and other small particles of matter circulating and evolving in space constitute an enormous aggregate of energy and material substance. Light has weight, is a real substance.

Planets are the larger aggregations of matter which follow an orbit around a sun or some other space body. In your solar system only three planets are at present suited to harbor life. An almost endless variety of creature life and other living manifestations characterizes the countless worlds of space.

15:7. The Architectural Spheres

The headquarters worlds are architectural spheres, space bodies specifically constructed for their special purpose. These spheres are independently lighted and heated. Each has a sun which gives forth light without heat.

The standard day of the superuniverse of Orvonton is equal to almost thirty days of Urantia time. The Uversa year equals one hundred standard days and it is twenty-two minutes short of three thousand days of Urantia time, about eight and one fifth of your years. *Jerusem*, the headquarters of your local system of Satania, is the location of the seven mansion worlds of morontia detention, man's first postmortal residence. *Edentia*, the headquarters of your constellation of Norlatiadek, has its seventy satellites of socializing culture and training. *Salvington*, the capital of Nebadon, is surrounded by ten university clusters of forty-nine spheres each; hereon is man spiritualized following his constellation socialization. *Uminor the third*, the headquarters of your minor sector, Ensa, is surrounded by the seven spheres of the higher physical studies of the ascendant life. *Umajor the fifth*, the headquarters of your major sector, Splandon, is surrounded by the seventy spheres of the advancing intellectual training of the superuniverse. *Uversa*, the headquarters of Orvonton, your superuniverse, is immediately surrounded by the seven higher universities of advanced spiritual training for ascending will creatures.

As mortal creatures ascend the universe, passing from the material to the spiritual realms, they never lose their appreciation for, and enjoyment of, their former levels of existence.

15:8. Energy Control and Regulation

The headquarters spheres of the superuniverses are so constructed that they are able to function as efficient power-energy regulators for their various sectors. The Universe Power Directors have the ability to condense and detain, or to expand and liberate, varying quantities of energy. As the larger physical systems become stabilized, they are swung into the balanced and established circuits of the superuniverses. Subsequent to this event no more collisions or other devastating catastrophes will occur in such systems. The farther out in the universe we go, the more certainly we encounter those variational and unpredictable phenomena which are so characteristic of the unfathomable presence-performances of the Absolutes and the experiential Deities. And these phenomena must be indicative of some universal overcontrol of all things. The living power directors and force organizers are the secret of the special control and intelligent direction of the endless metamorphoses of universe making, unmaking, and remaking. Nebulae may disperse, suns burn out, systems vanish, and planets perish, but the universes do not run down.

15:9. Circuits of the Superuniverses

The universal circuits of Paradise do actually pervade the realms of the seven superuniverses. These presence circuits are: the personality gravity of the Universal Father, the spiritual gravity of the Eternal Son, the mind gravity of the Conjoint Actor, and the material gravity of the eternal Isle. In addition there are the superuniverse circuits of the Seven Master Spirits, the Reflective Spirits, the Mystery Monitors, and the Eternal Son and Paradise Sons, as well as the flash presence of the Infinite Spirit, the broadcasts of Paradise, and the energy circuits of the power centers and physical controllers. The local universe circuits are: the Spirit of Truth, the Holy Spirit, and the intelligence-ministry circuit including the adjutant mind-spirits. Your local universe is not even reckoned as belonging to the settled physical order of the superuniverse, much less as holding membership in the recognized spiritual family of the supergovernment.

15:10. Rulers of the Superuniverses

Each superuniverse is presided over by three Ancients of Days. In addition to the Ancients of Days, the executive branch consists of three groups of Co-ordinate Trinity personalities—Perfectors of Wisdom, Divine Counselors, and Universal Censors—and three groups of glorified ascendant mortals—Mighty Messengers, Those High in Authority, and Those Without Name or Number. The coordinate council of the superuniverse also includes the following sector rulers and other regional overseers: Perfections of Days, Recents of Days, Unions of Days, Faithfuls of Days, Trinity Teacher Sons, Eternals of Days, and the Seven Reflective Image Aids. At almost all times it is possible to find representatives of all groups of created beings on the headquarters worlds of the superuniverses. The routine ministering work of the superuniverses is performed by the mighty seconaphim and by other members of the vast family of the Infinite Spirit.

15:11. The Deliberative Assembly

It is on such worlds as Uversa that the beings representative of the autocracy of perfection and the democracy of evolution meet face to face. The legislative or advisory council consists of seven houses, to each of which every local universe admitted to the superuniverse councils elects a native representative. The average term of service is about one hundred years of superuniverse standard time. Never have I known of a disagreement between the Orvonton executives and the Uversa assembly. The presence of the deliberative assemblies on the superuniverse headquarters reveals the wisdom, and foreshadows the ultimate triumph, of the whole vast evolutionary concept of the Universal Father and his Eternal Son.

15:12. The Supreme Tribunals

Our courts are presided over by an Ancient of Days, a Perfector of Wisdom, or a Divine Counselor. The evidence for or against an individual, a planet, system, constellation, or universe is presented and interpreted by the Censors. The defense of the children of time and the evolutionary planets is offered by the Mighty Messengers. The attitude of the higher government is portrayed by Those High in Authority. And ordinarily the verdict is formulated by a varying-sized commission consisting equally of Those without Name and Number and a group of understanding personalities chosen from the deliberative assembly. Mandates of judgment originate in the local universes, but sentences involving the extinction of will creatures are always formulated on, and executed from, the headquarters of the superuniverse.

15:13. The Sector Governments

The work of the major sector governments has chiefly to do with the intellectual status of a far-flung creation. The seventy satellites of Umajor the fifth are devoted to your superuniverse intellectual training and development.

The minor sector governments are presided over by three Recents of Days. These headquarters worlds are the grand rendezvous of the Master Physical Controllers. They are the centers of training for physical and administrative knowledge concerning the universe of universes. The courts of the Perfections of Days are constituted much as are those of the Ancients of Days except that they do not sit in spiritual judgment upon the realms.

15:14. Purpose of the Seven Superuniverses

There are seven major purposes which are being unfolded in the evolution of the seven superuniverses. Each major purpose in superuniverse evolution will find fullest expression in only one of the seven superuniverses, and therefore does each superuniverse have a special function and a unique nature. Orvonton is known chiefly because of its tremendous and lavish bestowal of merciful ministry. It is a universe demonstration of love and mercy. We feel that the six unique purposes of cosmic evolution are here being interassociated into a meaning-of-the-whole; and it is for this reason that we have sometimes conjectured that God the Supreme will rule the perfected seven superuniverses from Uversa in all the experiential majesty of his then attained almighty sovereign power.

Your world is called Urantia, and it is number 606 of Satania. Your system has at present 619 inhabited worlds. The grand universe number of your world, Urantia, is 5,342,482,337,666. Your planet is a member of an enormous cosmos; but your sphere is just as precisely administered and just as lovingly fostered as if it were the only inhabited world in all existence.

Paper 16: The Seven Master Spirits

Universal Censor

THE Seven Master Spirits of Paradise are the primary personalities of the Infinite Spirit. In this sevenfold creative act of self-duplication the Infinite Spirit exhausted the associative possibilities inherent in the existence of the three persons of Deity. In spirit character and nature these Seven Spirits of Paradise are as one, but in all other aspects of identity they are very unlike. The Master Spirits have many functions, but at the present time their particular domain is the central supervision of the seven superuniverses.

16:1. Relation to Triune Deity

The Seven Master Spirits are the eternal portrayal of sevenfold Deity. When they unite as sevenfold Deity, this union equivalates to a functional level associable with Trinity functions. To all practical intents and purposes the Seven Master Spirits do encompass the functional domain of the Supreme-Ultimate to and in the master universe. When associated, the Master Spirits represent the Paradise Deities in what may be roughly conceived as the finite domain of action. It might embrace much that is ultimate but not absolute.

16:2. Relation to the Infinite Spirit

At the center of centers the Infinite Spirit is approachable. Outside of Paradise and Havona the Infinite Spirit speaks only by the voices of the Seven Master Spirits. All of everything which has been told you concerning the divinity and personality of the Conjoint Actor applies equally and fully to the Seven Master Spirits, who so effectively distribute the Infinite Spirit to the seven segments of the grand universe in accordance with their divine endowment and in the manner of their differing and individually unique natures.

16:3. Identity and Diversity of the Master Spirits

The Seven Master Spirits are indescribable beings, but they are distinctly and definitely personal.

Master Spirit Number One (of the first superuniverse) is the direct representation of the Paradise Father and is the close associate and supernal adviser of the chief of Mystery Monitors.

Master Spirit Number Two (of the second superuniverse) portrays the matchless nature and charming character of the Eternal Son and is always in close association with all orders of the Sons of God.

Master Spirit Number Three (of the third superuniverse) especially resembles the Infinite Spirit and is closely associated with all personalities who take exclusive origin in the Third Source and Center.

Master Spirit Number Four (of the fourth superuniverse) partakes of the combined natures of the Father and the Son and is the chief director and adviser of those ascendant beings who have attained the Infinite Spirit and thus have become candidates for seeing the Son and the Father. He fosters that enormous group of personalities taking origin in the Father and the Son.

Master Spirit Number Five (of the fifth superuniverse) blends the character of the Universal Father and the Infinite Spirit and is the adviser of that enormous group of beings known as the power directors, power centers, and physical controllers. This Spirit also fosters all personalities taking origin in the Father and the Conjoint Actor.

Master Spirit Number Six (of the sixth superuniverse) seems to portray the combined character of the Eternal Son and the Infinite Spirit. Whenever the creatures jointly created by the Son and the Spirit forgather in the central universe, it is this Master Spirit who is their adviser.

Master Spirit Number Seven (of the seventh superuniverse) is a uniquely equal portrayal of the Universal Father, the Eternal Son, and the Infinite Spirit. The Seventh Spirit, the fostering adviser of all triune-origin beings, is also the adviser and director of all the ascending pilgrims of Havona. This Spirit discloses a personal and organic relationship to the spirit person of the evolving Supreme. He is the presiding head of the Paradise council of the Seven Master Spirits. The inability of the Havona pilgrims fully to find God the Supreme is compensated by the Seventh Master Spirit, whose triune nature in such a peculiar manner is revelatory of the spirit person of the Supreme.

16:4. Attributes and Functions of the Master Spirits

The Seven Master Spirits represent the Third Source and Center in the relationships of energy, mind, and spirit. The Master Spirits are unique in that they function on all universe levels of reality excepting the absolute. They combine and associate material and spiritual energies to produce a hitherto nonexistent phase of universe reality—morontia substance and morontia mind. Much of the reality of the spiritual worlds is of the morontia order. It is in this realm that the Master Spirits make their great contribution to the plan of man's Paradise ascension. They exert a decided influence on a wide range of universe activities.

16:5. Relation to Creatures

Each segment of the grand universe, each individual universe and world, enjoys the benefits of the united counsel and wisdom of all Seven Master Spirits but receives the personal touch and tinge of only one. The personal nature of each Master Spirit entirely pervades and uniquely conditions his superuniverse—each native creature, man or angel, will forever bear this badge of natal identification. Throughout all eternity an ascendant mortal will exhibit traits indicative of the presiding Spirit of his superuniverse of nativity.

16:6. The Cosmic Mind

The Master Spirits are the sevenfold source of the cosmic mind—the intellectual potential of the grand universe and the mind of the evolving Supreme Being. The fact of the cosmic mind explains the kinship of various types of human and superhuman minds. Not only are kindred spirits attracted to each other, but kindred minds are also very fraternal and inclined towards co-operation the one with the other. The cosmic mind unfailingly responds (recognizes response) on three levels of universe reality: *causation* (scientific), *duty* (moral), and *worship* (spiritual). These scientific, moral, and spiritual insights are innate in the cosmic mind. It is sad to record that so few persons on Urantia take delight in cultivating these qualities of courageous and independent cosmic thinking. But when they become unified in personality development, they produce a strong character. It is the purpose of education to develop and sharpen these innate endowments.

16:7. Morals, Virtue, and Personality

Man is able to exercise scientific, moral, and spiritual insight prior to all exploration or experimentation. Intelligence alone can discriminate as to the best means of attaining indiscriminate ends, but a moral being possesses an insight which enables him to discriminate between ends as well as between means. Virtue is righteousness—conformity with the cosmos. It is the attainment of ascending levels of cosmic achievement. Morality can never be advanced by law or by force. It is a personal and freewill matter and must be disseminated by the contagion of the contact of morally fragrant persons. Moral acts are those human performances which are characterized by the highest intelligence, directed by selective discrimination in the choice of superior ends as well as in the selection of moral means to attain these ends. Supreme virtue is to wholeheartedly choose to do the will of the Universal Father.

16:8. Urantia Personality

Personality is a unique endowment of original nature whose existence is independent of, and antecedent to, the bestowal of the Thought Adjuster. Persons of a given series, type, order, or pattern may and do resemble one another, but they are never identical. Personality is that feature of an individual which we know, and which enables us to identify such a being at some future time regardless of the nature and extent of changes in form, mind, or spirit status.

The relative free will which characterizes the self-consciousness of human personality is involved in moral wisdom, spiritual discernment, unselfish love, purposeful cooperation, cosmic insight, wholehearted devotion to doing the Father's will, and worship.

16:9. Reality of Human Consciousness

The cosmic-mind-endowed, Adjuster-indwelt, personal creature possesses innate recognition-realization of energy reality, mind reality, and spirit reality. The will creature is thus equipped to discern the fact, the law, and the love of God. The God-discerning mortal is able to sense the unification value of these three cosmic qualities in the evolution of the surviving soul, man's supreme undertaking in the physical tabernacle. Jesus not only revealed God to man, but he also made a new revelation of man to himself and to other men. Only a God-knowing individual can love another person as he loves himself. Inherent in human self-consciousness is the quest for knowledge, moral values, spiritual values, and personality values. You become conscious of man as your creature brother because you are already conscious of God as your Creator Father. We worship God, first, because he is, then, because he is in us, and last, because we are in him.

Paper 17: The Seven Supreme Spirit Groups
Divine Counselor

THE seven Supreme Spirit groups are: the Seven Master Spirits, the Seven Supreme Executives, the Reflective Spirits, the Reflective Image Aids, the Seven Spirits of the Circuits, the Local Universe Creative Spirits, and the Adjutant Mind-Spirits. The Seven Master Spirits are the coordinating directors of this far-flung administrative realm. The Seven Master Spirits do not directly and personally contact universe administration below the courts of the Ancients of Days. Your local universe is administered by the Creative Mother Spirit.

17:1. The Seven Supreme Executives

The Master Spirits maintain contact with the various divisions of the super- universe governments through these Supreme Executives who function as the administrative co-ordinators of the grand universe, carrying out the combined policies of all duly constituted rulers in the grand universe.

The immediate subordinates of the Supreme Executives consist for the greater part of the trinitized sons of Paradise-Havona personalities and of the trinitized offspring of the glorified mortal graduates.

17:2. Majeston—Chief of Reflectivity

The Reflective Spirits are of divine Trinity origin. After their creation, the Deity Absolute imparted new personality prerogatives to the Supreme Being which resulted in the creation of Majeston, the reflectivity chief and Paradise center of all the work of the forty-nine Reflective Spirits and their associates throughout the universe of universes. The Deity response to the creative wills of the Supreme Being and his associates was vastly beyond their purposeful intent and greatly in excess of their conceptual forecasts. We stand in awe of the possibility of what the future ages may witness when the Supreme and the Ultimate attain new levels of divinity and the deitization of still other unexpected and undreamed of beings appear who will possess unimagined powers of enhanced universe co-ordination.

17:3. The Reflective Spirits

The groups of seven dissimilar Reflective Spirits maintain headquarters on the capitals of the superuniverses. The attribute of reflectivity is transmissible to all beings concerned in the working of this vast scheme of universal intelligence. The Reflective Spirits of each superuniverse are the creators of their Reflective Image Aids, their personal voices to the courts of the Ancients of Days. The Reflective Spirits are not merely transmitting agents; they are retentive personalities as well. Their offspring, the seconaphim, are also retentive or record personalities. Everything of true spiritual value is registered in duplicate. The true spiritual records are assembled by reflectivity. These are the live records in contrast with the formal and dead records of the universe, and they are perfectly preserved in the living minds of the recording personalities of the Infinite Spirit. While Thought Adjusters do not participate in the operation of the universal reflectivity system, we have every reason to believe that all Father fragments are fully cognizant of these transactions and are able to avail themselves of their content.

17:4. The Reflective Image Aids

The Reflective Image Aids are true images and constantly function as the channel of communication between the Reflective Spirits and the superuniverse authorities. The Reflective Spirits themselves are true personalities but require the assistance of their Image Aids in all personal intercourse with the Ancients of Days and their associates. As a class, ascending mortals do not intimately contact with reflectivity. Always some being of the reflective nature will be interposed between you and the actual operation of the service.

17:5. The Seven Spirits of the Circuits

The Seven Spirits of the Havona Circuits are the joint impersonal representation of the Infinite Spirit and the Seven Master Spirits to the seven circuits of the central universe. They are in liaison with the Seven Supreme Executives, and they synchronize with the central universe presence of the Supreme Being. These Spirits of the Circuits make contact with those who sojourn in Havona through their personal offspring, the tertiary supernaphim. The Circuit Spirits are related to the native inhabitants of Havona much as the Thought Adjusters are related to the mortal creatures. Like the Thought Adjusters, the Circuit Spirits are impersonal, and they consort with the perfect minds of Havona beings much as the impersonal spirits of the Universal Father indwell the finite minds of mortal men. But the Spirits of the Circuits never become a permanent part of Havona personalities.

17:6. The Local Universe Creative Spirits

We are conversant with six phases of the career of a local universe Mother Spirit:

1. *Initial Paradise Differentiation.* When a Creator Son is personalized by the joint action of the Universal Father and the Eternal Son, simultaneously there occurs in the person of the Infinite Spirit what is known as the "supreme reaction of complement."

2. *Preliminary Creatorship Training.* During the long period of the preliminary training of a Michael Son in the organization and administration of universes, his future consort undergoes further development of entity and becomes group conscious of destiny.

3. *The Stage of Physical Creation.* At the time the creatorship charge is administered to a Michael Son by the Eternal Son, the Master Spirit gives expression to the "prayer of identification"; and for the first time, the entity of the subsequent Creative Spirit appears as differentiated from the person of the Infinite Spirit. When the Creator Son departs for the adventure of space the Master Spirit commits the new Spirit consort to the keeping of the Creator Son. And then occurs one of the most profoundly touching episodes which ever take place on Paradise. The Universal Father speaks in acknowledgment of the eternal union of the Creator Son and the Creative Spirit. The Father-united Creator Son and Creative Spirit then go forth on their adventure of universe creation.

4. *The Life-Creation Era:* Upon the declaration of intention to create life by the Creator Son, there ensue on Paradise the "personalization ceremonies," resulting in the Mother Spirit becoming a bona fide person.

5. *The Postbestowal Ages:* When the Creator Son returns to universe headquarters after his acquirement of full universe sovereignty, he elevates

the Universe Mother Spirit to cosovereignty and acknowledges the Spirit consort as his equal.

6. *The Ages of Light and Life*: Upon the establishment of the era of light and life the local universe cosovereign enters upon the sixth phase of a Creative Spirit's career. But we may not portray the nature of this great experience.

7. *The Unrevealed Career*: We conjecture that there awaits the Universe Mother Spirits some undisclosed career.

17:7. The Adjutant Mind-Spirits

These adjutant spirits are the sevenfold mind bestowal of a local universe Mother Spirit upon the living creatures of the conjoint creation of a Creator Son and such a Creative Spirit. This bestowal becomes possible at the time of the Spirit's elevation to the status of personality prerogatives. The narration of the nature and functioning of the seven adjutant mind-spirits belongs to the story of your local universe of Nebadon.

17:8. Functions of the Supreme Spirits

The activity of the Supreme Spirits is encountered everywhere in the central, super-, and local universes. The Supreme Spirit groups are the immediate creators of the vast creature family of the ministering spirits. They are the co-ordinators of the inhabited creation. A Creative Spirit is the mother of the angelic orders of a local creation. Functional unity, inherent in the Conjoint Actor, is disclosed to the evolving universes in the Seven Master Spirits, his primary personalities. But in the perfected superuniverses of the future this unity will undoubtedly be inseparable from the experiential sovereignty of the Supreme.

Paper 18: The Supreme Trinity Personalities
Divine Counselor

THERE are seven orders of the Supreme Trinity Personalities. These beings of administrative perfection are of definite and final numbers. They form an interrelated line of administrative perfection extending from the Paradise spheres of the Father to the headquarters worlds of the local universes and to the capitals of their component constellations.

18:1. The Trinitized Secrets of Supremacy

There are seven worlds in the innermost circuit of the Paradise satellites. This group of worlds is universally known as the personal circuit of the Universal Father. Each of these exalted worlds is presided over by a corps of ten

Trinitized Secrets of Supremacy. The ten supreme directors of Divinington affairs are reflective of the personal character and nature of the Universal Father. The ten directors who rule Ascendington are reflective of the combined nature of the Father, Son, and Spirit. I can reveal very little about the work of these high personalities. There are no arbitrary secrets associated with the approach to the Universal Father, the Eternal Son, or the Infinite Spirit. The Paradise Creators respect the privacy and sanctity of personality even in their lowly creatures. And this is true both of individuals and of the various separate orders of personalities.

18:2. The Eternals of Days

Each of the billion worlds of Havona is directed by an Eternal of Days. These beings are visible to all will creatures. The architecture, natural embellishment, morontia structures, and spirit creations are exclusive and unique on each sphere. Every world is a place of everlasting beauty and is wholly unlike any other world in the central universe. And you will spend a longer or shorter time on each of these unique and thrilling spheres on your way inward through Havona to Paradise.

18:3. The Ancients of Days

When mortals of time graduate from the training worlds of a local universe they have progressed in spiritual development to recognize and communicate with the high spiritual rulers, including the Ancients of Days. The Ancients of Days are all basically identical; they disclose the combined character and unified nature of the Trinity. They provide the uniform directorship of the otherwise differing seven superuniverses. They represent the beginning of the personality records of the universe of universes. These high beings always govern in groups of three. In power, scope of authority, and extent of jurisdiction the Ancients of Days are the most powerful and mighty of any of the direct rulers of the time-space creations. The Supreme Being is achieving the sovereignty of the seven superuniverses by experiential service. But during the present age of the unfinished evolution of the Supreme, the Ancients of Days provide the co-ordinated and perfect administrative overcontrol of the evolving universes of time and space.

18:4. The Perfections of Days

Three Perfections of Days preside over the governments of the ten major sectors of each superuniverse. You will early see the Perfections of Days when you advance to the headquarters of Splandon after your sojourn on the worlds of your minor sector, for these exalted rulers are closely associated with the seventy major sector worlds of higher training for the ascendant creatures of time. The Perfections of Days, in person, administer the group pledges to the ascending graduates of the major sector schools. The work of the pilgrims of time on the worlds surrounding a major sector headquarters is chiefly of an intellectual nature in contrast with the more physical and material character of the training on the seven educational spheres of a minor sector and with the spiritual undertakings on the four hundred ninety university worlds of a superuniverse headquarters.

18:5. The Recents of Days

The Recents of Days are the youngest of the supreme directors of the superuniverses; in groups of three they preside over the affairs of the minor sectors. The governments of the minor sectors are very largely, though not exclusively, concerned with the great physical problems of the superuniverses. The minor sector spheres are the headquarters of the Master Physical Controllers. On these worlds ascending mortals carry on studies and experiments having to do with an examination of the activities of the third order of the Supreme Power Centers and of all seven orders of the Master Physical Controllers.

18:6. The Unions of Days

The Unions of Days in the evolving local universes serve only as counselors and advisers. In a special manner these Trinity observers co-ordinate the administrative activities of all branches of the local universe government. Since they are Trinity- origin beings, all of the Paradise circuits are available to them for intercommunication. Aside from duties as an observer, a Union of Days acts only at the request of the local authorities. A local universe is directly ruled by a Creator Son, but he has constantly by his side a Trinity-origin Union of Days. In the event of the temporary absence of a Creator Son from the headquarters of his local universe, the acting rulers are largely guided in their major decisions by the counsel of their Union of Days.

18:7. The Faithfuls of Days

These high Trinity-origin personalities are the Paradise advisers to the rulers of the one hundred constellations in each local universe. All that a Union of Days is to a Creator Son of a local universe, the Faithfuls of Days are to the Vorondadek Sons who rule the constellations of that local creation. They act only as counselors. They do not have a far-flung system of intercommunication, being ordinarily self-limited to an interassociation within the limits of a local universe. The Faithfuls of Days are the last link in the long administrative-advisory chain which reaches from the sacred spheres of the Universal Father near the center of all things to the primary divisions of the local universes.

Paper 19: The Co-Ordinate Trinity Origin Beings
Divine Counselor

EXCEPTING the Trinity Teacher Sons and possibly the Inspired Trinity Spirits, these groups are of definite numbers; their creation is a finished and past event.

19:1. The Trinity Teacher Sons

The Trinity Teacher Sons (Daynals) are the only group of the Sons of God revealed to you whose origin is in the Paradise Trinity. They range the central and superuniverses, and an enormous corps is assigned to each local universe. They also serve the individual planets.

These Sons teach that when the human mind undertakes to follow the philosophic technique of starting from the lower to approach the higher, whether in biology or theology, it is always in danger of committing errors of reasoning. The true perspective of any reality problem can be had only by the full and unprejudiced study and correlation of three phases of universe reality: origin, history, and destiny.

19:2. The Perfectors of Wisdom

The Perfectors of Wisdom are designed to personify the wisdom of divinity in the superuniverses. One billion are assigned to each superuniverse. Wisdom is twofold in origin, being derived from the perfection of divine insight inherent in perfect beings and from the personal experience acquired by evolutionary creatures. The Perfectors of Wisdom are the divine wisdom of the Paradise perfection of Deity insight. Their administrative associates on Uversa, the Mighty Messengers, Those without Name and Number, and Those High in Authority, when acting together, *are* the universe wisdom of experience. The versatility of the Perfectors of Wisdom enables them to participate in practically all of the celestial services of the ascendant creatures.

It has been postulated that a high and hitherto unattained level of wisdom may possibly be achieved by the Paradise finaliters. If this inference is correct, then would such perfected beings of evolutionary ascent undoubtedly become the most effective universe administrators ever to be known in all creation.

19:3. The Divine Counselors

These Trinity-origin beings are the counsel of Deity to the realms of the seven superuniverses. Three billion are assigned to each superuniverse. Divine Counselors are the perfection of the divine counsel of the Paradise Trinity. One Perfector of Wisdom, seven Divine Counselors, and one Universal Censor constitute a tribunal of Trinity divinity, the highest mobile advisory body in the universes of time and space. Seven Divine Counselors in liaison with a trinitized evolutionary trio—a Mighty Messenger, One High in Authority, and One without Name and Number—represent the nearest superuniverse approach to the union of the human viewpoint and the divine attitude on near-paradisiacal levels of spiritual meanings and reality values.

19:4. The Universal Censors

These unique beings are the judgment of Deity. There are eight billion Universe Censors. Even the Ancients of Days do not sit in judgment except in association with the Universal Censors. One Censor is commissioned on each of the billion worlds of the central universe. Their present activities hardly account for their assignment in Havona, and we therefore suspect that they are there in anticipation of the needs of some future universe age in which the Havona population may partially change. The Censors act on all levels of the grand universe. The Censors are universe totaling personalities. When a thousand witnesses have given testimony—or a million—then the Censor functions, and there is immediately revealed an unerring and divine totaling of all that has transpired. When he speaks, there is no appeal. It seems likely that the Censors are in some manner in liaison with the Deity Absolute; we are otherwise unable to explain many of their decisions and rulings.

19:5. Inspired Trinity Spirits

I will be able to tell you very little concerning the Inspired Trinity Spirits. They may possibly belong to the category of superpersonal spirits. They have no clearly discernible place in the present economy or administration of the evolving seven superuniverses. The Inspired Spirits are the solitary Spirits of the universe of universes. As Spirits they are very much like the Solitary Messengers except that the latter are distinct personalities. The Inspired Spirits do not apparently belong to the evolutionary scheme of the individual planets or universes, and yet they seem to be almost everywhere. I have arrived at the settled conclusion that the Inspired Trinity Spirits, by superconscious techniques, are functioning as teachers of the realms. Excepting Solitary Messengers, and sometimes Trinity-origin beings, none of the celestial family have ever been conscious of the nearness of the Inspired Spirits. And from this, you mortals can well see that you must advance a long way before you will progress by "sight" and "material" assurance.

19:6. Havona Natives

It is not possible for Urantians to conceive of the inherent endowments of these divinely perfect creatures. You must await your arrival in Havona, when you can greet them as spirit comrades. During your long sojourn on the billion worlds of Havona culture you will develop an eternal friendship for these superb beings. The good to both ascending mortal and Havona native is great and mutual. We have entertained the thought that in the subsequent universe ages the central universe may be peopled by a mixed group of resident beings.

19:7. Paradise Citizens

There are resident on Paradise numerous groups of superb beings. They are not directly concerned with the scheme of perfecting ascending will creatures and are not, therefore, fully revealed to Urantia mortals.

Trinity-origin beings possess prerogatives of transit which make them independent of transport personalities, such as seraphim. It required 109 days of your time for me to journey from Uversa to Urantia. Through these same avenues we are enabled to intercommunicate instantaneously.

Paper 20: The Paradise Sons of God

Perfector of Wisdom

THE Sons of God are classified under three general heads: Descending Sons, Ascending Sons, and Trinitized Sons.

20:1. The Descending Sons of God

All descending Sons of God have high and divine origins. Those Sons who come forth from the Deities on the central Isle are called the *Paradise Sons of God* and embrace the following three orders: the Creator Sons—the Michaels; the Magisterial Sons—the Avonals; and the Trinity Teacher Sons—the Daynals. The remaining four orders of descending sonship are known as the *Local Universe Sons of God*: the Melchizedek Sons, the Vorondadek Sons—the Most Highs, the Lanonandek Sons—System Sovereigns and Planetary Princes, and the Life Carriers. The entire order of Michael, the Creator Sons, is so unique that the consideration of their natures and activities will be reserved to the next paper in this series.

20:2. The Magisterial Sons

Magisterial Sons are planetary ministers and judges, the magistrates of the time-space realms. Avonals are the Paradise Sons of service and bestowal to the individual planets where they are often incarnated in the likeness of mortal flesh and sometimes are born of earthly mothers on the evolutionary worlds. In judicial actions they may go to the same or to other worlds times without number as dispensation terminators, liberators of the sleeping survivors. On magisterial missions an Avonal appears as an adult of the realm by a technique of incarnation. On bestowal missions Avonals are born of woman as Michael of Nebadon was incarnated on Urantia. To all intents and purposes their work on the inhabited spheres is just as effective and acceptable as would have been the service of a Creator Son.

20:3. Judicial Actions

If a Magisterial Son comes solely as a dispensational adjudicator, he arrives on a planet as a spiritual being, invisible to the material creatures of the realm. Such technical visits occur repeatedly in the long history of an inhabited world.

20:4. Magisterial Missions

A planet may experience many magisterial visitations both before and after the appearance of a bestowal Son. Urantia has never been host to an Avonal Son on a magisterial mission. Urantia may yet be visited by an Avonal commissioned to incarnate on a magisterial mission.

20:5. Bestowal of the Paradise Sons of God

The bestowals of the Avonal and the Michael Sons are a necessary part of the experiential process designed to make these Sons safe and sympathetic magistrates and rulers of the peoples and planets of time and space. Though the possibility of disaster always attends these Paradise Sons during their bestowal incarnations, I have yet to see the record of the failure or default of either a Magisterial or a Creator Son on a mission of bestowal. The story of their bestowal and planetary service throughout Nebadon constitutes the most noble and fascinating chapter in the history of your local universe.

20:6. The Mortal-Bestowal Careers

On a mortal-bestowal mission a Paradise Son is always born of woman and grows up as a male child of the realm. From a material viewpoint, these human-divine Sons live ordinary lives with just one exception: They do not beget offspring on the worlds of their sojourn. As teachers, these Sons are exclusively devoted to the spiritual enlightenment of the mortal races on the worlds of their sojourn. A bestowal Son must encounter death, but it is not a requirement of the divine plan that this death be either violent or unusual.

20:7. The Trinity Teacher Sons

These highly personal and highly spiritual Daynals are the universal educators. In all universes they are the embodiment of service and the discretion of wisdom. Unlike their Paradise brethren, Michaels and Avonals, Trinity Teacher Sons receive no preliminary training in the central universe. They are dispatched directly to the headquarters of the superuniverses.

20:8. Local Universe Ministry of the Daynals

The Paradise Spiritual Sons are the only Trinity creatures to be so completely associated with the conduct of the dual-origin universes. They are affectionately devoted to the educational ministry to mortal creatures and the lower orders of spiritual beings. The Teacher Sons compose the faculties who administer all examinations and conduct all tests for the qualification and certification of all subordinate phases of universe service. They conduct an agelong course of training, ranging from the planetary courses up to the high College of Wisdom located on Salvington. The vast domain of Daynal-sonship activities will be better understood on Urantia when you are more advanced in intelligence, and after the spiritual isolation of your planet has been terminated.

20:9. Planetary Service of the Daynals

When the progress of events on an evolutionary world indicates that the time is ripe to initiate a spiritual age, the Trinity Teacher Sons always volunteer for this service. You are not familiar with this order of sonship because Urantia has never experienced a spiritual age. They will be due to appear on Urantia after its inhabitants have gained comparative deliverance from the shackles of animalism and from the fetters of materialism. The Teacher Sons usually remain on their visitation planets for one thousand years of planetary time. The Daynals do not incarnate or otherwise so materialize themselves as to be visible to mortal beings; therefore is contact with the world of visitation maintained through the activities of the Brilliant Evening Stars. On Uversa it is our belief that, when the superuniverses are finally settled in light and life, these Paradise Teacher Sons, who have become so thoroughly familiar with the problems of evolutionary worlds and have been so long associated with the career of evolutionary mortals, will probably be transferred to eternal association with the Paradise Corps of the Finality.

20:10. United Ministry of the Paradise Sons

These Sons of God are the divine ministers who are unceasingly devoted to the work of helping the creatures of time attain the high spiritual goal of eternity. In their divinely perfect co-operation, Michaels, Avonals, and Daynals are contributing to the actualization and revelation of the personality and sovereignty of God the Supreme.

Paper 21: The Paradise Creator Sons

Perfector of Wisdom

THE Creator Sons are the makers and rulers of the local universes of time and space. These universe creators and sovereigns are of dual origin, embodying the characteristics of God the Father and God the Son. But each Creator Son is different from every other; each is the "only-begotten Son" of the perfect deity ideal of his origin. Sometimes we refer to the sovereign of your universe of Nebadon as Christ Michael.

21:1. Origin and Nature of Creator Sons

Each Creator Son is the absolute of the united deity concepts which constitute his divine origin. Some Creator Sons appear to be more like God the Father, others more like God the Son. The trend of administration in the universe of Nebadon suggests that its Creator is one whose nature and character more resemble that of the Eternal Mother Son.

21:2. The Creators of Local Universes

A Creator Son is permitted to choose the space site of his future cosmic activity, but before he may begin even the physical organization of his universe, he must spend a long period of observation devoted to the study of the efforts of his older brothers in various creations located in the superuniverse of his projected action. And prior to all this, the Michael Son will have completed his long and unique experience of Paradise observation and Havona training.

When a Michael Son is absent from his universe, its government is directed by the first-born native being, the Bright and Morning Star, the local universe chief executive. The advice and counsel of the Union of Days is invaluable at such times. During these absences a Creator Son is able to invest the associated Mother Spirit with the overcontrol of his spiritual presence on the inhabited worlds and in the hearts of his mortal children.

21:3. Local Universe Sovereignty

Before the completion of his bestowal career a Creator Son rules with certain self-imposed limitations of sovereignty, but subsequent to his finished bestowal service he rules by virtue of his actual experience in the form and likeness of his manifold creatures. When a Creator has seven times sojourned among his creatures, when the bestowal career is finished, then is he supremely settled in universe authority; he has become a Master Son, a sovereign and supreme ruler. These primary Paradise Sons are the real revealers of the Father's loving nature and beneficent authority.

21:4. The Michael Bestowals

After each of his bestowals a Creator Son proceeds to the "right hand of the Father," there to gain the Father's acceptance of the bestowal and to receive instruction preparatory to the next episode of universe service. Following the seventh and final bestowal a Creator Son receives from the Universal

Father supreme authority and jurisdiction over his universe. Creator Sons, subsequent to the completion of their bestowal careers, are reckoned as a separate order, sevenfold Master Sons. Such beings embody all that can be secured from divine parentage and embrace everything to be derived from perfected-creature experience. Why should man bemoan his lowly origin and enforced evolutionary career when the very Gods must pass through an equivalent experience before they are accounted experientially worthy and competent finally and fully to rule over their universe domains!

21:5. Relation of Master Sons to the Universe

The Master Michaels are supreme in their own local universes when once they have been installed as sovereign rulers. This is the first step, the beginning, of a settled administration in any local universe. A Master Son may at will vary the order of the spiritual adjudication and evolutionary adjustment of the inhabited planets. And such Sons do make and carry out the plans of their own choosing in all matters of special planetary needs, in particular regarding the worlds of their creature sojourn and still more concerning the realm of terminal bestowal, the planet of incarnation in the likeness of mortal flesh.

21:6. Destiny of the Master Michaels

It is highly probable that the undisclosed creator powers may attain to absonite levels of service attended by the appearance of new things, meanings, and values on transcendental levels of ultimate universe significance. We believe that in eternity the Michaels are literally destined to be "the way, the truth, and the life," ever blazing the path for all universe personalities as it leads from supreme divinity through ultimate absonity to eternal deity finality.

Paper 22: The Trinitized Sons of God

Mighty Messenger

THE trinitized order of sonship is subdivided into three primary divisions: *Deity-trinitized Sons*, *Trinity-embraced Sons*, and *Creature-trinitized Sons*. The Deity-trinitized Sons are unrevealed in these narratives.

22:1. The Trinity-Embraced Sons

All Trinity-embraced sons are originally of dual or single origin. This corps embraces seven orders of personalities: *Mighty Messengers, Those High in Authority, Those without Name and Number, Trinitized Custodians, Trinitized Ambassadors, Celestial Guardians,* and *High Son Assistants*.

These seven groups of personalities are further classified, according to origin, nature, and function, into three major divisions: the *Trinitized Sons of Attainment*—the Mighty Messengers, Those High in Authority, and Those without Name and Number are all Adjuster-fused ascendant mortals who have attained Paradise and the Corps of the Finality. The *Trinitized Sons of Selection* embrace the Trinitized Custodians and the Trinitized Ambassadors. They are recruited from certain of the evolutionary seraphim and translated midway creatures as well as from certain of the Spirit-fused and the Son-fused mortals. The *Trinitized Sons of Perfection* include the Celestial Guardians and the High Son Assistants who comprise a unique group of twice-trinitized personalities.

22:2. The Mighty Messengers

These are a class of perfected mortals who have been rebellion tested or otherwise equally proved as to their personal loyalty. In the superuniverse courts, Mighty Messengers act as defenders of both individuals and planets when they come up for adjudication. They are fully conscious of their entire ascendant careers, and that is why they are such useful and sympathetic ministers, understanding messengers, for service on any world of space and to any creature of time. As soon as you are delivered from the flesh, you will communicate freely and understandingly with us.

22:3. Those High in Authority

These are the perfected mortals who have exhibited superior administrative ability and have shown extraordinary executive genius throughout their long ascending careers. They foster the execution of justice and the rectification of misadaptations in the evolutionary universes.

22:4. Those without Name and Number

Those without Name and Number are the ascendant souls who have developed the ability to worship beyond the skill of all the sons and daughters of the evolutionary races. They have acquired a spiritual concept of the eternal purpose of the Universal Father. They are superior spiritual minds of the survival races, and are especially qualified to sit in judgment and to render opinions when a spiritual viewpoint is desirable. They are the supreme jurors of Orvonton. If the viewpoint of a mortal creature is ever in doubt, the question is settled by appeal to an ascendant commission consisting of a Mighty Messenger, One High in Authority, and One without Name and Number.

22:5. The Trinitized Custodians

Trinitized Custodians are ascendant seraphim and translated midway creatures who have passed through Havona and have attained Paradise and the Corps of the Finality. The Trinitized Custodians administer group affairs and foster collective projects. They are the custodians of records, plans, and institutions; they act as the trustees of undertakings, personality groups, ascendant projects, morontia plans, universe projections, and innumerable other enterprises.

22:6. The Trinitized Ambassadors

Certain of these Spirit- and Son-fused mortals reach Havona and attain Paradise. From among these Paradise ascenders candidates are selected for the Trinity embrace. They represent the superior minds of their respective groups. Trinitized Ambassadors are the emissaries of the Ancients of Days for any and all purposes. They are the emergency or reserve corps of the Trinitized Sons of the supergovernments, and they are therefore available for a great range of duties.

22:7. Technique of Trinitization

The ascendant Adjuster-fused mortal finaliters who have attained certain levels of Paradise culture and spiritual development are among those who can essay to trinitize a creature being. Unbelievably long periods of time are sometimes consumed in these adventures. And not always do these devoted couples meet with success. Candidates for trinitization who thus fail are admitted to a special group of finaliters who have made the supreme effort and sustained the supreme disappointment.

The two ancestors of a creature-trinitized son become in a certain sense spiritually as one. During the current universe age, all trinitization-united parents are inseparable in assignment and function. The Seven Master Spirits have authority to sanction the trinitizing union of finaliters and Paradise-Havona personalities, and such mixed liaisons are always successful. The resultant magnificent creature-trinitized sons become the wards of the Architects of the Master Universe. These trinitized sons of destiny embody ideas, ideals, and experience which apparently pertain to a future universe age—certain aspects of the unrevealed master universe function of the Supreme-Ultimate.

22:8. The Creature-Trinitized Sons

When new ascender-trinitized and Paradise-Havona-trinitized sons are young and untrained, they are usually dispatched for long periods of service under the Supreme Executives, the Trinity Teacher Sons, the Master Spirits, or the local universe Mother Spirits. Excepting the Trinitized Sons of Perfection and those who are forgathering on Vicegerington, the supreme destiny of all creature-trinitized sons appears to be entrance into the Corps of Trinitized Finaliters, one of the seven Paradise Corps of the Finality.

22:9. The Celestial Guardians

These creature-trinitized Sons of Perfection are the officers of the courts of the Ancients of Days, functioning as court messengers and as bearers of the summonses and decisions of the various tribunals of the superuniverse governments. They are the apprehending agents of the Ancients of Days; they go forth from Uversa to bring back beings whose presence is required before the superuniverse judges. These twice-trinitized sons are marvelous beings, but they lack that tremendous and profound personal experience acquired by those who have actually ascended from the worlds of space. There is simply nothing in all universal existence which can take the place of personal experience.

22:10. High Son Assistants

The High Son Assistants are the superior group of the retrinitized trinitized sons of glorified ascendant beings of the Mortal Corps of the Finality and of their eternal associates, the Paradise-Havona personalities. They are assigned as personal aids to the high sons of the governments of the Ancients of Days. They might fittingly be denominated private secretaries. Let me call attention to their one point of great strength, the attribute which makes them almost invaluable to us. They show forth and actually embody the very wisdom of the divine Trinity as concerns the idea-ideal of their personality existence. They are in constant circulation, serving where the idea or ideal which they embody can best further the eternal purposes of the Paradise Trinity. They are touchingly affectionate, superbly loyal, exquisitely intelligent, supremely wise—regarding a single idea—and transcendently humble. It is well-nigh pathetic to observe them seeking knowledge and information on hosts of other subjects, even from the ascending mortals.

Paper 23: The Solitary Messengers

Divine Counselor

SOLITARY Messengers are the personal and universal corps of the Conjoint Creator; they are the first and senior order of the Higher Personalities of the Infinite Spirit.

23:1. Nature and Origin of Solitary Messengers

Immediately following the creation of the Seven Spirits of the Havona Circuits, the Infinite Spirit brought into being the vast corps of Solitary Messengers; they have functioned throughout the grand universe from near eternity. These solitary spirits start out at the center of all things and crave assignment to the remote creations, even to the individual worlds of the outermost local universes and even on beyond. Though denominated Solitary Messengers, they are not lonesome spirits, for they truly like to work alone. They are not isolated in their service; they are constantly in touch with the wealth of the intellect of all creation since they are capable of "listening in" on all the broadcasts of the realms of their sojourn. When they collaborate in a group they are altogether cut off from the sustenance and direction of their Paradise circuit. They possess inherent and automatic powers which detect and indicate the proximity of both the Inspired Trinity Spirits and the divine Thought Adjusters. There is practically no work of the universes in which they cannot engage; they assist us all, from the highest to the lowest.

23:2. Assignments of Solitary Messengers

Solitary Messengers are able to work in all aspects of the grand and master universe. The Deities can and do create perfect beings. The confusion and turmoil of Urantia do not signify that the Paradise Rulers lack either interest or ability to manage affairs differently. The Creators are possessed of full power to make Urantia a veritable paradise, but such an Eden would not contribute to the development of those strong, noble, and experienced characters which the Gods are so surely forging out on your world between the anvils of necessity and the hammers of anguish. Solitary Messengers are the only available type of spirit intelligence—aside, possibly, from the Inspired Trinity Spirits—that can be dispatched from the headquarters of one superuniverse directly to the headquarters of another. There is no limitation upon the service of Solitary Messengers in the superuniverses and the local universes. They delight to be dispatched as free and untrammeled explorers, to experience the thrill of finding the organizing nucleuses of new worlds and universes. They are constantly out on exploring expeditions to the uncharted regions of all outer space. When it develops that it will require hundreds of years for a native ambassador to reach a far-distant local universe, a Solitary Messenger is often asked to proceed there immediately. They can go in very short order, not independently of time and space as do the Gravity Messengers, but nearly so. The Solitary Messengers regard the assignment to reveal truth as the highest trust of their order.

23:3. Time and Space Services of Solitary Messengers

The Solitary Messengers are the highest type of perfect and confidential personality available for the quick transmission of important and urgent messages when it is inexpedient to utilize either the broadcast service or the reflectivity mechanism.

It is wholly beyond my ability to explain to the material type of mind how a spirit can be a real person and at the same time traverse space at such tremendous velocities. Of the myriads of beings who co-operate with us in the conduct of the affairs of the superuniverse, none are more important in practical helpfulness and time-saving assistance. I am at a loss to explain to Urantia mortals how the Solitary Messengers can be without form and yet possess real and definite personalities. The Solitary Messengers are the only class of beings who seem to be possessed of well-nigh all the advantages of a formless spirit coupled with all the prerogatives of a full-fledged personality.

23:4. Special Ministry of Solitary Messengers

The Solitary Messengers seem to be personality co-ordinators for all types of spirit beings. Their ministry helps to make all the personalities of the far-flung spiritual world akin, however dissimilar. When a finaliter and a Paradise Citizen co-operate in the trinitization of a "child of time and eternity" and when such an unclassified personality is dispatched to Vicegerington, a Solitary Messenger is always assigned as a guardian-companion and never leaves Vicegerington. What the future of such an extraordinary association may be, we do not know.

It appears to us that at some time in the remote future the supply of messengers will become exhausted. Are these extraordinary spirit personalities going to be eternally associated with these trinitized sons of unrevealed destiny? This transaction, together with many similar occurrences in universe administration, unmistakably indicates that the personnel of the grand universe, even that of Havona and Paradise, is undergoing a definite and certain reorganization in co-ordination with, and with reference to, the vast energy evolutions now taking place throughout the realms of outer space.

Paper 24:
Higher Personalities of the Infinite Spirit
Divine Counselor

THE Higher Personalities of the Infinite Spirit are: *Solitary Messengers, Universe Circuit Supervisors, Census Directors, Personal Aids of the Infinite Spirit, Associate Inspectors, Assigned Sentinels,* and *Graduate Guides.*

24:1. The Universe Circuit Supervisors

The four orders of Universe Circuit Supervisors direct and manipulate all spirit-energy circuits outside the Isle of Paradise. Whether acting in the local or higher universes, circuit supervisors direct all concerned as to the proper circuits to employ for the transmission of all spirit messages and for the transit of all personalities. They are able to throw any world out of certain universe circuits of the higher spiritual order, such as isolating an evolutionary world if its Planetary Prince should rebel against the Universal Father. They are truly personal beings, but they possess a type of other-than-Father-endowed personality not encountered in any other type of creature in all universal existence. Although you will recognize and know them as you journey inward towards Paradise, you will have no personal relations with them.

24:2. The Census Directors

These directors, by a not-fully-understood technique, are made immediately aware of the birth of will in any part of the grand universe. They are, therefore, always competent to give us the number, nature, and whereabouts of all will creatures in any part of the central creation and the seven superuniverses. One Census Director resides at the headquarters of each superuniverse, one on the capital of every local universe. Census Directors register the existence of a new will creature when the first act of will is performed; they indicate the death of a will creature when the last act of will takes place.

24:3. Personal Aids of the Infinite Spirit

The Personal Aids of the Infinite Spirit exist for the exclusive assistance of the Paradise presence of the Third Person of Deity. Wherever the circuits of the Conjoint Creator extend, there these Personal Aids may appear for the purpose of executing the bidding of the Infinite Spirit. They traverse space much as do the Solitary Messengers but are not persons in the sense that the messengers are.

24:4. The Associate Inspectors

The Associate Inspectors are the personal embodiment of the authority of the Seven Supreme Executives to the local universes. Associate Inspectors work under the direct supervision of the Supreme Executives, being their personal and powerful representatives to the local universes.

24:5. The Assigned Sentinels

The Assigned Sentinels are co-ordinating personalities and liaison representatives of the Seven Supreme Executives. They are among the highest ranking personalities stationed on a system capital. The sentinels are almost exclusively concerned in keeping the Associate Inspector of their universe fully informed on all matters relating to the welfare and state of the systems of their assignment.

24:6. The Graduate Guides

The Graduate Guides, as a group, sponsor and conduct the high university of technical instruction and spiritual training. They are exclusively devoted to the tasks of guiding the mortal graduates from the superuniverses of time through the Havona course of instruction and training which serves to prepare the ascending pilgrims for admission to Paradise and the Corps of the Finality. The guide who greets you upon your arrival on the receiving world of the outer Havona circuit will remain with you throughout your entire career on the heavenly circuits.

24:7. Origin of the Graduate Guides

We believe that the Graduate Guides are the perfected or more experienced members of another order of central universe creatures, the Havona Servitals. We believe that this transformation takes place in response to the will of the Infinite Spirit, undoubtedly acting in behalf of the Supreme. Graduate Guides are not created by the Supreme Being, but we all conjecture that experiential Deity is in some way concerned in those transactions which bring these beings into existence.

Paper 25: The Messenger Hosts of Space
One High in Authority

THE Messenger Hosts of Space are: *Havona Servitals, Universal Conciliators, Technical Advisers, Custodians of Records on Paradise, Celestial Recorders, Morontia Companions,* and *Paradise Companions.* The servitals, conciliators, and Morontia Companions are created as such; the remaining four represent attainment levels of the angelic orders.

25:1. The Havona Servitals

The Havona Servitals are the joint creative work of the Seven Master Spirits and their associates, the Seven Supreme Power Directors. Every fourth servital is more physical in type than the others. The newly created servitals, together with newly appearing Graduate Guides, all pass through the courses of training which the senior guides continuously conduct on each of the seven Havona circuits. In large numbers they are dispatched, from time to time, to serve on the study worlds encircling the headquarters spheres of the seven superuniverses, the worlds devoted to the final training and spiritual culture of the ascending souls of time who are preparing for advancement to the circuits of Havona. They are also designated assistants and associates of the Graduate Guides in helping and instructing the various orders of ascending creatures who have attained Havona, and who seek to attain Paradise.

25:2. The Universal Conciliators

For every Havona Servital created, seven Universal Conciliators are brought into being, one in each superuniverse. In each superuniverse the

Universal Conciliators find themselves segregated into groups of four, a conciliating commission: the *Judge-Arbiter*, the *Spirit-Advocate*, the *Divine Executioner*, and the *Recorder*. When in session a commission functions as a group of three since the advocate is detached during adjudication and participates in the formulation of the verdict only at the conclusion of the hearing. Hence these commissions are sometimes called referee trios. The conciliators are of great value in keeping the universe of universes running smoothly. When a commission has once accepted jurisdiction of a problem, its rulings are final and always unanimous; there is no appeal from the decision of the judge-arbiter.

25:3. The Far-Reaching Service of Conciliators

Conciliators operate progressively from worlds, systems, constellations, local universes, minor sectors, major sectors, and superuniverses. They prove to be the understanding friends of men, angels, and other spirit beings. The farther they ascend, the less misunderstanding there is to adjudicate and the more mysterious phenomena to explain and interpret. They become wonderful advisers and wise teachers of the ascending pilgrims who are in residence on the educational spheres surrounding the headquarters worlds of the superuniverses. By experiential ascent and Paradise training they have acquired a unique grasp of the emerging reality of the Supreme Being, and they roam the universe of universes on special assignment. They are eternally associated as the embodiment of the supreme justice of time and space.

25:4. Technical Advisers

From the early supernaphim and omniaphim, one million of the most orderly minds were chosen by the Infinite Spirit as the nucleus of this vast and versatile group. The Technical Advisers are recruited from various categories of angels, ascending mortals and midwayers. Those mortals and midwayers who serve transiently with the advisers are chosen for such work because of their expertness in the concept of universal law and supreme justice. These advisers are more than legal experts; they are students and teachers of applied law, the laws of the universe applied to the lives and destinies of all who inhabit the vast domains of the far-flung creation. Technical Advisers are dedicated to the work of preventing delay, facilitating progress, and counseling achievement. They are the advisers of all classes of beings regarding the proper usages and techniques of all spirit-world transactions. There is no known limit to the domain of their service. They even essay to elucidate the technique of the Ultimate.

As you journey toward your Paradise goal, you are continuously afforded the opportunity to give out to others the wisdom and experience you have already accumulated; all the way in to Havona you enact the role of a pupil-teacher. In the universal regime you are not reckoned as having possessed yourself of knowledge and truth until you have demonstrated your ability and your willingness to impart this knowledge and truth to others.

25:5. The Custodians of Records on Paradise

From among the tertiary supernaphim in Havona, certain of the senior chief recorders are chosen as Custodians of Records, keepers of the formal archives of the Isle of Light. The recording angels of the inhabited planets are the source of all individual records. Every occurrence of significance in the organized and inhabited creation is a matter of record.

25:6. The Celestial Recorders

These are the recorders who execute all records in duplicate, making an original spirit recording and a semimaterial counterpart. Celestial Recorders are ascendant seraphim from the local universes. In your transition experience, as you ascend from this material world, you will always be able to consult the records of, and to be otherwise conversant with, the history and traditions of your status sphere. On Uversa the senior Celestial Recorders can show the records of everything of cosmic import in all Orvonton since the far-distant times of the arrival of the Ancients of Days.

25:7. The Morontia Companions

These children of the local universe Mother Spirits are the friends and associates of all who live the ascending morontia life. The Morontia Companions are simply gracious hosts to those who are just beginning the long inward ascent. Though you will have earnest and progressively difficult tasks to perform on the morontia training worlds of Nebadon, you will always be provided with regular seasons of rest and reversion. At every stage of the ascending career all contactable personalities will be friendly and companionable, but not until you meet the Paradise Companions will you find another group so devoted to friendship and companionship.

25:8. The Paradise Companions

The Paradise Companions are a composite or assembled group recruited from the ranks of the seraphim, seconaphim, supernaphim, and omniaphim. Aside from permanent status on Paradise, this temporary service of Paradise companionship is the highest honor ever conferred upon the ministering spirits. You may be certain of being warmly welcomed by one of them when you experience the resurrection into eternity on the everlasting shores of Paradise. During your prefinaliter sojourn on Paradise, if for any reason you should be temporarily separated from your associate of the ascending career—mortal or seraphic—a Paradise Companion would be forthwith assigned for counsel and companionship. If an ascending mortal should reach the central universe alone and should fail in some phase of the Deity adventure, he would be remanded to the universes of time, and forthwith a call would be made to the reserves of the Paradise Companions. One of this order would be assigned to follow the defeated pilgrim, to be with him and to comfort and cheer him, and to remain with him until he returned to the central universe to resume the Paradise ascent.

Paper 26:
Ministering Spirits of the Central Universe

Perfector of Wisdom

SUPERNAPHIM are the ministering spirits of Paradise and the central universe. No major part of the organized and inhabited creation is without their services.

26:1. The Ministering Spirits

Angels are the ministering-spirit associates of the evolutionary and ascending will creatures of all space. The ministering spirits of the grand universe are: *Supernaphim, Seconaphim, Tertiaphim, Omniaphim, Seraphim, Cherubim* and *Sanobim*, and *Midway Creatures*. It is the supernaphim, seconaphim, and seraphim who, in large numbers, are employed in the furtherance of the ascending scheme of progressive perfection for the children of time. Seraphim can work singly as discrete and localized personalities, but they are able to encircuit only when polarized as liaison pairs. These brilliant creatures of light are sustained directly by the intake of the spiritual energy of the primary circuits of the universe.

26:2. The Mighty Supernaphim

The supernaphim are the skilled ministers to all types of beings who sojourn on Paradise and in the central universe. Primary supernaphim divide their ministry about equally between certain groups of the Paradise Citizens and the ever-enlarging corps of ascendant pilgrims. The work of the primary supernaphim is so unique and distinctive that it will be separately considered in the succeeding narrative. Secondary supernaphim are the directors of the affairs of ascending beings on the seven circuits of Havona. Tertiary supernaphim take origin in these Seven Spirits of the Circuits.

26:3. The Tertiary Supernaphim

The Tertiary Supernaphim serve as Harmony Supervisors, Chief Recorders, Broadcasters, Messengers, Intelligence Co-ordinators, Transport

Personalities, and the Reserve Corps. Intelligence Co-ordinators secure intelligence by the Havona graph method, which enables them automatically to assimilate as much information in one hour of Urantia time as would require a thousand years for your most rapid telegraphic technique to record.

26:4. The Secondary Supernaphim

According to their periodic assignment to the ministry of the ascending pilgrims, secondary supernaphim work in the following seven groups: Pilgrim Helpers, Supremacy Guides, Trinity Guides, Son Finders, Father Guides, Counselors and Advisers, and Complements of Rest.

The pilgrim lands on the receiving planet of Havona, with only one endowment of perfection, perfection of purpose. You are known to be disappointment proof. By the time you reach Havona, your sincerity has become sublime. Now must the pilgrim helpers begin the work of developing that perfection of understanding and that technique of comprehension which are so indispensable to Paradise perfection of personality. Ability to comprehend is the mortal passport to Paradise.

26:5. The Pilgrim Helpers

The first of the seven groups of secondary supernaphim to be encountered are the pilgrim helpers. They conduct their work for the ascending mortals in three major divisions: first, the supreme understanding of the Paradise Trinity; second, the spiritual comprehension of the Father-Son partnership; and third, the intellectual recognition of the Infinite Spirit. But long before reaching Havona, these ascendant children of time have learned to feast upon uncertainty, to fatten upon disappointment, to enthuse over apparent defeat, to invigorate in the presence of difficulties, to exhibit indomitable courage in the face of immensity, and to exercise unconquerable faith when confronted with the challenge of the inexplicable. Long since, the battle cry of these pilgrims became: "In liaison with God, nothing—absolutely nothing—is impossible."

The test of the seventh circle is the recognition of the Master Spirit of the pilgrim's superuniverse. Time is of little consequence on the Havona circles. Achievement is the final and supreme test.

26:6. The Supremacy Guides

The supremacy guides function only on the sixth circle of the central universe. It is in this circle that the ascenders achieve a new realization of God the Supreme. It appears as if God the Supreme were affectionately bestowing upon his experiential children, up to the very limits of their experiential capacities, those enhancements of intellectual grasp, of spiritual insight, and of personality outreach which they will so need, in all their efforts at penetrating the divinity level of the eternal and existential Deities of Paradise.

26:7. The Trinity Guides

Trinity guides are the tireless ministers of the fifth circle of the Havona. Here the pilgrims receive advanced instruction concerning the divine Trinity in preparation for the attempt to achieve the personality recognition of the Infinite Spirit. After the completion of the course of training on this circuit, the ascender is taken for a trial trip to Paradise. The ascender's companions of the transit trio afford all possible assistance to a pilgrim in his difficult task of recognizing, discerning, and comprehending the Infinite Spirit. Seldom does the quest for the Infinite Spirit fail of consummation.

26:8. The Son Finders

From the worlds of the fourth Havona circuit the ascending pilgrims go to Paradise to achieve an understanding contact with the Eternal Son. On the fourth circuit the pilgrims of time and the pilgrims of eternity arrive at their first truly mutual understanding of one another. The Son finders instruct their subjects first, in the adequate spiritual comprehension of the Son; second, in the satisfactory personality recognition of the Son; and third, in the proper differentiation of the Son from the personality of the Infinite Spirit. In the event of failure no reasons are ever assigned, neither are the candidates themselves nor their various tutors and guides ever chided or criticized. On Paradise, disappointment is never regarded as defeat; postponement is never looked upon as disgrace; the apparent failures of time are never confused with the significant delays of eternity.

26:9. The Father Guides

When the pilgrim soul attains the third circle of Havona, he comes under the tutelage of the Father guides. The attainment of the Universal Father is the passport to eternity. The transit trio announce that the last venture of time is about to ensue; that another creature of space seeks entry to Paradise through the portals of eternity. The test of time is almost over. Step by step, life by life, world by world, the ascendant career has been mastered, and the goal of Deity has been attained. Time is lost in eternity; space is swallowed up in worshipful identity and harmony with the Universal Father.

26:10. The Counselors and Advisers

The superaphic counselors and advisers of the second circle are the instructors of the children of time regarding the career of eternity. Those who are unsuccessful in the first effort at Deity attainment are advanced from the circle of failure directly to the second circle before they are returned to superuniverse service. For the successful pilgrims on the second circuit the stimulus of evolutionary uncertainty is over, but the traversal of the innermost circle lies just ahead, and soon thereafter the last transit sleep will terminate, and the new adventure of the eternal career will begin.

26:11. The Complements of Rest

Much of an ascender's time on the last circuit is devoted to a continuation of the study of the impending problems of Paradise residence. On this innermost circuit, both the ascending and the descending pilgrims fraternize with each other and with the creature-trinitized sons. The superaphic complements of rest are not so much concerned with their training as with promoting their understanding association with diverse groups. Beyond doubt, the Creator Sons and their mortal children are preparing for some future and unknown universe service. At the culmination of the Havona career, as you mortals go to sleep on the pilot world of the inner circuit, you go not alone to your rest as you did on the worlds of your origin. Now, as you prepare for the attainment rest, there moves over by your side your long-time associate of the first circle, the majestic complement of rest, who prepares to enter the rest as one with you. Your first transition was indeed death, the second an ideal sleep, and now the third metamorphosis is the true rest, the relaxation of the ages.

Paper 27:
Ministry of the Primary Supernaphim

Perfector of Wisdom

PRIMARY supernaphim are the supernal servants of the Deities on the eternal Isle of Paradise. Primary supernaphim are also placed in command of the seraphic hosts ministering on worlds isolated because of rebellion. On Urantia the present "chief of seraphim" is the second of this order to be on duty since the times of the bestowal of Christ Michael. These high angels now minister chiefly in the following seven orders of service: *Conductors of Worship, Masters of Philosophy, Custodians of Knowledge, Directors of Conduct, Interpreters of Ethics, Chiefs of Assignment,* and *Instigators of Rest.*

27:1. Instigators of Rest

These instigators of rest are the final instructors who make ready the pilgrims of time for their introduction to eternity. You enter the rest on the final Havona circuit and are eternally resurrected on Paradise. And as you there spiritually repersonalize, you will immediately recognize the instigator of rest who welcomes you to the eternal shores as the very primary supernaphim who produced the final sleep on the innermost circuit of Havona. The last rest of time has been enjoyed; the last transition sleep has been experienced; now you awake to life everlasting on the shores of the eternal abode.

27:2. Chiefs of Assignment

The angels of assignment have much to do with glorified mortal residents of Paradise before they are admitted to the Corps of the Finality. When you mortal ascenders attain Paradise, you must fraternize with upwards of three thousand different orders of Paradise Citizens, with the various groups of the Transcendentalers, and with numerous other types of Paradise inhabitants.

27:3. Interpreters of Ethics

The higher you ascend in the scale of life, the more attention must be paid to universe ethics. Every new group of colleagues met with adds one more level of ethics to be recognized and complied with until, by the time the mortals of ascent reach Paradise, they really need someone to provide helpful and friendly counsel regarding ethical interpretations. The interpreters of ethics are of inestimable assistance to the Paradise arrivals in helping them to adjust to numerous groups of majestic beings during that eventful period extending from the attainment of residential status to formal induction into the Corps of Mortal Finaliters.

27:4. Directors of Conduct

Having already been fully instructed in the ethics of Paradise relationships the ascendant mortals find it helpful to receive the counsel of the superaphic directors of conduct, who instruct the new members of Paradise society in the usages of the perfect conduct of the high beings who sojourn on the central Isle of Light and Life. Harmony is the keynote of the central universe. All Paradise conduct is wholly spontaneous, in every sense natural and free. But there still is a proper and perfect way of doing things on the eternal Isle. These directors of conduct are chiefly concerned with instructing the new mortal residents regarding the almost endless array of new situations and unfamiliar usages.

27:5. The Custodians of Knowledge

The superaphic custodians of knowledge are the higher "living epistles" known and read by all who dwell on Paradise. They are the divine records of truth, the living books of real knowledge. They are in reality living, automatic libraries. No longer must you seek enlightenment from engrossed pages; you now commune with living intelligence face to face. Supreme knowledge you thus obtain from the living beings who are its final custodians. These primary supernaphim who are inherently in possession of universe knowledge are also responsible for its organization and classification.

27:6. Masters of Philosophy

Next to the supreme satisfaction of worship is the exhilaration of philosophy. Never do you climb so high or advance so far that there do not remain a thousand mysteries which demand the employment of philosophy in an attempted solution. The master philosophers of Paradise delight to lead the minds of its inhabitants in the exhilarating pursuit of attempting to solve universe problems. With them knowledge attains to truth and experience ascends to wisdom. They may even seek to encompass the concepts of the Ultimate and attempt to grasp the techniques of the Absolutes. These Paradise philosophers teach by every possible method of instruction. One hour's instruction on Paradise would be the equivalent of ten thousand years of the word-memory methods of Urantia. When you have listened to these primary supernaphim discourse upon the unsolved problems of eternity and the performances of the Absolutes, you will feel a certain and lasting satisfaction concerning these unmastered questions.

27:7. Conductors of Worship

Worship is the highest privilege and the first duty of all created intelligences. Worship is the first and dominant passion of all who climb to the Isle of Paradise. It becomes necessary to direct and otherwise control its expression. It is the task of the conductors of worship so to teach the ascendant creatures how to worship that they may be enabled to gain this satisfaction of self-expression and at the same time be able to give attention to the essential activities of the Paradise regime. Sometimes all Paradise becomes engulfed in a dominating tide of spiritual and worshipful expression. Often the conductors of worship cannot control such phenomena until the appearance of the threefold fluctuation of the light of the Deity abode, signifying that the divine heart of the Gods has been fully and completely satisfied by the sincere worship of the residents of Paradise. After the attainment of the supreme satisfaction of the fullness of worship, you are qualified for admission to the Corps of the Finality. The endless service of the Paradise Trinity is about to begin; and now the finaliter is face to face with the challenge of God the Ultimate.

Paper 28: Ministering Spirits of the Superuniverses

Mighty Messenger

AS the supernaphim are the angelic hosts of the central universe and the seraphim of the local universes, so are the seconaphim the ministering spirits of the superuniverses. They embrace the following three orders: the *Seconaphim*, the *Tertiaphim*, and the *Omniaphim*.

28:1. The Tertiaphim

Throughout the early times of universe building, one thousand tertiaphim are the only personal staff of a Creator Son. They serve by the side of the Creator Son until the day of the personalization of the Bright and Morning Star. They then retire from active service in the local universe and become the liaison ministers between the Creator Son and the Ancients of Days.

28:2. The Omniaphim

The omniaphim are wholly occupied with the oversight of the superuniverses in the interests of administrative co-ordination from the viewpoint of the Seven Supreme Executives. Our colony on Uversa receives instructions from, and makes reports to, only the Supreme Executive of Orvonton.

28:3. The Seconaphim

The seconaphim of the superuniverses are the offspring of the Reflective Spirits, and therefore reflectivity is inherent in their nature.

28:4. The Primary Seconaphim

The primary seconaphim are living mirrors in the service of the Ancients of Days. Think what it means in the economy of a superuniverse to be able to turn to a living mirror and therein to see and to hear the certain responses of another being a thousand or a hundred thousand light-years distant and to do all this instantly and unerringly. The primary seconaphim are found to incline by inherent nature towards seven types of service: 1. The Voice of the Conjoint Actor; 2. The Voice of the Seven Master Spirits; 3. The Voice of the Creator Sons; 4. The Voice of the Angelic Hosts; 5. Broadcast Receivers; 6. Transport Personalities; and 7. The Reserve Corps. Their usual tasks are the performance of those generalized duties of a superuniverse which do not fall within the scope of the angels of specific assignment.

28:5. The Secondary Seconaphim

Seconaphim of the secondary order are no less reflective than their primary fellows. The seven reflective types of secondary seconaphim are assigned to the services of the co-ordinate Trinity-origin associates of the Ancients of Days: the Perfectors of Wisdom, the Divine Counselors, and the Universal Censors. Like the primary order, this group is created serially: 1. *The Voice of Wisdom*. Certain of these seconaphim are in perpetual liaison with the living libraries of Paradise; 2. *The Soul of Philosophy*. These teachers are in focal synchrony with the masters of philosophy on Paradise; 3. *The Union of Souls*. These seconaphim remain in reflective liaison with the interpreters of ethics on Paradise. These are the angels who foster and promote the teamwork of all Orvonton. One of the most important lessons to be learned during your mortal career is teamwork; 4. *The Heart of Counsel*. Seconaphim of this type are in possession of the facts and wise counsel of the high minds of Havona and even of Paradise; 5. *The Joy of Existence*. Their principal activities are directed toward promoting reactions of joy among the various orders of the angelic hosts and the lower will creatures; 6. *The Satisfaction of Service*. These angels are highly reflective of the attitude of the directors of conduct on Paradise; 7. *The Discerner of Spirits*. These discerners inform us as to the true motive, the actual purpose, and the real nature of the origin and nature of motive and purpose.

28:6. The Tertiary Seconaphim

All tertiary seconaphim are collectively assigned to the Trinitized Sons of Attainment, who use them interchangeably. These seven types of tertiary seconaphim are: 1. *The Significance of Origins*. These angels are the living ready-reference genealogies of the vast hosts of beings—men, angels, and others; 2. *The Memory of Mercy*. These are the actual, full and replete, living records of the mercy which has been extended to individuals and races; 3. *The Import of Time*. The Imports of Time must always afford testimony to show that every defendant has had ample time for making decisions, achieving choice. These time evaluators portray the element of time which will be required in the completion of any undertaking; 4. *The Solemnity of Trust*. They unerringly reflect to the governing authorities the exact trustworthiness of any candidate to discharge responsibility and fulfill missions; 5. *The Sanctity of Service*. The real nature of any service, be it rendered by man or angel, is fully revealed in the faces of these secoraphic service indicators. Service—more service, increased service, difficult service, adventurous service, and at last divine and perfect service—is the goal of time and the destination of space; 6 and 7. *The Secret of Greatness and the Soul of Goodness*. Greatness and goodness simply cannot be divorced. This truth is literally and strikingly illustrated by the reflective interdependence of the Secret of Greatness and the Soul of Goodness, for neither can function without the other.

28:7. Ministry of the Seconaphim

Of the three orders of seconaphim, the tertiary group, attached to the ascendant authorities, minister most extensively to the ascending creatures of time. These tertiary seconaphim are the timesavers, space abridgers, error detectors, faithful teachers, and everlasting guideposts. We are denied the full privilege of using these angels of the reflective order on Urantia. This sphere is still under partial spiritual quarantine, and some of the circuits essential to their services are not here at present. But we go on joyfully conducting our affairs with the instrumentalities at hand.

Paper 29: The Universe Power Directors

Universal Censor

OF all the universe personalities concerned in the regulation of interplanetary and interuniverse affairs, the power directors and their associates have been the least understood on Urantia. We are not permitted to give information about Primary Eventuated Master Force Organizers and Associate Transcendental Master Force Organizers. The Universe Power Directors include: 1. *The Seven Supreme Power Directors*, 2. *The Supreme Power Centers*, 3. *The Master Physical Controllers*, and 4. *The Morontia Power Supervisors*.

29:1. The Seven Supreme Power Directors

The Seven Supreme Power Directors are the physical-energy regulators of the grand universe. These power directors function singly in the power-energy regulation of the superuniverses but collectively in the administration of the central creation. These mighty beings are the physical ancestors of the vast host of the power centers and, through them, of the physical controllers scattered throughout the seven superuniverses.

29:2. The Supreme Power Centers

The Supreme Power Centers of the grand universe function in the following seven groups: 1. Supreme Center Supervisors, 2. Havona Centers, 3. Superuniverse Centers, 4. Local Universe Centers, 5. Constellation Centers, 6. System Centers, and 7. Unclassified Centers. The Supreme Center Supervisors are the regulators of the master energy circuits of the grand universe. Each Havona Center has the supervision of a thousand Havona worlds. Here in the divine universe there is perfection of energy control. The Superuniverse Centers convert the force-energies of nether Paradise into channels of useful electronic application. The Local Universe Centers downstep and otherwise modify the power circuits emanating from superuniverse headquarters, thus making them applicable to the services of the constellations and systems. The Constellation Centers send the power lines for communication and transport and for the energizing of those living creatures who are dependent upon certain forms of physical energy for the maintenance of life. System Centers dispatch the power circuits to the inhabited worlds of time and space. Unclassified Centers function in special local situations but not on the inhabited planets.

29:3. The Domain of Power Centers

The power centers are in some way closely associated with the cosmic overcontrol of the Supreme Being. They are always on duty; never for a fraction of a second can these beings relinquish their direct supervision of the energy circuits of time and space. In any local energy situation the centers and controllers exert near-supremacy, but they are always conscious of the superenergy presence and the unrecognizable performance of the Unqualified Absolute.

29:4. The Master Physical Controllers

These beings are the mobile subordinates of the Supreme Power Centers. They are able to traverse local space at velocities approaching the flight of Solitary Messengers. The physical controllers are chiefly occupied in the adjustment of basic energies undiscovered on Urantia. The Master Physical Controllers include the following: Associate Power Directors, Mechanical Controllers, Energy Transformers, Energy Transmitters, Primary Associators, Secondary Dissociators, and the Frandalanks and Chronoldeks. Associate Power Directors keep the whole vast living energy aggregation in harmonious synchrony. Mechanical Controllers possess the living endowment of antigravity in excess of all other beings. Ten of these controllers are now stationed on Urantia, and one of their most important planetary activities is to facilitate the departure of seraphic transports. Energy Transformers are powerful and effective living switches. The status of the physical realms seems to undergo a transformation under their skillful manipulation. Energy Transmitters can render a distant scene "visible" as well as a distant sound "audible." They provide the emergency lines of communication in the local systems and on the individual planets. Primary Associators are masterly energy conservators and custodians. Secondary Dissociators are endowed with the unique power of evolving limitless supplies of energy. The frandalanks function exclusively as living and automatic presence, pressure, and velocity gauges. The frandalanks that register time in addition to quantitative and qualitative energy presence are called chronoldeks.

29:5. The Master Force Organizers

The Master Force Organizers function mainly in the domains of unorganized space and comprise two divisions of service: Primary Eventuated Master Force Organizers and Associate Transcendental Master Force Organizers. Primary Master Force Organizers are the manipulators of the primordial or basic space-forces of the Unqualified Absolute; they are nebulae creators. They are succeeded by the associate force organizers, who continue the process of energy transmutation from the primary through the secondary or gravity-energy stage. Upon the completion of the plans for the creation of a local universe, signaled by the arrival of a Creator Son, the Associate Master Force Organizers give way to the orders of power directors acting in the superuniverse of astronomic jurisdiction. The only other types of revealed beings capable of functioning in these realms of outer space are the Solitary Messengers and the Inspired Trinity Spirits.

Paper 30: Personalities of the Grand Universe
Mighty Messenger

THE personalities and other-than-personal entities now functioning on Paradise and in the grand universe constitute a well-nigh limitless number of living beings.

30:1. The Paradise Classification of Living Beings

I. Triune-Origin Beings: *Supreme Spirits*—The Seven Master Spirits, the Seven Supreme Executives, and the Seven Orders of Reflective Spirits. *Stationary Sons*—Trinitized Secrets of Supremacy, Eternals of Days, Ancients of Days, Perfections of Days, Recents of Days, Unions of Days, Faithfuls of Days, Perfectors of Wisdom, Divine Counselors, and Universal Censors. *Trinity-origin and Trinitized Beings*—Trinity Teacher Sons, Inspired Trinity Spirits, Havona Natives, Paradise Citizens, Unrevealed Trinity-origin Beings, Unrevealed Deity-trinitized Beings, Trinitized Sons of Attainment, Trinitized Sons of Selection, Trinitized Sons of Perfection, and Creature-trinitized Sons.

II. Dual-Origin Beings: *The Descending Orders*—Creator Sons, Magisterial Sons, Bright and Morning Stars, Father Melchizedeks, the Melchizedeks, the Vorondadeks, the Lanonandeks, Brilliant Evening Stars, the Archangels, Life Carriers, Unrevealed Universe Aids, and Unrevealed Sons of God. *The Stationary Orders*—Abandonters, Susatia, Univitatia, Spironga, and Unrevealed Dual-origin Beings. *The Ascending Orders*—Adjuster-fused Mortals, Son-fused Mortals, Spirit-fused Mortals, Translated Midwayers, and Unrevealed Ascenders.

III. Single-Origin Beings: *The Supreme Spirits*—Gravity Messengers, the Seven Spirits of the Havona Circuits, the Twelvefold Adjutants of the Havona Circuits, the Reflective Image Aids, Universe Mother Spirits, the Sevenfold Adjutant Mind-Spirits, and Unrevealed Deity-origin Beings. *The Ascending Orders*—Personalized Adjusters, Ascending Material Sons, Evolutionary Seraphim, Evolutionary Cherubim, and Unrevealed Ascenders. *The Family of the Infinite Spirit*—Solitary Messengers, Universe Circuit Supervisors, Census Directors, Personal Aids of the Infinite Spirit, Associate Inspectors, Assigned Sentinels, Graduate Guides, Havona Servitals, Universal Conciliators, Morontia Companions, Supernaphim, Seconaphim, Tertiaphim, Omniaphim, Seraphim, Cherubim and Sanobim, Unrevealed Spirit-origin Beings, the Seven Supreme Power Directors, the Supreme Power Centers, the Master Physical Controllers, and the Morontia Power Supervisors.

IV. Eventuated Transcendental (absonite) Beings: The Architects of the Master Universe, Transcendental Recorders, Other Transcendentalers, Primary Eventuated Master Force Organizers, and Associate Transcendental Master Force Organizers.

V. Fragmented Entities of Deity: Thought Adjusters, Infinite Spirit fragments, individualized spirits of a Creator Son, and other fragmentations of Deity.

VI. Superpersonal Beings: There is a vast host of other-than-personal beings of divine origin and of manifold service in the universe of universes.

VII. Unclassified and Unrevealed Orders: These include the Consummator of Universe Destiny, the Qualified Vicegerents of the Ultimate, the Unqualified Supervisors of the Supreme, the Unrevealed Creative Agencies of the Ancients of Days, Majeston of Paradise, the Unnamed Reflectivator Liaisons of Majeston, and the Midsonite Orders of the Local Universes.

30:2. The Uversa Personality Register

I. The Paradise Deities: The Universal Father, the Eternal Son, and the Infinite Spirit.

II. The Supreme Spirits: The Seven Master Spirits, the Seven Supreme Executives, the Seven Groups of Reflective Spirits, the Reflective Image Aids, the Seven Spirits of the Circuits, Local Universe Creative Spirits, and Adjutant Mind-Spirits.

III. The Trinity-Origin Beings: Trinitized Secrets of Supremacy, Eternals of Days, Ancients of Days, Perfections of Days, Recents of Days, Unions of Days, Faithfuls of Days, Trinity Teacher Sons, Perfectors of Wisdom, Divine Counselors, Universal Censors, Inspired Trinity Spirits, Havona Natives, and Paradise Citizens.

IV. The Sons of God: *Descending*—Creator Sons (Michaels), Magisterial Sons (Avonals), Trinity Teacher Sons (Daynals), Melchizedek Sons, Vorondadek Sons, Lanonandek Sons, and Life Carrier Sons. *Ascending*—Father-fused Mortals, Son-fused Mortals, Spirit-fused Mortals, Evolutionary Seraphim, Ascending Material Sons, Translated Midwayers, and Personalized Adjusters. *Trinitized*—Mighty Messengers, Those High in Authority, Those without Name and Number, Trinitized Custodians, Trinitized Ambassadors, Celestial Guardians, High Son Assistants, Ascender-trinitized Sons, Paradise-Havona-trinitized Sons, and Trinitized Sons of Destiny.

V. Personalities of the Infinite Spirit: *Higher Personalities*—Solitary Messengers, Universe Circuit Supervisors, Census Directors, Personal Aids of the Infinite Spirit, Associate Inspectors, Assigned Sentinels, and Graduate Guides. *Messenger Hosts of Space*—Havona Servitals, Universal Conciliators, Technical Advisers, Custodians of Records on Paradise, Celestial Recorders, Morontia Companions, and Paradise Companions. *Ministering Spirits*—Supernaphim, Seconaphim, Tertiaphim, Omniaphim, Seraphim, Cherubim and Sanobim, and Midwayers.

VI. The Universe Power Directors: *The Seven Supreme Power Directors* and *Supreme Power Centers*—Supreme Center Supervisors, Havona Centers, Superuniverse Centers, Local Universe Centers, Constellation Centers, System Centers, and Unclassified Centers. *Master Physical Controllers*—Associate Power Directors, Mechanical Controllers, Energy Transformers, Energy Transmitters, Primary Associators, Secondary Dissociators, and Frandalanks and Chronoldeks. *Morontia Power Supervisors*—Circuit Regulators, System Co-ordinators, Planetary Custodians, Combined Controllers, Liaison Stabilizers, Selective Assorters, and Associate Registrars.

VII. The Corps of Permanent Citizenship: The Planetary Midwayers, the Adamic Sons of the Systems, the Constellation Univitatia, the Local Universe Susatia, Spirit-fused Mortals of the Local Universes, the Superuniverse Abandonters, Son-fused Mortals of the Superuniverse, the Havona Natives, Natives of the Paradise Spheres of the Spirit, Natives of the Father's Paradise Spheres, the Created Citizens of Paradise, and Adjuster-fused Mortal Citizens of Paradise.

Composite Personality Groups: *The Paradise Corps of the Finality*—Mortal Finaliters, Paradise Finaliters, Trinitized Finaliters, Conjoint Trinitized Finaliters, Havona Finaliters, Transcendental Finaliters, and the Corps of Unrevealed Sons of Destiny. *The Universe Aids*—Bright and Morning Stars, Brilliant Evening Stars, Archangels, Most High Assistants, High Commissioners, Celestial Overseers, and Mansion World Teachers. *The Seven Courtesy Colonies.*

30:3. The Courtesy Colonies

These include Star Students, Celestial Artisans, Reversion Directors, Extension-school Instructors, the Various Reserve Corps, Student Visitors, and Ascending Pilgrims.

30:4. The Ascending Mortals

Ascending Mortals follow seven stages in the ascending universe career:

1. *Planetary Mortals*—animal-origin evolutionary beings of ascendant potential.

2. *Sleeping Survivors*—mortals who have been unable to attain that level of intelligence mastery and endowment of spirituality which would entitle

them go directly to the mansion worlds and who must rest in unconscious sleep until the judgment day of a new epoch.

3. *Mansion World Students*—mortal survivors who have received a new morontia body as the new life vehicle for the immortal soul and for the indwelling of the returned Adjuster.

4. *Morontia Progressors*—those who are advancing through the spheres of the system, constellation, and the local universe before departing for the receiving worlds of the minor sectors of the superuniverse.

5. *Superuniverse Wards*—ascenders who have arrived on the training worlds of the superuniverse as accredited spirits to begin the same thorough course in superuniverse management that they received during their local universe experience.

6. *Havona Pilgrims*—Havona arrivals, spirits whose development is complete though not replete, who will now receive instruction that is personal and threefold in nature: intellectual, spiritual, and experiential.

7. *Paradise Arrivals*—perfected spirits who begin the progressive course in divinity and absonity, who have found God and are mustered into the Mortal Corps of the Finality.

The future ages of the evolution of the spheres of outer space will undoubtedly further elaborate, and with more repleteness divinely illuminate, the wisdom and loving-kindness of the Gods in the execution of their divine plan of human survival and mortal ascension.

Paper 31: The Corps of the Finality

Divine Counselor and One without Name or Number

THE Corps of Mortal Finaliters represents the present known destination of the ascending Adjuster-fused mortals of time. The primary finaliter corps is composed of the following: Havona Natives, Gravity Messengers, Glorified Mortals, Adopted Seraphim, Glorified Material Sons and Glorified Midway Creatures. Their future destination must be the now-organizing universes of outer space. One or more companies of the mortal finaliters are constantly in service on Urantia.

31:1. The Havona Natives

Havona natives provide the viewpoint of one born in perfection and divine repleteness but must achieve certain experiential developments in liaison with evolutionary beings in order to create reception capacity for a fragment of the spirit of the Universal Father These finaliters thus embrace both phases of experiential existence—perfect and perfected.

31:2. Gravity Messengers

Gravity Messengers are modified and personalized Adjusters. They are under the exclusive jurisdiction of Grandfanda, and are assigned only to the primary (mortal) Corps of the Finality. No other group of intelligent creatures possesses such a personalized messenger corps able to transcend time and space. They seem to be competent to utilize any and all energies, circuits, and even gravity. The Gravity Messenger in the Mortal Corps of the Finality has a permanent staff of 999 fellow messengers assigned to him and may call upon the reserves of the order for assistants in unlimited numbers.

31:3. Glorified Mortals

Ascendant Adjuster-fused mortals compose the bulk of the primary Corps of the Finality. Each company of one thousand finaliters has places for just ten nonmortal and nonseraphic personalities. These Adjuster-fused mortals are sixth-stage spirits.

There undoubtedly remains one more step in the career of the Mortal Corps of the Finality. We surmise that the bestowal of seventh-spirit classification upon the Mortal Corps of the Finality will be simultaneous with their advancement to eternal assignment for service on hitherto unrecorded and unrevealed spheres and concomitant with their attainment of God the Supreme. You are free to conjecture with us respecting the mystery of the ultimate destiny of the Paradise Corps of Finality. We all ask, "Why should the Gods be so concerned in so thoroughly training surviving mortals in the technique of universe management?"

31:4. Adopted Seraphim

These are the faithful seraphic guardians of mortals who are permitted to go through the ascendant career with their human wards. After becoming Father fused, they join their subjects in taking the finaliter oath of eternity and forever accept the destiny of their mortal associates.

31:5. Glorified Material Sons

When an advanced evolutionary world attains the later eras of the age of light and life, the Material Sons, the Planetary Adam and Eve, may elect to humanize, receive Adjusters, and embark upon the evolutionary course of universe ascent leading to the Corps of Mortal Finaliters. Their presence lends great potential to the possibilities of high service for such a group, and they are invariably chosen as its leaders.

31:6. Glorified Midway Creatures

Midwayers seldom tarry on their native world subsequent to its being settled in light and life. Then, or soon thereafter, they are released from permanent-citizenship status and start on the ascension to Paradise in company with the mortals of time and space. The secondary midwayers are all eventually Adjuster fused and are mustered into the mortal corps.

31:7. The Evangels of Light

Any celestial personality assigned to the service of any finaliter corps (which currently numbers 999 personalities) is denominated an Evangel of Light. These beings are not of permanent attachment. The finaliters, as might be expected, engage in much speculation as to the identity of their future comrades, but there is little agreement among them. We will most likely have to await the entrance of the finaliters upon their seventh stage of spirit attainment before we really know.

31:8. The Transcendentalers

Transcendentalers are eventuated beings of absonite attributes. Part of the perfected mortal's experience on Paradise as a finaliter consists in the effort to achieve comprehension of the nature and function of more than one thousand groups of the transcendental supercitizens of Paradise. The vast host of the Paradise Transcendentalers are concerned only with the superadministration of the affairs of the master universe. They are subject to God the Ultimate, and their present Paradise sojourn is in every way Trinity supervised and directed. Although all mortals who attain Paradise frequently fraternize with the Transcendentalers, it develops that man's first serious contact with a Transcendentaler occurs when the mortal ascender stands in the finaliter receiving circle as the Trinity oath of eternity is administered by the chief of Transcendentalers, the presiding head of the Architects of the Master Universe.

31:9. Architects of the Master Universe

The Architects of the Master Universe are the governing corps of the Paradise Transcendentalers. This governing corps numbers 28,011 personalities possessing master minds, superb spirits, and supernal absonites. These Master Architects exist in seven levels of the absonite: 1. *The Paradise Level*—The senior Architect, 2. *The Havona Level*—Three Architects, 3. *The Superuniverse Level*—Seven Architects, 4. *The Primary Space Level*—Seventy Architects, 5. *The Secondary Space Level*—490 Architects, 6. *The Tertiary Space Level*—3,430 Architects, 7. *The Quartan Space Level*—24,010 Architects. The Architects of the Master Universe have at their disposal numerous groups of assistants and helpers, including two vast orders of Master Force Organizers. Only Solitary Messengers and Inspired Trinity Spirits maintain any organic association with the Transcendentalers and the Architects of the Master Universe. The Master Architects contribute technical approval of the assignment of the Creator Sons to their space sites for the organization of the local universes.

31:10. The Ultimate Adventure

The senior Master Architect has the oversight of the seven Corps of the Finality: 1. The Corps of Mortal Finaliters. 2. The Corps of Paradise Finaliters. 3. The Corps of Trinitized Finaliters. 4. The Corps of Conjoint Trinitized Finaliters. 5. The Corps of Havona Finaliters. 6. The Corps of Transcendental Finaliters. and 7. The Corps of Unrevealed Sons of Destiny. These seven finaliter corps probably signify the present activity of the Ultimate Trinity engaged in mustering the forces of the finite and the absonite in preparation for inconceivable developments in the universes of outer space.

These outer universes will all enjoy the matchless ministry and supernal overcontrol of the Supreme Being, but the very fact of his active presence precludes their participation in the actualization of the Supreme Deity. But those of us who have acquired this unique experience during the youth of the universe will treasure it throughout all future eternity. We anticipate that something new and unrevealed is approaching culmination in the master universe. Evolutionary mortals are born on the planets of space, pass through the morontia worlds, ascend the spirit universes, traverse the Havona spheres, find God, attain Paradise, and are mustered into the primary Corps of the Finality, therein to await the next assignment of universe service. As we view this sublime spectacle, we all exclaim: What a glorious destiny for the animal-origin children of time, the material sons of space!

PART II
THE LOCAL UNIVERSE

Paper 32: The Evolution of the Local Universes
Mighty Messenger

A LOCAL universe is the handiwork of a Creator Son of the Paradise order of Michael. It comprises one hundred constellations, each embracing one hundred systems of inhabited worlds. Each system will eventually contain approximately one thousand inhabited spheres.

32:1. Physical Emergence of Universes

There is no opportunity for a Creator Son to begin universe organization until the power directors have effected the mobilization of the space-energies sufficiently to provide suns and material spheres for the emerging universe. When energy-matter has attained a certain stage in mass materialization, a Paradise Creator Son appears upon the scene, accompanied by a Creative Daughter of the Infinite Spirit. Simultaneously with the arrival of the Creator Son, work is begun upon the architectural sphere which is to become the headquarters world of the projected local universe.

32:2. Universe Organization

The first completed act of physical creation in Nebadon consisted in the organization of the headquarters world, the architectural sphere of Salvington. This was immediately followed by the creation of the one hundred headquarters worlds of the projected constellations and the ten thousand headquarters spheres of the projected local systems. Presently, the physical plan of a universe is completed, and the Creator Son, in association with the Creative Spirit, projects his plan of life creation. When this first creative act is formulated and executed, there springs into being the Bright and Morning Star, the chief executive of the universe. There ensues the bringing into existence of a vast and wonderful array of diverse creatures: the fathers of the constellations, the sovereigns of the local systems, and the Planetary Princes presiding over the individual worlds. And then does the Creator Son enter into the Father's proposal to create mortal man in their divine image.

The organization of planetary abodes is still progressing in Nebadon. Satania, the local system of your world, has 619 inhabited worlds. From Jerusem, the headquarters of Satania, it is over two hundred thousand light-years to the physical center of the superuniverse of Orvonton.

32:3. The Evolutionary Idea

The only creation that is perfectly settled is Havona, the central universe. The creations of the seven superuniverses are finite, evolutionary, and consistently progressive. In the central universe the Father is personally present as such but absent in the minds of the children of that perfect creation; in the universes of space the Father is absent in person, being represented by his Sovereign Sons, while he is intimately present in the minds of his mortal children. The surest safeguard for the creature throughout the long struggle to attain the Father, during this time when inherent conditions make such attainment impossible, is tenaciously to hold on to the truth-fact of the Father's presence in his Sons. It is a fact: He who has seen a Creator Son has seen the Father. With those who entertain the Mystery Monitors, there is no limit to the possible heights of their spiritual ascent and universe attainment. When the heights of perfection and eternity are attained, those who began at the bottom and joyfully climbed the ladder of life will have gained a personal experience which embodies an actual knowledge of every phase of life from the bottom to the top. The divinely perfect creature and the evolutionary perfected creature are equal in degree of divinity potential, but they differ in kind. Each requires the other to achieve completion of function, service, and destiny.

32:4. God's Relation to a Local Universe

Do not entertain the idea that, since the Universal Father has delegated so much of himself and his power to his ordained agencies and personalities, he is a silent or inactive member of the Deity partnership. There is on God's part an actual, literal, and personal participation in these events. The law of the Creator Son, the rule of the Constellation Fathers, the System Sovereigns, and the Planetary Princes always prevail. But such a plan does not mean that the Universal Father may not in his own way intervene and do aught that pleases the divine mind with any individual creature throughout all creation. Through the personality circuit the Father is cognizant of all the thoughts and acts of all the beings in all the systems of all the universes of all creation. The Universal Father has truly divested himself of every function which it is possible for another being to perform. God has given us himself that we may be like him, and he has reserved for himself of power and glory only that which is necessary for the maintenance of all things.

32:5. The Eternal and Divine Purpose

There is a great and glorious purpose in the march of the universes through space. All of your mortal struggling is not in vain. We are all part of an immense plan, a gigantic enterprise, and it is the vastness of the undertaking that renders it impossible to see very much of it at any one time and during any one life. There is in the mind of God a plan which embraces every creature of all his vast domains, and this plan is an eternal purpose of boundless opportunity, unlimited progress, and endless life. And the infinite treasures of such a matchless career are yours for the striving! The goal of eternity is ahead! The adventure of divinity attainment lies before you! The race for perfection is on! whosoever will may enter, and certain victory will crown the efforts of every human being who will run the race of faith and trust, depending every step of the way on the leading of the indwelling Adjuster and on the guidance of that good spirit of the Universe Son, which so freely has been poured out upon all flesh.

Paper 33: Administration of the Local Universe
Chief of Archangels

WHILE the Universal Father most certainly rules over his vast creation, he functions in a local universe administration through the person of the Creator Son. Michael and the local universe Mother Spirit delegate executive power to Gabriel and jurisdictional authority to the Constellation Fathers, System Sovereigns, and Planetary Princes.

33:1. Michael of Nebadon

The Michael of Nebadon is the "only-begotten Son" personalizing the 611,121st universal concept of the Universal Father and the Eternal Son. His headquarters is in the threefold mansion of light on Salvington. And this dwelling is so ordered because Michael has experienced the living of all three phases of intelligent creature existence: spiritual, morontial, and material. Because of the name associated with his seventh and final bestowal on Urantia, he is sometimes spoken of as Christ Michael. Creator Sons are the final power-personality focalizations of the mighty time-space attributes of God the Sevenfold. To our universe and all its inhabited worlds the Sovereign Son is, to all practical intents and purposes, God. In the person of the Creator Son we have a ruler and divine parent who is just as mighty, efficient, and beneficent as would be the Universal Father and the Eternal Son if both were present on Salvington and engaged in the administration of the affairs of the universe of Nebadon.

33:2. The Sovereign of Nebadon

Our Creator Son very definitely manifests traits and attributes which more resemble the Eternal Son. Michael is the personification of the Paradise Father-Son to and in the local universe of Nebadon. When the Creative Mother Spirit subordinated herself to Christ Michael upon the return from his final bestowal on Urantia, the Master Son thereby acquired jurisdiction over "all power in heaven and on earth." The creature-bestowal experiences of the Michaels qualify them to portray the experiential divinity of the Supreme Being. No other beings in the universes have thus personally exhausted the potentials of present finite experience for solitary sovereignty.

33:3. The Universe Son and Spirit

As concerns a local universe, the administrative authority of a Creator Son is supreme; the Infinite Spirit, as the Divine Minister, is wholly co-operative though perfectly co-ordinate. The Son functions as a father in his local universe. The Spirit enacts the role of a mother, always assisting the Son and being everlastingly indispensable to the administration of the universe. After the pledge of subordination by the Creative Mother Spirit, Michael of Nebadon nobly acknowledged his eternal dependence on his Spirit companion and there went forth the final "Proclamation of Equality." The Son and the Spirit now preside over the universe much as a father and mother watch over, and minister to, their family of sons and daughters. The Son initiates the creation of certain of the universe children, while the Spirit is solely responsible for bringing into existence the numerous orders of spirit personalities. In the creation of other types of universe personalities, both the Son and the Spirit function together, and in no creative act does the one do aught without the counsel and approval of the other.

33:4. Gabriel—The Chief Executive

The Bright and Morning Star is the personalization of the first concept of identity and ideal of personality conceived by the Creator Son and the local universe Daughter of the Infinite Spirit. Only one such being of wisdom and majesty is brought forth in each local universe. Gabriel of Salvington is like the Universe Son in divinity of nature though considerably limited in the attributes of Deity. This first-born of the parents of a new universe is a unique personality possessing many wonderful traits not visibly present in either ancestor, a being of unprecedented versatility and unimagined brilliance. Gabriel of Salvington is the chief executive of the universe of Nebadon and the arbiter of all executive appeals respecting its administration. He may employ any and all of the orders of celestial beings functioning in Nebadon, and he is also the commander in chief of "the armies of heaven." Mortals will seldom encounter him as they ascend through the local universe until they are inducted into the administrative work of the local creation. As administrators, of whatever order or degree, you will come under the direction of Gabriel.

33:5. The Trinity Ambassadors

The ambassador of the Paradise Trinity—Immanuel of Salvington—the Union of Days, is assigned to the local universe of Nebadon. He bears the distinction of being the only personality in all Nebadon who has never acknowledged subordination to his brother Michael. He functions as adviser to the Sovereign Son but gives counsel only on request. He does not exercise authoritative jurisdiction in the executive affairs of an evolving local universe except in the supervision of his liaison brethren, the Faithfuls of Days, serving on the headquarters of the constellations. The Faithfuls of Days, like the Union of Days, never proffer advice or offer assistance to the constellation rulers unless it is asked for.

33:6. General Administration

Gabriel is the chief executive and actual administrator of Nebadon. The Father Melchizedek is Gabriel's first assistant.

A system government is more particularly concerned with the physical status of living beings. The constellation rulers pay especial attention to the social and governmental conditions and are chiefly exercised over unification and stabilization. The local universe rulers are more occupied with the spiritual status of the realms. From Salvington, broadcasts are simultaneously directed to the constellation headquarters, the system headquarters, and to individual planets. Planetary intercommunication is denied only those worlds under spiritual quarantine.

The standard day of Nebadon is equal to eighteen days and six hours of Urantia time, plus two and one-half minutes. The Nebadon year is equal to about five years of Urantia time. Nebadon time, broadcast from Salvington, is the standard for all constellations and systems in this local universe. Each constellation conducts its affairs by Nebadon time, but the systems maintain their own chronology, as do the individual planets. The day in Satania, is a little less (1 hour, 4 minutes, 15 seconds) than three days of Urantia time.

33:7. The Courts of Nebadon

The Master Son, Michael, is supremely concerned with but three things: creation, sustenance, and ministry. The entire judicial mechanism of Nebadon is under the supervision of Gabriel. The high courts, located on Salvington, are occupied with problems of general universe import and with the appellate cases coming up from the system tribunals. In all matters of adjudication there presides a dual magistracy consisting of one judge of perfection antecedents and one magistrate of ascendant experience.

As regards jurisdiction, the local universe courts are final and supreme except for in the following matters: 1. The universe tribunals are denied the right to pass upon those cases involving the question of eternal life and death. 2. The default or defection of any of the Local Universe Sons of God which jeopardizes their status and authority as Sons is never adjudicated in the tribunals of a Son; such a misunderstanding would be immediately carried to the superuniverse courts. 3. The question of the readmission of any constituent part of a local universe—such as a local system—to the fellowship of full spiritual status in the local creation subsequent to spiritual isolation must be concurred in by the high assembly of the superuniverse.

33:8. The Legislative and Executive Functions

On Salvington, the headquarters of Nebadon, there are no true legislative bodies. The legislative assemblies of the local universe are located on the headquarters of the one hundred constellations. The System Sovereigns and their associates enforce the legislative mandates of the constellation rulers and execute the judicial decrees of the high courts of the universe. The supreme council of the local universe is made up of three members from each system and seven representatives from each constellation. Systems in isolation do not have representation in this assembly, but they are permitted to send observers who attend and study all its deliberations. The one hundred councils of supreme sanction are also situated on Salvington. The presidents of these councils constitute the immediate working cabinet of Gabriel. All findings of the high universe advisory councils are referred either to the Salvington judicial bodies or to the legislative assemblies of the constellations. These high councils are without authority or power to enforce their recommendations. If their advice is founded on the fundamental laws of the universe, then will the Nebadon courts issue rulings of execution; but if their recommendations have to do with local or emergency conditions, they must pass down to the legislative assemblies of the constellation for deliberative enactment and then to the system authorities for execution. These high councils are, in reality, the universe superlegislatures.

Paper 34: The Local Universe Mother Spirit

Mighty Messenger

WHEN a Creator Son is personalized by the Universal Father and the Eternal Son, then does the Infinite Spirit individualize a new and unique representation of himself to accompany this Creator Son to the realms of space.

34:1. Personalization of the Creative Spirit

After the completion of the physical organization of a starry and planetary cluster and the establishment of the energy circuits by the superuniverse power centers there goes forth the proclamation of the Michael Son that life is next to be projected in the newly organized universe. Upon the Paradise approval in the Paradise Trinity there occurs what is known as a "primary eruption" in the superuniverse Master Spirit, after which occurs a marked change in the nature of the creative spirit presence—a new personalization of the local universe Creative Mother Spirit. This personalized presence of the Infinite Spirit is known in Satania as the Divine Minister.

34:2. Nature of the Divine Minister

Having undergone marked personality metamorphosis at the time of life creation, the Divine Minister thereafter functions as a person and cooperates in a very personal manner with the Creator Son in the planning and management of the extensive affairs of their local creation. The Universe Spirit possesses all the physical-control attributes of the Infinite Spirit, including the full endowment of antigravity. Upon the attainment of personal status the Universe Spirit exerts full and complete control of mind gravity. The Creative Spirit is coresponsible with the Creator Son in producing the creatures of the worlds.

While the seventh segment of the grand universe may, in many respects, be tardy in development, we predict a high degree of symmetry in Orvonton because the presiding Spirit of this superuniverse is the chief of the Master Spirits on high, being a spirit intelligence embodying the balanced union and perfect co-ordination of the traits and character of all three of the eternal Deities. There undoubtedly awaits us a transcendent development and an unprecedented achievement sometime in the eternal ages of the future.

34:3. The Son and the Spirit in Time and Space

In personal prerogatives a Creative Spirit is wholly and entirely independent of space, but not of time. A Creator Son acts instantaneously throughout his universe; but the Creative Spirit must reckon with time in the ministration of the universal mind except as she consciously and designedly avails herself of the personal prerogatives of the Universe Son. A Creator Son is not handicapped by time, but he is conditioned by space; he cannot personally be in two places at the same time. The Divine Minister is the understanding helper of the Creator Son, enabling him to overcome and atone for his inherent limitations regarding space, for when these two function in administrative union, they are practically independent of time and space within the confines of their local creation.

34:4. The Local Universe Circuits

There are three distinct spirit circuits in the local universe of Nebadon: 1. The bestowal spirit of the Creator Son, the Comforter, the Spirit of Truth. 2. The spirit circuit of the Divine Minister, the Holy Spirit. 3. The intelligence-ministry circuit of the seven adjutant mind-spirits. The Creator Sons are endowed with the Spirit of Truth which is poured out upon a world by a bestowal Son after he receives spiritual title to such a sphere. This bestowed Comforter is the spiritual force which ever draws all truth seekers towards the Creator Son. The Universe Mother Spirit never leaves the local universe headquarters world. She acts as the universe focus and center of the Spirit of Truth as well as of her own personal influence, the Holy Spirit. The seven adjutant mind-spirits are the creation of the Divine Minister of a local universe. The adjutants are the spirits of: wisdom, worship, counsel, knowledge, courage, understanding, and intuition. The four points of the compass are universal and inherent in the life of Nebadon. All living creatures possess bodily units which are sensitive and responsive to these directional currents.

34:5. The Ministry of the Spirit

On the inhabited worlds the Spirit begins the work of evolutionary progression, starting with the lifeless material of the realm, first endowing vegetable life, then the animal organisms, then the first orders of human existence. Mortal man first experiences the ministry of the Spirit when the purely animal mind of evolutionary creatures develops reception capacity for the adjutants of worship and of wisdom. And immediately are such minds included in the spiritual circuits of the Divine Minister. The Holy Spirit is partly independent of human attitude and partially conditioned by the decisions and co-operation of the will of man. After a bestowal Son has liberated the Spirit of Truth for planetary ministry, all normal minds are automatically prepared for the reception of the Thought Adjusters. The Thought Adjusters ever work in perfect harmony with the combined spirits of the Creator Son and Creative Spirit.

34:6. The Spirit in Man

With the advancing evolution of an inhabited planet and the further spiritualization of its inhabitants, additional spiritual influences may be received by such mature personalities. Although Divinity may be plural in manifestation, in human experience Deity is singular, always one. From the heights of eternal glory the divine Spirit descends, by a long series of steps, to meet you as you are and where you are and then, in the partnership of faith, lovingly to embrace the soul of mortal origin and to embark on the sure and certain retracement of those steps of condescension, never stopping until the evolutionary soul is safely exalted to the very heights of bliss from which the divine Spirit originally sallied forth on this mission of mercy and ministry.

The dead theory of even the highest religious doctrines is powerless to transform human character or to control mortal behavior. The seed of theoretical truth is dead, the highest moral concepts without effect, unless and until the divine Spirit breathes upon the forms of truth and quickens the formulas of righteousness. Such divinely watered souls are all but independent of material environment as regards the joys of living and the satisfactions of earthly existence. The divine Spirit must dominate and control every phase of human experience. The Spirit never drives, only leads. The fruits of the spirit are love, joy, peace, long-suffering, gentleness, goodness, faith, meekness, and temperance. There truly exists within you a conspiracy of spiritual forces, a confederation of divine powers, whose exclusive purpose is to effect your final deliverance from material bondage and finite handicaps.

34:7. The Spirit and the Flesh

Evolutionary mortals inhabiting normal worlds of spiritual progress do not experience the acute conflicts between the spirit and the flesh which characterize the present-day Urantia races. The Caligastia upheaval and the Adamic default deprived the races of that superior type of physical nature which would have been more consonant with spiritual aspirations. Those God-knowing men and women who have been born of the Spirit experience no more conflict with their mortal natures than do the inhabitants of the most normal of worlds. Having started out on the way of life everlasting, having accepted the assignment and received your orders to advance, do not fear the dangers of human forgetfulness and mortal inconstancy, do not be troubled with doubts of failure or by perplexing confusion, do not falter and question your status and standing, for in every dark hour, at every crossroad in the forward struggle, the Spirit of Truth will always speak, saying, "This is the way."

Paper 35: The Local Universe Sons of God

Chief of Archangels

THE types of Sons about to be considered are of local universe origin; they are the offspring of a Paradise Creator Son with the Universe Mother Spirit. The following orders are: *Melchizedek Sons, Vorondadek Sons, Lanonandek Sons,* and *Life Carrier Sons.*

35:1. The Father Melchizedek

The original Melchizedek—the Father Melchizedek—is that unique being who subsequently collaborates with the Creator Son and the Creative Spirit to bring into existence the entire group of Melchizedek Sons. Father Melchizedek acts as the first executive associate of Gabriel. The Melchizedeks do not function extensively outside the local universe except when they are called as witnesses in matters pending before the tribunals of the superuniverse, and when designated special ambassadors.

35:2. The Melchizedek Sons

The Melchizedeks are the first order of divine Sons to approach sufficiently near the lower creature life to be able to function directly in the ministry of mortal uplift. All forms of intelligent life find in these Sons understanding friends, sympathetic teachers, and wise counselors. The Melchizedeks are a self-governing order. They are the hope of every universe group which aspires to self-government. They maintain an autonomous organization devoted to universe intelligence, making periodical reports to the Creator Son. The Melchizedeks function as mobile and advisory review courts of the realms. These eldest Sons of a universe are the chief aids of the Bright and Morning Star in carrying out the mandates of the Creator Son. There is no phase of planetary spiritual need to which they do not minister. The Melchizedeks are well-nigh perfect in wisdom, but they are not infallible in judgment. But minor misadaptations in Melchizedek function have rarely occurred in Nebadon.

35:3. The Melchizedek Worlds

The Melchizedeks occupy a world of their own near Salvington. This sphere is the pilot world of the Salvington circuit of seventy primary spheres, each of which is encircled by six tributary spheres devoted to specialized activities. These marvelous spheres are often spoken of as the Melchizedek University. Ascending mortals from all the constellations of Nebadon pass through training on all 490 worlds in the acquirement of residential status on Salvington. To an ascender the pilot world, Melchizedek, is probably the most interesting place in all Nebadon. And never will you forget your reactions to the first day of life on this unique world, not even after you have reached your Paradise destination. On the six tributary worlds of the Melchizedek sphere mortals study: 1. The initial planetary life, 2. A review of the experiences passed through on the mansion worlds, 3. Experiences on the capital of the local system, 4. A review of the experiences of the seventy tributary worlds of the constellation, 5. A review of the ascendant sojourn on the constellation headquarters world, and 6. An attempt to correlate these five epochs and enter the Melchizedek primary schools of universe training. The schools of universe administration and spiritual wisdom are located on the Melchizedek home world. The College of High Ethics here is presided over by the original Father Melchizedek. It is to these schools that the various universes send exchange students. The Melchizedeks in Nebadon are renowned throughout all Splandon.

35:4. Special Work of the Melchizedeks

A highly specialized branch of Melchizedek activities has to do with the supervision of the progressive morontia career of the ascending mortals. While the Melchizedek orders are chiefly devoted to the vast educational system, they also function in unique assignments and in unusual circumstances. On Edentia they are known as emergency Sons. In a planetary crisis these Melchizedek Sons serve in many unique capacities. It is easily possible for such a Son to make himself visible to mortal beings. Seven times in Nebadon has a Melchizedek served on an evolutionary world in the similitude of mortal flesh. The Melchizedek who lived on Urantia did foster the truth of his day and safely pass it on to Abraham and his associates.

35:5. The Vorondadek Sons

After the creation of the versatile Melchizedeks, the Creator Son and the local universe Creative Spirit brought into existence the second great and diverse order of universe sonship, the Vorondadeks. They are more generally known as Constellation Fathers because a Son of this order is uniformly found at the head of each constellation government. They do not equal their Melchizedek brethren in brilliant versatility, but they are even more reliable and efficient as rulers and farseeing administrators. They excel all orders of universe sonship in stability of purpose and in divinity of judgment. These Sons rarely fall into error, and they have never gone into rebellion. The service of the Vorondadeks in the local universes is extensive and varied. They are often entrusted with sovereign powers in critical universe situations. Their work more largely pertains to the legislative functions indigenous to the constellation governments. As a result of all these services, the Vorondadek Sons have become the historians of the local universes.

35:6. The Constellation Fathers

At least three Vorondadeks are assigned to the rulership of each of the one hundred constellations of a local universe. The reigning Most High, the Constellation Father, has two associates, a senior and a junior. At each change of administration the senior associate becomes the head of the government, the junior assumes the duties of the senior, while the unassigned Vorondadeks resident on the Salvington worlds nominate one of their number as candidate for selection to assume the responsibilities of junior associate. The one hundred Constellation Fathers constitute the supreme advisory cabinet of the Creator Son. Norlatiadek, your own constellation, is at present administered by twelve Vorondadek Sons.

35:7. The Vorondadek Worlds

The second group of seven worlds in the circuit of seventy primary spheres surrounding Salvington comprise the Vorondadek planets. Each of these spheres, with its six encircling satellites, is devoted to a special phase of Vorondadek activities. On these forty-nine realms the ascending mortals secure the acme of their education. The instruction to be had in the Vorondadek schools is unexcelled even on Uversa. The ascending pilgrims will be introduced to numerous new activities on these worlds of study and practical work. But we despair of being able to portray these undertakings to the material mind of mortal beings.

35:8. The Lanonandek Sons

After the creation of the Vorondadeks, the Creator Son and the Universe Mother Spirit unite for the purpose of bringing into existence the third order of universe sonship, the Lanonandeks. They are best known as System Sovereigns and as Planetary Princes. They were the first students in the Melchizedek University and were classified and certified by their Melchizedek teachers and examiners according to ability, personality, and attainment. They were divided in the final tests into three classes:

1. *Primary Lanonandeks.* These are the Sons designated as System Sovereigns and assistants to the supreme councils of the constellations and as counselors in the higher administrative work of the universe.
2. *Secondary Lanonandeks.* They are assigned as Planetary Princes and to the reserves of that order.
3. *Tertiary Lanonandeks.* These Sons function as subordinate assistants, messengers, custodians, commissioners, observers, and prosecute the miscellaneous duties of a system.

The Lanonandeks are of great service in the subordinate units of the universe, for they are capable of drawing nearer the lower creatures of the intelligent races. They also stand in greater danger of going astray. In executive ability they are excelled only by Gabriel and his unrevealed associates.

35:9. The Lanonandek Rulers

The Lanonandeks are the continuous rulers of the planets and the rotating sovereigns of the systems. The System Sovereigns rule in commissions of two or three on the headquarters of each system of inhabited worlds. The Constellation Father names one of these Lanonandeks as chief every deka-millennium. They are well-nigh sovereign in the local affairs of the inhabited worlds. They are the executive division of the local universe and present the one place in all universe administration where personal disloyalty to the will of the Michael Son could most easily and readily entrench itself and seek to assert itself.

Our local universe has been unfortunate in that over seven hundred Sons of the Lanonandek order have rebelled. We have had so much administrative trouble in Nebadon because our Sons of the Lanonandek order have been created with such a large degree of personal liberty. When things are fully sifted and finally settled, the gains of higher loyalty and fuller volitional service on the part of these thoroughly tested Sons will far more than compensate for the confusion and tribulations of earlier times. In the event of rebellion on a system headquarters, a new sovereign is usually installed within a comparatively short time, but not so on the individual planets. Successor Planetary Princes do not assume active rulership of such worlds until the results of insurrection are partially overcome. Only a bestowal Son can re-establish interplanetary lines of communication on such a spiritually isolated world.

35:10. The Lanonandek Worlds

The third group of seven worlds in the Salvington circuit of seventy planets constitute the Lanonandek cluster of administrative spheres. On these realms the experienced Lanonandeks belonging to the ex-System Sovereign corps officiate as administrative teachers of the ascending pilgrims and the seraphic hosts. These executive colleges are excelled only by the administrative schools of Ensa. The universe educational system sponsored by the Melchizedeks is practical, progressive, meaningful, and experiential. It embraces training in things material, intellectual, morontial, and spiritual.

Paper 36: The Life Carriers

Vorondadek Son

LIFE Carriers are entrusted with designing and carrying creature life to the planetary spheres. And after planting this life on such new worlds, they remain there for long periods to foster its development.

36:1. Origin and Nature of Life Carriers

The Life Carriers are the offspring of three pre-existent personalities: the Creator Son, the Universe Mother Spirit, and one of the three Ancients of Days. They are directed by the life-determining trio, consisting of Gabriel, the Father Melchizedek, and Nambia, the original and first-born Life Carrier of Nebadon. Life Carriers are graded into three grand divisions: The first division is the senior Life Carriers, the second, assistants, and the third, custodians. When an evolutionary planet is finally settled in light and life, the Life Carriers of that world are organized into the higher deliberative bodies of advisory capacity.

36:2. The Life Carrier Worlds

The Melchizedeks have the general oversight of the fourth group of seven primary spheres in the Salvington circuit. These worlds of the Life Carriers are designated as follows: the Life Carrier headquarters, the life-planning sphere, the life-conservation sphere, the sphere of life evolution, the sphere of life associated with mind, the sphere of mind and spirit in living beings, and the sphere of unrevealed life.

The domain of life is characterized by three, seven, and twelve or by multiples and combinations of these basic numbers. On Urantia there are forty-eight units of pattern control—trait determiners—in the sex cells of human reproduction. Urantia is a decimal planet, a life-experiment world. On planets such as yours the highest form of life is reproduced by a life-carrying bundle which possesses twenty-four pattern units. Mind is an endowment of the seven adjutant mind-spirits.

36:3. Life Transplantation

Life Carriers are the carriers, disseminators, and guardians of life. The corps of Life Carriers commissioned to plant life upon a new world usually consists of one hundred senior carriers, one hundred assistants, and one thousand custodians. The Life Carriers often carry actual life plasm to a new world, but they sometimes organize the life patterns after arriving on the planet of assignment. The vital spark is bestowed through the Life Carriers by the Universe Mother Spirit. The Life Carriers are given approximately one-half million years to establish life. During the ages intervening between life establishment and the emergence of human creatures of moral status, the Life Carriers are permitted to manipulate the life environment and otherwise favorably directionize the course of biologic evolution. Upon the arrival of a Planetary Prince they prepare to leave, though two of the senior carriers and twelve custodians may volunteer to remain indefinitely on the planet. Two such Sons and their twelve associates are now serving on Urantia.

36:4. Melchizedek Life Carriers

In every local system of inhabited worlds throughout Nebadon there is a single sphere whereon the Melchizedeks have functioned as life carriers. On each of them a materially modified Melchizedek Son has mated with a selected Material Daughter. The progeny of a Melchizedek life carrier and a Material Daughter are known as *midsoniters*. The Melchizedek father and the Mother Eve depart upon the appearance of the seventh generation of planetary offspring. The midsonite creatures live and function as reproducing beings on their magnificent worlds until they are one thousand standard years of age, whereupon they are translated by seraphic transport. The Melchizedek life carriers, as well as the associated Mother Eves, go from the system midsonite spheres to the finaliters' worlds of the Salvington circuit, where their offspring are also destined to forgather. The purpose of the midsonite creatures is not at present known. It is the belief of the Melchizedek life carriers that their midsonite children will someday be endowed with the transcendental and eternal spirit of absonity by God the Ultimate.

36:5. The Seven Adjutant Mind-Spirits

The adjutants are the children of the Universe Mother Spirit and are called by names which are the equivalents of the following designations: intuition, understanding, courage, knowledge, counsel, worship, and wisdom. The first five adjutant mind-spirits function in the animal orders. The function of the first five in the animal orders is to a certain extent essential to the function of all seven in the human intellect. The final two mind-spirits, worship and wisdom, function only in mortals that have the potential of spiritual ascension. Wisdom is the acme of intellectual performance. With the appearance of the spiritual response, such minds are instantly encircuited in the spirit cycles of the local universe Mother Spirit. Human mind has no survival qualities apart from spirit identification.

36:6. Living Forces

Ever will Urantia physicists and chemists progress in their understanding of the protoplasmic forms of vegetable and animal life, but never will they be able to produce living organisms. Life Carriers can organize the material forms but the Spirit provides the initial spark of life and bestows the endowment of mind. The survival of mortal creatures is wholly predicated on the evolvement of an immortal soul within the mortal mind. Life, as such, constitutes the animation of some pattern-configured or otherwise segregated system of energy—material, mindal, or spiritual. There are some things connected with the elaboration of life on the evolutionary planets which are not altogether clear to us. We do not wholly understand the nature and source of the life-activation spark. We know that life flows from the Father through the Son and by the Spirit. We do know that the Universe Mother Spirit actually vitalizes the lifeless patterns and imparts to such activated plasm the prerogatives of organismal reproduction.

Paper 37: Personalities of the Local Universe
Brilliant Evening Star

AT the head of all personality in Nebadon stands the Creator and Master Son, Michael, the universe father and sovereign. Co-ordinate in divinity and complemental in creative attributes is the local universe Mother Spirit, the Divine Minister of Salvington.

37:1. The Universe Aids

The Universe Aids include the following seven orders: *Bright and Morning Stars, Brilliant Evening Stars, Archangels, Most High Assistants, High Commissioners, Celestial Overseers,* and *Mansion World Teachers.* The Bright and Morning Star is Gabriel, the chief executive of Nebadon.

37:2. The Brilliant Evening Stars

These brilliant creatures were planned by the Melchizedeks and were then brought into being by the Creator Son and the Creative Spirit. They serve chiefly as liaison officers of Gabriel. Gabriel maintains contact with all phases of universe life and affairs through the Brilliant Evening Stars. Their head is Gavalia; since the return of Christ Michael from Urantia, he has been assigned to the ascendant mortal ministry. The Brilliant Evening Stars are a unique twofold order, embracing some of created dignity and others of attained service. One of the high duties of the Evening Stars is to accompany the Avonal bestowal Sons on their planetary missions, and they may be assigned as liaisons for the Trinity Teacher Sons.

37:3. The Archangels

Archangels are the highest type of high spirit being produced in large numbers in a local universe. They are dedicated to the work of creature survival and to the furtherance of the ascending career of the mortals of time and space.

A divisional headquarters of the archangels is maintained on Urantia. Do you grasp the significance of the fact that your lowly and confused planet has become a divisional headquarters for the universe administration and direction of certain archangel activities having to do with the Paradise ascension scheme?

A corps of one hundred accompanies every Paradise bestowal Son to an inhabited world. In general, the archangels are assigned to the service and ministry of the Avonal order of sonship. They also serve as record keepers, keeping straight the record of each mortal of time from the moment of birth up through the universe career until such an individual leaves Salvington for the superuniverse.

37:4. The Most High Assistants

The Most High Assistants are a group of volunteering beings of origin outside the local universe. They include: Perfectors of Wisdom, Divine Counselors, Universal Censors, Inspired Trinity Spirits, Trinitized Sons, Solitary Messengers, supernaphim, seconaphim, tertiaphim, and other gracious ministers. They sojourn with us helping to bring all Nebadon into fuller harmony with the ideas of Orvonton and the ideals of Paradise.

37:5. High Commissioners

The High Commissioners are Spirit-fused ascendant mortals. On the mansion worlds you will meet and fraternize with them as they ascend the Paradise path with you as far as Salvington, where they stop. The High Commissioners begin their service on the planets as race commissioners. In this capacity they interpret the viewpoints and portray the needs of the various human races. We invariably find these commissioners in all the tribunals of justice advising the presiding magistrates respecting the antecedents, environment, and inherent nature of those concerned in the adjudication. These beings may not attain Paradise, but they achieve an experiential wisdom in the mastery of Nebadon problems that utterly surpasses anything attained by the transient ascenders.

37:6. Celestial Overseers

The Nebadon educational system is jointly administered by the Trinity Teacher Sons and the Melchizedek teaching corps, but much of the work designed to effect its maintenance and upbuilding is carried on by the Celestial Overseers. These beings are a recruited corps embracing all types of individuals connected with the scheme of educating and training the ascending mortals.

The entire universe is one vast school. Fundamentally, the Nebadon educational system provides for your assignment to a task and then affords you opportunity to receive instruction as to the ideal and divine method of best performing that task. The purpose of all this training and experience is to prepare you for admission to the higher and more spiritual training spheres of the superuniverse. Before leaving the universe of Nebadon, most Urantia mortals will be afforded opportunity to serve for a longer or shorter time as members of the Nebadon corps of Celestial Overseers.

37:7. Mansion World Teachers

The Mansion World Teachers are recruited and glorified cherubim. They will receive further consideration in the next paper, while as teachers playing an important part in the morontia life, they will be more extensively discussed in the paper of that name.

37:8. Higher Spirit Orders of Assignment

Certain of the higher-origin spirit beings of the family of the Infinite Spirit are of permanent assignment to the local universe. The *Solitary Messengers* render invaluable service to us in our efforts to overcome the handicaps of time and space. Andovontia, the *Universe Circuit Supervisor*, is concerned only with spirit and morontia circuits. In sending greetings to the mortals of Urantia, he expresses pleasure in the anticipation of your sometime restoration to the universe circuits of his supervision. The Nebadon *Census Director*, Salsatia, is automatically cognizant of the birth and death of will and currently registers the exact number of will creatures functioning in the local universe. An *Associate Inspector* is the personal representative of the Supreme Executive of Orvonton. His associates in the local systems, the *Assigned Sentinels*, are also representatives of the Supreme Executive of Orvonton. The *Universal Conciliators* are the traveling courts of the universes of time and space. The *Technical Advisers* are the legal minds of the universe. The *Celestial Recorders* are the senior or supervising recorders. The ministry of the *Morontia Companions* is described in those narratives dealing with the transition planets of the pilgrims of time.

37:9. Permanent Citizens of the Local Universe

The local universe orders of permanent citizenship are: Susatia, Univitatia, Material Sons, and Midway Creatures. The *Susatia* are closely associated with the ascendant citizens of the local universe, the Spirit-fused mortals of the Nebadon Corps of Perfection. The *Univitatia* accomplish for ascending mortals during the traversal of the constellation spheres what the Havona natives contribute to the pilgrim spirits passing through the central creation. The *Material Sons* are a reproducing order of sonship, being created male and female. Their progeny function as the relatively permanent citizens of a system capital, though some are commissioned as Planetary Adams to found the Adamic race of that world. The *Midway Creatures* serve from the early days of the arrival of a Planetary Prince to the far-distant time of the settling of the planet in light and life, they are the only group of intelligent beings to remain continuously on the sphere.

37:10. Other Local Universe Groups

Besides the seraphic and mortal orders, who will be considered in later papers, there are numerous additional beings concerned in the maintenance and perfecting of the universe of Nebadon. The *Spironga* are the spirit offspring of the Bright and Morning Star and the Father Melchizedek. They are the spirit helpers of the local universe, executing the routine spirit tasks of Nebadon. The *Spornagia* are devoted to the care and culture of the material phases of the headquarters worlds. Spornagia are an animal order of existence, but if you could see them, you would agree that they seem to be perfect animals. We especially profit from the ministry of the celestial artisans on the constellations and benefit from the activities of the reversion directors, who operate chiefly on the capitals of the local systems. The mortal ascenders, after attaining Salvington, are used in an almost endless variety of activities in the conduct of universe affairs as helpers, students, observers, and teachers. There are still other types of intelligent life concerned with the administration of a local universe. Further experience in your advancing careers will increasingly reveal these interesting and charming beings.

Paper 38:
Ministering Spirits of the Local Universe
Melchizedek

AS the supernaphim in the central universe and the seconaphim in a superuniverse, so the seraphim, with the associated cherubim and sanobim, constitute the angelic corps of a local universe. The seraphim are all fairly uniform in design.

38:1. Origin of Seraphim

Seraphim are created by the Universe Mother Spirit. The creation of seraphim dates from the attainment of relative personality by the Universe Mother Spirit. Seraphim are still being periodically created.

38:2. Angelic Natures

Angels are of spirit nature and origin. Though invisible to mortals, they perceive you as you are in the flesh. They appreciate and greatly enjoy your efforts in music, art, and real humor. They are fully cognizant of your moral struggles and spiritual difficulties. Seraphim are very affectionate and sympathetic beings. They are much as you will be on the mansion worlds. The seraphim are so created as to function on both spiritual and literal levels. They possess many powers far beyond human comprehension; you would truly regard a seraphim as a mathematical prodigy. You do well to love them. In nature and personality endowment the seraphim are just a trifle ahead of mortal races in the scale of creature existence. Throughout the whole morontia and subsequent spirit ascent, your fraternity with the seraphim will be ideal; your companionship will be superb.

38:3. Unrevealed Angels

Numerous orders of spirit beings function throughout the domains of the local universe that are unrevealed to mortals. There are six other orders of related beings who are wholly occupied with the administrative and other affairs of Nebadon.

38:4. The Seraphic Worlds

These headquarters worlds are among the magnificent realms of Nebadon; the seraphic estates are characterized by both beauty and vastness. Here each seraphim has a real home, and "home" means the domicile of two seraphim; they live in pairs. In the majority of assignments it requires two angels to accomplish the task. Besides designated homes, seraphim also have group, company, battalion, and unit headquarters.

38:5. Seraphic Training

The Melchizedeks have a large part in the education and training of all local universe angels—seraphim, cherubim, and sanobim. Seraphim are initiated as ministering spirits by serving as observers on the lowest of the evolutionary worlds. On the system architectural worlds our seraphim complete their training and are commissioned as ministering spirits of time. When once seraphim are commissioned, they may range all Nebadon, even Orvonton, on assignment. Their work in the universe is without bounds and limitations.

38:6. Seraphic Organization

After the second millennium of sojourn at seraphic headquarters the seraphim are organized under chiefs into groups of twelve (12 pairs, 24 seraphim). Twelve groups constitute a company, twelve companies a battalion, twelve battalions a seraphic unit, twelve units a legion, twelve legions a host, twelve such hosts (35,831,808 pairs or 71,663,616 individuals) make up the largest operating organization of seraphim, an angelic army. Gabriel is the supreme commander of the armies of heaven.

38:7. Cherubim and Sanobim

In all essential endowments cherubim and sanobim are similar to seraphim. They are wonderfully intelligent, marvelously efficient, touchingly affectionate, and almost human. One is an energy positive personality; the other, energy negative. Each type of angel is very limited in solitary function; hence they usually serve in pairs. Cherubim and sanobim are the faithful and efficient aids of the seraphic ministers. When assigned to a planet, cherubim enter the local courses of training, including a study of planetary usages and languages. Every fourth cherubim and every fourth sanobim are quasi-material, very definitely resembling the morontia level of existence. They are to the morontia spheres about what the midway creatures are to the evolutionary planets. They frequently work in liaison with the midway creatures.

38:8. Evolution of Cherubim and Sanobim

There are three great classes of cherubim and sanobim with regard to evolutionary potential: 1. *Ascension Candidates* are by nature candidates for seraphic status. 2. *Mid-phase Cherubim* are the inherently limited beings of the angelic creations, although the more gifted individuals may achieve limited seraphic service. 3. *Morontia Cherubim* always retain their quasi-material characteristics. They will continue on as cherubim and sanobim pending the completed factualization of the Supreme Being. Many of the more experienced of these cherubim are attached to the seraphic guardians of destiny and are thus placed in direct line for advancement to the status of Mansion World Teachers. These Teachers may eventually be re-embraced by the Universe Mother Spirit and emerge as full-fledged seraphim.

38:9. The Midway Creatures

Primary Midwayers are uniformly derived from the modified ascendant-mortal staffs of the Planetary Princes. *Secondary Midwayers* are variously derived from the Adams and Eves, or from their immediate progeny. Primary midwayers are energized intellectually and spiritually by the angelic technique. Secondary midwayers are physically energized by the Adamic technique, spiritually encircuited by the seraphic, and intellectually endowed with the morontia transition type of mind. Primary midwayers resemble angels more than mortals; the secondary orders are much more like human beings.

The gap between the material and spiritual worlds is perfectly bridged by the serial association of mortal man, secondary midwayer, primary midwayer, morontia cherubim, mid-phase cherubim, and seraphim. On only three other worlds in Satania do the midwayers function as one group under unified leadership as do the united midway ministers of Urantia. The primary midwayers are the planetary historians. Sooner or later all accredited midway creatures will be mustered into the ranks of the ascending Sons of God.

Paper 39: The Seraphic Hosts
Melchizedek

HUMAN beings sometimes find it hard to understand that a created capacity for higher-level ministry does not necessarily imply ability to function on relatively lower service levels. Seraphim must acquire knowledge and gain experience much as do human beings. They are not far removed from you in certain personality attributes. And they all crave to start at the bottom, on the lowest possible level of ministry; thus may they hope to achieve the highest possible level of experiential destiny.

39:1. Supreme Seraphim

These seraphim are the highest of the seven revealed orders of local universe angels. They function in seven groups: 1. *Son-Spirit Ministers,* 2. *Court Advisers,* 3. *Universe Orientators,* 4. *The Teaching Counselors,* 5. *Directors of Assignment,* 6. *The Recorders,* and 7. *Unattached Ministers.*

Seraphim equally crave assignment to the missions of the incarnated Sons and attachment as destiny guardians to the mortals of the realms; the latter is the surest seraphic passport to Paradise. The seraphic court advisers serve extensively as defenders of mortals. It is the task of the universe orientators to help pilgrims in making those kaleidoscopic adjustments in the comprehension of meanings and values inherent in the realization of a first-stage spirit.

39:2. Superior Seraphim

The superior seraphim function in the following seven groups: 1. *The Intelligence Corps,* 2. *The Voice of Mercy,* 3. *Spirit Co-ordinators,* 4. *Assistant Teachers,* 5. *The Transporters,* 6. *The Recorders,* and 7. *The Reserves.* Mercy is the keynote of seraphic service and angelic ministry. A marvelous corps of Assistant Teachers functions on Urantia for the purpose of fostering and furthering the cause of truth and righteousness.

The angels cannot transport combustion bodies—flesh and blood—such as you now have, but they can transport all others. After awakening on Paradise you will not be dependent on angels for transport from universe to universe.

39:3. Supervisor Seraphim

This versatile order of universe angels is assigned to the exclusive service of the constellations in the following seven groups: 1. *Supervising Assistants,* 2. *Law Forecasters,* 3. *Social Architects,* 4. *Ethical Sensitizers,* 5. *The Transporters,* 6. *The Recorders,* and 7. *The Reserves.*

The intellectual foundation of justice is law, and in a local universe law originates in the legislative assemblies of the constellations. Social architects do everything within their province and power to bring together suitable individuals that they may constitute efficient and agreeable working groups on earth.

39:4. Administrator Seraphim

Administrator Seraphim are mainly occupied with the affairs of the local systems and their component worlds. They are organized for service as follows: 1. *Administrative Assistants,* 2. *Justice Guides,* 3. *Interpreters of Cosmic Citizenship,* 4. *Quickeners of Morality,* 5. *The Transporters,* 6. *The Recorders,* and 7. *The Reserves.*

The present acting ruler of Urantia is assisted by a corps of one thousand Administrative Seraphim. In the Lucifer rebellion in Satania very few of the justice guides were lost.

The Quickeners of Morality teach that ever and anon there is a pause in the Paradise ascent during which the personality tastes the sweetness of goal fulfillment. As you ascend the personality scale, first you learn to be loyal, then to love, then to be filial, and then may you be free. They point out the fruitfulness of patience: That stagnation is certain death, but that overrapid growth is equally suicidal. It is not so much what you learn in this first life; it is the experience of living this life that is important. The keys of the kingdom of heaven are: sincerity, more sincerity, and more sincerity. The highest moral choice is to choose to do the will of God. If man thus chooses, he is great, though he be the humblest citizen on Urantia.

39:5. Planetary Helpers

On Urantia the majority of the planetary helpers were removed upon the collapse of the Adamic regime; but these seraphic aids of your defaulting Material Sons still serve Urantia in the following groups: 1. *The Voices of the Garden,* 2. *The Spirits of Brotherhood,* 3. *The Souls of Peace,* 4. *The Spirits of Trust,* 5. *The Transporters,* 6. *The Recorders,* and 7. *The Reserves.*

The Spirits of Trust teach that uncertainty is the secret of contented continuity. We must learn the sweetness of uncertainty, the charm of the indefinite and unknown future.

Human beings have sometimes been permitted to observe seraphim that were being prepared for transport service. In observing a transport seraphim being made ready to receive a passenger for interplanetary transit, there may be seen what are apparently double sets of wings extending from the head to the foot of the angel. In reality these wings are energy insulators—friction shields.

39:6. Transition Ministers

As their name might suggest, transition ministers serve wherever they can contribute to creature transition from the material to the spiritual estate. This ministry is diversified in accordance with the following seven orders of assignment: *Seraphic Evangels, Racial Interpreters, Mind Planners, Morontia Counselors, Technicians, Recorder-Teachers,* and *Ministering Reserves.* You will learn more about these seraphic ministers to transitional ascenders in the narratives dealing with the mansion worlds and the morontia life.

39:7. Seraphim of the Future

These angels do not minister extensively except in older realms and on the more advanced planets of Nebadon. Inasmuch as these angels are not now directly concerned with either Urantia or Urantians, it is deemed best to withhold the description of their fascinating activities.

39:8. Seraphic Destiny

Seraphington is the angelic threshold to Paradise and Deity attainment, the transition sphere from the ministry of time to the exalted service of eternity. Seraphim may attain Paradise in scores—hundreds—of ways. None but successful destiny guardians can be sure of proceeding to Paradise by a progressive path of evolutionary ascent. Destiny guardians of Havona-circle experience usually enter the Mortal Finaliter Corps. Others enter the various nonmortal finaliter corps, and many are mustered into the Corps of Seraphic Completion.

39:9. The Corps of Seraphic Completion

Angels of the Seraphic Corps of Completion serve as associates of the superuniverse seconaphim and as assistants to the high Paradise-Havona orders of supernaphim. Large numbers of the completion seraphim return to their native universes. Your world enjoys the extensive ministry of twelve specialized groups of the Seraphic Corps of Completion. Many fascinating avenues of ministry are open to the completion seraphim. Throughout the whole mortal adventure of finding God and of achieving divine perfection, these spirit ministers of seraphic completion are always and forever your true friends and unfailing helpers.

Paper 40: The Ascending Sons of God

Mighty Messenger

SINCE the greater part of this narrative will be devoted to a discussion of the three basic orders of ascending mortals, consideration will first be given to the nonmortal ascending orders of sonship—seraphic, Adamic, midwayer, and Adjuster.

40:1. Evolutionary Seraphim

Guardian seraphim, through experience and service with the ascending mortals of time also achieve the status of ascendant sonship. Such angels attain Paradise through Seraphington, and many are even mustered into the Corps of Mortal Finality.

40:2. Ascending Material Sons

When an Adam and Eve are wholly successful in their joint planetary mission as biologic uplifters, they share the destiny of the inhabitants of their world. When such a world is settled in the advanced stages of light and life, this faithful Material Son and Daughter are permitted to resign all planetary administrative duties and register themselves as ascending Sons of God and may immediately begin the long journey to Havona and Paradise.

40:3. Translated Midwayers

Soon after an evolutionary planet has attained the intermediate epochs of light and life (if not before), both groups of midway creatures are released from planetary duty and are registered in the local universe as ascending Sons of God, immediately beginning the long Paradise ascent. The primary group are destined to various finaliter corps, but the secondary or Adamic midwayers are all routed for enrollment in the Mortal Corps of Finality.

40:4. Personalized Adjusters

When the mortals of time fail to achieve eternal survival, such deserted Monitors return to Divinington and subsequently are personalized by the Universal Father. Personalized Adjusters are beings of a unique and unfathomable order and are classified as ascending Sons of God, the highest of all such orders of sonship.

40:5. Mortals of Time and Space

The Mighty Messenger author reminds us that the Father, who is the farthest from you in personality and in spirit, draws the nearest to you in the personality circuit and in the indwelling Thought Adjusters.

The classification is as follows: 1. Mortals of the transient or experiential Adjuster sojourn, 2. Mortals of the non-Adjuster-fusion types (many of the nonbreathers belong to this series), and 3. Mortals of Adjuster-fusion potential. The Adjusters contribute much to the advancement of primitive men but are unable to form eternal unions with such mortals. The transient sojourn of the Adjusters contributes much towards preparing their mortal subjects for possible subsequent Spirit fusion. When you encounter these modified mortal types on the mansion worlds, you will find no difficulty in communicating with them.

Mortals of Adjuster-fusion potential embrace mortals of the one-brained, two-brained, and three-brained types. Urantians are of the intermediate or two-brained type.

40:6. The Faith Sons of God

The mortal races stand as the representatives of the lowest order of intelligent and personal creation. You will be reckoned as ascending sons the instant fusion takes place, but the status of the mortals of time and space is that of faith sons. You are faith sons because you have received the Spirit of Truth and the Holy Spirit, and there dwells within you a fragment of the Universal Father.

40:7. Father-Fused Mortals

The indwelling of Adjusters is indeed one of the unfathomable mysteries of God the Father. When you and your Adjuster are finally and forever fused, you become ascending sons of God. To the Adjuster-fused mortal the career of universal service is wide open. What dignity of destiny and glory of attainment await every one of you! Do you comprehend the grandeur of the heights of eternal achievement which are spread out before you?—even you who now trudge on in the lowly path of life through your so-called "vale of tears"?

40:8. Son-Fused Mortals

When it becomes apparent that some synchronizing difficulty is inhibiting Father fusion, and it is finally determined that the ascending mortal is not guilty of any discoverable cause for failure to attain fusion, the morontia mortal is fused with an individualized gift of the spirit of the Creator Son. These Son-fused creatures share the services of Orvonton with their Adjuster-fused brethren. They are truly your brethren, and you will greatly enjoy their association as you pass through the training worlds of the superuniverse. Aside from not having residential destiny on Paradise they are in every way the equals of their Adjuster-fused associates. They frequently journey to Paradise on superuniverse assignment but seldom permanently reside there, being, as a class, confined to the superuniverse of their nativity.

40:9. Spirit-Fused Morals

Mortals may be temporarily indwelt by Adjusters. When such sleeping survivors are repersonalized on the mansion worlds, the place of the departed Adjuster is filled by an individualization of the spirit of the Divine Minister. This spirit infusion constitutes these surviving creatures Spirit-fused mortals. Such beings are in every way your equals in mind and spirit. There is, however, one particular in which Spirit-fused mortals differ from their ascendant brethren: They awaken in the resurrection halls of the morontia spheres of Nebadon as if they were newly created beings, creatures without consciousness of former existence. They are enabled to repossess themselves of much of their former human memory experience through having it retold by the associated seraphim and cherubim. Spirit-fused mortals are the permanent citizens of the local universes.

40:10. Ascendant Destinies

Spirit-fused mortals are, generally speaking, confined to a local universe; Son-fused survivors are restricted to a superuniverse; Adjuster-fused mortals are destined to penetrate the universe of universes. Does all this represent an intended part of the all-wise plans of the Architects of the Master Universe designed to provide the Creator Sons and the Ancients of Days with a permanent ascendant population with evolved orders of citizenship that will become increasingly competent to carry forward the affairs of these realms in the universe ages to come? In the final analysis, it would be hardly proper to use the words "greater" or "lesser" in contrasting the destinies of the ascending orders of sonship. The Father loves each of his sons individually, personally, and exclusively. And such a love utterly eclipses all other facts.

Paper 41: Physical Aspects of the Local Universe
Archangel

THAT space which is pervaded by our local universe Mother Spirit is Nebadon.

41:1. The Nebadon Power Centers

Within the domain of the Paradise Son of God, the Supreme Power Centers and the Master Physical Controllers collaborated with the later appearing Morontia Power Supervisors and others to produce that vast complex of communication lines, energy circuits, and power lanes which firmly bind the manifold space bodies of Nebadon into one integrated administrative unit. Architectural spheres, such as Salvington, Edentia, and Jerusem, are lighted, heated, and energized by methods which make them quite independent of the suns of space.

41:2. The Satania Physical Controllers

A Master Physical Controller, stationed on Jerusem, works in co-ordination with the system power center, serving as liaison chief of the power inspectors functioning throughout the local system. The circuitizing and channelizing of energy is supervised by the five hundred thousand living and intelligent energy manipulators scattered throughout Satania. The power-energy supervision of the evolutionary inhabited worlds is the responsibility of the Master Physical Controllers, but these beings are not responsible for all energy misbehavior on Urantia, which is in the lines of tremendous energies. They have trouble insulating against the powerful Norlatiadek currents.

41:3. Our Starry Associates

There are upward of two thousand brilliant suns pouring forth light and energy in Satania, and your own sun is an average blazing orb. The stars have just as much comparative elbow room in space as one dozen oranges would have if they were circulating about throughout the interior of Urantia, and were the planet a hollow globe. The most recent of the major cosmic eruptions in Orvonton was the extraordinary double star explosion, the light of which reached Urantia in A.D. 1572. This conflagration was so intense that the explosion was clearly visible in broad daylight. Your sun has eleven and one-half year sunspot cycles.

41:4. Sun Density

The mass of your sun is about one and one-half times the density of water. But your sun is neither a liquid nor a solid—it is gaseous—and this is true notwithstanding the difficulty of explaining how gaseous matter can attain this and even much greater densities.

41:5. Solar Radiation

That the suns of space are not very dense is proved by the steady streams of escaping light-energies. Light is real. As you value energy and power on your world, sunlight would be economical at a million dollars a pound. The interior of your sun is a vast X-ray generator. The X rays of a sun's interior charge the highly heated and agitated electrons with sufficient energy to carry them out through space until they encounter considerable masses of matter, whereupon they are quickly transformed into heat with the liberation of other energies.

41:6. Calcium—The Wanderer of Space

Space is not empty; calcium is the chief element of the matter-permeation of space throughout Orvonton. Our whole superuniverse is sprinkled with minutely pulverized stone. Stone is literally the basic building matter for the planets and spheres of space. Local space-permeation by calcium is due to the fact that ionized calcium atoms escape from the solar photosphere by literally riding the outgoing sunbeams.

41:7. Sources of Solar Energy

The surface temperature of your sun is almost 6,000 degrees F., but it rapidly increases until it attains the unbelievable height of about 35,000,000 degrees F. The sources of solar energy are annihilated atoms and various other space-energies.

One drop of ordinary water contains over one billion trillions of atoms. This is the energy of more than one hundred horsepower exerted continuously for two years. The total heat now given out by the solar system sun each second is sufficient to boil all the water in all the oceans on Urantia in just one second of time.

41:8. Solar-Energy Reactions

In those suns which are encircuited in the space-energy channels, solar energy is liberated by various complex nuclear-reaction chains. Reduction of hydrogen content increases the luminosity of a sun. In large suns, when hydrogen is exhausted and gravity contraction ensues, then a sudden collapse occurs. It was such an emigration of these "runaway particles" that occasioned the collapse of the giant nova of the Andromeda nebula about fifty years ago [from A.D. 1934] This vast stellar body collapsed in forty minutes of Urantia time.

41:9. Sun Stability

The larger suns maintain such a gravity control over their electrons that light escapes only with the aid of the powerful X rays. Atoms and electrons are subject to gravity. The ultimatons are not subject to local gravity but they are fully obedient to absolute or Paradise gravity. Your own solar center radiates almost one hundred billion tons of actual matter annually. Your sun is now passing out of its six billionth year. At the present time it is functioning through the period of greatest economy. It will shine on as of present efficiency for more than twenty-five billion years.

41:10. Origin of Inhabited Worlds

Your sun was in a state of mighty pulsation when the massive Angona system swung into near approach, and the outer surface of the sun began to erupt veritable streams of matter—the ancestor of the solar system. The force of gravity coalesced the disgorged matter into planets.

Your solar system, and thus Urantia, is comparatively isolated on the outskirts of Satania. You were truly among the least of all creation until Michael's bestowal elevated your planet to a position of honor and great universe interest. Sometimes the last is first, while truly the least becomes greatest.

Paper 42: Energy—Mind and Matter

Mighty Messenger

THE foundation of the universe is material in the sense that energy is the basis of all existence, and pure energy is controlled by the Universal Father, and modified by the co-ordinate acts and decisions of the Eternal Son and Conjoint Actor. These divine beings act personally and as individuals; they also function in the persons and powers of an almost unlimited number of subordinates, each variously expressive of the eternal and divine purpose in the universe of universes.

42:1. Paradise Forces and Energies

The foundation of the universe is material, but the essence of life is spirit. The ultimaton, the first measurable form of energy, has Paradise as its nucleus. There is innate in matter and present in universal space a form of energy not known on Urantia. The river of energy and life is a continuous outpouring from the Deities. The force organizers initiate those changes and institute those modifications of space-force which eventuate in energy; the power directors transmute energy into matter; thus the material worlds are born.

42:2. Universal Nonspiritual Energy Systems (Physical Energies)

It is difficult to find suitable words in the English language whereby to designate and describe the various levels of force and energy. I will endeavor to lessen conceptual confusion by suggesting the following classification for cosmic force, emergent energy, and universe power: 1. Space potency—the domain of the Unqualified Absolute—is prereality known as *absoluta*. 2. Primordial force represents the first basic change in space potency, known as *segregata*. 3. Emergent energies include puissant and gravity energies—*ultimata*—making available universe power. 4. Universe power—*gravita*—is physical energy made to serve the universe Creators. 5. Havona energy—*triata*—is characteristic of the central universe. 6. Transcendental energy—*tranosta*—is used by absonite peoples. 7. *Monota* is the living, nonspirit energy of Paradise.

The Nebadon Melchizedeks long since denominated the phenomenon of the transmutation of cosmic force into universe power as one of the seven "infinities of divinity."

42:3. Classification of Matter

Matter in all universes, excepting in the central universe, is identical. In the varied suns, planets, and space bodies there are ten grand divisions of matter: ultimatonic matter, subelectronic matter, electronic matter, subatomic matter, shattered atoms, ionized matter, atomic matter, the molecular stage of matter, radioactive matter, and collapsed matter. The foregoing classification of matter pertains to its organization rather than to the forms of its appearance to created beings.

42:4. Energy and Matter Transmutations

Light, heat, electricity, magnetism, chemism, energy, and matter are—in origin, nature, and destiny—one and the same thing, together with other material realities as yet undiscovered on Urantia. We do not fully comprehend the almost endless changes to which physical energy may be subject. The power centers and their associates are much concerned in the work of transmuting the ultimaton into the circuits and revolutions of the electron. Throughout all space, cold and other influences are at work creatively organizing ultimatons into electrons. Low temperatures favor certain forms of electronic construction and atomic assembly, while high temperatures facilitate all sorts of atomic breakup and material disintegration. The relative integrity of matter is assured by the fact that energy can be absorbed or released only in those exact amounts which Urantia scientists have designated *quanta*.

42:5. Wave-Energy Manifestations

In the superuniverse of Orvonton there are one hundred octaves of wave energy. Of these one hundred groups of energy manifestations, sixty-four are wholly or partially recognized on Urantia. Wavelike energy manifestations may be classified into the following ten groups: infraultimatonic rays, ultimatonic rays, the short space rays, the electronic stage, gamma rays, the X-ray group, the ultraviolet, the white light, infrared rays, and Hertzian waves—those energies utilized on Urantia for broadcasting. Of all these ten phases of wavelike energy activity, the human eye can react to just one octave, the whole light of ordinary sunlight. The so-called ether is merely a collective name to designate a group of force and energy activities occurring in space.

42:6. Ultimatons, Electrons, and Atoms

Local or linear gravity becomes fully operative with the appearance of the atomic organization of matter. The ultimatons, unknown on Urantia, slow down through many phases of physical activity before they attain the revolutionary-energy prerequisites to electronic organization. Mutual attraction holds one hundred ultimatons together in the constitution of the electron.

If the mass of matter should be magnified until that of an electron equaled one tenth of an ounce, then were size to be proportionately magnified, the volume of such an electron would become as large as that of the earth. If the volume of a proton—eighteen hundred times as heavy as an electron—should be magnified to the size of the head of a pin, then, in comparison, a pin's head would attain a diameter equal to that of the earth's orbit around the sun.

42:7. Atomic Matter

Within the atom the electrons revolve about the central proton with about the same comparative room the planets have as they revolve about the sun in the space of the solar system. The electronic axial revolutions and their orbital velocities about the atomic nucleus are both beyond the human imagination, not to mention the velocities of their component ultimatons. There are just one hundred distinguishable atomic elements in a dual universe.

42:8. Atomic Cohesion

There is a powerful and unknown energy, the secret of the atomic energy system's basic constitution and ultimate behavior, which remains to be discovered on Urantia. The charged protons and the uncharged neutrons of the nucleus of the atom are held together by the reciprocating function of the mesotron.

42:9. Natural Philosophy

Religion is not alone dogmatic; natural philosophy equally tends to dogmatize. The number seven is basic to the central universe and the spiritual system of inherent transmissions of character, but the number ten, the decimal system, is inherent in energy, matter, and the material creation. There is in all the physical universes of time and space the ever-present reminder of the reality of the sevenfold electronic organization of prematter. When the Urantia chemical elements are arranged in a row, any given quality or property tends to recur by sevens. Man should also note that there are seven colors in the natural spectrum.

42:10. Universal Nonspiritual Energy Systems (Material Mind Systems)

Energy-matter is being progressively subjected to the overcontrol of living and divine spirit through the experiential striving of living and personal mind. The universal nonspiritual energies are reassociated in the living systems of non-Creator minds on various levels: 1. *Preadjutant-spirit mind* is nonexperiencing, mechanical mind. 2. *Adjutant-spirit minds* are teachable; animal intellect in the first five adjutants; human intellect in the seven adjutants; midwayer intellect in the last two adjutants. 3. *Evolving morontia minds* function differentially in response to the 570 levels of morontia life. *The cosmic mind* encompasses all finite-mind levels and co-ordinates experientially with the evolutionary-deity levels of the Supreme Mind and transcendentally with the existential levels of absolute mind—the direct circuits of the Conjoint Actor. On Paradise, mind is absolute; in Havona, absonite; in Orvonton, finite. Paradise mind is beyond human understanding; it is existential, nonspatial, and nontemporal.

42:11. Universe Mechanisms

The universe of universes in toto is mind planned, mind made, and mind administered. But the divine mechanism of the universe of universes is altogether too perfect for the scientific methods of the finite mind of man to discern even a trace of the dominance of the infinite mind. The phenomenon of progressive evolution associated with cosmic self-maintenance is universal. The evolutionary capacity of the universe is inexhaustible in the infinity of spontaneity. Progress towards harmonious unity, a growing experiential synthesis superimposed on an ever-increasing complexity of relationships, could be effected only by a purposive and dominant mind.

42:12. Pattern and Form—Mind Dominance

The evolution of mechanisms implies and indicates the concealed presence and dominance of creative mind. The personality form is the pattern aspect of a living being; it connotes the arrangement of energies. Nearly all beings encountered in the seven superuniverses are possessed of forms. But there are a few exceptions: Solitary Messengers, Inspired Trinity Spirits, Personal Aids of the Infinite Spirit, Gravity Messengers, Transcendental Recorders, and certain others. The morontia form will be highly individual and adequately characteristic of the creative mind which dominates it. Spirit forms are equally diverse, personal, and characteristic of their respective spirit-mind indwellers. Mind universally dominates matter, even as it is in turn responsive to the ultimate overcontrol of spirit.

Paper 43: The Constellations
Malavatia Melchizedek

URANTIA is commonly referred to as 606 of Satania in Norlatiadek of Nebadon, meaning the six hundred sixth inhabited world in the local system of Satania, situated in the constellation of Norlatiadek, one of the one hundred constellations of the local universe of Nebadon. All these architectural worlds are fully administered by the various groups of native life, for the greater part unrevealed but including the efficient spironga and the beautiful spornagia. Being the mid-point in the morontia-training regime, the morontia life of the constellations is both typical and ideal.

43:1. The Constellation Headquarters

Edentia abounds in fascinating highlands crowned with morontia life and overspread with spiritual glory. There are tens of thousands of sparkling lakes. Edentia can be circumnavigated via these various water routes, though the chief channel of transportation is the atmosphere. The sea of glass, the receiving area of Edentia, is one enormous circular crystal about one hundred miles in circumference and about thirty miles in depth. The Melchizedeks maintain two special colleges on Edentia. One, the emergency school, is devoted to the study of problems growing out of the Satania rebellion. The other, the bestowal school, is dedicated to the mastery of the new problems arising out of the fact that Michael made his final bestowal on one of the worlds of Norlatiadek.

43:2. The Constellation Government

The constellations are the autonomous units of a local universe. They function as the legislative or lawmaking units, while the local systems serve as the executive or enforcement units. The Salvington government is the supreme judicial and co-ordinating authority. There are three legislative groups: the lower house of ascenders, the mid-chamber of seraphic hosts, and the advisory house of the divine Sons. The latter are the fact-finding and timesaving group which very effectively serves both of the lower divisions of the legislative assembly. The combined council of legislators sanctions the final form of all enactments and authorizes their promulgation by the broadcasters.

43:3. The Most Highs of Norlatiadek

At least three Vorondadek Sons are commissioned by Gabriel as the Most Highs of each of the Nebadon constellations. A Constellation Father reigns for ten thousand standard years (about 50,000 Urantia years), having previously served as junior associate and as senior associate for equal periods. Urantia is closely related to the constellation rulers because of certain system and planetary conditions growing out of the Lucifer rebellion.

43:4. Mount Assembly—The Faithful of Days

The most holy mount of assembly is the dwelling place of the Faithful of Days, the representative of the Paradise Trinity who functions on Edentia. On this consecrated highland the ascending mortals periodically assemble to hear this Son of Paradise tell of the long and intriguing journey of progressing mortals through the one billion perfection worlds of Havona and on to the indescribable delights of Paradise. After the Satania rebellion the archrebels of Jerusem were wont to come up to these Edentia councils until after the bestowal of Michael on Urantia and his subsequent assumption of unlimited sovereignty throughout all Nebadon. Since the triumph of Christ, all Norlatiadek is being cleansed of sin and rebels.

43:5. The Edentia Fathers Since the Lucifer Rebellion

The rotation of the Most Highs on Edentia was suspended at the time of the Lucifer rebellion. The present government of the constellation, however, has been expanded to include twelve Sons of the Vorondadek order. Ever since the Lucifer rebellion the Edentia Fathers have exercised a special care over Urantia and the other isolated worlds of Satania.

43:6. The Gardens of God

The extraordinarily beautiful places on the inhabited worlds of Norlatiadek are often called "the gardens of Eden." The architectural worlds enjoy ten forms of life: three vegetable, three animal, and four unrevealed types. The morontia vegetation is purely an energy growth; when eaten there is no residual portion. If you enjoy the flowers, shrubs and trees of Urantia, then will you feast your eyes upon the botanical beauty and the floral grandeur of the supernal gardens of Edentia. All the animal life is most intelligent and exquisitely serviceable, and all the various species are surprisingly gentle and touchingly companionable. Centrally located in this magnificent garden is the worship shrine of the Most Highs. At this shrine the Most Highs, on every tenth day of relaxation, lead all Edentia in the worshipful contemplation of God the Supreme.

43:7. The Univitatia

Univitatia are the permanent citizens of Edentia and its associated worlds. The natives of each of the seventy major spheres of Edentia possess different visible forms, and the morontia mortals have their morontia forms attuned to correspond with the ascending scale of the univitatia each time they change residence from one Edentia sphere to another. In all Orvonton no extra-Havona beings excepting the Uversa abandonters can equal the univitatia in artistic skill, social adaptability, and co-ordinating cleverness.

43:8. The Edentia Training Worlds

Your sojourn on Edentia and its associated spheres will be chiefly occupied with the mastery of group ethics. On the constellation training worlds you are to achieve the real socialization of your evolving morontia personality. This supernal cultural acquirement consists in learning how to, among other things, live happily and work effectively with ten diverse fellow morontians and with ten univitatia.

Intellectually, socially, and spiritually two moral creatures do not merely double their personal potentials of universe achievement by partnership technique; they more nearly quadruple their attainment and accomplishment possibilities.

43:9. Citizenship on Edentia

After graduation from world number seventy, ascending mortals take up residence on Edentia. This entire sojourn on the constellation training worlds, culminating in Edentia citizenship, is a period of true and heavenly bliss for the morontia progressors. On that day when you are prepared to leave Edentia for the Salvington career, you will pause and look back on one of the most beautiful and most refreshing of all your epochs of training this side of Paradise.

Paper 44: The Celestial Artisans

Archangel

THESE beings are the master artists and artisans of the morontia and lower spirit realms. The celestial artisans are not created as such; they are a selected and recruited corps of beings drawn from the ascending mortals and numerous other celestial groups. To spirit beings the material world is almost entirely unreal. After attainment of the higher spirit levels the ascenders are able to recognize material, morontia, and spirit realities. I almost despair of being able to convey to the material mind the nature of the work of the celestial artisans.

44:1. The Celestial Musicians

With the limited range of mortal hearing, you can hardly conceive of morontia melodies. There are over one hundred thousand different modes of sound, color, and energy manipulation, techniques analogous to the human employment of musical instruments. Some day a real musician may appear on Urantia, and whole peoples will be enthralled by the magnificent strains of his melodies. One such human being could forever change the course of the entire civilized world. Forever, music will remain the universal language of men, angels, and spirits. Harmony is the speech of Havona.

44:2. The Heavenly Reproducers

Mortal man can hardly hope for more than a meager and distorted concept of the functions of the heavenly reproducers. The higher intellectual teachers and the transition ministers freely and effectively utilize these various groups of reproducers in their morontia educational activities. So versatile are these artisans that, when they function en masse, they are able to re-enact an age, and in collaboration with the seraphic ministers they can actually portray the eternal values of the spirit world to the mortal seers of time.

44:3. The Divine Builders

For every material satisfaction which humans are capable of enjoying, we have thousands of spiritual realities that serve to enrich and enlarge our existence. There are home, vocation, play, worship, and public builders. While neither these structures nor their embellishment would be exactly real to the sensory comprehension of material mortals we clearly discern them and just as fully enjoy them.

44:4. Thought Recorders

These artisans are devoted to the preservation and reproduction of the superior thought of the realms. All of the higher orders of Nebadon are bilingual, speaking both the language of Nebadon and the tongue of Uversa. The ability to translate thought into language in the morontia and spirit spheres is beyond mortal comprehension. Using concept recorders, I could gain more knowledge in one hour of your time than you could gain in one hundred years of perusing ordinary written language. In the language of Nebadon we could, in a half hour's address, cover the subject matter of the entire lifetime of a Urantia mortal.

44:5. Energy Manipulators

These interesting and effective artisans are concerned with every kind of energy: physical, mindal, and spiritual. These artisans are the keen students of the mind circuits of the Infinite Spirit. They are seeking to discover the universe presence of God the Supreme. Urantia is served by a corps of seventy transport advisers and by twelve technicians of interplanetary and interuniverse communication.

Divine rest is associated with the technique of spiritual-energy intake. Morontia and spirit energy must be replenished just as certainly as physical energy. Spiritual energy acts in accordance with established laws, just as does physical energy.

44:6. The Designers and Embellishers

This corps embraces over one thousand subdivisions of activity working with color, sound, emotion, joyous arrangements, taste; and when all others have made their respective contributions, the designers and embellishers then add the culminating and finishing touches to the morontia ensemble achieving an inspiring portrayal of the divinely beautiful. But you must await your deliverance from the animal body before you can begin to conceive of the artistic glories and aesthetic beauties of the morontia and spirit worlds.

44:7. The Harmony Workers

The Harmony workers point out that beauty, rhythm, and harmony are intellectually associated and spiritually akin. Truth, fact, and relationship are intellectually inseparable and associated with the philosophic concepts of beauty. Goodness, righteousness, and justice are philosophically interrelated and spiritually bound up together with living truth and divine beauty. These expressions of the divine urge within the evolving creature may be intellectually true, emotionally beautiful, and spiritually good; but the real soul of expression is absent unless these realities of truth, meanings of beauty, and values of goodness are unified in the life experience of the artisan, the scientist, or the philosopher. These divine qualities are perfectly and absolutely unified in God. The Harmony workers attempt to actualize these truths in their work.

44:8. Mortal Aspirations and Morontia Achievements

Celestial artisans do come, from time to time, from the headquarters of the system to proffer help to the naturally gifted individuals of the mortal races to act as harmonizers of these talents and otherwise to assist and inspire these mortals to seek for ever-perfecting ideals and to attempt their enhanced portrayal for the edification of the realm. No matter how lowly your origin, if you have ability and the gift of expression, you will gain adequate recognition and receive due appreciation as you ascend upward in the scale of morontia experience and spiritual attainment. Before ascending mortals leave the local universe to embark upon their spirit careers, they will be satiated respecting every intellectual, artistic, and social longing or true ambition which ever characterized their mortal or morontia planes of existence.

Paper 45: The Local System Administration
Melchizedek

THE administrative center of Satania consists of a cluster of architectural spheres, fifty-seven in number—Jerusem itself, the seven major satellites, and the forty-nine subsatellites. The seven mansion worlds are the seven subsatellites of transition world number one.

45:1. Transitional Culture Worlds

The seven major worlds swinging around Jerusem are generally known as the transitional culture spheres. These spheres are: 1. *the Finaliter World*, headquarters of the finaliter corps and surrounded by the seven mansion worlds; 2. *the Morontia World*, headquarters of the supervisors of morontia life; 3. *the Angelic World*, headquarters of all the seraphic hosts; 4. *the Superangel World*, home of the Brilliant Evening Stars; 5. *the World of the Sons*, headquarters of the divine Sons of all orders; 6. *the World of the Spirit*, the system rendezvous of the high personalities of the Infinite Spirit; 7. *the World of the Father*, the silent sphere of the system as no groups are domiciled on it. Its seven satellites are now used as the detention spheres for the interned groups of the Lucifer rebellion.

45:2. The System Sovereign

The present System Sovereign, Lanaforge, is a tried and tested administrator. He presides over the system council of world rulers, the Planetary Princes and the resident governors general of the isolated worlds and is a frequent visitor on Urantia. Once a week, every ten days on Jerusem, the

Sovereign holds a conclave with some one group of the various orders of personalities. These are the charmingly informal hours of Jerusem. Ascending mortals come together at these times merely to enjoy themselves and to meet their fellow Jerusemites.

45:3. The System Government

The System Sovereign, is always supported by two or three Lanonandek Sons, but at the present time the system of Satania is administered by a staff of seven Lanonandeks. This executive group of seven Lanonandeks constitutes the expanded emergency administration made necessary by the exigencies of the Lucifer rebellion. The Lanonandek administration is supported by the Jerusem executive council, the supreme advisory body of Satania. This council consists of twelve members. Since the bestowal of Michael the system has resumed the election of ten members to the Edentia legislature.

45:4. The Four and Twenty Counselors

At the center of the seven angelic residential circles on Jerusem is located the headquarters of the Urantia advisory council, the personal agents of Michael on Jerusem, composed of: 1. *Onagar*, the master mind of the pre-Planetary Prince age; 2. *Mansant*, the great teacher of the post-Planetary Prince age; 3. *Onamonalonton*, a far-distant leader of the red man; 4. *Orlandof*, a prince of the blue men; 5. *Porshunta*, the oracle of the extinct orange race; 6. *Singlangton*, who taught the yellow men; 7. *Fantad*, the deliverer of the green men; 8. *Orvonon*, the enlightener of the indigo races; 9. *Adam* and 10. *Eve* the rehabilitated planetary parents of Urantia; 11. *Enoch*, the first of the mortals of Urantia to fuse with his Thought Adjuster; 12. *Moses*, the emancipator of a remnant of the submerged violet race; 13. *Elijah*, a translated soul of brilliant spiritual achievement; 14. *Machiventa Melchizedek*, the only Son of this order to bestow himself upon the Urantia races and presently proclaimed vicegerent Planetary Prince of Urantia; 15. *John the Baptist*, the forerunner of Michael's mission; 16. 1-2-3 *the First*, the leader of the loyal midway creatures. Seats 17-24 and not permanently occupied.

45:5. The Material Sons

The domain of the Adams is the center of attraction to all new arrivals on Jerusem. These Material Sons are the highest type of sex-reproducing beings to be found on the training spheres of the evolving universes. These Material Sons are the last and physical link in the chain of personalities extending from divinity and perfection above down to humanity and material existence below. These Sons provide the inhabited worlds with a mutually contactable intermediary between the invisible Planetary Prince and the material creatures of the realms.

45:6. Adamic Training of Ascenders

The Material Sons and Daughters, together with their children, present an engaging spectacle which never fails to arouse the curiosity and intrigue the attention of all ascending mortals. These citizens of Jerusem are the immediate sponsors and mentors of the mortal survivors from the time they attain citizenship on the headquarters world until they take leave for Edentia. Sex experience in a physical sense is past for ascenders, but in close association with the Material Sons and Daughters, both individually and as members of their families, these sex-deficient mortals are enabled to compensate the social, intellectual, emotional, and spiritual aspects of their parental deficiency. No mortal, midwayer, or seraphim may ascend to Paradise without having passed through the experience of a parental relationship.

45:7. The Melchizedek Schools

The Melchizedek Sons conduct upward of thirty different educational centers on Jerusem. These training schools begin with the college of self-evaluation and end with the schools of Jerusem citizenship. Representative government is the divine ideal of self-government among nonperfect beings. Every one hundred years of universe time each system selects its ten representatives to sit in the constellation legislature. All representatives must be graduates of the highest school of the Melchizedek College of Administration. Suffrage is universal on Jerusem but the vote is differentially cast in accordance with the recognized and duly registered personal possession of mota—morontia wisdom. The vote cast at a Jerusem election by any one personality has a value ranging from one up to one thousand. Jerusem citizens are thus classified in accordance with their mota achievement.

Paper 46: The Local System Headquarters
Archangel

JERUSEM, the headquarters of Satania, is truly the heaven visualized by the majority of twentieth-century religious believers.

46:1. Physical Aspects of Jerusem

The sphere has seven major capitals and seventy minor administrative centers. The Satania day equals a little less than three days of Urantia time. The system year consists of one hundred Jerusem days. The full-light temperature is maintained at about 70 degrees Fahrenheit, while during the period of light recession it falls to a little lower than 50 degrees. Light intensity is about like Urantia sunlight at ten o'clock in the morning. At the time of minimum illumination, the light is about that of your full moon on a clear night.

46:2. Physical Features of Jerusem

There are thousands upon thousands of small lakes. The atmosphere of Jerusem is a three-gas mixture. By adjustment of physical mechanisms the material beings of the planet can proceed at a pace varying from two to five hundred miles per hour. The manufacturing or laboratory sector of Jerusem is an extensive domain. There is a perfection of mechanical technique and physical achievement which would astonish and even awe your most experienced chemists and inventors. Mount Seraph is the highest elevation on Jerusem, almost fifteen thousand feet, and is the point of departure for all transport seraphim. Transports arrive on the crystal field, the so-called sea of glass.

46:3. The Jerusem Broadcasts

All broadcasts are automatically displayed so as to be discernible by all types of beings present in the central broadcast amphitheater. It is the favorite diversion for all Jerusem to spend their leisure at the broadcast station, there to learn of the welfare and state of the universe. All broadcasts to the individual worlds are relayed from the system capitals except the Michael messages, which sometimes go direct to their destinations over the archangels' circuit.

46:4. Residential and Administrative Areas

Considerable portions of Jerusem are assigned as residential areas. These arrangements are designed as follows: 1. *The circles*—the nonnative residential areas. 2. *The squares*—the system executive-administrative areas. 3. *The rectangles*—the rendezvous of the lower native life. 4. *The triangles*—the local or Jerusem administrative areas. Jerusem enjoys the efficient services of the spironga. These beings are devoted to spiritual ministry in behalf of the supermaterial residents and visitors. Jerusem has great buildings of both material and morontia types, while the embellishment of the purely spiritual zones is no less exquisite and replete.

46:5. The Jerusem Circles

The residential circles include: 1. *Circles of the Sons of God*—The central region is now occupied by the Michael memorial. When this temple was dedicated, Michael was present in person, and all Jerusem heard the touching story of the Master Son's bestowal on Urantia. 2. *The circles of the angels*—These seven circles are surrounded by the exhibit panorama of Jerusem, five thousand standard miles in circumference, which is devoted to the presentation of the advancing status of the peopled worlds of Satania. 3. *The circles of the Universe Aids*—The headquarters of the Evening Stars. 4. *The circles of the Master Physical Controllers.* 5. *The circles of the ascending mortals*—The central area is occupied by memorials representative of the inhabited worlds of the system. Many changes are even now being made in the Urantia structures. 6. *The circles of the courtesy colonies*—Many of these buildings are constructed wholly of crystal gems. 7. *The circles of the finaliters* have a unique structure at the center that bears this inscription: "Undedicated to the seventh stage of spirit—to the eternal assignment."

46:6. The Executive-Administrative Squares

The one thousand squares are clustered in ten grand divisions, thus constituting the following ten administrative departments: 1. Physical maintenance and material improvement. 2. Arbitration and ethics. 3. Planetary and local affairs. 4. Constellation and universe affairs. 5. Education and other Melchizedek activities. 6. Planetary and system physical progress. 7. Morontia affairs. 8. Pure spirit activities and ethics. 9. Ascendant ministry. 10. Grand universe philosophy. These structures are transparent; hence all system activities can be viewed even by student visitors.

46:7. The Rectangles—The Spornagia

On Jerusem you will be amazed by the agricultural achievements of the wonderful spornagia. They utilize both animals and numerous mechanical contrivances in the culture of the soil. Although spornagia neither possess nor evolve survival souls they do evolve an individuality which can experience reincarnation. They are bisexual and procreate as they are required to meet the needs of a growing population. They embrace the combined traits of a faithful horse and an affectionate dog and manifest an intelligence exceeding that of the highest type of chimpanzee. They are most appreciative of the attentions shown them.

46:8. The Jerusem Triangles

The purely local and routine affairs of Jerusem are directed from the one hundred triangles which are surrounded by the panoramic depiction of the system headquarters history. This sector will be restored upon the readmission of Satania into the constellation family. Every provision for this event has been made by the decrees of Michael. But ere long, the adjudication of Lucifer and his associates will restore the Satania system to the Norlatiadek constellation, and subsequently, Urantia and the other isolated spheres will be restored to the Satania circuits, and again will such worlds enjoy the privileges of interplanetary communication and intersystem communion.

Paper 47: The Seven Mansion Worlds

Brilliant Evening Star

IN a certain sense, all fifty-six of the encircling worlds of Jerusem are devoted to the transitional culture of ascending mortals, but the seven satellites of world number one are more specifically known as the mansion worlds.

47:1. The Finaliters' World

Finaliters and certain groups of salvaged children and their caretakers are resident on transitional world number one. The temple of the finaliters is not visible to the unaided material or early morontia vision. But the energy transformers are able to visualize many of these realities to ascending mortals and from time to time they do thus function. On the first mansion world all survivors must pass the requirements of the parental commission. No ascending mortal can escape the experience of rearing children—their own or others.

47:2. The Probationary Nursery

The infant-receiving schools of Satania are situated on the finaliter world. These infants of ascending mortals are always personalized as of their exact physical status at the time of death except for reproductive potential. Any time after sixteen, if final choice has been made, they translate to the first mansion world and begin their Paradise ascent.

47:3. The First Mansion World

On the mansion worlds the resurrected mortal survivors resume their lives just where they left off when overtaken by death. The mortal-mind transcripts and the active creature-memory patterns as transformed from the material levels to the spiritual are the individual possession of the detached Thought Adjusters. The creature mind-matrix and the passive potentials of identity are present in the morontia soul entrusted to the keeping of the seraphic destiny guardians. And it is the reuniting of the morontia-soul trust of the seraphim and the spirit-mind trust of the Adjuster that reassembles creature personality and constitutes resurrection of a sleeping survivor. Throughout all eternity you will recall the profound memory impressions of your first witnessing of these resurrection mornings. From the resurrection halls you proceed to the Melchizedek sector, where you are assigned permanent residence. Then you enter upon ten days of personal liberty. You have time to consult the registry and call upon your loved ones and other earth friends. If you are not to be detained on mansion world number one, at the end of ten days you will enter the translation sleep and proceed to world number two, and every ten days thereafter you will thus advance until you arrive on the world of your assignment. Morontia Companions are assigned to ascending mortals. These beautiful and versatile beings are companionable associates and charming guides.

47:4. The Second Mansion World

A newly developed and suitably adjusted morontia body is acquired at the time of each advance from one mansion world to another. You partake of the morontia order of food; both food and water are fully utilized in the morontia body; there is no residual waste. From sphere to sphere you grow less material, more intellectual, and slightly more spiritual. Mansonia number two provides for the removal of all phases of intellectual conflict and for the cure of all varieties of mental disharmony. The development on mansonia number two compares with the intellectual status of the post-Magisterial Son culture of the ideal evolutionary worlds.

47:5. The Third Mansion World

Mansonia the third is the headquarters of the Mansion World Teachers. On the third mansion world the survivors really begin their progressive morontia culture. The chief purpose of this training is to enhance the understanding and co-ordination of morontia mota and human philosophy. The culture of the third mansion world partakes of the nature of the post-bestowal Son age of a normal inhabited planet.

47:6. The Fourth Mansion World

It is during the period of training on world number four that the ascending mortals are really first introduced to the demands and delights of the true social life of morontia creatures. Ascenders are all becoming self-conscious of God-knowing, God-revealing, God-seeking, and God-finding. The intellectual and social culture of this fourth mansion world is comparable to the mental and social life of the post-Teacher Son.

47:7. The Fifth Mansion World

Transport to the fifth mansion world represents a tremendous forward step in the life of a morontia progressor. The culture of this mansion world corresponds in general to that of the early era of light and life on the planets of normal evolutionary progress. Having mastered the local universe language before leaving the fourth mansion world, you now devote more time to the perfection of the tongue of Uversa to the end that you may be proficient in both languages before arriving on Jerusem with residential status. A real birth of cosmic consciousness takes place on mansonia number five.

You are becoming universe minded. Study is becoming voluntary, unselfish service natural, and worship spontaneous.

47:8. The Sixth Mansion World

The first lessons embracing the affairs of a whole universe are now imparted. This is a brilliant age for ascending mortals and usually witnesses the perfect fusion of the human mind and the divine Adjuster. Immediately upon the confirmation of Adjuster fusion the new morontia being is introduced to his fellows for the first time by his new name and is granted the forty days of spiritual retirement from all routine activities wherein to commune with himself and to choose some one of the optional routes to Havona and to select from the differential techniques of Paradise attainment.

47:9. The Seventh Mansion World

The experience on this sphere is the crowning achievement of the immediate postmortal career. Any discernible differences between those mortals hailing from the isolated and retarded worlds and those survivors from the more advanced and enlightened spheres are virtually obliterated. Now begins the formation of classes for graduation to Jerusem. You will soon be welcomed on the receiving field of the headquarters world as Jerusem citizens.

47:10. Jerusem Citizenship

The reception of a new class of mansion world graduates is the signal for all Jerusem to assemble as a committee of welcome. After mortals have attained residence on the system headquarters, no more literal resurrections will be experienced. Changes will be made from time to time, but you will retain this same form until you bid it farewell when you emerge as first-stage spirits preparatory for transit to the superuniverse worlds of ascending culture and spirit training.

Paper 48: The Morontia Life

Archangel

THE morontia life, extending as it does over the various stages of the local universe career, is the only possible approach whereby material mortals could attain the threshold of the spirit world.

48:1. Morontia Materials

The morontia realms are the local universe liaison spheres between the material and spiritual levels of creature existence. Morontia materials have exactly one hundred forms of a unique energy organization called morontia material. When you traverse the morontia life of Nebadon, these patient and skillful Morontia Power Supervisors will successively provide you with 570 morontia bodies. Eight of these occur in the system, seventy-one in the constellation, and 491 during the sojourn on the spheres of Salvington.

48:2. Morontia Power Supervisors

These unique beings are exclusively concerned with the supervision of those activities which represent a working combination of spiritual and physical energies. They are the channels of morontia power which sustain and energize the morontia phases of the transition worlds. Each morontia world has a separate order of morontia energy. When mansion world ascenders pass from one sphere to another the necessary changes in creature form are skillfully effected by the system co-ordinators. The early morontia-form changes require about seven days of standard time for their accomplishment. As you progress from one class or phase of a morontia world to another, you must be re-keyed or advance-tuned.

48:3. Morontia Companions

These hosts of the mansion and morontia worlds are the offspring of a local universe Mother Spirit and are trained for service by the Melchizedeks. These companions are touchingly affectionate and charmingly social beings. One of them will certainly be on hand to welcome you when you awaken on the initial mansion world from the first transit sleep of time. These brilliant beings will be your language teachers. The first study on the mansion worlds will be the tongue of Satania and then the language of Nebadon. These beings are probably going to contribute much to your enjoyment of the mansion worlds.

48:4. The Reversion Directors

There is a morontial and a spiritual equivalent of mirth and laughter. The ascendant life is about equally divided between work and freedom from assignment. Our humor embraces three general levels of appreciation: reminiscent jests, current humor, and prophetic joy. The reversion directors are occupied with the leadership of diversion, spiritual recreation and morontia entertainment. When partially exhausted by the efforts of attainment there is agreeable pleasure in living over again the enactments of other days and ages. You are to be congratulated on a comparatively keen sense of humor. One of the functions of humor is to help all of us take ourselves less seriously. Humor is the divine antidote for exaltation of ego. Humor also functions to lessen the shock of the unexpected impact of fact or of truth. It is the recalling of past experiences that provides the basis for present diversion and amusement.

48:5. The Mansion World Teachers

The Mansion World Teachers are a corps of deserted but glorified cherubim and sanobim. On the mansion worlds schools are organized in three general groups: the schools of thinking, the schools of feeling, and the schools of doing. When you reach the constellation, there are added the schools of ethics, the schools of administration, and the schools of social adjustment. On the universe headquarters worlds you will enter the schools of philosophy, divinity, and pure spirituality. The mansonia life early teaches the young morontia pupils that postponement is in no sense avoidance. After the life in the flesh, time is no longer available as a technique of dodging situations or of circumventing disagreeable obligations.

Mansion World Teachers are practical and sympathetic teachers, wise and understanding instructors, able and efficient guides. Many of the older of these teachers are re-embraced by the Universe Mother Spirit, and emerge with the status of seraphim.

48:6. Morontia World Seraphim—Transition Ministers

These angels are devoted to facilitating the transit of material and mortal creatures from the temporal life in the flesh on into the early stages of morontia existence on the seven mansion worlds. You should understand that the morontia life of an ascending mortal is really initiated on the inhabited worlds at the conception of the soul. You will not, however, be conscious of the ministry of the transition seraphim until you attain the mansion worlds. On the mansion worlds the seraphic evangels will help you to choose wisely among the optional routes to Edentia, Salvington, Uversa, and Havona. They proclaim the great law of the conservation and dominance of goodness: No act of good is ever wholly lost. Mota is more than a superior philosophy; it is to philosophy as two eyes are to one. The shadow of a hair's turning premeditated for an untrue purpose constitute falseness. One can be technically right as to fact and everlastingly wrong in the truth. Sometimes your most disappointing disappointments have become your greatest blessings. You will learn that you increase your burdens and decrease the likelihood of success by taking yourself too seriously. Nothing can take precedence over the work of your status sphere. Self-importance, not work-importance, exhausts immature creatures; it is the self element that exhausts, not the effort to achieve. You can do important work if you do not become self-important; you can do several things as easily as one if you leave yourself out. Variety is restful; monotony is what wears and exhausts.

48:7. Morontia Mota

The lower planes of morontia mota join directly with the higher levels of human philosophy. On the first mansion world it is the practice to teach the less advanced students by the parallel technique, i.e.: 2. Few persons live up to the faith which they really have. 11. The weak indulge in resolutions, but the strong act. 12. The greatest affliction of the cosmos is never to have been afflicted. 18. Impatience is a spirit poison; anger is like a stone hurled into a hornet's nest. 19. Anxiety must be abandoned. The disappointments hardest to bear are those which never come. 28. The argumentative defense of any proposition is inversely proportional to the truth contained. Such is the work of the beginners on the first mansion world while the more advanced pupils on the later worlds are mastering the higher levels of cosmic insight and morontia mota.

48:8. The Morontia Progressors

Being a morontia progressor is the evolutionary portal to spirit life and the eventual attainment of creature perfection by which ascenders achieve the goal of time—the finding of God on Paradise. There is a definite and divine purpose in all this morontia and subsequent spirit scheme of mortal progression. If the Gods designed merely to take you on one long and eternal joy excursion, they certainly would not so largely turn the whole universe into one vast and intricate practical training school and then spend ages upon ages piloting you, one by one, through this gigantic universe school of experiential training. If the future destiny of the Paradise finaliters is service in new universes now in the making, it is assured that in this new and future creation there will be no created orders of experiential beings whose lives will be wholly different from those which mortal finaliters have lived on some world as a part of their ascending training, as one of the stages of their agelong progress from animal to angel and from angel to spirit and from spirit to God.

Paper 49: The Inhabited Worlds

Melchizedek

ALL mortal-inhabited worlds are evolutionary in origin and nature. These spheres are the spawning ground of the mortal races of time and space. Satania is an unfinished system containing only 619 inhabited worlds. Urantia is number 606 of Satania. The oldest inhabited world of Satania is Anova, which is in an advanced stage of progressive civilization.

49:1. The Planetary Life

Life is sometimes initiated in one center, sometimes in three, as it was on Urantia. In the development of planetary life the vegetable form always precedes the animal. The process of planetary evolution is orderly and controlled. The selected and superior strains of living protoplasm initiated by the Life Carriers should be jealously and intelligently guarded. On most of the inhabited worlds these superior potentials of life are valued much more highly than on Urantia.

49:2. Planetary Physical Types

There is a standard and basic pattern of vegetable and animal life in each system. There are seven distinct physical types: 1. *The atmospheric types*—There are subbreather, mid-breather, and superbreather planets. Beings such as the Urantia races are classified as mid-breathers. A planet devoid of air would belong to the separate order of nonbreathers. 2. *The elemental types*—These differentiations have to do with the relation of mortals to water, air, and land. It is both amazing and amusing to observe the early civilization of a primitive race of human beings taking shape, in one case, in the air and treetops and, in another, amidst the shallow waters of sheltered tropic basins. 3. *The gravity types*—The various planetary types of mortals vary in height, the average in Nebadon being a trifle under seven feet with a range between two and one-half feet and ten feet. 4. *The temperature types*—It is possible to create living beings who can withstand temperatures both much higher and much lower than the life range of the Urantia races. 5. *The electric types*—The electric, magnetic, and electronic behavior of the worlds varies greatly. 6. *The energizing types*—Not all worlds are alike in the manner of taking in energy, air and food. 7. *The unnamed types*—There are numerous additional physical variations in planetary life.

49:3. Worlds of the Nonbreathers

On the nonbreathing worlds the advanced races must do much to protect themselves from meteor damage by making electrical installations which operate to consume or shunt the meteors. Life on the worlds of the nonbreathers is radically different from what it is on Urantia. The nonbreathers do not eat food or drink water. In survival their peoples are candidates for Spirit fusion. Such a race of beings inhabits a sphere in close proximity to Urantia.

49:4. Evolutionary Will Creatures

There are six basic evolutionary races: three primary—red, yellow, and blue; and three secondary—orange, green, and indigo. Many of the three-brained planets harbor only the three primary types. We do not regard a planet as having emerged from barbarism so long as one sex seeks to tyrannize over the other. The length of life varies on the different planets from twenty-five years on the primitive worlds to near five hundred on the more advanced and older spheres.

49:5. The Planetary Series of Mortals

Mortal creatures may be studied from numerous viewpoints, among which are the following: 1. *Adjustment to planetary environment*—normal, radical, and experimental. Many forms of life have appeared on Urantia that are not found elsewhere. 2. *Brain-type series*—the one-, the two-, and the three-brained types. Urantians are of the two-brained type. These three orders stand on an equal footing in the ascension career. 3. *Spirit-reception series*—different gland chemistry. 4. *Planetary-mortal epochs*—reception of celestial ministry. Your Planetary Prince joined the Lucifer rebellion. Your Material Son and Daughter, Adam and Eve, defaulted; however, your planet enjoyed the signal honor of becoming the mortal home planet of the Sovereign Son, Michael of Nebadon. There has never been a magisterial mission on your world. 5. *Creature-kinship serials*—according to type, series, and other relationships. 6. *Adjuster-fusion series*—Almost ninety per cent of the inhabited worlds of Nebadon are peopled with Adjuster-fusion candidates. 7. *Techniques of terrestrial escape*—There are numerous techniques whereby man escapes natural death.

49:6. Terrestrial Escape

From time to time special resurrections of the sleeping survivors are conducted. 1. *Mortals of the dispensational or group order of survival*—The sleeping survivors of a planetary age are repersonalized on the mansion worlds in the dispensational roll calls. 2. *Mortals of the individual orders of ascension*—all who have attained the third cosmic circle may be repersonalized on the third day after natural death. 3. *Mortals of the probationary-dependent orders of ascension*—many die in youth before choosing the Paradise career; they follow the parent of most advanced spiritual status, going to the probationary nursery on the third day. 4. *Mortals of the secondary modified orders of ascension*. These progressive human beings reawaken on the headquarters of their local system. The intermediate group go to the constellation training worlds. 5. *Mortals of the primary modified order of ascension*. These mortals belong to the Adjuster-fused type of evolutionary life; they are translated from among the living and appear immediately in the presence of the Sovereign Son on the headquarters of the local universe.

Paper 50: The Planetary Princes
Secondary Lanonandek

WHILE belonging to the order of Lanonandek Sons, the Planetary Princes are so specialized in service that they are commonly regarded as a distinct group.

50:1. Mission of the Princes

On a newly inhabited world the Planetary Prince is the sole representative of complete divinity. This effort to provide sympathetic rulership for the evolutionary worlds entails the increased liability that these near-human personalities may be led astray by the exaltation of their own minds over and above the will of the Supreme Rulers. Nebadon has suffered the misfortune of several rebellions. But not often do these world princes fail in their missions of organizing and administering the inhabited spheres.

50:2. Planetary Administration

The Planetary Princes may at any time seek the counsel of the Melchizedeks. The rule of the evolutionary planets in their early and unsettled careers is largely autocratic. The princes usually surround themselves with a supreme council of twelve. The staff of a world ruler consists largely of personalities of the Infinite Spirit. On special occasions the seraphic helpers and even the Melchizedeks can and do make themselves visible to the inhabitants of the evolutionary worlds..

50:3. The Prince's Corporeal Staff

On going to a young world, a Planetary Prince usually takes with him a group of volunteer ascending mortals from the local system headquarters. Caligastia had a corps of one hundred such helpers; none of them had fused with their indwelling Adjusters. These assistants to the Planetary Prince seldom mate with the world races, but they do always mate among themselves. Two classes of beings result from these unions: the primary type of midway creatures and certain high types of material beings.

50:4. The Planetary Headquarters and Schools

The prince's corporeal staff early organize the planetary schools of training and culture. The students and teachers in the Prince's schools were all agriculturists and horticulturists. The time is about equally divided between the following pursuits: Physical labor, Social activities, Educational application, Vocational training, and Spiritual culture. On Urantia these plans for planetary progress and cultural advancement were well under way, when the whole enterprise was brought to a rather sudden and most inglorious end by Caligastia's adherence to the Lucifer rebellion. The wreck of these schools was speedy and complete. Many of the offspring of the ascenders of the Prince's materialized staff remained loyal, which did much to uphold the planetary concepts of truth and righteousness.

50:5. Progressive Civilization

The mortal races on an average world of time and space will successively pass through the following seven developmental epochs: The nutrition epoch, The security age, The material-comfort era, The quest for knowledge and wisdom, The epoch of philosophy and brotherhood, The age of spiritual striving, and The era of light and life. After serving their spheres through successive dispensations of world history and the progressing epochs of planetary progress, the Planetary Princes are elevated to the position of Planetary Sovereigns upon the inauguration of the era of light and life.

50:6. Planetary Culture

When compared with the loyal worlds of the universe, your planet seems most confused and greatly retarded in all phases of intellectual progress and spiritual attainment. It will require age upon age to retrieve the resultant handicaps of sin and secession. Your world still continues to pursue an irregular and checkered career as a result of the double tragedy of a rebellious Planetary Prince and a defaulting Material Son.

50:7. The Rewards of Isolation

It may turn out, eventually, that mortal creatures hailing from the worlds quarantined in consequence of rebellion are extremely fortunate. We have discovered that such ascenders are very early entrusted with numerous special assignments to cosmic undertakings where unquestioned faith and sublime confidence are essential to achievement. On Jerusem the ascenders from these isolated worlds occupy a residential sector by themselves and are known as the *agondonters*, meaning evolutionary will creatures who can believe without seeing, persevere when isolated, and triumph over insuperable difficulties even when alone. Tabamantia is an agondonter of finaliter status, having survived from one of the quarantined spheres involved in the first rebellion ever to take place in the universes of time and space.

Paper 51: The Planetary Adams
Secondary Lanonandek

THESE Sons are the biologic uplifters. usually known on a planet as Adam and Eve. While there was a miscarriage of the ideal plans for improving your native races, still, Adam's mission was not in vain; Urantia has profited immeasurably from the gift of Adam and Eve.

51:1. Origin and Nature of the Material Sons of God

The material or sex Sons and Daughters are the offspring of the Creator Son. Material Sons vary in height from eight to ten feet, and their bodies glow with the brilliance of radiant light of a violet hue. They are surcharged with divine energy and saturated with celestial light. The Material Sons enjoy a dual nutrition; they partake of materialized energy, while their immortal existence is fully maintained by the direct and automatic intake of certain sustaining cosmic energies. These unique and wonderfully useful beings are the connecting links between the spiritual and physical worlds.

51:2. Transit of the Planetary Adams

They must undergo dematerialization on the system capital before they can be enseraphimed for transport to the world of assignment. Upon arrival at their planetary destination the Material Son and Daughter are rematerialized under the direction of the Life Carriers, to all intents and purposes just as they were before submitting to the dematerializing process on Jerusem.

51:3. The Adamic Missions

On the inhabited worlds the Material Sons and Daughters construct their own garden homes with the help of many of the higher types of native races. Such Garden of Eden homes are usually located in a secluded section and in a near-tropic zone. They are wonderful creations. A Planetary Adam and Eve are, in potential, the full gift of physical grace to the mortal races. Caligastia, the traitorous Planetary Prince, did succeed in compromising your Adam and Eve, but he failed in his effort to involve them in the Lucifer rebellion. The seraphim, Solonia, proclaimed the miscarriage of the divine plan and requisitioned the return of the Melchizedek receivers to Urantia. The secondary midway creatures are indigenous to the Adamic missions. These planetary ministers contribute much to the advancement of civilization and even to the subjection of insubordinate minorities. On the day of Pentecost the loyal primary and the secondary midwayers effected a voluntary union and have functioned as one unit in world affairs ever since.

51:4. The Six Evolutionary Races

The race of dominance during the early ages of the inhabited worlds is the red man. On those worlds having all six evolutionary races the superior peoples are the red, the yellow, and the blue. It is a misfortune on Urantia that you so largely lost your superior blue men, except as they persist in your amalgamated "white race." The more backward humans are usually employed as laborers by the more progressive races. This accounts for the origin of slavery on the planets during the early ages. On most normal worlds involuntary servitude does not survive the dispensation of the Planetary Prince. On these normal worlds the inferior and unfit are largely eliminated under the direction of the Planetary Prince and the Material Son. It seems that you ought to be able to agree upon the biologic disfellowshiping of your more markedly unfit, defective, degenerate, and antisocial stocks.

51:5. Racial Amalgamation—Bestowal of the Adamic Blood

Usually the violet peoples do not begin to amalgamate with the planetary natives until their own group numbers over one million. On most worlds it is considered the highest honor to be selected as a candidate for mating with the sons and daughters of the garden. This whole scheme of race improvement was early wrecked on Urantia. It would not prove beneficial for the higher strains of Urantia mortals to mate with the lower races. You must now work out your planetary problem of race improvement by other and largely human methods of adaptation and control.

51:6. The Edenic Regime

On normal worlds the garden headquarters of the violet race becomes the second center of world culture and, jointly with the headquarters city of the Planetary Prince, sets the pace for the development of civilization. Think what it would mean on your world if somewhere in the Levant there were a world center of civilization, a great planetary university of culture, which had functioned uninterruptedly for 37,000 years. And not far distant still another and older headquarters of celestial ministry whose traditions would exert a cumulative force of 500,000 years of integrated evolutionary influence. It is custom and tradition which eventually spreads the ideals of Eden to a whole world.

51:7. United Administration

Before the first Magisterial Son concludes his mission on a normal evolutionary world, there has been effected the union of the educational and administrative work of the Planetary Prince and the Material Son. The Planetary Prince and his staff still foster the spiritual and philosophic domains of activity. Adam and Eve pay particular attention to the physical, scientific, and economic status of the realm. Both groups equally devote their energies to the promotion of the arts, social relations, and intellectual achievements. By the time of the inauguration of the fifth dispensation of world affairs, a magnificent administration of planetary activities has been achieved.

Paper 52: Planetary Mortal Epochs
Mighty Messenger

FROM the inception of life on an evolutionary planet to the time of its final flowering in the era of light and life, there appear upon the stage of world action at least seven epochs of human life.

52:1. Primitive Man

The length of time consumed in early life evolution varies ranging from one hundred and fifty thousand years to over one million years of Urantia time. The evolutionary races of color—red, orange, yellow, green, blue, and indigo—begin to appear about the time that primitive man is developing a simple language. Primitive men are mighty hunters and fierce fighters. The law of this age is the physical survival of the fittest.

52:2. Post-Planetary Prince Man

With the arrival of the Planetary Prince a new dispensation begins. Government appears on earth, and the advanced tribal epoch is attained. The inhabitants of a world so changed by rebellion can have little or no idea of such a regime on a normal planet. The average length of this dispensation is around five hundred thousand years. This dispensation witnesses a spiritual dawn; and specialized systems of religious and philosophic thought develop. In some respects Urantians do not seem to have wholly emerged from this stage of planetary evolution. Color is the basis of tribal and national groupings, and the different races often develop separate languages. This is the dispensation of the realization of sex equality. This is the dawn of the golden age of the home. During this age agriculture makes its appearance. The races are purified and brought up to a high state of physical perfection—promoting the increase of the higher types of mortals with proportionate curtailment of the lower. This is something which the Urantia peoples have not even yet seriously undertaken. It is the false sentiment of your partially perfected civilizations that fosters, protects, and perpetuates the hopelessly defective strains of evolutionary human stocks.

52:3. Post-Adamic Man

When the highest possible level of evolutionary life has been attained, when primitive man has ascended as far as possible in the biologic scale, a Material Son and Daughter always appear on the planet. Twenty-five thousand years of such an administration of the conjoint wisdom of the Planetary Prince and the Material Sons usually ripens the sphere for the advent of a

Magisterial Son. On an average world the post-Adamic dispensation is an age of great invention, energy control, and mechanical development; it is the golden age of exploration and the final subduing of the planet—just such an epoch as Urantia is now experiencing. Your world is a full dispensation and more behind the average planetary schedule. Universal peace and co-operation are seldom attained until the races are fairly well blended, and until they speak a common language. Truth is revealed up to the administration of the constellations. World-wide peace is the indicator of planetary ripeness for the advent of the third order of sonship, the Magisterial Son.

52:4. Post-Magisterial Son Man

When an evolutionary world becomes thus ripe for the magisterial age, one of the high order of Avonal Sons makes his appearance on a magisterial mission. The Magisterial Sons extend the revelation of truth to portray the affairs of the local universe and all its tributaries. The daily work required to sustain one's independence would be represented by two and one-half hours of your time. Such worlds advance and honor only those leaders and rulers who are most fit to bear social and political responsibilities. During this epoch the majority of the world mortals are Adjuster indwelt. This is the age of the flowering of art, music, and higher learning. The termination of this age, on an ideal world, witnesses the fullness of a great religious awakening, a world-wide spiritual enlightenment. These dispensations of the Magisterial Sons cover anywhere from twenty-five thousand to fifty thousand years of Urantia time. But in the fullness of time one of these same Magisterial Sons will be born as the Paradise bestowal Son.

52:5. Post-Bestowal Son Man

On Urantia the bestowal Son, even your own Creator Son, appeared at the close of the Adamic dispensation, but that is not the usual order of events on the worlds of space. This is an age characterized by the world-wide pursuit of moral culture and spiritual truth. The revelations of truth are extended to include the superuniverse. Ever since the day of Pentecost, Urantia mortals again may proceed directly to the morontia spheres. All normal-minded will creatures of that world will receive Adjusters as soon as they attain the age of moral responsibility, of spiritual choice. The post-bestowal Son age may extend from ten thousand to a hundred thousand years. This is a time of great ethical and spiritual progress. Under the spiritual influence of these ages, human character undergoes tremendous transformations and experiences phenomenal development. During this era the problems of disease and delinquency are virtually solved. The average length of life, during this period, climbs well above the equivalent of three hundred years of Urantia time. There are many nations, mostly determined by land distribution, but only one race, one language, and one religion. Mortal affairs are almost, but not quite, utopian.

52:6. Urantia's Post-Bestowal Age

Urantia is not proceeding in the normal order. On a confused and disordered planet like Urantia such an achievement requires a much longer time and necessitates far greater effort. Religious revelation is essential to the realization of brotherhood on Urantia. Your world depends much on the achievement of the following personal transformations and planetary adjustments: 1. *Social fraternity*—a common language, interchange of students, teachers, and religious philosophers. 2. *Intellectual cross-fertilization*—exchange of national and racial literature. 3. *Ethical awakening*—development of moral consciousness that condemns the evils of national envy and racial jealousy. 4. *Political wisdom*—Substitution of international techniques of civilized adjudication for the barbarous arbitrament of war. 5. *Spiritual insight*—spiritual transformation that realizes the brotherhood of man predicated on the recognition of the Fatherhood of God. If you could be transplanted from your backward and confused world to some normal planet now in the post-bestowal Son age, you would think you had been translated to the heaven of your traditions.

52:7. Post-Teacher Son Man

The Sons of the next order to arrive on the average evolutionary world are the Trinity Teacher Sons. Jesus has promised to return but no one knows whether his second coming will precede or follow the appearances of Magisterial or Teacher Sons on Urantia. The Teacher Sons come in groups to the spiritualizing worlds. They remain for some time on the world to effect the transition from the evolutionary ages to the era of light and life, not less than one thousand years of planetary time. The revelation of truth is now extended to the central universe and to Paradise. This is the dispensation when many mortals are translated from among the living. The length of life approaches five hundred Urantia years. Representative government is vanishing, and the world is passing under the rule of individual self-control. The physical administration of a world during this age requires about one hour each day. Sooner or later, in connection with the termination of one of the Teacher Sons missions, the Planetary Prince is elevated to the position of Planetary Sovereign, and the System Sovereign appears to proclaim the entrance of such a world upon the era of light and life.

Paper 53: The Lucifer Rebellion

Manovandet Melchizedek

LUCIFER was a brilliant primary Lanonandek Son of Nebadon. He was designated as one of the one hundred most able and brilliant personalities in more than seven hundred thousand of his kind. From such a magnificent beginning, he embraced sin and now is numbered as one of three System Sovereigns in Nebadon who have succumbed to the urge of self and surrendered to the sophistry of spurious personal liberty.

53:1. Leaders of the Rebellion

Lucifer was a magnificent being, a brilliant personality; he stood next to the Most High Fathers of the constellations in the direct line of universe authority. Lucifer is now the fallen and deposed Sovereign of Satania. His first lieutenant, Satan, advocated his cause on your planet. The "devil" is none other than Caligastia, the deposed Planetary Prince of Urantia. Abaddon, the chief of the staff of Caligastia, has acted as chief executive of the Urantia rebels. Beelzebub was the leader of the disloyal midway creatures. The dragon eventually became the symbolic representation of all these evil personages.

53:2. The Causes of Rebellion

It is our belief that the idea took origin and form in Lucifer's mind. For more than one hundred years of standard time the Union of Days on Salvington had been reflectivating to Uversa that all was not at peace in Lucifer's mind. Throughout this period Lucifer became increasingly critical of the entire plan of universe administration. His first outspoken disloyalty was manifested on the occasion of a visit of Gabriel to Jerusem just a few days before the open proclamation of the Lucifer Declaration of Liberty. It is very difficult to point out the exact cause or causes which finally culminated in the Lucifer rebellion. At some point in this experience Lucifer became insincere, and evil evolved into deliberate and willful sin. He was long offered opportunity for repentance, but only some of his subordinates ever accepted the proffered mercy.

53:3. The Lucifer Manifesto

The cause of the rebels was stated under three heads: 1. *The reality of the Universal Father.* Lucifer charged that the Universal Father did not really exist. He even intimated that the finaliters were in collusion with the Paradise Sons to foist fraud upon all creation. 2. *The universe government of the Creator Son*—Michael. Lucifer contended that the local systems should be autonomous. Most bitterly did he attack the right of the Ancients of Days—

"foreign potentates," he branded them—to interfere in the affairs of the local systems and universes. 3. *The attack upon the universal plan of ascendant mortal training.* Lucifer maintained that far too much time and energy were expended upon the scheme of so thoroughly training ascending mortals. He intimated that the finaliters were co-operating with the scheme of enslaving all creation to the fictions of a mythical eternal destiny for ascending mortals.

53:4. The Outbreak of the Rebellion

The Lucifer manifesto was issued at the annual conclave of Satania in the presence of the assembled hosts of Jerusem, about two hundred thousand years ago. Self-assertion was the battle cry of the Lucifer rebellion. He maintained that all government should be limited to the local planets. He promised the Planetary Princes that they should rule the worlds as supreme executives. He was given a free hand to prosecute his seductive plan without let or hindrance. Gabriel was personally present on Jerusem throughout all these disloyal proceedings and only announced that he would, in due time, speak for Michael, and that all beings would be left free and unmolested in their choice. This period of delay was a time of great trial and testing to the loyal beings of all Satania. All was chaotic for a few years, and there was great confusion on the mansion worlds.

53:5. Nature of the Conflict

Upon the outbreak of the Satania rebellion, Michael took counsel of his Paradise brother, Immanuel. Following this momentous conference, Michael announced that he would pursue the same policy which had characterized his dealings with similar upheavals in the past, an attitude of noninterference. From the outbreak of rebellion to the day of his enthronement as sovereign ruler of Nebadon, Michael never interfered with the rebel forces of Lucifer. Gabriel called his personal staff together on Edentia and, in counsel with the Most Highs, elected to assume command of the loyal hosts of Satania. He displayed the banner of Michael, the material emblem of the Trinity government of all creation, the three azure-blue concentric circles on a white background. The Lucifer emblem was a banner of white with one red circle, in the center of which was a black solid circle. The various personalities present on the sphere who were in doubt as to their attitude would journey back and forth between these discussions until they arrived at a final decision. This war in heaven was very terrible and very real fought in terms of life eternal.

53:6. A Loyal Seraphic Commander

There were many noble and inspiring acts of devotion and loyalty which were performed by numerous personalities, but the most thrilling of all these daring feats of devotion was the courageous conduct of Manotia, the second in command of the Satania headquarters' seraphim. Not long since, in describing the experiences associated with the onset of the Lucifer rebellion, Manotia said: "But my most exhilarating moment was the thrilling adventure connected with the Lucifer rebellion when, as second seraphic commander, I refused to participate in the projected insult to Michael. I was morally upheld by the Melchizedeks, ably assisted by a majority of the Material Sons, deserted by a tremendous group of my own order, but magnificently supported by the ascendant mortals on Jerusem. We were able to carry on until the arrival of the new System Sovereign." This angel is still in service on Urantia, functioning as associate chief of seraphim.

53:7. History of the Rebellion

The Lucifer rebellion was system wide. Thirty-seven seceding Planetary Princes swung their world administrations largely to the side of the archrebel. Only on Panoptia did the Planetary Prince fail to carry his people with him. On this world, under the guidance of the Melchizedeks, the people rallied to the support of Michael. Ellanora, a young woman of that mortal realm, grasped the leadership of the human races, and not a single soul on that strife-torn world enlisted under the Lucifer banner. Upon the actual outbreak of the insurrection the entire system of Satania was isolated in both the constellation and the universe circuits. Of the supreme order of seraphim, not an angel was lost, but a considerable group of the next order were deceived and ensnared. The greatest loss occurred in the angelic ranks. Of the 681,217 Material Sons lost in Satania, ninety-five per cent were casualties of the Lucifer rebellion. Large numbers of midway creatures were lost on those individual planets whose Planetary Princes joined the Lucifer cause. In many respects this rebellion was the most widespread and disastrous of all such occurrences in Nebadon. It was over two years of system time from the beginning of the "war in heaven" until the installation of Lucifer's successor. The first message of Lanaforge to the Constellation Father of Norlatiadek read: "Not a single [Adjuster-indwelled] Jerusem citizen was lost." And on to Salvington, Uversa, and Paradise went this message of assurance that the survival experience of mortal ascension is the greatest security against rebellion and the surest safeguard against sin. The archrebels were allowed to roam the entire system to seek further penetration for their doctrines of discontent and self-assertion. But in almost two hundred thousand Urantia years they have been unable to deceive another world.

53:8. The Son of Man on Urantia

The bestowal of Michael terminated the Lucifer rebellion in all Satania aside from the planets of the apostate Planetary Princes. The Uversa tribunals have not yet rendered the executive decision regarding the appeal of Gabriel praying for the destruction of the rebels, but such a decree will, no doubt, be forthcoming in the fullness of time since the first step in the hearing of this case has already been taken. Caligastia, your apostate Planetary Prince, is still free on Urantia to prosecute his nefarious designs, but he has absolutely no power to enter the minds of men. The devil has been given a great deal of credit for evil which does not belong to him. Caligastia has been comparatively impotent since the cross of Christ.

53:9. Present Status of the Rebellion

Early in the days of the Lucifer rebellion, salvation was offered all rebels by Michael. None of the leaders accepted this merciful proffer. But thousands of the angels and the lower orders of celestial beings, including hundreds of the Material Sons and Daughters, accepted the mercy proclaimed by the Panoptians and were given rehabilitation at the time of Jesus' resurrection. Upon Michael's becoming the settled head of the universe of Nebadon, Lucifer was taken into custody by the agents of the Uversa Ancients of Days and has since been a prisoner on satellite number one of the Father's group of the transition spheres of Jerusem. Satan did periodically visit Caligastia and others of the fallen princes right up to the time of the presentation of these revelations, when there occurred the first hearing of Gabriel's plea for the annihilation of the archrebels. Satan is now unqualifiedly detained on the Jerusem prison worlds. We do not look for a removal of the present Satania restrictions until the Ancients of Days make final disposition of the archrebels. We anticipate the verdict of Uversa will be announced by the executionary broadcast which will effect the annihilation of these interned rebels.

Paper 54: Problems of the Lucifer Rebellion

Mighty Messenger

POTENTIAL evil is time-existent in a universe embracing differential levels of perfection meanings and values. Sin is potential in all realms where imperfect beings are endowed with the ability to choose between good and evil. The deliberate choice of evil constitutes sin; the persistent pursuit of sin and error is iniquity.

54:1. True and False Liberty

Of all the perplexing problems growing out of the Lucifer rebellion, none has occasioned more difficulty than the failure of immature evolutionary mortals to distinguish between true and false liberty. True liberty is the quest of the ages and the reward of evolutionary progress. True liberty is progressively related to reality and is ever regardful of social equity, cosmic fairness, universe fraternity, and divine obligations. Liberty without the associated and ever-increasing conquest of self is a figment of egoistic mortal imagination. Self-motivated liberty is a conceptual illusion, a cruel deception. License masquerading in the garments of liberty is the forerunner of abject bondage. True liberty is the associate of genuine self-respect; false liberty is the consort of self-admiration. True liberty is the fruit of self-control. Self-control leads to altruistic service. There is no error greater than that species of self-deception which leads intelligent beings to crave the exercise of power over other beings for the purpose of depriving these persons of their natural liberties.

54:2. The Theft of Liberty

Every creature of every evolving universe who aspires to do the Father's will is destined to become the partner of the time-space Creators in the magnificent adventure of experiential perfection attainment. Lucifer's folly was the attempt to do the nondoable, to short-circuit time in an experiential universe. The Lucifer rebellion threatened to deprive every personality in Satania of the thrilling experience of contributing something personal and unique to the slowly erecting monument to experiential wisdom which will sometime exist as the perfected system of Satania. In short, what God had given men and angels Lucifer would have taken away from them, that is, the divine privilege of participating in the creation of their own destinies and of the destiny of this local system of inhabited worlds.

54:3. The Time Lag of Justice

The all-wise Creators permit evil and sin because both are inevitable if the creature is to be truly free. Man's ability to choose good or evil is a universe reality. Although conscious and wholehearted identification with evil (sin) is the equivalent of nonexistence (annihilation), there must always intervene between the time of such personal identification with sin and the execution of the penalty. A period of time of sufficient length is afforded to win the approval of the sinner himself. The Ancients of Days refuse to annihilate any being until all moral values and all spiritual realities are extinct, both in the evildoer and in all related supporters and possible sympathizers.

54:4. The Mercy Time Lag

Another problem somewhat difficult of explanation in the constellation of Norlatiadek pertains to the reasons for permitting Lucifer, Satan, and the fallen princes to work mischief so long before being apprehended, interned, and adjudicated. Parents, those who have borne and reared children, are better able to understand why Michael, a Creator-father, might be slow to condemn and destroy his own Sons. Most of the liberties which Lucifer sought he already had; others he was to receive in the future. There are many reasons known to us why the Supreme Rulers did not immediately destroy or intern the leaders of the Lucifer rebellion. The ministry of mercy to the children of time and space always provides for this time lag between seedtime and harvest. Justice in a mercy-dominated universe may be slow, but it is certain.

54:5. The Wisdom of Delay

Of the many reasons known to me as to why Lucifer and his confederates were not sooner interned or adjudicated, I am permitted to recite the following: 1. Mercy requires that every wrongdoer have sufficient time to fully consider the implications of his position. 2. Supreme justice is dominated by a Father's love. 3. No affectionate father is ever precipitate in visiting punishment. 4. Wisdom and love admonish the upright children to bear with an erring brother. 5. Michael had not then attained unqualified sovereignty of Nebadon. 6. The Ancients of Days seldom execute wrongdoers without a full hearing. 7. It is evident that Immanuel counseled Michael to remain aloof from the rebels and allow rebellion to pursue a natural course of self-obliteration. 8. The Faithful of Days on Edentia advised the Constellation Fathers to allow the rebels free course. 9. The Supreme Executive of Orvonton counseled Gabriel to foster full opportunity for every living creature to mature a deliberate choice. 10. The Divine Minister of Salvington issued a mandate directing that nothing be done to half cure or otherwise hide the hideous visage of rebels and rebellion. 11. An emergency council of ex-mortals consisting of Mighty Messengers advised Gabriel that at least three times the number of beings would be led astray if arbitrary or summary methods of suppression were attempted. 12. The relative lapse of time from the viewpoint of Uversa, where the litigation is pending, could be indicated by saying that the crime of Lucifer was being brought to trial within two and a half seconds of its commission.

54:6. The Triumph of Love

The technique of dealing with the rebels is a vindication of divine love. In all their dealings with intelligent beings, both the Creator Son and his Paradise Father are love-dominated. If you are made to suffer the evil consequences because of the wrongdoing of your associates, fellows, or superiors, you may rest secure in the eternal assurance that such tribulations are transient afflictions. And there is compensation for these trials, delays, and disappointments. At first the Lucifer upheaval appeared to be an unmitigated calamity to the system and to the universe. The Melchizedeks now teach that the good resulting from the Satania rebellion is more than a thousand times the sum of all the evil. Shortsighted and time-bound mortal minds should be slow to criticize the time delays of the farseeing and all-wise administrators of universe affairs. As you ascend Paradiseward, you will increasingly learn that many problematic features of universe administration can only be comprehended subsequent to the acquirement of increased experiential capacity and to the achievement of enhanced spiritual insight. Cosmic wisdom is essential to the understanding of cosmic situations.

Paper 55: The Spheres of Light and Life
Mighty Messenger

THE age of light and life is the final evolutionary attainment of a world of time and space. This era of light and life, inaugurated by the Teacher Sons at the conclusion of their final planetary mission, continues indefinitely on the inhabited worlds. There are seven stages in the unfoldment of the era of light and life.

55:1. The Morontia Temple

The presence of a morontia temple at the capital of an inhabited world is the certificate of the admission of such a sphere to the settled ages of light and life. This event, signaling the dawn of the era of light and life, is always honored by the personal presence of the Paradise bestowal Son of that planet. The average morontia temple seats about three hundred thousand spectators. These edifices are used for special ceremonies of the planet. The schools of cosmic philosophy here conduct their graduation exercises. Such a morontia temple also serves as the place of assembly for witnessing the translation of living mortals to the morontia existence. On planets without morontia temples these fusion flashes many times occur in the planetary atmosphere, where the material body of a translation candidate is elevated by the midway creatures and the physical controllers.

55:2. Death and Translation

The majority of advanced evolutionary beings are translated directly from the life in the flesh to the morontia existence. When the family, friends, and working group of such a fusion candidate have forgathered in the morontia temple, they are distributed around the central stage whereon the fusion candidates are resting. What a beautiful occasion when mortals thus forgather to witness the ascension of their loved ones in spiritual flames. The scenes of weeping and wailing characteristic of earlier epochs of human evolution are now replaced by ecstatic joy and the sublimest enthusiasm. And it would be decidedly helpful if less advanced mortals could only learn to view natural death with something of this same cheerfulness and lightheartedness. The translated souls of the flowering ages of the settled spheres do not pass through the mansion worlds. They go back as teachers to the very worlds they passed by.

55:3. The Golden Ages

During this age of light and life the world increasingly prospers under the fatherly rule of the Planetary Sovereign. By this time the worlds are progressing under the momentum of one language, one religion, and, on normal spheres, one race. But there still remain the problems of caring for accidental injuries and the inescapable infirmities attendant upon the decrepitude of old age. Disease has not been entirely vanquished. Human government in the conduct of material affairs continues to function throughout this age of relative progress and perfection.

The public activities of a world in the first stage of light and life which I recently visited were financed by the tithing technique. The natural resources of this planet were administered as social possessions, community property.

Nevertheless, there is a certain, inevitable penalty attaching to mortal existence on such advanced evolutionary planets. When a settled world progresses beyond the third stage of light and life, all ascenders are destined, before attaining the minor sector, to receive some sort of transient assignment on a planet passing through the earlier stages of evolution.

The great handicap confronting Urantia in the matter of attaining the high planetary destiny of light and life is embraced in the problems of disease, degeneracy, war, multicolored races, and multilingualism.

55:4. Administrative Readjustments

The finaliters are active in co-operation with the Trinity Teacher Sons, but they do not begin their real participation in world affairs until the morontia temple appears on earth. From the first to the seventh stages of light and life successive administrative adjustments are made. One of the last acts of the Trinity Teacher Sons on their terminal mission is to liberate the midwayers of the realm and to promote them to responsible places in the new administration. A Life Carrier becomes the volunteer adviser of the planetary rulers regarding the further efforts to purify and stabilize the mortal race. In each succeeding age of settled existence the finaliters function in ever-increasing capacities. The Planetary Adam and Eve can petition the Sovereign Creator Son for release from planetary duties in order to begin their Paradise ascent.

55:5. The Acme of Material Development

Poverty and social inequality have all but vanished. Science, art, and industry flourish, and society is a smoothly working mechanism of high material, intellectual, and cultural achievement. War has become a matter of history, and there are no more armies or police forces. Schools are vastly improved and are devoted to the training of mind and the expansion of soul. A special feature of the competitive activities on such a highly cultured world concerns the efforts of individuals and groups to excel in the sciences and philosophies of cosmology. Life is refreshingly simple; man has at last co-ordinated a high state of mechanical development with an inspiring intellectual attainment and has overshadowed both with an exquisite spiritual achievement. The pursuit of happiness is an experience of joy and satisfaction.

55:6. The Individual Mortal

On a normal world the biologic fitness of the mortal race was long since brought up to a high level during the post-Adamic epochs. Both vision and hearing are extended. By now the population has become stationary in numbers. These mortals are increasingly able to commune with the indwelling Father fragment. We conjecture that there can never be a limit to intellectual evolution and the attainment of wisdom. We observe that human beings fully learn the local universe language before they are translated.

55:7. The First or Planetary Stage

This epoch extends from the appearance of the morontia temple at the new planetary headquarters to the time of the settling of the entire system in light and life. When such an era is attained on your world, no doubt Machiventa Melchizedek, now the vicegerent Planetary Prince of Urantia, will occupy the seat of the Planetary Sovereign; and it has long been conjectured on Jerusem that he will be accompanied by a son and daughter of the Urantia Adam and Eve.

55:8. The Second or System Stage

When an entire system becomes settled in life, a new order of government is inaugurated. Such a system of inhabited worlds becomes virtually self-governing. The system legislative assembly is constituted on the headquarters world. For the first time midsoniters come from the universe headquarters. What the Material Sons did for the mortal races biologically, the midsonite creatures now do for these unified and glorified humans in the ever-advancing realms of philosophy and spiritualized thinking. The Most Highs are proclaimed the unqualified rulers of the newly perfected family of one hundred settled systems of inhabited worlds.

55:9. The Third or Constellation State

The unification of a whole constellation of settled systems is attended by new distributions of executive authority and additional readjustments of universe administration. During this age many constellation and universe activities are transferred to the system capitals. Now administrative groups deal directly with the superuniverse government in matters pertaining to Havona and Paradise relationships. As the ages pass, the Constellation Fathers take over more and more of the detailed administrative functions which were formerly centered on the universe headquarters.

55:10. The Fourth or Local Universe Stage

When a universe becomes settled in light and life, it swings into the established superuniverse circuits, and the Ancients of Days proclaim the establishment of the supreme council of unlimited authority. The first act of this supreme council is to acknowledge the continued sovereignty of the Master Creator Son. New relationships extend down to the constellations and systems. The local universe Mother Spirit experiences new liaison relations with the Master Spirit of the superuniverse. The finaliter corps now, for the first time, acknowledges the jurisdiction of an extra-Paradise authority, the supreme council. The Creator Sons of such settled universes spend much of their time on Paradise. If the Creator Sons are destined to the outer universes, the Divine Ministers will undoubtedly accompany them. We hold that the Melchizedeks are destined to play ever-increasingly responsible parts in local universe government and administration.

55:11. The Minor and Major Sector States

Minor and major sectors of the superuniverse do not figure directly in the plan of being settled in light and life. The minor sector stage of stabilization has exclusively to do with physical status. We infer that major sector unification will be concerned with certain new intellectual levels of attainment.

Environmental limitations, even on an isolated world, cannot thwart the personal attainment of the individual mortal; Jesus of Nazareth, as a man among men, personally achieved the status of light and life over nineteen hundred years ago on Urantia.

55:12. The Seventh or Superuniverse Stage

We cannot positively forecast what would occur when a superuniverse becomes settled in light because such an event has never factualized. We infer that sweeping changes would be made in the entire organization and administration of every unit of the creations of time and space.

None of us entertains a satisfactory concept of what will happen when the grand universe becomes entirely settled in light and life. That event will undoubtedly be the most profound occurrence in the annals of eternity since the appearance of the central universe. There are those who hold that the Supreme Being himself will emerge from the Havona mystery enshrouding his spirit person and will become residential on the headquarters of the seventh superuniverse as the almighty and experiential sovereign of the perfected creations of time and space. But we really do not know.

Paper 56: Universal Unity
Mighty Messenger and Machiventa Melchizedek

GOD is unity. Deity is universally co-ordinated. The universe of universes is one vast integrated mechanism which is absolutely controlled by one infinite mind. The perfect and imperfect are truly interrelated, and therefore may the finite evolutionary creature ascend to Paradise in obedience to the Universal Father's mandate: "Be you perfect, even as I am perfect."

56:1. Physical Co-ordination

Paradise is the source of all material universes. The Unqualified Absolute upholds the physical universe, while the Deity Absolute motivates the exquisite overcontrol of all material reality; and both Absolutes are functionally unified by the Universal Absolute. All gravity centers in the personal presence of the Paradise Father of pure energy and pure spirit. Pure energy is the ancestor of all relative, nonspirit functional realities, while pure spirit is the potential of the divine and directive overcontrol of all basic energy systems. These realities, so diverse in space and time, are both centered in the person of the Paradise Father. In him they are one because God is one. The moment you depart from the unqualified concept of the infinite personality of the Paradise Father, you must postulate MIND as the inevitable technique of unifying the ever-widening divergence of these dual universe manifestations of the original monothetic Creator personality.

56:2. Intellectual Unity

The primal thought of the Universal Father eternalizes in dual expression: the Isle of Paradise and his Deity equal, the spiritual and Eternal Son. Such duality of eternal reality renders the mind God, the Infinite Spirit, inevitable. Mind is the indispensable channel of communication between spiritual and material realities. This infinite and universal mind is ministered in the universes of time and space as the cosmic mind. All mind activity is perfectly correlated with the all-embracing mind of the Infinite Spirit.

56:3. Spiritual Unification

As the universal mind gravity is centered in the Paradise personal presence of the Infinite Spirit, so does the universal spirit gravity center in the

Paradise personal presence of the Eternal Son. The spirit ministry to the evolving worlds is more directly unified in the personalities resident on the headquarters of the local universes and in the persons of the presiding Divine Ministers, who are in turn well-nigh perfectly correlated with the Paradise gravity circuit of the Eternal Son, wherein occurs final unification of all time-space spirit manifestations. The mortal mind when fused with the Thought Adjuster partakes of the threefold spirit endowment of the evolutionary realms. Spirit must always and ultimately become threefold in expression (Father, Son, & Spirit) and Trinity-unified in final realization.

56:4. Personality Unification

The Universal Father is a divinely unified personality; hence will all his ascendant children likewise be fully unified personalities before they reach Havona. Personality inherently reaches out to unify all constituent realities. Philosophically, cosmically, you may and perforce must conceive of the functioning of plural Deities and postulate the existence of plural Trinities; but in the worshipful experience of the personal contact of every worshiping personality, God is one; and that unified and personal Deity is our Paradise parent, God the Father.

56:5. Deity Unity

The oneness, the indivisibility, of Paradise Deity is existential and absolute. There are three eternal personalizations of Deity—the Universal Father, the Eternal Son, and the Infinite Spirit—but in the Paradise Trinity they are actually one Deity, undivided and indivisible. On Paradise and in the central universe, Deity unity is a fact of existence. Throughout the evolving universes of time and space, Deity unity is an achievement.

56:6. Unification of Evolutionary Deity

God the Supreme as a person existed in Havona before the creation of the seven superuniverses, but he functioned only on spiritual levels. The material-minded creatures of the evolutionary worlds of the seven superuniverses can comprehend Deity unity only as it is evolving in this power-personality synthesis of the Supreme Being. Mortal man must, through the recognition of truth, the appreciation of beauty, and the worship of goodness, evolve the recognition of a God of love and then progress through ascending deity levels to the comprehension of the Supreme. While ascending mortals achieve power comprehension of the Almighty on the capitals of the superuniverses and personality comprehension of the Supreme on the outer circuits of Havona, they do not actually find the Supreme Being. The finaliters are not likely to until they have achieved seventh-stage-spirit status, and until the

Supreme has become actually functional in the activities of the future outer universes.

56:7. Universal Evolutionary Repercussions

The steady progress of evolution in the time-space universes is accompanied by ever-enlarging revelations of Deity to all intelligent creatures. It should be noted that ascending mortals may experience the impersonal presence of successive levels of Deity long before they become sufficiently spiritual and adequately educated to attain experiential personal recognition of, and contact with, these Deities as personal beings. It is a fact that, as the creations of time and space are progressively settled in evolutionary status, there is observed a new and fuller functioning of God the Supreme concomitant with a corresponding withdrawing of the first three manifestations of God the Sevenfold. We all conjecture that the Michaels, the Creator Sons, are destined to function in these outer universes. We have not the slightest concept of what technique of deity approach may become operative in the future universes of outer space. Nevertheless, we deem that the perfected superuniverses will in some way become a part of the Paradise-ascension careers of those beings who may inhabit these outer creations. It is quite possible that in that future age we may witness outer-spacers approaching Havona through the seven superuniverses, administered by God the Supreme with or without the collaboration of the Seven Master Spirits.

56:8. The Supreme Unifier

The Supreme Being has a threefold function in the experience of mortal man: First, he is the unifier of time-space divinity; second, he is the maximum of Deity which finite creatures can actually comprehend; third, he is mortal man's only avenue of approach to the transcendental experience of consorting with absonite mind, eternal spirit, and Paradise personality. Ascendant finaliters by techniques of experience come really to know the Supreme Being, and they are destined to the service and the revelation of this Supreme Deity in and to the future universes of outer space. In eternity you may be permitted to make increasing revelations of this God of evolutionary creatures on supreme levels—even ultimate—as seventh-stage finaliters.

56:9. Universal Absolute Unity

The Unqualified Absolute and the Deity Absolute are unified in the Universal Absolute. The Absolutes are co-ordinated in the Ultimate, conditioned in the Supreme, and time-space modified in God the Sevenfold. To all personality intelligences of the grand universe the Paradise Trinity forever stands in finality, eternity, supremacy, and ultimacy and, for all practical purposes of personal comprehension and creature realization, as absolute. Spiritual personality is absolute only on Paradise, and the concept of the Absolute is unqualified only in infinity. The universe of universes is altogether unified. There is co-ordination of all levels of energy and all phases of personality. Philosophically and experientially, in concept and in reality, all things and beings center in the Paradise Father.

56:10. Truth, Beauty, and Goodness

The chief pursuit of the ever-advancing mortals is the quest for a better understanding and a fuller realization of the comprehensible elements of Deity—truth, beauty, and goodness. This represents man's effort to discern God in mind, matter, and spirit. And as the mortal pursues this quest, he finds himself increasingly absorbed in the experiential study of philosophy, cosmology, and divinity.

Beauty, art, is largely a matter of the unification of contrasts. Truth is the basis of science and philosophy, presenting the intellectual foundation of religion. Goodness embraces the sense of ethics, morality, and religion—experiential perfection-hunger. The fact of progressive evolution indicates the dominance of the Supreme Mind. The possession of goodness, greatness, is the measure of real divinity attainment. To finite man truth, beauty, and goodness embrace the full revelation of divinity reality. As this love-comprehension of Deity finds spiritual expression in the lives of God-knowing mortals, there are yielded the fruits of divinity: intellectual peace, social progress, moral satisfaction, spiritual joy, and cosmic wisdom. Love is the greatest thing in the universe—God is love. Love is the desire to do good to others.

PART III
THE HISTORY OF URANTIA

Paper 57: The Origin of Urantia
Life Carrier

IN presenting the records of Urantia we reckon time in terms of current usage—the present leap-year calendar of 365¼ days to the year. As a rule, no attempt will be made to give exact years. We will depict these far-distant events as occurring in even periods of thousands, millions, and billions of years.

57:1. The Andronover Nebula

Urantia is of origin in your sun, and your sun is one of the multifarious offspring of the Andronover nebula. 875,000,000,000 years ago the enormous Andronover nebula number 876,926 was duly initiated. Only the presence of the force organizer and the liaison staff was required to inaugurate the energy whirl which eventually grew into this vast cyclone of space. In reality the story has its proper beginning at the point when the Paradise force organizers made the space-energy conditions ready for the action of the power directors and physical controllers of the superuniverse of Orvonton.

57:2. The Primary Nebular Stage

800,000,000,000 years ago the Andronover creation was well established as one of the magnificent primary nebulae of Orvonton. 600,000,000,000 years ago the height of the Andronover energy-mobilization period was attained. Gravity and other influences were about to begin their work of converting space gases into organized matter.

57:3. The Secondary Nebular Stage

500,000,000,000 years ago the first Andronover sun was born. It was scarcely a million years subsequent to this epoch that Michael of Nebadon, a Creator Son of Paradise, selected this disintegrating nebula as the site of his adventure in universe building. Almost immediately the architectural worlds of Salvington and the one hundred constellation headquarters groups of planets were begun. It required almost one million years to complete these clusters of specially created worlds. The local system headquarters planets were constructed over a period extending from that time to about five billion years ago.

300,000,000,000 years ago the staff of Michael arrived on Salvington, and the Uversa government of Orvonton extended physical recognition to the local universe of Nebadon. 200,000,000,000 years ago some planets revolving around the newborn suns had cooled sufficiently to be suitable for life implantation. The oldest inhabited planets of Nebadon date from these times. 100,000,000,000 years ago the spectacular period of sun dispersion began.

57:4. Tertiary and Quartan Stages

75,000,000,000 years ago the Andronover nebula had attained the height of its sun-family stage. 50,000,000,000 years ago the first period of sun dispersion was completed, during which it gave origin to 876,926 sun systems. 8,000,000,000 years ago the terrific terminal eruption began. And this was the beginning of the end of the nebula. This final sun disgorgement extended over a period of almost two billion years. 6,000,000,000 years ago marks the end of the terminal breakup and the birth of your sun. This final eruption of the nebular nucleus gave birth to 136,702 suns. The total number of suns and sun systems having origin in the Andronover nebula was 1,013,628. The number of the solar system sun is 1,013,572.

57:5. Origin of Monmatia—The Urantia Solar System

5,000,000,000 years ago your sun was a comparatively isolated blazing orb, having gathered to itself most of the near-by circulating matter of space. Today, your sun has achieved relative stability, but its eleven and one-half year sunspot cycles betray that it was a variable star in its youth. 4,500,000,000 years ago the enormous Angona system began its approach to the neighborhood of this solitary sun. As the Angona system drew nearer, the solar extrusions grew larger and larger. The solar gases which were separated from the sun subsequently evolved into the twelve planets of the solar system. Jupiter and Saturn contained so much highly heated sun material that they shone with a brilliant light and have remained largely gaseous to this day.

57:6. The Solar System Stage—The Planet-Forming Era

The planets nearest the sun were the first to have their revolutions slowed down by tidal friction. When the tidal frictions of the moon and the earth become equalized, the earth will always turn the same hemisphere toward the moon. In the far-distant future when the moon approaches to within about eleven thousand miles of the earth, the gravity action of the latter will cause the moon to shatter into small particles, which may assemble about the world as rings of matter resembling those of Saturn or may be gradually drawn into the earth as meteors. 3,000,000,000 years ago the solar system was functioning much as it does today. About this time your solar system was placed on the physical registry of Nebadon and given its name, Monmatia.

57:7. The Meteoric Era—The Volcanic Age—The Primitive Planetary Atmosphere

Throughout these early times in the absence of a protective combustion atmosphere meteors crashed directly on the surface of Urantia. 2,000,000,000 years ago Urantia was then about one fifth its present size and had become large enough to hold the primitive atmosphere which had begun to appear as a result of the internal elemental contest between the heated interior and the cooling crust. Definite volcanic action dates from these times. The study of radioactive elements will reveal that Urantia is more than one billion years old on its surface. A crust, consisting chiefly of the comparatively lighter granite, is gradually forming. The stage is being set for a planet which can someday support life. Presently, the atmosphere became more settled and cooled sufficiently to start precipitation of rain on the hot rocky surface of the planet. For thousands of years Urantia was enveloped in one vast and continuous blanket of steam. There was virtually no free oxygen in the atmosphere until it was later generated by the seaweeds and other forms of vegetable life.

57:8. Crustal Stabilization—The Age of Earthquakes—The World Ocean and the First Continent

1,000,000,000 years ago is the date of the actual beginning of Urantia history. The planet had attained approximately its present size, and about this time it was placed upon the physical registries of Nebadon and given its name, Urantia. The real geologic history of Urantia begins with the cooling of the earth's crust sufficiently to cause the formation of the first ocean. By the end of this period the ocean was world-wide, covering the entire planet to an average depth of over one mile. 950,000,000 years ago Urantia presents the picture of one great continent of land and one large body of water, the Pacific Ocean. It was then that Urantia was assigned to the system of Satania for planetary administration and was placed on the life registry of Norlatiadek. 900,000,000 years ago witnessed the arrival on Urantia of the first Satania scouting party to examine the planet and make a report on its adaptation for a life-experiment station. 750,000,000 years ago the first breaks in the continental land mass began. Urantia was approaching the ripening of conditions suitable for the support of life. 650,000,000 years ago witnessed a further extension of the continental seas. And these waters were rapidly attaining that degree of saltiness which was essential to Urantia life. These inland seas of olden times were truly the cradle of evolution.

Paper 58: Life Establishment on Urantia
Life Carrier

IN all Satania there are only sixty-one worlds similar to Urantia, life modification planets. On such planets the Life Carriers are permitted to undertake certain life experiments in an effort to modify or possibly improve the standard universe types of living beings.

58:1. Physical-Life Prerequisites

600,000,000 years ago the commission of Life Carriers sent out from Jerusem arrived on Urantia and began the study of physical conditions preparatory to launching life on world number 606 of the Satania system. The Satania Life Carriers had projected a sodium chloride pattern of life; therefore no steps could be taken toward planting it until the ocean waters had become sufficiently briny. The Urantia type of protoplasm can function only in a suitable salt solution. Today this same salty solution freely circulates about in your bodies, bathing each individual cell. On a planet where life has a marine origin the ideal conditions for life implantation are provided by a large number of inland seas. And it was from such seashores of the mild and equable climes of a later age that primitive plant life found its way onto the land. The atmosphere was then ideal for plant growth; it contained such a high degree of carbon dioxide that no animal could have lived on the face of the earth.

58:2. The Urantia Atmosphere

If the light falling upon North America were paid for at the rate of two cents per kilowatt-hour, the annual light bill would be upward of 800 quadrillion dollars. Vast solar energies pour in upon Urantia embracing wave lengths ranging both above and below the recognition range of human vision. Your sun pours forth a veritable flood of death-dealing rays, and your pleasant life on Urantia is due to the "fortuitous" influence of more than two-score apparently accidental protective operations similar to the action of this unique ozone layer. Were it not for the "blanketing" effect of the atmosphere at night, heat would be lost by radiation so rapidly that life would be impossible of maintenance except by artificial provision.

58:3. Spatial Environment

Much of the organized matter which the blazing suns break down and disperse as radiant energy was originally built up in the early appearing hydrogen clouds of space. All of the phenomena of atom building and atom dissolution are attended by the emergence of flood tides of short space rays of radiant energy. Accompanying these diverse radiations is a form of space-energy unknown on Urantia. The vast hydrogen clouds are veritable cosmic chemical laboratories, harboring all phases of evolving energy and metamorphosing matter. All of these essential cosmic conditions had to evolve to a favorable status before the Life Carriers could actually begin the establishment of life on Urantia.

58:4. The Life-Dawn Era

Urantia life is unique, original with the planet. 550,000,000 years ago the Life Carriers, in co-operation with spiritual powers and superphysical forces, organized and initiated the original life patterns of this world and made three original, identical, and simultaneous marine-life implantations: the central or Eurasian-African, the eastern or Australasian, and the western, embracing Greenland and the Americas. Our purpose was to insure that each great land mass would carry this life with it. We foresaw that in the later era of the emergence of land life large oceans of water would separate these drifting continental land masses.

58:5. The Continental Drift

The outer one thousand miles of the earth's mass consists principally of different kinds of rock. Underneath are the denser and heavier metallic elements. This outer shell was supported by a molten sea of basalt. Even today the continents continue to float upon this noncrystallized cushiony sea of molten basalt. The lava layers of the earth's crust, when cooled, form granite. The sea bottoms are more dense than the land masses, and this is what keeps the continents above water. But all continents tend to creep into the oceans.

58:6. The Transition Period

450,000,000 years ago the transition from vegetable to animal life occurred. This development, all of which was inherent in the original life patterns, came about gradually. There were many transitional stages between the early primitive vegetable forms of life and the later well-defined animal organisms.

From era to era radically new species of animal life arise. They do not evolve as the result of the gradual accumulation of small variations; they appear as full-fledged and new orders of life, and they appear *suddenly*. The sudden appearance of new species and diversified orders of living organisms is wholly biologic, strictly natural. There is nothing supernatural connected with these genetic mutations. But the subsequent endowment of mind is a bestowal of the adjutant mind-spirits in accordance with innate brain capacity.

58:7. The Geologic History Book

The vast group of rock systems which constituted the outer crust of the world during the life-dawn or Proterozoic era does not now appear at many points on the earth's surface. In North America this ancient and primitive fossil-bearing stone layer comes to the surface over the eastern, central, and northern regions of Canada. The lava flows of this age brought much iron, copper, and lead up near the planetary surface. There are few places on the earth where such activities are more graphically shown than in the St. Croix valley of Wisconsin. This era witnesses the spread of life throughout the waters of the world; marine life has become well established on Urantia. All of this story is graphically told within the fossil pages of the vast "stone book" of world record. And the pages of this gigantic biogeologic record unfailingly tell the truth if you but acquire skill in their interpretation.

Paper 59: The Marine-Life Era on Urantia
Life Carrier

WE reckon the history of Urantia as beginning about one billion years ago and extending through five major eras: 1. *The prelife era* extends over the initial four hundred and fifty million years—Archeozoic. 2. *The life-dawn era* extends over the next one hundred and fifty million years—Proterozoic. 3. *The marine-life era* covers the next two hundred and fifty million years—Paleozoic. 4. *The early land-life era* extends over the next one hundred million years—Mesozoic. 5. *The mammalian era* occupies the last fifty million years—Cenozoic. The marine-life era thus covers about one quarter of your planetary history. The continent of North America is wonderfully rich in the fossil-bearing deposits of the entire marine-life era.

59:1. Early Marine Life in the Shallow Seas: The Trilobite Age

400,000,000 years ago marine life, both vegetable and animal, is fairly well distributed over the whole world. Vegetation now for the first time crawls out upon the land and soon makes considerable progress in adaptation to a nonmarine habitat. Suddenly and without gradation ancestry the first multicellular animals make their appearance. The trilobites have evolved, and for ages they dominate the seas. Periodically land masses throughout various parts of the world would sink into the ocean and rise again. Because of the pressure of land masses in many places, sandstone has been turned into quartz, shale has been changed to slate, while limestone has been converted into marble. The marine life was much alike the world over and consisted of the seaweeds, one-celled organisms, simple sponges, trilobites, and other crustaceans—shrimps, crabs, and lobsters. This was the biogeologic picture of Urantia, embracing fifty million years, designated by your geologists as the Cambrian.

59:2. The First Continental Flood Stage: The Invertebrate-Animal Age

The periodic phenomena of land elevation and land sinking characteristic of these times were all gradual. 350,000,000 years ago saw the beginning of the great flood period of all the continents except central Asia. 330,000,000 years ago marked the eruption of the great North American volcano of eastern Kentucky, one of the greatest single volcanic activities the world has ever known. 310,000,000 years ago was the great age of individual animal organismal evolution. The bivalve gastropods have come on down through the intervening millions of years and embrace the mussels, clams, oysters, and scallops. So ends the evolutionary story of the second great period of marine life, which is known to your geologists as the Ordovician.

59:3. The Second Great Flood Stage: The Coral Period—The Brachiopod Age

300,000,000 years ago another great period of land submergence began. 290,000,000 years ago the sea had largely withdrawn from the continents. It is in the deposits of this age that much of the gas, oil, zinc, and lead are found. The center of the stage was occupied by the larger mollusks, or cephalopods. This species of animal appeared suddenly and assumed dominance of sea life. 280,000,000 years ago the continents had largely emerged from the second Silurian inundation. The rock deposits of this submergence are known in North America as Niagara limestone because this is the stratum of rock over which Niagara Falls now flows. During this age the true scorpions—actual air breathers—*suddenly* made their appearance. These developments terminate the third marine-life period, covering twenty-five million years and known to your researchers as the Silurian.

59:4. The Great Land-Emergence Stage: The Vegetative Land-Life Period, The Age of Fishes

In the agelong struggle between land and water, for long periods the sea has been comparatively victorious, but times of land victory are just ahead. It is the dawn of a new age on earth. The naked and unattractive landscape of former times became clothed with luxuriant verdure, and the first magnificent forests appeared. 250,000,000 years ago witnessed the appearance of the fish family, the vertebrates, one of the most important steps in all prehuman evolution. The present-day sharks are the survivors of these ancient fishes. Now, and suddenly, the prolific fern family appeared and quickly spread over the face of the rapidly rising land in all parts of the world. And thus drew to a close one of the longest periods of marine-life evolution, almost fifty million years—the Devonian.

59:5. The Crustal-Shifting Stage: The Fern-Forest Carboniferous Period—The Age of Frogs

This period opens with the stage almost ideally set for the appearance of the first land animals. 220,000,000 years ago many of the continental land areas, including most of North America, were above water. The land was overrun by luxurious vegetation; this was indeed the age of ferns. Abruptly, the first of the land animals appeared. From the briny waters of the seas there crawled out upon the land snails, scorpions, and frogs. This period could well be known as the age of frogs. Very soon thereafter the insects first appeared. The large shell-feeding sharks were also highly evolved, and for more than five million years they dominated the oceans. The finer building limestones were laid down during this epoch. 200,000,000 years ago the really active stages of the Carboniferous period began. The length of the actual coal-deposition epoch was a little over twenty-five million years. 180,000,000 years ago brought the close of the Carboniferous period, during which coal had been formed all over the world. In general, these were the epochs of development for fresh-water organisms. The life features of the coal age were ferns and frogs.

59:6. The Climatic Transition Stage: The Seed-Plant Period—The Age of Biologic Tribulation

This was a time of biologic tribulation. Toward the close of the long marine-life era there were more than one hundred thousand species of living things on earth. At the close of this period of transition less than five hundred had survived. 170,000,000 years ago great evolutionary changes and adjustments were taking place over the entire face of the earth. Two new climatic factors appeared—glaciation and aridity. The seed plants first appeared, and they afforded a better food supply for the subsequently increased land-animal life. The insects underwent a radical change. The first step in the evolution of the frog into the reptile occurred. 160,000,000 years ago the land was largely covered with vegetation adapted to support land-animal life, and the atmosphere had become ideal for animal respiration. The vast oceanic nursery of life on Urantia has served its purpose. Now the biologic importance of the sea progressively diminishes as the second stage of evolution begins to unfold on the land.

Paper 60:
Urantia During the Early Land-Life Era
Life Carrier

THE era of exclusive marine life has ended. Land elevation, cooling crust and cooling oceans all conspired greatly to change the world's climate in all regions far removed from the equatorial zone.

60:1. The Early Reptilian Age

150,000,000 years ago the early land-life periods of the world's history began. 140,000,000 years ago, *suddenly* the reptiles appeared in full-fledged form. They developed rapidly, soon yielding crocodiles, scaled reptiles, and eventually both sea serpents and flying reptiles. These rapidly evolving reptilian dinosaurs soon became the monarchs of this age. They were egg layers and are distinguished from all animals by their small brains. Several million years later the first mammals appeared. They were nonplacental and proved a speedy failure; none survived. This was an experimental effort to improve mammalian types. The life changes of this period were indeed revolutionary notwithstanding that they were transitional and gradual. This period extended over twenty-five million years and is known as the Triassic.

60:2. The Later Reptilian Age

120,000,000 years ago a new phase of the reptilian age began. The great event of this period was the evolution and decline of the dinosaurs. The largest of the dinosaurs originated in western North America. These massive creatures became less active and strong as they grew larger and larger; but they required such an enormous amount of food and the land was so overrun by them that they literally starved to death and became extinct. 110,000,000 years ago marked changes occurred in the fish family, a sturgeon type first appearing, but the ferocious sea serpents still infested all the seas. This continued to be, pre-eminently, the age of the dinosaurs. Two species of dinosaurs migrated to the water in a futile attempt at self-preservation, two other types were driven to the air by the bitter competition of life on land. These latter represent the nonsurviving strains of bird ancestry. One hundred million years ago the reptilian age was drawing to a close. The dinosaurs, for all their enormous mass, were all but brainless animals. Henceforth, planetary evolutionary progress will follow the increase in brain size. This period extended nearly twenty-five million years and is known as the Jurassic.

60:3. The Cretaceous Stage: The Flowering-Plant Period— The Age of Birds

This period brings Urantia to near the end of the long reptilian dominance and witnesses the appearance of flowering plants and bird life on land. As the continental land drift continued, it met with the first great obstruction on the deep floor of the Pacific, giving impetus to the formation of the whole vast north and south mountain range extending from Alaska down through Mexico to Cape Horn. 90,000,000 years ago seed-bearing plants emerged from these early Cretaceous seas and soon overran the continents. These land plants *suddenly* appeared along with fig trees, magnolias, and tulip trees. 85,000,000 years ago Bering Strait closed, shutting off the cooling waters of the northern seas. 75,000,000 years ago marks the end of the continental drift. 65,000,000 years ago great plant-life evolution was taking place. Many present-day trees first appeared, including beech, birch, oak, walnut, sycamore, maple, and modern palms. 55,000,000 years ago the evolutionary march was marked by the sudden appearance of the first of the true birds, a small pigeonlike creature which was the ancestor of all bird life. And so this becomes known as the age of birds as well as the declining age of reptiles.

60:4. The End of the Chalk Period

The great Cretaceous period was drawing to a close, and its termination marks the end of the great sea invasions of the continents. These alternate periods of land and sea dominance have occurred in million-year cycles. And these same rhythmical crustal movements will continue from this time on throughout the earth's history but with diminishing frequency and extent. Biologically as well as geologically this was an eventful and active age on land and under water. On land the fern forests were largely replaced by pine and other modern trees, including the gigantic redwoods. By the end of this period the biologic stage is fully set for the appearance of the early ancestors of the future mammalian types. And thus ends a long era of world evolution, the Cretaceous age, which covers fifty million years and is known as the Mesozoic.

Paper 61: The Mammalian Era on Urantia
Life Carrier

THE era of mammals extends from the times of the origin of placental mammals to the end of the ice age, covering a little less than fifty million years. During this Cenozoic age the world's landscape presented an attractive appearance—rolling hills, broad valleys, wide rivers, and great forests. The animal types were both many and varied. The trees swarmed with birds, and the whole world was an animal paradise.

61:1. The New Continental Land Stage: The Age of Early Mammals

Early in this period and in North America the placental type of mammals *suddenly* appeared. The father of the placental mammals was a small, highly active, carnivorous, springing type of dinosaur. Mammals possess an immense survival advantage over all other forms of animal life in that they can bring forth relatively mature and well-developed offspring and use superior intelligence in environmental adjustment and adaptation. 45,000,000 years ago mammalian life was evolving rapidly. Soon there were small horses, fleet-footed rhinoceroses, tapirs with proboscises, primitive pigs, squirrels, lemurs, opossums, and several tribes of monkeylike animals. A large ostrich-like land bird developed to a height of ten feet. These were the ancestors of the later gigantic passenger birds that were so highly intelligent, and that onetime transported human beings through the air. North America was then connected by land with every continent except Australia.

61:2. The Recent Flood Stage: The Age of Advanced Mammals

This period was characterized by the further and rapid evolution of placental mammals. 35,000,000 years ago marks the beginning of the age of placental-mammalian world domination. Brains and agility had replaced armor and size in the progress of animal survival. Various groups of mammals had their origin in a unique animal now extinct. This carnivorous creature was something of a cross between a cat and a seal; it could live on land or in water and was highly intelligent and very active. In Europe the ancestor of the canine family evolved, soon giving rise to many species of small dogs. The horse lived during these times in both North America and Europe. Camels and llamas had their origin in North America but soon both were extinct in North America. A whole tribe of placental mammals deserted the land and took up their residence in the oceans. And they have ever since remained in the sea, yielding the modern whales, dolphins, porpoises, seals, and sea lions. By the close of this Oligocene period, covering ten million years, the plant and animal life was present on earth much as today.

61:3. The Modern Mountain Stage: Age of the Elephant and the Horse

20,000,000 years ago was indeed the golden age of mammals. The Bering Strait land bridge was up, and many groups of animals migrated to North America from Asia. The first deer appeared, and North America was soon overrun by deer, oxen, camels, and bison. The huge elephants of this and subsequent periods possessed large brains as well as large bodies, and they soon overran the entire world except Australia. In intelligence and adaptation the elephant is approached only by the horse and is surpassed only by man himself. Enormous herds of horses joined the camels on the western plains of North America. The horse has long served mankind and has played an important part in the development of human civilization. In central Asia the true types of both the primitive monkey and the gorilla evolved. The dog family was represented by wolves and foxes; the cat tribe by panthers and large saber-toothed tigers, the latter first evolving in North America. This age of the elephant and the horse is known as the Miocene.

61:4. The Recent Continental-elevation Stage: The Last Great Mammalian Migration

This is the period of preglacial land elevation in North America, Europe, and Asia. 10,000,000 years ago for a short time all the land of the world was again joined excepting Australia, and the last great world-wide animal migration took place. The cat family dominated the animal life. Before the continents were finally isolated the mastodons migrated everywhere except to Australia. 5,000,000 years ago the horse evolved as it now is and from North America migrated to all the world. But the horse had become extinct on the continent of its origin long before the red man arrived. This is the time usually designated as the Pliocene.

61:5. The Early Ice Age

By the close of the preceding period the lands of the northeastern part of North America and of northern Europe were rising up to 30,000 feet and more. Simultaneously with these land elevations the ocean currents shifted, and the seasonal winds changed their direction. Snow began to fall on these elevated regions to a depth of 20,000 feet, which soon metamorphosed into solid but creeping ice. 2,000,000 years ago the first North American glacier started its southern advance. The central ice sheet extended south as far as Kansas. During these early epochs of the ice age North America was overrun with mastodons, woolly mammoths, horses, camels, deer, musk oxen, bison, giant beavers, saber-toothed tigers, and many groups of the cat and dog families. Toward the close of the ice age the majority of these animal species were extinct in North America.

61:6. Primitive Man in the Ice Age

The great event of this glacial period was the evolution of primitive man. Slightly to the west of India, on land now under water and among the offspring of North American lemur types, the dawn mammals *suddenly* appeared. They possessed large brains in proportion to their size. In the seventieth generation a new and higher group of animals suddenly differentiated. These new mid-mammals—almost twice the size and height of their ancestors and possessing proportionately increased brain power—had only well established themselves when the Primates, the third vital mutation, suddenly appeared. (At this same time a retrograde development within the mid-mammal stock gave origin to some of the simian ancestry.) 1,000,000 years ago Urantia was registered as an inhabited world when a mutation within the stock of the progressing Primates *suddenly* produced two primitive human beings, the actual ancestors of mankind. This event occurred in a stimulating, invigorating, and difficult environment. The sole survivors of these Urantia aborigines, the Eskimos, even now prefer to dwell in frigid northern climes.

61:7. The Continuing Ice Age

A glacier, as it advances, displaces rivers and changes the whole face of the earth. 750,000 years ago the fourth ice sheet at its height reached to southern Illinois, displacing the Mississippi River fifty miles to the west. In the east it extended as far south as the Ohio River and central Pennsylvania. 500,000 years ago *suddenly* and in one generation the six colored races mutated from the aboriginal human stock. This is a doubly important date since it also marks the arrival of the Planetary Prince. 250,000 years ago the sixth and last glaciation began. This was the largest of all ice invasions coming down into Kansas, Missouri, and Illinois. At this time the horse, tapir, llama, and saber-toothed tiger became extinct in North America. During its retreat the North American system of Great Lakes was produced. Those animals which followed the glaciers back and forth over the land were the bear, bison, reindeer, musk ox, mammoth, and mastodon. The mastodon persisted in North America until exterminated by the red man. 35,000 years ago marks the termination of the great ice age excepting in the polar regions of the planet.

Paper 62: The Dawn Races of Early Man
Life Carrier

ABOUT one million years ago the immediate ancestors of mankind made their appearance by three successive and sudden mutations stemming from early stock of the lemur type of placental mammal.

62:1. The Early Lemur Types

In the lands to the west of India in this then almost paradisiacal area, and from the superior descendants of a lemur type of mammal there sprang two great groups, the simian tribes of modern times and the present-day human species.

62:2. The Dawn Mammals

A little more than one million years ago the Mesopotamian dawn mammals *suddenly* appeared. They were active little creatures, almost three feet tall. They were flesh eaters and had a primitive opposable thumb as well as a highly useful grasping big toe. The members of this new species had large brains for their size. They experienced many of the emotions and shared numerous instincts which later characterized primitive man. The beginning of the fear tendencies of mankind dates from these days. These aggressive little animals multiplied and spread over the Mesopotamian peninsula for more than one thousand years, constantly improving in physical type and general intelligence.

62:3. The Mid-Mammals

Early in the career of the dawn mammals, in the treetop abode of a superior pair of these agile creatures, twins were born, one male and one female. These children grew to be a little over four feet in height. They had almost perfectly opposable thumbs and walked upright. Their brains were superior and much larger than those of their ancestors. This brother and sister mated and soon enjoyed the society of twenty-one children. This new group formed the nucleus of the mid-mammals. When the numbers of this new and superior group grew great war broke out and when the terrible struggle was over, not a single individual of this race of dawn mammals remained alive. And now for almost fifteen thousand years this creature became the terror of this part of the world. Their potential life span was about twenty-five years. A number of rudimentary human traits appeared in this new species. These mid-mammals were the first to exhibit a definite construction propensity. As time passed serious food competition and sex rivalry culminated in a series of internecine battles that nearly destroyed the entire species. After lightning struck the tree in which the prospective mother of the Primates twins was sleeping, they moved away and began the construction of new treetop abodes and new ground shelters.

Soon after the completion of their home, this couple found themselves the proud parents of twins, the first of the new species of Primates constituting the next vital step in prehuman evolution. Contemporaneously with the birth of these Primates twins, a couple that were both mentally and physically inferior gave birth to twins. These retarded twins became the founders of the modern simian tribes.

62:4. The Primates

These Primates twins stood erect and attained a height of over five feet. They learned to communicate with each other by means of signs and sounds. When about fourteen years of age they fled from the tribe and raised their family, establishing the new species of Primates. The Primates were more human and less animal than their mid-mammal predecessors. They had a natural life span of about forty years. After about twenty-one thousand years from the origin of the dawn mammals, the Primates suddenly gave birth to two remarkable creatures, the first true human beings. In less than five thousand years not a single individual of these extraordinary Primate tribes was left.

62:5. The First Human Beings

From the year A.D. 1934 back to the birth of the first two human beings is just 993,419 years. These first human beings reached full maturity at twelve years of age and possessed a potential life span of about seventy-five years. They nearly lost their lives on numerous occasions before they were eight years old. Very early they learned to engage in verbal communication. When about nine years of age, they held a momentous conference and arrived at an understanding to live with and for each other. This finally culminated in the decision to flee from their inferior animal associates and to journey northward, little knowing that they were thus to found the human race.

The most remarkable advance in emotional development was the sudden appearance of a new group of really human feelings, the worshipful group, embracing awe, reverence, humility, and even a primitive form of gratitude.

62:6. Evolution of the Human Mind

We, the Life Carriers on Urantia, were overjoyed with the advent of the first really intelligent and volitional beings. We had been watching the twins develop mentally through our observation of the functioning of the seven adjutant mind-spirits. Imagine our joy one day—the twins were about ten years old—when the spirit of worship made its first contact with the mind of the female twin and shortly thereafter with the male. About a year later, when they finally decided to flee from home and journey north, then did the spirit of wisdom begin to function on the planet and in these two now-recognized human minds.

62:7. Recognition as an Inhabited World

At noon, the day after the runaway of the twins, there occurred the initial test flash of the universe circuit signals. On the third day after the elopement of the twins there arrived the Nebadon archangel of initial planetary circuit establishment. It was an eventful day when our small group gathered about the planetary pole of space communication and received the first message from Salvington: "To the Life Carriers on Urantia—greetings! We transmit assurance of great pleasure on Salvington, Edentia, and Jerusem in honor of the registration of the signal of the existence on Urantia of mind of will dignity...." These messages from Salvington, Edentia, and Jerusem formally marked the termination of the Life Carriers' agelong supervision of the planet. Urantia being a life-modification world, permission was granted to leave behind two senior Life Carriers with twelve assistants. It is just 993,408 years ago (from the year A.D. 1934) that Urantia was formally recognized as a planet of human habitation in the universe of Nebadon.

Paper 63: The First Human Family
Life Carrier

ARCHANGEL message: "Man-mind has appeared on 606 of Satania, and these parents of the new race shall be called Andon and Fonta." (First Fatherlike and Sonlike creatures to exhibit perfection hunger.) Andon and Fonta never knew these names until they were bestowed on them at the time of fusion with their Thought Adjusters.

63:1. Andon and Fonta

In many respects, Andon and Fonta were the most remarkable pair of human beings that have ever lived on the earth. Their vague feeling of being something more than mere animals was due to the possession of personality and was augmented by the indwelling presence of their Thought Adjusters.

63:2. The Flight of the Twins

One night after they had been awakened by a violent storm, they finally and fully made up their minds to flee from the tribal habitat and the home treetops. They had already prepared a crude treetop retreat some half-day's journey to the north. While it required unusual courage for them to undertake this night journey, they safely made their previously prepared rendezvous shortly after midnight. As they journeyed northward, the nights grew cooler and cooler. Andon signified to his mate that he thought he could make fire with the flint. It occurred to Fonta to climb a near-by tree to secure an abandoned bird's nest. The nest was dry and highly inflammable and consequently flared right up into a full blaze the moment the spark fell upon it. All night long they sat up watching their fire burn, vaguely realizing that they had made a discovery which would make it possible for them to defy climate.

63:3. Andon's Family

It was almost two years from the night of the twins' departure from home before their first child, Sontad, was born. Andon and Fonta had nineteen children in all, and they lived to enjoy the association of almost half a hundred grandchildren and half a dozen great-grandchildren. The family was domiciled in four adjoining rock shelters, or semicaves. These early Andonites evinced a very marked clannish spirit; they hunted in groups and never strayed very far from the homesite. Andon and Fonta labored incessantly for the nurture and uplift of the clan. They lived to the age of forty-two, when both were killed at the time of an earthquake by the falling of an overhanging rock. This family of Andon and Fonta held together until the twentieth generation, when combined food competition and social friction brought about the beginning of dispersion.

63:4. The Andonic Clans

Primitive man had black eyes and a swarthy complexion. They smiled occasionally, but never indulged in hearty laughter. These early human beings were not very sensitive to pain. Childbirth was not a painful or distressing ordeal to Fonta and her immediate progeny. They were very loyal to their families; they would die without question in defense of their children. Before the extensive dispersion of the Andonic clans a well-developed language had evolved from their early efforts to intercommunicate. Only two things came to occupy the minds of these peoples: hunting to obtain food and fighting to avenge themselves against some real or supposed injustice. Family feuds increased, tribal wars broke out, and serious losses were sustained among the very best elements of the more able and advanced groups. It is impossible to induce such primitive beings long to live together in peace. The Life Carriers know this and accordingly make provision for the separation of developing human beings into at least three, and more often six, distinct and separate races.

63:5. Dispersion of the Andonites

These Andonic tribes were the early river dwellers of France; they lived along the river Somme for tens of thousands of years. They very early became remarkably clever in disguising their partially sheltered abodes and showed great skill in constructing stone sleeping chambers. The Andonites were fearless and successful hunters and, with the exception of wild berries and certain fruits of the trees, lived exclusively on flesh. These early humans became highly skillful in the fashioning of flint tools. They traveled far and wide in search of flint. These Andon tribes manifested a degree of intelligence which their retrogressing descendants did not attain in half a million years.

63:6. Onagar—The First Truth Teacher

As the Andonic dispersion extended, the cultural and spiritual status of the clans retrogressed for nearly ten thousand years until the days of Onagar. He assumed the leadership of the tribes near the Caspian Sea, brought peace among them, and led them in the worship of the "Breath Giver to men and animals." Very early the Andonic peoples formed the habit of refraining from eating the flesh of the animal of tribal veneration. Still later this developed into the more elaborate sacrificial ceremonies of their descendants. The prayer taught by Onagar was: "O Breath of Life, give us this day our daily food, deliver us from the curse of the ice, save us from our forest enemies, and with mercy receive us into the Great Beyond." The emissaries of Onagar were the world's first missionaries; they were also the first human beings to cook meat. Onagar was born 983,323 years ago (from A.D. 1934), and he lived to be sixty-nine years of age. Never again, until the arrival of the Planetary Prince, was there such a high spiritual civilization on earth. This was, indeed, the golden age of primitive man.

63:7. The Survival of Andon and Fonta

Andon and Fonta in due time emerged from the regime of the mansion worlds with citizenship status on Jerusem. Although they have never been permitted to return to Urantia, they are cognizant of the history of the race they founded. On Jerusem both Andon and Fonta were fused with their Thought Adjusters, Shortly after their arrival on Jerusem, they received permission from the System Sovereign to return to the first mansion world to welcome the pilgrims of time from Urantia to the heavenly spheres. They sought to send greetings to Urantia in connection with these revelations, but this request was wisely denied them.

Paper 64: The Evolutionary Races of Color
Life Carrier

THIS is the story of the evolutionary races of Urantia from the days of Andon and Fonta, almost one million years ago, down through the times of the Planetary Prince to the end of the ice age.

64:1. The Andonic Aborigines

Many of man's earliest religious emotions grew out of his feeling of helplessness in the shut-in environment of this geographic situation—mountains to the right, water to the left, and ice in front. In the forests man has always deteriorated; human evolution has made progress only in the open and in the higher latitudes. The cold and hunger of the open lands stimulate action, invention, and resourcefulness. 950,000 years ago the descendants of Andon and Fonta had migrated far to the east and to the west. The groups going west became less contaminated with the backward stocks of mutual ancestral origin than those going east, who mingled so freely with their retarded animal cousins. And thus it has ever been on Urantia. Civilizations of great promise have successively deteriorated and have finally been extinguished by the folly of allowing the superior freely to procreate with the inferior.

64:2. The Foxhall Peoples

900,000 years ago the arts of Andon and Fonta and the culture of Onagar were vanishing from the face of the earth. Later a somewhat superior and prolific people arrived in Europe, the Heidelberg race. The Foxhall peoples of England and the Badonan tribes northwest of India continued to hold on to some of the traditions of Andon and certain remnants of the culture of Onagar. Many of the more intelligent and spiritual of the Foxhall peoples maintained their racial superiority and perpetuated their primitive religious customs. And these people, as they were later admixed with subsequent stocks, journeyed on west from England after a later ice visitation and have survived as the present-day Eskimos.

64:3. The Badonan Tribes

The Badonan tribes in the foothills of the northwestern Indian were the only descendants of Andon who never practiced human sacrifice. 850,000 years ago the superior Badonan tribes began a warfare of extermination directed against their inferior and animalistic neighbors. This campaign for the extermination of inferiors brought about a slight improvement in the hill tribes of that age. And the mixed descendants of this improved Badonite stock appeared on the stage of action as an apparently new people—the Neanderthal race.

64:4. The Neanderthal Races

The Neanderthalers were excellent fighters, and they traveled extensively. They dominated the world for almost half a million years until the times of the migration of the evolutionary races of color. The Neanderthalers were great hunters, and the tribes in France were the first to adopt the practice of giving the most successful hunters the choice of women for wives. For almost a quarter of a million years these primitive peoples drifted on hunting and fighting and, on the whole, steadily retrogressing as compared with their superior Andonic ancestors. During these spiritually dark ages the culture of superstitious mankind reached its lowest levels. Attempts to placate the invisible forces behind the natural elements culminated in the sacrificing of humans. And this terrible practice of human sacrifice has been perpetuated by the more backward peoples of Urantia right on down to the twentieth century.

64:5. Origin of the Colored Races

500,000 years ago the Badonan tribes of the northwestern highlands of India became involved in another great racial struggle; the survivors were the most intelligent and desirable of all the then living descendants of Andon and Fonta. A man and woman of these Badonan tribes began *suddenly* to produce a family of unusually intelligent children. This was the Sangik family, the ancestors of all of the six colored races of Urantia. Among these nineteen Sangik children there were five red, two orange, four yellow, two green, four blue, and two indigo.

64:6. The Six Sangik Races of Urantia

The simultaneous emergence of all six races on Urantia, and in one family, was most unusual.

1. *The red men* were remarkable people. They were a most intelligent group and were always monogamous. About eighty-five thousand years ago the comparatively pure remnants of the red race went en masse across the Bering isthmus to North America. The red men seemed doomed when, about sixty-five thousand years ago, Onamonalonton appeared as their leader and spiritual deliverer. He brought temporary peace and revived their worship of the "Great Spirit." Onamonalonton lived to be ninety-six years of age and maintained his headquarters among the great redwood trees of California. Increasingly the more intelligent strains perished in tribal struggles; otherwise a great civilization would have been built in North America.

2. *The orange man.* The outstanding characteristic of this race was their peculiar urge to build. This people lost much cultural and spiritual ground, but there was a great revival of higher living as a result of the wise leadership of Porshunta. The last great struggle between the orange and the green men occurred in the region of the lower Nile valley in Egypt. At its close very few of the orange race were left alive. The shattered remnants of these people were absorbed by the green and by the later arriving indigo men. But as a race the orange man ceased to exist about one hundred thousand years ago.

3. *The yellow man.* The primitive yellow tribes were the first to establish settled communities and to develop a home life based on agriculture. They proved themselves superior to all of the Sangik peoples in the matter of fostering racial civilization. They drifted into great darkness following the Caligastia apostasy; but there occurred one brilliant age among this people when Singlangton, about one hundred thousand years ago, assumed the leadership of these tribes and proclaimed the worship of the "One Truth." The yellow race has been numbered among the more peaceful of the nations of Urantia. This race received a small but potent legacy of the later imported Adamic stock.

4. *The green man.* The green race was one of the less able groups of primitive men. These tribes experienced a great revival of culture under the leadership of Fantad. The green race was subdued, enslaved, and absorbed by the yellow and blue races. They were also amalgamated with the Indian peoples of those days. The green men carried strains of the giant order, many of their leaders being eight and nine feet in height. The remnants of the green men were subsequently absorbed by the indigo race.

5. *The blue man.* The blue men were a great people. They early invented the spear and subsequently worked out the rudiments of many of the arts of modern civilization. The blue man had the brain power of the red man associated with the soul and sentiment of the yellow man. Orlandof became a great teacher among the blue race and led many of the tribes back to the worship of the true God under the name of the "Supreme Chief." The so-called white races of Urantia are the descendants of these blue men as they were first modified by slight mixture with yellow and red, and as they were later greatly upstepped by assimilating the greater portion of the violet race.

6. *The indigo race.* As the red men were the most advanced of all the Sangik peoples, so the black men were the least progressive. Isolated in Africa, the indigo peoples received little or none of the race elevation of the Adamic stock. Under the leadership of Orvonon who proclaimed the "God of Gods." Notwithstanding their backwardness, these indigo peoples have exactly the same standing before the celestial powers as any other earthly race. Mansant was a great teacher of the post-Planetary Prince days. There are many good and sufficient reasons for the plan of evolving either three or six colored races on the worlds of space: variety affords the survival of superior strains; interbreeding eventually carries superior inheritance factors; competition is healthfully stimulated; differences are essential for the development of tolerance and altruism.

64:7. Dispersion of the Colored Races

Between the times of the Planetary Prince and Adam, India became the home of the most cosmopolitan population ever to be found on the face of the earth. The primary Sangik peoples, the superior races, avoided the tropics, the red man going northeast to Asia, closely followed by the yellow man, while the blue race moved northwest into Europe. As the Sangik migrations drew to a close, the green and orange races were gone, the red man held North America, the yellow man eastern Asia, the blue man Europe, and the indigo race had gravitated to Africa. India harbored a blend of the secondary Sangik races. The brown man, a blend of the red and yellow, held the islands off the Asiatic coast. An amalgamated race of rather superior potential occupied the highlands of South America. The purer Andonites lived in the extreme northern regions of Europe and in Iceland, Greenland, and northeastern North America.

The struggles of these early ages were characterized by courage, bravery, and even heroism. And we all regret that so many of those sterling and rugged traits of your early ancestors have been lost to the later-day races.

Paper 65: The Overcontrol of Evolution
Life Carrier

BASIC evolutionary material life is the formulation of the Master Physical Controllers and the life-impartation ministry of the Seven Master Spirits in conjunction with the active ministration of the ordained Life Carriers. There are, then, three distinct levels of life production and evolution: 1. The physical-energy domain. 2. The mind ministry of the adjutant spirits. 3. The spirit endowment of mortal mind—culminating in Thought Adjuster bestowal. It is the integrated functioning of the Life Carriers, the physical controllers, and the spirit adjutants that conditions the course of organic evolution on the inhabited worlds. And this is why evolution is always purposeful and never accidental.

65:1. Life Carrier Functions

The Life Carriers are endowed with potentials of personality metamorphosis which but few orders of creatures possess. Life Carriers can and do function on the following three levels: 1. The physical level of electrochemistry. 2. The usual mid-phase of quasi-morontial existence. 3. The advanced semispiritual level. When the Life Carriers make ready to engage in life implantation, they summon the archangel commission of Life Carrier transmutation. When the commissioners are properly encircuited, they can effect such modifications in the Life Carriers as will enable them immediately to function on the physical levels of electrochemistry.

After the life patterns have been formulated and the material organizations have been duly completed, the supermaterial forces concerned in life propagation become forthwith active, and life is existent. After organic evolution has run a certain course and free will of the human type has appeared, the Life Carriers must either leave the planet or must pledge themselves to refrain from all attempts further to influence the course of organic evolution. These Life Carriers are then transmuted to the third phase of personality existence—the semispiritual level of being. And I have functioned on Urantia in this third phase of existence ever since the times of Andon and Fonta.

65:2. The Evolutionary Panorama

The story of man's ascent from seaweed to the lordship of earthly creation is indeed a romance of biologic struggle and mind survival.

The bacteria are very little changed from the early dawn of life. The majority of disease-causing bacteria and their auxiliary virus bodies really belong to the group of renegade parasitic fungi. The higher protozoan type of animal life soon appeared *suddenly*. Hundreds upon hundreds of species intervened and perished. The fish was the first backboned animal. The frog is one of the earliest of surviving human-race ancestors. The human race has no surviving ancestry between the frog and the Eskimo. Probably the greatest single leap of all prehuman evolution was executed when the reptile became a bird. It was from an agile little reptilian dinosaur of carnivorous habits but having a comparatively large brain that the placental mammals suddenly sprang. In this way the life that was planted on Urantia evolved until the ice age, when man himself first appeared and began his eventful planetary career. The rigors and climatic severity of the glacial era were in every way adapted to the purpose of fostering the production of a hardy type of human being with tremendous survival endowment.

65:3. The Fostering of Evolution

Urantia mortals evolved by way of primitive frog development that narrowly escaped extinction on a certain occasion. But it should not be inferred that the evolution of mankind would have been terminated by such an accident. At that very moment we were observing and fostering no less than one thousand different and remotely situated mutating strains of life. This particular ancestral frog represented our third selection. Even the loss of Andon and Fonta before they had offspring, though delaying human evolution, would not have prevented it. There evolved no less than seven thousand favorable strains which could have achieved some sort of human type of development.

Mankind on Urantia must solve its problems of mortal development with the human stocks it has. But this fact does not preclude the possibility of the attainment of vastly higher levels of human development through the intelligent fostering of the evolutionary potentials still resident in the mortal races. In a general way, man's evolutionary destiny is in his own hands, and scientific intelligence must sooner or later supersede the random functioning of uncontrolled natural selection.

65:4. The Urantia Adventure

Do not overlook the fact that Urantia was assigned to us as a life-experiment world. On Urantia we worked out and have satisfactorily demonstrated not less than twenty-eight features of life modification which will be of service to all Nebadon throughout all future time. The chemical action and reaction concerned in wound healing and cell reproduction represents the choice of the Life Carriers of a formula embracing over one hundred thousand phases and features of possible chemical reactions and biologic repercussions. More than half a million specific experiments were made by the Life Carriers in their laboratories before they finally settled upon this formula for the Urantia life experiment. When Urantia scientists know more of these healing chemicals, they will become more efficient in the treatment of injuries, and indirectly they will know more about controlling certain serious diseases.

It was our intention to produce an early manifestation of will in the evolutionary life of Urantia, and we succeeded. Ordinarily, will does not emerge until the colored races have long been in existence.

65:5. Life-Evolution Vicissitudes

Throughout all of the biologic adventure our greatest disappointment grew out of the reversion of certain primitive plant life to the prechlorophyll levels of parasitic bacteria on such an extensive and unexpected scale. This eventuality in plant-life evolution caused many distressful diseases in the higher mammals, particularly in the human species. We knew that the subsequent admixture of the Adamic life plasm would so reinforce the resisting powers of the resulting blended race as to make it practically immune to all diseases produced by the vegetable type of organism. But our hopes were doomed to disappointment owing to the misfortune of the Adamic default. The wise and all-powerful beings who are responsible for universe management undoubtedly know exactly what they are about; and so it becomes Life Carriers and behooves mortal minds to enlist in patient waiting and hearty co-operation with the rule of wisdom, the reign of power, and the march of progress. There are, of course, certain compensations for tribulation, such as Michael's bestowal on Urantia.

65:6. Evolutionary Techniques of Life

It is impossible accurately to determine, simultaneously, the exact location and the velocity of a moving object; any attempt at measurement of either inevitably involves change in the other. The same sort of a paradox confronts mortal man when he undertakes the chemical analysis of protoplasm. The chemist can elucidate the chemistry of dead protoplasm, but he cannot discern either the physical organization or the dynamic performance of living protoplasm. Ever will the scientist come nearer and nearer the secrets of life, but never will he find them.

The process of evolution is still actively and adaptatively in progress on this planet. The mind becomes increasingly adjustive, creative, co-ordinative, and dominative. Intellectual, social, moral, and spiritual evolution are dependent on the mind ministry of the seven adjutant spirits and their superphysical associates.

65:7. Evolutionary Mind Levels

The seven adjutant mind-spirits are the versatile mind ministers to the lower intelligent existences of a local universe. The seven adjutant spirits are more circuitlike than entitylike. On life-experiment planets they are relatively isolated. The acquisition of the potential of the ability to learn from experience marks the beginning of the functioning of the adjutant spirits. The adjutants function exclusively in the evolution of experiencing mind up to the level of the sixth phase, the spirit of worship. At this level there occurs that inevitable overlapping of ministry—the phenomenon of the higher reaching down to co-ordinate with the lower in anticipation of subsequent attainment of advanced levels of development. And still additional spirit ministry accompanies the action of the seventh and last adjutant, the spirit of wisdom. Throughout the ministry of the spirit world the individual never experiences abrupt transitions of spirit co-operation; always are these changes gradual and reciprocal. The domains of physical, mental, and spiritual gravity are distinct realms of cosmic reality, notwithstanding their intimate interrelations.

65:8. Evolution in Time and Space

Time and space are indissolubly linked. The delays of time are inevitable in the presence of certain space conditions. We are all under the jurisdiction of the Supreme Rulers of Paradise, and time is nonexistent on Paradise. All creatures are time conditioned, and therefore do they regard evolution as being a long-drawn-out process. As mind evolution is dependent on, and delayed by, the slow development of physical conditions, so is spiritual progress dependent on mental expansion. But this does not mean that spiritual evolution is dependent on education, culture, or wisdom. The soul may evolve regardless of mental culture but not in the absence of mental capacity and desire—the choice of survival and the decision to achieve ever-increasing perfection—to do the will of the Father in heaven. Although survival may not depend on the possession of knowledge and wisdom, progression most certainly does. When physical conditions are ripe, sudden mental evolutions may take place; when mind status is propitious, sudden spiritual transformations may occur; when spiritual values receive proper recognition, then cosmic meanings become discernible, and increasingly the personality is released from the handicaps of time and delivered from the limitations of space.

Paper 66: The Planetary Prince of Urantia

Melchizedek

THE advent of a Lanonandek Son on an average world signifies that will has developed in the mind of primitive man. But on Urantia the Planetary Prince arrived almost half a million years after the appearance of human will. About five hundred thousand years ago Caligastia, the Planetary Prince, arrived on Urantia.

66:1. Prince Caligastia

Caligastia was a Lanonandek Son of the secondary order. He was experienced in the administration of the affairs of the local universe. Caligastia very early sought a commission as Planetary Prince, but repeatedly, when his request came up for approval in the constellation councils, it would fail to receive the assent of the Constellation Fathers. No prince of the planets ever embarked upon a career of world rulership with a richer preparatory experience or with better prospects than did Caligastia, notwithstanding a certain characteristic restlessness coupled with a tendency to disagree with the established order in certain minor matters. I really regarded Urantia as being among the five or six most fortunate planets in all Satania in that it was to have such an experienced, brilliant, and original mind at the helm of world affairs. I did not then comprehend that Caligastia was insidiously falling in love with himself.

66:2. The Prince's Staff

The Planetary Prince of Urantia was not sent out on his mission alone but was accompanied by the usual corps of assistants and administrative helpers. At the head of this group was Daligastia, the associate-assistant of the Planetary Prince. From your standpoint the most interesting group of all were the corporeal members of the Prince's staff. These one hundred rematerialized members of the Prince's staff were chosen by Caligastia from over 785,000 ascendant citizens of Jerusem who volunteered for embarkation on the Urantia adventure. Each one of the chosen one hundred was from a different planet. The one hundred were given a portion of the life plasm of selected descendants of Andon and Fonta. The entire transaction of repersonalization, from the time of the arrival of the seraphic transports bearing the one hundred Jerusem volunteers until they became conscious, threefold beings of the realm, consumed exactly ten days.

66:3. Dalamatia—The City of the Prince

The headquarters of the Planetary Prince was situated in the Persian Gulf. The climate and landscape in the Mesopotamia of those times were in every way favorable. The nucleus of the Prince's settlement was a very simple but beautiful city, enclosed within a wall forty feet high. Centermost in the city was the temple of the unseen Father. The buildings of Dalamatia were brick and all one story except the council headquarters, which were two stories, and the central temple which was small but three stories in height. Near the Prince's headquarters there dwelt all colors and strata of human beings.

It was from these near-by tribes that the first students of the Prince's schools were recruited. The Prince's corporeal staff continuously gathered about them the superior individuals of the surrounding tribes and, after training and inspiring these students, sent them back as teachers and leaders of their respective peoples.

66:4. Early Days of the One Hundred

The arrival of the Prince's staff created a profound impression. The one hundred were superhuman beings but unfused with their Thought Adjusters. They were corporeal and relatively human. In skin color and language they followed the Andonic race. The re-created bodies of this group were fully satisfied by a nonflesh diet. Circulating through their material forms were the antidotal complements of the life currents of the Satania system, which were derived from the fruit of the tree of life, a shrub of Edentia which was sent to Urantia by the Most Highs of Norlatiadek. This supersustenance was quite sufficient to confer continuous life upon the Caligastia one hundred and also upon the one hundred modified Andonites who were associated with them.

It was during the thirty-third year of their sojourn that two of their number accidentally discovered a phenomenon attendant upon the liaison of their morontia selves (supposedly nonsexual and nonmaterial); and the result of this adventure proved to be the first of the primary midway creatures. Upon authority of the Planetary Prince, 50,000 primary midwayers were produced. These mid-type creatures were of great service in carrying on the affairs of the world's headquarters.

66:5. Organization of the One Hundred

The one hundred were organized for service in ten autonomous councils of ten members each:

1. *The council on food and material welfare*, presided over by Ang. Food, water, clothes, and the material advancement of the human species were fostered by this able corps.

2. *The board of animal domestication and utilization*, directed by Bon. This council was dedicated to the task of selecting and breeding those ani-

mals best adapted to help human beings. This corps first taught men to use the wheel and also trained the great fandors as passenger birds.

3. *The advisers regarding the conquest of predatory animals,* captained by Dan. By employing improved techniques and the use of traps, this group made great progress in animal subjugation.

4. *The faculty on dissemination and conservation of knowledge,* presided over by Fad. This group organized and directed the purely educational endeavors of those early ages. Fad formulated the first alphabet and introduced a writing system. The Dalamatia library comprised more than two million separate records.

5. *The commission on industry and trade,* under the leadership of Nod. This council was employed in fostering industry within the tribes and in promoting trade between the various peace groups.

6. *The college of revealed religion,* headed by Hap. This group provided seven chants of worship and also gave them the daily praise-phrase and eventually taught them "the Father's prayer."

7. *The guardians of health and life,* led by Lut. This council was concerned with the introduction of sanitation and the promotion of primitive hygiene. They taught mankind that cooking, boiling and roasting, was a means of avoiding sickness. They also sought to introduce handshaking in place of saliva exchange or blood drinking as a seal of personal friendship.

8. *The planetary council on art and science,* led by Mek. This group taught the rudiments of physics and chemistry and finally persuaded the fearful Dalamations to work with metals and fire. Mek's council also did a great deal to advance the culture and improve the art of the blue man. Their teachings led to great progress in the home arts.

9. *The governors of advanced tribal relations,* under the leadership of Tut. These leaders contributed much to bringing about intertribal marriages. They labored to promote group associations of a peaceful nature.

10. *The supreme court of tribal co-ordination and racial co-operation,* directed by Van. This supreme council was the court of appeals for all of the other nine special commissions. It was one of wide function, being entrusted with all matters of earthly concern which were not specifically assigned to the other groups.

66:6. The Prince's Reign

The degree of a world's culture is wholly determined by the ability of its inhabitants to comprehend new and advanced ideas. Tradition produces stability but it likewise stifles initiative. Custom and fashion still unduly dominates Urantia. The Caligastia one hundred wisely refrained from any radical attempts at modifying man's mode of life on earth. Those who labored for the uplift and advancement of a given tribe or race were always natives of that tribe or race. The process was slow but very effectual. Their motive was progression by evolution and not revolution by revelation. Confusion and dismay always results when enlightened and superior beings undertake to uplift the backward races by overteaching and overenlightenment.

66:7. Life in Dalamatia

The Prince's headquarters, though exquisitely beautiful and designed to awe the primitive men of that age, was altogether modest. While the residential buildings were models of neatness and cleanliness, everything was very simple. The Prince's staff lived together as fathers and mothers. The fifty pattern homes of Dalamatia never sheltered less than five hundred adopted little ones. The Dalamatia plan of teaching was carried out as an industrial school in which the pupils learned by doing.

Hap presented the following seven commands: You shall not fear nor serve any God but the Father of all; you shall not disobey the Father's Son; you shall not speak a lie; you shall not kill; you shall not steal; you shall not touch your friend's wife; you shall not show disrespect to your parents or to the elders of the tribe. This was the law of Dalamatia for almost three hundred thousand years.

The time measurement of these days was the lunar month, and the seven-day week was introduced by the Dalamatia teachers.

The cultivation of the soil is inherent in the establishment of an advancing civilization and this injunction was the center of all teaching of the Planetary Prince and his staff. Work with the soil is the highest blessing to all who are thus permitted to enjoy this most human of all human activities.

66:8. Misfortunes of Caligastia

Caligastia was inclined to take sides with almost every party of protest. We detect the early appearance of this tendency to be restless under authority, to mildly resent all forms of supervision. Nonetheless, whenever a test had come, he had always proved loyal to the universe rulers and obedient to the mandates of the Constellation Fathers. It should be noted that both Lucifer and Caligastia had been patiently instructed and lovingly warned respecting their critical tendencies and the subtle development of their pride of self.

The Prince of Urantia went into darkness at the time of the Lucifer rebellion. The power of the fallen Prince to disturb human affairs was enormously curtailed by the mortal incarnation of Machiventa Melchizedek in the days of Abraham; and subsequently, during the life of Michael in the flesh, this traitorous Prince was finally shorn of all authority on Urantia.

Paper 67: The Planetary Rebellion
Melchizedek

THE problems associated with human existence on Urantia are impossible of understanding without a knowledge of certain great epochs of the past, notably the occurrence and consequences of the planetary rebellion. Although this upheaval did not seriously interfere with the progress of organic evolution, the entire superphysical history of the planet was profoundly influenced by this devastating calamity.

67:1. The Caligastia Betrayal

For three hundred thousand years Caligastia had been in charge of Urantia when Satan, Lucifer's assistant, made one of his periodic inspection calls. In the course of this inspection Satan informed Caligastia of Lucifer's then proposed "Declaration of Liberty," and as we now know, the Prince agreed to betray the planet upon the announcement of the rebellion. In committing this deliberate sin, Caligastia so completely distorted his personality that his mind has never since been able fully to regain its equilibrium.

Evil is a partial realization of, or maladjustment to, universe realities. But sin is a purposeful resistance to divine reality while iniquity consists in an open and persistent defiance of recognized reality and signifies such a degree of personality disintegration as to border on cosmic insanity. While all manner of sins may be forgiven, we doubt whether the established iniquiter would ever sincerely experience sorrow for his misdeeds or accept forgiveness for his sins.

67:2. The Outbreak of Rebellion

Caligastia held a prolonged conference with his associate, Daligastia, after which the latter called the ten councils of Urantia in session extraordinary demanding that all administrative groups abdicate by resigning all of their functions and powers into the hands of Daligastia as trustee. The presentation of this astounding demand was followed by the masterly appeal of Van, chairman of the supreme council of co-ordination who branded the proposed course of Caligastia as an act bordering on planetary rebellion. Appeal was made to Lucifer who designated Caligastia as the supreme sovereign of Urantia. And it was in reply to this amazing message that the noble Van made his memorable address of seven hours' length in which he formally drew his indictment of Daligastia, Caligastia, and Lucifer as standing in contempt of the sovereignty of the universe of Nebadon. The system circuits were severed; Urantia was isolated. Each group drew off by itself and began deliberations to choose between the ways of Lucifer and the will of the unseen Father. For more than seven years this struggle continued. Not until every personality concerned had made a final decision, would or did the authorities of Edentia interfere or intervene.

67:3. The Seven Crucial Years

Forty members of the corporeal staff of one hundred (including Van) refused to join the insurrection. There was a terrible loss of personalities among seraphim and cherubim. Forty thousand one hundred and nineteen of the primary midway creatures joined hands with Caligastia. During the times of this struggle the loyalists dwelt in an unwalled and poorly protected settlement a few miles to the east of Dalamatia, but their dwellings were guarded day and night by the alert and ever-watchful loyal midway creatures, and they had possession of the priceless tree of life. This seven years of waiting was a time of heart searching and soul discipline.

Amadon is the outstanding human hero of the Lucifer rebellion. Caligastia, with a maximum of intelligence and a vast experience in universe affairs, went astray. Amadon, with a minimum of intelligence and utterly devoid of universe experience, remained steadfast.

67:4. The Caligastia One Hundred After Rebellion

Those who refused to join the rebellion were transferred to Jerusem, where they resumed their Paradise journey. The sixty members who went into rebellion chose Nod as their leader. They soon discovered that they were deprived of the sustenance of the system life circuits and awakened to the fact that they had been degraded to the status of mortal beings, doomed to suffer extinction by death. In an effort to increase their numbers, Daligastia ordered immediate resort to sexual reproduction. Their descendants were long known as the Nodites, and their dwelling place as "the land of Nod." The presence of these extraordinary supermen and superwomen originated the thousand and one legends of a mythical nature which later found a place in the folk tales and traditions of various peoples.

We know not the fate of the sixty staff rebels. The vast majority of all human and superhuman beings have long since heartily repented of their folly and will be restored to some phase of universe service when the Ancients of Days finally complete the adjudication of the affairs of the Satania rebellion, which they have so recently begun.

67:5. Immediate Results of Rebellion

Great confusion reigned in Dalamatia. Liberty was quickly translated into license by the half-evolved primitive men of those days. Very soon after the rebellion the entire staff of sedition were engaged in energetic defense of the city against the hordes of semisavages who drove the secession staff and their associates northward. The Caligastia scheme for the immediate reconstruction of human society in accordance with his ideas of individual freedom and group liberties proved a swift and more or less complete failure, leaving the world in confusion worse confounded. One hundred and sixty-two years after the rebellion a tidal wave swept up over Dalamatia, and the planetary headquarters sank beneath the waters of the sea.

67:6. Van—the Steadfast

The followers of Van early withdrew to the highlands west of India. Van placed the administration of human affairs in the hands of ten commissions of four each. The senior resident Life Carriers assumed temporary leadership of this council of forty. Van was left on Urantia until the time of Adam, remaining as titular head of all superhuman personalities functioning on the planet for over one hundred and fifty thousand years.

The affairs of Urantia were for a long time administered by a council of twelve Melchizedeks. They preserved the remnants of civilization, and their planetary policies were faithfully executed by Van. Within one thousand years after the rebellion he had more than three hundred and fifty advanced groups scattered abroad in the world.

Van now serves in behalf of Urantia while awaiting the order to go forward on the long, long trail to Paradise perfection. It should be recorded that the Constellation Fathers dispatched an immediate decision sustaining Van on every point of his contention. This verdict failed to reach him because the planetary circuits of communication were severed while it was in transit. The technical status of Van on the legal records of Satania was not actually and finally settled until this ruling of the Edentia Fathers was recorded on Jerusem.

67:7. Remote Repercussions of Sin

Sin on Urantia did very little to delay biologic evolution, but it did operate to deprive the mortal races of the full benefit of the Adamic inheritance. But it does not prevent the highest spiritual achievement by any individual who chooses to know God and sincerely do his divine will. Every mortal born on Urantia since Caligastia's rebellion has been in some manner time-penalized, but the future welfare of such souls has never been in the least eternity-jeopardized.

67:8. The Human Hero of the Rebellion

The records of Salvington portray Amadon as the outstanding character of the entire system in his glorious rejection of the flood tides of sedition and in his unswerving devotion to Van; he and Van stood together in their loyalty to the supremacy of the invisible Father and his Son Michael. From

Edentia up through Salvington and even on to Uversa, for seven long years the first inquiry of all subordinate celestial life regarding the Satania rebellion, ever and always, was: "What of Amadon of Urantia, does he still stand unmoved?"

Let me assure you, the loyalty of Amadon and Van has already done more good in the universe of Nebadon and the superuniverse of Orvonton than can ever be outweighed by the sum total of all the evil and sorrow of the Lucifer rebellion.

Paper 68: The Dawn of Civilization
Melchizedek

CIVILIZATION is a racial acquirement; hence must all children be reared in an environment of culture, while each succeeding generation of youth must receive anew its education. In more times the yellow race and the white race have presented the most advanced social development on Urantia.

68:1. Protective Socialization

Association early became the price of survival. Primitive society was thus founded on the reciprocity of necessity and on the enhanced safety of association. The modern phrase, "back to nature," is a delusion of ignorance, a belief in the reality of the onetime fictitious "golden age." The lack of natural brotherly attraction stands in the way of immediate realization of the brotherhood of man on Urantia.

68:2. Factors in the Social Progression

Two great influences which contributed to the early association of human beings were food hunger and sex love. Primitive man only thought when he was hungry. From earliest times, where woman was has always been regarded as the home. Woman early became indispensable to the evolving social scheme; she was an essential partner in self-maintenance. She was a food provider, a beast of burden, and a companion who would stand great abuse without violent resentment, and in addition to all of these desirable traits, she was an ever-present means of sex gratification. Almost everything of lasting value in civilization has its roots in the family. The family was the first successful peace group, with the man and woman learning how to adjust their antagonisms, while at the same time teaching the pursuits of peace to their children.

Vanity contributed mightily to the birth of society. Pleasure-want has long since superseded hunger-want. Self-maintenance builds society; unbridled self-gratification unfailingly destroys civilization.

68:3. Socializing Influence of Ghost Fear

Primitive desires produced the original society, but ghost fear held it together and imparted an extrahuman aspect to its existence. Probably the greatest single factor in the evolution of human society was the ghost dream. The ghost dream drove these early peoples into each other's arms for mutual protection against the vague and unseen imaginary dangers of the spirit world. Hunger and love drove men together; vanity and ghost fear held them together.

68:4. Evolution of the Mores

The mores were man's first social institution. The origin of folkways, like the origin of languages, is always unconscious and unintentional and therefore always shrouded in mystery. The one thing which early established and crystallized the mores was the belief that the dead were jealous of the ways by which they had lived and died. Ancient man was a slave to the tyranny of usage; his life contained nothing free, spontaneous, or original. Custom has been the thread of continuity which has held civilization together. The survival of a society depends chiefly on the progressive evolution of its mores. But this does not mean that each separate and isolated change in the composition of human society has been for the better. No! for there have been many, many retrogressions in the long forward struggle of Urantia civilization.

68:5. Land Techniques—Maintenance Arts

The evolution of the mores is always dependent on the land-man ratio. Man's land technique, or maintenance arts, plus his standards of living, equal the sum total of the folkways, the mores. There were four great steps in the forward march of civilization. They were: 1. *The collection stage.* 2. *The hunting stage.* 3. *The pastoral stage.* When man entered the pastoral era, woman's dignity fell greatly. She had become scarcely more than a human animal, consigned to work and to bear human offspring. 4. *The agricultural stage.* The growing of plants exerts an ennobling influence on all races of mankind. Agriculture and industrialism are the activities of peace. But the weakness of both, as world social activities, is that they lack excitement and adventure. An industrial era cannot hope to survive if its leaders fail to recognize that even the highest social developments must ever rest upon a sound agricultural basis.

68:6. Evolution of Culture

The land-man ratio underlies all social civilization. The improvement of the land yield, the extension of the mechanical arts, and the reduction of population all tend to foster the development of the better side of human nature. Cities always multiply the power of their inhabitants for either good or evil. The size of the family has always been influenced by the standards of living. When standards of living become too complicated or too highly luxurious, they speedily become suicidal. The early races often resorted to practices designed to restrict population.

Multiple births were believed to be caused either by magic or by infidelity. The Andonite peoples always regarded twins as omens of good luck. Many races learned the technique of abortion. Many primitive clans were virtually exterminated by the practice of both abortion and infanticide.

Overpopulation may become a serious problem in the near future. The normal man should be fostered; he is the backbone of civilization and the source of the mutant geniuses of the race.

Paper 69: Primitive Human Institutions
Melchizedek

EMOTIONALLY, man transcends his animal ancestors in his ability to appreciate humor, art, and religion. Socially, man exhibits his superiority in that he is a toolmaker, a communicator, and an institution builder.

69:1. Basic Human Institutions

All human institutions minister to some social need, past or present. Man should control his institutions rather than permit himself to be dominated by these creations of advancing civilization. Human institutions are of three general classes: 1. *The institutions of self-maintenance.* These include industry, property, war for gain, and all the regulative machinery of society. 2. *The institutions of self-perpetuation.* These embrace the social safeguards of the home and the school, of family life, education, ethics, and religion. 3. *The institutions of self-gratification.* These embrace customs in dress and personal adornment, social usages, war for glory, dancing, amusement, games, and other phases of sensual gratification.

69:2. The Dawn of Industry

Primitive industry slowly grew up as an insurance against the terrors of famine. Primitive savages never did any real work cheerfully or willingly. Primitive man disliked hard work, and he would not hurry unless confronted by grave danger.

The necessity for labor is man's paramount blessing. The Hebrews were the first tribe to put a supreme premium on industry; they were the first people to decree that "he who does not work shall not eat." But there was a long, long struggle between the lazy devotees of magic and the apostles of work—those who exercised foresight.

The first human foresight was directed toward the preservation of fire, water, and food. But primitive man was a natural-born gambler; he always wanted to get something for nothing, and all too often during these early times the success which accrued from patient practice was attributed to charms. Magic was slow to give way before foresight, self-denial, and industry.

69:3. The Specialization of Labor

The divisions of labor in primitive society were determined first by natural and then by social circumstances. The early order of specialization in labor was: 1. *Specialization based on sex.* Woman became the routine worker, while man became the hunter and fighter. Man has most selfishly chosen the more agreeable work. 2. *Modification consequent upon age and disease.* The old men and cripples were early set to work making tools and weapons. 3. *Differentiation based on religion.* The medicine men were the first human beings to be exempted from physical toil. The smiths were a small group who competed with the medicine men as magicians. They were regarded as neutrals during war, and this extra leisure led to their becoming, as a class, the politicians of primitive society. 4. *Master and slave.* This differentiation of labor grew out of the relations of the conqueror to the conquered, and that meant the beginning of human slavery. 5. *Differentiation based on diverse physical and mental endowments.* Whole families and clans dedicated themselves to certain sorts of labor. The early traders were women; they were employed as spies, carrying on commerce as a sideline.

69:4. The Beginnings of Trade

The first barter was conducted by armed traders who would leave their goods on a neutral spot. Women held the first markets. Very early the trading counter was developed, a wall wide enough to prevent the traders reaching each other with weapons. A fetish was used to stand guard over the deposits of goods. For ages silent barter continued before men would meet, unarmed, on the sacred market place. Any fugitive reaching the market place was safe and secure against attack. Modern writing originated in the early trade records. New ideas and better methods were carried around the inhabited world by the ancient traders. Commerce, linked with adventure, led to exploration and discovery. Commerce has been the great civilizer through promoting the cross-fertilization of culture.

69:5. The Beginnings of Capital

Savings represent a form of maintenance and survival insurance. The early banker was the valorous man of the tribe. He held the group treasures on deposit. The accumulation of individual capital and group wealth immediately led to military organization. The basic urges which led to the accumulation of capital were: 1. *Hunger associated with foresight*—food saving and preservation meant power and comfort for those with sufficient foresight thus to provide for future needs. 2. *Love of family*—desire to provide for their wants. 3. *Vanity*—longing to display one's property accumulations. 4. *Position*—eagerness to buy social and political prestige. 5. *Power*—the craving to be master. The moneylenders made themselves kings by creating a standing army of debtors. 6. *Fear of the ghosts of the dead*—priest fees for protection. The priesthoods thus became very rich. 7. *Sex urge*—the desire to buy one or more wives. 8. *Numerous forms of self-gratification.* Early man tended to squander his resources on luxury.

As civilization developed, men acquired new incentives for saving. Rich men endow great institutions of philanthropy and learning. Man's technique varies, but his disposition remains quite unchanged. Through capital and invention the present generation enjoys a higher degree of freedom than any that ever preceded it on earth.

69:6. Fire in Relation to Civilization

Primitive society with its four divisions—industrial, regulative, religious, and military—rose through the instrumentality of fire, animals, slaves, and property. Fire enabled man to stay on the ground at night as all animals are afraid of it. The household fire, which was attended by the mother or eldest daughter, was the first educator, requiring watchfulness and dependability. When a son founded a new home, he carried a firebrand from the family hearth. It was a sin to extinguish a flame. The fires of the temples and shrines were sacred. Ideas of supernatural origin led directly to fire worship. Fire opened the doors to metalwork and led to the subsequent discovery of steam power and the present-day uses of electricity.

69:7. The Utilization of Animals

The domestication of animals came about accidentally. It was discovered that certain species of animals would submit to man's presence, and that they would reproduce in captivity. This led to selective breeding. The dog was the first animal to be domesticated. The dog's keen sense of smell led to the notion it could see spirits. It became the custom to employ watchdogs to protect the home against spirits as well as material enemies.

When man was a hunter he was fairly kind to women, but after the domestication of animals, coupled with the Caligastia confusion, many tribes shamefully treated their women. Man's brutal treatment of woman constitutes one of the darkest chapters of human history.

69:8. Slavery as a Factor in Civilization

Primitive man never hesitated to enslave his fellows. Woman was the first slave, a family slave. Enslavement was a forward step in the merciful treatment of war captives. The hunter, like the American red man, did not enslave. He either adopted or killed his captives. The Mosaic code contained specific directions for making wives of women captives. The Africans could easily be taught to till the soil; hence they became the great slave race.

Slavery was an indispensable link in the chain of human civilization. It compelled backward and lazy peoples to work and thus provide wealth and leisure for the social advancement of their superiors. Slavery creates an organization of culture and social achievement but soon insidiously attacks society internally as the gravest of all destructive social maladies. Modern mechanical invention rendered the slave obsolete. Today involuntary slavery has given way to a new and improved form of modified industrial servitude. While the ideal of society is universal freedom, idleness should never be tolerated.

69:9. Private Property

Communism was indispensable scaffolding in the growth of primitive society, but it gave way to the evolution of a higher social order because it ran counter to four strong human proclivities: 1. *The family*. Man desires to bequeath his capital goods to his progeny. 2. *Religious tendencies*. Primitive man also wanted to save up property as a nucleus for starting life in the next existence. 3. *The desire for liberty and leisure*. The improvident habitually lived off the thrifty. 4. *The urge for security and power*. Private ownership brought increased liberty and enhanced stability.

At first, all property, including tools and weapons, was the common possession of the tribe. Sleeping space was one of man's earliest properties. Water holes and wells were among the first private possessions. Private ownership brought increased liberty and enhanced stability.

The right to property is not absolute; it is purely social. The present social order is not necessarily right—not divine or sacred—but mankind will do well to move slowly in making changes. Do not be persuaded to experiment with the discarded formulas of your forefathers.

Paper 70: The Evolution of Human Government
Melchizedek

NO sooner had man partially solved the problem of making a living than he was confronted with the task of regulating human contacts. The development of industry demanded law, order, and social adjustment; private property necessitated government.

70:1. The Genesis of War

War is the natural state and heritage of evolving man; peace is the social yardstick measuring civilization's advancement. War is an animalistic reaction to misunderstandings and irritations. Among the early causes of war were: 1. hunger, 2. woman scarcity, 3. vanity, 4. slaves, 5. revenge. 6. recreation, and 7. religion.

Only in recent times has religion begun to frown upon war. One of the great peace moves of the ages has been the attempt to separate church and state. The first refinement of war was the taking of prisoners. Next, women were exempted from hostilities, though they have always fed and nursed the soldiers and urged them on to battle. This was followed by the gradual development of the rules of "civilized" warfare.

70:2. The Social Value of War

The constant necessity for national defense creates many new and advanced social adjustments. War has had a social value to past civilizations because it: 1. imposed discipline, 2. put a premium on courage, 3. fostered nationalism, 4. destroyed weak and unfit peoples, 5. dissolved the illusion of primitive equality.

War is rapidly becoming culturally bankrupt. Industrialism is more civilized and should be so carried on as to promote initiative and to encourage individualism. Its dangers are: strong drift toward materialism, glorifying wealth, vices of luxury, increasing dangers of indolence, racial softness resulting in biologic deterioration, and the threat of standardized industrial slavery.

Man will never accept peace as a normal mode of living until he has been thoroughly and repeatedly convinced that peace is best for his material welfare. Do not make the mistake of glorifying war.

70:3. Early Human Associations

In the most primitive society the horde is everything; even children are its common property. The evolving family displaced the horde in child rearing, while the emerging clans and tribes took its place as the social unit.

The first treaties of peace were the "blood bonds." The earliest peace missions consisted of delegations of men bringing their choice maidens for the sex gratification of their onetime enemies. And soon intermarriages between the families of the chiefs were sanctioned.

The peace of Urantia will be promoted far more by international trade organizations than by all the sentimental sophistry of visionary peace planning.

70:4. Clans and Tribes

The first peace group was the family, then the clan, the tribe, and later on the nation. The clans were blood-tie groups within the tribe, and they owed their existence to certain common interests, such as a common ancestor, religious totem, dialect, dwelling place or military experience. The clan headmen were always subordinate to the tribal chief and served at his court. The clan peace chiefs usually ruled through the mother line; the tribal war chiefs established the father line. The clans served a valuable purpose in local self-government, but they greatly delayed the growth of large and strong nations.

70:5. The Beginnings of Government

From the early clans and primitive tribes there gradually developed the successive orders of human government. The first real governmental body was the council of the elders. This group was composed of old men who had distinguished themselves in some efficient manner. In the early council of the elders there resided the potential of all governmental functions: executive, legislative, and judicial. The chairman of the council was one of the forerunners of the later tribal chief. Some tribes had female councils. At first the war chiefs were chosen only for military service; in later times some chiefs were chosen for other than military service. The peace rulers were also judges and teachers. And it was by these steps that the executive branch of government gradually came into existence. The clan and tribal councils continued in an advisory capacity and as forerunners of the later appearing legislative and judicial branches.

70:6. Monarchial Government

Effective state rule only came with the arrival of a chief with full executive authority. Hereditary kingship avoided the anarchy which had previously wrought such havoc between the death of a king and the election of a successor. The succession of kings was eventually regarded as supernatural, too sacred to be viewed except on feast days and holy days. Ordinarily a representative was chosen to impersonate him, and this is the origin of prime ministers. The assistants of the early kings became the accepted nobility. Unscrupulous rulers gained great power by the discovery of poison. The medicine men, witch doctors, and priests have always been a powerful check on the kings. Deposed rulers, when sentenced to death, were often given the option of committing suicide.

70:7. Primitive Clubs and Secret Societies

Blood kinship determined the first social groups. Then there developed religious cults and the political clubs. Religious cults and political clubs, first appearing as secret societies, then developed. The secrecy of these societies conferred on all members the power of mystery over the rest of the tribe. Secrecy also appeals to vanity; the initiates were the social aristocracy of their day.

Primitive people very early taught their adolescent youths sex control, their education and training being entrusted to the men's secret societies. The puberty initiation ceremonies involved much self-torture. Circumcision was first practiced as a rite of initiation into one of these secret fraternities. One of the chief purposes of the puberty ceremonies was to impress upon the boy that he must leave other men's wives alone. Many later tribes sanctioned the formation of women's secret clubs. Presently nonsecret clubs made their appearance. These societies gave rise to the first political parties. By and by these secret associations grew into the first charitable organizations—the forerunners of churches. Finally some of these societies became the first international fraternities.

70:8. Social Classes

The mental and physical inequality of human beings insures that social classes will appear. The mental and physical inequality of human beings insures that social classes will appear for the following reasons: 1. Natural-sex and relationships; 2. Personal-ability, knowledge, and intelligence; 3. Chance-war and emigration; 4. Economic-rich and poor; 5. Geographic-urban and rural; 6. Social-social worth of groups; 7, Vocational-professional, skilled, and unskilled; 8. Religious-lay persons and priests; 9. Racial-different races; 10. Age-youth and maturity.

Social caste solves the problem of finding one's place in industry, but it sharply curtails individual development and virtually prevents social cooperation. Classes in society will persist until man gradually achieves their evolutionary obliteration through intelligent manipulation of the biologic, intellectual, and spiritual resources of a progressing civilization.

70:9. Human Rights

Nature confers no rights on man, only life and a world in which to live it. Society's prime gift to man is security through: 1. food supply, 2. military defense, 3. internal peace preservation, 4. sex control—the family institution, 5. property—the right to own, 6. fostering of individual and group competition, 7. provision for educating and training youth, 8. promotion of trade and commerce, 9. improvement of labor conditions and rewards, and 10. the guarantee of the freedom of religious practices.

Human rights are entirely social. They are relative and ever changing. Society cannot offer equal rights to all, but it can promise to administer the varying rights of each with fairness and equity.

70:10. Evolution of Justice

Natural justice is a man-made theory. Nature provides but one kind of justice—inevitable conformity of results to causes. Justice is a matter of progressive evolution.

In the earliest primitive society public opinion operated directly. Society was regulated on the theory that the group membership should have some degree of control over the behavior of each individual. It was very early believed that ghosts administered justice through the medicine men and priests. Their early methods of detecting crime consisted in conducting ordeals of poison, fire, and pain. It is not to be wondered that the Hebrews practiced such primitive techniques of justice, but it is most amazing that thinking men would subsequently retain such a relic of barbarism within the pages of a collection of sacred writings.

Suicide was a common mode of retaliation. If one were unable to avenge himself in life, he died entertaining the belief that, as a ghost, he could return and visit wrath upon his enemy. Hunger strikes are a modern analogue of this old-time method of retaliation.

Punishment by burning alive was once a common practice. Treason was the first capital crime. Cattle stealing was universally punished by summary death. When society fails to punish crimes, group resentment usually asserts itself as lynch law. Lynching and dueling represent the unwillingness of the individual to surrender private redress to the state.

70:11. Laws and Courts

Law is always at first negative and prohibitive; in advancing civilizations it becomes increasingly positive and directive. Society could not have held together during early times had not rights had the sanction of religion; superstition was the moral and social police force of the long evolutionary ages. Law is a codified record of long human experience, public opinion crystallized and legalized.

Property disputes were handled in many ways, such as: 1. by destroying the disputed property; 2. by force, 3. by arbitration, 4. by appeal to the elders, later to the courts.

The first courts were regulated fistic encounters; the judges were merely umpires or referees. The status of any civilization may be very accurately determined by the thoroughness and equity of its courts and by the integrity of its judges.

70:12. Allocation of Civil Authority

The evolutionary peoples on the inhabited worlds are best regulated by the representative type of civil government when there is maintained proper balance of power between the executive, legislative, and judicial branches. Urantia mortals are entitled to liberty; they should create their systems of government. And having done this, they should select their most competent and worthy fellows as chief executives. For representatives in the legislative branch they should elect only those who are qualified intellectually and morally to fulfill such sacred responsibilities. As judges of their high and supreme tribunals only those who are endowed with natural ability and who have been made wise by replete experience should be chosen. If men would maintain their freedom, they must prevent: 1. usurpation of unwarranted power; 2. machinations of ignorant and superstitious agitators; 3. retardation of scientific progress; 4. the dominance of mediocrity; 5. domination by vicious minorities, 6. control by ambitious and clever would-be dictators; 7. disastrous disruption of panics; 8. exploitation by the unscrupulous; 9. taxation enslavement; 10. failure of social and economic fairness; 11. union of church and state; 12. loss of personal liberty.

While there is a divine and ideal form of government, such cannot be revealed but must be slowly and laboriously discovered by the men and women of each planet throughout the universes of time and space.

Paper 71: Development of the State

Melchizedek

THE state is not of divine genesis; it was not even produced by volitionally intelligent human action; it is purely an evolutionary institution and was wholly automatic in origin.

71:1. The Embryonic State

The early states were small and were all the result of conquest. The northern tribes of the American red men never attained real statehood. The red men were too democratic; they had a good government, but it failed. The successful Roman state was based on: the father family, agriculture, cities, private property, conquest, roads, and strong leaders. The great weakness in Roman civilization was the supposed liberal and advanced provision for the emancipation of the boy at twenty-one and the unconditional release of the girl so that she was at liberty to marry a man of her own choosing. The harm to society consisted not in these reforms themselves but rather in the sudden and extensive manner of their adoption. During the European Middle Ages the territorial state collapsed, and there was a reversion to the small castle groups.

71:2. The Evolution of Representative Government

Democracy, while an ideal, is a product of civilization, not of evolution. Go slowly! select carefully! for the dangers of democracy are: mediocrity, ignorant rulers, universal suffrage of uneducated majorities, and slavery to public opinion. Education of public opinion is the only safe and true method of accelerating civilization.

There are ten steps to the evolution of an efficient form of representative government, and these are: 1. freedom of the person, 2. freedom of the mind, 3. the reign of law, 4. freedom of speech, 5. security of property, 6. the right of petition, 7. the right to rule, 8. universal suffrage, 9. control of public servants, 10. intelligent and trained representation—electing to public offices only those individuals who are technically trained, intellectually competent, socially loyal, and morally fit.

71:3. The Ideals of Statehood

The ideal state functions under the impulse of three mighty and co-ordinated drives: 1. love loyalty derived from the realization of human brotherhood, 2. intelligent patriotism based on wise ideals, and 3. cosmic insight interpreted in terms of planetary facts, needs, and goals.

The laws of the ideal state are few in number. That state is best which co-ordinates most while governing least. No society has progressed very far when it permits idleness or tolerates poverty. In advanced states, political service is esteemed as the highest devotion of the citizenry. Such governments confer their highest honors of recognition for service upon their civil and social servants. Honors are next bestowed, in the order named, upon philosophers, educators, scientists, industrialists, and militarists. Religious leaders receive their real rewards in another world.

71:4. Progressive Civilization

The progressive program of an expanding civilization embraces preservation of individual liberties, protection of the home, promotion of economic security, prevention of disease, compulsory education, compulsory employment, profitable utilization of leisure, care of the unfortunate, race improvement, promotion of science and art, promotion of philosophy—wisdom, and augmentation of cosmic insight—spirituality.

The appearance of genuine brotherhood signifies that a social order has arrived in which all men delight in bearing one another's burdens. Idealism can never survive on an evolving planet if the idealists in each generation permit themselves to be exterminated by the baser orders of humanity. National survival demands preparedness, and religious idealism alone can prevent the prostitution of preparedness into aggression. Only love, brotherhood, can prevent the strong from oppressing the weak.

71:5. The Evolution of Competition

Competition is essential to social progress. The ideal state undertakes to regulate social conduct only enough to take violence out of individual competition and to prevent unfairness in personal initiative. As the evolution of man progresses, co-operation becomes increasingly effective. In advanced civilizations co-operation is more efficient than competition. Later civilizations are better promoted by intelligent co-operation, understanding fraternity, and spiritual brotherhood.

71:6. The Profit Motive

Present-day profit-motivated economics is doomed unless profit motives can be augmented by service motives. But the profit motive must not be suddenly destroyed or removed; it keeps many otherwise slothful mortals hard at work. Profit motivation must not be taken away from men until they have firmly possessed themselves of superior types of nonprofit motives for economic striving and social serving—the transcendent urges of superlative wisdom, intriguing brotherhood, and excellency of spiritual attainment.

71:7. Education

The enduring state is founded on culture, dominated by ideals, and motivated by service. The purpose of education should be acquirement of skill, pursuit of wisdom, realization of selfhood, and attainment of spiritual values. In the ideal state, education continues throughout life, and philosophy eventually becomes the chief pursuit of its citizens.

Education has too long been localistic, militaristic, ego exalting, and success seeking; it must eventually become world-wide, idealistic, self-realizing, and cosmic-grasping. Teachers must be free beings, real leaders, to the end that philosophy, the search for wisdom, may become the chief educational pursuit. And then many will ascend to the mortal ultimate of mind attainment, God-consciousness.

71:8. The Character of Statehood

The only sacred feature of any human government is the division of statehood into the three domains of executive, legislative, and judicial functions. The evolution of statehood entails progress from level to level, as follows: freedom of social, political, and religious activities; control of the levying of taxes; establishment of universal education; the fostering of science; the recognition of sex equality; a universal language; the ending of war; the pursuit of wisdom, and the evolution of a world religion. These are the prerequisites of progressive government and the earmarks of ideal statehood. Urantia is far from the realization of these exalted ideals.

Paper 72: Government on a Neighboring Planet
Melchizedek

BY permission of Lanaforge and with the approval of the Most Highs of Edentia, I am authorized to narrate something of the social, moral, and political life of the most advanced human race living on a not far-distant planet belonging to the Satania system. This planet has experienced a history most like that of Urantia.

72:1. The Continental Nation

A very superior civilization is evolving on an isolated continent about the size of Australia. Its people are a mixed race, predominantly blue and yellow, having a slightly greater proportion of violet than the so-called white race of Urantia. These people are self-sustaining, that is, they can live indefinitely without importing anything from the surrounding nations. The development from the tribal stage to the appearance of strong rulers and kings occupied thousands of years. The transition from monarchy to a representative form of government was gradual, the kings remaining as mere social or sentimental figureheads. The present republic has now been in existence just two hundred years, during which time there has been a continuous progression toward progressive governmental techniques.

72:2. Political Organization

The central government of this continental nation consists of a strong federation of one hundred comparatively free states. These states elect their governors and legislators for ten years, and none are eligible for re-election. There are five different types of metropolitan government. No city is permitted to have more than one million inhabitants.

The federal government embraces three co-ordinate divisions: executive, legislative, and judicial. The federal chief executive is elected every six years by universal territorial suffrage. He is advised by a supercabinet composed of all living ex-chief executives. The legislative division embraces three houses: the upper house, the lower house, and the house of elder statesmen—the scope of this latter body is purely advisory. This nation is adjudicated by two major court systems—the law courts and the socioeconomic courts.

72:3. The Home Life

These people regard the home as the basic institution of their civilization. On this continent it is against the law for two families to live under the same roof. The smallest homesite permitted must provide fifty thousand square feet of land. Attendance of parents, both fathers and mothers, at the parental schools of child culture is compulsory. All sex instruction is administered in the home by parents and religious training is the exclusive privilege of parents. Purely religious instruction is given publicly only in the temples of philosophy. Children remain legally subject to their parents until they are fifteen, when the first initiation into civic responsibility is held. Suffrage is conferred at twenty, the right to marry without parental consent is not bestowed until twenty-five, and children must leave home on reaching the age of thirty. Permission to marry is only granted after one year's notice of intention, and after both bride and groom present certificates showing that they have been duly instructed in the parental schools regarding the responsibilities of married life. Divorce regulations are somewhat lax, but notwithstanding their easy divorce laws, the rate of divorce is only one tenth that of the civilized races of Urantia.

72:4. The Educational System

The educational system of this nation is compulsory and the student attends from the ages of five to eighteen. These schools are vastly different from those of Urantia. There are no classrooms, only one study is pursued at a time, and after the first three years all pupils become assistant teachers. Books are used only to secure information. The feeble-minded are trained only in agriculture and animal husbandry, and are segregated by sex to prevent parenthood. Everyone takes one month's vacation each year. One quarter of the school time is devoted to play—competitive athletics. The chief object of education on this continent is to make every pupil a self-supporting citizen. Every child graduating from the precollege school system at eighteen is a skilled artisan. Then begins the study of books and the pursuit of special knowledge.

72:5. Industrial Organization

On this unique continent the workers are increasingly becoming shareholders in all industrial concerns. Abolition of slavery was effected gradually by the liberation of two per cent of the slaves each year. Many years ago they deported the last of their inferior slaves. Wages, profits, and other economic problems are not rigidly regulated, but they are in general controlled by the industrial legislatures, while all disputes arising out of industry are passed upon by the industrial courts. Every ten years the regional executives adjust and decree the lawful hours of daily gainful toil. Industry now operates on a five-day week, working four and playing one. These people labor six hours each working day. Vacation is usually spent in travel. Among this people public service is rapidly becoming the chief goal of ambition. These people are also beginning to foster a new form of social disgust—disgust for both idleness and unearned wealth. Slowly but certainly they are conquering their machines.

72:6. Old-Age Insurance

This nation is making dignified government-insurance guarantees of security in old age. All persons must retire from gainful pursuit at sixty-five. This age limit does not apply to government servants or philosophers. The funds for old-age pensions are derived from four sources: one day's earnings each month, bequests, the earnings of compulsory labor in the state mines, and the income from natural resources. Old-age pensions are solely administered by the federal government. Social and political disloyalty are now looked upon as being the most heinous of all crimes.

72:7. Taxation

Cities have no taxing power, neither can they go in debt. They receive per capita allowances from the state treasury and must supplement such revenue from the earnings of their socialistic enterprises and by licensing various commercial activities. The city fire departments are supported by the fire-prevention and insurance foundations. The police forces are recruited almost entirely from the unmarried men between twenty-five and fifty.

There is little or no uniformity among the taxation schemes of the one hundred comparatively free and sovereign states. Basic constitutional provisions prevent levying a tax of more than one per cent on the value of any property in any one year, homesites being exempted.

The federal government cannot go in debt except for purposes of war. Income to support the federal government is derived from the following five sources: import duties, royalties, inheritance tax, leasing military equipment, and natural resources.

72:8. The Special Colleges

There are five special schools: 1. *Statesmanship schools*—national, regional, and state. Various office holders at different levels must hold degrees from these schools of statesmanship. 2. *Schools of philosophy*—these schools are affiliated with the temples of philosophy and are more or less associated with religion. 3. *Institutions of science*—these technical schools are co-ordinated with industry. 4. *Professional training schools*—these special institutions provide the technical training for the various learned professions. 5. *Military and naval schools*—these institutions are devoted to the military training of volunteer citizens from eighteen to thirty years of age. Parental consent is required before twenty-five in order to gain entrance to these schools.

72:9. The Plan of Universal Suffrage

Every man and woman of twenty years and over has one vote. Variously qualified individuals may acquire up to ten votes. All individuals sentenced to compulsory labor in the mines and all governmental servants supported by tax funds are, for the periods of such services, disenfranchised. This does not apply to aged persons who may be retired on pensions at sixty-five. Heavy taxpayers are permitted up to five extra votes. All citizens vote as members of industrial, social, or professional groups, regardless of their residence. There is one exception to this scheme of functional or group suffrage: The election of a federal chief executive every six years is by nation-wide ballot, and no citizen casts over one vote.

These people recognize that, when fifty per cent of a nation is inferior or defective and possesses the ballot, such a nation is doomed. Voting is compulsory, heavy fines being assessed against all who fail to cast their ballots.

72:10. Dealing with Crime

The methods of this people in dealing with crime, insanity, and degeneracy will, no doubt, prove shocking to most Urantians. Ordinary criminals and the defectives are placed, by sexes, in different agricultural colonies. The more serious habitual criminals and the incurably insane are sentenced to death. Recently the country has gone so far as to attempt the prevention of crime by sentencing those who are believed to be potential murderers and major criminals to life service in the detention colonies. If such convicts subsequently demonstrate that they have become more normal, they may be either paroled or pardoned. Efforts to prevent the breeding of criminals and defectives were begun over one hundred years ago and have already yielded gratifying results. There are no prisons or hospitals for the insane—there are only about ten per cent as many of these groups as are found on Urantia.

72:11. Military Preparedness

Graduates of the federal military schools may be commissioned as "guardians of civilization" in seven ranks. The courses pursued by such commissioned officers are four years in length and are invariably correlated with the mastery of some trade or profession. In this way the creation of a professional military class is avoided. Military service during peacetime is purely voluntary, and the enlistments in all branches of the service are for four years. Although these people maintain a powerful war establishment, they have not in over one hundred years employed these military resources in an offensive war. During the last two centuries these people have been called upon to wage nine fierce defensive conflicts, three of which were against mighty confederations of world powers. When at peace with the world, all mobile defense mechanisms are quite fully employed in trade, commerce, and recreation. When war is declared, the entire nation is mobilized. Throughout the period of hostilities military pay obtains in all industries.

72:12. The Other Nations

For the first time in this superior nation a great religious leader has arisen who advocates the sending of missionaries to the inferior surrounding nations. We fear this nation is about to make the mistake that so many others have made when they have endeavored to force a superior culture and religion upon other races. What a wonderful thing could be done on this world if this continental nation of advanced culture would only go out and bring to itself the best of the neighboring peoples and then, after educating them, send them back as emissaries of culture to their benighted brethren!

Urantia is far better prepared for the more immediate realization of a planetary government, which could contribute so mightily to the establishment of world-wide peace under law and could lead to the sometime dawning of a real age of spiritual striving.

Paper 73: The Garden of Eden
Solonia

ALMOST forty thousand years ago, the Life Carriers, the Melchizedek receivers, and Tabamantia, sovereign supervisor of the series of decimal or experimental worlds, recommended that Urantia be granted Material Sons. In a little less than one hundred years, Adam and Eve arrived and began the difficult task of attempting to untangle the confused affairs of a planet retarded by rebellion and resting under the ban of spiritual isolation.

73:1. The Nodites and The Amadonites

The Nodites were the descendants of the rebel members of the Prince's staff. The Amadonites were the descendants of those Andonites who chose to remain loyal with Van and Amadon. There existed a traditional enmity between the Nodites and the Amadonites. In the vicinity of Lake Van and the southern Caspian Sea region, the Nodites mingled and mixed with the Amadonites, and they were numbered among the "mighty men of old." Prior to the arrival of Adam and Eve these groups—Nodites and Amadonites—were the most advanced and cultured races on earth.

73:2. Planning for the Garden

Van told his nearest associates the story of the Material Sons on Jerusem; what he had known of them before ever he came to Urantia. He well knew that these Adamic Sons always lived in simple but charming garden homes and proposed, eighty-three years before the arrival of Adam and Eve, that they devote themselves to the proclamation of their advent and to the preparation of a garden home for their reception. Van and Amadon recruited a corps of over three thousand willing and enthusiastic workers. Van divided his volunteers into one hundred companies with a captain over each. These commissions all began in earnest their preliminary work, and the committee on location for the Garden sallied forth in search of the ideal spot.

73:3. The Garden Site

The committee on location was absent for almost three years. It reported favorably concerning three possible locations: the first was an island in the Persian Gulf; the second, the river location subsequently occupied as the second garden; the third, a long narrow peninsula—almost an island—projecting westward from the eastern shores of the Mediterranean Sea. The committee almost unanimously favored the third selection. This site was chosen, and two years were occupied in transferring the world's cultural headquarters, including the tree of life, to this Mediterranean peninsula. The site chosen for the Garden was probably the most beautiful spot of its kind in all the world, and the climate was then ideal.

73:4. Establishing the Garden

The first task was the building of the brick wall across the neck of the peninsula. This once completed, the real work of landscape beautification and home building could proceed unhindered. A zoological garden was created by building a smaller wall just outside the main wall; the intervening space, occupied by all manner of wild beasts, served as an additional defense against hostile attacks. All flesh eaten by the Garden workers throughout all the years of construction was brought in from the herds maintained under guard on the mainland. This great enterprise was carried through to completion in spite of the difficulties attendant upon the confused status of the world during these troublous times.

73:5. The Garden Home

At the center of the Edenic peninsula was the exquisite stone temple of the Universal Father, the sacred shrine of the Garden. The architectural plans for Eden provided homes and abundant land for one million human beings. At the time of Adam's arrival, though the Garden was only one-fourth finished, it had thousands of miles of irrigation ditches and more than twelve thousand miles of paved paths and roads. The sanitary arrangements of the Garden were far in advance of anything that had been attempted theretofore on Urantia. Before the disruption of the Adamic regime a covered brick-conduit disposal system had been constructed which ran beneath the walls and emptied into the river of Eden almost a mile beyond the outer or lesser wall of the Garden. Although the work of embellishment was hardly finished at the time of Adam's arrival, the place was already a gem of botanic beauty. Never before this time nor after has Urantia harbored such a beautiful and replete exhibition of horticulture and agriculture.

73:6. The Tree of Life

In the center of the Garden temple Van planted the long-guarded tree of life. Van well knew that Adam and Eve would also be dependent on this gift of Edentia for their life maintenance after they appeared on Urantia in material form. This form of sustenance was wholly useless to the ordinary evolutionary beings on Urantia, but was serviceable to the one hundred materialized members of Caligastia's staff and to the one hundred modified Andonites, who were made possessors of that complement of life which made it possible for them to utilize the fruit of the tree of life for an indefinite extension of their otherwise mortal existence. When the plans of the Material Son went astray, Adam and his family were not permitted to carry the core of the tree away from the Garden. It was eventually destroyed by fire.

73:7. The Fate of Eden

The Edenic peninsula had been overrun by lower-grade Nodites for almost four thousand years after Adam left the Garden when, in connection with the violent activity of the surrounding volcanoes and the submergence of the Sicilian land bridge to Africa, the eastern floor of the Mediterranean Sea sank, carrying down beneath the waters the whole peninsula. We do not regard the submergence of Eden as anything but a natural occurrence.

The Melchizedeks counseled Adam not to initiate the program of racial uplift and blending until his own family had numbered one-half million. It was never intended that the Garden should be the permanent home of the Adamites. The instructions given Adam by the Melchizedeks implied that he was to establish racial, continental, and divisional headquarters, while he and Eve were to divide their time among these various world capitals as advisers and co-ordinators of the world-wide ministry of biologic uplift, intellectual advancement, and moral rehabilitation.

Paper 74: Adam and Eve

Solonia

ADAM and Eve arrived on Urantia, from the year A.D. 1934, 37,848 years ago. From the time of their arrival ten days passed before they were re-created for presentation as the world's new rulers.

74:1. Adam and Eve on Jerusem

Adam and Eve belonged to the third physical series and were a little more than eight feet in height. Before embarking for Urantia, they were called before the System Sovereign and his entire cabinet for examination and instruction. The details of Urantia affairs were fully presented; they were exhaustively instructed as to the plans to be pursued in accepting the responsibilities of rulership on such a strife-torn world.

This Jerusem pair left behind them fifty sons and fifty daughters. These children accompanied their parents to the dematerialization headquarters of their order and were the last to bid them farewell and divine speed as they fell asleep in the personality lapse of consciousness which precedes the preparation for seraphic transport. They went forth to their new responsibilities adequately equipped and fully instructed concerning every duty and danger to be encountered on Urantia.

74:2. Arrival of Adam and Eve

When Adam and Eve awakened in the Father's temple on Urantia in the presence of the mighty throng assembled to welcome them, they were face to face with Van and his faithful associate Amadon. (Adam and Eve had fully mastered Van and Amadon's dialect before they departed from Jerusem.) And on that day the runners went in great haste to the rendezvous of the carrier pigeons, shouting: "Let loose the birds; the promised Son has come." Adam and Eve were escorted to the formal reception on the great mound to the north of the temple. Here, at noon, the Urantia reception committee, chaired by Amadon, welcomed them. The next act was the delivery of the charge of planetary custody to Adam and Eve by the senior Melchizedek. Then was heard the archangels' proclamation, and the broadcast voice of Gabriel decreed the second judgment roll call of Urantia and the resurrection of the sleeping survivors. The age of Adam, the third planetary epoch, opens and the new rulers of Urantia start their reign under seemingly favorable conditions.

74:3. Adam and Eve Learn About the Planet

And now, after their formal installation, Adam and Eve became painfully aware of their planetary isolation. It was a serious and disillusioned Son and Daughter of Jerusem who walked that night through the Garden under the shining of the full moon.

The second day Adam and Eve learned more about the details of the Caligastia rebellion and the folly of attempting to achieve planetary advancement independently of the divine plan of progression. The third day was devoted to an inspection of the Garden from the large passenger birds. On the fourth day Adam and Eve addressed the Garden assembly. The fifth day was occupied with the organization of the temporary government. The sixth day was devoted to an inspection of the numerous types of men and animals. The instant Adam glanced at an animal, he would indicate its nature and behavior. When the sixth day of their sojourn on earth was over, Adam and Eve rested for the first time in their new home.

74:4. The First Upheaval

That night strange things were transpiring in the vicinity of the Father's temple. Hundreds of enthusiastic and excited men and women decided that Divinity had descended to earth in bodily form, that Adam and Eve were in reality gods or else so near such an estate as to be worthy of reverent worship. Van protested and made his way out through the throng and, being able to communicate with the midwayers, sent their leader in great haste to Adam. It was early on the morning of this seventh day that Adam held forth and made it clear that only the Father and those whom he designates may be worshiped. Adam and Eve pointed to the Father's temple and said: "Go you now to the material emblem of the Father's invisible presence and bow down in worship of him." And this was the origin of the Sabbath-day tradition.

74:5. Adam's Administration

For almost seven years after Adam's arrival the Melchizedek receivers remained on duty, but the time finally came when they turned the administration of world affairs over to Adam and returned to Jerusem, along with Van and Amadon.

All went fairly well for a time on Urantia. Pursuant to the advice of the Melchizedeks, Adam began to foster the arts of manufacture with the idea of developing trade relations with the outside world. Only a few groups, here and there, were at all ready for the reception of the Adamic culture. The moment Adam's associates began to work outside the Garden, they met the direct and well-planned resistance of Caligastia and Daligastia. For the time being Adam abandoned all effort to establish representative government, but he succeeded in establishing almost one hundred outlying trade and social centers where strong individuals ruled in his name. The sending of ambassadors from one tribe to another dates from the times of Adam.

74:6. Home Life of Adam and Eve

Eve was the mother of five children before the Melchizedeks left. She bore sixty-three children before the default. When Adam and Eve left the Garden, their family consisted of four generations numbering 1,647 pure-line descendants. The Adamic children did not take milk from animals when they ceased to nurse the mother's breast at one year of age; Eve fed them nut milk and juices. There was no cooking in Adam's household. They found their foods—fruits, nuts, and cereals—ready prepared as they ripened. They ate once a day. Adam and Eve also imbibed "light and energy" direct from certain space emanations in conjunction with the ministry of the tree of life.

Their bodies gave forth a shimmer of light, which is the origin of the traditional halo encircling the heads of supposed holy men. Adam and Eve could communicate with each other and with their immediate children over a distance of about fifty miles. The Adamic children attended their own schools until they were sixteen, the younger being taught by the older. The average age of betrothal was eighteen, and at twenty they were eligible for marriage with one another.

74:7. Life in the Garden

The children of Adam from sixteen to twenty were taught in the Urantia schools at the other end of the Garden, serving there also as teachers in the lower grades. The teaching in these schools included instruction regarding health, social relationships, vocational potentials, and athletics. The laws of the Garden were based on the older codes of Dalamatia. Adam endeavored to teach the races sex equality. The public worship hour of Eden was noon; sunset was the hour of family worship. Adam taught his contemporaries all they could comprehend, but it was a difficult task to lead these mixed peoples in the better way.

74:8. The Legend of Creation

The story of the creation of Urantia in six days was based on the tradition that Adam and Eve had spent just six days in their initial survey of the Garden.

The fact of evolution is not a modern discovery; the ancients understood the slow and evolutionary character of human progress. The Old Testament account of creation dates from long after the time of Moses. Because Moses endeavored to trace the lineage of Abraham back to Adam, the Jews assumed that Adam was the first of all mankind, with the result that almost a thousand years after Moses the tradition of creation in six days was written out and subsequently credited to him.

Paper 75: The Default of Adam and Eve
Solonia

AFTER more than one hundred years of effort on Urantia, Adam was able to see very little progress outside the Garden. The situation seemed so desperate as to demand something for relief not embraced in the original plans. Adam and his mate were loyal, but they were sorely distressed by the sorry plight of their world.

75:1. The Urantia Problem

The Adamic mission on experimental, rebellion-seared, and isolated Urantia was a formidable undertaking. No Adam was ever set down on a more difficult world; the obstacles seemed insuperable and the problems beyond creature solution. But Adam and Eve would have sometime met with success had they been more farseeing and patient. They were not willing to settle down to the long, long endurance test. They wanted to see some immediate results, and they did, but the results thus secured proved most disastrous both to themselves and to their world.

75:2. Caligastia's Plot

Caligastia paid frequent visits to the Garden. He soon gave up trying to corrupt Adam deciding to try a wily flank attack on Eve.

The Melchizedeks, before departing, had especially enjoined Eve never to attempt personal or secret methods of furthering her and Adam's mutual undertakings. It did not occur to her that any danger would attach to the increasingly private and confidential visits she was enjoying with a certain Nodite leader named Serapatatia. The whole affair developed so gradually and naturally that she was taken unawares. The Garden dwellers had received much valuable help and co-operation from the Nodites and through them the Edenic regime was now to meet its complete undoing and final overthrow.

75:3. The Temptation of Eve

Serapatatia had made several visits to the Garden and had become deeply impressed with the righteousness of Adam's cause. Shortly after assuming the leadership of the Syrian Nodites, he announced his intention of establishing an affiliation with the work of Adam and Eve in the Garden. Serapatatia became one of the most able and efficient of all of Adam's lieutenants. He contended that if his tribe could have a leader born to them of part origin in the violet stock, it would constitute a powerful tie binding these peoples more closely to the Garden. Serapatatia was altogether honest and wholly sincere in all that he proposed. For more than five years these plans were secretly matured. At last they had developed to the point where Eve consented to have a secret conference with Cano, the most brilliant mind and active leader of the near-by colony of friendly Nodites. Influenced by flattery, enthusiasm, and great personal persuasion, Eve then and there consented to embark upon the much-discussed enterprise. Before she quite realized what was transpiring, the fatal step had been taken. It was done.

75:4. The Realization of Default

The celestial life of the planet was astir. Adam recognized that something was wrong, and he asked Eve to come aside with him in the Garden. And now, for the first time, Adam heard the entire story. They were informed by Solonia, the seraphic voice in the garden, that they had defaulted in the execution of their oaths of trust to the sovereign of the universe. Even though this project of modifying the divine plan had been conceived and executed with entire sincerity and with only the highest motives concerning the welfare of the world, it constituted evil because it represented the wrong way to achieve righteous ends, because it departed from the right way, the divine plan.

75:5. Repercussions of Default

Eve's disillusionment was truly pathetic. It was in the despair of the realization of failure that Adam, the day after Eve's misstep, sought out Laotta and with premeditation committed the folly of Eve. He deliberately chose to share the fate of Eve. When the inhabitants of the Garden learned what had happened to Eve, they became furious and declared war on the nearby Nodite settlement. They swept out through the gates of Eden and down upon these unprepared people, utterly destroying them—not a man, woman, or child was spared. Serapatatia was overcome with consternation and beside himself with fear and remorse. The next day he drowned himself in the great river. The children of Adam sought to comfort their distracted mother while their father wandered in solitude for thirty days. Time passed, but Adam was not certain of the nature of their offense until seventy days after the default of Eve, when the Melchizedek receivers returned to Urantia and assumed jurisdiction over world affairs. And then he knew they had failed.

75:6. Adam and Eve Leave the Garden

When Adam learned that the Nodites were on the march, he sought the counsel of the Melchizedeks, but they refused to advise him. Adam held an all-night conference with some twelve hundred loyal followers and the next day at noon they all went forth from Eden in quest of new homes. On the third day out from the Garden, the Edenic caravan was halted by the arrival of the seraphic transports from Jerusem. The children who had arrived at the age of choice (twenty years) were given the option of remaining on Urantia with their parents or of becoming wards of the Most Highs of Norlatiadek. All children of prechoice age were taken to Edentia. We do not know what disposition is to be made of them.

It was a sad caravan that prepared to journey on. Could anything have been more tragic! To have come to a world in such high hopes, to have been so auspiciously received, and then to go forth in disgrace from Eden, only to lose more than three fourths of their children even before finding a new abiding place!

75:7. Degradation of Adam and Eve

Gabriel appeared, telling them they were adjudged in default but not guilty of rebellion. The Edenic pair were informed that they had degraded themselves to the status of the mortals of the realm. Caligastia did succeed in trapping Adam and Eve, but he did not accomplish his purpose of leading them into open rebellion against the universe government.

75:8. The So-Called Fall of Man

Adam and Eve did fall from their high estate of material sonship down to the lowly status of mortal man. But that was not the fall of man. There never has been a "fall of man." The mortal races have profited enormously from the limited contribution which Adam and his descendants made to the Urantia races.

The history of the human race is one of progressive evolution. Never, in all your ascent to Paradise, will you gain anything by impatiently attempting to circumvent the established and divine plan by shortcuts, personal inventions, or other devices for improving on the way of perfection, to perfection, and for eternal perfection.

Paper 76: The Second Garden

Solonia

THE Edenic company journeyed eastward toward the then pleasant regions between the Tigris and Euphrates rivers. Cain (son of Eve and Cano) and Sansa (daughter of Adam and Laotta) were both born before the Adamic caravan had reached its destination. Laotta perished at the birth of Sansa. Eve took Sansa to her bosom and reared her along with Cain.

76:1. The Edenites Enter Mesopotamia

It required almost a full year for the caravan of Adam to reach the Euphrates River. This site was known to Adam as one of the three original selections of the committee assigned to choose possible locations for the Garden. Now were the new settlers compelled to wrest a living from unprepared soil and to cope with the realities of life in the face of the natural hostilities and incompatibilities of mortal existence.

76:2. Cain and Abel

Less than two years after Cain's birth, Abel was born. When Abel grew up to the age of twelve years, he elected to be a herder; Cain had chosen to follow agriculture. The two boys never got along well, and this matter of sacrifices further contributed to the growing hatred between them. The boys were respectively eighteen and twenty years of age when the tension between them was finally resolved, one day, when Abel's taunts so infuriated his bellicose brother that Cain turned upon him in wrath and slew him.

To Adam and Eve, Cain was fast becoming the grim reminder of their folly. Cain now went to Eve, his mother, and asked for spiritual help and guidance, and when he honestly sought divine assistance, he received a Thought Adjuster. Cain eventually departed for the land of Nod where he married his distant cousin Remona. He became a great leader among one group of his father's people and did promote peace between this division of the Nodites and the Adamites throughout his lifetime.

76:3. Life in Mesopotamia

Adam wisely spent most of the time training his children and their associates in civil administration, educational methods, and religious devotions. The civil rulers of the Adamites were derived hereditarily from the sons of the first garden. The religious rulers, or priesthood, originated with Seth, the eldest surviving son of Adam and Eve born in the second garden. The Sethite priesthood was a threefold undertaking, embracing religion, health, and education. The Adamites greatly excelled the surrounding peoples in cultural achievement and intellectual development. Here in the lands between the Tigris and Euphrates they maintained the arts of writing, metalworking, pottery making, and weaving, and produced a type of architecture that was not excelled in thousands of years. The home life of the violet peoples was, for their day and age, ideal. Their religious concepts of Deity and the universe were advanced and more or less accurate, their health provisions were, for their time, excellent, and their methods of education have never since been surpassed.

76:4. The Violet Race

Adam and Eve were the founders of the violet race of men, the ninth human race to appear on Urantia. Adam and his offspring had blue eyes, and the violet peoples were characterized by fair complexions and light hair color—yellow, red, and brown. Eve did not suffer pain in childbirth. Adam and Eve and their first generation of children did not use the flesh of animals for food. Both the physical and spiritual visions of Adam and Eve were far superior to those of the present-day peoples; they were able to see the midwayers and the angelic hosts. They retained the ability to see these celestial beings for over one hundred years after the default. Their body cells were far more resistant to disease than those of the indigenous evolutionary beings.

After becoming established in the second garden on the Euphrates, Adam elected to leave behind as much of his life plasm as possible to benefit the world after his death. Accordingly, Eve was made the head of a commission of twelve on race improvement, and before Adam died this commission had selected 1,682 of the highest type of women on Urantia, and these women were impregnated with the Adamic life plasm. Their children constituted the early beginnings of the mighty Andite race.

76:5. Death of Adam and Eve

After their default, and shortly after their reduction to mortal status, Adam and Eve were given Thought Adjusters. It was this knowledge of being Adjuster indwelt that greatly heartened them throughout the remainder of their lives. The Edenic pair always proclaimed that a Son of God would sometime come. It seemed too good to be true, but Adam did entertain the thought that strife-torn Urantia might, after all, turn out to be the most fortunate world in the system of Satania, the envied planet of all Nebadon.

Adam lived for 530 years; he died of what might be termed old age. Eve had died nineteen years previously of a weakened heart.

No comprehensive plan for far-reaching world welfare was promulgated to the mortals of earth until the arrival of Machiventa Melchizedek who, with the power, patience, and authority of a Son of God, did lay the foundations for the further uplift and spiritual rehabilitation of unfortunate Urantia. Misfortune has not, however, been the sole lot of Urantia; this very background of darkness did so appeal to Michael of Nebadon that he selected this world as the arena wherein to reveal the loving personality of the Father in heaven.

76:6. Survival of Adam and Eve

Adam and Eve did not long rest in the oblivion of the unconscious sleep of the mortals of the realm. On the third day after Adam's death, supermortals directed the special roll call of the distinguished survivors of the Adamic default on Urantia, and Adam and Eve were repersonalized and reassembled in the resurrection halls of the mansion worlds of Satania together with 1,316 of their associates. Adam and Eve quickly passed through the worlds of progressive ascension until they attained citizenship on Jerusem. They were immediately attached to the Urantia service on the system capital, later being assigned membership among the four and twenty counselors who constitute the present advisory-control body of Urantia. And thus ends the story of the Planetary Adam and Eve of Urantia, a story of trial, tragedy, and triumph, and in the end, a story of ultimate victory for their world and its rebellion-tossed and evil-harassed inhabitants.

Paper 77: The Midway Creatures
Archangel

ON Urantia there function two distinct orders of midwayers: the primary or senior corps, who came into being back in the days of Dalamatia, and the secondary or younger group, whose origin dates from the times of Adam.

77:1. The Primary Midwayers

The primary midwayers have their genesis in a unique interassociation of the material and the spiritual on Urantia. A nonsexual liaison of a male and a female member of the Planetary Prince's corporeal staff resulted in the appearance of the first-born of the primary midwayers. It was immediately discovered that a creature of this order would be of great service in carrying on the affairs of the Prince's headquarters. After a year of observation the Prince authorized the reproduction of midwayers without restriction. When one thousand such beings had been born to each couple, no more were ever forthcoming. The original corps of 50,000 was brought into being.

77:2. The Nodite Race

When the sixty rebel members of the staff of Prince Caligastia, the followers of Nod, actually engaged in sexual reproduction, their children proved to be far superior in almost every way to both the Andonite and the Sangik peoples. Thus did the Nodite peoples arise out of certain peculiar and unexpected modifications occurring in the life plasm which had been transferred from the bodies of the Andonite contributors to those of the corporeal staff members by the Avalon surgeons

The Nodites furnished one half of the ancestry for the secondary order of midway creatures. The Life Carriers had planned a new type of mortal embracing the union of the conjoint offspring of the Prince's staff with the first-generation offspring of Adam and Eve, whom they hoped would become the teacher-rulers of human society, beings designed for social sovereignty, not civil sovereignty. This project almost completely miscarried.

The pure-line Nodites were a magnificent race, but they gradually mingled with the evolutionary peoples of earth, and their average length of life was little more than that of the evolutionary races. The records of long-lived individuals are also due to the confusion of months and years as time periods.

77:3. The Tower of Babel

After the submergence of Dalamatia the Nodites moved north and east, presently founding the new city of Dilmun as their racial and cultural headquarters. About fifty thousand years after the death of Nod, when the offspring of the Prince's staff had become too numerous to find subsistence in the lands immediately surrounding, and after they had reached out to intermarry with the Andonite and Sangik tribes adjoining their borders, it occurred to their leaders that something should be done to preserve their racial unity. After much deliberation the plan of Bablot (Babel), to erect a pretentious temple of racial glorification, was endorsed. After four and a half years of work a great dispute arose about the object and motive for the erection of the tower, and the contentions became so bitter that all work stopped. They fell to fighting until well-nigh obliterated. About twelve thousand years ago a second attempt to erect the tower of Babel was made but there was not sufficient support for the enterprise. This region was long known as the land of Babel.

77:4. Nodite Centers of Civilization

The dispersion of the Nodites was an immediate result of the internecine conflict over the tower of Babel. There were four great Nodite centers: *the western or Syrian Nodites*, remnants of the nationalistic or racial memorialists who journeyed northward; *the eastern or Elamite Nodites*, the culture and commerce advocates who migrated in large numbers eastward into Elam and there united with the mixed Sangik tribes; *the central or pre-Sumerian Nodites* who blended with the Adamites to found the Sumerian peoples of historic times; and *the northern Nodites and Amadonites—the Vanites*, descendants of those who had forsaken the leadership of Nod and his successors for that of Van and Amadon and who settled about the shores of Lake Van.

Ten thousand years ago the Vanite ancestors of the Assyrians taught that their moral law of seven commandments had been given to Van by the Gods upon Mount Ararat. Since much of your tradition of these ancient times was acquired in connection with the Babylonian story of the flood, it is not surprising that Mount Ararat and its region were woven into the later Jewish story of Noah and the universal flood.

Even in the times of Adam the Nodites were still an able people. Some of the most capable minds serving on Adam's staff were of this race.

77:5. Adamson and Ratta

Adamson, the eldest son of Adam and Eve, was among that group of the children who elected to remain on earth with their father and mother. Adamson was 120 years old at the time of the Adamic default and had been the father of thirty-two pure-line children of the first garden. His mate and children elected to go to Edentia. He did much to forward the early activities of defense and construction, but decided to leave for the north at the earliest opportunity. A company of twenty-seven followed Adamson northward in quest of the people he had heard Van and Amadon tell about. In a little over three years Adamson's party actually found the object of their adventure, and among these people he discovered a wonderful and beautiful woman, twenty years old, who claimed to be the last pure-line descendant of the Prince's staff. This woman, Ratta, had about decided not to mate, but she lost her heart to the majestic Adamson. In a little more than three months they were married.

Adamson and Ratta had a family of sixty-seven children. Every fourth child born to them was of a unique order. It was often invisible. When the second strangely behaving offspring arrived, Adamson decided to mate them, since one was male and the other female, and this is the origin of the secondary order of midwayers. Within one hundred years, before this phenomenon ceased, almost two thousand were brought into being. Adamson and Ratta thus had at their command this corps of marvelous helpers, who labored with them throughout their long lives to assist in the propagation of advanced truth and in the spread of higher standards of spiritual, intellectual, and physical living.

77:6. The Secondary Midwayers

Among the children of Adamson there were just sixteen of the peculiar progenitors of the secondary midwayers. These sixteen children lived and died as mortals of the realm, but their electrically energized offspring live on and on, not being subject to the limitations of mortal flesh. Thirty-three of these secondary midwayers, the chiefs of their organization at the death of Adamson, endeavored to swing the whole order over to the service of the Melchizedeks. But failing to accomplish this, they deserted their companions and went over in a body to the service of the planetary receivers. The remainder of the secondary midwayers became a strange, unorganized, and unattached influence on Urantia. They were productive of much mischief up to the days of Christ Michael. During his sojourn on earth they all made final decisions as to their future destiny, the loyal majority then enlisting under the leadership of the primary midwayers.

77:7. The Rebel Midwayers

The majority of the primary midwayers went into sin at the time of the Lucifer rebellion; of the original 50,000, 40,119 joined the Caligastia secession. The original number of secondary midwayers was 1,984, and of these 873 failed to align themselves with the rule of Michael. No one can forecast the future of these fallen creatures. Both groups of rebel midwayers are now held in custody awaiting the final adjudication of the affairs of the system rebellion. On no world can evil spirits possess any mortal mind subsequent to the life of a Paradise bestowal Son. Since the day of Pentecost there never again can be such a thing as demoniacal possession.

77:8. The United Midwayers

The primary and secondary midwayers now function as a single corps numbering 10,992. Both orders are indispensable to the seraphim who serve as personal guardians to mortals. The United Midwayers of Urantia are organized for service in the following groups: 1. midway messengers; 2. planetary sentinels—observers for supernatural beings; 3. contact personalities—such as with the subject through whom these communications were transmitted; and 4. progress helpers.

The secondary midwayers exist just outside the range of mortal vision and can make physical contact with "material things." Their chief work today is that of unperceived personal-liaison associates of those men and women who constitute the planetary reserve corps of destiny. It should be made clear that the midway creatures are not involved in the sordid performances of "spiritualism" or "mediumship."

77:9. The Permanent Citizens of Urantia

As actual citizens of Urantia, the midwayers have a kinship interest in the destiny of this sphere. Their determination is suggested by the motto of their order: "What the United Midwayers undertake, the United Midwayers do." 1-2-3 the first, a primary midwayer, serves at present on Jerusem as a member of the twenty-four counselors. Midwayers never cease to grow in wisdom and experience. There are many great minds and mighty spirits among the Urantia midway corps. Midwayers are the skillful ministers who bridge the gap between the material and spiritual affairs of Urantia.

Paper 78:
The Violet Race After the Days of Adam

Archangel

THE second Eden was the cradle of civilization for almost thirty thousand years. The planetary history of the violet race began about 35,000 B.C., and extended down through its amalgamation with the Nodite and Sangik races, about 15,000 B.C., to form the Andite peoples, and on to its final disappearance from the Mesopotamian homelands, about 2000 B.C.

78:1. Racial and Cultural Distribution

Thirty-five thousand years ago the world at large possessed little culture. Certain centers of civilization existed here and there, but most of Urantia languished in savagery. Racial and cultural distribution was as follows:

1. *The violet race—Adamites and Adamsonites* had their chief center in the second garden; their secondary or northern center was the Adamsonite headquarters situated east of the southern shore of the Caspian Sea.

2. *Pre-Sumerians and other Nodites* were also present in Mesopotamia and became thoroughly admixed with the Adamites to the north.

3. *The Andonites* had settlements to the north and east of the Adamson headquarters, were scattered throughout Turkestan and the northlands of the Eurasian continent, together with Iceland and Greenland.

4. *The red man* occupied the Americas, having been driven out of Asia.

5. *The yellow race* were in control of eastern Asia.

6. *The blue race* was scattered all over Europe, with centers of culture in the then fertile valleys of the Mediterranean basin and in northwestern Europe.

7. *Pre-Dravidian India* embraced every race on earth, but especially the green, orange, and black.

8. *The Sahara civilization* consisted of superior elements of the indigo race which carried extensive strains of the submerged orange and green races.

9. *The Mediterranean basin* harbored the most highly blended race outside of India. Here blue men from the north and Saharans from the south met and mingled with Nodites and Adamites from the east.

This was the picture of the world prior to the beginnings of the great expansions of the violet race, about twenty-five thousand years ago. Adam and Eve contributed much that was of value to the biological, social, moral, and intellectual progress of mankind.

78:2. The Adamites in the Second Garden

For thousands of years the sons of Adam labored along the rivers of Mesopotamia. The heroism displayed in the leadership of the second garden constitutes one of the amazing and inspiring epics of Urantia's history. But the civilization of the second Eden was an artificial structure; it had not been evolved and was therefore doomed to deteriorate until it reached a natural evolutionary level. The civilization of the violet race was predicated on the presence of Adam and on the traditions of the first Eden.

The Adamites were a real nation around 19,000 B.C., numbering four and a half million, and already they had poured forth millions of their progeny into the surrounding peoples.

78:3. Early Expansions of the Adamites

The violet race retained the Edenic traditions of peacefulness for many millenniums, which explains their long delay in making territorial conquests. The mass movement of the Adamites of the later days was extensively northward and thence westward into Europe. From about 30,000 to 10,000 B.C., epoch-making racial mixtures were taking place throughout southwestern Asia. The highland inhabitants of Turkestan and the best of the early Andonites were absorbed by the northward-moving Adamites. This amalgamation led to the adoption of many new ideas; it facilitated the progress of civilization and greatly advanced all phases of art, science, and social culture.

As the period of the early Adamic migrations ended, about 15,000 B.C., there were already more descendants of Adam in Europe and central Asia than anywhere else in the world. These racial distributions, associated with extensive climatic changes, set the world stage for the inauguration of the Andite era of Urantia civilization.

78:4. The Andites

The Andite races were the primary blends of the pure-line violet race and the Nodites plus the evolutionary peoples. The Andites were the best all-round human stock to appear on Urantia since the days of the pure-line violet peoples. It is Andite inheritance that gives to the polyglot mixture of the so-called white races that generalized homogeneity which has been called Caucasoid. As the Adamites united with the Nodite stocks, who were by this time a belligerent race, their Andite descendants became the most skillful and sagacious militarists ever to live on Urantia. These Andites were adventurous; they had roving dispositions. Their later descendants never stopped until they had circumnavigated the globe and discovered the last remote continent.

78:5. The Andite Migrations

The Andites inaugurated new advances throughout Eurasia and North Africa. The so-called Aryan mother tongue was in process of formation in the highlands of Turkestan; it was a blend of the Andonic dialect of that region with the language of the Adamsonites and later Andites.

By 12,000 B.C. three quarters of the Andite stock of the world was resident in northern and eastern Europe. The Andites not only migrated to Europe but to northern China and India. From time to time small groups made their way into Japan, Formosa [Taiwan], the East Indies, and southern China. One hundred and thirty-two of this race, embarking in a fleet of small boats from Japan, eventually reached South America and by intermarriage with the natives of the Andes established the ancestry of the later rulers of the Incas. The migratory conquests of the Andites continued on down to their final dispersions, from 8000 to 6000 B.C. And to every nation to which they journeyed, they contributed humor, art, adventure, music, and manufacture. The culture of Mesopotamia quietly spread out over Europe, India, China, northern Africa, and the Pacific Islands.

78:6. The Last Andite Dispersions

The last three waves of Andites poured out of Mesopotamia between 8000 and 6000 B.C. Sixty-five per cent entered Europe by the Caspian Sea route to conquer and amalgamate with the newly appearing white races—the blend of the blue men and the earlier Andites. Ten per cent moved to the Iranian plateau and Turkestan. Ten per cent of the Mesopotamians turned eastward, where they blended with the Andite-yellow inhabitants. Another ten per cent made their way across Arabia and entered Egypt. Five per cent refused to leave their homes. This group represented the survival of many superior Nodite and Adamite strains. The cultural age of the second garden was terminated by the increasing infiltration of the surrounding inferior stocks. Civilization moved westward to the Nile and the Mediterranean islands.

78:7. The Floods in Mesopotamia

The river dwellers were accustomed to rivers overflowing their banks at certain seasons; these periodic floods were annual events in their lives. These spring floods grew increasingly worse so that eventually the inhabitants of the river regions were driven to the eastern highlands.

The traditions of a time when water covered the whole of the earth's surface are universal. There has never been a universal flood since life was established on Urantia. The Biblical story of Noah, the ark, and the flood is an invention of the Hebrew priesthood during the Babylonian captivity. But Noah really lived; he kept a written record of the days of the river's rise from year to year. He would go to the neighboring river settlements every year and warn them that in so many days the floods would come. Finally a year came in which the annual floods were greatly augmented so that the sudden rise of the waters wiped out the entire village; only Noah and his immediate family were saved in their houseboat. These floods completed the disruption of Andite civilization.

78:8. The Sumerians—Last of the Andites

A small minority of the Andites, the Sumerians, remained in their homeland near the mouths of the Tigrus and Euphrates. The peaceful grain growers of these valleys had long been harassed by the raids of the barbarians of Turkestan and the Iranian plateau. The possession of horses gave these barbarians a tremendous military advantage and in a short time they overran all Mesopotamia. They did not conquer the Sumerians because of the latter's superior intelligence, better weapons, and extensive system of military canals. After the breakup of the early Sumerian confederation the later city-states were ruled by the apostate descendants of the Sethite priests. About 2500 B.C. the Sumerians suffered severe reverses and their capital fell.

This is the story of the violet race after the days of Adam and of the fate of their homeland between the Tigris and Euphrates. Their ancient civilization spread to Asia, Africa, and Europe and produced the ferments which have resulted in the twentieth-century civilization of Urantia.

Paper 79: Andite Expansion in the Orient
Archangel

ASIA is the homeland of the human race. It was on a southern peninsula of this continent that Andon and Fonta were born. Southwestern Asia witnessed the successive civilizations of Dalamatians, Nodites, Adamites, and Andites, and from these regions the potentials of modern civilization spread to the world.

79:1. The Andites of Turkestan

For over twenty-five thousand years, on down to nearly 2000 B.C., the heart of Eurasia was predominantly, though diminishingly, Andite. In the lowlands of Turkestan the Andites made the westward turning around the inland lakes into Europe. Eastern Turkestan and Tibet were the ancient gateways through which these peoples of Mesopotamia penetrated the mountains to the northern lands of the yellow men. The Andite infiltration into India proceeded from the Turkestan highlands into the Punjab. By 8000 B.C. the slowly increasing aridity drove them to the valleys of the Nile, Euphrates, Indus, and Yellow rivers. There was a tremendous exodus of Andites from Turkestan and a new class of men, the traders, began to appear in large numbers.

This is the terminal movement of the so-called Aryans into the Levant and India. The last great manifestation of the submerged military genius of the central Asiatic Andites was in A.D. 1200, when the Mongols under Genghis Khan began the conquest of the greater portion of the Asiatic continent.

79:2. The Andite Conquest of India

India is the only locality where all the Urantia races were blended. The earliest race mixtures in India were a blending of the migrating red and yellow races with the aboriginal Andonites. This group was later weakened by absorbing the greater portion of the green peoples, the orange race, and large numbers of the indigo race. About 15,000 B.C. increasing population pressure throughout Turkestan and Iran occasioned the first really extensive Andite movement toward India. The Andite pressure drove many of the southern and eastern inferiors into Burma [Myanmar] and southern China but not sufficiently to save the invaders from racial obliteration. The Andite conquerors made a desperate attempt to preserve their identity and stem the tide of racial engulfment by the establishment of rigid restrictions regarding intermarriage. Had the Andite conquerors been in numbers three times what they were, then would India have become one of the world's leading centers of cultural civilization.

79:3. Dravidian India

The blending of the Andite conquerors of India with the native stock eventually resulted in that mixed people which has been called Dravidian. The superior culture and religious leanings of the peoples of India date from the early times of Dravidian domination and are due, in part, to the fact that so many of the Sethite priesthood entered India. During these times India bid fair to produce the leading cultural, religious, philosophic, and commercial civilization of the world. But their religion did not persist. Within five thousand years their doctrines of the Paradise Trinity had degenerated into the triune symbol of the fire god. The Dravidians were among the earliest peoples to build cities and to engage in an extensive export and import business. Despite biologic limitations, the Dravidians founded a superior civilization. It was well diffused throughout all India and has survived on down to modern times in the Deccan.

79:4. The Aryan Invasion of India

The second Andite penetration of India was the Aryan invasion during a period of almost five hundred years in the middle of the third millennium before Christ. The early Aryan centers were scattered over the northern half of India. The Aryans made very little racial impression on India except in the northern provinces. In India many types of social organizations flourished from time to time, but the most characteristic feature of society was the persistence of the great social castes that were instituted by the Aryans in an effort to perpetuate racial identity. The people of the premier caste are the lineal cultural descendants of the priests of the second garden. But the Brahman priests were never able to withstand the pagan momentum built up by the sudden contact with the inferior religions of the Deccan. So it was that India failed to produce the high civilization which had been foreshadowed in earlier times. But someday a greater Gautama may arise to lead all India in the search for the living God, and then the world will observe the fruition of the cultural potentialities of a versatile people so long comatose under the benumbing influence of an unprogressing spiritual vision.

79:5. Red Man and Yellow Man

The narrative of eastern Asia is essentially that of the red man and the yellow man. The tribal organization of the red races was formed earlier than that of any other peoples. The red man had reigned supreme in eastern Asia for almost one hundred thousand years before the yellow tribes arrived. More than three hundred thousand years ago the main body of the yellow race entered China. Growing population pressure caused the northward-moving yellow race to begin to push into the hunting grounds of the red man. This encroachment, coupled with natural racial antagonism, culminated in increasing hostilities. In the earlier struggles the red men were generally successful, but the yellow man was an apt pupil in the art of warfare. The red race began to suffer repeated defeats at the aggressive hands of the relentless Chinese. When the land passage to the east, over the Bering isthmus, became passable, these tribes were not slow in forsaking the inhospitable shores of the Asiatic continent. The story of this agelong contest between the red and yellow races is an epic of Urantia history.

It is eighty-five thousand years since the last of the pure red men departed from Asia. The North American Indians never came in contact with even the Andite offspring of Adam and Eve. The red and the yellow races are the only human stocks that ever achieved a high degree of civilization apart from the influences of the Andites.

79:6. The Dawn of Chinese Civilization

Sometime after driving the red man across to North America, the expanding Chinese cleared the Andonites from the river valleys of eastern Asia. In Burma and the peninsula of Indo-China the cultures of India and China mixed and blended to produce the successive civilizations of those regions. Many different races occupied the islands of the Pacific. In general, the southern islands were occupied by peoples carrying a heavy percentage of green and indigo blood. The northern islands were held by Andonites. The ancestors of the Japanese people were not driven off the mainland until 12,000 B.C. Their final exodus was due to the initiative of a chieftain whom they came to regard as a divine personage.

The superiority of the ancient yellow race was due to four great factors: 1. genetic—superior red and Andonic strains; 2. social—peaceableness; 3. spiritual—worship of the One Truth proclaimed by Singlangton; 4. geographic—protected by the mountains to the west and the Pacific to the east.

79:7. The Andites Enter China

About fifteen thousand years ago the Andites, in considerable numbers, entered China. The northern Chinese were more progressive than their brethren in the south. The later waves of Andites brought with them certain of the cultural advances of Mesopotamia. The infusion of this new blood did not add so much to the civilization of the yellow man as it stimulated the further and rapid development of the latent tendencies of the superior Chinese stocks.

The Chinese people did not begin to build cities and engage in manufacture until after 10,000 B.C. The similarities between certain of the early Chinese and Mesopotamian methods of time reckoning, astronomy, and governmental administration were due to the commercial relationships between these two remotely situated centers.

79:8. Later Chinese Civilization

Consciousness of past achievements, the conservatism of an overwhelmingly agricultural people, and a well-developed family life equaled the birth of ancestor veneration. Slowly the genius of the yellow race became diverted from the pursuit of the unknown to the preservation of the known. And this is the reason for the stagnation of what had been the world's most rapidly progressing civilization. The great weakness of ancestor veneration is that it promotes a backward-looking philosophy. Truth is relative and expanding; it lives always in the present, achieving new expression in each generation of men—even in each human life.

The ancient civilization of the yellow race has persisted down through the centuries. The mechanical and religious developments of the white races have been of a high order, but the whites have never excelled the Chinese in family loyalty, group ethics, or personal morality. This ancient culture is even now reawakening to envision anew the transcendent goals of mortal existence, once again to take up the unremitting struggle for never-ending progress.

Paper 80: Andite Expansion in the Occident

Archangel

THE European blue man supplied the biologic foundation which, when its Adamized strains were blended with the later Andite invaders, produced one of the most potent stocks for the attainment of aggressive civilization ever to appear on Urantia since the times of the violet race and their Andite successors.

80:1. The Adamites Enter Europe

Before the last Andites were driven out of the Euphrates valley, many of their brethren had entered Europe as adventurers, teachers, traders, and warriors. In the eastern trough of the Mediterranean the Nodites had established one of their most extensive cultures, and from these centers they had penetrated somewhat into southern Europe and northern Africa. Adam's blood has been shared with most of the human races, but the Adamites very naturally chose union with the blue races of Europe. This technique of race blending, combined with the elimination of inferior strains, produced a dozen or more virile and progressive groups of superior blue men, one of which you have denominated the Cro-Magnons. These circumstances determined the antecedents of modern European civilization.

80:2. Climatic and Geologic Changes

The early expansion of the violet race into Europe was cut short by certain rather sudden climatic and geologic changes. The water-laden winds from the west shifted to the north, gradually turning the great open pasture regions of the Sahara into a barren desert. About the time of these climatic changes in Africa, the isthmus of Gibraltar gave way, quickly raising this inland lake to the level of the Atlantic Ocean. Presently the Sicilian land bridge submerged, creating one sea of the Mediterranean. This cataclysm of nature flooded scores of human settlements and occasioned the greatest loss of life by flood in all the world's history. The descendants of Adam extended their territory into Europe to find the culture of the blue man thousands of years behind that of Asia since this region has been almost entirely out of touch with Mesopotamia.

80:3. The Cro-Magnoid Blue Man

The ancient centers of the culture of the blue man were located along all the rivers of Europe. Thirty-five thousand years ago the European blue races were already a highly blended people. The European civilization of this early post-Adamic period was a unique blend of the vigor and art of the blue men with the creative imagination of the Adamites. It was very difficult for the Adamites to impress their religion upon the Cro-Magnoids because of the tendency of so many to cheat and to debauch the maidens. These Cro-Magnon peoples were a brave and farseeing race. They had courage, but above all they were artists.

The great and relatively sudden climatic modifications drove the races of Europe to change from open-space hunters to herders, and in some measure to fishers and tillers of the soil. These changes, while resulting in cultural advances, produced certain biologic retrogressions. Inferior slaves subsequently greatly deteriorated the whole Cro-Magnon type. A fresh impetus occurred when the final invasion of the Mesopotamians swept over Europe, quickly absorbing the Cro-Magnon type and culture and initiating the civilization of the white races.

80:4. The Andite Invasions of Europe

While the Andites poured into Europe in a steady stream, there were seven major invasions, the last arrivals coming on horseback in three great waves. The Adamites were pacific; the Nodites were belligerent. The union of these stocks produced the able, aggressive Andites who made military conquests. The horse was the evolutionary factor which determined the dominance of the Andites in the Occident. As they moved westward across the Russian plains, absorbing the best of the blue man and exterminating the worst, they became blended into one people. These were the ancestors of the so-called Nordic races, the forefathers of the Scandinavian, German, and Anglo-Saxon peoples.

80:5. The Andite Conquest of Northern Europe

When the last waves of Andite cavalry swept over Europe, there were already more men with Andite inheritance in that region than were to be found in all the rest of the world. For three thousand years the military headquarters of the northern Andites was in Denmark. From this central point there went forth successive waves of conquest, which grew decreasingly Andite and increasingly white with the blending of the conquered peoples. The decisive struggles between the white man and the blue man were fought out in the valley of the Somme. Thor, the victorious commander of the armies of the north in the final battle of the Somme, became the hero of the northern white tribes and later on was revered as a god by some of them. By 5000 B.C. the evolving white races were dominant throughout all of northern Europe.

80:6. The Andites Along the Nile

Egypt became the successor of Mesopotamia as the headquarters of the most advanced group on earth. When the last exodus from the Euphrates valley occurred, Egypt was fortunate in gaining so many of the most skillful artists and artisans. The Egyptians very early assembled their municipal deities into an elaborate national system of gods and developed an extensive theology with a burdensome priesthood. Imhotep, an Andite architectural genius, built the first stone pyramid. This brilliant epoch of culture was cut short by internal warfare, and the country was soon overrun by the inferior tribes from inhospitable Arabia and by the blacks from the south.

80:7. Andites of the Mediterranean Isles

During the decline of culture in Mesopotamia there persisted for some time a superior civilization on the islands of the eastern Mediterranean. About 12,000 B.C. a brilliant tribe of Andites migrated to Crete. It was in Crete that the mother cult of the descendants of Cain, glorifying Eve, attained its greatest vogue. Almost two thousand years after the settlement of Crete a group of the tall descendants of Adamson made their way over the northern islands to Greece. These later sons of Adamson carried the then most valuable strains of the emerging white races. The Greeks were not only great teachers and artists, they were also the world's greatest traders and colonizers. They succeeded in planting so many outposts of culture to the west that a great many of the advances in early Greek civilization persisted in the later peoples of southern Europe. By about 6500 B.C. there occurred a great decline in the spiritual heritage of the Andites.

80:8. The Danubian Andonites

The Andite peoples of the Euphrates valley migrated north to Europe to mingle with the blue men and west into the Mediterranean regions to mix with the remnants of the commingled Saharans and the southern blue men. These two branches of the white race were widely separated by the survivors of the earlier Andonite tribes who were dispersed through most of the mountainous regions of central and southeastern Europe. The ancient Hittites stemmed directly from the Andonite stock; their pale skins and broad heads were typical of that race and of their later Jewish descendants who, while having a culture and religion derived from the Andites, spoke a distinctly Andonite tongue. The Danubian Andonites became mother worshipers as the result of the work of the missionaries from Crete. Much of central Europe was thus early settled by these mixed types of the broad-headed white races which practiced mother worship and the religious rite of cremating the dead.

80:9. The Three White Races

The racial blend in Europe toward the close of the Andite migrations, around 3000 B.C., became generalized into the three white races as follows: 1. *The northern white race,* the so-called Nordic race, consisted primarily of the blue man plus the Andite, considerable Andonite, together with smaller amounts of the red and yellow Sangik. These Nordics were typically long-headed, tall, and blond. 2. *The central white race* was predominantly Andonite but included strains of blue, yellow and Andite. They are driven like a wedge between the Nordic and the Mediterranean races. These Alpine people are broad-headed, swarthy, and stocky. 3. *The southern white race* consisted of a blend of the Andite and the blue man, with a smaller Andonite strain than in the north. This Mediterranean race also absorbed a considerable amount of secondary Sangik blood. In general its members were short, long-headed, and brunet.

But it is a fallacy to presume to classify the white peoples as Nordic, Alpine, and Mediterranean. For a long time European culture has been experiencing its best opportunity for blending in the cosmopolitan population of North America; and the future of that continent will be determined by the quality of the racial factors which are permitted to enter into its present and future populations, as well as by the level of the social culture which is maintained.

Paper 81: Development of Modern Civilization
Archangel

EVOLUTION can be delayed but it cannot be stopped. The influence of the violet race, though in numbers smaller than planned, produced an advance in civilization which has far exceeded the progress of mankind throughout its entire previous existence of almost a million years.

81:1. The Cradle of Civilization

For about thirty-five thousand years after the days of Adam, the cradle of civilization was in southwestern Asia. Around 15,000 B.C. climatic evolution compelled Eurasian man to abandon hunting for the more advanced callings of herding and farming. The evolutionary peoples (notably the Chinese) early learned to plant seeds and to cultivate crops through observation of the sprouting of seeds accidentally moistened or which had been put in graves as food for the departed. But throughout southwest Asia the Andites were carrying out the improved agricultural techniques inherited from their ancestors, who had made farming and gardening the chief pursuits.

The enforced changes in living conditions caused a large proportion of the human race to become omnivorous; the combination of wheat, rice, and vegetables with the flesh of the herds marked a great forward step in the health and vigor of the ancient peoples.

81:2. The Tools of Civilization

The growth of culture is predicated upon the development of the tools of civilization. The first four great advances in human civilization were the taming of fire, the domestication of animals, the enslavement of captives, and private property.

The ancients sought a supernatural explanation for all natural phenomena not within the range of their personal comprehension; and many moderns continue to do this. The frank, honest, and fearless search for true causes gave birth to modern science.

Domestication of animals prepared the way for both agriculture and transportation. The Andites of Turkestan were the first peoples to extensively domesticate the horse. Through animals, fire, wind, water, electricity, and other undiscovered sources of energy, man has liberated himself from the necessity for unremitting toil. Civilization can never flourish, much less be established, until man has *leisure* to think, to plan, to imagine new and better ways of doing things.

81:3. Cities, Manufacture, and Commerce

The climatic destruction of the rich, open grasslands around 12,000 B.C. compelled the men of those regions to resort to new forms of industry and crude manufacturing. The chief business of the superior tribes became the cultivation of the soil, with commerce as a sideline. Trade brought into fellowship different sorts of human beings, thus contributing to a more speedy cross-fertilization of culture.

About this time the era of the independent cities was dawning. These primitive trading and manufacturing cities were always surrounded by zones of agriculture and cattle raising. While industry was promoted by the elevation of the standards of living, the early races were not overly neat and clean, and the average primitive community rose from one to two feet every twenty-five years as the result of accumulation of dirt and trash.

The Andites early learned to work in iron, gold, and copper. The discovery of mixing copper and tin to make bronze was made by one of the Adamsonites of Turkestan. By 5000 B.C. the horse was in general use throughout civilized and semicivilized lands. The traveling trader and the roving explorer did more to advance historic civilization than all other influences combined.

81:4. The Mixed Races

At the dawn of historic times, all of Eurasia, northern Africa, and the Pacific Islands is overspread with the composite races of mankind. The Urantia races were originally distinguished by five distinct types of skeletal structure: Andonic, Primary Sangik, Secondary Sangik, Nodite, and Adamic. Mankind was now divided into approximately three classes: the Caucasoid, the Mongoloid, and the Negroid. In North China was a certain blending of Caucasoid and Mongoloid types; in the Levant the Caucasoid and Negroid intermingled; in India, as in South America, all three types were represented.

81:5. Cultural Society

Biologic evolution and cultural civilization are not necessarily correlated. But when lengthy periods of human history are surveyed, it will be observed that eventually evolution and culture become related. Through agriculture, animal domestication and improved architecture, mankind gradually escaped the worst of the incessant struggle to live. Through manufacture and industry, man gradually augmented the pleasure content of mortal life.

Social association is a form of survival insurance which human beings have learned is profitable. Society thus becomes a co-operative scheme for securing various forms of human freedom. Every human right is associated with a social duty. Group and individual rights must be protected, including the regulation of the sex propensity. Liberty subject to group regulation is the legitimate goal of social evolution.

81:6. The Maintenance of Civilization

Culture has slowly spread throughout the world. And this civilization must be maintained and fostered, for there exist today no new sources of culture, no Andites to invigorate and stimulate the slow progress of the evolution of civilization.

The civilization which is now evolving on Urantia is predicated on the following factors:

1. *Natural circumstances.* Climate, weather, and numerous physical conditions are factors in the evolution of culture. The configuration of continents and other land-arrangement situations are very influential in determining peace or war. Very few Urantians have ever had such a favorable opportunity for continuous and unmolested development as has been enjoyed by the peoples of North America, protected on practically all sides by vast oceans.

2. *Capital goods.* Culture is never developed under conditions of poverty. Cultural civilization is only derived from those conditions of material prosperity which foster leisure combined with ambition.

3. *Scientific knowledge.* The material aspects of civilization must always await the accumulation of scientific data. Science, guided by wisdom, may become man's great social liberator.

4. *Human resources.* Man power is indispensable to the spread of civilization; but there comes a point in population increase where further growth is suicidal. Wisdom can be secured only through experience and by men and women who are innately intelligent.

5. *Effectiveness of material resources.* Much depends on the wisdom displayed in the utilization of natural resources, scientific knowledge, capital goods, and human potentials.

6. *Effectiveness of language.* Language is man's greatest and most serviceable thinking tool. Language differences have ever been the great barrier to the extension of peace. Today, there is great need for further linguistic development. A universal language promotes peace, insures culture, and augments happiness.

7. *Effectiveness of mechanical devices.* The progress of civilization is directly related to the development and possession of tools, machines, and channels of distribution.

8. *Character of torchbearers.* Social inheritance enables man to stand on the shoulders of all who have preceded him. The home is basic to passing on culture. The improvement in education has not kept pace with the expanding social structure. The greatest twentieth-century influences contributing to the furtherance of civilization and culture are the marked increase in world travel and communication.

9. *The racial ideals.* The ideals of one generation carve out the channels of destiny for immediate posterity. Spiritual idealism is the energy which really uplifts and advances human culture.

10. *Co-ordination of specialists.* Civilization is now dependent on the effective co-ordination of specialists.

11. *Place-finding devices.* Some technique for directing individuals to suitable employment must be devised. People should be trained in one or more methods of commonplace labor, trades or callings which could be utilized when they were transiently unemployed in their specialized work.

12. *The willingness to co-operate.* The maintenance of world-wide civilization is dependent on human beings learning how to live together in peace and fraternity.

13. *Effective and wise leadership.* The teamwork of social co-operation is dependent on wise and progressives leadership.

14. *Social changes.* Man should be unafraid to experiment with the mechanisms of society. *No great social or economic change should be attempted suddenly.*

15. *The prevention of transitional breakdown.* The great danger of civilization is the threat of breakdown during the time of transition. Civilization is never really jeopardized until able leadership begins to vanish, and the quantity of such wise leadership has never exceeded one per cent of the population. Now human society is plunging forward under the force of the accumulated momentum of all the ages through which civilization has struggled.

Paper 82: The Evolution of Marriage

Chief of Seraphim

MARRIAGE has given mankind the home, and the home is the crowning glory of the whole long and arduous evolutionary struggle. While religious, social, and educational institutions are all essential to the survival of cultural civilization, the family is the master civilizer.

82:1. The Mating Instinct

Notwithstanding the personality gulf between men and women, the sex urge is sufficient to insure their coming together for the reproduction of the species. The all-absorbing sex passion of the more highly civilized peoples is chiefly due to race mixtures, especially the influence of the Nodites and Adamites. Of the evolutionary races, the red man had the highest sex code.

The mating instinct is one of the dominant physical driving forces of human beings. This great biologic urge becomes the impulse hub for all sorts of associated instincts, emotions, and usages physical, intellectual, moral, and social. No human emotion or impulse, when unbridled and overindulged, can produce so much harm and sorrow as this powerful sex urge. Self-control, more and more self-control, is the ever-increasing demand of advancing mankind and the supreme test of any civilization.

82:2. The Restrictive Taboos

The story of the evolution of marriage is simply the history of sex control. This social conflict consists in the unending war between basic instincts and evolving ethics. Mating has progressed through a multitude of transitions from a state of almost complete sex license to the twentieth-century standards of relatively complete sex restriction. It was long the practice to suspend all sex regulations on high festival days, especially May Day. Women have always been subject to more restrictive taboos than men. Married women have always borne some mark which set them apart as a class by themselves.

82:3. Early Marriage Mores

In primitive times marriage was the price of social standing. Many early tribes required feats of stealing as a qualification for marriage; later peoples substituted athletic contests and competitive games. The winners of these contests were given the choice of the season's brides. Some marriage tests required the groom to enter the bride's family for at least one year, there to live and labor and prove that he was worthy of the wife he sought. If the bride had borne a child before marriage, she was all the more valuable; her fertility was thus assured. Many primitive tribes sanctioned trial marriage until the woman became pregnant; the contracting individuals married permanently just as soon as fertility was established.

It was also a general belief that unmarried persons could not enter spiritland, which was an incentive for child marriages. The ancients believed that even the dead must be married. This was arranged by the parents of the two dead people. Under certain mores widowhood was greatly to be feared, widows being either killed or allowed to commit suicide on their husbands' graves to go to spiritland with their spouses.

82:4. Marriage Under the Property Mores

Marriage has always been closely linked with both property and religion. Property has been the stabilizer of marriage. The ancients married for the advantage and welfare of the group, wherefore their marriages were planned and arranged by the group, their parents and elders. Woman started out as the property of her father, who transferred his title to her husband. As chastity came more into demand, it became the practice literally to cage up girls in order to assure their virginity. Those women who were found by the grooms' mothers not to be virgins gave origin to the professional prostitute classes.

82:5. Endogamy and Exogamy

Very early the savage observed that race mixture improved the quality of the offspring. Woman has usually favored the practice of in-marriage; man, outmarriage. In an effort to conserve property, women were required to choose husbands within their fathers' tribes. In-mating was also practiced in an effort to preserve craft secrets. The Nodites were one of the great in-marriage groups. The violet race, among whom matings at first were between brother and sister, influenced such marriages in early Egypt, Syria, and Mesopotamia. There were many steps in the evolution of in-marriage into the modern practice of outmarriage. Even after the taboo rested upon in-marriages for the common people, chiefs and kings were permitted to marry those of close kin. Outmarriage was a peace promoter and a nation builder.

82:6. Racial Mixtures

There are no pure races in the world today. While the so-called white race is predominantly descended from the ancient blue man, it is admixed more or less with all other races much as is the red man of the Americas. If the present-day races of Urantia could be freed from the curse of their lowest strata of deteriorated, antisocial, feeble-minded, and outcast specimens, there would be little objection to a limited race amalgamation. Hybridization of superior and dissimilar stocks is the secret of the creation of new and more vigorous strains, as is shown in the present population of the United States of North America. Interbreeding between the highest types of the white, red, and yellow races would immediately bring into existence many new and biologically effective characteristics.

Paper 83: The Marriage Institution

Chief of Seraphim

THE safeguard of marriage and the resultant family is the simple and innate biologic fact that men and women positively will not live without each other. Sex has been the unrecognized and unsuspected civilizer of the savage; it unerringly compels man to think and eventually leads him to love.

83:1. Marriage as a Societal Institution

Marriage is society's mechanism designed to regulate and control those many human relations which arise out of the physical fact of bisexuality. The human family is a distinctly human institution. Marriage is an institution of society, not a department of the church. Marriage is slowly becoming mutual, romantic, parental, poetical, affectionate, ethical, and even idealistic. Among the ancients, personal affection was not strongly linked to sex attraction; men and women became fond of one another largely because of living and working together.

83:2. Courtship and Betrothal

Primitive marriages were always planned by the parents. The transition stage to the times of free choosing was occupied by the marriage broker. These matchmakers were at first the barbers; later, the priests. Marriage was originally a group affair, then a family matter; only recently has it become an individual adventure. Marriage by capture preceded marriage by contract. An early type of wedding ceremony was the mimic flight, a sort of elopement rehearsal which was once a common practice. As civilization has progressed, women have had an increasing part in all phases of courtship and marriage. Increasing love, romance, and personal selection in premarital courtship are an Andite contribution to the world races.

83:3. Purchase and Dowry

The ancients mistrusted love and promises; they thought that abiding unions must be guaranteed by some tangible security, property. Bride purchase was not always just a cold-blooded money transaction; service was equivalent to cash in the purchase of a wife. If an otherwise desirable man could not pay for his wife, he could be adopted as a son by the girl's father and then could marry. As civilization progressed, fathers, while continuing to accept the bride purchase price, initiated the custom of giving the pair valuable presents which about equaled the value of the purchase money. The idea of a dowry was to convey the impression of the bride's independence. A man could not divorce a dowered wife without paying back the dowry in full.

83:4. The Wedding Ceremony

The wedding ceremony grew out of the fact that marriage was originally a community affair. Early marriage was a factor in property interests, even as it is today, and therefore required a legal ceremony. The red man was the first to develop the more elaborate celebration of weddings. Lucky days were sought out, Thursday being most favorably regarded, and weddings celebrated at the full of the moon were thought to be exceptionally fortunate.

The custom of throwing grain upon the newlyweds was to insure fecundity. The wearing of the bridal veil is a relic of the times when it was considered necessary to disguise the bride so that jealous and envious spirits might not recognize her. One of the most ancient forms of the wedding ceremony was to have a priest bless the wedding bed to insure the fertility of the union. Primitive man sought protection against marriage failure, which led him to go in quest of priests and magic. And this movement culminated directly in modern church weddings.

83:5. Plural Marriages

The next step from the promiscuity of the herd was group marriage. Following group marriage came the practice of polygyny, with one man and many wives. In the early stages of monogamy, a man might have only one wife, but he could maintain sex relations with any number of concubines. Concubinage was the steppingstone to true monogamy. The purpose of a harem was to build up a strong and numerous body of blood kin.

83:6. True Monogamy—Pair Marriage

Monogamy is cultural and societal, artificial and unnatural to evolutionary man. It was wholly natural to the purer Nodites and Adamites and has been of great cultural value to all advanced races. It is always best for the children. Monogamy always has been, now is, and forever will be the idealistic goal of human sex evolution. This ideal of true pair marriage entails the acme of all human virtues, rugged self-control. It contributes to a delicacy of sentiment, a refinement of moral character, and spiritual growth. Pair marriage favors and fosters that intimate understanding and effective co-operation which is best for parental happiness, child welfare, and social efficiency. Marriage is gradually evolving into a magnificent institution of self-culture, self-control, self-expression, and self-perpetuation.

83:7. The Dissolution of Wedlock

The inauguration of wife purchase and wife dowry, by introducing a property penalty for marriage failure, did much to lessen separation. The social pressure of community standing and property privileges has always been potent in the maintenance of the marriage mores. Down through the ages marriage has made steady progress and stands on advanced ground in the modern world. The new and sudden substitution of the more ideal but extremely individualistic love motive in marriage for the older and long-established property motive, has unavoidably caused the marriage institution to become temporarily unstable. Just so long as society fails to provide adequate premarital training, and so long as unwise and immature youthful idealism is to be the arbiter of the entrance upon marriage, just so long will divorce remain prevalent.

83:8. The Idealization of Marriage

Marriage which culminates in the home is indeed man's most exalted institution, but it is essentially human. The likening of human associations to divine associations is most unfortunate. It is also unfortunate that certain groups of mortals have conceived of marriage as being consummated by divine action. Nevertheless, there is an ideal of marriage exhibited by the Material Sons and Daughters of God. After all, the ideal mortal marriage is humanly sacred. Marriage always has been and still is man's supreme dream of temporal ideality. But young men and women should be taught something of the realities of marriage before they are plunged into the exacting demands of the interassociations of family life. The ideals of marriage have made great progress in recent times; among some peoples woman enjoys practically equal rights with her consort. The home institution is now undergoing a serious testing because of the problems so suddenly thrust upon the social organization by the precipitate augmentation of woman's liberties.

Paper 84: Marriage and Family Life

Chief of Seraphim

MATERIAL necessity founded marriage, sex hunger embellished it, religion sanctioned and exalted it, the state demanded and regulated it. Home building should be the center and essence of all educational effort.

84:1. Primitive Associations

Woman, because of physical and emotional attachment to her offspring, is dependent on co-operation with the male. It was food hunger which first attracted savage man to woman and the primitive shelter shared by her children.

Primitive man comprehended no connection between sex indulgence and the subsequent birth of a child. Pregnancy was believed to be the result of a woman's being entered by a spirit. Both diet and the evil eye were also believed to be capable of causing pregnancy in a virgin or unmarried woman.

The mother and child relation is natural, strong, and instinctive. A man and a woman, co-operating, are vastly superior in most ways to either two men or two women. This pairing of the sexes enhanced survival and was the very beginning of human society. The sex division of labor also made for comfort and increased happiness.

84:2. The Early Mother-Family

The woman's periodic hemorrhage and her further loss of blood at childbirth early suggested blood as the creator of the child and gave origin to the blood-bond concept of human relationships. In early times all descent was reckoned in the female line. The persistence of the mother-family among the North American red men is one of the chief reasons why the otherwise progressive Iroquois never became a real state. The earliest races gave little credit to the father, looking upon the child as coming altogether from the mother. Later on, when the switch came from the mother-family to the father-family, the father took all credit for the child. The stupendous change from the mother-family to the father-family is one of the most radical and complete right-about-face adjustments ever executed by the human race. This change led at once to greater social expression and increased family adventure.

84:3. The Family Under Father Dominance

Pastoral living tended to create the patriarchal type of family life. All society passed through the stage of the autocratic authority of a patriarchal order. Primitive women unintentionally created their dependence on the male by their admiration and applause for his pugnacity and virility. Woman early learned to trade upon her sex charms. She became more alert and conservative than man. At home woman has usually outgeneraled even the most primitive of men. She has always been the burden bearer, leaving the man's hands free for fighting or hunting. The coming of agriculture enhanced woman's prestige and social standing. In hunting and war man had learned the value of organization, and he introduced these techniques into industry; later, when taking over much of woman's work in the tilling of the soil, he greatly improved on her loose methods of labor.

84:4. Woman's Status in Early Society

Woman's status has always been a social paradox; she has always been a shrewd manager of men. By trading subtly upon her sex charms, she has often been able to exercise dominant power over man. The sexes have had great difficulty in understanding each other. Man found it hard to understand woman, regarding her with a strange mixture of ignorant mistrust and fearful fascination. At one time there was a universal distrust of woman. Childbearing was once generally looked upon as rendering a woman dangerous and unclean.

Under the mores of olden times, every woman, from adolescence to the end of the childbearing period, was subjected to complete family and social quarantine one full week each month. For overworked females it was a period of welcome rest and profitable meditation.

Woman eventually gained the legal right to own, control, and dispose of property and then to hold office in the church and state. She has not yet gained world-wide freedom from seclusion under man's control.

84:5. Woman Under the Developing Mores

In self-perpetuation woman is man's equal, but in the partnership of self-maintenance she labors at a decided disadvantage because of her enforced maternity. Science, not religion, really emancipated woman. Evolution has succeeded in doing what even revelation failed to accomplish. In the ideals of pair marriage, woman has finally won recognition, dignity, independence, equality, and education; but will she prove worthy of this accomplishment? Today woman is undergoing the crucial test of her long world existence!

Civilization never can obliterate the behavior gulf between the sexes. Forever each sex will remain supreme in its own domain, domains determined by biologic differentiation and by mental dissimilarity. Only socially will men and women compete on equal terms.

84:6. The Partnership of Man and Woman

Marriage, the basis of home building, is the highest manifestation of that antagonistic co-operation which so often characterizes the contacts of nature and society. Male and female are, practically regarded, two distinct varieties of the same species living in close and intimate association. Woman has always been the moral standard-bearer and the spiritual leader of mankind. The differences of nature, reaction, viewpoint, and thinking between men and women should be regarded as highly beneficial to mankind. Many orders of universe creatures are created in dual phases of personality manifestation. Such dual associations greatly multiply versatility and overcome inherent limitations. Always, even in the Corps of the Finality, will these two basic variations of humankind continue to intrigue, stimulate, encourage, and assist each other. The family is man's greatest purely human achievement.

84:7. The Ideals of Family Life

Families reflect the quality of society. If the families are good, the society is likewise good. Marriage is now passing out of the property stage into the personal era. The higher the civilization, the greater the joy of parents in the children's advancement and success. The advancing ideals of family life are leading to the concept that bringing a child into the world entails the supreme responsibility of human existence. Any attempt to shift parental responsibility to state or church will prove suicidal to the welfare and advancement of civilization. The family is the fundamental unit of fraternity in which parents and children learn those lessons of patience, altruism, tolerance, and forbearance which are so essential to the realization of brotherhood among all men. But even more, a true family a good family reveals to the parental procreators the attitude of the Creator to his children, while at the same time such true parents portray to their children the first of a long series of ascending disclosures of the love of the Paradise parent of all universe children.

84:8. Dangers of Self-Gratification

The great threat against family life is the menacing rising tide of self-gratification, the modern pleasure mania. Marriage is the only institution of human society which embraces all three of the great incentives for living—self-maintenance, self-perpetuation and self-gratification. The evolving mores have failed to build any distinct institution of self-gratification. And it is due to this failure that all human institutions are so completely shot through with this pleasure pursuit. The hunger of the soul cannot be satisfied with physical pleasures.

All efforts to obtain wholesome diversion and to engage in uplifting play are sound. Let man enjoy himself; let the human race find pleasure in a thousand and one ways; let evolutionary mankind explore all forms of legitimate self-gratification. But look you well to the goal of destiny! Pleasures are indeed suicidal if they succeed in destroying property; self-gratifications have cost a fatal price if they bring about the collapse of marriage, the decadence of family life, and the destruction of the home—man's supreme evolutionary acquirement and civilization's only hope of survival.

Paper 85: The Origins of Worship
Brilliant Evening Star

MAN creates his primitive religions out of his fears and by means of his illusions. As nature worship developed, man's concepts envisioned nature spirits for lakes, trees, waterfalls, rain, and hundreds of other ordinary terrestrial phenomena. At one time or another mortal man has worshiped everything on the face of the earth, including himself. Primitive man worshiped every natural phenomenon he could not comprehend. The inexplicable things of life are still termed "acts of God."

85:1. Worship of Stones and Hills

The first object to be worshiped by evolving man was a stone. Jacob slept on a stone because he venerated it. All ancient clans and tribes had their sacred stones, and most modern peoples manifest a degree of veneration for certain types of stones—their jewels. In India even to this day a stone can be used as a witness. The ancients had a peculiar regard for holes in stones.

Such porous rocks were supposed to be unusually efficacious in curing diseases. Stone worship is even now widespread over the world. The tombstone is a surviving symbol of images and idols which were carved in stone in connection with the spirits of departed fellow beings. Hill worship followed stone worship, and the first hills to be venerated were large stone formations. It presently became the custom to believe that the gods inhabited the mountains. As time passed, certain mountains were associated with certain gods and therefore became holy.

85:2. Worship of Plants and Trees

Plants were first feared and then worshiped because of the intoxicating liquors which were derived therefrom. Primitive man believed that intoxication rendered one divine. Even in modern times alcohol is known as "spirits."

The cults of tree worship are among the oldest religious groups. All early marriages were held under the trees. The Finns believed that most trees were occupied by kind spirits. The inhabitants of India and eastern Russia regarded the tree spirits as being cruel. Except in China, there once existed a universal cult of the tree of life. The belief that water or precious metals beneath the earth's surface can be detected by a wooden divining rod is a relic of the ancient tree cults. The Maypole, the Christmas tree, and the superstitious practice of rapping on wood perpetuate certain of the ancient customs of tree worship and the later-day tree cults.

85:3. The Worship of Animals

Primitive man had a peculiar and fellow feeling for the higher animals. In southern Asia it was early believed that the souls of men came back to earth in animal form. Animals have all been worshiped by one race or another at one time or another. The Hebrews worshiped serpents down to the days of King Hezekiah. The Chinese worship of the dragon is a survival of the snake cults. The wisdom of the serpent was a symbol of Greek medicine and is still employed as an emblem by modern physicians. Early in evolutionary religion the lamb became the typical sacrificial animal and the dove the symbol of peace and love. In religion, symbolism may be either good or bad just to the extent that the symbol does or does not displace the original worshipful idea.

85:4. Worship of the Elements

Mankind has worshiped earth, air, water, and fire. Baptism became a religious ceremonial in Babylon. It was easy for the ancients to imagine that the spirits dwelt in the bubbling springs, gushing fountains, flowing rivers, and raging torrents. A rainbow is worshiped by many of the hill tribes of India; Hebrews and Christians regard it as "the bow of promise." Windstorms with thunder and lightning overawed early man. Fire was mixed up with magic in the minds of primitive fear-ridden mortals. Fire reverence reached its height in Persia, where it long persisted. Vestal virgins were charged with the duty of watching sacred fires, and in the twentieth century candles still burn as a part of the ritual of many religious services

85:5. Worship of the Heavenly Bodies

Moon worship preceded sun worship. Veneration of the moon was at its height during the hunting era, while sun worship became the chief religious ceremony of the subsequent agricultural ages. In Persia sun veneration gave rise to the later Mithraic cult. Later civilizations honored the sun by giving its name to the first day of the week. The sun god was supposed to be the mystic father of the virgin-born sons of destiny who ever and anon were thought to be bestowed as saviors upon favored races. These supernatural infants were always put adrift upon some sacred river to be rescued in an extraordinary manner, after which they would grow up to become miraculous personalities and the deliverers of their peoples.

85:6. Worship of Man

Early man regarded all unusual persons as superhuman. Lunatics, epileptics, and the feeble-minded were often worshiped by their normal-minded fellows, who believed that such abnormal beings were indwelt by the gods. Priests, kings, and prophets were worshiped; the holy men of old were looked upon as inspired by the deities. Later, distinguished souls passed on and were sainted. The worship of man by man reached its height when temporal rulers commanded such veneration from their subjects and, in substantiation of such demands, claimed to have descended from deity. Evolutionary religion creates its gods in the image and likeness of mortal man; revelatory religion seeks to evolve and transform mortal man into the image and likeness of God.

85:7. The Adjutants of Worship and Wisdom

Although nature worship developed naturally, there was operating all this time in primitive minds the sixth adjutant spirit, which had been bestowed upon these peoples as a directing influence of this phase of human evolution. The spirit of worship gave definite origin to the human impulse to worship, notwithstanding that animal fear motivated the expression of this worship. Feeling, not thinking, was the guiding and controlling influence in all evolutionary development. To the primitive mind there was little difference between fearing, shunning, honoring, and worshiping.

When the worship urge is admonished and directed by wisdom—meditative and experiential thinking—it then begins to develop into the phenomenon of real religion. When the seventh adjutant spirit, the spirit of wisdom, achieves effective ministration, then in worship man begins to turn away from nature and natural objects to the God of nature and to the eternal Creator of all things natural.

Paper 86: Early Evolution of Religion
Brilliant Evening Star

THE evolution of religion from the preceding and primitive worship urge is not dependent on revelation. The normal functioning of the human mind under the directive influence of the sixth and seventh mind-adjutants of universal spirit bestowal is wholly sufficient to insure such development.

86:1. Chance: Good Luck and Bad Luck

Aside from the natural worship urge, early evolutionary religion had its roots of origin in the human experiences of chance—so-called luck. Superstitious savages lived lives of peril in which chance played an important role. They always feared a run of good luck, viewing such good fortune as a certain harbinger of calamity. Early man lived in uncertainty and in constant fear of chance—bad luck. He alternated between two potent interests: the passion of getting something for nothing and the fear of getting nothing for something. This notion of chance and luck strongly pervaded the philosophy of all ancient peoples.

86:2. The Personification of Chance

Anxiety was a natural state of the savage mind. Religion was born of the fear of the mysterious, the awe of the unseen, and the dread of the unknown. If one event followed another, the savage considered them to be cause and effect. The savage strives to personalize everything intangible and abstract, and thus both nature and chance become personalized as spirits and later on as gods. Chance is a word which signifies that man is too ignorant or too indolent to determine causes. Primitive man never regarded anything as accidental; always was everything intentional. Exploration of the phenomena of life sooner or later destroys man's belief in chance and luck, substituting therefor a universe of law and order.

86:3. Death—The Inexplicable

Death was the supreme shock to evolving man, the most perplexing combination of chance and mystery. Early man accepted life as a fact, while he regarded death as a visitation of some sort. All human disease and natural death were at first believed to be due to spirit influence. The savage sought help from the supermaterial world, which he vaguely visualized as the source of these mysterious vicissitudes of life.

86:4. The Death-Survival Concept

Early man was much concerned about his breath which was regarded as the one phenomenon which differentiated the living and the dead. Eventually the savage conceived of himself as a double-body and breath. The breath minus the body equaled a spirit. Disembodied spirits seemed to explain the occurrence of the unusual, the extraordinary, and the inexplicable.

The Chinese and Egyptians once believed that soul and body remained together. Among the Egyptians this led to careful tomb construction and efforts at body preservation. Even modern peoples seek to arrest the decay of the dead. The Hebrews made an important advance in the doctrine of the evolution of the soul.

86:5. The Ghost-Soul Concept

The nonmaterial part of man has been variously termed ghost, spirit, shade, phantom, specter, and latterly soul. The belief in dream doubles led directly to the notion that all things animate and inanimate had souls as well as men. Death was finally regarded as "giving up the ghost." As civilization advanced man has become dependent on revelation and personal religious experience for his idea of the soul as the joint creation of the God-knowing mortal mind and its indwelling divine spirit, the Thought Adjuster.

The ancients believed that the soul could leave the body in various ways. The savage looked upon sneezing as an abortive attempt of the soul to escape from the body. The ancients made a practice of awaking sleepers gradually so that the soul might have time to get back into the body. The Hebrews believed that God spoke to them in dreams. The ancients believed that souls could enter animals, which culminated in the werewolf ideas of animal identification. Primitive men thought that the soul qualities could be transferred by the breath. It was long the custom of the eldest son to try to catch the last breath of his dying father.

86:6. The Ghost-Spirit Environment

Very early in the history of mankind the realities of the imaginary world of ghosts and spirits became universally believed, and this newly imagined spirit world became a power in primitive society. The mental and moral life of all mankind was modified for all time by the appearance of this new factor in human thinking and acting. Today many of the world's races have only this crude religion of evolution. Each passing generation smiles at the foolish superstitions of its ancestors while it goes on entertaining those fallacies of thought and worship which will give cause for further smiling on the part of enlightened posterity. The appearance of crude superstitions in evolutionary religion initiated the long and wasteful struggle associated with tombs, temples, sacrifices, and priesthoods. It was a terrible and frightful price to pay, but it was worth all it cost, for man therein achieved a natural consciousness of relative right and wrong; human ethics was born!

86:7. The Function of Primitive Religion

Modern society is removing the business of insurance from the realm of priests and religion to the domain of economics. The religion of ghost fear impressed upon men that they must regulate their conduct, that there was a supermaterial world which was in control of human destiny. But while men are giving up the erroneous doctrine of a spirit cause of the vicissitudes of life, they exhibit a surprising willingness to accept an almost equally fallacious teaching which bids them attribute all human inequalities to political misadaptation, social injustice, and industrial competition. But new legislation will not remedy the facts of birth and the accidents of living. Scientific knowledge, leading to scientific action, is the only antidote for so-called accidental ills. Primitive religion prepared the soil of the human mind, by the powerful and awesome force of false fear, for the bestowal of a bona fide spiritual force of supernatural origin, the Thought Adjuster. And the divine Adjusters have ever since labored to transmute God-fear into God-love. Evolution may be slow, but it is unerringly effective.

Paper 87: The Ghost Cults

Brilliant Evening Star

THE ghost cult evolved as an offset to the hazards of bad luck. Man has had a long and bitter struggle with the ghost cult. Nothing in human history is designed to excite more pity than this picture of man's abject slavery to ghost-spirit fear.

87:1. Ghost Fear

Death was feared because death meant the liberation of another ghost from its physical body. Many tricks and stratagems were practiced in an effort to hoodwink and deceive the ghosts. The primitives feared sickness because they observed it was often a harbinger of death. The sick man was usually removed from the family hut, being taken to a smaller one or left in the open air to die alone. A house in which death had occurred was usually destroyed. If the death hut was not destroyed, the corpse was removed through a hole in the wall. The savages sat up all night and talked when a member of the clan died. In the twentieth century, candles are still burned in death chambers, and men still sit up with the dead. Mourners also returned from a funeral by a different road, lest the ghost follow.

87:2. Ghost Placation

The funeral service originated in man's effort to induce the ghost soul to depart for its future home, and the funeral sermon was originally designed to instruct the new ghost how to get there. It was the custom to provide food and clothes for the ghost's journey. The savage believed that it required from three days to a year for the ghost to get away from the vicinity of the grave. The Eskimos still believe that the soul stays with the body three days. Fasting and other forms of self-denial were thought to be pleasing to the ghosts. The names of the dead were never spoken.

Ghosts wanted wives and servants; a well-to-do savage expected that at least one slave wife would be buried alive at his death. It later became the custom for a widow to commit suicide on her husband's grave. Property sacrifices were also made by burning or burying. Ancient funeral wastes were enormous. Modern man is not supposed to fear ghosts, but custom is strong, and much terrestrial wealth is still consumed on funeral rituals and death ceremonies.

87:3. Ancestor Worship

The advancing ghost cult made ancestor worship inevitable since it became the connecting link between common ghosts and the higher spirits. Ancestor worship was originally more of a fear than a worship. The savage lived in fear of the ghosts of his fellows and spent his spare time planning for the safe conduct of his own ghost after death. Most tribes instituted an all-souls' feast at least once a year. Regardless of varying beliefs in more advanced spirits, all tribes and races once believed in ghosts.

87:4. Good and Bad Ghosts

Ghost fear was the fountainhead of all world religion. When the doctrine of good and bad spirits finally matured, it became the most widespread and persistent of all religious beliefs. Man was at last able to conceive of supermortal forces that were consistent in behavior, and this was one of the most momentous discoveries of truth in the entire history of the evolution of religion and in the expansion of human philosophy. The concept of good and evil as cosmic co-ordinates is, even in the twentieth century, very much alive in human philosophy; most of the world's religions still carry this cultural birthmark of the long-gone days of the emerging ghost cults.

87:5. The Advancing Ghost Cult

Human prosperity was supposed to be especially provocative of the envy of evil spirits. Pretty women were veiled to protect them from the evil eye.

The early prayers always included the petition, "Deliver us from the evil eye." The Koran contains a whole chapter devoted to the evil eye and magic spells, and the Jews fully believed in them. The whole phallic cult grew up as a defense against the evil eye. The custom of depreciating complimentary remarks regarding oneself or family had its origin in pleasing the spirits. During these times, dreams were regarded as prophetic, while everything out of the ordinary was considered an omen. And even today the civilized races are cursed with the belief in signs, tokens, and other superstitious remnants of the advancing ghost cult of old.

87:6. Coercion and Exorcism

In the early days of the cult, man's efforts to influence ghost action were confined to propitiation, attempts by bribery to buy off ill luck, later to win good luck. Ghosts were supposed to be disturbed and frightened by noise; shouting, bells, and drums drove them away from the living. Water was regarded as the best protection against ghosts. Holy water was superior to all other forms, water in which the priests had washed their feet. Through religious ritual and other practices man was soon attempting to compel spirit action. Exorcism was the employment of one spirit to control or banish another. It was long believed that by reverting to the usages of the more ancient mores the spirits and demigods could be forced into desirable action. Modern man is guilty of the same procedure. You address one another in common, everyday language, but when you engage in prayer, you resort to the older style of another generation, the so-called solemn style. The practice of religious pledges and sacred oaths were accompanied by self-torture, later by fasting and prayer. Modern man no longer attempts openly to coerce the spirits, though he still evinces a disposition to bargain with Deity. And he still swears, knocks on wood, and crosses his fingers.

87:7. Nature of Cultism

The cult type of social organization persisted because it provided a symbolism for the preservation and stimulation of moral sentiments and religious loyalties. Notwithstanding that the cult has always retarded social progress, it is regrettable that so many modern believers in moral standards and spiritual ideals have no adequate symbolism—no cult of mutual support—nothing to belong to. Every new revelation of truth has given rise to a new cult, and even the restatement of the religion of Jesus must develop a new and appropriate symbolism. No cult can endure and contribute to the progress of social civilization and individual spiritual attainment unless it is based on the biologic, sociologic, and religious significance of the home. No cult can survive unless it embodies some masterful mystery and conceals some worthful unattainable. But a cult will not function if it is too complex.

No cult can survive if it retards moral growth and fails to foster spiritual progress. The cult is the skeletal structure around which grows the living and dynamic body of personal spiritual experience—true religion.

Paper 88: Fetishes, Charms, and Magic
Brilliant Evening Star

THE concept of a spirit's entering into an inanimate object, an animal, or a human being, is a very ancient belief. This doctrine of spirit possession is nothing more nor less than fetishism. The fetish cult eventually incorporated all of the primitive ideas of ghosts, souls, spirits, and demon possession.

88:1. Belief in Fetishes

Primitive man always wanted to make anything extraordinary into a fetish. The first fetishes were peculiarly marked pebbles, and "sacred stones." The Kaaba and the Stone of Scone are very old fetish stones. Fire and water were also among the early fetishes. fire worship, together with belief in holy water, still survives. When plants and fruits became fetishes, they were taboo as food; the apple was among the first to fall into this category. The serpent was revered in Palestine; the Jews considered it to be the mouthpiece of evil spirits. Even many moderns believe in the charm powers of reptiles. For ages Friday has been regarded as an unlucky day and the number thirteen as an evil numeral. Saliva was a potent fetish; devils could be driven out by spitting on a person. The umbilical cord was a highly prized fetish. Many people looked upon geniuses as fetish personalities possessed by a wise spirit—even infallible. Thus did chiefs, kings, priests, prophets, and church rulers eventually wield great power and exercise unbounded authority.

88:2. Evolution of the Fetish

The ancients always revered the bones of their leaders. Even today, pilgrimages are made to the tombs of great men. Words eventually became fetishes, more especially those which were regarded as God's words; in this way the sacred books of many religions have become fetishistic prisons incarcerating the spiritual imagination of man—the most terrible of all tyrants which enslave men. To take an oath on a "holy book" or to swear by some object of supreme veneration is a form of refined fetishism. To become fetishes, words had to be considered inspired, and the invocation of supposed divinely inspired writings led directly to the establishment of the authority of the church.

88:3. Totemism

Totemism is a combination of social and religious observances. Totems were at one and the same time symbols of the group and their god. The totem eventually evolved into the flag, or national symbol. The medicine man of old never allowed his fetish bag to touch the ground. Civilized peoples in the twentieth century see to it that their flags likewise never touch the ground. The insignia of priestly and kingly office were eventually regarded as fetishes. Fetish kings have ruled by "divine right." Men have also made a fetish of democracy, the exaltation and adoration of the common man's ideas when collectively called "public opinion."

88:4. Magic

Civilized man attacks the problems of a real environment through his science; savage man attempted to solve the real problems of an illusory ghost environment by magic. Magic was the art of obtaining voluntary spirit cooperation and of coercing involuntary spirit aid through the use of fetishes or other and more powerful spirits. Magic gained such a strong hold upon the savage because he could not grasp the concept of natural death. It was at one time not at all uncommon for ten innocent persons to be put to death because of supposed responsibility for one natural death. Magic is natural to a savage. He believes that an enemy can actually be killed by practicing sorcery on his shingled hair or fingernail trimmings. The difficulty in combating magic arises from the fact that fear can kill.

88:5. Magical Charms

Since anything connected with the body could become a fetish, the earliest magic had to do with hair and nails. All excreta of the body were carefully buried; spittle was always covered. Magical charms were concocted from a great variety of things: human flesh, tiger claws, crocodile teeth, poison plant seeds, snake venom, and human hair. The milk of a black cow was highly magical; so also were black cats. The staff or wand was magical, along with drums, bells, and knots. Primitive man believed that names must be treated with respect. Names were pawned for loans. Nowadays one signs his name to a note. The savage had two names; the important one was regarded as too sacred to use on ordinary occasions. He never told his real name to strangers. Any experience of an unusual nature caused him to change his name. Men still invest in titles and degrees.

88:6. The Practice of Magic

Women outnumbered the men among primitive magicians. The savage never doctored himself except on the advice of the specialists in magic. The voodoo doctors of the twentieth century are typical of the magicians of old.

The concept of dual spiritism, good and bad spirits, gave rise to the later beliefs in white and black magic. Word combinations, the ritual of chants and incantations, were highly magical. The sex festivities of May Day were simply imitative magic. Belief in astrology led to the development of astronomy.

In the days of barbarism it was dangerous to know very much; there was always the chance of being executed as a black artist. Gradually science is removing the gambling element from life. But superstitions still linger in the minds of many intelligent human beings who still believe in good luck, the evil eye, and astrology. Ancient magic was the cocoon of modern science. Today, Urantia is in the twilight zone of this intellectual evolution. One half the world is grasping eagerly for the light of truth and the facts of scientific discovery, while the other half languishes in the arms of ancient superstition and but thinly disguised magic.

Paper 89: Sin, Sacrifice, and Atonement

Brilliant Evening Star

THE savage was early possessed with the notion that spirits derive supreme satisfaction from the sight of human misery, suffering, and humiliation. At first, man was only concerned with sins of commission, but later he became exercised over sins of omission. The whole subsequent sacrificial system grew up around these two ideas.

89:1. The Taboo

Observance of a taboo was man's effort to dodge ill luck. It was the earliest form of societal regulation. The seven commandments of Dalamatia and Eden, as well as the ten injunctions of the Hebrews, were definite taboos. But these newer codes were truly emancipating in that they took the place of thousands of pre-existent taboos. The Egyptian taboo on pork has been perpetuated by the Hebraic and Islamic faiths. Methods of eating soon became taboo, and so originated ancient and modern table etiquette. There would be no civilized society to sit in criticism upon primitive man except for these far-flung and multifarious taboos, and the taboo would never have endured but for the upholding sanctions of primitive religion. These achievements of self-control were the real rungs on which man climbed civilization's ascending ladder.

89:2. The Concept of Sin

It was only by the concept of sin that natural death became logical to the primitive mind. Sin was the transgression of taboo, and death was the penalty of sin. The tradition of Adam and the Garden of Eden lent substance to the belief that man started his career in perfection, and that transgression of the taboos—sin—brought him down to his later sorry plight. Community calamity was always regarded as punishment for tribal sin. The idea of confession and forgiveness early appeared in primitive religion. Men would ask forgiveness at a public meeting for sins they intended to commit the following week. Then followed all the ritualistic schemes of purification. All ancient peoples practiced these meaningless ceremonies. Many apparently hygienic customs of the early tribes were largely ceremonial.

89:3. Renunciation and Humiliation

Renunciation came as the next step in religious evolution; fasting was a common practice. These notions of the spiritual dangers of material possession were widely entertained in the times of Philo and Paul, and became incorporated into the writings and teachings of many religions, notably Christianity. The priests of the mother cult were especially active in teaching the virtue of physical suffering, setting the example by submitting themselves to castration. It was only natural that the cult of renunciation and humiliation should have paid attention to sexual gratification. The Apostle Paul was a devotee of this cult, and his personal views are reflected in the teachings which he fastened onto Christian theology. The pity of it all is that his personal opinions have long influenced the teachings of a great world religion. And it is not to be wondered at that all such beliefs fostered the formation of celibate priesthoods.

Someday man should learn how to enjoy liberty without license, nourishment without gluttony, and pleasure without debauchery. Self-control is a better human policy of behavior regulation than is extreme self-denial. Nor did Jesus ever teach these unreasonable views to his followers.

89:4. Origins of Sacrifice

It is but one step from the impulse of worship to the act of sacrifice. Primitive man gauged the value of his sacrifice by the pain which he suffered. The doctrine of original sin, or racial guilt, started every person out in serious debt to the spirit powers. At first man sacrificed the best of everything. As time passed, man became shrewd in his sacrificing, ceasing to offer up his work animals. Sheer necessity eventually drove these semisavages to eat the material part of their sacrifices, the gods having enjoyed the soul thereof. And this custom found justification under the pretense of the ancient sacred meal, a communion service according to modern usage.

89:5. Sacrifices and Cannibalism

Cannibalism was a social, economic, religious, and military custom. Early man enjoyed human flesh, and therefore he offered it as a food gift to his primitive gods. Cannibalism was once well-nigh universal among the evolving races. It was considered an honor to the soul of a friend or fellow tribesman if his body were eaten. The taboo on man-eating originated in Dalamatia and slowly spread over the world.

89:6. Evolution of Human Sacrifice

Human sacrifice was an indirect result of cannibalism as well as its cure. Human sacrifice has been virtually universal. It was less than a thousand years ago that these sacrifices died out in northern Europe. In olden times, when a new building of any importance was started, it was customary to slay a human being as a "foundation sacrifice." Moses had forbidden these foundation sacrifices, but the Israelites reverted to them soon after his death. The spectacle of Abraham constrained to sacrifice his son Isaac, while shocking to civilized susceptibilities, was not a new or strange idea to the men of those days. It was long a prevalent practice for fathers, at times of great emotional stress, to sacrifice their first-born sons. There once existed a world-wide and profound belief that it was necessary to offer a human sacrifice when anything extraordinary or unusual happened.

89:7. Modifications of Human Sacrifice

Moses attempted to end human sacrifices by inaugurating the ransom as a substitute. Those groups which ceased to sacrifice their first-born soon possessed great advantages over less advanced neighbors who continued these atrocious acts. It was then the custom to put an infant away by itself. If the child survived, it was thought that the gods had intervened to preserve him, as in the traditions of Sargon, Moses, Cyrus, and Romulus. First-born sons were then dedicated to colonization. Later, a maiden consecrated to the gods as a sacrifice might elect to redeem her life by the sacred sex service of the temple. It was a religious ceremony to consort with these sacred maidens. Temple harlotry eventually spread throughout southern Europe and Asia. The highest types of women thronged the temple sex marts and devoted their earnings to all kinds of sacred services and works of public good. Many of the highest classes of women thronged the temple sex marts and devoted their earnings to all kinds of sacred services and works of public good. Most men preferred to have such women for wives.

89:8. Redemption and Covenants

Men eventually conceived the idea that the offering of some part of the body could take the place of the older and complete human sacrifice. Men were circumcised; women had their ears pierced. Shaving the head and cutting the hair were likewise forms of religious devotion. The making of eunuchs was at first a modification of the idea of human sacrifice. Evolutionary man eventually acquired such moral dignity that he dared to bargain with his gods.

Early prayer was hardly worship; it was a bargaining petition for health, wealth, and life. And in many respects prayers have not much changed with the passing of the ages.

89:9. Sacrifices and Sacrament

The early rituals of sacrifice bred the later ceremonies of sacrament, and all this ceremonial evolution has exerted a mighty socializing influence. The Hebrews long practiced a sacrament of cakes and wine, and it was from this ceremonial that the later Christian version of the sacrament took its origin. The early Jewish fraternity was a sacrificial blood affair. Paul started out to build a new Christian cult on "the blood of the everlasting covenant." His theologic compromises indicate that even revelation must submit to the graduated control of evolution. According to Paul, Christ became the last and all-sufficient human sacrifice; the divine Judge is now fully and forever satisfied. Many still depend upon blood for salvation, but it has at least become figurative, symbolic, and mystic.

89:10. Forgiveness of Sin

Sin must be redefined as deliberate disloyalty to Deity. The sense or feeling of guilt is the consciousness of the violation of the mores; it is not necessarily sin. There is no real sin in the absence of conscious disloyalty to Deity.

The forgiveness of sin by Deity is the renewal of loyalty relations following a period of the human consciousness of the lapse of such relations as the consequence of conscious rebellion. The forgiveness does not have to be sought, only received as the consciousness of re-establishment of loyalty relations between the creature and the Creator. And all the loyal sons of God are happy, service-loving, and ever-progressive in the Paradise ascent.

Paper 90:
Shamanism—Medicine Men and Priests

Melchizedek

IN response to man's increasingly complex concept of the supermaterial realms, it was inevitably dominated by medicine men, shamans, and priests. Religion thus enters upon a new phase, a stage wherein it gradually becomes secondhand; always does a medicine man, a shaman, or a priest intervene between the religionist and the object of worship. Today most Urantia systems of organized religious belief are passing through this level of evolutionary development.

90:1. The First Shamans—The Medicine Men

The shaman was the ranking medicine man. In many groups the shaman outranked the war chief. Many of these shamans were epileptic, many of the women hysteric. The great majority of the shamans believed in the fact of their spirit possession. Many were shrewd and able tricksters. Sleight-of-hand feats were regarded as supernatural by the common folk, and ventriloquism was first used by shrewd priests. Many of the olden shamans unwittingly stumbled onto hypnotism. When a shaman failed in his undertakings he was either demoted or killed. Thus the honest shamans early perished; only the shrewd actors survived. It was shamanism that took the exclusive direction of tribal affairs out of the hands of the old and the strong and lodged it in the hands of the shrewd, the clever, and the farsighted.

90:2. Shamanistic Practices

The human race very early sought for superhuman help, for revelation; and men believed that the shaman actually received such revelations. In the early development of their profession the shamans began to specialize in such vocations as rain making, disease healing, and crime detecting. Primitive astrology was a world-wide belief and practice; dream interpreting also became widespread. Thousands of supposedly intelligent people still believe that the juxtaposition of the heavenly bodies determines the outcome of various terrestrial adventures. Fortunetellers are still patronized by the credulous. In many ways and by devious methods the olden shamans established their reputations as voices of God and custodians of providence. The shamans dressed well and usually had a number of wives; they were the original aristocracy, being exempt from all tribal restrictions. Ever and anon, true prophets and teachers arose to denounce and expose shamanism.

90:3. The Shamanic Theory of Disease and Death

Since all diseases and death itself were originally regarded as spirit phenomena, it was inevitable that the shamans, while functioning as medicine men and priests, should also have labored as doctors and surgeons. In comparatively recent times it has been believed that sickness is a punishment for sin. The ancient Greeks were among the first to recognize that all disease is the result of natural causes. Slowly and certainly the unfolding of a scientific era is destroying man's age-old theories of sickness and death.

90:4. Medicine Under the Shamans

The entire life of ancient men was prophylactic. They had unbounded faith in their methods of treatment, and that, in itself, is a powerful remedy. It was a great advance in humanitarianism when the evolution of shamancraft produced priests and medicine men who consented to treat disease. The usual method of diagnosing disease was to examine the entrails of an animal. The shamans learned to treat fractures and dislocations, to open boils and abscesses; the shamanesses became adept at midwifery. Cupping and sucking the affected parts, together with bloodletting, were thought to be of value in getting rid of a disease-producing spirit. Vapor baths were highly regarded. Fasting, dieting, and counterirritants were often used as remedial measures. The shamans believed that disease spirits could be driven out of the body by foul-smelling and bad-tasting medicines. The values of raw cocoa and quinine were among the earliest pharmaceutical discoveries. The Greeks were the first to evolve truly rational methods of treating the sick.

90:5. Priests and Rituals

Ritual is the technique of sanctifying custom and myths. The essence of the ritual is the perfection of its performance; among savages it must be practiced with exact precision. Ritual finally developed into the modern types of social ceremonials and religious worship. For tens of thousands of years endless rituals have hampered society and cursed civilization.

The priests have always sought to impress and awe the common people by conducting the religious ritual in an ancient tongue and by sundry magical passes. When religion became institutionalized, these priests claimed to "hold the keys of heaven." The priesthoods have done much to delay scientific development and to hinder spiritual progress. It is not denied that the priests have been a millstone about the neck of the races, but the true religious leaders have been invaluable in pointing the way to higher and better realities.

Paper 91: The Evolution of Prayer

Chief of Midwayers

PRAYER, as an agency of religion, evolved from previous nonreligious monologue and dialogue expressions. With the attainment of self-consciousness by primitive man there occurred the inevitable corollary of other-consciousness, the dual potential of social response and God recognition.

91:1. Primitive Prayer

Religion and its agencies, the chief of which is prayer, are allied only with those values which have general social recognition. Prayer very early became a mighty promoter of social evolution, moral progress, and spiritual attainment. Early men did not perceive that material things were not the province of prayer. True prayer does not appear until the agency of religious ministry is visualized as personal.

91:2. Evolving Prayer

The first prayers were merely verbalized wishes, the expression of sincere desires. Prayer next became a technique of achieving spirit co-operation. And then it attained to the higher function of assisting religion in the conservation of all worth-while values. The truest prayer is in reality a communion between man and his Maker.

In the day-by-day experience of the average mortal, prayer is very much a phenomenon of man's intercourse with his own subconscious. But there is also a domain of prayer wherein the intellectually alert and spiritually progressing individual attains more or less contact with the superconscious levels of the human mind. Prayer contributes greatly to the development of the religious sentiment of an evolving human mind. It is a mighty influence working to prevent isolation of personality.

91:3. Prayer and the Alter Ego

Children, with the dawn of creative imagination, evince a tendency to converse with imaginary companions. In this way a budding ego seeks to hold communion with a fictitious alter ego. When the alter-ego concept is exalted to a superior status of divine dignity, prayer as an agency of religion has appeared. Prayer is always a socializing, moralizing, and spiritualizing practice. Prayer ever has been and ever will be a twofold human experience: a psychologic procedure interassociated with a spiritual technique. Enlightened prayer must recognize the factual presence of the Adjuster so that man can talk face to face, as it were, with a real and genuine and divine alter ego that indwells him—the very presence and essence of the living God, the Universal Father.

91:4. Ethical Praying

Selfish praying transgresses the spirit of all ethics founded on loving justice. Prayer must never be so prostituted as to become a substitute for action. In all your praying be fair; do not expect God to show partiality. When the prayer seeks nothing for the one who prays nor anything for his fellows, then such attitudes of the soul tend to the levels of true worship. The real prayer of faith always contributes to the augmentation of the technique of living.

Remember, even if prayer does not change God, it very often effects great and lasting changes in the one who prays. Prayer has been the ancestor of much peace of mind, cheerfulness, calmness, courage, self-mastery, and fair-mindedness in the men and women of the evolving races.

91:5. Social Repercussions of Prayer

Prayer, as a feature of Deity worship, transcends all other such practices since it leads to the cultivation of divine ideals. Such praying is the enhancement of human character and the profound unification of human personality. Group or congregational praying is very effective in that it is highly socializing in its repercussions. For a prayer to be effective, the person who is prayed for should know that he is being prayed for, and the person who prays should come into intimate social contact with the person for whom he is praying. Those who are God-conscious without symbolism must not deny the grace-ministry of the symbol to those who find it difficult to worship Deity without form and ritual. In prayerful worship, most mortals envision some symbol of the object-goal of their devotions.

91:6. The Province of Prayer

Prayer is not a technique for curing real and organic diseases, but it has contributed enormously to the enjoyment of abundant health and to the cure of numerous mental, emotional, and nervous ailments. And even in actual bacterial disease, prayer has many times added to the efficacy of other remedial procedures. Prayer has turned many an irritable and complaining invalid into a paragon of patience and made him an inspiration to all other human sufferers. Prayer is a sound psychologic practice, aside from its religious implications and its spiritual significance.

Never hesitate to ask God for wisdom and spiritual strength to guide and sustain you while you yourself resolutely and courageously attack the problems at hand. Pray in the light of scientific facts, philosophic wisdom, intellectual sincerity, and spiritual faith. Pray as Jesus taught his disciples—honestly, unselfishly, with fairness, and without doubting. The psychic and spiritual concomitants of the prayer of faith are immediate, personal, and experiential.

91:7. Mysticism, Ecstasy, and Inspiration

The great religious teachers and the prophets of past ages were not extreme mystics. They were God-knowing men and women who best served their God by unselfish ministry to their fellow mortals. Genuine spiritual ecstasy is usually associated with great outward calmness and almost perfect emotional control. The practical test of all these strange religious experiences of mysticism, ecstasy, and inspiration is to observe whether these phenomena cause an individual to: enjoy better and more complete physical health; function more efficiently and practically in his mental life; more completely to spiritualize his day-by-day living; enhance his love for, and appreciation of, truth, beauty, and goodness; conserve social, moral, ethical, and spiritual values; and increase his spiritual insight—God-consciousness.

91:8. Praying as a Personal Experience

Prayer is the effort to adjust the personality to the will of Deity. Prayer may be a spontaneous expression of God-consciousness or a meaningless recitation of theologic formulas. Real praying does attain reality. Prayer elevates man because it is a technique of progressing by the utilization of the ascending spiritual currents of the universe. Genuine prayer adds to spiritual growth, modifies attitudes, and yields that satisfaction which comes from communion with divinity. It is the most potent spiritual-growth stimulus. Words are irrelevant to prayer. God answers the soul's attitude, not the words. Prayer is not a technique of escape from conflict but rather a stimulus to growth in the very face of conflict. Pray only for values, not things; for growth, not for gratification.

91:9. Conditions of Effective Prayer

If you would engage in effective praying, you should bear in mind the laws of prevailing petitions: 1. You must sincerely and courageously face the problems of universe reality. 2. You must have honestly exhausted the human capacity for human adjustment. 3. You must be dedicated to the transforming embrace of spiritual growth. 4. You must make a wholehearted choice of the divine will. 5. You must make an unqualified consecration, and a dynamic dedication, to the actual doing of the Father's will. 6. Your prayer will be directed exclusively for divine wisdom. 7. And you must have faith—living faith.

Paper 92: The Later Evolution of Religion
Melchizedek

MAN possessed a religion of natural origin as a part of his evolutionary experience long before any systematic revelations were made on Urantia. Through the ministry of the adjutants of worship and wisdom along with the Holy Spirit and later the Thought Adjusters, seraphim, and the Spirit of Truth, religious development has been accelerated. Much of the potential of these divine agencies has never yet had opportunity for expression; much will be revealed in the ages to come as mortal religion ascends, level by level, toward the supernal heights of morontia value and spirit truth.

92:1. The Evolutionary Nature of Religion

Religion progressed from nature worship up through ghost worship to fetishism throughout the savage childhood of the races. With the dawn of civilization the human race espoused the more mystic and symbolic beliefs, while now, with approaching maturity, mankind is ripening for the appreciation of real religion, even a beginning of the revelation of truth itself. Religion is society's adjustment, in any age, to that which is mysterious.

Mystery and power have always stimulated religious feelings and fears. Fear has always been the basic religious stimulus. As civilization advances, fear becomes modified by reverence and admiration. Jesus, the revelation of the highest type of religious living, proclaimed that "God is love."

92:2. Religion and the Mores

Religion is the most rigid and unyielding of all human institutions, but it does tardily adjust to changing society. Religion clings to the mores—that which is ancient and supposedly sacred. Novelty has always been regarded as sacrilege. A great deal that one generation might look upon as obscene, preceding generations have considered a part of their accepted mores, even as approved religious rituals.

It is foolish to attempt the too sudden acceleration of religious growth. Races of men only superficially accept a strange and new religion; they actually adjust it to their mores and old ways of believing. Religion has at one time or another sanctioned all that is now regarded as immoral or sinful.

Conscience is not a divine voice speaking to the human soul. It is merely the sum total of the moral and ethical content of the mores of any current stage of existence.

92:3. The Nature of Evolutionary Religion

Always remember that cults are formed, not to discover truth, but to promulgate their beliefs and creeds. Evolutionary religion makes no provision for change or revision. Evolved religion commands respect because its followers believe it is The Truth. Only two influences can modify and uplift the dogmas of natural religion: the pressure of the slowly advancing mores and the periodic illumination of epochal revelation.

While calling attention to the fact that religion was essential to the development and preservation of civilization, it should be recorded that natural religion has also done much to cripple and handicap civilization. Evolutionary religion has been man's most expensive but incomparably effective institution. Religion has been the moral police force of all time. Evolutionary religion, must ever continue to be refined and ennobled by the continuous censorship of revealed religion and by the fiery furnace of genuine science.

92:4. The Gift of Revelation

Revelation is evolutionary but always progressive. It is the mission of revelation to sort and censor the successive religions of evolution. There have been many events of religious revelation but only five of epochal significance. These were as follows:

1. *The Dalamatian teachings.* Except for the work of Van, the influence of the Dalamatian revelation was practically lost to the whole world.

2. *The Edenic teachings.* The aborted teachings of Adam were carried on by the Sethite priests, and some of these truths have never been entirely lost to the world.

3. *Melchizedek of Salem.* The cardinal precepts of his teachings were trust and faith.

4. *Jesus of Nazareth.* The essence of his teaching was love and service.

5. *The Urantia Papers.* These constitute the most recent presentation of truth to the mortals of Urantia. But no revelation short of the attainment of the Universal Father can ever be complete. All other celestial ministrations are no more than partial, transient, and practically adapted to local conditions in time and space.

92:5. The Great Religious Leaders

Most great religious epochs have been inaugurated by the life and teachings of some outstanding personality. In considering the teachers of recent times, it may prove helpful to group them into the seven major religious epochs of post-Adamic Urantia:

1. *The Sethite period.* The influence of the Sethite priests persisted longest among the Greeks, Sumerians, and Hindus.

2. *Era of the Melchizedek missionaries.* Urantia religion was in no small measure regenerated by the efforts of these teachers.

3. *The post-Melchizedek era.* Though Amenemope and Ikhnaton both taught in this period, the outstanding religious genius of the post-Melchizedek era was Moses.

4. *The sixth century before Christ* was one of the greatest centuries of religious awakening ever witnessed on Urantia. Among its teachers was Gautama Buddha, Confucius, Lao-tse, Zoroaster, and the Jainist teachers.

5. *The first century after Christ.* Paul of Tarsus and Philo of Alexandria were the greatest teachers of this era.

6. *The sixth century after Christ.* Mohammed founded a religion which was superior to many of the creeds of his time.

7. *The fifteenth century after Christ.* This period witnessed two religious movements: the disruption of the unity of Christianity (Reformation) in the Occident and the synthesis of a new religion in the Orient. In the Orient the combined teachings of Islam, Hinduism, and Buddhism were synthesized by Nanak and his followers into Sikhism, one of the most advanced religions of Asia.

The future of Urantia will doubtless be characterized by the appearance of teachers of religious truth. But it is to be hoped that the ardent and sincere efforts of these future prophets will be directed toward the augmentation of the religious brotherhood of spiritual worship among the many followers of the differing intellectual theologies which so characterize Urantia of Satania.

92:6. The Composite Religions

Twentieth-century Urantia religions present an interesting study of the social evolution of man's worship impulse. Many faiths have progressed very little since the days of the ghost cult. On Urantia, evolutionary and revelatory religion are progressing side by side. The religions of twentieth-century Urantia, may be enumerated as follows: 1. Hinduism—the most ancient, 2. The Hebrew religion, 3. Buddhism, 4. the Confucian teachings, 5. the Taoist beliefs, 6. Zoroastrianism, 7. Shinto, 8. Jainism, 9. Christianity, 10. Islam, and 11. Sikhism—the most recent. The most advanced religions of ancient times were Judaism and Hinduism. The great international, interracial faiths are the Hebraic, Buddhist, Christian, and Islamic. The Christian religion was formulated primarily by three individuals: Philo, Peter, and Paul.

92:7. The Further Evolution of Religion

New religions cannot be invented; they are either evolved, or else they are *suddenly revealed*. The many religions of Urantia are all good to the extent that they bring man to God and bring the realization of the Father to man. It is a fallacy for any group of religionists to conceive of their creed as The Truth. There is not a Urantia religion that could not profitably study and assimilate the best of the truths contained in every other faith, for all contain truth. They can never hope to attain a uniformity of creeds, but they can, and someday will, realize a unity in true worship of the Father of all.

Man has been profoundly influenced, not only by his concepts of Deity, but also by the character of the heroes whom he has chosen to honor. It is most unfortunate that those who have come to venerate the divine and risen Christ should have overlooked the man—the valiant and courageous hero—Joshua ben Joseph.

Modern man is confronted with the task of making more readjustments of human values in one generation than have been made in two thousand years. True religion must ever be, at one and the same time, the eternal foundation and the guiding star of all enduring civilizations.

Paper 93: Machiventa Melchizedek
Melchizedek

THE Melchizedeks are widely known as emergency Sons. When any extraordinary problem arises, it is quite often a Melchizedek who accepts the assignment. The Melchizedek order of universe sonship has been exceedingly active on Urantia. A corps of twelve served in conjunction with the Life Carriers. A later corps of twelve became receivers for your world shortly after the Caligastia secession and continued in authority until the time of Adam and Eve. These twelve Melchizedeks returned to Urantia upon the default of Adam and Eve, and they continued thereafter as planetary receivers on down to the day when Jesus of Nazareth, as the Son of Man, became the titular Planetary Prince of Urantia.

93:1. The Machiventa Incarnation

Revealed truth was threatened with extinction during the millenniums which followed the miscarriage of the Adamic mission on Urantia. The twelve Melchizedek receivers already on Urantia were told that they should continue to uphold truth in the manner of their own election. Machiventa Melchizedek, one of the twelve, volunteered to do that which had been done only six times in all the history of Nebadon: to personalize on earth as a temporary man of the realm. Permission was granted for this adventure by the Salvington authorities, and the actual incarnation of Machiventa Melchizedek was consummated near what was to become the city of Salem, in Palestine.

93:2. The Sage of Salem

It was 1,973 years before the birth of Jesus that Machiventa was bestowed upon the human races of Urantia. He was first observed by mortal man when he entered the tent of Amdon and proclaimed to this shepherd, "I am Melchizedek, priest of El Elyon, the Most High, the one and only God." Within a few years Melchizedek had gathered around himself a group of disciples who formed the nucleus of the later community of Salem, subsequently being called Jerusalem. In personal appearance, Melchizedek resembled the then blended Nodite and Sumerian peoples, being almost six feet in height and possessing a commanding presence. On his breast he wore an emblem of three concentric circles, the Satania symbol of the Paradise Trinity. He spoke Chaldean and a half dozen other languages. Melchizedek received a Thought Adjuster, which enabled this spirit of the Father to function so valiantly in the human mind of the later Son of God, Michael. During his incarnation in the flesh, Machiventa was in full contact with his eleven fellows of the corps of planetary custodians.

93:3. Melchizedek's Teachings

With the passing of a decade, Melchizedek organized his schools at Salem, patterning them on the olden system which had been developed by the early Sethite priests of the second Eden. Melchizedek taught the concept of one God, a universal Deity, but he allowed the people to associate this teaching with the Constellation Father, whom he termed El Elyon—the Most High. But to some, Melchizedek taught advanced truth, embracing the conduct and organization of the local universe, while to his brilliant disciple Nordan the Kenite and his band of earnest students he taught the truths of the superuniverse and even of Havona. Melchizedek taught that at some future time another Son of God would come in the flesh as he had come.

93:4. The Salem Religion

The ceremonies of the Salem worship were very simple. Every person of the Melchizedek church committed to memory, and subscribed to, the threefold creed of the Salem colony and the seven commandments of Melchizedek. But even such a short and simple declaration of faith was altogether too advanced for the men of those days. Melchizedek well knew how difficult it is to suddenly uproot long-established customs and accordingly had wisely offered these people the substitute of a sacrament of bread and wine for the older sacrifice of flesh and blood. But Melchizedek never did succeed in fully eradicating this proclivity to sacrifice from the religious practices of his followers. Like Jesus, Melchizedek attended strictly to the fulfillment of the mission of his bestowal. He did not attempt to reform the mores or to change the habits of the world. He came to achieve two tasks: to keep alive on earth the truth of the one God and to prepare the way for the subsequent mortal bestowal of a Paradise Son of that Universal Father.

93:5. The Selection of Abraham

Melchizedek laid upon Abraham the responsibility of keeping alive the truth of one God. For some time the Melchizedek receivers had been observing the ancestors of Abraham, and they confidently expected offspring in a certain generation who would be characterized by intelligence, initiative, sagacity, and sincerity. Observing the ancestors of Abraham had considerable to do with the appearance of Machiventa at Salem, rather than in Egypt, China, India, or among the northern tribes.

Abraham had kingly ambitions. When Melchizedek heard of Abraham's declaration of war against neighboring rulers, he went forth to dissuade him but only caught up with his former disciple as he returned victorious from the battle. Abraham insisted that the God of Salem had given him victory over his enemies and persisted in giving a tenth of his spoils to the Salem treasury. Abraham became leader of a second confederation of eleven tribes and not only paid tithes to Melchizedek but saw to it that all others in that vicinity did the same. Abraham was really well on the way to establishing a powerful state in Palestine.

93:6. Melchizedek's Covenant with Abraham

Melchizedek persuaded Abraham to abandon his scheme of material conquest and temporal rule in favor of the spiritual concept of the kingdom of heaven. Said he to Abraham: "Look now up to the heavens and number the stars if you are able; so numerous shall your seed be." It was not long after the establishment of this formal covenant that Isaac, the son of Abraham, was born in accordance with the promise of Melchizedek. After the birth of Isaac, Abraham took a very solemn attitude toward his covenant with Melchizedek, changing his name from Abram to Abraham. He assumed the civil and military leadership of the Salem colony, which at its height carried over one hundred thousand regular tithe payers on the rolls of the Melchizedek brotherhood. Abraham not only extended the tithing system but instituted many improved methods of conducting the business of the school, and of handling of the department of missionary propaganda. Abraham was a shrewd and efficient business man; he was not overly pious, but he was thoroughly sincere, and he did believe in Machiventa Melchizedek.

93:7. The Melchizedek Missionaries

Melchizedek continued for some years to instruct his students and to train the Salem missionaries, who penetrated to all the surrounding tribes and eventually to all of the known world. The lives and experiences of the men and women who ventured forth from Salem, Mesopotamia, and Lake Van to enlighten the tribes of the Eastern Hemisphere present a heroic chapter in the annals of the human race. But the task was so great and the tribes were so backward that the results were vague and indefinite. Long before the coming of Jesus the teachings of the early Salem missionaries had become generally submerged in the older and more universal superstitions and beliefs. You who today enjoy the advantages of the art of printing little understand how difficult it was to perpetuate truth during these earlier times. A new revelation is always contaminated by the older evolutionary beliefs.

93:8. Departure of Melchizedek

It was shortly after the destruction of Sodom and Gomorrah that Machiventa decided to end his emergency bestowal on Urantia. Melchizedek's decision to terminate his sojourn in the flesh was influenced by numerous conditions, chief of which was the growing tendency to look upon him as a supernatural being, which indeed he was; but his followers were beginning to reverence him unduly. In addition to these reasons, Melchizedek wanted to leave the scene of his earthly activities a sufficient length of time before Abraham's death to insure that the truth of the one and only God would become strongly established in the minds of his followers. Accordingly Machiventa retired one night to his tent at Salem, having said good night to his human companions, and when they went to call him in the morning, he was not there, for his fellows had taken him.

93:9. After Melchizedek's Departure

It was a great trial for Abraham when Melchizedek so suddenly disappeared. Although he had fully warned his followers that he must sometime go as he had come, they were not reconciled to the loss of their wonderful leader. The great organization built up at Salem nearly disappeared. But Abraham was not long to be deterred in his mission as the successor of Melchizedek. He again become a great leader in Palestine. His last act was to send trusty servants to secure a woman of his own people as a wife for his son Isaac. And Abraham died confident in that faith in God which he had learned from Melchizedek.

It was hard for the next generation to comprehend the story of Melchizedek; within five hundred years many regarded the whole narrative as a myth. Abraham was not so old as the records indicate, and his wife was much younger. These ages were deliberately altered in order to provide for the subsequent alleged miraculous birth of Isaac.

The Jews distorted and perverted their traditions with the view of exalting themselves above all races as the chosen people of God. The Hebrew scribes destroyed every record of the times of Melchizedek which they could find. Thus, in losing sight of Melchizedek, they also lost sight of the teaching of this emergency Son regarding the spiritual mission of the promised bestowal Son. Very few of their progeny were able or willing to recognize and receive Michael when he appeared on earth and in the flesh as Machiventa had foretold.

93:10. Present Status of Machiventa Melchizedek

Machiventa continued as a planetary receiver up to the times of the triumph of Michael on Urantia. Subsequently, he was attached to the Urantia service on Jerusem as one of the four and twenty directors, recently having been elevated to the position of personal ambassador on Jerusem of the Creator Son, bearing the title Vicegerent Planetary Prince of Urantia. Recent rulings handed down from the Most Highs of Edentia, and later confirmed by the Ancients of Days of Uversa, strongly suggest that this bestowal Melchizedek is destined to take the place of the fallen Planetary Prince, or else appear on earth to function as vicegerent Planetary Prince representing Christ Michael, who now actually holds the title of Planetary Prince of Urantia. All speculations associated with the certainty of future appearances of both Magisterial and Trinity Teacher Sons, in conjunction with the explicit promise of the Creator Son to return sometime, make Urantia a planet of future uncertainty and render it one of the most interesting and intriguing spheres in all the universe of Nebadon.

Paper 94:
The Melchizedek Teachings in the Orient
Melchizedek

URANTIA has never had more enthusiastic and aggressive missionaries of any religion than the noble men and women who carried the teachings of Melchizedek over the entire Eastern Hemisphere. These missionaries were recruited from many peoples and races, and they largely spread their teachings through the medium of native converts.

94:1. The Salem Teachings in Vedic India

In the days of Melchizedek, India was a cosmopolitan country which had recently come under the political and religious dominance of the Aryan-Andite invaders from the north and west. The Vedic cult was then in process of growth and metamorphosis under the direction of the Brahman caste of teacher-priests. Never would the Brahman priests accept the Salem teaching of salvation through faith. The rejection of the Melchizedek gospel of trust in God and salvation through faith marked a vital turning point for India. The Brahmans culled the sacred writings of their day in an effort to combat the Salem teachers, and this compilation, as later revised, has come on down to modern times as the Rig-Veda, one of the most ancient of sacred books. An examination of the Vedas will disclose some of the highest and some of the most debased concepts of Deity ever to be conceived.

94:2. Brahmanism

The Brahman priest caste greatly retarded the progress of the Salem teachers. This caste system failed to save the Aryan race, but it did succeed in perpetuating the Brahmans, who, in turn, have maintained their religious hegemony in India to the present time. They proclaimed that, of the two essential divine principles of the universe, one was Brahman the deity, and the other was the Brahman priesthood. Among no other Urantia peoples did the priests presume to exalt themselves above even their gods. Of all the contaminating beliefs which could have become fastened upon what may have been an emerging monotheism, none was so stultifying as the belief in transmigration—the doctrine of the reincarnation of souls. The Brahmans emerged with a distant and metaphysical idea of an all-encompassing Absolute. For more than two thousand years cults have virtually shackled the souls of many Hindu peoples in the chains of spiritual hopelessness. Of all civilizations, the Vedic-Aryan paid the most terrible price for its rejection of the Salem gospel.

94:3. Brahmanic Philosophy

While the highest phase of Brahmanism was hardly a religion, it was truly one of the most noble reaches of the mortal mind into the domains of philosophy and metaphysics. In the concept of Brahman the minds of those days truly grasped at the idea of some all-pervading Absolute, but they failed to recognize the existence of the Universal Father. In certain phases the concept of the One Universal Oversoul led the Indian philosophers very close to the truth of the Supreme Being. The philosophy of Brahmanism also came very near to the realization of the indwelling of the Thought Adjusters. Brahmanic philosophy has approximated many of the facts of the universe and has approached numerous cosmic truths, but has failed to differentiate between the several levels of reality and to discern the personality of the Universal Father.

94:4. The Hindu Religion

With the passing of the centuries in India, the populace returned in measure to the ancient rituals of the Vedas as they had been modified by the teachings of the Melchizedek missionaries, the Brahman priesthood, Buddhism, Jainism, Mohammedanism, and Christianity. Hindu theology, at present, depicts four descending levels of deity and divinity: 1. the Brahman, the Absolute—the IT IS; 2. the Trimurti, the supreme trinity of Hinduism—Brahma, Siva, and Vishnu; 3. Vedic and post-Vedic deities such as Agni, Indra, and Soma; 4. the demigods—supermen, semigods, and saints of the later-day cults. The great strength of Hinduism lies in the fact that it has proved to be the most adaptive religion to appear on Urantia.

Today, in India, the great need is for the portrayal of the Jesusonian gospel which is personally realized in loving ministry and social service. In India the philosophical framework is existent, the cult structure is present; all that is needed is the vitalizing spark of the dynamic love portrayed in the original gospel of the Son of Man, divested of the Occidental dogmas and doctrines which have tended to make Michael's life bestowal a white man's religion.

94:5. The Struggle for Truth in China

It was in the middle of the second millennium before Christ that the Salem missionaries arrived in China. At See Fuch, for more than one hundred years, the Salemites maintained their headquarters, there training Chinese teachers who taught throughout all the domains of the yellow race. It was in direct consequence of this teaching that the earliest form of Taoism arose in China. The composite belief of the lingering teachings of Singlangton, the Salem religion, and the Brahman-Absolute concept spread through the lands of the yellow and brown races. In Japan this proto-Taoism was known as Shinto. In China all of these beliefs were later confused and compounded with the ever-growing cult of ancestor worship. China met her defeat because she failed to progress beyond her early emancipation from priests; she fell into an almost equally calamitous error, the worship of ancestors. The moral atmosphere and the spiritual sentiments of the times of Lao-tse and Confucius grew up out of the teachings of the Salem missionaries of an earlier age.

94:6. Lao-Tse and Confucius

In the sixth century before Christ, through an unusual co-ordination of spiritual agencies, not all of which are understood even by the planetary supervisors, Urantia witnessed a most unusual presentation of manifold religious truth. This unique century of spiritual progress was characterized by great religious, moral, and philosophic teachers all over the civilized world. In China, the two outstanding teachers were Lao-tse and Confucius. Lao-tse built directly upon the concepts of the Salem traditions. Lao was a man of great spiritual vision. He taught that "man's eternal destiny was everlasting union with Tao, Supreme God." Lao also visualized the Trinity and taught returning good for evil. He saw death as a returning home of our personality. Confucius based his doctrines upon the better moral traditions of the long history of the yellow race, and he was also somewhat influenced by the lingering traditions of the Salem missionaries. But he built too well; he made a new fetish out of order and established a respect for ancestral conduct that is still venerated by the Chinese at the time of this writing. And so China, once at the head of human society because of an advanced religion, fell behind because of temporary failure to progress in the true path of the development of God-consciousness.

94:7. Gautama Siddhartha

Gautama Siddhartha was born in the sixth century before Christ. Amid the confusion and extreme cult practices of India teachings of Gautama came as a refreshing relief. He denounced gods, priests, and their sacrifices, but he too failed to perceive the personality of the One Universal. While Siddhartha did not have a very clear concept of the Universal Father, he took an advanced stand on salvation through faith. When proclaimed at its best, Gautama's gospel of universal salvation was a revolutionary and amazing doctrine for its time. It came surprisingly near to being a revival of the Salem gospel. Siddhartha taught far more truth than has survived in the modern cults bearing his name. Modern Buddhism is no more the teachings of Gautama Siddhartha than is Christianity the teachings of Jesus of Nazareth.

94:8. The Buddhist Faith

The original gospel of Gautama was based on the doctrine of suffering and the escape therefrom and was linked to the philosophy of the Eightfold

Path: right views, aspirations, speech, conduct, livelihood, effort, mindfulness, and contemplation. His teaching was a designed look beyond the associations of this material world to the realities of the eternal future. The moral commandments of Gautama's preachment were: You shall not kill, steal, be unchaste, lie, or drink intoxicating liquors. Siddhartha hardly believed in the immortality of the human personality. His doctrine of Nirvana implied a condition of supreme enlightenment and supernal bliss wherein all fetters binding man to the material world had been broken. Salvation is achieved by human effort alone. The great truth of Siddhartha's teaching was his proclamation of a universe of absolute justice. He taught the best godless philosophy ever invented by mortal man. The great weakness in the original gospel of Buddhism was that it did not produce a religion of unselfish social service. Gautama himself was highly social; indeed, his life was much greater than his preachment.

94:9. The Spread of Buddhism

Buddhism did not become widespread as a religion until it was espoused by the low-caste monarch Asoka, who, next to Ikhnaton in Egypt, was one of the most remarkable civil rulers between Melchizedek and Michael. During a period of twenty-five years he trained and sent forth more than seventeen thousand missionaries to the farthest frontiers of all the known world. The spread of Buddhism to all of Asia is one of the thrilling stories of the spiritual devotion and missionary persistence of sincere religionists. The Chinese and north Indian groups of Gautama's followers began the development of the Mahayana teaching of the "Great Road" to salvation in contrast with the purists of the south who held to the Hinayana, or "Lesser Road." Buddhism is a living, growing religion today because it succeeds in conserving many of the highest moral values of its adherents. It promotes calmness and self-control, augments serenity and happiness, and does much to prevent sorrow and mourning.

94:10. Religion in Tibet

In Tibet may be found the strangest association of the Melchizedek teachings combined with Buddhism, Hinduism, Taoism, and Christianity. Examination of the religious ceremonials of present-day Tibetan rituals reveals an overgrown brotherhood of priests with shaven heads who practice an elaborate ritual embracing bells, chants, incense, processionals, rosaries, images, charms, pictures, holy water, gorgeous vestments, and elaborate choirs. The Tibetans have rigid dogmas and crystallized creeds. Their hierarchy embraces monks, nuns, abbots, and the Grand Lama. Their monasteries are extensive and their cathedrals magnificent. Among no other people of modern times can be found the observance of so much from so many religions. The Tibetans have something of all the leading world religions except the simple teachings of the Jesusonian gospel.

94:11. Buddhist Philosophy

Buddhism entered China in the first millennium after Christ, and it fitted well into the religious customs of the yellow race. The religion of the great Indian protestant eventually found itself shackled with those very ceremonial practices and ritualistic incantations against which he had so fearlessly fought, and which he had so valiantly denounced. The great advance made in Buddhist philosophy consisted in its comprehension of the relativity of all truth. This philosophy also held that the Buddha (divine) nature resided in all men. This teaching is one of the clearest presentations of the truth of the indwelling Adjusters ever to be made by a Urantian religion. It was believed that mankind in the future would be blessed by other teachers which led to the concept of many Buddhas. These Buddhas were the manifestation of a higher essence, the Absolute Buddha—the infinite I AM. Such concepts, though helpful to philosophy, are not vital to religious development. These speculations were of little comfort to the hungry multitudes who craved to hear the simple gospel of Salem, that faith in God would assure divine favor and eternal survival.

94:12. The God Concept of Buddhism

Gradually the concept of God, as contrasted with the Absolute, began to appear in Buddhism. Step by step the God concept has evolved and finally came to fruit in the belief in Amida Buddha. The Amidists teach that the soul, upon experiencing death, may elect to enjoy a sojourn in Paradise prior to entering Nirvana, the ultimate of existence. They hold to an Infinite Reality which is beyond all finite mortal comprehension. Amida assures us that all who call on his name in true faith and with a pure heart will attain the supernal happiness of Paradise.

The great strength of Buddhism is that its adherents are free to choose truth from all religions. In this respect the Shin sect of Japan has become one of the most progressive religious groups in the world. Buddhism itself is undergoing a twentieth-century renaissance. At the time of this writing, much of Asia rests its hope in Buddhism. Will this noble faith once again receive the truth of new concepts of God for which it has so long searched?

All Urantia is waiting for the proclamation of the ennobling message of Michael, unencumbered by the accumulated doctrines and dogmas of nineteen centuries of contact with the religions of evolutionary origin. The hour is striking for presenting to Buddhism, to Christianity, to Hinduism, even to the peoples of all faiths, not the gospel about Jesus, but the living, spiritual reality of the gospel of Jesus.

Paper 95:
The Melchizedek Teachings in the Levant
Melchizedek

AS India gave rise to many of the religions and philosophies of eastern Asia, so the Levant was the homeland of the faiths of the Occidental world. The Salem missionaries spread out through Palestine, Mesopotamia, Egypt, Iran, and Arabia, everywhere proclaiming the good news of the gospel of Machiventa Melchizedek.

95:1. The Salem Religion in Mesopotamia

Although the Salem teachers did much to refine and uplift the religions of Mesopotamia, they did not succeed in bringing the various peoples to the permanent recognition of one God. Never did the Salem teachers fully overcome the popularity of Ishtar, the mother of gods and the spirit of sex fertility. It had become a universal practice throughout Mesopotamia for all women to submit, at least once in early life, to the embrace of strangers; this was thought to be a devotion required by Ishtar. Melchizedek had warned his followers to teach about the one God, the Father and Maker of all. But as has often been the error of the teachers of new truth, they attempted too much, attempted to supplant slow evolution by sudden revolution, and their noble cause went down in defeat. It was the Salem missionaries who wrote many of the Old Testament Psalms. The Book of Job is a fairly good reflection of the teachings of the Salem school at Kish.

95:2. Early Egyptian Religion

The original Melchizedek teachings took their deepest root in Egypt, where it fostered the most thoroughly blended type of religious philosophy to be found on Urantia. The Egyptians believed that preservation of the body facilitated one's passage through the future life. Their superstitions included the belief in the efficacy of spittle as a healing agent. They long believed that the stars twinkling in the night sky represented the survival of the souls of the worthy dead. The sloping entrance passage of the great pyramid pointed directly toward the Pole Star, so that the soul of the King could go directly to the supposed abode of the kings. They believed that a disembodied soul could make its way to the judgment hall of Osiris. This concept of judgment in the hereafter for the sins of one's life in the flesh on earth was carried over into Hebrew theology.

95:3. Evolution of Moral Concepts

Although the culture and religion of Egypt were chiefly derived from Andite Mesopotamia and largely transmitted to subsequent civilizations through the Hebrews and Greeks, much of the social and ethical idealism of the Egyptians arose in the valley of the Nile as a purely evolutionary development. Thousands of years before the Salem gospel penetrated to Egypt, its moral leaders taught justice, fairness, and the avoidance of avarice. In the soil of these evolving ethical ideas and moral ideals the surviving doctrines of the Salem religion flourished. Egypt was intellectual and moral but not overly spiritual. In six thousand years only four great prophets arose among the Egyptians: Amenemope, Okhban, Ikhnaton, and Moses. It was political rather than religious circumstances that made it easy for Abraham and Joseph to exert great influence throughout Egypt in behalf of the Salem teachings of one God.

95:4. The Teachings of Amenemope

Amenemope taught that riches and fortune were the gift of God, and this concept thoroughly colored the later appearing Hebrew philosophy. In substance he taught: Man proposes but God disposes. His teachings, translated into Hebrew, determined the philosophy of the Old Testament Book of Proverbs. Translated into Greek, they gave color to all subsequent Hellenic religious philosophy. Amenemope functioned to conserve the ethics of evolution and the morals of revelation and in his writings passed them on both to the Hebrews and to the Greeks. The first psalm of the Hebrew Book of Psalms was written by Amenemope and is the heart of the teachings of Ikhnaton.

95:5. The Remarkable Ikhnaton

Since the disappearance of Melchizedek in the flesh, no human being had possessed as clear a concept of the revealed religion of Salem as Ikhnaton. In some respects this young Egyptian king is one of the most remarkable persons in human history. With the most amazing determination he broke with the past, changed his name, abandoned his capital, built an entirely new city, and created a new art and literature for a whole people. But he went too fast; he built too much, more than could stand when he had gone. Very wisely Ikhnaton sought to establish monotheism under the guise of the sun-god, Aton. This young teacher-king was a prolific writer, being author of the exposition entitled "The One God," which the priests, when returned to power, utterly destroyed. Ikhnaton also wrote one hundred and thirty-seven hymns, twelve of which are now preserved in the Old Testament Book of Psalms. The fatal weakness of Ikhnaton's gospel was its greatest truth, the teaching that Aton was not only the creator of Egypt but also of the whole world. The repercussions of Ikhnaton's work became the agent for transmitting the combined evolutionary culture of the Nile and the revelatory religion of the Euphrates to all of the subsequent peoples of the Occident.

95:6. The Salem Doctrines in Iran

Zoroaster on his first pilgrimage to Ur in Mesopotamia learned of the traditions of the Caligastia and the Lucifer rebellion. As the result of a dream while in Ur, he settled upon a program of returning to his northern home to undertake the remodeling of the religion of his people. He had learned of the story of the Seven Master Spirits and, accordingly, created a galaxy of seven supreme gods with Ahura-Mazda at its head. This new religion was one of action. It was a militant religious philosophy which dared to battle with evil. Zoroaster did not teach the worship of fire but sought to utilize the flame as a symbol. Finally, upon the conversion of an Iranian prince, this new religion was spread by the sword. Zoroaster heroically died in battle for that which he believed was the "truth of the Lord of light." Original Zoroastrianism was not a pure dualism; it taught that evil was eternity-submerged in the ultimate reality of the good. The teachings of Zoroaster came successively to impress three great religions: Judaism and Christianity and, through them, Mohammedanism.

95:7. The Salem Teachings in Arabia

The Melchizedek teachings of the one God became established in the Arabian desert at a comparatively recent date. Not even in China or Rome did the Melchizedek teachings fail more completely than in this desert region so very near Salem itself. There were numerous centers that might have responded to the Jesusonian gospel, but the Christian missionaries of the desert lands were an austere and unyielding group.

The only factor of a tribal, racial, or national nature about the primitive and unorganized beliefs of the desert was the peculiar and general respect which almost all Arabian tribes were willing to pay to a certain black stone fetish in a certain temple at Mecca. This point of common contact and reverence subsequently led to the establishment of the Islamic religion. The strength of Islam has been its clear-cut and well-defined presentation of Allah as the one and only Deity; its weakness, the association of military force with its promulgation, together with its degradation of woman.

Paper 96: Yahweh—God of the Hebrews
Melchizedek

FACTUALLY the Hebrew religion is predicated upon the covenant between Abraham and Machiventa Melchizedek, evolutionally it is the outgrowth of many unique situational circumstances, but culturally it has borrowed freely from the religion, morality, and philosophy of the entire Levant.

96:1. Deity Concepts Among the Semites

The early Semites regarded everything as being indwelt by a spirit. The progress of the Hebrews from polytheism through henotheism to monotheism was not an unbroken and continuous conceptual development. From time to time numerous terms were applied to their varying concepts of God: *Yahweh* (associated with Mount Horeb), *El Elyon* (associated with Melchizedek), *El Shaddai* (a composite Egyptian concept which held that God bestowed material prosperity on the faithful), *El* (a composite Deity), *Elohim* (a Trinity concept). The Semites disliked to speak the name of their Deity and used numerous appellations. The term *Jehovah* did not come into use until fifteen hundred years after the times of Jesus. The idea of Yahweh has undergone the most extensive development of all the mortal theories of God.

96:2. The Semitic Peoples

Racially the Semites were among the most blended of Urantia peoples. It was only after the days of Machiventa Melchizedek and Abraham that certain tribes of Semites, because of their peculiar religious beliefs, were called the children of Israel and later on Hebrews, Jews, and the "chosen people." The Melchizedek teaching concerning El Elyon, the Most High, and the covenant of divine favor through faith, had been largely forgotten by the time of the Egyptian enslavement of the Semite peoples who were shortly to form the Hebrew nation.

96:3. The Matchless Moses

The beginning of the evolution of the Hebraic concepts and ideals dates from the departure of the Semites from Egypt under that great leader, teacher, and organizer, Moses. His mother was of the royal family of Egypt; his father was a Semitic liaison officer. Moses possessed qualities derived from superior racial sources. No leader ever undertook to reform and uplift a more forlorn, downcast, dejected, and ignorant group of human beings. Moses endeavored to negotiate diplomatically for the freedom of his fellow Semites. But the king later saw fit to repudiate this treaty. But Moses was not discouraged; in less than a year, when the Egyptian military forces were fully occupied, this intrepid organizer led his compatriots out of Egypt in a spectacular night flight.

96:4. The Proclamation of Yahweh

Moses had heard of the teachings of Machiventa Melchizedek from both his father and his mother. Moses was educated an El Shaddaist; through the influence of his father-in-law he became an El Elyonist; and by the time of the Hebrew encampment about Mount Sinai he had formulated a new and enlarged concept of Deity. The fact that Yahweh was the god of the fleeing

Hebrews explains why they tarried so long before the holy mountain of Sinai and there received the Ten Commandments. Moses proclaimed that Yahweh was the Lord God of Israel, who had singled out the Hebrews as his chosen people. Moses taught that Yahweh was a covenant-keeping God and made a heroic effort to uplift Yahweh to the dignity of a supreme Deity.

96:5. The Teachings of Moses

Moses was an extraordinary combination of military leader, social organizer, and religious teacher. He was the most important individual world teacher and leader between the times of Machiventa and Jesus. Moses and his father-in-law, Jethro, gathered up the residue of the traditions of the days of Melchizedek, and these teachings, joined to the learning of the Egyptians, guided Moses in the creation of the improved religion and ritual of the Israelites. Moses made a brave and partly successful stand against fetishes and idolatry. He also forbade the making of images of any sort. While Moses presented fleeting glimpses of a universal and beneficent Deity to the children of Israel, on the whole, their day-by-day concept of Yahweh was that of a God but little better than the tribal gods of the surrounding peoples. When Moses turned over the command of the Hebrews to Joshua, he had already gathered up thousands of the collateral descendants of Abraham, Nahor, Lot, and other of the related tribes and had whipped them into a self-sustaining and partially self-regulating nation of pastoral warriors.

96:6. The God Concept After Moses' Death

Upon the death of Moses his lofty concept of Yahweh rapidly deteriorated. During the times of the beginning of the transmutation of the austere, crude, exacting, and thunderous desert god of Sinai into the later appearing concept of a God of love, justice, and mercy, the Hebrews almost lost sight of Moses' lofty teachings. Desperately Joshua sought to hold the concept of a supreme Yahweh in the minds of the tribesmen. But even in this dark age, every now and then a solitary teacher would arise proclaiming the Mosaic concept of divinity.

96:7. Psalms and the Book of Job

The Psalms are the work of a score or more of authors; many were written by Egyptian and Mesopotamian teachers. No collection of religious writings gives expression to such a wealth of devotion and inspirational ideas of God as the Book of Psalms. In the Psalms God is depicted in all phases of conception, from the crude idea of a tribal deity to the vastly expanded ideal of the later Hebrews, wherein Yahweh is pictured as a loving ruler and merciful Father. The worshipful spirit of this collection of hymns transcends that of all other sacred books of the world.

The variegated picture of Deity presented in the Book of Job was the product of more than a score of Mesopotamian religious teachers. In Palestine the wisdom and all-pervasiveness of God was often grasped but seldom his love and mercy. Not since the times of Melchizedek had the Levantine world heard such a ringing and cheering message of human salvation as this extraordinary teaching of Elihu, the prophet of Ur and priest of the Salem believers. And thus did the remnants of the Salem missionaries in Mesopotamia maintain the light of truth until the appearance of the first of that long line of the teachers of Israel who never stopped as they built, concept upon concept, until they had achieved the realization of the ideal of the Universal and Creator Father of all.

Paper 97: Evolution of the God Concept Among the Hebrews

Melchizedek

THE spiritual leaders of the Hebrews did what no others before them had ever succeeded in doing—they deanthropomorphized their God concept without converting it into an abstraction of Deity comprehensible only to philosophers.

97:1. Samuel—First of the Hebrew Prophets

Samuel sprang from a long line of the Salem teachers who had persisted in maintaining the truths of Melchizedek as a part of their worship forms. This teacher was a virile and resolute man. He did little preaching, less teaching, but he did act. One day he was mocking the priest of Baal; the next, chopping in pieces a captive king. He devotedly believed in the one God, and he had a clear concept of that one God as creator of heaven and earth. But the great contribution which Samuel made to the development of the concept of Deity was his ringing pronouncement that Yahweh was changeless. And he preached anew the story of God's sincerity, his covenant-keeping reliability. This gradual development of the concept of the character of Yahweh continued under the ministry of Samuel's successors.

97:2. Elijah and Elisha

In the tenth century before Christ the Hebrew nation became divided into two kingdoms. Elijah restored to the northern kingdom a concept of God comparable with that held in the days of Samuel. Elijah carried forward his reforms in the face of the opposition of an idolatrous monarch; his task was even more gigantic and difficult than that which Samuel had faced. When

Elijah was called away, Elisha, his faithful associate, took up his work and kept the light of truth alive in Palestine. The era of Elijah and Elisha closed with the better classes returning to the worship of the supreme Yahweh and witnessed the restoration of the idea of the Universal Creator to about that place where Samuel had left it.

97:3. Yahweh and Baal

The long-drawn-out controversy between the believers in Yahweh and the followers of Baal was a socioeconomic clash of ideologies rather than a difference in religious beliefs. The southern or wandering Arabian tribes (the Yahwehites) looked upon land as an inalienable gift of Deity to the clan. The northern and more settled Canaanites (the Baalites) freely bought, sold, and mortgaged their lands. The word Baal means owner. This socioeconomic controversy did not become a definite religious issue until the times of Elijah. From the days of this aggressive prophet the issue was fought out on more strictly religious lines—Yahweh vs. Baal—and it ended in the triumph of Yahweh and the subsequent drive toward monotheism.

97:4. Amos and Hosea

A great step in the transition of the tribal god to a God who would punish crime and immorality among even his own people, was taken by Amos, who appeared from among the southern hills to denounce the criminality, drunkenness, oppression, and immorality of the northern tribes. Not since the times of Moses had such ringing truths been proclaimed in Palestine. Amos proclaimed Yahweh the "God of all nations" and warned the Israelites that ritual must not take the place of righteousness. Before this courageous teacher was stoned to death, he had spread enough leaven of truth to save the doctrine of the supreme Yahweh. Hosea followed Amos and his doctrine of a universal God of justice by the resurrection of the Mosaic concept of a God of love. He struck the opening notes in the later merciful chords of divine compassion and loving-kindness which were so exquisitely sung by Isaiah and his associates.

97:5. The First Isaiah

Isaiah preached the eternal nature of God, his infinite wisdom and unchanging perfection of reliability. He represented the God of Israel as saying: "'Come now and let us reason together,' says the Lord, 'though your sins be as scarlet, they shall be as white as snow.'" "The spirit of the Lord is upon me because he has anointed me to preach good tidings to the meek. . . ." This Isaiah was followed by Micah and Obadiah, who confirmed and embellished this soul-satisfying gospel. These two brave messengers boldly denounced the priest-ridden ritual of the Hebrews and fearlessly attacked the whole sacrificial system. Micah's message was: "He has shown me, O man, what is good; and what does the Lord require of you but to do justly and to love mercy and to walk humbly with your God." And but for the stubborn resistance of the priests, these teachers would have overthrown the whole bloody ceremonial of the Hebrew ritual of worship.

97:6. Jeremiah the Fearless

Jeremiah fearlessly declared that Yahweh was not on the side of the Hebrews in their military struggles with other nations. He asserted that Yahweh was God of all the earth, of all nations and of all peoples. Jeremiah also preached the just and loving God described by Isaiah. It was considered blasphemous treason when, during the siege of Jerusalem, Jeremiah counseled the surrender of the city, and the priests and civil rulers cast him into the miry pit of a dismal dungeon.

97:7. The Second Isaiah

The Jewish priests went to great lengths in the invention of fables and the multiplication of miraculous appearing events in Hebrew history in an effort to restore the Jews as the chosen people. They were greatly hindered in their influence over their fellow captives by the presence of a young and indomitable prophet, Isaiah the second, who was a full convert to the elder Isaiah's God of justice, love, righteousness, and mercy, which may be found in chapters forty to fifty-five inclusive of the Book of Isaiah. No prophet or religious teacher from Machiventa to the time of Jesus attained the high concept of God that Isaiah the second proclaimed. Listen to the gospel of this new revelation of the God of Salem: "He shall feed his flock like a shepherd; he shall gather the lambs in his arms and carry them in his bosom. He gives power to the faint, and to those who have no might he increases strength. Those who wait upon the Lord shall renew their strength; they shall mount up with wings as eagles; they shall run and not be weary; they shall walk and not faint." In superb language and with matchless grace this great teacher portrayed the all-powerful Creator as the all-loving Father. No more beautiful pronouncements about the heavenly Father have ever been made.

97:8. Sacred and Profane History

After the priests of the Babylonian exile had prepared their new record of God's supposedly miraculous dealings with the Hebrews, the sacred history of Israel as portrayed in the Old Testament, they carefully and completely destroyed the existing records of Hebrew affairs. This fictionalized history so confused the Jewish leaders that they failed to recognize and accept the mission and ministry of the divine Son of Paradise when he came to them as the incarnated Son of Man. Secular Hebrew history has been converted into a fiction of sacred history and has become inextricably bound up with the moral concepts and religious teachings of the so-called Christian nations.

97:9. Hebrew History

There never were twelve tribes of the Israelites—only three or four tribes settled in Palestine. The Hebrew nation came into being as the result of the union of the so-called Israelites and the Canaanites. Pretentious Hebrew history begins with Saul's rallying the northern clans to withstand an attack by the Ammonites. With an army of a little more than three thousand he defeated the enemy, and it was this exploit that led the hill tribes to make him king.

The description of the reign of David is a distortion of Jewish history. David's army was a polyglot assortment of malcontents and fugitives from justice. Presently his compatriots proclaimed him king of the new kingdom of Judah. David's corrupt political machine began to take possession of land in the north. Then came a series of atrocities climaxed by the murder of Uriah. After David's death Solomon bankrupted the nation by his lavish court and by his elaborate building program. His harem numbered almost one thousand.

It was during the period of Babylonian captivity, following the destruction of Judah, that Judaism was shocked into a return to monotheism and the service of Yahweh as a chosen people. The Jewish religion of the Old Testament really evolved in Babylon during the captivity. The truth about the Jewish people discloses that much which has been regarded as sacred history turns out to be little more than the chronicle of ordinary profane history. The Jews were not a miraculous people.

97:10. The Hebrew Religion

Their leaders had taught the Israelites that they were a chosen people; if they would fulfill this destiny, they would become the spiritual leaders of all peoples, and the coming Messiah would reign over them and all the world as the Prince of Peace. National egotism, false faith in a misconceived promised Messiah, and the increasing bondage and tyranny of the priesthood forever silenced the voices of the spiritual leaders. But the Jews never lost the concept of the Universal Father. Though Hebrew theology refused to expand, it played an important part in the development of two other world religions, Christianity and Mohammedanism. The Jewish religion persisted also because of its institutions. It is difficult for religion to survive as the private practice of isolated individuals. This has ever been the error of the religious leaders: Seeing the evils of institutionalized religion, they seek to destroy the technique of group functioning. In place of destroying all ritual, they would do better to reform it. The Hebraic concept of God was the highest human visualization of the Universal Father until it was enlarged and exquisitely amplified by the personal teachings and life example of his Son, Michael of Nebadon.

Paper 98:
The Melchizedek Teachings in the Occcident
Melchizedek

THE Melchizedek teachings entered Europe along many routes, but chiefly they came by way of Egypt and were embodied in Occidental philosophy after being thoroughly Hellenized and later Christianized. Among those who maintained the Salem teachings in the purest form must be mentioned the Cynics.

98:1. The Salem Religion Among the Greeks

The Salem missionaries might have built up a great religious structure among the Greeks had it not been for their strict interpretation of their oath of ordination, a pledge imposed by Machiventa which forbade the organization of exclusive congregations for worship. The early influence of the Salem teachers was nearly destroyed by the so-called Aryan invasion. This importation inaugurated the evolution of the Greek family of gods and goddesses. The Hellenic Greeks found the Mediterranean world largely dominated by the mother cult, and they imposed upon these peoples their man-god, Dyaus-Zeus. The Greeks would have eventually achieved a true monotheism in the concept of Zeus except for their retention of the overcontrol of Fate. The intelligent Greeks never did regard these gods very seriously. The Hellenes became so impregnated with the antipriestcraft doctrines of the earlier Salem teachers that no priesthood of any importance ever arose in Greece. Greek morals, ethics, and philosophy presently advanced far beyond the god concept, and this imbalance between intellectual and spiritual growth was as hazardous to Greece as it had proved to be in India.

98:2. Greek Philosophic Thought

The Greeks were without a national religion, the gods of Olympus having long lost their hold upon the better minds during the sixth century before Christ. They, however, did engage in a magnificent intellectual advancement. They sought for the solace of the soul in deep thinking—philosophy and metaphysics. The philosophers practically all held loosely to the background of a belief in the Salem doctrine of "the Intelligence of the universe," "the idea of God," and "the Great Source." The cardinal virtues of Socrates and his successors, Plato and Aristotle, were: wisdom, courage, temperance, and justice. In Greece, believing was subordinated to thinking. But the average men of these times could not grasp, nor were they much interested in, the Greek philosophy of self-realization and an abstract Deity; they rather craved promises of salvation, coupled with a personal God who could hear their prayers. They exiled the philosophers, persecuted the remnants of the Salem cult, and made ready for that terrible orgiastic plunge into the follies of the mystery cults. All Greece became involved in these new methods of attaining salvation, these emotional and fiery ceremonials.

Philosophy is to religion as conception is to action. The ideal human estate is that in which philosophy, religion, and science are welded into a meaningful unity by the conjoined action of wisdom, faith, and experience.

98:3. The Melchizedek Teachings in Rome

The religion of the earlier Latin tribes was for the most part an observance of mere forms, vows, and taboos. Roman religion was greatly influenced by extensive cultural importations from Greece. Eventually most of the Olympian gods were transplanted and incorporated into the Latin pantheon. The religious initiation of Roman youths was the occasion of their solemn consecration to the service of the state. This formal and unemotional form of pseudoreligious patriotism was doomed to collapse. It was followed by the deeply emotional worship of the mystery cults. These imported cults continued to flourish throughout the Roman state up to the time of Augustus, who, purely for political and civic reasons, made a heroic and somewhat successful effort to destroy the mysteries and revive the older political religion. He reorganized the state priesthood, re-established the state religion, appointed himself acting high priest of all, and as emperor did not hesitate to proclaim himself the supreme god. The last stand of the dwindling band of Salem believers was made by an earnest group of preachers, the Cynics. But the people at large rejected the Cynics; they preferred to plunge into the rituals of the mysteries, which not only offered hopes of personal salvation but also gratified the desire for diversion, excitement, and entertainment.

98:4. The Mystery Cults

The majority of people in the Greco-Roman world turned their attention to the spectacular and emotional mystery cults from Egypt and the Levant. The most popular were the Phrygian cult of Cybele and her son Attis, the Egyptian cult of Osiris and his mother Isis, and the Iranian cult of the worship of Mithras. The Phrygian and Egyptian mysteries taught that the divine son (respectively Attis and Osiris) had experienced death and had been resurrected by divine power, and that all who were properly initiated into the mystery would become partakers of his divine nature and his immortality. The frenzy of the observance of these mystery cults and the orgies of their ceremonials were sometimes most revolting.

98:5. The Cult of Mithras

The cult of Mithras arose in Iran and long persisted in its homeland despite the militant opposition of the followers of Zoroaster. It was chiefly through the Mithraic cult that Zoroaster's religion exerted an influence upon later appearing Christianity. Mithras was conceived as the surviving champion of the sun-god in his struggle with the god of darkness. In recognition of his slaying the mythical sacred bull, Mithras was made immortal. The annual festival of Mithras was December twenty-fifth. It was taught that when a man died, he went before Mithras for judgment, and that at the end of the world Mithras would summon all the dead from their graves to face the last judgment. The wicked would be destroyed by fire, and the righteous would reign with Mithras forever. At first it was a religion only for men; later on, the wives and daughters of believers were admitted to the temples of the Great Mother.

98:6. Mithraism and Christianity

During the third century after Christ, Mithraic and Christian churches were very similar both in appearance and in the character of their ritual. Always had it been the practice of Mithraic worshipers, on entering the temple, to dip their fingers in holy water. Both religions employed baptism and partook of the sacrament of bread and wine. The one great difference between Mithraism and Christianity, aside from the characters of Mithras and Jesus, was that the one encouraged militarism while the other was ultrapacific. But the deciding factor in the struggle between the two was the admission of women into the full fellowship of the Christian faith.

98:7. The Christian Religion

A Creator Son bestowed himself upon the humanity of Urantia to win all mankind to the recognition of the Father's love and to the realization of their sonship with God. Christianity was spread throughout the Levant and Occident by the followers of this Galilean, and their missionary zeal equaled that of their illustrious predecessors, the Sethites and Salemites. The Christian religion arose through the compounding of the following teachings, influences, beliefs, cults, and personal individual attitudes: 1. the Melchizedek teachings, 2. the Hebraic system, 3. the Zoroastrian beliefs, 4. the mystery cults, 5. the historic fact of the human life of Jesus of Nazareth, 6. the personal viewpoint of Paul of Tarsus (Paul little dreamed that his well-intentioned letters would someday be regarded as the "word of God."), and 7. the philosophic thought of the Hellenistic peoples. As the original teachings of Jesus penetrated the Occident, they became Occidentalized, and lost their potentially universal appeal. Christianity has long since ceased to be the religion of Jesus—the gospel of the Fatherhood of God and the universal brotherhood of all men.

Paper 99: The Social Problems of Religion
Melchizedek

RELIGION achieves its highest social ministry when it has least connection with the secular institutions of society. Religion should not be directly concerned either with the creation of new social orders or with the preservation of old ones.

99:1. Religion and Social Reconstruction

Mechanical inventions and the dissemination of knowledge are modifying civilization. This new and oncoming social order will not settle down complacently for a millennium. The new social relations and economic upheavals can result in lasting brotherhood only by the ministry of religion. Religion must not become organically involved in the secular work of social reconstruction and economic reorganization. The spirit of religion is eternal, but the form of its expression must be restated every time the dictionary of human language is revised.

99:2. Weakness of Institutional Religion

Institutional religion is now caught in the stalemate of a vicious circle. It cannot reconstruct society without first reconstructing itself; and being so much an integral part of the established order, it cannot reconstruct itself until society has been radically reconstructed. Religionists must function in society, in industry, and in politics as individuals, not as groups, parties, or institutions. Religious collectivism must confine its efforts to the furtherance of religious causes. Its only proper attitude consists in the teaching of nonviolence. Modern religion finds it difficult to adjust its attitude toward the rapidly shifting social changes only because it has permitted itself to become so thoroughly traditionalized, dogmatized, and institutionalized. The religion of living experience finds no difficulty in keeping ahead of all these social developments and economic upheavals, amid which it ever functions as a moral stabilizer, social guide, and spiritual pilot.

99:3. Religion and the Religionist

Early Christianity was entirely free from all civil entanglements, social commitments, and economic alliances. The kingdom of heaven is an exclusively spiritual brotherhood of God-knowing individuals. Religion influences social reconstruction directly because it spiritualizes and idealizes the individual citizen. Overmuch false sentiment on the part of the church has led to the unwise perpetuation of racially degenerate stocks which have tremendously retarded the progress of civilization. Religion does not grow unless it is disciplined by constructive criticism, amplified by philosophy, purified by science, and nourished by loyal fellowship. Religionists, as a group, must never concern themselves with anything but religion, albeit any one such religionist, as an individual citizen, may become the outstanding leader of some social, economic, or political reconstruction movement.

99:4. Transition Difficulties

Religion puts new meaning into all group associations—families, schools, and clubs. But if religion is to stimulate individual development of character it must not be standardized, stereotyped, or formalized. During the psychologically unsettled times of the twentieth century thousands upon thousands of men and women have become humanly dislocated; they need the consolation and stabilization of sound religion. Modern science, particularly psychology, has weakened only those religions which are so largely dependent upon fear, superstition, and emotion. Transition is always accompanied by confusion, and there will be little tranquility in the religious world until the great struggle between the three partial approaches to the reality of the cosmos—the spiritistic belief, the humanistic and idealistic belief, and the mechanistic and naturalistic scientific conceptions—are harmonized through the revelatory presentation of religion, philosophy, and cosmology which portrays the triune existence of spirit, mind, and energy.

99:5. Social Aspects of Religion

Religion is first an inner or personal adjustment, and then it becomes a matter of social service or group adjustment. What happens to these religious groups depends very much on intelligent leadership. True religion is to know God as your Father and man as your brother. The religion of Jesus is the most dynamic influence ever to activate the human race. Jesus shattered tradition, destroyed dogma, and called mankind to the achievement of its highest ideals in time and eternity—to be perfect, even as the Father in heaven is perfect. Religious experience unfailingly yields the "fruits of the spirit" in the daily life of the spirit-led mortal. Someday religionists will get together and actually effect co-operation on the basis of unity of ideals and purposes rather than attempting to do so on the basis of psychological opinions and theological beliefs. It is high time that man had a religious experience so personal and so sublime that it could be realized and expressed only by "feelings that lie too deep for words."

99:6. Institutional Religion

Sectarianism is a disease of institutional religion, and dogmatism is an enslavement of the spiritual nature. It is the purpose of group religious activities to dramatize the loyalties of religion; to magnify the lures of truth, beauty, and goodness; to provide wise counsel and spiritual guidance; and to encourage group worship. But as religion becomes institutionalized, its power for good is curtailed. The dangers of formalized religion are: the fixation of beliefs and crystallization of sentiments; the accumulation of vested interests with increase of secularization; the tendency to standardize and fossilize truth; the diversion of religion from the service of God to the service of the church; the inclination of leaders to become administrators instead of ministers; the tendency to form sects and competitive divisions; the establishment of oppressive ecclesiastical authority; the creation of the aristocratic "chosen people" attitude; the fostering of false and exaggerated ideas of sacredness; the routinizing of religion and the petrification of worship; the tendency to venerate the past while ignoring present demands; the failure to make up-to-date interpretations of religion; the entanglement with functions of secular institutions; the evil discrimination of religious castes; the intolerant judge of orthodoxy; the failure to hold the interest of adventurous youth, and the gradual loss of the saving message of the gospel of eternal salvation.

99:7. Religion's Contribution

Though churches and all other religious groups should stand aloof from all secular activities, they must do nothing to hinder or retard the social co-ordination of human institutions. In all social reconstruction religion provides a stabilizing loyalty to a transcendent object, a steadying goal beyond and above the immediate and temporal objective. Religion inspires man to live courageously and joyfully; it joins patience with passion, insight to zeal, sympathy with power, and ideals with energy. Man is naturally a dreamer, but science is sobering him so that religion can presently activate him with far less danger of precipitating fanatical reactions.

Paper 100: Religion in Human Experience
Melchizedek

THE experience of dynamic religious living transforms the mediocre individual into a personality of idealistic power. Spiritual growth is mutually stimulated by intimate association with other religionists. And religion ennobles the commonplace drudgery of daily living.

100:1. Religious Growth

Some persons are too busy to grow and are therefore in grave danger of spiritual fixation. The chief inhibitors of growth are prejudice and ignorance. Give every developing child a chance to grow his own religious experience. Remember, year-by-year progress through an established educational regime does not necessarily mean intellectual progress, much less spiritual growth. Real educational growth is indicated by enhancement of ideals and values. Children are permanently impressed only by the loyalties of their adult associates. Live loyally today—grow—and tomorrow will attend to itself. The quickest way for a tadpole to become a frog is to live loyally each moment as a tadpole. Religion cannot be bestowed, received, loaned, learned, or lost; it is a personal experience. The factors of religious growth may be intentional, but the growth itself is unvaryingly unconscious.

100:2. Spiritual Growth

Spiritual growth is first an awakening to needs, next a discernment of meanings, and then a discovery of values. Spirituality enhances the ability to discover beauty in things, recognize truth in meanings, and discover goodness in values. The goal of human self-realization should be spiritual, not material. Jesus portrayed the profound surety of the God-knowing mortal when he said: "To a God-knowing kingdom believer, what does it matter if all things earthly crash?" Temporal securities are vulnerable, but spiritual sureties are impregnable. Every human being who has dedicated the keeping of his soul to the indwelling spirit of the eternal God can calmly stand by while his fondest ambitions perish and his keenest hopes crash; he positively knows that such catastrophes are preliminary to the rearing of the more noble and enduring realities of a new and more sublime level of universe attainment.

100:3. Concepts of Supreme Value

Religion is an impulse for organizing the soul for dynamic service. It is the enlistment of the totality of selfhood in the loyal service of loving God and serving man. Values can never be static; reality signifies change, growth. The association of actuals and potentials equals growth, the experiential realization of values. The supreme value of human life consists in growth of values and progress in meanings. And such an experience is the equivalent of God-consciousness. Man cannot cause growth, but he can supply favorable conditions. Growth is always unconscious. Love thus grows; it cannot be created, manufactured, or purchased; it must grow. Evolution is a cosmic technique of growth. Social growth cannot be secured by legislation, and moral growth is not had by improved administration. Man's sole contribution to growth is the mobilization of the total powers of his personality—living faith.

100:4. Problems of Growth

New religious insights arise out of conflicts which initiate the choosing of new and better reaction habits. Religious perplexities are inevitable; there can be no growth without psychic conflict and spiritual agitation. Loyalties are not exercised in behalf of the great, the good, the true, and the noble without a struggle. But the great problem of religious living consists in the task of unifying the soul powers of the personality by the dominance of LOVE. Health, mental efficiency, and happiness arise from the unification of physical systems, mind systems, and spirit systems. The highest happiness is indissolubly linked with spiritual progress.

You can best discover values in your associates by discovering their motivation. If some one irritates you, causes feelings of resentment, you should sympathetically seek to discern his viewpoint, his reasons for such objectionable conduct. If once you understand your neighbor, you will become tolerant, and this tolerance will grow into friendship and ripen into love. Love is infectious, and when human devotion is intelligent and wise, love is more catching than hate. If each mortal could only become a focus of dynamic affection, all civilization would be encompassed by love, and that would be the realization of the brotherhood of man.

100:5. Conversion and Mysticism

The world is filled with lost souls wandering about in confusion among the isms and cults of a frustrated philosophic era. Too few have learned how to install a philosophy of living in the place of religious authority. Most of the spectacular phenomena associated with so-called religious conversions are entirely psychologic in nature, but now and then there do occur experiences which are also spiritual in origin. The great danger in psychic speculations is that visions and other so-called mystic experiences, along with extraordinary dreams, may be regarded as divine communications to the human mind. The better approach to the morontia zones of possible contact with the Thought Adjuster would be through living faith and sincere worship, wholehearted and unselfish prayer. Under no circumstances should the trancelike state of visionary consciousness be cultivated as a religious experience. The mystic status is favored by such things as: physical fatigue, fasting, psychic dissociation, profound aesthetic experiences, vivid sex impulses, fear, anxiety, rage, and wild dancing. It should be clearly understood that Jesus of Nazareth never resorted to such methods for communion with the Paradise Father.

100:6. Marks of Religious Living

True religion is a wholehearted devotion to some reality which the religionist deems to be of supreme value to himself and for all mankind. The accepted supreme value of the religionist may be base or even false, but it is nevertheless religious. A religion is genuine to just the extent that the value which is held to be supreme is truly a cosmic reality of genuine spiritual worth. The intense striving for the attainment of supermortal ideals is always characterized by increasing patience, forbearance, fortitude, and tolerance. True religion is a living love, a life of service. It generates new types of enthusiasm, zeal, and courage. One of the most amazing earmarks of religious living is dynamic and sublime peace. The characteristic difference between evolved and revealed religion is that the latter produces a new quality of divine wisdom which is added to purely experiential human wisdom.

100:7. The Acme of Religious Living

Although the average mortal of Urantia cannot hope to attain the high perfection of character which Jesus of Nazareth acquired, it is altogether possible for every mortal believer to develop a strong and unified personality along the perfected lines of the Jesus personality. The unique feature of the Master's personality was not so much its perfection as its symmetry and balanced unification. The unfailing kindness of Jesus touched the hearts of men, but his stalwart strength of character amazed his followers. He was unquestioningly loyal to all truth. He was surcharged with divine enthusiasm, but he never became fanatical. He frankly faced the realities of life, but he was never dull or prosaic. Jesus was very broad in his outlook. He was immune to disappointment and impervious to persecution. His constant word of exhortation was, "Be of good cheer." He was candid, but always kind. His courage was equaled only by his patience. His watchword was, "Fear not." He was gentle and unassuming in his personal life, and yet he was the perfected man of a universe. And today he unifies life, ennobles character, and simplifies experience. He enters the human mind to elevate, transform, and transfigure it. It is literally true: "If any man has Christ Jesus within him, he is a new creature."

Paper 101: The Real Nature of Religion

Melchizedek

RELIGION, as a human experience, transcends the reason of the mind, even the logic of philosophy. Religion *is* faith, trust, and assurance.

101:1. True Religion

True religion is the experiencing of divinity in the consciousness of a moral being; it represents true experience with eternal realities in time. These experiences are made available through the naturally ordained mechanism of mortal mind. The divine spirit makes contact with mortal man, not by feelings or emotions, but in the realm of the highest and most spiritualized thinking. Religion lives and prospers by faith and insight. It is ever more or less mysterious and always indefinable and inexplicable in terms of purely intellectual reason and philosophic logic. Man finally reaches that position of mind and that attitude of soul where he concludes that he *has no right not to believe in God*. To doubt God or distrust his goodness would be to prove untrue to the realest and deepest thing within the human mind and soul—the divine Adjuster.

101:2. The Fact of Religion

The fact of religion consists wholly in the religious experience of human beings. Reason is the method of science; faith is the method of religion; logic is the attempted technique of philosophy. Revelation compensates for the absence of the morontia viewpoint. True revelation never renders science unnatural, religion unreasonable, or philosophy illogical. Revelation is validated only by human experience and confirms the experiential harmony of science, philosophy, and religion. Revelation as an epochal phenomenon is periodic; as a personal human experience it is continuous. The realization of religion never has been, and never will be, dependent on great learning or clever logic. Religious faith is available alike to the learned and the unlearned. Your only assurance of a personal God consists in your own insight and experience. Only theology, the province of faith and the technique of revelation, can afford any sort of intelligent account of the nature and content of religious experience.

101:3. The Characteristics of Religion.

Religion is so vital that it persists in the absence of learning. Faith-insight and spiritual philosophy constitute man a spirit personality in potential destiny. Genuine spiritual faith is revealed in that it: produces a sublime trust in the goodness of God even in the face of bitter disappointment and crushing defeat; exhibits inexplicable poise and sustaining tranquility notwithstanding baffling diseases and even acute physical suffering; persists in the unswerving belief in God despite all contrary demonstrations of logic and successfully withstands all other intellectual sophistries; steadfastly adheres to a sublime belief in universe unity and divine guidance regardless of the perplexing presence of evil and sin; goes right on worshiping God in spite of anything and everything. It is just such a vital and vigorous performance of faith that entitles mortal man to affirm the personal possession and spiritual reality of the crowning endowment of human nature, religious experience.

101:4. The Limitations of Revelation

Any cosmology presented as a part of revealed religion is destined to be outgrown in a very short time. Mankind should understand that we who participate in the revelation of truth are very rigorously limited by the instructions of our superiors. We full well know that, while the historic facts and religious truths of this series of revelatory presentations will stand on the records of the ages to come, within a few short years many of our statements regarding the physical sciences will stand in need of revision. Nevertheless, such revelations are of immense value in that they at least transiently clarify knowledge by presenting cosmic data in such a manner as to illuminate the spiritual teachings contained in the accompanying revelation. While divine or spiritual insight is a gift, human wisdom must evolve.

101:5. Religion Expanded by Revelation

Revelation is a technique whereby ages upon ages of time are saved in the necessary work of sorting and sifting the errors of evolution from the truths of spirit acquirement. It is a part of the plan of the universe that, sooner or later, evolutionary religion is destined to receive the spiritual expansion of revelation. Evolved religion rests wholly on faith. Revelation has the additional assurance of its expanded presentation of the truths of divinity and reality. Such a working union of human faith and divine truth constitutes the possession of a character well on the road to the actual acquirement of a morontial personality. Increasingly throughout the morontia progression the assurance of truth replaces the assurance of faith. When you are finally mustered into the actual spirit world, then will the assurances of pure spirit insight be superimposed upon these former techniques of personality assurance.

101:6. Progressive Religious Experience

Morontia insight entails an ever-expanding consciousness of the Sevenfold, the Supreme, and even the Ultimate. Throughout all religious experience, the Adjuster is the secret of the personal realization of the reality of the existence of the Supreme, and also holds the secrets of your faith in the transcendental attainment of the Ultimate. The faith of Jesus pointed the way to finality of human salvation since it provided for salvation from: material fetters, intellectual bondage, spiritual blindness, incompleteness of self, and finite time through the perfected oneness with Deity in and through the Supreme. Through the appropriation of the faith of Jesus, mortal man can foretaste in time the realities of eternity. Jesus was and is the new and living way whereby man can come into the divine inheritance which the Father has decreed shall be his for but the asking.

101:7. A Personal Philosophy of Religion

The materials out of which to build a personal philosophy of religion are derived from both the inner and the environmental experience of the individual. The soundness of philosophic conclusions depends on keen, honest, and discriminating thinking in connection with sensitivity to meanings and accuracy of evaluation. There are four phases in the evolution of religious philosophy: submission to tradition and authority; satisfaction with slight attainments; progression to the level of logical intellectuality but there stagnating in cultural slavery; and attainment of freedom from all conventional and traditional handicaps, daring to think, act, and live honestly, loyally, fearlessly, and truthfully. The acid test for any religious philosophy consists in whether or not it distinguishes between the realities of the material and the spiritual worlds while at the same moment recognizing their unification in intellectual striving and in social serving.

101:8. Faith and Belief

Belief has attained the level of faith when it motivates life and shapes the mode of living. Belief is always limiting and binding; faith is expanding and releasing. Belief fixates, faith liberates. Living religious faith is more than the association of noble beliefs; it is more than an exalted system of philosophy; it is a living experience concerned with spiritual meanings, divine ideals, and supreme values; it is God-knowing and man-serving. Beliefs may become group possessions, but faith must be personal. Living faith does not foster bigotry, persecution, or intolerance. Faith does not shackle the creative imagination, neither does it maintain an unreasoning prejudice toward the discoveries of scientific investigation. Faith vitalizes religion and constrains the religionist heroically to live the golden rule. The zeal of faith is according to knowledge, and its strivings are the preludes to sublime peace.

101:9. Religion and Morality

Revelation unfailingly enlarges the ethical horizon of evolved religion while it simultaneously and unfailingly expands the moral obligations of all prior revelations. Do not make the mistake of judging another's religion by your own standards of knowledge and truth. True religion is that sublime and profound conviction within the soul which compellingly admonishes man that it would be wrong for him not to believe in his highest ethical and moral concepts and in the universe's deepest realities. The search for beauty is a part of religion only in so far as it is ethical. Religion creates for the human mind a spiritualized consciousness of divine reality. Religion thereby becomes a censor in moral affairs. It also establishes confidence in the enhanced realities of time and the more enduring realities of eternity. Faith becomes the connection between moral consciousness and the spiritual concept of enduring reality.

101:10. Religion As Man's Liberator

The exhaustion of the possibilities of logic and reason will never reveal to the reasoner the eternal truth of the survival of personality. Nor can there be either scientific or logical proofs of divinity. It is only through the morontial avenue leading to spiritual insight that man can ever break the fetters inherent in his mortal status in the universe. Mankind can never discover divinity except through the avenue of religious experience and by the exercise of true faith. But it will always remain true: Whosoever wills to do the will of God shall comprehend the validity of spiritual values. Religion effectually cures man's sense of isolation by identifying him with the plan of the Infinite and the purpose of the Eternal. Such a liberated soul immediately begins to feel at home in this new universe, his universe. Now are the sons of God enlisted together in fighting the battle of reality's triumph over the partial shadows of existence. The divine hosts of a well-nigh limitless universe are on their side in the supernal struggle to attain eternity of life and divinity of status; and all is transformed from the uncertainties of material isolation to the sureties of eternal spiritual progression.

Paper 102: The Foundations of Religious Faith
Melchizedek

TO the unbelieving materialist, man is simply an evolutionary accident; the devotional labors and inspirational genius of the best of men are doomed to be extinguished by death. Nameless despair is man's only reward for living and toiling under the temporal sun of mortal existence. But such is not man's end and eternal destiny; such a vision is but the cry of despair uttered by some wandering soul blinded by the confusion and distortion of a complex learning. And all this doom of darkness and all this destiny of despair are forever dispelled by one brave stretch of faith on the part of the most humble and unlearned of God's children on earth.

102:1. Assurances of Faith

If any man chooses to do the divine will, he shall know the way of truth. It is literally true, "Human things must be known in order to be loved, but divine things must be loved in order to be known." What knowledge and reason cannot do for us, true wisdom admonishes us to allow faith to accomplish through religious insight and spiritual transformation. Truth remains unchanged from generation to generation. The certainties of science proceed entirely from the intellect; the certitudes of religion spring from the very foundations of the entire personality. The indwelling Thought Adjuster unfailingly arouses in man's soul a true and searching hunger for perfection together with a far-reaching curiosity which can be adequately satisfied only by communion with God. Whatever more God may be than a high and perfect moral personality, he cannot be anything less.

102:2. Religion and Reality

Religion is the property of the human race; it is not a child of culture. True, one's perception of religion is still human and therefore subject to the bondage of ignorance, the slavery of superstition, and the delusions of false philosophy. The wisdom of religious experience is something of a paradox in that it is both humanly original and Adjuster derivative. Religionists exhibit a stabilization of personality and a tranquility of character not explained by the laws of physiology, psychology, and sociology. It is the mission of religion to prepare man for bravely, even heroically, facing the vicissitudes of life. The mind perspective can and sometime will portray to man the experiential synthesis of energy, mind, and spirit in and as the Supreme Being. Unity is best found in human experience through philosophy. There is no real religion apart from a highly active personality. True religion must act. We are not blind to the fact that religion often acts unwisely, even irreligiously, but it acts, it is dynamic!

102:3. Knowledge, Wisdom, and Insight

Religion must continually labor under a paradoxical necessity: the necessity of making effective use of thought while at the same time discounting the spiritual serviceableness of all thinking. Speculation tends to translate religion into something material or humanistic. Real religion leads to increased social service. Science, knowledge, leads to fact consciousness; religion, experience, leads to value consciousness; philosophy, wisdom, leads to co-ordinate consciousness; revelation (the substitute for morontia mota) leads to the consciousness of true reality. Philosophy attempts the identification of the material segments of science with the spiritual-insight concept of the whole. In science, the idea precedes the expression of its realization; in religion, the experience of realization precedes the expression of the idea. Evolution tends to make God manlike; revelation tends to make man Godlike. Science is only satisfied with first causes, religion with supreme personality, and philosophy with unity. Revelation affirms that these three are one, and that all are good.

102:4. The Fact of Experience

Because of the presence in your minds of the Thought Adjuster, it is no more of a mystery for you to know the mind of God than for you to be sure of the consciousness of knowing any other mind. What is human experience? It is simply any interplay between an active and questioning self and any other active and external reality. The fact of experience is found in self-consciousness plus other-existences—things, minds, and spiritual reality. Faith translates this natural experience into religion, the recognition of God as the reality—source, nature, and destiny—of other-mindedness.

The element of error present in human religious experience is directly proportional to the content of materialism which contaminates the spiritual concept of the Universal Father. Deity is more than spirit but the spiritual approach is the only one possible to ascending man.

The reflective powers of the mind are deepened and broadened by worship. Prayer may enrich the life, but worship illuminates destiny. Revealed religion is the unifying element of human existence. Revelation unifies history, co-ordinates geology, astronomy, physics, chemistry, biology, sociology, and psychology. Spiritual experience is the real soul of man's cosmos.

102:5. The Supremacy of Purposive Potential

In the time universes, potential is always supreme over the actual. In the evolving cosmos the potential is what is to be, and what is to be is the unfolding of the purposive mandates of Deity. Human morality may recognize values, but only religion can conserve, exalt, and spiritualize such values. Religion is to morality as love is to duty, as essence is to substance. Morality discloses an almighty Controller; religion discloses an all-loving Father, a God to be worshiped and loved. Indeed the spiritual potentiality of religion is dominant over the duty actuality of the morality of evolution.

102:6. The Certainty of Religious Faith

The philosophic elimination of religious fear and the steady progress of science add greatly to the mortality of false gods; they eventually destroy that ignorance and superstition which so long obscured the living God of eternal love. The religionist of philosophic attainment has faith in a personal God of love and personal salvation. Love is the essence of religion and the wellspring of superior civilization. Convictions about God may be arrived at through wise reasoning, but the individual becomes God-knowing only by faith, through personal experience. The God-knowing soul dares to say, "I know." God is the first truth and the last fact; therefore does all truth take origin in him, while all facts exist relative to him. The positive always has the advantage over the negative, truth over error, experience over theory, spiritual realities over the isolated facts of time and space. The higher any scientist progresses in his chosen science, the more will he abandon the theories of materialistic fact in favor of the cosmic truth of the dominance of the Supreme Mind. Materialism cheapens human life; the gospel of Jesus tremendously enhances and supernally exalts every mortal.

102:7. The Certitude of the Divine

God is the one and only self-caused fact in the universe. He is the secret of the order, plan, and purpose of the whole creation of things and beings. Man can, intellectually, deny God and yet be morally good, loyal, filial, honest, and even idealistic. In such a mortal experience only social fruits are forthcoming, not spiritual. The God-knowing individual is not one who is blind to the difficulties which stand in the way of finding God in the maze of superstition, tradition, and materialistic tendencies of modern times. He has encountered all these deterrents and surmounted them by living faith, and attained the highlands of spiritual experience in spite of them. Only an unqualified reality, an absolute, could dare consistently to be dogmatic. Those who assume to be dogmatic must, if consistent, sooner or later be driven into the arms of the Absolute of energy, the Universal of truth, and the Infinite of love. Of God, the most inescapable of all presences, the most real of all facts, the most living of all truths, the most loving of all friends, and the most divine of all values, we have the right to be the most certain of all universe experiences.

102:8. The Evidences of Religion

The highest evidence of the reality and efficacy of religion consists in the fact of human experience—that power and person designated by his faith as God. Regarding the status of any religion in the evolutionary scale, it may best be judged by its moral judgments and its ethical standards. Many of the world's most notable religious teachers have been virtually unlettered. The wisdom of the world is not necessary to an exercise of saving faith in eternal realities. It is regretfully recorded that institutional religion has invariably lagged behind the slowly changing mores of the human races. The prophets have usually led the people in religious development; the theologians have usually held them back. Religion, being a matter of inner or personal experience, can never develop very far in advance of the intellectual evolution of the races. Religion is never enhanced by an appeal to the so-called miraculous. The highest religion yet revealed in the universe of Nebadon is the earth life of Jesus of Nazareth.

Paper 103: The Reality of Religious Experience
Melchizedek

THE Thought Adjuster is the cosmic window through which the finite creature may faith-glimpse the certainties and divinities of limitless

Deity, the Universal Father. As natural religious experience continues to progress, periodic revelations of truth punctuate the otherwise slow-moving course of planetary evolution.

103:1. Philosophy of Religion

The unity of religious experience among a social or racial group derives from the identical nature of the God fragment indwelling the individual. But since personality is unique it inevitably follows that no two human beings can similarly interpret the leadings and urges of the spirit of divinity which lives within their minds. A group of mortals can experience spiritual unity, but they can never attain philosophic uniformity. It is most important that you should be exposed to the knowledge of a vast number of other religious experiences to the end that you may prevent your religious life from becoming egocentric and circumscribed. It is much easier for men to agree on religious values (goals) than on beliefs (interpretations). A given person can maintain his religious experience in the face of giving up or changing many of his religious beliefs.

103:2. Religion and the Individual

The "birth" of religion is not sudden; it is rather a gradual emergence. You do not enter the kingdom of heaven unless you have been "born again"— born of the Spirit. No religious development occurs without conscious effort and positive and individual determinations. The first promptings of a child's moral nature are impulses of justice, fairness, and urges to kindness. Every human being very early experiences something of a conflict between his self-seeking and his altruistic impulses. The psychology of a child is naturally positive, not negative. When the growing child fails of personality unification, the altruistic drive may become so overdeveloped as to work serious injury to the welfare of the self. A misguided conscience can become responsible for much conflict, worry, sorrow, and no end of human unhappiness.

103:3. Religion and the Human Race

In the evolutionary origin of primitive religions, you should not overlook the influence of the clan or tribal spirit of solidarity. But the social group is not the source of religious experience. The true religious impulse has its origin in genuine spirit presences activating the will to be unselfish. Religion is designed to change man's environment, but much of the religion found among mortals today has become helpless to do this. Environment has all too often mastered religion. In the religion of all ages the experience which is paramount is the feeling regarding moral values and social meanings, not the thinking regarding theologic dogmas or philosophic theories. Religion evolves favorably as the element of magic is replaced by the concept of morals. Powerful influences—one human and the other divine—insured the survival of religion throughout the vicissitudes of the ages and that notwithstanding it was so often threatened with extinction by a thousand subversive tendencies and hostile antagonisms.

103:4. Spiritual Communion

The characteristic difference between a social occasion and a religious gathering is that religious groups are pervaded by the atmosphere of communion. Even in Christianity the Lord's Supper retains this mode of communion. The hunger and thirst for righteousness leads to the discovery of truth and ideals, and this creates new problems, for our ideals tend to grow by geometrical progression, while our ability to live up to them is enhanced only by arithmetical progression. Man cannot hope to live up to his highest ideals, but he can be true to his purpose of finding God and becoming more and more like him. Jesus swept away all of the ceremonials of sacrifice and atonement. He destroyed the basis of all this fictitious guilt and sense of isolation in the universe by declaring that man is a child of God. God the Father deals with man his child on the basis, not of actual virtue or worthiness, but in recognition of the child's motivation—the creature purpose and intent. The relationship is one of parent-child association and is actuated by divine love.

103:5. The Origin of Ideals

Primitive man regards as neighbor only those very close to him. Jesus enlarged the neighbor scope to embrace the whole of humanity, even that we should love our enemies. Human happiness is achieved only when the ego desire of the self and the altruistic urge of the higher self (divine spirit) are co-ordinated and reconciled by the unified will of the integrating and supervising personality. The attempt to secure equal good for the self and for the greatest number of other selves presents a problem which cannot always be satisfactorily resolved in a time-space frame.

The life after death is no different in the essentials than the mortal existence. Everything we do in this life which is good contributes directly to the enhancement of the future life. Man is most truly the architect of his own eternal destiny.

Spiritual growth is greatest where all external pressures are at a minimum. But this must not be construed as meaning that there is no place in a progressive society for home, social institutions, church, and state.

The security of a religious group depends on spiritual unity, not on theological uniformity. There is great hope for any church that worships the living God, validates the brotherhood of man, and dares to remove all creedal pressure from its members.

103:6. Philosophical Co-ordination

Theology is always the study of *your* religion; the study of another's religion is psychology. When man approaches the study and examination of his universe from the outside, he brings into being the various physical sciences; when he approaches the research of himself and the universe from the inside, he gives origin to theology and metaphysics. Philosophy strives to harmonize the many discrepancies which are destined at first to appear between the findings and teachings of these two diametrically opposite avenues of approaching the universe of things and beings. Never can either science or religion, in and of themselves, standing alone, hope to gain an adequate understanding of universal truths and relationships without the guidance of human philosophy and the illumination of divine revelation. Metaphysics stands for man's well-meant but futile effort to compensate for the absence of the mota of morontia. The highest attainable philosophy of mortal man must be logically based on the reason of science, the faith of religion, and the truth insight afforded by revelation. By this union man can compensate somewhat for his failure to develop an adequate metaphysics and for his inability to comprehend morontia mota.

103:7. Science and Religion

True salvation is the technique of the divine evolution of the mortal mind from matter identification through the realms of morontia liaison to the high universe status of spiritual correlation. As ascending man reaches inward and Paradiseward for the God experience, he will likewise be reaching outward and spaceward for an energy understanding of the material cosmos. The union of the scientific attitude and the religious insight by the mediation of experiential philosophy is part of man's long Paradise-ascension experience. The teachers of both science and religion are often altogether too self-confident and dogmatic. Revelation functions to co-ordinate both science and religion with the truth of reality. It affords a common meeting ground for the discoveries of both science and religion and makes possible the human attempt logically to correlate these separate but interdependent domains of thought into a well-balanced philosophy. Science discovers the material world, religion evaluates it, and philosophy endeavors to interpret its meanings while co-ordinating the scientific material viewpoint with the religious spiritual concept. But history is a realm in which science and religion may never fully agree.

103:8. Philosophy and Religion

Although both science and philosophy may assume the probability of God by their reason and logic, only the personal religious experience of a spirit-led man can affirm the certainty of such a supreme and personal Deity. The experiencing of God may be wholly valid, but the discourse *about* God, being intellectual and philosophical, is divergent and oftentimes confusingly fallacious. The certainty of the God-knowing religionist should not be disturbed by the uncertainty of the doubting materialist. Philosophy, to be of the greatest service to both science and religion, should avoid the extremes of both materialism and pantheism. Revelation is a compensation for the frailties of evolving philosophy.

103:9. The Essence of Religion

Religion has to do with feeling, acting, and living, not merely with thinking. No matter how illusory and erroneous one's theology, one's religion may be wholly genuine and everlastingly true. Buddhism in its original form is one of the best religions without a God which has arisen throughout all the evolutionary history of Urantia. Jesus' life and teachings finally divested religion of the superstitions of magic, the illusions of mythology, and the bondage of traditional dogmatism.

Although religious experience is a purely spiritual subjective phenomenon, such an experience embraces a positive and living faith attitude toward the highest realms of universe objective reality. When theology masters religion, religion dies; it becomes a doctrine instead of a life. Reason, wisdom, and faith are man's highest human attainments. Faith most willingly carries reason along as far as reason can go and then goes on with wisdom to the full philosophic limit; and then it dares to launch out upon the limitless and never-ending universe journey in the sole company of TRUTH. There is a reality in religious experience that is proportional to the spiritual content, and such a reality is transcendent to reason, science, philosophy, wisdom, and all other human achievements. The convictions of such an experience are unassailable, and the destinies final.

Paper 104: Growth of the Trinity Concept
Melchizedek

THE Trinity concept of revealed religion must not be confused with the triad beliefs of evolutionary religions. Sometimes the concept of an evolutionary triad has become mixed with that of a revealed Trinity; in these instances it is often impossible to distinguish one from the other.

104:1. Urantia Trinity Concepts

The first Urantian revelation leading to the comprehension of the Paradise Trinity was made by the staff of Prince Caligastia about one-half million years ago. The second presentation of the Trinity was made by Adam and Eve in the first and second gardens. The third presentation of the Trinity was made by Machiventa Melchizedek. Through the activities of the Salem missionaries the Melchizedek teachings of the Trinity gradually spread throughout much of Eurasia and northern Africa. Among the Hindus the trinitarian concept took root as Being, Intelligence, and Joy—later as Brahma, Siva, and Vishnu. The Buddhist faith developed two doctrines of a trinitarian nature: The earlier was Teacher, Law, and Brotherhood; the later idea embraced Supreme Lord, Holy Spirit, and Incarnate Savior. The Hebrews knew about the Trinity from the Kenite traditions of the days of Melchizedek, but by the time of Jesus' appearance the Elohim doctrine had been practically eradicated from Jewish theology. The followers of the Islamic faith likewise failed to grasp the idea of the Trinity. Jesus taught his apostles the truth regarding the persons of the Paradise Trinity, but they thought he spoke figuratively and symbolically. Paul confused Jesus, the Creator Son of the local universe, with the Second Person of Deity, the Eternal Son of Paradise. Not since the times of Jesus has the factual identity of the Paradise Trinity been known on Urantia (except by a few individuals to whom it was especially revealed) until its presentation in these revelatory disclosures.

104:2. Trinity Unity and Deity Plurality

Personality in Deity demands that such Deity exist in relation to other personalities of equal Deity quality. Through the recognition of the Trinity concept the mind of man can hope to grasp something of the interrelationship of love and law in the time-space creations. He should recognize the Trinity sovereignty extending outward from Paradise.

The Paradise Trinity is a real entity—not a personality but nonetheless compatible with coexistent personalities—the personalities of the Father, the Son, and the Spirit. Trinity functions are something unique, original, and not wholly predictable from an analysis of the attributes of Father, Son, and Spirit. The Gods, as persons, do not administer justice, but they perform this very function as a collective whole, as the Paradise Trinity. The Trinity concept prepares the human mind for the further presentation of certain other threefold relationships.

104:3. Trinities and Triunities

All that is true of the Paradise Trinity is not necessarily true of a triunity. A triunity is not an entity as is the Trinity. The relationship of its members is functional rather than organic. Its functions are something other than the discernible sum of the attributes of the component members, Through them the Universal Father exercises immediate and personal control over the master functions of infinity.

104:4. The Seven Triunities

In attempting the description of seven triunities, attention is directed to the fact that the Universal Father is the primal member of each. The Universal Father is the personal cause of the Absolutes; he is the absolute of Absolutes. The nature and meaning of the seven triunities may be suggested as: *The First Triunity*—the personal-purposive triunity: the Universal Father, the Eternal Son, the Infinite Spirit. This is the threefold union of love, mercy, and ministry. *The Second Triunity*—the power-pattern triunity: The Father-Son, The Paradise Isle, The Conjoint Actor. Whether it be a tiny ultimaton or a superuniverse, the physical pattern is derived from the function of this triunity. *The Third Triunity*—the spirit-evolutional triunity: the Universal Father, the Son-Spirit, the Deity Absolute. The entirety of spiritual manifestation has its beginning and end in this association. *The Fourth Triunity*—the triunity of energy infinity: the Father-Spirit, the Paradise Isle, the Unqualified Absolute. Within this triunity there eternalizes the beginnings and the endings of all energy reality. *The Fifth Triunity*—the triunity of reactive infinity: the Universal Father, the Universal Absolute, the Unqualified Absolute. This grouping yields the eternalization of the functional infinity of all that is actualizable within the domains of nondeity reality. *The Sixth Triunity*—the triunity of cosmic-associated Deity: the Universal Father, the Deity Absolute, the Universal Absolute. This is the immanence of Deity in conjunction with the transcendence of Deity. *The Seventh Triunity*—the triunity of infinite unity: the Universal Father, the Conjoint Actor, the Universal Absolute. This is the unity of infinity functionally manifest in time and eternity. The triunities are the functional balance wheel of infinity, the unification of the uniqueness of the Seven Infinity Absolutes.

104:5. Triodities

The Triodity of Actuality: the Eternal Son, the Paradise Isle, the Conjoint Actor. This triodity consists in the interrelationship of the three absolute actuals. The Eternal Son is the absolute of spirit reality, the absolute personality. The Paradise Isle is the absolute of cosmic reality, the absolute pattern. The Conjoint Actor is the absolute of mind reality, the co-ordinate of absolute spirit reality, and the existential Deity synthesis of personality and power. *The Triodity of Potentiality*: the Deity Absolute, the Universal Absolute, the Unqualified Absolute. This triodity consists in the association of the three Absolutes of potentiality. Thus are interassociated the infinity reservoirs of all latent energy reality—spirit, mindal, or cosmic. The triunities are indirectly concerned, but the triodities are directly concerned, in the experiential Deities—Supreme, Ultimate, and Absolute. They appear in the emerging power-personality synthesis of the Supreme Being. And to the time creatures of space the Supreme Being is a revelation of the unity of the I AM.

Paper 105: Deity and Reality
Melchizedek

THE human mind can hardly form an adequate concept of eternity existences. Nevertheless, we may attempt such a presentation, although we are fully aware that our concepts must be subjected to profound distortion in the process of translation-modification to the comprehension level of mortal mind.

105:1. The Philosophic Concept of the I AM

Absolute primal causation in infinity the philosophers of the universes attribute to the Universal Father functioning as the infinite, the eternal, and the absolute I AM. No qualification can be applied to the Infinite except to state that the I AM is. When we speak of the Father, we mean God as he is understandable by his creatures both high and low, but there is much more of Deity which is not comprehensible to universe creatures. When you stand in awe of the magnitude of the master universe, pause to consider that even this inconceivable creation can be no more than a partial revelation of the Infinite. Unqualified infinity is meaningless to the finite creature. But the face which the Infinite turns toward all universe personalities is the face of a Father, the Universal Father of love.

105:2. The I AM as Triune and as Sevenfold

In considering the genesis of reality, ever bear in mind that all absolute reality is from eternity and is without beginning of existence. By absolute reality we refer to the three existential persons of Deity, the Isle of Paradise, and the three Absolutes.

The self-metamorphoses of the I AM establishes the sevenfold nature of reality: 1. *The Universal Father*, the I AM father of the Eternal Son, the primal personality relationship of actualities. 2. *The Universal Controller*, the I AM cause of eternal Paradise, the master pattern from which all copies are made. 3. *The Universal Creator*, the I AM one with the Eternal Son. This union of the Father and the Son initiates the creative cycle, which is consummated in the appearance of the conjoint personality and the eternal universe. From the finite mortal's viewpoint, reality has its true beginnings with the eternity appearance of the Havona creation. 4. *The Infinite Upholder*, the I AM self-associative. This phase of the I AM is best understood as the Universal Absolute—the unifier of the Deity and the Unqualified Absolutes. 5. *The Infinite Potential*, the I AM self-qualified. This is the volitional self-limitation of the I AM by virtue of which there was achieved threefold self-expression and self-revelation, understood as the Deity Absolute. 6. *The Infinite Ca-*

pacity, the I AM static-reactive. This is the possibility for all future cosmic expansion in the presence of the Unqualified Absolute. 7. *The Universal One of Infinity*, the I AM as I AM. This is the self-relationship of Infinity, the divine Father of all personality, the absolute coherence of pure energy and of pure spirit in the presence of the Universal Father.

105:3. The Seven Absolutes of Infinity

The seven prime relationships within the I AM eternalize as the Seven Absolutes of Infinity: 1. *The First Source and Center*, the First Person of Deity, the Universal Father, creator, controller, and upholder; universal love, eternal spirit, and infinite energy. 2. *The Second Source and Center*, the Second Person of Deity, the Eternal and Original Son, the absolute personality. 3. *The Paradise Source and Center*, second nondeity pattern. Paradise is the absolute of patterns. 4. *The Third Source and Center*, the Third Person of Deity, the Conjoint Actor; infinite integrator of Paradise cosmic energies with the spirit energies of the Eternal Son, and the source of mind. 5. *The Deity Absolute*, the causational, potentially personal possibilities of universal reality, the totality of all Deity potential. 6. *The Unqualified Absolute*, static, reactive, and abeyant; the unrevealed cosmic infinity of the I AM; totality of nondeified reality and finality of all nonpersonal potential. 7. *The Universal Absolute*, the Unifier of the deified and the undeified; correlator of the absolute and the relative. It is both fact and truth that all reality is predicated upon the eternity existence and infinity relationships of the Seven Absolutes of Infinity.

105:4. Unity, Duality, and Triunity

The universe philosophers postulate the eternity existence of the I AM as the primal source of all reality. And concomitant therewith they postulate the self-segmentation of the I AM into the primary self-relationships—the seven phases of infinity. And simultaneous with this assumption is the third postulate—the eternity appearance of the Seven Absolutes of Infinity and the eternalization of the duality association of the seven phases of the I AM and these seven Absolutes. The I AM is unqualified infinity as unity. The dualities eternalize reality foundations. The triunities eventuate the potential of all reality.

105:5. Promulgation of Finite Reality

The promulgation of finite reality is the result of the volitional acts of Paradise Deity and the repercussional adjustments of the functional triunities. It should be borne in mind that transcendentals both preceded and succeeded all that is finite. With the appearance of relative and qualified reality there comes into being a new cycle of reality—the growth cycle. These inconceivable transactions mark the beginning of universe history, mark the coming into existence of time itself. This newly appearing finite reality exists in two original phases: the constitutively perfect and the evolutionally perfected. But these differences, which are so important this side of Paradise, are nonexistent in eternity. There is still another type: Trinitizing and other relationships result in the appearance of tertiary maximums—things, meanings, and values that are neither perfect nor perfected yet are co-ordinate with both ancestral factors.

105:6. Repercussions of Finite Reality

Among the repercussions to the creative actualization of the finite, are the appearance of supremacy activities and the physical organization of the seven superuniverses. The divinity response to the imperfection in the evolutionary creations is disclosed in the compensating presence of God the Sevenfold. The time lag of evolution makes possible creature participation in divine creation. Even the material mind of the mortal creature thus becomes partner with the divine Adjuster. God the Sevenfold also provides techniques of compensation for the experiential limitations of inherent perfection as well as compensating the preascension limitations of imperfection.

105:7. Eventuation of Transcendentals

Transcendentals are subinfinite and subabsolute but superfinite and supercreatural. Transcendentals eventuate as an integrating level correlating the supervalues of absolutes with the maximum values of finites. That which is transcendental is not necessarily nondevelopmental, but it is superevolutional in the finite sense; neither is it nonexperiential, but it is superexperience as such is meaningful to creatures. Perhaps the best illustration of such a paradox is Havona—something which is not exactly finite nor yet absolute. As the Supreme is associated with finites, so the Ultimate is identified with transcendentals. The Ultimate is an eventuation of new Deity realities, such as absonite qualities and realities. The universe in which we now live may be thought of as existing on finite, transcendental, and absolute levels. It is altogether possible that the continued diversification of the original reality of the First Source and Center may proceed onward and outward throughout age upon age, on and on, into the faraway and inconceivable stretches of absolute infinity.

Paper 106: Universe Levels of Reality
Melchizedek

THE ascending mortal should know something of the relationships existing between himself and the numerous levels of existential and experiential realities: 1. *Incomplete finites*. This is the present status of the ascending creatures of the grand universe. 2. *Maximum finites.* Some phases of Havona appear to be on the maximum order. 3. *Transcendentals.* This superfinite level (antecedently) follows finite progression. 4. *Ultimates.* This level encompasses that which is of master universe significance. 5. *Coabsolutes.* This level implies the projection of experientials upon a supermaster universe field of creative expression. 6. *Absolutes.* This level connotes the eternity presence of the seven existential Absolutes. 7. *Infinity.* This level is pre-existential and postexperiential. These concepts are entirely relative and limited by mortal language, mortal mind, and other limitations which we encounter in attempting to present a unified concept of the cosmic growth of things, meanings, and values and of their synthesis on ever-ascending levels of reality.

106:1. Primary Association of Finite Functionals

The primary or spirit-origin phases of finite reality find immediate expression on creature levels as perfect personalities and on universe levels as the perfect Havona creation. Even experiential Deity is expressed in the spirit person of God the Supreme in Havona. But the secondary, evolutionary, time-and-matter-conditioned phases of the finite become cosmically integrated only as a result of growth and attainment. It is thus possible for the creature to enter into partnership with the Creator. During these times of expanding growth the incomplete is correlated with the perfect through the ministry of God the Sevenfold. All is destined to be eternally unified in the emerging personality of the Supreme Being.

106:2. Secondary Supreme Finite Integration

As God the Sevenfold functionally co-ordinates finite evolution, so does the Supreme Being eventually synthesize destiny attainment. The concept of the Supreme must provide for the differential recognition of spirit person, evolutionary power, and power-personality synthesis—the unification of evolutionary power with, and its dominance by, spirit personality. Thus does the Supreme Being eventually attain to the embrace of all of everything evolving in time and space while investing these qualities with spirit personality. When ascenders attain the postulated seventh stage of spirit existence, they will therein experience the realization of a new meaning-value of the absoluteness and infinity of the triodities as such is revealed on subabsolute levels in the Supreme Being. But the attainment of these stages of maximum development will probably await the co-ordinate settling of the entire grand universe in light and life.

106:3. Transcendental Tertiary Reality Association

The absonite architects eventuate the plan; the Supreme Creators bring it into existence; the Supreme Being will consummate its fullness. The appearance of the Almighty Supreme at the termination of the present universe age will lead to the completed function of the first experiential Trinity—the union of the Supreme Creators, the Supreme Being, and the Architects of the Master Universe. This Trinity is destined to effect the further evolutionary integration of the master creation. In the ages to come, after the seven superuniverses have been settled in light and life, the Corps of the Finality will doubtless be promulgating the purposes of the Paradise Deities as they are dictated by the Trinity Ultimate, and as they are power-personality unified in the Supreme Being.

106:4. Ultimate Quartan Integration

While the Trinity Ultimate is destined to co-ordinate the master creation, God the Ultimate is the transcendental power-personalization of the directionization of the entire master universe. What changes will be inaugurated by the full emergence of the Ultimate we do not know. But irrespective of the administrative repercussions attendant upon the emergence of Ultimate Deity, the personal values of his transcendental divinity will be experiencible by all personalities who have been participants in the actualization of this Deity level. God the Ultimate transcends time and space, but is nonetheless subabsolute.

106:5. Coabsolute or Fifth-Phase Association

The Ultimate is the apex of transcendental reality even as the Supreme is the capstone of evolutionary-experiential reality. And the actual emergence of these two experiential Deities lays the foundation for the second experiential Trinity. This is the Trinity Absolute, the union of God the Supreme, God the Ultimate, and the unrevealed Consummator of Universe Destiny. Trinities are, in and of themselves, not personal, but neither do they contravene personality. The three Absolutes—Deity, Universal, and Unqualified—are not trinity, for all are not deity. Only the deified can become trinity; all other associations are triunities or triodities.

106:6. Absolute or Sixth-Phase Integration

If we assume a cosmos-infinite, then it becomes possible to conjecture that the completed function of the Trinity Absolute will achieve final expression in the creations of infinity and will consummate the absolute actualization of all potentials. The eternity action of the Trinity Absolute may be thought of as culminating in some kind of experientialization of the Absolutes of potentiality. But in regard to the conceivable values of divinity and personality, these conjectured happenings imply the personalization of the Deity Absolute and the appearance of the superpersonal values and ultrapersonal meanings inherent in the personality completion of God the Absolute.

106:7. Finality of Destiny

It is inconceivable that quantitative infinity could ever be completely realized in finality. Destiny is probably consummated by the act of the Consummator of Universe Destiny, and this act is probably involved with the Supreme and the Ultimate in the Trinity Absolute. The improbability of attaining such a finality of destiny does not, however, prevent philosophical theorizing about it. Mortals, morontians, spirits, finaliters, Transcendentalers, and others, together with the universes themselves and all other phases of reality, certainly do have a potentially final destiny that is absolute in value; but we doubt that any being or universe will ever completely attain all of the aspects of such a destiny. The infinity of God should be the supreme assurance that an ascending personality will have before him the possibilities of personality development and Deity association which even eternity will neither exhaust nor terminate.

106:8. The Trinity of Trinities

The nature of the Trinity of Trinities is difficult to portray to the human mind. In the Trinity of Trinities the experiential infinite attains to identity with the existential infinite, and both are as one in the pre-experiential, pre-existential I AM. The Trinity of Trinities consists of the Paradise Trinity, the Ultimate Trinity, and the Absolute Trinity, which includes God the Supreme, God the Ultimate, and God the Absolute. Theoretically, if such a unity event could take place, we should witness the experiential unification of the three Absolutes as one. If the Trinity of Trinities could ever achieve trinity unity, we are confident that it would lead directly to the realization of the I AM as an experiential attainable as the Father-Infinite.

106:9. Existential Infinite Unification

In the concept of the Trinity of Trinities we postulate the possible experiential unification of limitless reality. Time, space, and experience constitute barriers to creature concept; and yet they are man's greatest aids to relative reality perception. On the absolute level there is neither time nor space; all potentials may be there perceived as actuals. The total integration of reality is unqualifiedly and eternally and existentially present in the Paradise Trinity, within which, at this very universe moment, infinite reality is absolutely unified. All creature growth is proportional to Father identification. A Father-identified life is predicated on truth, sensitive to beauty, and dominated by goodness. A God-knowing person is inwardly illuminated by worship and outwardly devoted to the wholehearted service of the universal brotherhood of all personalities. All these life qualities are unified in the evolving personality on ever-ascending levels of cosmic wisdom, self-realization, God-finding, and Father worship.

Paper 107:
Origin and Nature of Thought Adjusters

Solitary Messenger

THE Universal Father is present on the worlds of space in the minds of his countless children of time. The eternal Father is at one and the same time farthest removed from, and most intimately associated with, his planetary mortal sons. Eternal fusion of the Thought Adjuster with the evolutionary soul of man actualizes a new order of being for unending universe service. The Adjuster is man's infallible cosmic compass, always and unerringly pointing the soul Godward.

From the arrival of the Adjuster to comparative full growth, about twenty years of age on Urantia, the Monitors are sometimes designated Thought Changers. From this time to the attainment of the age of discretion, about forty years, the Mystery Monitors are called Thought Adjusters. From the attainment of discretion to deliverance from the flesh, they are often referred to as Thought Controllers.

107:1. Origin of Thought Adjusters

Since Thought Adjusters are of the essence of original Deity, no one may presume to discourse authoritatively upon their nature and origin. They proceed direct from the Universal Father—fragmentized entities constituting the factual presence of the infinite God. The technique of the origin of the Thought Adjusters is one of the unrevealed functions of the Universal Father. In the last analysis, the Father fragments must be the gift of the absolute God to those creatures whose destiny encompasses the possibility of the attainment of God as absolute.

107:2. Classification of Adjusters

Adjusters are individuated as virgin entities, and all are destined to become either liberated, fused, or Personalized Monitors. There are seven orders of Thought Adjusters: 1. *Virgin Adjusters*, those on initial assignment. 2. *Advanced Adjusters*—those who have served with will creatures on worlds where fusion takes place with an individualized portion of the local universe Mother Spirit. 3. *Supreme Adjusters*—those whose human partners declined eternal survival and have been subsequently assigned to other adventures in other mortals on other evolving worlds. 4. *Vanished Adjusters*—those who are possibly on detached assignments, roaming the universe of universes. 5. *Liberated Adjusters*, those who have been eternally liberated from the service of time; what functions may be theirs, we do not know. 6. *Fused Adjusters*—the eternity partners of the Paradise Corps of the Finality. 7. *Personalized*

Adjusters, those who have served with the incarnated Paradise Sons, together with many who have achieved unusual distinction during the mortal indwelling, but whose subjects rejected survival.

107:3. The Divinington Home of Adjusters

All universe activities related to the dispatch, management, and direction of the Mystery Monitors seem to be centered on the sacred sphere of Divinington. Although we know something of all the seven secret spheres of Paradise, we know less of Divinington than of the others. Beings of high spiritual orders are directed not to go there. I am very sure there is nothing on Divinington of real value or profit to me. The valor and wisdom exhibited by Thought Adjusters suggest that they have undergone a training of tremendous scope and range. We really know very little about the nonpersonalized Adjusters; we only contact and communicate with the personalized orders. The Personalized Adjusters are permanently domiciled on Divinington.

107:4. Nature and Presence of Adjusters

The reality of the Adjuster must border on absoluteness. In intensiveness of meaning, value, and fact they are absolute. They are supreme and infallible in their supernal sphere of creature ministry and universe function. Nonpersonalized Adjusters are visible only to Personalized Adjusters. My order, the Solitary Messengers, together with Inspired Trinity Spirits, can detect the presence of Adjusters by means of spiritual reactive phenomena. The universal invisibility of the Adjusters is strongly suggestive of their high and exclusive divine origin and nature. There is a characteristic light, a spirit luminosity, which accompanies this divine presence. To all beings who have attained the Universal Father, the Personalized Thought Adjusters are visible.

When mortal man fuses with an actual fragment of the existential Cause of the total cosmos, no limit can ever be placed upon the destiny of such an unprecedented and unimaginable partnership. In eternity the Adjuster will be revealing to the mortal personality the wonder of God, and never can this supernal revelation come to an end. Can you really realize the true significance of the Adjuster's indwelling?

107:5. Adjuster Mindedness

Thought Adjusters have minds which are not only prepersonal but also prior to all energy and spirit divergence. Since Adjusters can plan, work, and love, they must have powers of selfhood which are commensurate with mind.

They are possessed of unlimited ability to communicate with each other. The mindedness of the Thought Adjuster is like the mindedness of the Universal Father and the Eternal Son. When a Thought Adjuster is fused with the evolving immortal morontia soul of the surviving human, the mind of the Adjuster can only be identified as persisting apart from the creature's mind until the ascending mortal attains spirit levels of universe progression.

107:6. Adjusters as Pure Spirits

The Adjuster is man's eternal possibility; man is the Adjuster's personality possibility. The Adjusters truly and divinely love you. They long for the divinity attainment of your mortal minds that their loneliness may end, that they may be delivered with you from the limitations of material investiture and the habiliments of time. The Adjuster is indeed a spirit, pure spirit. It is a fact that the Adjusters traverse space over the instantaneous and universal gravity circuits of the Paradise Isle. It is entirely possible that they may even penetrate the outer space levels. Thought Adjusters do not require energy intake; they are energy, energy of the highest and most divine order.

107:7. Adjusters and Personality

Thought Adjusters are not personalities, but they are real entities. We have often speculated that Adjusters must have volition on all prepersonal levels of choice. They volunteer to indwell human beings, they lay plans for man's eternal career, they adapt, modify, and substitute in accordance with circumstances, and these activities connote genuine volition. They unquestionably exhibit conduct which betokens the exercise of powers in every sense the equivalent of will. Why then are they subservient to the mortal will? We believe it is because Adjuster volition, though absolute in nature, is prepersonal in manifestation.

The Adjusters have direct and unlimited communication with any and all material creatures. There are no created beings that would not delight to be hosts to the Mystery Monitors, but no orders of beings are thus indwelt excepting evolutionary will creatures of finaliter destiny.

Paper 108:
Mission and Ministry of Thought Adjusters
Solitary Messenger

THE mission of the Thought Adjusters is that of elevating the mortal minds and of translating the immortal souls of men up to the divine heights and spiritual levels of Paradise perfection. The Adjusters bring into existence a unique type of being which it would be impossible to create by any other universe technique. Nothing in the entire universe can substitute for the fact of experience on nonexistential levels. God cannot experientially know what he has never personally experienced. Therefore does the spirit of the Father descend from Paradise to participate with finite mortals in every bona fide experience of the ascending career. It is only by such a method that the existential God could become in truth and in fact man's experiential Father.

108:1. Selection and Assignment

We cannot explain the basis of Adjuster assignment, but we conjecture that these divine gifts are bestowed in accordance with some wise and efficient policy of eternal fitness of adaptation to the indwelt personality. Adjusters are in possession of full data respecting the candidate for indwelling. This forecast covers not only the hereditary antecedents of the mortal candidate but also the estimate of probable intellectual endowment and spiritual capacity. The volunteering Adjuster is particularly interested in three qualifications of the human candidate: intellectual capacity, spiritual perception, and combined intellectual and spiritual powers. A working pattern is utilized in instructing the assigned Adjuster as to the most effective plans for personality approach and mind spiritization. When once the Adjusters are actually dispatched from Divinington, practically no time intervenes between that moment and the hour of their appearance in the minds of their chosen subjects.

108:2. Prerequisites of Adjuster Indwelling

The Adjusters are not actually assigned until the human subjects make their first moral personality decision. Adjusters reach their human subjects on Urantia, on the average, just prior to the sixth birthday. Before the times of the pouring out of the Spirit of Truth upon the inhabitants of an evolutionary world, the Adjusters' bestowal appears to be determined by many spirit influences and personality attitudes. Among these factors are the attainment of the third circle of intellectual and spiritual achievement, the making of a superior decision of unusual spiritual import, and the declaration of intention to do the will of God.

108:3. Organization and Administration

As far as we know, Adjusters are organized as an independent working unit in the universe of universes and are apparently administered directly from Divinington. Adjusters are of complete record (outside of Divinington) only on the headquarters of the seven superuniverses. Human subjects are often known by the numbers of their Adjusters; mortals do not receive real universe names until after Adjuster fusion, which union is signalized by the bestowal of the new name upon the new creature by the destiny guardian.

Recently Urantia underwent a periodic inspection by Tabamantia, the sovereign supervisor of all life-experiment planets in the universe of Nebadon, who said to the chief of Adjusters: "Now to you, superiors far above me . . . I come to express admiration and profound respect for this magnificent group of celestial ministers . . . No matter how trying the crises, you never falter. . . . You are marvelous beings, guardians of the good in the souls of this backward realm. . . . I honor you! I all but worship you!"

108:4. Relation to Other Spiritual Influences

The Father has reserved to himself the unchallengeable right to be present in the minds and souls of his evolving creatures to the end that he may draw all creature creation to himself. Mystery Monitors are continually assisting in the establishment of the spiritual dominion of Michael throughout the universe of Nebadon while mysteriously contributing to the stabilization of the sovereignty of the Ancients of Days in Orvonton. Thought Adjusters function in the human mind in perfect synchrony and co-ordination with all other spirit ministries. When a world is isolated by rebellion, there remains but one possibility of direct interplanetary or universe communication, and that is through the liaison of the Adjusters of the spheres. The isolation of a planet in no way affects the Adjusters and their ability to communicate with any part of the local universe, superuniverse, or the central universe.

108:5. The Adjuster's Mission

As a result of the Lucifer and Caligastia rebellion and the Adamic default, the Adjusters accept a difficult assignment when they volunteer to indwell such composite beings as live on Urantia. The Mystery Monitors labor with the material mind for the purpose of constructing, by adjustment and spiritualization, a new mind for the new worlds and the new name of your future career. Their mission chiefly concerns the future life, not this life. They are not interested in making the mortal career easy; rather are they concerned in making your life reasonably difficult and rugged, so that decisions will be stimulated and multiplied. The presence of a great Thought Adjuster does not bestow ease of living and freedom from strenuous thinking, but such a divine gift should confer a sublime peace of mind and a superb tranquility of spirit. The Thought Adjusters would like to change your feelings of fear to convictions of love and confidence, but they cannot mechanically and arbitrarily do such things; that is your task. In doing so, you literally supply the psychic fulcrum on which the Adjuster may subsequently apply a spiritual lever of uplifting and advancing illumination.

108:6. God in Man

It is indeed a marvel of divine condescension for the exalted and perfect Adjusters to offer themselves for actual existence in the minds of the mortals of Urantia. The indwelling Adjusters are particularly tormented by those of man's thoughts which are purely sordid and selfish; and they are virtually thwarted in their work by many of man's foolish animal fears and childish anxieties.

The Adjuster is the wellspring of spiritual attainment and the hope of divine character within you. They are slowly and surely re-creating you as you really are (only spiritually) for resurrection on the survival worlds. And how they do enjoy communicating with their subjects in more or less direct channels! You humans have begun an endless unfolding of an almost infinite panorama, a limitless expanding of never-ending, ever-widening spheres of opportunity for exhilarating service, matchless adventure, sublime uncertainty, and boundless attainment.

Paper 109:
Relation of Adjusters to Universe Creatures
Solitary Messenger

THE Thought Adjusters are the children of the universe career, and indeed the virgin Adjusters must gain experience while mortal creatures grow and develop.

109:1. Development of Adjusters

There must be a comprehensive and elaborate plan for the training and development of virgin Adjusters before they are sent forth from Divinington. Actual living experience has no cosmic substitute. Therefore, in common with all beings living and functioning within the present sphere of the Supreme, Thought Adjusters must acquire experience; they must evolve from the lower, inexperienced, to the higher, more experienced, groups. They are equal partners of the human mind in fostering the evolution of the immortal soul of survival capacity. The first stage of Adjuster evolution is attained in fusion with the surviving soul of a mortal being. The final product of this union of divinity and humanity will eternally be the son of man and the son of God.

109:2. Self-Acting Adjusters

You have been informed of the classification of Adjusters in relation to experience—virgin, advanced, and supreme. You should also recognize a certain functional classification—the self-acting Adjusters. A self-acting Adjuster is one who: 1. has had certain requisite experience in the life of a will creature; 2. has a subject who has made the third psychic circle; 3. has a subject who has made a sincere betrothal with the Adjuster; 4. has a subject who has been mustered into one of the reserve corps of destiny; 5. has been detached during human sleep for some exploit of service; 6. has served in a time of crisis of some human being who was the complement of a spiritual personality intrusted with the enactment of some essential cosmic achievement.

Undoubtedly these higher and more experienced types of Adjusters can communicate with those in other realms. Supreme and self-acting Adjusters can leave the human body at will. Nevertheless it should be recorded that they very rarely, even temporarily, leave their mortal tabernacles after they once take up their indwelling.

109:3. Relation of Adjusters to Mortal Types

The character of the detailed work of Mystery Monitors varies in accordance with the nature of their assignments. On certain primitive worlds (the series one group) the Adjuster indwells the mind of the creature as an experiential training. On another type of world (the series two group) the Adjusters are merely loaned to mortal beings. These surviving mortals attain eternal life through Spirit fusion. On worlds such as Urantia (the series three group) there is a real betrothal with the divine gifts, a life and death engagement. In the three-brained mortals of this series of worlds, the Adjusters are able to gain far more actual contact with their subjects during the temporal life than in the one- and two-brained types. But in the career after death, the three-brained type proceed just as do the one-brained type and the two-brained types. It is our belief that on two-brain worlds practically all Adjusters indwelling intelligent men and women of survival capacity belong to the advanced or to the supreme type.

109:4. Adjusters and Human Personality

The higher forms of intelligent intercommunication between human beings are greatly helped by the indwelling Adjusters. The type of Adjuster has much to do with the potential for expression of the human personality. On down through the ages, many of the great intellectual and spiritual leaders of Urantia have exerted their influence chiefly because of the superiority and previous experience of their indwelling Adjusters. I have observed a Thought Adjuster indwelling a mind on Urantia who has, according to the records on Uversa, indwelt fifteen minds previously in Orvonton. This is a marvelous Adjuster and one of the most useful and potent forces on Urantia during this present age. Adjusters are seldom given two indwelling experiences on the same planet; there is no Adjuster now serving on Urantia who has been on this world previously.

109:5. The Material Handicaps to Adjuster Indwelling

Supreme and self-acting Adjusters are often able to contribute factors of spiritual import to the human mind when it flows freely in the liberated but controlled channels of creative imagination. It is sometimes possible to have the mind illuminated, to hear the divine voice that continually speaks within you, so that you may become partially conscious of the wisdom, truth, goodness, and beauty of the potential personality constantly indwelling you. Their work is interfered with by the innate natures of the mortal races, and is greatly retarded by your own preconceived opinions, settled ideas, and long-standing prejudices. If you will co-operate with your Adjuster, the divine gift will, sooner or later, evolve the immortal morontia soul and, subsequent to fusion therewith, will present the new creature to the sovereign Master Son of the local universe and eventually to the Father of Adjusters on Paradise.

109:6. The Persistence of True Values

Adjusters never fail; nothing worth surviving is ever lost. When Adjusters of long universe experience volunteer to indwell divine Sons on bestowal missions, they full well know that personality attainment can never be achieved through this service. But often does the Father of spirits grant personality to these volunteers and establish them as directors of their kind. The activities of Adjusters in your local universe are directed by the Personalized Adjuster of Michael of Nebadon, that very Monitor who guided him step by step when he lived his human life as Joshua ben Joseph. This same Adjuster now reflects in the inscrutable nature of his mighty personality the prebaptismal humanity of Joshua ben Joseph, the eternal and living transcript of the eternal and living values which the greatest of all Urantians created out of the humble circumstances of a commonplace life as it was lived to the complete exhaustion of the spiritual values attainable in mortal experience. Everything of permanent value which is intrusted to an Adjuster is assured eternal survival.

109:7. Destiny of Personalized Adjusters

Personalized Thought Adjusters combine the Creator and creature experience—existential and experiential. They are the all-wise and powerful executives of the Architects of the Master Universe. They are the personal agents of the full ministry of the Universal Father—personal, prepersonal, and superpersonal. They are the personal ministers of the extraordinary, the unusual, and the unexpected throughout all the realms of the transcendental absonite spheres of the domain of God the Ultimate, even to the levels of God the Absolute.

When the planetary Vorondadek observer of Urantia recently assumed an emergency regency of your world he began with a full staff of his own choosing. But he did not choose the three Personalized Adjusters who appeared in his presence the instant he assumed the regency. He did not even know they would thus appear. And the Most High regent did not assign service or designate duties for these volunteer Personalized Adjusters. Nevertheless, these three omnipersonal beings were among the most active of the numerous orders of celestial beings then serving on Urantia. These extraordinary human divinities are among the most remarkable personalities of the entire grand universe, and no one dares to predict what their future missions may be.

Paper 110: Relation of Adjusters to Individual Mortals

Solitary Messenger

AS far as I am conversant with the affairs of a universe, I regard the love and devotion of a Thought Adjuster as the most truly divine affection in all creation. The Paradise Father has apparently reserved this form of personal contact with his individual creatures as an exclusive Creator prerogative.

110:1. Indwelling the Mortal Mind

The Thought Adjuster may be envisaged as indwelling the mortal mind of man. And indirectly and unrecognized the Adjuster is constantly communicating with the human subject. These Monitors are efficient ministers to the higher phases of men's minds; they are wise and experienced manipulators of the spiritual potential of the human intellect. The Adjusters are loving leaders, your safe and sure guides through the dark and uncertain mazes of your short earthly career. I wish you could love them more, co-operate with them more fully, and cherish them more affectionately.

Although the divine indwellers are chiefly concerned with your spiritual preparation for the next stage of the never-ending existence, they are also deeply interested in your temporal welfare and in your real achievements on earth. They are delighted to contribute to your health, happiness, and true prosperity. All physical poisons greatly retard the efforts of the Adjuster to exalt the material mind, while the mental poisons of fear, anger, envy, jealousy, suspicion, and intolerance likewise tremendously interfere with the spiritual progress of the evolving soul. If you only prove faithful to the trust reposed in you by the divine spirit who seeks your mind and soul in eternal union, there will eventually ensue such a perfect fusion that even the most experienced personalities can never segregate or recognize as separate identities the fusion partners—mortal man and divine Adjuster.

110:2. Adjusters and Human Will

When Thought Adjusters indwell human minds, they bring with them the model careers, the ideal lives, as determined and foreordained by themselves and the Personalized Adjusters of Divinington. The Adjusters respect your sovereignty of personality; they are always subservient to your will. The Adjuster is not trying to control your thinking, as such, but rather to spiritualize it, to eternalize it. The Adjusters are devoted to the work of building up spiritual counterparts of your careers, morontia transcripts of your true advancing selves, for survival purposes. If you so fully conform to the Adjuster's mind that you see eye to eye, then your minds become one, and you receive the reinforcement of the Adjuster's mind. To the extent that this identity is realized, you are mentally approaching the morontia order of existence. Morontia mind is a term signifying the substance and sum total of the co-operating minds of diversely material and spiritual natures. Morontia intellect, therefore, connotes a dual mind in the local universe dominated by one will.

110:3. Co-operation with the Adjuster

Adjusters are playing the sacred and superb game of the ages. And how happy they are when your co-operation permits them to lend assistance in your short struggles of time. The success of your Adjuster in the enterprise of piloting you through the mortal life and bringing about your survival depends not so much on the theories of your beliefs as upon your decisions, determinations, and steadfast faith. I cannot but observe that so many of you spend so much time and thought on mere trifles of living, while you almost wholly overlook the more essential realities of everlasting import. But a devoted and determined effort to realize eternal destiny is wholly compatible with a light-hearted and joyous life and with a successful and honorable career on earth.

You must not regard co-operation with your Adjuster as a particularly conscious process, for it is not. You can consciously augment Adjuster harmony by choosing to respond to divine leading, loving God and desiring to be like him, loving man and sincerely desiring to serve him, and joyfully accepting cosmic citizenship.

110:4. The Adjuster's Work in the Mind

Adjusters are able to receive the continuous stream of cosmic intelligence coming in over the master circuits of time and space; but these mighty indwellers are unable to transmit very much of this wealth of wisdom and truth to the minds of their mortal subjects. The Thought Adjuster is engaged in a constant effort so to spiritualize your mind as to evolve your morontia soul. Trust all matters of mind beyond the dead level of consciousness to the custody of the Adjusters. The Urantia races are so largely electrically and chemically controlled, so highly animallike in their common behavior, that it becomes exceedingly difficult for the Monitors to guide and direct them. You are so devoid of courageous decisions and consecrated co-operation that your indwelling Adjusters find it next to impossible to communicate directly with the human mind. Many a new religion and strange "ism" has arisen from the aborted, imperfect, misunderstood, and garbled communications of the Thought Adjusters. For many thousands of years in each generation there have lived fewer and fewer beings who could function safely with self-acting Adjusters.

110:5. Erroneous Concepts of Adjuster Guidance

Do not confuse and confound the mission and influence of the Adjuster with what is commonly called conscience. Conscience, rightly, admonishes you to *do* right; but the Adjuster endeavors to tell you what truly *is* right. The Adjusters simply cannot, in a single lifetime, arbitrarily co-ordinate and synchronize two such unlike and diverse types of thinking as the human and the divine. While their mortal hosts are asleep, the Adjusters try to register their creations in the higher levels of the material mind. It is extremely dangerous to postulate as to the Adjuster content of the dream life. Every human being must settle these problems for himself in accordance with his natural human wisdom and superhuman insight.

The Adjuster of the human being through whom this communication is being made enjoys almost complete indifference to any outward manifestations of the Adjuster's inner presence. And all this constitutes a favorable co-ordination of influences, favorable both to the Adjuster in the higher sphere of action and to the human partner from the standpoints of health, efficiency, and tranquility.

110:6. The Seven Psychic Circles

Entrance upon the seventh circle marks the beginning of true human personality function. Completion of the first circle denotes the relative maturity of the mortal being. The successful traversal of these levels demands the harmonious functioning of the entire personality. Every decision you make either impedes or facilitates the function of the Adjuster. Persons become more real as they ascend from the seventh to the first level of mortal existence. The Adjuster's work is much more effective after the human ascender attains the third circle and receives a personal seraphic guardian of destiny. From the third circle onward the influence of the seven adjutant mind spirits progressively diminishes.

The circle attainments are only relatively related to God-consciousness. The mastery of the cosmic circles is related to the quantitative growth of the morontia soul. The Adjuster cannot, ordinarily, speak directly and immediately with you until you attain the first and final circle of progressive mortal achievement. The great days in the individual careers of Adjusters are: first, when the human subject breaks through into the third psychic circle; second, when the human partner attains the first psychic circle and they are thereby enabled to intercommunicate to some degree; and third, when they are finally and eternally fused.

110:7. The Attainment of Immortality

The achievement of the seven cosmic circles does not equal Adjuster fusion. There are many mortals living on Urantia who have attained their circles; but fusion depends on yet other greater and more sublime spiritual achievements. After the fusion of the immortal morontia soul and the associated Adjuster, all of the experience and all of the values of the one eventually become the possession of the other, so that the two are actually one entity. An absolute oneness with the divine Monitor, a complete exhaustion of the endowment of an Adjuster, can only be achieved in eternity subsequent to the final attainment of the Universal Father. So few mortals are real thinkers; you do not spiritually develop and discipline your minds to the point of favorable liaison with the divine Adjusters.

Not long since on Urantia a message was transmitted by a self-acting Adjuster to the human associate. Among other things, the Adjuster pleaded "that he more faithfully give me his sincere co-operation, more cheerfully endure the tasks of my emplacement, more faithfully carry out the program of my arrangement, more patiently go through the trials of my selection, more persistently and cheerfully tread the path of my choosing, more humbly receive credit that may accrue as a result of my ceaseless endeavors. . . . I await with pleasure and without apprehension the roll call of destiny; I am prepared to submit all to the tribunals of the Ancients of Days."

Paper 111: The Adjuster and the Soul
Solitary Messenger

THE morontia soul is the child of the universe and may be really known only through cosmic insight and spiritual discovery. The concept of a soul and of an indwelling spirit is not new to Urantia; it has frequently appeared in the various systems of planetary beliefs. The Chinese recognized two aspects of a human being, the *yang* and the *yin*, the soul and the spirit. The Egyptians and many African tribes also believed in two factors, the *ka* and the *ba*.

111:1. The Mind Arena of Choice

Mind is the human soil from which the spirit Monitor must evolve the morontia soul with the cooperation of the indwelt personality. Material mind is the arena in which human personalities live, are self-conscious, make decisions, choose God or forsake him, eternalize or destroy themselves. It is not so much what mind comprehends as what mind desires to comprehend that insures survival. What you are today is not so important as what you are becoming day by day and in eternity. Mind is your ship, the Adjuster is your pilot, the human will is captain. With your consent, this faithful pilot will safely carry you across the barriers of time and the handicaps of space to the very source of the divine mind and on beyond, even to the Paradise Father of Adjusters.

111:2. Nature of the Soul

The material mind of mortal man is the cosmic loom that carries the morontia fabrics on which the indwelling Thought Adjuster threads the spirit patterns of a surviving soul of ultimate destiny and unending career, a potential finaliter. The soul is a morontial reality. The midway creatures have long denominated this evolving soul of man the mid-mind in contradistinction to the lower or material mind and the higher or cosmic mind. And thus does the material and mortal reality of the self transcend the temporal limitations of the physical-life machine and attain a new expression and a new identification in the evolving vehicle for selfhood continuity, the morontia and immortal soul.

111:3. The Evolving Soul

At any time before fusion with the Adjuster, the evolving and ascending creature can choose to forsake the will of the Paradise Father. Fusion with the Adjuster signalizes the fact that the ascending mortal has eternally and unreservedly chosen to do the Father's will. As terrestrial mortal growth proceeds, this self, with its priceless powers of choice, becomes increasingly identified with the emerging morontia-soul entity; after death and following the mansion world resurrection, the human personality is completely identified with the morontia self. The soul is thus the embryo of the future morontia vehicle of personality identity. This immortal soul is at first wholly morontia in nature, but it possesses such a capacity for development that it invariably ascends to the true spirit levels of fusion value with the spirits of Deity. In so far as man's evolving morontia soul becomes permeated by truth, beauty, and goodness as the value-realization of God-consciousness, such a resultant being becomes indestructible.

111:4. The Inner Life

Meanings are derived from a combination of recognition and understanding. Meanings and values are only perceived in the inner or supermaterial spheres of human experience. The advances of true civilization are all born in this inner world of mankind. Civilization can hardly progress when the majority of the youth of any generation devote their interests and energies to the materialistic pursuits of the sensory or outer world. Personality is inherently creative, but it thus functions only in the inner life of the individual. Happiness and joy take origin in the inner life. You cannot experience real joy all by yourself. It is the creativity of the inner world that is most subject to your direction because there your personality is so largely liberated from the fetters of the laws of antecedent causation. How can a creative imagination produce worthy children when the stage whereon it functions is already preoccupied by prejudice, hate, fears, resentments, revenge, and bigotries? Inner creativity contributes to ennoblement of character through personality integration and selfhood unification. Only the future can be changed by the ministry of the present creativity of the inner self.

111:5. The Consecration of Choice

The doing of the will of God is nothing more or less than an exhibition of creature willingness to share the inner life with God. The imitation of God is the key to perfection—the secret of survival. Such a creature choice is not a surrender of will. It is a consecration of will, an expansion of will, a glorification of will, a perfecting of will. And if this choice is made, sooner or later will the God-choosing son find inner union (fusion) with the indwelling God fragment, while this same perfecting son will find supreme personality satisfaction in the worship communion of the personality of man and the personality of his Maker, two personalities whose creative attributes have eternally joined in self-willed mutuality of expression—the birth of another eternal partnership of the will of man and the will of God.

111:6. The Human Paradox

Many of the temporal troubles of mortal man grow out of his twofold relation to the cosmos. Man is a part of nature and yet he is able to transcend nature. Such a paradox is inseparable from temptation, potential evil, decisional errors; and when self becomes proud and arrogant, sin may evolve. The fact of finiteness is not evil or sinful; it is the misuse, distortion, and perversion of the finite that gives origin to evil and sin. Man can never begin to appreciate the infinite symmetry, the supernal harmony, the exquisite repleteness of the all-inclusive nature of the First Source and Center until he has found divine law and divine love and has experientially unified these in his own evolving cosmic philosophy. When man wishes to modify physical reality, be it himself or his environment, he succeeds to the extent that he has discovered the ways and means of controlling matter and directing energy.

Of all the dangers which beset man's mortal nature and jeopardize his spiritual integrity, pride is the greatest. Courage is valorous, but egotism is vainglorious and suicidal. Pride is deceitful, intoxicating, and sin-breeding whether found in an individual, a group, a race, or a nation. It is literally true, "Pride goes before a fall."

111:7. The Adjuster's Problem

Uncertainty with security is the essence of the Paradise adventure. May I admonish you to heed the distant echo of the Adjuster's faithful call to your soul? The indwelling Adjuster cannot stop or even materially alter your career struggle of time. You could, if you only would, permit the valiant Adjuster to fight with you and for you. Why do you not aid the Adjuster in the task of showing you the spiritual counterpart of all these strenuous material efforts?

Not long since I was present on Salvington and heard a guardian of destiny present a formal statement in extenuation of the difficulties of ministering to her mortal subject: "Much of my difficulty was due to the unending conflict between the two natures of my subject: the urge of ambition opposed by animal indolence; . . . the gladness of anticipation disillusioned by the bitterness of realization; the joys of living ever threatened by the sorrows of death. Such a life on such a planet! And yet, because of the ever-present help and urge of the Thought Adjuster, this soul did achieve a fair degree of happiness and success and has even now ascended to the judgment halls of mansonia."

Paper 112: Personality Survival
Solitary Messenger

URANTIA is your starting point; here you and your divine Thought Adjuster are joined in temporary union. You have been endowed with a perfect guide; therefore, if you will sincerely run the race of time and gain the final goal of faith, you will be eternally united with your indwelling Adjuster. Then will begin your real life, the ascending life, and throughout all of the successive ages and stages of evolutionary growth there is one part of you that remains absolutely unaltered, and that is personality. Personality is that quality in reality which is bestowed by the Universal Father. It is not wholly subject to the fetters of antecedent causation and is relatively creative. It causes spirit to strive for the mastery of energy-matter through the mediation of mind and can unify the identity of any living energy system. Personality is unique, absolutely unique, and responds directly to other-personality presence. Personality may survive mortal death with identity in the surviving soul.

112:1. Personality and Reality

Personality is bestowed by the Universal Father upon his creatures as a potentially eternal endowment. Personality performs effectively on the levels of the finite, the absonite, and even as impinging upon the absolute. The type of personality bestowed upon Urantia mortals has a potentiality of seven dimensions of self-expression or person-realization. Personality cannot very well perform in isolation. Man is dominated by the craving of belongingness. Personality signifies the unification of all factors of reality as well as co-ordination of relationships. In the human system it is the personality which unifies all activities and in turn imparts the qualities of identity and creativity.

112:2. The Self

It would be helpful in the study of selfhood to remember that the indwelling spiritual force is potentially directive. In the cosmic economy insight precedes foresight. The universe fact of God's becoming man has forever changed all meanings and altered all values of human personality. Everything nonspiritual in human experience, excepting personality, is a means to an end. Every true relationship of mortal man with other persons—human or divine—is an end in itself. The possession of personality identifies man as a spiritual being since the unity of selfhood and the self-consciousness of personality are endowments of the supermaterial world. The purpose of cosmic evolution is to achieve unity of personality through increasing spirit dominance. Selfhood of survival value is only evolved by establishing a potential transfer of the seat of the identity of the evolving personality from the material body to the more enduring and immortal nature of the morontia soul and on beyond to those levels whereon the soul becomes infused with, and eventually attains the status of, spirit reality. This actual transfer is effected by the sincerity, persistence, and steadfastness of the God-seeking decisions of the human creature.

112:3. The Phenomenon of Death

Urantians generally recognize only one kind of death, the physical cessation of life energies; but concerning personality survival there are really three kinds: spiritual (soul) death, when mortal man has finally rejected survival; intellectual (mind) death, when the vital circuits of higher adjutant ministry are disrupted; and physical (body and mind) death. After death two nonmaterial factors of surviving personality persist: the pre-existent Thought Adjuster with the memory transcription of the mortal career which proceeds to Divinington; and the immortal morontia soul of the deceased human, which is kept by the destiny guardian. Those who go to the mansion worlds are not permitted to send messages back to their loved ones.

112:4. Adjusters After Death

When death of a material, intellectual, or spiritual nature occurs, the Adjuster bids farewell to the mortal host and departs for Divinington. If the mortal associate belongs to a group that will be repersonalized at the end of a dispensation, the Adjuster will not immediately return to the mansion world of the former system of service but will, according to choice, enter upon some temporary assignment. If, when death overtakes you, you have attained the third circle or a higher realm and therefore have had assigned to you a personal guardian of destiny, and if the final transcript of the summary of survival character submitted by the Adjuster is unconditionally certified by the destiny guardian, the tribunals of the Sovereign of Nebadon will decree the immediate passage of the surviving soul to the resurrection halls of the mansion worlds. The Adjuster returns to indwell the actual personality form made ready for the reception of the surviving soul of the earth mortal as that form has been projected by the guardian of destiny.

112:5. Survival of the Human Self

Human beings, from a cosmic perspective, are born, live, and die in a relative instant of time. If ever there is doubt as to the advisability of advancing a human identity to the mansion worlds, the universe governments invariably rule in the personal interests of that individual. During the transit of surviving mortals from the world of origin to the mansion worlds the record of personality constitution is faithfully preserved by the archangels.

The reassembly of the constituent parts of a onetime material personality involves: the fabrication of a suitable form; the return of the Adjuster to the waiting morontia creature; and the bestowal of the morontia soul by the seraphic custodian upon and in the awaiting morontia mind-body form. This completes the repersonalization, reassembly of memory, insight, and consciousness—identity. When you thus awaken on the mansion worlds of Jerusem, you will be so changed, the spiritual transformation will be so great that, were it not for your Thought Adjuster and the destiny guardian, you would at first have difficulty in connecting the new morontia consciousness with the reviving memory of your previous identity. Much of your past life and its memories, having neither spiritual meaning nor morontia value, will perish with the material brain. But personality and the relationships between personalities are never scaffolding; mortal memory of personality relationships has cosmic value and will persist. On the mansion worlds you will know and be known, and more, you will remember, and be remembered by, your onetime associates in your short but intriguing life on Urantia.

112:6. The Morontia Self

Just as a butterfly emerges from the caterpillar stage, so will the true personalities of human beings emerge on the mansion worlds. In the physical life, mortals may be outwardly beautiful though inwardly unlovely; in the morontia life, and increasingly on its higher levels, the personality form will vary directly in accordance with the nature of the inner person. The morontia soul does not retain self-consciousness without the Adjuster. The evolving soul possesses a continuing character derived from the decisions of its former associated adjutant mind. The persistence of memory is proof of the retention of the identity of original selfhood. When a creature leaves his native planet, he leaves the adjutant ministry behind and becomes solely dependent on morontia intellect. When an ascender leaves the local universe, he has attained the spiritual level of existence, having passed beyond the morontia level. This newly appearing spirit entity then becomes attuned to the direct ministry of the cosmic mind of Orvonton.

112:7. Adjuster Fusion

Thought Adjuster fusion imparts eternal actualities to personality which were previously only potential: fixation of divinity quality, past-eternity experience and memory, immortality, and a phase of qualified potential absoluteness. Fusion is the secret of the sacred sphere of Ascendington. It is usually effected while the ascender is resident within his local system. The Adjuster and human being together have achieved the evolution of a member of one of the unique orders of the ascending personalities of the Supreme. We believe that the mortals of Adjuster fusion, together with their finaliter associates, are destined to function in some manner in the administration of the universes of the first outer space level. We conceive that such amalgamated beings, such partnerships of Creator and creature, will become superb rulers, matchless administrators, and understanding and sympathetic directors of the first outer space level. True it is, you mortals are of earthly, animal origin; your frame is indeed dust. But if you actually will, if you really desire, surely the heritage of the ages is yours, and you shall someday serve throughout the universes in your true characters—children of the Supreme God of experience and divine sons of the Paradise Father of all personalities. What an adventure! What a romance!

Paper 113: Seraphic Guardians of Destiny
Chief of Seraphim

SERAPHIM are the traditional angels of heaven; they are the ministering spirits who live so near you and do so much for you. They have ministered on Urantia since the earliest times of human intelligence.

113:1. The Guardian Angels

Originally, the seraphim were definitely assigned to the separate Urantia races. But since the bestowal of Michael, they are assigned in accordance with human intelligence, spirituality, and destiny. No matter in what circle a human happens to be, if such an individual becomes enrolled in any of the several reserve corps of destiny a personal seraphim are assigned. Also, when any human being makes the supreme decision of betrothal with the Adjuster, a personal guardian is immediately assigned to that soul. Seraphic assignments are ordinarily made in accordance with the human attainment of the circles of intellectuality and spirituality. One thousand humans of seventh circle attainment share one pair of seraphim and a company of cherubim. Five hundred sixth circlers share a pair of seraphim and a company of cherubim. By the fourth circle, mortals are supervised in groups of ten. Once the third circle is attained, a personal seraphic pair is exclusively devoted to a single person; such seraphim are known as guardians of destiny.

113:2. The Destiny Guardians

All angelic assignments are made from a group of volunteering seraphim, and these appointments are always in accordance with human needs and with regard to the experience, skill and wisdom of the angelic pair. Only the more experienced and tested types of seraphim are assigned as destiny guards.

The seraphim develop a sentimental regard for individual worlds and entertain a special affection for certain races and types of mortal creatures with whom they have been closely associated. The only emotion actuating you which is somewhat difficult for them to comprehend is the legacy of animal fear that bulks so large in the mental life of the average inhabitant of Urantia.

Like cherubim, seraphim usually serve in pairs, but unlike their less advanced associates, the seraphim sometimes work singly, in which case one of the two angels becomes the recorder of the undertaking. For purposes of rest and recharging with the life energy of the universe circuits, the guardian is periodically relieved by her complement.

113:3. Relation to Other Spirit Influences

One of the most important things a destiny guardian does for her mortal subject is to effect a personal co-ordination of the numerous impersonal spirit influences which indwell, surround, and impinge upon the mind and soul of the evolving material creature. Having unified and made more personal these vast ministries of the Infinite Spirit, the seraphim then undertakes to correlate this integrated influence of the Conjoint Actor with the spirit presences of the Father and the Son. On the spiritual level, seraphim make personal many otherwise impersonal and prepersonal ministries of the universe; they are co-ordinators; on the physical level they manipulate terrestrial environment through their liaison with the Master Physical Controllers and through the co-operative ministry of the midway creatures. We conjecture that this phenomenal ministry is in some undisclosed manner facilitated by the unrecognized and unrevealed working of the Supreme Being. Throughout the entire realm of progressive survival in and through the Supreme Being, seraphim are an essential part of continuing mortal progression.

113:4. Seraphic Domains of Action

Seraphim are mind stimulators; they continually seek to promote circle-making decisions in human mind. Seraphim function as the personal agency of the ministry of the Infinite Spirit. The Adjuster is the essence of man's eternal nature; the seraphim is the teacher of man's evolving nature. To accept the guidance of a seraphim you are sure to encounter the rugged hills of moral choosing and spiritual progress. While there is apparently no communication between the indwelling Adjusters and the encompassing seraphim, they always seem to work in perfect harmony and exquisite accord. The ministering personality of the guardian seraphim, the God presence of the indwelling Adjuster, the encircuited action of the Holy Spirit, and the Son-consciousness of the Spirit of Truth are all divinely correlated into a meaningful unity of spiritual ministry in and to a mortal personality.

113:5. Seraphic Ministry to Mortals

The guardian of destiny influences you in every possible manner consistent with the dignity of your personality. Angels are near you and care so feelingly for you. The seraphim act in your behalf quite independent of your direct appeals; they are executing the mandates of their superiors. You must chart your own course, but these angels then act to make the best possible use of the course you have chosen. They do not (ordinarily) arbitrarily intervene in the routine affairs of human life except in emergencies and then usually on the direct orders of their superiors. They are going to follow you for many an age and are thus receiving an introduction to their future work and personality association. Seraphim are able to function as material ministers to human beings under certain circumstances with the assistance of the midway creatures and the physical controllers, even to make actual contact with mankind, but such occurrences are very unusual.

113:6. Guardian Angels After Death

After reporting to superiors, the guardian of destiny proceeds to the first mansion world to await the consciousizing of her former ward in the flesh. The guardian seraphim is the custodial trustee of the survival values of mortal man's slumbering soul as the absent Adjuster is the identity of such an immortal universe being. When the Adjuster and the seraphim collaborate in the resurrection halls of mansonia in conjunction with the newly fabricated morontia form, there occurs the reassembly of the constituent factors of the personality of the mortal ascender. The Adjuster will identify you; the guardian seraphim will repersonalize you.

113:7. Seraphim and the Ascendant Career

It is indeed an epoch in the career of an ascending mortal to awaken on the mansion world and to see your long-loved and ever-present angelic companions of earth days; there also to become truly conscious of the identity and presence of the divine Monitor who so long indwelt your mind on earth. Your first assignment of the morontia life will be as assistants to the seraphim. And as you ascend the heavenly spheres the seraphic guardians accompany you through Jerusem, Edentia, Salvington, and Uversa, remaining with you until you finally enseconaphim for the long Havona flight. Some of the destiny guardians follow the course of the ascending pilgrims through Havona. The others will be in waiting on the shores of Paradise when their mortal associates awaken. Man and angel may or may not be reunited in eternal service, but wherever seraphic assignment may take them, the seraphim are always in communication with their former wards of the evolutionary worlds.

Paper 114: Seraphic Planetary Government
Chief of Seraphim

THE Most Highs rule in the kingdoms of men through many celestial forces and agencies but chiefly through the ministry of seraphim. The angels, ably assisted by the midwayers, function on Urantia as the actual supermaterial ministers who execute the mandates of the resident governor general. Urantia's planetary government is unlike that of any other world in all Nebadon.

114:1. The Sovereignty of Urantia

Michael is the Planetary Prince of Urantia. He has established a Jerusem commission of twenty-four former Urantians with authority to represent him in the government of Urantia and on all other quarantined planets in the system. One of this council is now always resident on Urantia as resident governor general. Vicegerent authority to act for Michael as Planetary Prince has been recently vested in Machiventa Melchizedek. Some believe that Machiventa will not come to take personal direction of Urantian affairs until the end of the current dispensation. Others hold that the vicegerent Prince may not come, as such, until Michael sometime returns to Urantia. Still others, including this narrator, look for Melchizedek's appearance any day or hour.

114:2. The Board of Planetary Supervisors

The general management of Urantia has been intrusted to a special group on Jerusem of twenty-four one-time Urantians. Members are nominated to the twenty-four by the cabinet of Lanaforge, and appointed by Gabriel of Salvington in accordance with the mandate of Michael. At the present time John the Baptist is chairman of this council when it is in session on Jerusem. The members of this commission also act as advisory supervisors of the thirty-six other rebellion-isolated worlds of Satania, each of which is advised by similar and varying sized commissions of its onetime inhabitants. No one knows how long these twenty-four Urantia counselors will continue in their present status. The present resident governor general of Urantia seems inclined to the opinion that all but Machiventa may be released for Paradise ascension the moment Satania is restored to the constellation circuits. Other opinions are also current.

114:3. The Resident Governor General

Every one hundred years of Urantia time, the Jerusem corps of twenty-four planetary supervisors designate one of their number to sojourn on your world to act as their executive representative. He acts as the co-ordinator of superhuman administration and is the respected head and universally recognized leader of the celestial beings functioning on Urantia. He is much more of a fatherly adviser than a technical ruler. The Urantia government is represented in the councils of Jerusem in accordance with an arrangement whereby the returning governor general sits as a temporary member of the System Sovereign's cabinet of Planetary Princes.

114:4. The Most High Observer

The sovereignty of Urantia is complicated by the onetime arbitrary seizure of planetary authority by the government of Norlatiadek shortly after the planetary rebellion. There is still resident on Urantia a Vorondadek Son, an observer for the Most Highs of Edentia. In a crisis the actual head of Urantia's government, excepting in certain purely spiritual matters, would be this Vorondadek Son of Edentia. It is of record that this Son has had to assume emergency leadership thirty-three times in the history of Urantia. Vorondadek regencies are not peculiar to rebellion-isolated planets, for the Most Highs may intervene at any time in the affairs of the inhabited worlds.

114:5. The Planetary Government

The actual administration of Urantia is indeed difficult to describe. The twenty-four counselors come the nearest to being the legislative branch of the planetary government. The governor general is a provisional and advisory chief executive, with veto power resident in the Most High observer. There are no absolutely authoritative judicial powers operative on the planet, only the conciliating commissions. The absence of the Planetary Prince is effectively compensated by the triune presence of the archangels, the Most High observer, and the governor general. This rather loosely organized and somewhat personally administered planetary government is more than expectedly effective because of the time-saving assistance of the archangels and their ever-ready circuit. The direct administrative cabinet of the governor general consists of twelve seraphim, the acting chiefs of the twelve groups of special angels functioning as the immediate superhuman directors of planetary progress and stability.

114:6. The Master Seraphim of Planetary Supervision

Twelve groups of angels, functioning under the general supervision of the resident governor general, are immediately directed by the seraphic council of twelve, the acting chiefs of each group. This council also serves as the volunteer cabinet of the resident governor general. As planetary chief of seraphim, I preside over this council of seraphic chiefs.

The twelve corps of the master seraphim of planetary supervision are functional on Urantia as follows: 1. *the epochal angels* are entrusted with the oversight of the current age; 2. *the progress angels* are entrusted with the task of initiating the evolutionary progress; 3. *the religious guardians*, the angels of the churches, are the checkmates of the angels of progress; 4. *the angels of nation life* are the directors of the political performances; 5. *the angels of the races* work for the conservation of the evolutionary races of time; 6. *the angels of the future* are the architects of the successive eras; 7. *the angels of enlightenment* foster planetary education; 8. *the angels of health* are dedicated to the promotion of health; 9. *the home seraphim* are dedicated to the preservation and advancement of the home; 10. *the angels of industry* foster industrial development; 11. *the angels of diversion* foster the values of play, humor, and rest; and 12. *the angels of superhuman ministry* foster all superhuman life on the planet. None of these groups are able to inject new and higher conceptions into human minds, although they often act to intensify some higher ideal which has already appeared within a human intellect. They also insure planetary progress through the mobilization, training, and maintenance of the reserve corps of destiny. They are the guarantees against disaster.

114:7. The Reserve Corps of Destiny

The reserve corps of destiny consists of living men and women who have been admitted to the special service of the superhuman administration of world affairs. All reservists have self-conscious Adjusters, and most of them function in the higher cosmic circles of intellectual achievement and spiritual attainment. They are secretly rehearsed for numerous possible emergency missions in the conduct of various activities of world affairs, coupled with willingness to serve without human recognition and rewards. Most of this unique group are wholly unconscious of their preparation for possible function in certain planetary crises. (The cosmic reserve corps of universe-conscious citizens on Urantia now [in 1934] numbers over one thousand mortals but I am forbidden to reveal the real nature of the function of this unique group of living human beings.)

You mortals now dwelling on Urantia are just as lovingly cherished and just as faithfully watched over as if the sphere had never been betrayed by a faithless Planetary Prince, even more so. It is eternally true, "the Father himself loves you."

Paper 115: The Supreme Being

Mighty Messenger

WITH God the Father, sonship is the great relationship. With God the Supreme, achievement is the prerequisite to status—one must do something as well as be something.

115:1. Relativity of Concept Frames

Conceptual frames of the universe are only relatively true; they are serviceable scaffolding which must eventually give way to enlarged cosmic comprehension. In order to facilitate mortal comprehension of the universe of universes, the diverse levels of cosmic reality have been designated as finite, absonite, and absolute. Of these only the absolute is unqualifiedly eternal, truly existential. The realms of the finite exist by virtue of the eternal purpose of God.

115:2. The Absolute Basis for Supremacy

From the existential standpoint, nothing new can happen throughout the galaxies, for the completion of infinity inherent in the I AM is eternally present in the seven Absolutes. But the fact that infinity is thus existentially present in these absolute associations in no way makes it impossible to realize new cosmic experientials. To the experiential universes even divine values are increased as actualities by enlarged comprehension of reality meanings, the conversion of potentialities into actualities. The apparent method whereby the possibilities of the cosmos are brought into actual existence varies from level to level, being experiential evolution in the finite and experiential eventuation in the absonite. Existential infinity is inclusive of the possibility for evolutionary finite experiencing. And the possibility for such experiential growth becomes a universe actuality through triodity relationships impinging upon and in the Supreme.

115:3. Original, Actual, and Potential

The absolute cosmos is conceptually without limit. There is no language in the past, present, or future of Urantia adequate to express the reality of infinity or the infinity of reality. Man, a finite creature in an infinite cosmos, must content himself with distorted reflections and attenuated conceptions of that limitless, boundless, never-beginning, never-ending existence. The triodity of the Eternal Son, the Infinite Spirit, and the Paradise Isle constitutes the *actual* revelation of the originality of the First Source and Center. The triodity of the three Absolutes of potentiality, the Deity, Unqualified, and Universal Absolutes, constitutes the *potential* revelation of the originality of the First Source and Center.

The will of God does ultimately prevail, not always concerning the individual but invariably concerning the total. Always will actuals be opening up new avenues to the realization of hitherto impossible potentials. The final penetration of the truth, beauty, and goodness of the Supreme Being could only open up to the progressing creature those absonite qualities of ultimate divinity which lie beyond the finite concept levels of truth, beauty, and goodness.

115:4. Sources of Supreme Reality

Any consideration of the origins of God the Supreme must begin with the Paradise Trinity. The Supreme is first of all a spirit person. Supreme reality, which is total finite reality, is in process of dynamic growth between the unqualified potentials of outer space and the unqualified actuals at the center of all things. The growth of Supremacy derives from the triodities, actual and potential; the spirit person of the Supreme, from the Trinity; but the power prerogatives of the Almighty are predicated on the divinity successes of God the Sevenfold, while the conjoining of the power prerogatives of the Almighty Supreme with the spirit person of God the Supreme takes place by virtue of the ministry of the Conjoint Actor, who bestowed the mind of the Supreme as the conjoining factor in this evolutionary Deity.

115:5. Relation of the Supreme to the Paradise Trinity

The Supreme Being is absolutely dependent on the existence and action of the Paradise Trinity for the reality of his personal and spirit nature, while the growth of the Supreme is a matter of triodity relationships—the creative acts of God the Sevenfold, the children of the Paradise Deities.

115:6. The Relation of the Supreme to the Triodities

The Supreme Being embraces possibilities for cosmic ministry that are not apparently manifested in the Eternal Son, the Infinite Spirit, or the nonpersonal realities of the Isle of Paradise. The growth of the Supreme is not only predicated on these absolute actualities but is also involved in developments within the Deity, Universal, and Unqualified Absolutes. The Supreme grows as the Creators and creatures of the evolving universes attain to Godlikeness. The motion of the Supreme is twofold: intensively toward Paradise and Deity and extensively toward the limitlessness of the Absolutes of potential. Though we are not sure, we believe that, as a finite reflection of Paradise Deity, the Supreme is engaged in an eternal progression into outer space; but as a qualification of the three Absolute potentials of outer space, this Supreme Being is forever seeking for Paradise coherence. And these dual motions seem to account for most of the basic activities in the presently organized universes.

115:7. The Nature of the Supreme

In the Deity of the Supreme the Father-I AM has achieved relatively complete liberation from the limitations inherent in infinity of status, eternity of being, and absoluteness of nature. But God the Supreme has been freed from all existential limitations only by having become subject to experiential qualifications. In achieving liberation from eternity, the Almighty encounters the barriers of time; and the Supreme could only know growth and development as a consequence of partiality of existence and incompleteness of nature. He is the indispensable focalizer, summarizer, and encompasser of evolutionary experience for the purpose of contributing to the appearance of the *inevitable eventuation*, the superexperience and superfinite manifestation of God the Ultimate. The Supreme connects the finite with the absonite. By ordaining the experience-evolution of the Supreme, the Father has made it possible for finite creatures to exist in the universes and, by experiential progression, sometime to attain the divinity of Supremacy.

Paper 116: The Almighty Supreme
Mighty Messenger

THE Almighty Supreme is a living and evolving Deity of power and personality. His present domain, the grand universe, is also a growing realm of power and personality. His destiny is perfection, but his present experience encompasses the elements of growth and incomplete status. Some believe that, when the superuniverses are settled in light and life, the Supreme will become functional from Uversa as the almighty and experiential sovereign of the grand universe while expanding in power as the superalmighty of the outer universes. But none of us really know.

116:1. The Supreme Mind

The experience of every evolving creature personality is a phase of the experience of the Almighty Supreme. The creative synthesis of power and personality is a part of the creative urge of the Supreme Mind and is the very essence of the evolutionary growth of unity in the Supreme Being. The completed evolution of the Almighty Supreme will result in one unified and personal Deity. Throughout the evolutionary ages the physical power potential of the Supreme is vested in the Seven Supreme Power Directors, and the mind potential reposes in the Seven Master Spirits. We really know less about the mind of Supremacy than about any other aspect of this evolving Deity. It is unquestionably active throughout the grand universe and is believed to have a potential destiny of master universe function. Mind is the experiential technique of endless progress. The Supreme is an experiential Deity and therefore never achieves completion of mind attainment.

116:2. The Almighty and God the Sevenfold

God the Supreme derives his spirit and personality attributes from the Paradise Trinity, but he is power-actualizing in the doings of the Supreme Creators—the Creator Sons, the Ancients of Days, and the Master Spirits. The Supreme Being is the maximum revelation of Deity to the seven superuniverses and for the present universe age. In God the Sevenfold we encounter the Supreme Being between the Supreme Creators (Creator Sons, Ancients of Days, Master Spirits) and the Paradise Deities (Father, Son, Spirit).

116:3. The Almighty and Paradise Deity

The finite domains of energy and spirit are literally held together by the mind presences of the Conjoint Actor. The mind bestowal of the Third Source and Center unifies the spirit person of God the Supreme with the experiential power of the evolutionary Almighty. The Mystery Monitors are to human beings what the Paradise Trinity is to the Supreme Being. The Paradise Deities participate in the evolutions of time as they unfold on the circling planets of space, and as they culminate in the emergence of the Supreme personality consequence of all evolution.

116:4. The Almighty and the Supreme Creators

During those ages in which the sovereignty of Supremacy is undergoing its time development, the almighty power of the Supreme is dependent on the divinity acts of God the Sevenfold, while there seems to be a particularly close relationship between the Supreme Being and the Conjoint Actor together with his primary personalities, the Seven Master Spirits—especially with Master Spirit Number Seven, who speaks for the Supreme. These Master Spirits are not only the supporters and augmenters of the sovereignty of Supremacy, but they are in turn affected by the creative purposes of the Supreme. The Ancients of Days are the field fulcrums for the mobilizing almighty power of the Supreme. But the local universes are the actual foundation upon which the Supreme is achieving deity evolution in and by experience.

116:5. The Almighty and the Sevenfold Controllers

The Almighty Supreme is evolving as the overcontroller of the physical power of the grand universe. In the present universe age this potential of physical power appears to be centered in the Seven Supreme Power Directors. It is conjectured that the final attainment of material equilibrium will signify the completed evolution of the physical control of the Almighty. The total evolution of the entire grand universe is a matter of the personality unification of the energy-controlling mind with the spirit-co-ordinated intellect and will be revealed in the full appearance of the almighty power of the Supreme.

116:6. Spirit Dominance

In the evolutionary superuniverses energy-matter is dominant except in personality, where spirit through the mediation of mind is struggling for the mastery. Thus, in relation to personality, do physical systems become subordinate; mind systems, co-ordinate; and spirit systems, directive. This union of power and personality is expressive on deity levels in and as the Supreme. The spirit person of Supremacy requires the evolutionary power of the Almighty to achieve completion of Deity. The dominance of spirit becomes an evolutionary experience on finite levels from mortal man to the Supreme Being. All strive, personally strive, in this destiny.

116:7. The Living Organism of the Grand Universe

The grand universe is not only a material creation of physical grandeur, spirit sublimity, and intellectual magnitude, it is also a magnificent and responsive living organism. There is actual life pulsating throughout the mechanism of the vast creation of the vibrant cosmos. This living organism is penetrated by intelligence circuits and permeated by energy lanes and co-ordinating centers of magnificent overcontrol. Much as mortals look to solar energy for life maintenance, so does the grand universe depend upon the unfailing energies emanating from nether Paradise. The Supreme Mind has been bestowed upon the totality of the finite whereby the spirit of this emerging personality of the cosmos ever strives for the mastery of energy-matter. The Supreme everlastingly depends on the absolute stability of Original Deity, the Paradise Trinity. When all creatures and all Creators in the grand universe strive for God-attainment and divine perfection, there is built up a profound cosmic tension which can only find resolution in the sublime synthesis of almighty power with the spirit person of the evolving God of all creatures, the Supreme Being.

Paper 117: God the Supreme

Mighty Messenger

GOD the Supreme is becoming the highest finite manifestation of the total will of God. If all grand universers should ever relatively achieve the full living of the will of God, then would the time-space creations be settled in light and life, and then would the Almighty, the deity potential of Supremacy, become factual in the emergence of the divine personality of God the Supreme.

117:1. Nature of the Supreme Being

The Supreme is the beauty of physical harmony, the truth of intellectual meaning, and the goodness of spiritual value. He is the oversoul of the grand universe, the consciousness of the finite cosmos. In the Supreme Being, Creator and creature are united in one Deity whose will is expressive of one divine personality. God the Supreme is truth, beauty, and goodness, for these concepts of divinity represent finite maximums of ideational experience. The Supreme is both actual and potential, a being of personal supremacy and of almighty power, responsive alike to creature effort and Creator purpose. The Deity of Supremacy is thus expressive of the sum total of the entire finite.

117:2. The Source of Evolutionary Growth

The Supreme is God-in-time; his is the secret of creature growth in time; his also is the conquest of the incomplete present and the consummation of the perfecting future. The final fruits of all finite growth are: power controlled through mind by spirit by virtue of the unifying and creative presence of personality, culminating in the Supreme Being. There will come an end sometime to the growth of the Supreme. This termination of the evolution of the Supreme will also witness the ending of creature evolution as a part of Supremacy. Creatures and universes are evolving within the Supreme, and as they evolve, there is appearing the unified summation of the entire finite activity of this universe age. What kind of growth may characterize the universes of outer space, we do not know. It will undoubtedly be the function of the evolutionary citizens of the grand universe to compensate the outer-spacers for the deprivation of the growth of Supremacy.

117:3. Significance of the Supreme to Universe Creatures

The cosmic reality variously designated as the Supreme Being, God the Supreme, and the Almighty Supreme, is the complex and universal synthesis of the emerging phases of all finite realities. The Supreme is the living way from finite consciousness to transcendence of consciousness, even to the insight of absonity. Man consciously grows from the material toward the spiritual by the strength, power, and persistency of his own decisions. The human morontial soul is a volitional, cocreative partner in its own immortalization.

God the Supreme is not only Creator-evolved and Trinity-derived; he is also self-evolved and self-derived. God the Supreme is himself a volitional, creative participant in his own deity actualization. What the Trinity is to God the Supreme, the Adjuster is to evolving man. From the finite standpoint, we actually live, move, and have our being within the immanence of the Supreme. The Supreme culminates the total finite and establishes its relationship with the destiny of the absonite.

117:4. The Finite God

God the Supreme is the finite Deity, and he must cope with the problems of the finite in the total sense of that word. Throughout the grand universe the Supreme struggles for expression. His divine evolution is in measure predicated on the wisdom-action of every personality in existence. Will you fail the God of time, who is so dependent upon the decisions of the finite mind? Will you fail the great brother of all creatures, who is so dependent on each creature? The more closely man approaches God through love, the greater the reality—actuality—of that man. When man consecrates his will to the doing of the Father's will, when man gives God all that he has, then does God make that man more than he is.

117:5. The Oversoul of Creation

The great Supreme is the cosmic oversoul of the grand universe and embraces an evolving universe purpose. When the creature submits to the will of the Creator, he participates in this great Deity adventure; by such union with divinity man exalts, enriches, spiritualizes, and unifies his evolving self to the very threshold of supremacy. The evolving immortal soul of man, when mustered into the Corps of the Finality, becomes a candidate for experiential recognition as a personality of God the Supreme.

As the ascending mortal passes beyond the boundaries of his local universe of origin, he is not entirely deprived of the ministry of the Spirit of Truth. Through the ministry of the spirit of the emerging Supreme Being and through the provisions of superuniverse reflectivity, you will still be guided in your Paradise ascent by the comforting directive of the Spirit of Truth.

The finite of time contains within itself the seeds of eternity; and we are taught that, when the fullness of evolution witnesses the exhaustion of the capacity for cosmic growth, the total finite will embark upon the absonite phases of the eternal career in quest of the Father as Ultimate.

117:6. The Quest for the Supreme

The Supreme is your universe home, and when you find him, it will be like returning home. He is your experiential parent. As God is your divine Father, so is the Supreme your divine Mother, in whom you are nurtured. What Michael is to Nebadon, the Supreme is to the finite cosmos. When men search for God, they are searching for everything. When they find God, they have found everything. All true love is from God, and man receives the divine affection as he himself bestows this love upon his fellows. Love is dynamic.

God the Supreme will never be personally discovered by any one creature until that far-distant time when, through the universal attainment of perfection, all creatures will simultaneously find him. Man can discover the Father in his heart, but he will have to search for the Supreme in the hearts of all other men. No God-knowing mortal can ever be lonely in his journey through the cosmos, for he knows that the Father walks beside him each step of the way, while the very way that he is traversing is the presence of the Supreme.

117:7. The Future of the Supreme

The completed realization of all finite potentials equals the completion of the realization of all evolutionary experience. This suggests the final emergence of the Supreme as an almighty Deity presence in the universes. It is conjectured that at this far-distant time the Supreme Being will be observable by all creature intelligences, and experienced by all universe personalities. This concept implies the actual sovereignty of the Supreme in the grand universe. We believe that the present demarcations between the seven superuniverses will gradually disappear, and that the entire grand universe will function as a perfected whole. It is possible that the Supreme may then be personally resident on Uversa, from which he will direct the administration of the time creations. And perhaps for a space there will be rest, relaxation from the agelong struggle for evolutionary perfection. But not for long! The curtain of cosmic destiny will draw back to reveal the transcendent grandeur of the alluring absonite quest for the attainment of the Universal Father on those new and higher levels revealed in the ultimate of creature experience.

Paper 118:
Supreme and Ultimate—Time and Space

Mighty Messenger

WHILE God the Sevenfold is indispensable to the evolutionary attainment of the Supreme, the Supreme is also indispensable to the eventual emergence of the Ultimate. Together they constitute the experiential bridge linking the beginnings and the completions of all creative growth in the master universe. Each successive universe age is the antechamber of the following era of cosmic growth, and each universe epoch provides immediate destiny for all preceding stages.

118:1. Time and Eternity

The personality of the mortal creature may eternalize by self-identification with the indwelling spirit through the technique of choosing to do the will of the Father. In the maturity of the developing self, the past and future are brought together to illuminate the true meaning of the present. As the self matures, it reaches further and further back into the past for experience, while its wisdom forecasts seek to penetrate deeper and deeper into the unknown future. And as the conceiving self extends this reach ever further into both past and future, so does judgment become less and less dependent on the momentary present. Patience is exercised by those mortals whose time units are short; true maturity transcends patience by a forbearance born of real understanding. To become mature is to live more intensely in the present, at the same time escaping from the limitations of the present. On the levels of the infinite and the absolute the moment of the present contains all of the past as well as all of the future. To God, as absolute, an ascending mortal who has made the eternal decision is already a Paradise finaliter. But the Universal Father can also know of, and participate in, every temporal struggle with the problems of the creature ascent from animallike to Godlike levels of existence.

118:2. Omnipresence and Ubiquity

The ubiquity of Deity must not be confused with the ultimacy of the divine omnipresence. It is volitional with the Universal Father that the Supreme, the Ultimate, and the Absolute should compensate, co-ordinate, and unify his time-space ubiquity and his time-space-transcended omnipresence with his timeless and spaceless universal and absolute presence. As mortal and morontia ascenders you progressively discern God through the ministry of God the Sevenfold. Through Havona you discover God the Supreme, a manifestation of divine ubiquity. On Paradise you find him as a person, then as finaliters you will presently attempt to know him as Ultimate, and finally begin the quest of the Absolute. Will the emergence of God the Ultimate in the postulated universes of outer space be attended by an enhanced revelation of God the Absolute? But we really do not know.

118:3. Time-Space Relationships

Only by ubiquity could Deity unify time-space manifestations to the finite conception. You perceive time by analysis and space by synthesis, and co-ordinate and associate these two dissimilar conceptions by the integrating insight of personality. Things are time conditioned, but truth is timeless. The more truth you know, the more truth you are, the more of the past you can understand and of the future you can comprehend. Truth is never dead and formal; it is always vibrant and adaptable—radiantly alive. But when truth becomes linked with fact, then both time and space condition its meanings and correlate its values. Such realities of truth wedded to fact become concepts and are accordingly relegated to the domain of relative cosmic realities. Space comes the nearest of all nonabsolute things to being absolute. Space is a property of all material bodies. All patterns of reality occupy space on the material levels, but spirit patterns only exist in relation to space. Does the pattern—the reality—of an idea occupy space? We really do not know, albeit we are sure that an idea pattern does not contain space. But it would hardly be safe to postulate that the immaterial is always nonspatial.

118:4. Primary and Secondary Causation

The vital distinction between first causes and second causes is that first causes produce original effects which are free from inheritance of any fact or derived from any antecedent causation. Secondary causes yield effects which invariably exhibit inheritance from other and preceding causation. It is upon the matured absolute potentials that the creators and controllers of the grand universe enact the never-ending drama of cosmic evolution. Causation, disregarding existentials, is threefold in its basic constitution: 1. activation of static potentials, in consequence of the volitional mandates of the Paradise

Trinity; 2. eventuation of universe capacities, by the manifold agencies of the transcendental level; 3. creation and evolution of universe actuals, effected by the Supreme Creators.

118:5. Omnipotence and Compossibility

The omnipotence of Deity does not imply the power to do the nondoable. God cannot do the ungodlike thing. Compossibility is innate in divine power. Human beings are to become God's partners in the realization of finality of destiny. No limitation can be placed upon the future possibilities of such a partnership. Always must God first find man that man may later find God. Always must there be a Universal Father before there can ever be universal sonship and consequent universal brotherhood.

118:6. Omnipotence and Omnificence

God is truly omnipotent, but he is not omnificent—he does not personally do all that is done. There is but one uncaused Cause in the whole universe. Within a local frame, volition may appear to function as an uncaused cause, but it unfailingly exhibits inheritance factors which establish relationship with the unique, original, and absolute First Causes.

Mortal man is endowed with free will, the power of choice, and though such choosing is not absolute, nevertheless, it is relatively final on the finite level and concerning the destiny of the choosing personality. The entire range of human will is strictly finite-limited except in one particular: When man chooses to find God and to be like him, such a choice is superfinite; only eternity can disclose whether this choice is also superabsonite. To recognize Deity omnipotence is to enjoy security in your experience of cosmic citizenship, to possess assurance of safety in the long journey to Paradise. But to accept the fallacy of omnificence is to embrace the colossal error of Pantheism.

118:7. Omniscience and Predestination

Ultimate foreknowledge does not abrogate finite volition. A mature and farseeing human being might be able to forecast the decision of some younger associate most accurately, but this foreknowledge takes nothing away from the freedom and genuineness of the decision itself. Error in finite choosing is time bound and time limited. The bestowal of personality imparts to living organisms the prerogatives of self-determination, self-evolution, and self-identification with a fusion spirit of Deity. The possibility of cosmic self-destruction cannot be avoided if the evolving personality is to be truly free in the exercise of finite will. Therefore is there increased safety in narrowing the limits of personality choice throughout the lower levels of existence. Choice becomes increasingly liberated as the universes are ascended; choice eventually approximates divine freedom when the ascending personality achieves divinity of status, supremacy of consecration to the purposes of the universe, completion of cosmic-wisdom attainment, and finality of creature identification with the will and the way of God.

118:8. Control and Overcontrol

In the time-space creations, free will is hedged about with restraints, with limitations. Mortal man is much more than a machine; he is mind endowed and spirit indwelt; and though he can never throughout his material life escape the chemical and electrical mechanics of his existence, he can increasingly learn how to subordinate this physical-life machine to the directive wisdom of experience by the process of consecrating the human mind to the execution of the spiritual urges of the indwelling Thought Adjuster. The slowness of evolution, of human cultural progress, testifies to the effectiveness of that brake—material inertia—which so efficiently operates to retard dangerous velocities of progress. The iniquity of Caligastia was the by-passing of the time governor of progressive human liberation. Lucifer similarly sought to disrupt the time governor operating in restraint of the premature attainment of certain liberties in the local system. Man's great universe adventure consists in the transit of his mortal mind from the stability of mechanical statics to the divinity of spiritual dynamics, and he achieves this transformation by the force and constancy of his own personality decisions, in each of life's situations declaring, "It is my will that your will be done."

118:9. Universe Mechanisms

Time and space are a conjoined mechanism of the master universe. They are the devices whereby finite creatures are enabled to coexist in the cosmos with the Infinite. Mechanisms produced by higher minds function to liberate their creative sources but to some degree unvaryingly limit the action of all subordinate intelligences. The life mechanism of the mortal personality, the human body, is the product of supermortal creative design; therefore it can never be perfectly controlled by man himself.

The grand universe is mechanism as well as organism. The basic universe mechanisms have come into existence in response to the absolute will of the First Source and Center, and they will therefore eternally function in perfect harmony with the plan of the Infinite. God the Supreme will, in the eternal future, synthesize the manifold finite diversities into one experientially meaningful whole, even as they are now existentially united on absolute levels in the Paradise Trinity.

118:10. Functions and Providence

It would appear that, in the Supreme Being, all phases of universe activity are being partially reunited by the personality of this experiential Deity.

Providence is a function, the composite of the other-than-personal overcontrol of the universe of universes. Providence functions with regard to the total and deals with the function of any creature as such function is related to the total. But what man calls providence is all too often the product of his own imagination. Much of what a mortal would call good luck might really be bad luck. The apparent cruelty of tribulation may in reality be the tempering fire that is transmuting the soft iron of immature personality into the tempered steel of real character. To realize providence in time, man must accomplish the task of achieving perfection. Providence becomes increasingly discernible as men reach upward from the material to the spiritual. Providence is the sure and certain march of the galaxies of space and the personalities of time toward the goals of eternity, first in the Supreme, then in the Ultimate, and perhaps in the Absolute.

Paper 119: The Bestowals of Christ Michael

Chief of Evening Stars

I, GAVALIA, chief of the Evening Stars of Nebadon, have been assigned to report on the seven bestowals of the Universe Sovereign, Michael of Nebadon.

The attribute of bestowal is inherent in the Paradise Sons of the Universal Father. A Creator Son makes a solemn oath to the eternal Trinity not to assume full sovereignty of his new creation until his seven creature bestowals shall have been successfully completed and certified by the Ancients of Days. In this way such Sons become intelligent and understanding rulers. Michael of Nebadon is the 611,121st bestowal of the Eternal Son upon the universes of time and space, and he began the organization of your local universe about four hundred billion years ago. His bestowals have occurred about one hundred and fifty million years apart.

119:1. The First Bestowal

It was a solemn occasion on Salvington almost one billion years ago when the assembled directors and chiefs of the universe of Nebadon heard Michael announce that his elder brother, Immanuel, would presently assume authority in Nebadon while he (Michael) would be absent on an unexplained mission. Michael did not reappear for twenty years of standard time. Only the Divine Minister, Immanuel, and Gabriel knew what was taking place. Not until the third day after Michael's departure was any message of possible significance received: "At noon today there appeared on the receiving field of this world (Melchizedek headquarters sphere) a strange Melchizedek Son, not of our number, but wholly like our order. He was assigned to twenty-four missions of universe emergency and he faithfully performed all of his assignments. By universal consent he has become chief of Melchizedeks, having earned our love and adoration by his matchless wisdom, supreme love, and superb devotion to duty."

119:2. The Second Bestowal

Almost one hundred and fifty million years after the Melchizedek bestowal, trouble began to brew in system 11 (Palonia) of constellation 37. The System Sovereign, Lutentia, led his associates in one of the most widespread and disastrous rebellions against the sovereignty of the Creator Son ever instigated in the universe of Nebadon. The Most Highs ordered his segregation and requested a new System Sovereign. Three days after Michael's unexplained leave-taking there appeared a new and unknown Lanonandek Son who was assigned as the successor of the deposed Lutentia. For more than seventeen years of universe time this temporary ruler administered the affairs and wisely adjudicated the difficulties of the confused and demoralized local system—the most noble and the most benign system ruler that Nebadon had ever known. No System Sovereign was ever more ardently loved or more widespreadly honored and respected. Even his erring predecessor sent this message: "Just and righteous are you in all your ways. While I continue in rejection of the Paradise rule, I am compelled to confess that you are a just and merciful administrator."

119:3. The Third Bestowal

A request of the Life Carriers for a Material Son to help a planet, world 217, where the System Sovereign had rebelled, came to Salvington. After the usual procedure in a system, Michael vanished and the third day thereafter a strange Material Son appeared on the system headquarters. Immediately the acting System Sovereign appointed this new and mysterious Material Son acting Planetary Prince of world 217. Working alone for one whole generation of planetary time on this quarantined world, he effected the repentance and reclamation of the defaulting Planetary Prince and his entire staff. I regret that I do not have permission to narrate the patience, fortitude, and skill with which this Material Son met the trying situations on this confused planet. The reclamation of this isolated world is one of the most beautifully touching chapters in the annals of salvation throughout Nebadon.

119:4. The Fourth Bestowal

At the end of one of the periodic millennial roll calls of Uversa, Michael proceeded to place the government of Nebadon in the hands of Immanuel and Gabriel. On the third day after his departure we observed in the universe broadcasts to Uversa, the unannounced arrival of an unknown seraphim.

Michael was absent from Salvington during his seraphic bestowal for a period of over forty standard universe years. During this time he was attached as a seraphic teaching counselor to twenty-six different master teachers, functioning on twenty-two different worlds. His last or terminal assignment was as counselor and helper attached to a bestowal mission of a Trinity Teacher Son.

As Michael's successive bestowals partook increasingly of the nature of the lower forms of universe life, Gabriel became more and more an associate of these incarnation adventures.

119:5. The Fifth Bestowal

A little over three hundred million years ago, as time is reckoned on Urantia, we witnessed another of those transfers of universe authority to Immanuel and observed the preparations of Michael for departure. Michael announced that his destination was Uversa. Shortly after he left there appeared in the Uversa broadcasts this significant statement: "There arrived today an unannounced and unnumbered ascendant pilgrim of mortal origin accompanied by Gabriel of Nebadon." This ascending mortal, Eventod, lived and functioned on Uversa for a period of eleven years of Orvonton standard time. He received the assignments and performed the duties of a spirit and on all occasions proved worthy of the confidence and trust of his superiors, while he unfailingly commanded the respect and loyal admiration of his fellow spirits. The technique of these successive bestowals has remained a mystery.

119:6. The Sixth Bestowal

Now that all Salvington was familiar with the preliminaries of an impending bestowal, Michael announced that he was soon to leave Salvington for the purpose of assuming the career of a morontia mortal at the courts of the Most High Fathers on the headquarters planet of the fifth constellation. Michael appeared on the headquarters of constellation five as a full-fledged morontia mortal of ascending status. I regret that I am forbidden to reveal the details of the career of this unnumbered morontia mortal of Endantum, for it was one of the most extraordinary and amazing epochs in Michael's bestowal experience. We were informed in advance by Gabriel of the time of Michael's release from the morontia bestowal, and accordingly we arranged a suitable reception for him on Salvington.

119:7. The Seventh and Final Bestowal

The public announcement that Michael had selected Urantia as the theater for his final bestowal was made shortly after we learned about the default of Urantia's Adam and Eve. Thus, for more than thirty-five thousand years, your world occupied a very conspicuous place in the councils of the entire universe. From first to last there was the fullest universe publicity of all that transpired on your small but highly honored world. It was a thrilling announcement broadcast from Salvington telling of the birth of the babe of Bethlehem on Urantia. Joshua ben Joseph, the Jewish baby, was conceived and born into the world just as all other babies before and since except that this particular baby was the incarnation of Michael of Nebadon.

Certain wise men of earth knew of Michael's impending arrival; the seraphim, through the midway creatures, had made the announcement to a group of Chaldean priests whose leader was Ardnon, and these men of God visited the newborn child.

119:8. Michael's Postbestowal Status

After Michael's final and successful bestowal on Urantia, he was recognized by the Universal Father as the established director of the local universe of his own creation. The Union of Days and the Faithfuls of Days were directed to signify their intention of withdrawing to Paradise. But Michael would not consent to the withdrawal of the Trinity Sons of counsel and cooperation. He assembled them on Salvington and personally requested them forever to remain on duty in Nebadon. They signified their desire to comply with this request to their directors on Paradise, and shortly thereafter there were issued those mandates of Paradise divorcement which forever attached these Sons of the central universe to the court of Michael of Nebadon.

It required almost one billion years of Urantia time to complete the sevenfold bestowal career of Michael. Urantia is the sentimental shrine of all Nebadon, the chief of ten million inhabited worlds. Your record tells the truth when it says that this same Jesus has promised sometime to return to the world of his terminal bestowal, the World of the Cross.

PART IV
THE LIFE AND TEACHINGS OF JESUS

Paper 120: The Bestowal of Michael on Urantia

ASSIGNED by Gabriel to supervise the restatement of the life of Michael when on Urantia and in the likeness of mortal flesh, I, the Melchizedek director of the revelatory commission intrusted with this task, am authorized to present this narrative of certain events which immediately preceded the Creator Son's arrival on Urantia to embark upon the terminal phase of his universe bestowal experience. Michael desired to become qualified to rule his universe and administer its affairs with that perfection of insight and wisdom of execution which will sometime be characteristic of the exalted rule of the Supreme Being. This was the setting of the momentous occasion when Immanuel presented the seventh bestowal commission.

120:1. The Seventh Bestowal Commission

"My Creator brother, I am about to witness your seventh and final universe bestowal. Most faithfully and perfectly have you executed the six previous commissions, and I entertain no thought but that you will be equally triumphant on this, your terminal sovereignty bestowal. Heretofore you have appeared on your bestowal spheres as a fully developed being of the order of your choosing. Now you are about to appear upon Urantia, the disordered and disturbed planet of your choice, not as a fully developed mortal, but as a helpless babe."

120:2. The Bestowal Limitations

"1. You will grow up on Urantia as a child of the realm, complete your human education, live your life on Urantia as you have determined, terminate your planetary sojourn, and prepare for ascension to your Father to receive from him the supreme sovereignty of your universe.

"2. I counsel that you assume the additional task of technically terminating the Lucifer rebellion in the system of Satania.

"3. When you have succeeded in terminating the Urantia secession, as you undoubtedly will, I counsel you to accept from Gabriel the conference of the title of 'Planetary Prince of Urantia.'

"4. In accordance with your request, Gabriel and all concerned will co-operate with you in the expressed desire to end your Urantia bestowal with the pronouncement of a dispensational judgment of the realm, and the establishment of the dispensation of the bestowed Spirit of Truth.

"5. I counsel you to function largely in the role of a teacher. Give attention, first, to the liberation and inspiration of man's spiritual nature. Next, illuminate the darkened human intellect, heal the souls of men, and emancipate their minds from age-old fears. Live the ideal religious life for the inspiration and edification of all your universe.

"6. On the planet of your bestowal, set rebellion-segregated man spiritually free, and make a further contribution to the sovereignty of the Supreme.

"7. Bear constantly in mind that you are living a life for the instruction and edification of all your universe. Your life in the flesh on Urantia shall be the inspiration for all lives upon all Nebadon worlds throughout all generations in the ages to come.

"8. Your great mission is embraced in your decision to live a life wholeheartedly motivated to do the will of your Paradise Father.

"9. You should refrain from the formulation of any super-human achievement or power apart from the will of the Paradise Father."

120:3. Further Counsel and Advice

"1. Give some attention to things practical and immediately helpful to your fellow men.

"2. Give precedence to the accepted customs of family life.

"3. Confine your efforts largely to spiritual regeneration and intellectual emancipation.

"4. Under no circumstances should you interfere with the normal and orderly progressive evolution of the Urantia races.

"5. You are to identify yourself with existing religious and spiritual movements but seek to avoid the formal establishment of an organized cult. Your life and teachings are to become the common heritage of all religions and all peoples.

"6. Leave no writings behind you on the planet.

"7. You will probably not enter the marriage relation; and I must remind you that one of the incarnation mandates of Sonarington forbids the leaving of human offspring behind.

"8. In all other details of your oncoming bestowal we would commit you to the leading of the indwelling Adjuster."

120:4. The Incarnation—Making Two One

Christ Michael, while truly a dual-origin being, was not a double personality. He was not God in association *with* man but, rather, God *incarnate* in man. And he was always just that combined being. The only progressive factor in such a nonunderstandable relationship was the progressive self-conscious realization and recognition (by the human mind) of this fact of being God and man. Urantia mortals have varying concepts of the miraculous, but to us who live as citizens of the local universe there are few miracles, and of these by far the most intriguing are the incarnational bestowals of the Paradise Sons. The appearance in and on your world, by apparently natural processes, of a divine Son, we regard as a miracle—the operation of universal laws beyond our understanding. Jesus of Nazareth was a miraculous person.

Paper 121: The Times of the Bestowal

Midwayer Commission

ACTING under the supervision of a commission of twelve members of the United Brotherhood of Urantia Midwayers, conjointly sponsored by the presiding head of our order and the Melchizedek of record, I am the secondary midwayer of onetime attachment to the Apostle Andrew, and I am authorized to place on record the narrative of the life transactions of Jesus of Nazareth.

121:1. The Occident of the First Century After Christ

Jesus did not come to this world during an age of spiritual decadence; at the time of his birth Urantia was experiencing such a revival of spiritual thinking and religious living as it had not known in all its previous post-Adamic history nor has experienced in any era since. When Jesus was born, the entire Mediterranean world was a unified empire. Good roads, for the first time in the world's history, interconnected many major centers. The small upper class was rich; a miserable and impoverished lower class embraced the rank and file of humanity. There was no happy and prosperous middle class in those days.

121:2. The Jewish People

At the time of Jesus, the Jews were the most influential group of the Semitic peoples, and they occupied a peculiarly strategic geographic position in the world. Many of the great highways joining the nations of antiquity passed through Palestine. Greece provided a language and a culture, Rome built the roads and unified an empire, but the dispersion of the Jews, with their more than two hundred synagogues, provided the cultural centers in which the new gospel of the kingdom of heaven found initial reception. There was very close connection between the culture, commerce, and worship of Jerusalem and Antioch. It was also in Antioch Paul's disciples were first called "Christians." The friendly relations of Herod with the Roman rulers made the world safe for Jewish travel, and thus opened the way for increased Jewish penetration even to distant portions of the Roman Empire.

Galilee was more gentile than Jewish when Jesus was born, and the Galileans were not regarded with full favor by the Jerusalem religious leaders and rabbinical teachers.

121:3. Among the Gentiles

The widespread domestic peace and prosperity of the Roman state was propitious for the bestowal of Michael. In the first century after Christ the society of the Mediterranean world consisted of five well-defined strata: the aristocracy, the business groups, the small middle class, the free proletariat, and the slaves. The early Christian church was largely composed of the lower classes and slaves. There was no widespread social problem in the Roman Empire at that time. There was always the open door through which talented and able individuals could ascend from the lower to the higher strata of Roman society. Although woman enjoyed more freedom throughout the Roman Empire than in her restricted position in Palestine, the family devotion and natural affection of the Jews far transcended that of the gentile world.

121:4. The Gentile Philosophy

The gentile world was dominated by four great philosophies: 1. *Epicureanism*, a school of thought dedicated to the pursuit of happiness, which taught that men could do something to improve their terrestrial status. It did effectually combat ignorant superstition. 2. *Stoicism*, the superior philosophy of the better classes. It taught that the soul of man was divine; that it was imprisoned in the evil body of physical nature. Stoicism ascended to a sublime morality, ideals never since transcended by any purely human system of philosophy. Paul leaned heavily toward Stoicism when he wrote, "I have learned in whatsoever state I am, therewith to be content." 3. *Cynicism*, which derived much of its doctrine from the remnants of the teachings of Machiventa Melchizedek. The Cynics preached their doctrine that "man could save himself if he would." They preached simplicity and virtue and urged men to meet death fearlessly. They did much to prepare the spiritually hungry populace for the later Christian missionaries. Their plan of popular preaching was much after the pattern, and in accordance with the style, of Paul's Epistles. 4. *The Skeptic*—skepticism asserted that knowledge was fallacious, and that conviction and assurance were impossible. It was a purely negative attitude and never became widespread.

These philosophies were semireligious; they were often invigorating, ethical, and ennobling but were usually above the common people.

121:5. The Gentile Religions

In the times of Jesus the religions of the Occident included: 1. *the pagan cults*, a combination of Hellenic and Latin mythology, patriotism, and tradition; 2. *emperor worship*, the deification of man as the symbol of the state that was seriously resented by the Jews and the early Christians leading directly to the bitter persecutions of both churches by the Roman government; 3. *astrology*, the pseudo science of Babylon that developed into a religion throughout the Greco-Roman Empire, a superstitious belief which even today man has not been fully delivered from; 4. *The mystery religions*, new and strange religions from the Levant, with secret rites and rituals that were sometimes gruesome and revolting, but which enamored the common people because it promised them *individual* salvation. These mystery religions did much to prepare the way for the rapid spread of the vastly superior Christian teachings. Paul made certain adaptations of the teachings of Jesus so as to render them more acceptable to a larger number of prospective mystery religion converts. The mysteries were built upon myths; Christianity, as Paul preached it, was founded upon a historic fact: the bestowal of Michael, the Son of God, upon mankind.

121:6. The Hebrew Religion

By the close of the first century before Christ the religious thought of Jerusalem had been tremendously influenced by Greek cultural teachings and philosophy. In the days of Jesus three languages prevailed in Palestine; the common people spoke some dialect of Aramaic, the priests and rabbis spoke Hebrew, and the educated classes and the better strata of Jews in general spoke Greek. The early translation of the Hebrew scriptures into Greek was responsible in no small measure for the subsequent drift of Paul's Christian cult toward the West instead of toward the East. The Hellenized Jewish beliefs were little influenced by the Epicurian teachings but very materially affected by the philosophy of Plato and the self-abnegation doctrines of the Stoics. The Hellenized Jews brought to the Hebrew scriptures such an allegorical interpretation that they found no difficulty in conforming Hebrew theology with their revered Aristotelian philosophy. But this all led to disastrous confusion until these problems were taken in hand by Philo of Alexandria, who proceeded to harmonize and systemize Greek philosophy and Hebrew theology into a compact and fairly consistent system of religious belief and practice. And it was this teaching that prevailed in Palestine when Jesus lived and taught, and which Paul utilized as the foundation on which to build his more advanced and enlightening cult of Christianity.

Philo was a great teacher. In the matter of combining the better elements in contemporaneous systems of ethical and religious teachings, there have been seven outstanding human teachers: Sethard, Moses, Zoroaster, Lao-tse, Buddha, Philo, and Paul. In only one matter did Paul fail to keep pace with Philo and that was the doctrine of the atonement. The Gospel of John presents its story much in the light of the viewpoint of the later Alexandrian Christians, who were disciples of the teachings of Philo.

121:7. Jews and Gentiles

By the times of Jesus the Jews had arrived at a settled concept of their origin, history, and destiny. They had built up a rigid wall of separation between themselves and the gentile world; they looked upon all gentile ways with utter contempt. For generations the Jews had nourished an attitude toward the outside world which made it impossible for them to accept the Master's teachings about the spiritual brotherhood of man. The scribes, the Pharisees, and the priesthood held the Jews in a terrible bondage of ritualism and legalism. These circumstances rendered it impossible for the Jews to fulfill their divine destiny as messengers of the new gospel of religious freedom and spiritual liberty. And so a different people were called upon to carry an advancing theology to the world, a system of teaching embodying the philosophy of the Greeks, the law of the Romans, the morality of the Hebrews, and the gospel of personality sanctity and spiritual liberty formulated by Paul and based on the teachings of Jesus. This was an enchanted age; everybody believed in miracles as commonplace occurrences.

121:8. Previous Written Records

As far as possible, consistent with our mandate, we have endeavored to utilize and to some extent co-ordinate the existing records having to do with the life of Jesus on Urantia:

1. *The Gospel by Mark* was the earliest (excepting the notes of Andrew), the briefest, and most simple record of Jesus' life. John Mark presented the Master as a minister, as man among men. His record is in reality the Gospel according to Simon Peter and was completed near the end of A.D. 68. It has since been considerably changed.

2. *The Gospel of Matthew* was written by Isador, one of Matthew's disciples, in the year A.D. 71. This record of the Master's life was written for the edification of Jewish Christians. It portrays Jesus as a son of David, picturing him as showing great respect for the law and the prophets. The record by Matthew was written in Aramaic; Isador wrote in Greek.

3. *The Gospel by Luke,* was written by Luke, the physician of Antioch, a gentile convert of Paul. Luke wrote quite a different story of the Master's life;

he preserved much of the "grace of the Lord Jesus Christ" as he gathered up these facts from Paul and others, and presented the Master as "the friend of publicans and sinners." Luke wrote in the year 82 in Achaia. He planned three books dealing with the history of Christ and Christianity but died in A.D. 90, just before he finished the second of these works, the "Acts of the Apostles." Luke depended primarily on Paul's account, so in some ways this is a Gospel according to Paul, but Luke had many other sources including eyewitnesses to episodes in Jesus' life, a copy of Mark's Gospel, Isador's narrative, a brief record by a believer named Cedes, and a copy of some notes purported to have been made by Andrew.

4. *The Gospel of John* relates much of Jesus' work in Judea and around Jerusalem which is not contained in the other records. John the son of Zebedee did not write it but he did inspire it. In the year A.D. 101 John encouraged his associate, Nathan, a Greek Jew from Caesarea, to begin the writing. The Epistle known as "First John" was written by John himself as a covering letter for the work which Nathan executed under his direction.

All these writers presented honest pictures of Jesus as they saw, remembered, or had learned of him, and these records, imperfect as they are, have been sufficient to change the course of the history of Urantia for almost two thousand years.

[*Acknowledgment*: In carrying out my commission to restate the teachings and retell the doings of Jesus of Nazareth, I have drawn freely upon all sources of record and planetary information. Only when such sources failed, have I resorted to those records which are superhuman. The memoranda which I have collected embrace thought gems and superior concepts of Jesus' teachings assembled from more than two thousand human beings who have lived on earth from the days of Jesus down to the time of the inditing of these revelations, more correctly restatements. While I, with the collaboration of my eleven associate fellow midwayers and under the supervision of the Melchizedek of record, have portrayed this narrative in accordance with my concept of its effective arrangement, in many ways I have served more as a collector and editor than as an original narrator. In behalf of the Brotherhood of the United Midwayers of Urantia, I most gratefully acknowledge our indebtedness to all sources of record and concept which have been hereinafter utilized in the further elaboration of our restatement of Jesus' life on earth.]

Paper 122: Birth and Infancy of Jesus

AFTER a study of the special report on the status of segregated worlds prepared by the Melchizedeks, Michael finally chose Urantia as the planet whereon to enact his final bestowal. Gabriel decided that the Hebrews possessed those relative advantages which warranted their selection as the bestowal race. Upon Michael's approval of this decision, Gabriel appointed and dispatched to Urantia the Family Commission of Twelve. When this commission ended its labors, Gabriel was present on Urantia and received the report nominating three prospective unions as being equally favorable as bestowal families for Michael's projected incarnation. From the three couples nominated, Gabriel made the personal choice of Joseph and Mary, subsequently appearing to Mary to impart to her the glad tidings that she had been selected to become the earth mother of the bestowal child.

122:1. Joseph and Mary

Joseph was a Hebrew of the Hebrews, albeit he carried many non-Jewish racial strains in his ancestry, which went back to the days of Abraham and through this venerable patriarch to the Sumerians and Nodites and, through the southern tribes of the ancient blue man, to Andon and Fonta. Joseph's immediate ancestors were mechanics; Joseph himself was a carpenter and later a contractor. His family belonged to a long and illustrious line of the nobility of the common people, accentuated ever and anon by the appearance of unusual individuals who had distinguished themselves in connection with the evolution of religion on Urantia.

Mary was a descendant of a long line of unique ancestors embracing many of the most remarkable women in the racial history of Urantia, reckoning among her ancestors such well-known women as Annon, Tamar, Ruth, Bathsheba, Ansie, Cloa, Eve, Enta, and Ratta. Mary's ancestry was characterized by the predominance of strong but average individuals, relieved now and then by numerous outstanding personalities in the march of civilization and the progressive evolution of religion. Racially considered, it is hardly proper to regard Mary as a Jewess. In culture and belief she was a Jew, but in hereditary endowment she was more a composite of Syrian, Hittite, Phoenician, Greek, and Egyptian stocks, her racial inheritance being more general than that of Joseph.

122:2. Gabriel Appears to Elizabeth

Jesus' lifework on Urantia was really begun by John the Baptist. Zacharias, John's father, belonged to the Jewish priesthood, while his mother, Elizabeth, was a member of the same large family group to which Mary the mother of Jesus belonged. Zacharias and Elizabeth, though they had been married many years, were childless. Late in June, 8 B.C., Gabriel appeared to Elizabeth, saying, " I, Gabriel, have come to announce that you will shortly bear a son who shall be the forerunner of this divine teacher, and you shall call your son John. Your kinswoman Mary shall be the mother of this child of promise, and I will also appear to her." For five months Elizabeth withheld her secret even from her husband. Upon her disclosure of the story, Zacharias was very skeptical and doubted the entire experience; it was not until about six weeks before John's birth that, as the result of an impressive dream, Zacharias became fully convinced that Elizabeth was to become the mother of a son of destiny. John was born in the City of Judah, March 25, 7 B.C. From his earliest infancy John was judiciously impressed by his parents with the idea that he was to grow up to become a spiritual leader and religious teacher.

122:3. Gabriel's Announcement to Mary

One evening about sundown, November 8 B.C., Gabriel appeared to Mary and said, "To you, Mary, I bring glad tidings when I announce that the conception within you is ordained by heaven, and you will become the mother of a son; you shall call him Joshua, and he shall inaugurate the kingdom of heaven on earth." Gabriel's announcement was made the day following the conception of Jesus and was the only event of supernatural occurrence connected with her entire experience of carrying and bearing the child of promise. At first Joseph had doubts about the Gabriel visitation, but after several weeks of thought, both he and Mary reached the conclusion that they had been chosen to become the parents of the Messiah.

122:4. Joseph's Dream

Joseph did not become reconciled to the idea that Mary was to become the mother of an extraordinary child until after he had experienced a very impressive dream in which a brilliant celestial messenger appeared to him and, among other things, said, "Joseph, I appear by command of Him who now reigns on high, and I am directed to instruct you concerning the son whom Mary shall bear, and who shall become a great light in the world." Nothing was said about the house of David, of Jesus' becoming a "deliverer of the Jews," nor that he was to be the long-expected Messiah. Jesus was not such a Messiah as the Jews had anticipated, but he was the *world's deliverer*. His mission was to all races and peoples, not to any one group.

Most of the so-called Messianic prophecies of the Old Testament were made to apply to Jesus long after his life had been lived on earth. Many figurative passages found throughout the Hebrew scriptures were subsequently misapplied to the life mission of Jesus. The early followers of Jesus all too often succumbed to the temptation to make all the olden prophetic utterances appear to find fulfillment in the life of their Lord and Master.

122:5. Jesus' Earth Parents

Joseph was a mild-mannered man, extremely conscientious, and in every way faithful to the religious conventions and practices of his people. He talked little but thought much. He was subject to periods of mild spiritual discouragement. These temperamental manifestations were greatly improved just before his untimely death by his advancement from the rank of carpenter to the role of a prosperous contractor.

Mary's temperament was quite opposite to that of her husband. She was usually cheerful and possessed an ever-sunny disposition. Mary was never observed to be sorrowful until after the sudden death of Joseph. And she had hardly recovered from this shock when she had thrust upon her the anxieties and questionings aroused by the extraordinary career of her eldest son. But throughout all this unusual experience Mary was composed, courageous, and fairly wise in her relationship with her strange and little-understood first-born son and his surviving brothers and sisters.

Jesus derived much of his unusual gentleness and marvelous sympathetic understanding of human nature from his father; he inherited his gift as a great teacher and his tremendous capacity for righteous indignation from his mother. Joseph and Mary were educated far above the average for their day and station in life. He was a thinker; she was a planner, expert in adaptation and practical in immediate execution. Joseph was a black-eyed brunet; Mary, a brown-eyed well-nigh blond type. Joseph held vigorously to the Eastern, or Babylonian, views of the Jewish religion; Mary leaned strongly toward the more liberal and broader Western, or Hellenistic, interpretation of the law and the prophets. Had Joseph lived, he undoubtedly would have become a firm believer in the divine mission of his eldest son

122:6. The Home at Nazareth

The home of Jesus was not far from the high hill in the northerly part of Nazareth. Jesus' family dwelt in the outskirts of the city, and this made it all the easier for him subsequently to enjoy frequent strolls in the country. It was a one-room stone structure with a flat roof and an adjoining building for housing the animals. The furniture consisted of a low stone table, earthenware and stone dishes and pots, a loom, a lampstand, several small stools, and mats for sleeping on the stone floor. In the back yard, near the animal annex, was the shelter which covered the oven and the mill for grinding grain. In later years, when the family grew in size, they would all squat about an enlarged stone table to enjoy their meals, helping themselves from a common dish, or pot, of food After the birth of Martha, Joseph built an addition to this house, a large room, which was used as a carpenter shop during the day and as a sleeping room at night.

122:7. The Trip to Bethlehem

In March, 8 B.C., Caesar Augustus decreed that all inhabitants of the Roman Empire should be numbered, that a census should be made which could be used for effecting better taxation. It was not necessary that Mary should accompany Joseph to Bethlehem to register his family, but, being an adventurous and aggressive person, she insisted on going. On August 18, 7, B.C. they left Nazareth. Being poor, they had only one beast of burden, and Mary, being large with child, rode on the animal while Joseph walked, leading the beast. Arriving at Bethlehem on August 20, they found the inn overcrowded and every room filled to overflowing. On returning to the courtyard of the inn, Joseph was informed that the caravan stables had been cleared of animals and cleaned up for the reception of lodgers. They found themselves located in what had been a grain storage room to the front of the stalls and mangers. Tent curtains had been hung, and they counted themselves fortunate to have such comfortable quarters. Joseph had thought to go out at once and enroll, but Mary was weary; she was considerably distressed and besought him to remain by her side, which he did.

122:8. The Birth of Jesus

All that night Mary was restless so that neither of them slept much. By the break of day the pangs of childbirth were well in evidence, and at noon, August 21, 7 B.C., with the help and kind ministrations of women fellow travelers, Jesus of Nazareth was born into the world. He was wrapped in the clothes which Mary had brought along for such a possible contingency and laid in a near-by manger.

At the noontide birth of Jesus the seraphim of Urantia, assembled under their directors, sang anthems of glory over the Bethlehem manger, but this was not heard by human ears. No shepherds nor any other mortal creatures came to pay homage to the babe of Bethlehem until the day of the arrival of certain priests from Ur, who were sent down from Jerusalem by Zacharias. They had been informed by a strange religious teacher of their country that "the light of life" was about to appear on earth as a babe and among the Jews.

The next day, while making his enrollment, Joseph met a man who took him to a well-to-do friend who had a room at the inn, and who said he would gladly exchange quarters with the Nazareth couple. That afternoon they moved up to the inn, where they lived for almost three weeks until they found lodgings in the home of a distant relative of Joseph. On the eighth day after his birth, Jesus was circumcised and formally named Joshua (Jesus). Zacharias, Elizabeth, and Mary were convinced that Jesus was the Messiah, so it was not difficult to prevail upon Joseph to remain in Bethlehem, the City of David, so that Jesus might grow up to become the successor of David on the throne of all Israel. Accordingly, they remained in Bethlehem more than a year.

122:9. The Presentation in the Temple

Moses had taught the Jews that every first-born son belonged to the Lord, and that, in lieu of his sacrifice as was the custom among the heathen nations, such a son might live provided his parents would redeem him by the payment of five shekels to any authorized priest. Accordingly, Joseph and Mary went up to the temple at Jerusalem in person to present Jesus to the priests and effect his redemption and also to make the proper sacrifice to insure Mary's ceremonial purification from the alleged uncleanness of childbirth.

There lingered constantly about the courts of the temple two remarkable characters, Simeon a singer and Anna a poetess. Both were intimates of the priest Zacharias, who had confided the secret of John and Jesus to them. Zacharias knew the day Joseph and Mary were expected to appear at the temple with Jesus, and he had prearranged with Simeon and Anna to indicate, by the salute of his upraised hand, which one in the procession of first-born children was Jesus. For this occasion Anna had written a poem that proclaimed Jesus to be the expected deliverer of the Jewish people, which Simeon proceeded to sing, much to the astonishment of Joseph, Mary, and all who were assembled in the temple courts. On the way back to Bethlehem, Joseph and Mary were silent—confused and overawed. Mary was much disturbed and Joseph was not in harmony with this premature effort to make Jesus out to be the expected Messiah.

122:10. Herod Acts

But the watchers for Herod were not inactive. When they reported to him the visit of the priests of Ur to Bethlehem, Herod summoned these Chaldeans to appear before him. He sent them forth with a purse and directed that they should find the child. But when the wise men did not return, Herod grew suspicious. He then dispatched searchers to locate Joseph and Mary. When, after more than a year of searching, Herod's spies had not located Jesus, Herod prepared an order directing that a systematic search be made of every house in Bethlehem, and that all boy babies under two years of age should be killed. A believer among Herod's court attachés communicated with Zacharias, who in turn dispatched a messenger to Joseph; and the night before the massacre Joseph and Mary departed from Bethlehem with the babe for Alexandria in Egypt. They sojourned in Alexandria with relatives for two full years before returning to Bethlehem until after the death of Herod.

Paper 123: The Early Childhood of Jesus

ASIDE from a few friends and relatives no one was told about Jesus' being a "child of promise," but one of Joseph's relatives revealed this to a few friends in Memphis, and they, with a small group of Alexandrian believers, assembled at the palatial home of Joseph's relative-benefactor a short time before the return to Palestine and presented Jesus with a complete copy of the Greek translation of the Hebrew scriptures.

Joseph and Mary took leave of Alexandria in August of 4 B.C., going directly to Bethlehem. Mary had never fully given up the idea that Jesus ought to grow up in Bethlehem, the City of David, but Joseph did not really believe that their son was to become a kingly deliverer of Israel and finally convinced Mary and all their friends that it was best for them to return to Nazareth. Accordingly, early in October, 4 B.C., they departed from Bethlehem for Nazareth.

123:1. Back in Nazareth

Jesus was about three years and two months old at the time of their return to Nazareth. He was full of childish glee and excitement at having premises of his own to run about in and to enjoy, but he greatly missed the association of his Alexandrian playmates. Jesus' entire fourth year was a period of normal physical development and of unusual mental activity.

In the early morning hours of April 2, 3 B.C., the second child, James, was born. Jesus was thrilled by the thought of having a baby brother. It was midsummer of this same year that Joseph built a small workshop close to the village spring and near the caravan tarrying lot. And Jesus, as he grew up, when not at school, spent his time about equally between helping his mother with home duties and watching his father work at the shop, meanwhile listening to the conversation and gossip of the caravan conductors and passengers from the four corners of the earth.

123:2. The Fifth Year

In something more than a year after the return to Nazareth, Jesus arrived at the age of his first personal and wholehearted moral decision, and there came to abide with him a Thought Adjuster which had aforetime served with Machiventa Melchizedek. This event occurred on February 11, 2 B.C. In this year, a little more than one month before his fifth birthday, Jesus was made very happy by the coming of his sister Miriam, who was born on the night of July 11. During the evening of the following day Jesus had a long talk with his father concerning how living things are born into the world as separate individuals. Joseph never failed to do his full duty in taking pains and spending time answering the boy's numerous questions.

These Jews had a systematic program for rearing and educating their children. It was the custom of the Galilean Jews for the mother to bear the responsibility for a child's training until the fifth birthday, and then, if the child were a boy, to hold the father responsible for the lad's education from that time on.

123:3. Events of the Sixth Year (1 B.C.)

Already, with his mother's help, Jesus had mastered the Galilean dialect of the Aramaic tongue; and now his father began teaching him Greek. The textbook for the study of the Greek language was the copy of the Hebrew Scriptures which had been presented to them on leaving Egypt. Before this year ended, Jesus had assumed custody of this priceless manuscript. And in a very short time he could read it readily.

The first great shock of Jesus' young life occurred when he was not quite six years old. It had seemed to the lad that his parents knew everything. Imagine his surprise when he asked his father the cause of a mild earthquake which had just occurred, to hear Joseph say, "My son, I really do not know." Thus began that long and disconcerting disillusionment in the course of which Jesus found out that his earthly parents were not all-wise and all-knowing.

In the early summer, Zacharias and Elizabeth and their son John came to visit the Nazareth family. While the parents talked over many things, including the future plans for their sons, Jesus and John played with blocks in the sand on top of the house and in many other ways enjoyed themselves in true boyish fashion.

During this year Joseph and Mary had trouble with Jesus about his prayers. Jesus insisted on talking to his heavenly Father much as he would talk to Joseph, his earthly father. There was no persuading him to change; he would say his prayers just as he had been taught, after which he insisted on having "just a little talk with my Father in heaven." This year Jesus made great progress in adjusting his strong feelings to the demands of family co-operation and home discipline.

123:4. The Seventh Year (A.D. 1)

This year snow fell two feet deep at Nazareth, the heaviest snowfall in a hundred years.

The only real accident Jesus had up to this time was a fall down the backyard stone stairs which led up to the canvas-roofed bedroom. Jesus was blinded by an unexpected sandstorm when descending the stairs and fell. There was no way in which this accident could have been prevented; material accidents, commonplace occurrences of a physical nature, are not arbitrarily interfered with by celestial personalities. After this accident Joseph built a balustrade up both sides of the stairway.

The fourth member of the Nazareth family, Joseph, was born on March 16, A.D. 1.

123:5. School Days in Nazareth

In August of this year Jesus entered upon his eventful school life at Nazareth. He was now to acquaint himself with the task of learning to read, write, and speak the Hebrew language. For three years he attended the elementary school of the Nazareth synagogue. He also began to make contact with human nature from the four quarters of the earth as men from many lands passed in and out of his father's repair shop.

It was the custom for Joseph to take Jesus out for walks on Sabbath afternoons, one of their favorite jaunts being to climb the high hill near their home, from which they could obtain a panoramic view of all Galilee. Jesus' earliest training had to do with a reverent and sympathetic contact with nature. This year he learned to milk the family cow and care for the other animals, to make cheese and to weave. He also enjoyed playing with clay at the potter's shop with his friend Jacob.

As his "birthday text" Jesus chose from Isaiah: "The spirit of the Lord God is upon me, for the Lord has anointed me; he has sent me to bring good news to the meek, to bind up the brokenhearted, to proclaim liberty to the captives, and to set the spiritual prisoners free."

123:6. His Eighth Year (A.D. 2)

Jesus belonged to the more progressive third of the class, doing his work so well that he was excused from attendance one week out of each month, a week he usually spent either with his fisherman uncle on the shores of the Sea of Galilee or on the farm of another uncle five miles south of Nazareth.

About this time Jesus met a teacher of mathematics from Damascus; he developed a keen sense of numbers, distances, and proportions. This year Jesus made arrangements to exchange dairy products for lessons on the harp. In school he persisted in asking many embarrassing questions concerning both science and religion.

In February, Nahor, one of the teachers in a Jerusalem academy of the rabbis, came to Nazareth to observe Jesus. He advised Joseph and Mary to allow him to take Jesus back with him to Jerusalem. Because of a difference of opinion between Joseph and Mary, Nahor requested permission to lay the whole matter before Jesus. Jesus, not feeling competent to assume the responsibility for such a decision, finally decided to "talk with my Father who is in heaven"; and while he was not perfectly sure about the answer, he rather felt he should remain at home "with my father and mother," adding, "they who love me so much should be able to do more for me and guide me more safely than strangers who can only view my body and observe my mind but can hardly truly know me."

His third brother, Simon, was born on April 14, A.D. 2.

Paper 124: The Later Childhood of Jesus

ALTHOUGH Jesus might have enjoyed a better opportunity for schooling at Alexandria than in Galilee, he could not have had such a splendid environment for working out his own life problems with a minimum of educational guidance, at the same time enjoying the great advantage of constantly contacting with such a large number of all classes of men and women hailing from every part of the civilized world.

124:1. Jesus' Ninth Year (A.D. 3)

The most serious trouble as yet to come up at school occurred in late winter when Jesus dared to challenge the chazan regarding the teaching that all images, pictures, and drawings were idolatrous in nature. Trouble was again stirred up at school when one of the more backward pupils discovered Jesus drawing a charcoal picture of the teacher on the floor of the schoolroom. A committee of the elders went to call on Joseph to demand that something be done to suppress the lawlessness of his eldest son. Jesus listened to the indictment of his artistic efforts for some time then marched in and fearlessly confronted his accusers. He courageously defended his viewpoint, and with consummate self-control announced that he would abide by the decision of his father. Joseph felt impelled to rule that the rabbinical interpretation of the second commandment should prevail, but Jesus was unconvinced of the wrong of what he had done.

Jesus' second sister, Martha, was born on September 13. Three weeks later, Joseph, who was home for awhile, started building an addition to their house, a combined workshop and bedroom. A small workbench was built for Jesus.

Jesus continued to grow physically, intellectually, socially, and spiritually. Before he was ten years old, he had become the leader of a group of seven lads who formed themselves into a society for promoting the acquirements of manhood—physical, intellectual, and religious.

124:2. The Tenth Year (A.D. 4)

It was the fifth of July when Jesus, while strolling through the countryside with his father, first gave expression to feelings and ideas which indicated that he was becoming self-conscious of the unusual nature of his life mission. In August, he entered the advanced school of the synagogue where he constantly created trouble by the questions he persisted in asking.

Jesus' playmates saw nothing supernatural in his conduct; in most ways he was altogether like themselves. Perhaps his most unusual and outstanding trait was his unwillingness to fight for his rights. As it happened, he did not suffer much on account of this trait because of the friendship of Jacob, a neighbor boy, who was one year older. Jacob made it his business to see that no one was permitted to impose upon Jesus because of his aversion to physical combat.

Jesus was the generally accepted leader of the Nazareth lads who stood for the higher ideals of their day and generation. He had just about made up his mind to become a fisherman but close association with his father's vocation later on influenced him to become a carpenter, while still later a combination of influences led him to the final choice of becoming a religious teacher of a new order.

124:3. The Eleventh Year (A.D. 5)

Jesus spent considerable time at the caravan supply shop, and by conversing with the travelers from all parts of the world, he acquired a store of information about international affairs. This was the last year in which he enjoyed much free play and youthful joyousness.

On Wednesday evening, June 24, A.D. 5, Jude was born. Complications attended the birth of this, the seventh child. Mary was so very ill for several weeks that Joseph remained at home. Jesus was very much occupied with errands for his father and with many duties occasioned by his mother's illness. He was compelled to assume the responsibilities of the first-born son and to do all this one or two full years before these burdens should normally have fallen on his shoulders.

About the middle of May Jesus accompanied his father on a business trip to Scythopolis. When Jesus expressed approval of the competitive games that were in progress, Joseph, hearing his son express such un-Jewish sentiments, seized Jesus by the shoulder and angrily exclaimed, "My son, never again let me hear you give utterance to such an evil thought as long as you live." And ever again did Jesus allude to the games and other athletic activities of the Greeks as long as his father lived.

From this year on Jesus was more and more given to peculiar seasons of profound meditation and serious contemplation, thinking about how he was to carry out his obligations to his family and at the same time be obedient to the call of his mission to the world; already he had conceived that his ministry was not to be limited to the betterment of the Jewish people.

124:4. The Twelfth Year (A.D. 6)

Jesus continued to make progress at school and was indefatigable in his study of nature, while increasingly he prosecuted his study of the methods whereby men make a living. He began doing regular work in the home carpenter shop and was permitted to manage his own earnings, a very unusual arrangement to obtain in a Jewish family. He was becoming conscious of the way in which he had caused trouble in the village, and henceforth he became increasingly discreet in concealing everything which might cause him to be regarded as different from his fellows.

Increasingly Jesus' parents realized that there was something superhuman resident within this eldest son, but they never even faintly dreamed that this son of promise was indeed and in truth the actual creator of this local universe. More and more Jesus inclined to the view of his father, so that his mother was destined to be hurt by the realization that her son was gradually rejecting her guidance in matters having to do with his life career. He suffered great mental distress as the result of his constant effort to adjust his personal views of religious practices and social amenities to the established beliefs of his parents. However, he never shirked the responsibility of making the necessary daily adjustments based upon loyalty, fairness, tolerance, and love.

Throughout this year Jesus experienced many seasons of uncertainty, if not actual doubt, regarding the nature of his mission. His naturally developing human mind did not yet fully grasp the reality of his dual nature.

124:5. His Thirteenth Year (A.D. 7)

On Sunday night, January 9, A.D. 7, Jesus' baby brother, Amos, was born.

In this year Jesus passed from boyhood to the beginning of young manhood. It was about the middle of February that Jesus became humanly assured that he was destined to perform a mission on earth for the enlightenment of man and the revelation of God. Momentous decisions, coupled with far-reaching plans, were formulating in the mind of this youth.

On March 20 Jesus graduated from the course of training in the local school connected with the Nazareth synagogue. This was a great day in the life of any ambitious Jewish family, the day when the first-born son was pronounced a "son of the commandment" and the ransomed first-born of the Lord God of Israel, a "child of the Most High" and servant of the Lord of all the earth. Joseph had come over from Sepphoris to be present on this glad occasion. The elders were very proud of Jesus and had already begun laying plans which would enable him to go to Jerusalem to continue his education in the renowned Hebrew academies, but Jesus became increasingly sure that he would never study with the rabbis.

124:6. The Journey to Jerusalem

Having been formally graduated from the synagogue schools, Jesus was qualified to proceed to Jerusalem with his parents to participate with them in the celebration of his first Passover feast, which fell this year on Saturday, April 9, A.D. 7. A considerable company (103) departed from Nazareth early

Monday morning, April 4, for Jerusalem, going by way of the Jordan Valley to avoid passing through Samaria.

By the fourth and last day's journey the road was a continuous procession of pilgrims. As they neared the hills leading up to Jerusalem, they paused for rest on the eastern slopes of Olivet in the borders of a little village called Bethany, stopping near the house of one Simon, who had three children about the same age as Jesus: Mary, Martha, and Lazarus. They invited the Nazareth family in for refreshment, and a lifelong friendship sprang up between the two families.

They pressed on, soon standing on the brink of Olivet, and Jesus saw for the first time (in his memory) the Holy City. At no time in his life did Jesus ever experience such a purely human thrill as that which at this time so completely enthralled him. But they hurried on to Jerusalem. Soon they reached the place prearranged for their accommodation during the Passover week, the large home of a well-to-do relative of Mary's.

This was one of the most extraordinary days that the Son of God spent in the flesh; and during the night, for the first time in his earth career, there appeared to him an assigned messenger from Salvington, commissioned by Immanuel, who said, "The hour has come. It is time that you began to be about your Father's business."

Paper 125: Jesus at Jerusalem

NO incident in all Jesus' eventful earth career was more engaging, more humanly thrilling, than this, his first remembered visit to Jerusalem. All through a joyful childhood he had reverently heard of Jerusalem and its temple; now he was soon to behold them in reality. From the Mount of Olives and from the outside, on closer inspection, the temple had been all and more than Jesus had expected; but when he once entered its sacred portals, the great disillusionment began.

In company with his parents Jesus passed through the temple precincts, and the first great shock of the day came when his mother took leave of them on her way to the women's gallery. It had never occurred to Jesus that his mother was not to accompany him to the consecration ceremonies, and he was thoroughly indignant that she was made to suffer from such unjust discrimination. He passed through the consecration rituals but was disappointed by their perfunctory and routine natures. He then returned to greet his mother and prepared to accompany his father on his first trip about the temple.

Jesus simply would not accept explanations of worship and religious devotion which involved belief in the wrath of God or the anger of the Almighty.

After the conclusion of the temple visit, when his father became mildly insistent that he acknowledge acceptance of the orthodox Jewish beliefs, Jesus turned suddenly upon his parents and, looking appealingly into the eyes of his father, said, "My father, it cannot be true; the Father in heaven cannot so regard his erring children on earth. The heavenly Father cannot love his children less than you love me. And I well know, no matter what unwise thing I might do, you would never pour out wrath upon me nor vent anger against me. If you, my earthly father, possess such human reflections of the Divine, how much more must the heavenly Father be filled with goodness and overflowing with mercy. I refuse to believe that my Father in heaven loves me less than my father on earth." Never again did Joseph and Mary seek to change his mind about the love of God.

125:1. Jesus Views the Temple

Everywhere Jesus went throughout the temple courts, he was shocked and sickened by the spirit of irreverence which he observed. But he received the shock of his young life when his father escorted him into the court of the gentiles with its noisy jargon, loud talking and cursing, the presence of the money-changers, and the vendors of sacrificial animals. When they stood near the altar to observe the killing of the droves of animals and the washing away of the blood from the hands of the officiating slaughter priests, the terrible sight sickened this boy of Nazareth; he clutched his father's arm and begged to be taken away. Jesus had had enough for his first visit at the temple. They returned to the upper court for Mary then went to their lodgings and made ready for the celebration of the Passover.

125:2. Jesus and the Passover

It had been the plan to eat the Passover with Mary's relatives, but Jesus persuaded his parents to accept the invitation to go to Bethany. That night, eating the roasted flesh with unleavened bread and bitter herbs, Jesus, being a new son of the covenant, was asked to recount the origin of the Passover, and this he well did, but he somewhat disconcerted his parents by the inclusion of numerous remarks mildly reflecting the impressions made on his youthful but thoughtful mind by the things which he had so recently seen and heard. Jesus had begun to turn over in his mind the propriety of celebrating the Passover without the slaughtered lamb.

Jesus slept very little that night. His mind was distraught and his heart torn by the inconsistencies and absurdities of the theology of the whole Jewish ceremonial system. The next day's services at the temple were more acceptable to him and did much to relieve the unpleasant memories of the previous day.

The following morning young Lazarus took Jesus in hand, and they began a systematic exploration of Jerusalem and its environs. Before the day was over, Jesus discovered the various places about the temple where teaching and question conferences were in progress, and here he spent most of his time. On Wednesday, Jesus was permitted to go home with Lazarus to spend the night at Bethany. This evening, Lazarus, Martha, and Mary heard Jesus discuss things temporal and eternal, human and divine, and from that night on they all three loved him as if he had been their own brother.

125:3. Departure of Joseph and Mary

While his parents awaited the assembly of their fellow travelers in preparation for the return journey to Nazarth, Jesus had gone into the temple to listen to the discussions. Presently the company prepared to depart, the men going in one group and the women in another. On the way up to Jerusalem, Jesus had gone in company with his mother and the women; being now a young man, he was supposed to journey back to Nazareth in company with his father and the men. But as the Nazareth party moved on toward Bethany, Jesus was completely absorbed in the discussion of angels and he did not realize that he had been left behind until the noontime adjournment. Mary and Joseph did not discover Jesus' absence until they reached Jericho, Mary surmising he journeyed with the men and Joseph thinking he traveled with the women. Learning that none of the party had seen their son, they spent a sleepless night, recounting many of Jesus' unusual reactions to the Passover events and mildly chiding each other for not seeing to it that he was in the group before they left Jerusalem.

125:4. First and Second Days in the Temple

In the meantime, Jesus had remained in the temple listening to the discussions. At the conclusion he went over to Bethany, arriving just as Simon's family made ready to partake of their evening meal. He visited very little during the evening, spending much of the time alone in the garden meditating.

Early next day Jesus was up and on his way to the temple. On the brow of Olivet he paused and wept over the sight his eyes beheld—a spiritually impoverished people, tradition bound and living under the surveillance of the Roman legions. At the second conference he had made bold to ask questions, and in a very amazing way he participated in the temple discussions but always in a manner consistent with his youth. Sometimes his pointed questions embarrassed the learned teachers of the Jewish law, but he evinced such a spirit of candid fairness, coupled with an evident hunger for knowledge, that the majority of the temple teachers were disposed to treat him with every consideration.

When this, his second day in the temple, was finished, again he went to Bethany for the night. Meanwhile, Joseph and Mary also had arisen with the early dawn and retraced their steps to the house of their relatives where they had lodged in Jerusalem. After searching all day and finding no trace of Jesus, they returned to their relatives for the night.

125:5. The Third Day in the Temple

Jesus' third day with the scribes and teachers in the temple witnessed the gathering of many spectators who, having heard of this youth from Galilee, came to enjoy the experience of seeing a lad confuse the wise men of the law. The entire attention had become focused upon the questions being asked by Jesus, among them: 1. What really exists in the holy of holies, behind the veil?; 2. Why should mothers in Israel be segregated from the male temple worshipers?; 3. If God is a father who loves his children, why all this slaughter of animals to gain divine favor—has the teaching of Moses been misunderstood?; 4. Since the temple is dedicated to the worship of the Father in heaven, is it consistent to permit the presence of those who engage in secular barter and trade?; 5. Is the expected Messiah to become a temporal prince to sit on the throne of David, or is he to function as the light of life in the establishment of a spiritual kingdom?

Those who listened marveled at his many questions, and none was more astonished than Simon, who had come down from Bethany to see what the boy was up to. By the deft and subtle phrasing of a question Jesus would at one and the same time challenge the Jewish teachings and suggest his own. When the day was over, Simon and Jesus wended their way back to Bethany. After the evening meal Jesus again went to the garden, where he lingered long into the night, vainly endeavoring to think out some definite plan of approach to the problem of his lifework. But the clear light did not come to the truth-seeking lad.

Throughout this day Joseph and Mary had continued their anxious search for Jesus, even going several times into the temple but never thinking to scrutinize the several discussion groups.

125:6. The Fourth Day in the Temple

Jesus was strangely unmindful of his earthly parents; even at breakfast, when Lazarus's mother remarked that his parents must be about home by that time, Jesus did not seem to comprehend that they would be worried about his having lingered behind.

Again he journeyed to the temple, where the leader invited the lad to come forward and, sitting beside him, bade Jesus state his own views regarding prayer and worship. The evening before, Jesus' parents had heard about this strange youth who so deftly sparred with the expounders of the law, but it had not occurred to them that this lad was their son. Thinking that Zacharias might have seen Jesus, they went to the temple, and, as they strolled through the temple courts, they were surprised and amazed to recognize the voice of the missing lad and to behold him seated among the temple teachers. Joseph was speechless, but Mary gave vent to her long-pent-up fear and anxiety and rushed up to the lad, now standing to greet his astonished parents, saying, "My child, why have you treated us like this? It is now more than three days that your father and I have searched for you sorrowing. Whatever possessed you to desert us?" After a moment's thought, Jesus answered, saying, "Why is it that you have so long sought me? Would you not expect to find me in my Father's house since the time has come when I should be about my Father's business?" Presently Jesus said, "Come, my parents, none has done aught but that which he thought best. Our Father in heaven has ordained these things; let us depart for home."

As they were returning to Nazareth, they paused on the brow of Olivet, when Jesus raised his staff and said with intense emotion, "O Jerusalem, Jerusalem, and the people thereof, what slaves you are—subservient to the Roman yoke and victims of your own traditions—but I will return to cleanse yonder temple and deliver my people from this bondage! " On the three days' journey to Nazareth Jesus said little; neither did his parents say much in his presence. Upon reaching home, Jesus assured them of his affection, saying, "While I must do the will of my Father in heaven, I will also be obedient to my father on earth. I will await my hour."

Paper 126: The Two Crucial Years

OF all Jesus' earth-life experiences, the fourteenth and fifteenth years were the most crucial. These two years, after he began to be self-conscious of divinity and destiny, and before he achieved a large measure of communication with his indwelling Adjuster, were the most trying of his eventful life on Urantia.

More and more was Jesus in the company of his father; less and less did he come to Mary with his problems, while increasingly both parents failed to comprehend his frequent alternation between the affairs of this world and the contemplation of his relation to his Father's business. As he grew older, Jesus' pity and love for the Jewish people deepened, along with a growing righteous resentment of the presence in the Father's temple of the politically appointed priests; he looked with disdain upon all those religious leaders who were not sincere. When he scrutinized the leadership of Israel, he was sometimes tempted to look with favor on the possibility of his becoming the Messiah of Jewish expectation, but he never yielded to such a temptation.

126:1. His Fourteenth Year (A.D. 8)

Jesus was rapidly developing into an expert carpenter and cabinetmaker. This summer he made frequent trips to the top of the hill to the northwest of Nazareth for prayer and meditation. He was gradually becoming more self-conscious of the nature of his bestowal on earth. He continued to carry on his advanced courses of reading under the synagogue teachers, and he also continued with the home education of his brothers and sisters as they grew up to suitable ages.

Scores of times Mary stood in breathless anticipation, expecting to see her son engage in some superhuman or miraculous performance, but always were her hopes dashed down in cruel disappointment. The devout people of those days truly believed that men of promise always demonstrated their calling by performing miracles, but Jesus did none of these things; wherefore was the confusion of his parents steadily increased as they contemplated his future.

Throughout this year it can truly be said that Jesus "grew in favor with man and with God." The prospects of the family seemed good; the future was bright.

126:2. The Death of Joseph

All did go well until that fateful day of Tuesday, September 25, when a runner from Sepphoris brought to this Nazareth home the tragic news that Joseph had been severely injured by the falling of a derrick. Mary insisted in going to Sepphoris accompanied by James while Jesus remained home with the younger children, but Joseph died of his injuries before Mary arrived. This lad of Nazareth now became the sole support and comfort of this so suddenly bereaved family. Jesus cheerfully accepted the responsibilities so suddenly thrust upon him, and he carried them faithfully to the end. He proved to be a wise and efficient administrator of his father's estate. But in spite of all that Jesus and the Nazareth neighbors could do to bring cheer into the home, Mary, and even the children, were overcast with sadness. Joseph was an unusual husband and father, and they all missed him.

126:3. The Fifteenth Year (A.D. 9)

By the middle of this fifteenth year Jesus had taken a firm grasp upon the management of his family. Before this year had passed, their savings had about disappeared and they had to dispose of one of the properties Joseph had owned. They bought a second cow and began the sale of milk to their Nazareth neighbors.

On April 17, A.D. 9, Ruth, the baby of the family, was born, and to the best of his ability Jesus endeavored to take the place of his father in comforting and ministering to his mother. For almost a score of years no father could have loved and nurtured his daughter any more affectionately and faithfully than Jesus cared for little Ruth. And he was an equally good father to all the other members of his family.

During this year Jesus first formulated the prayer which he subsequently taught to his apostles, and which to many has become known as "The Lord's Prayer." He also found a passage in the so-called Book of Enoch which influenced him in the later adoption of the term "Son of Man" as a designation for his bestowal mission on Urantia. From this year on, Jesus' disclosures about what was going on in his mind steadily diminished. To all appearances he became commonplace and conventional, though he did long for someone who could understand his problems. The uniqueness of the unusual situation compelled him to bear his burdens alone.

126:4. First Sermon in the Synagogue

On the first Sabbath after his fifteenth birthday the chazan arranged for Jesus to conduct the morning service of the synagogue. Jesus read selected passages from Isaiah, Amos, and Micah: "The spirit of the Lord God is upon me, for the Lord has anointed me; he has sent me to bring good news to the meek, to bind up the brokenhearted, to proclaim liberty to the captives, and to set the spiritual prisoners free; to proclaim the year of God's favor and the day of our God's reckoning; to comfort all mourners, to give them beauty for ashes, the oil of joy in the place of mourning, a song of praise instead of the spirit of sorrow, that they may be called trees of righteousness, the planting of the Lord, wherewith he may be glorified."

Never had his townspeople seen him so magnificently solemn; never had they heard his voice so earnest and so sincere; never had they observed him so manly and decisive, so authoritative.

126:5. The Financial Struggle

Gradually Jesus and his family returned to the simple life of their earlier years. They had plenty of milk, butter, and cheese. In season they enjoyed the produce of their garden, but each passing month necessitated the practice of greater frugality. Apparently all Jesus' plans for a career were thwarted. The future did not look bright as matters now developed. But he did not falter; he was not discouraged. He lived on, day by day, doing well the present duty and faithfully discharging the *immediate* responsibilities of his station in life. Jesus' life is the everlasting comfort of all disappointed idealists.

Fearing that the copy of the Greek scriptures might be discovered and confiscated by the tax collectors, Jesus, on his fifteenth birthday, presented it to the Nazareth synagogue library as his maturity offering to the Lord.

The great shock of this year came when Jesus went over to Sepphoris to receive the decision of Herod regarding the appeal taken to him in the dispute about the amount of money due Joseph at the time of his accidental death. Herod decreed that his father had nothing due him at the time of his death. And for such an unjust decision Jesus never again trusted Herod Antipas. It is not surprising that he once alluded to Herod as "that fox."

The family supply shop had been taken over by his uncle, and Jesus worked altogether in the home shop, where he was near to help Mary with the family. During this year Jesus rented a piece of land near their home which was divided up as a family garden plot. They contrived to enjoy much of the experience of farm life as they now had three cows, four sheep, a flock of chickens, a donkey, and a dog, in addition to the doves.

With the close of this fifteenth year Jesus completed the transition between the more complacent years of childhood and the consciousness of approaching manhood. The growth period of mind and body had ended, and now began the real career of this young man of Nazareth.

Paper 127: The Adolescent Years

AS Jesus entered upon his adolescent years, he found himself the head and sole support of a large family. As time passed, he became increasingly conscious of his pre-existence; he began more fully to realize that he was present on earth and in the flesh for the express purpose of revealing his Paradise Father to the children of men. No adolescent youth who has lived or ever will live on this world or any other world has had or ever will have more weighty problems to resolve or more intricate difficulties to untangle. Slowly, but certainly and by actual experience, this divine Son is *earning* the right to become sovereign of his universe.

127:1. The Sixteenth Year (A.D. 10)

This year Jesus attained his full physical growth and was a virile and comely youth. He became increasingly sober and serious, but he was kind and sympathetic. His eye was kind but searching; his voice was musical but authoritative. Always, even in the most commonplace of contacts, there seemed to be in evidence the touch of a twofold nature, the human and the divine. His well-proportioned body and keen and analytical mind were becoming organized into a strong, striking, and attractive personality.

Jesus maintained (and his mother agreed) that girls should go to school the same as boys, and since the synagogue school would not receive them, there was nothing to do but conduct a home school especially for them. He was a real though youthful father to the family; he spent every possible hour with the youngsters, and they truly loved him. While there was much about her son that Mary could not understand, she did love him, and she most thoroughly appreciated the willing manner in which he shouldered the responsibility of the home.

127:2. The Seventeenth Year (A.D. 11)

At about this time there was considerable agitation against the payment of taxes to Rome. The Zealots political party arrived in Galilee and were making good headway until they reached Nazareth. Jesus listened carefully to them but refused to join the party. Mary did her best to induce him to enlist. Jesus also refused to join a more moderate political group because of his heavy family responsibilities. The situation was still further complicated when a wealthy Jew, Isaac, came forward agreeing to support Jesus' family if he would lay down his tools and assume leadership of these Nazareth patriots. His mother and uncle, and even his younger brother James, all urged him to join the nationalist cause. After consulting with his chazan, Jesus reiterated that loyalty to a dead father forbade his leaving the family no matter how much money was forthcoming, for "money cannot love." James, with the help of the chazan, made a speech stating that if they would only consent to allow Jesus to remain "with us, to be our father and teacher, then you will have not just one leader from Joseph's family, but presently you will have five loyal nationalists, for are there not five of us boys to grow up and come forth from our brother-father's guidance to serve our nation?" The crisis for the time being was over, but never was this incident forgotten in Nazareth.

127:3. The Eighteenth Year (A.D. 12)

In the course of this year all the family property, except the home and garden, was disposed of. With the financial pressure thus eased for the time being, Jesus decided to take James to the Passover. After attending the temple services and being received into the commonwealth of Israel, James wanted to hear Jesus participate in the temple discussions, as he had heard his mother tell about, but Jesus asked no questions. It all seemed so puerile and insignificant to his awakening mind and he could only pity them. James was disappointed, and to his inquiries Jesus only made reply, "My hour has not yet come."

Upon returning to Nazareth, Jesus began work in the old family repair shop and was greatly cheered by being able to meet so many people each day from all parts of the country and surrounding districts.

In September, Elizabeth and John came to visit the Nazareth family. John, having lost his father, intended to return to the Judean hills to engage in agriculture and sheep raising. Jesus and John had many talks together over some very intimate and personal matters. After this visit they decided not to see each other again until they should meet in their public service.

On December 3 death for the second time struck at this Nazareth family. Little Amos, their baby brother, died. After passing through this time of sorrow with her first-born son as her only support, Mary at last and in the fullest sense recognized Jesus as the real head of the family; and he was truly a worthy head.

127:4. The Nineteenth Year (A.D. 13)

By the beginning of this year Jesus had fully won his mother to the acceptance of his methods of child training—the positive injunction to do good in the place of the older Jewish method of forbidding to do evil. Prayer time in this household was the occasion for discussing anything and everything relating to the welfare of the family. On three occasions when it was deemed wise to punish Jude for self-confessed and deliberate violations of the family rules of conduct, his punishment was fixed by the unanimous decree of the older children and was assented to by Jude himself before it was inflicted.

As time passed, Jesus did much to liberalize and modify the family teachings and practices related to Sabbath observance and many other phases of religion. By this time Jesus had become the unquestioned head of the house. This year Jude started to school, and it was necessary for Jesus to sell his harp in order to defray these expenses. Thus disappeared the last of his recreational pleasures.

127:5. Rebecca, the Daughter of Ezra

Although Jesus was poor, his social standing in Nazareth was in no way impaired, and since he was such a splendid specimen of robust and intellectual manhood, and considering his reputation as a spiritual leader, it was not strange that Rebecca, the eldest daughter of Ezra, a wealthy merchant and trader of Nazareth, should discover that she was slowly falling in love with him. She first confided her affection to Miriam, Jesus' sister, and Miriam in turn talked it over with her mother. Mary and Miriam sought to stop it, honestly telling Rebecca about their belief that Jesus was a son of destiny; that he was to become a great religious leader, perhaps the Messiah. Rebecca was thrilled with the recital and more than ever determined to cast her lot with this man of her choice, interpreting Mary's efforts to dissuade her as a natural reaction to the dread of losing the head and sole support of her family.

In cooperation with her father Rebecca worked out a plan to supply the family with sufficient income fully to compensate for the loss of Jesus' earnings, and when she failed to win Mary and Miriam's support, she went directly to Jesus and invited him to their home for the celebration of her seventeenth birthday. After listening attentively and sympathetically to both father and daughter, Jesus kindly replied that no amount of money could take the place of his obligation personally to rear his father's family, to "fulfill the most sacred of all human trusts—loyalty to one's own flesh and blood." He sincerely thanked Rebecca for her expressed admiration, adding, "it shall cheer and comfort me all the days of my life." He explained that he was not free to enter into relations with any woman other than those of simple brotherly regard and pure friendship.

Rebecca was heartbroken. She refused to be comforted and begged her father to leave Nazareth until he finally consented to move to Sepphoris. She followed Jesus devotedly through his eventful years of public labor, and was present by the side of Mary on that fateful and tragic afternoon when the Son of Man hung upon the cross.

127:6. His Twentieth Year (A.D. 14)

Although they could hardly afford it, Jesus had a strange longing to go up to Jerusalem for the Passover. His mother, knowing of his recent experience with Rebecca, wisely urged him to make the journey. He wanted most of all to see Lazarus, Martha, and Mary. Next to his own family he loved these three most of all, and Jesus was the idolized ideal of all three of them.

On this visit occurred one of those periodic outbreaks of rebellion against tradition. Jesus proposed that they celebrate the feast at Lazarus's house. "But," said Lazarus, "we have no paschal lamb." And then Jesus entered upon a prolonged and convincing dissertation to the effect that the Father in heaven was not truly concerned with such childlike and meaningless rituals, that "those who have seen the light of life no longer need to approach our Father by the darkness of death." That evening about twilight these four sat down and partook of the first Passover feast ever to be celebrated by devout Jews without the paschal lamb.

It was during this year that Mary had a long talk with Jesus about marriage. She frankly asked him if he would get married if he were free from his family responsibilities. Jesus expressed himself as doubting that he would ever enter the marriage state. Having settled already in his mind that he was not to become the father of children in the flesh, he gave very little thought to the subject of human marriage.

This year he began anew the task of further weaving his mortal and divine natures into a simple and effective *human individuality*. He is rapidly becoming a man, not just a young man but an adult. He has learned well to bear responsibility. He knows how to carry on in the face of disappointment. He bears up bravely when his plans are thwarted and his purposes temporarily defeated. He has very nearly mastered the technique of utilizing the energy of the spiritual drive to turn the mechanism of material achievement. And all this human experience is an eternal possession of the Universe Sovereign. He is our understanding brother, sympathetic friend, experienced sovereign, and merciful father. And now as a full-grown man he prepares to continue his supreme mission of revealing God to men and leading men to God.

Paper 128: Jesus' Early Manhood

AS Jesus of Nazareth entered upon the early years of his adult life, he had lived, and continued to live, a normal and average human life on earth. Always be mindful of the twofold purpose of Michael's bestowal on Urantia: the mastering of the experience of living the full life of a human creature—the completion of his sovereignty in Nebadon—and the revelation of the Universal Father to the mortal dwellers on the worlds of time and space.

128:1. The Twenty-First Year (A.D. 15)

This year Jesus went up to Jerusalem with his brother Joseph to celebrate the Passover. Joseph asked Jesus many leading questions concerning his life mission, but to most of these inquiries Jesus would only reply, "My hour has not yet come." Jesus, with Joseph, spent this Passover with his three friends at Bethany, as was his custom when in Jerusalem attending these festival commemorations.

Joshua ben Joseph obtained knowledge, gained experience, and combined these into wisdom, just as do other mortals of the realm. Until after his baptism he availed himself of no supernatural power. We have a Sovereign who was in all points tested and tempted as we are, yet without sin. And since he himself has suffered, being tested and tried, he is abundantly able to understand and minister to those who are confused and distressed. The self-realization of divinity was a slow and, from the human standpoint, a natural evolutionary revelation. And yet, throughout all these years of his life in the flesh he was truly divine. He was actually a Creator Son of the Paradise Father.

128:2. The Twenty-Second Year (A.D. 16)

This was one of several years during which Jesus was kept busy helping his brothers and sisters to adjust themselves to the new awakenings of their adolescence lives. This year Simon graduated from school and began work with Jesus' old boyhood playmate, Jacob the stone mason. As a result of several family conferences it was decided that it was unwise for all the boys to take up carpentry; that by diversifying their trades they would be prepared to take contracts for putting up entire buildings.

The latter part of this year Jesus left James in charge of the repair shop while he went over to Sepphoris to work with a smith. Before taking up his new employment, Jesus held one of his periodic family conferences and solemnly installed James as acting head of the family, and never again did he take the reins out of James's hands. Living much of the time in Sepphoris for six months afforded Jesus a new opportunity to become better acquainted with the gentile viewpoint of life. When he returned to the repair shop, he did not again assume the personal direction of family affairs. It was by just such wise and thoughtful planning that Jesus prepared the way for his eventual withdrawal from active participation in the affairs of his family.

128:3. The Twenty-Third Year (A.D. 17)

This year the financial pressure was slightly relaxed as four were at work. The situation was such that Jesus stopped work for three weeks to take Simon to Jerusalem for the Passover. At Philadelphia Jesus and Simon became acquainted with a merchant from Damascus who proposed that Jesus come to Damascus to enter his Oriental import business, but Jesus explained that he could not be so far away from his family just then.

While Simon attended the Passover ceremonies, Jesus began a casual conversation with a young Hellenist named Stephen which led to a four-hour discussion of the way of life and the true God and his worship. Stephen was tremendously impressed with what Jesus said and subsequently became a believer in the teachings of Jesus, never surmising that the Galilean he had talked with some fifteen years previously was the very same person whom he later proclaimed the world's Savior. When Stephen yielded up his life there stood by one named Saul who eventually espoused the cause for which Stephen died; later on he became the aggressive and indomitable Paul, the founder of the Christian religion.

Simon never forgot what Jesus taught him on this trip. When they arrived home he kept the family up late relating his experiences.

More and more the Nazareth family became engrossed with their immediate and human problems. Mary was slowly giving up the idea that Jesus was to fulfill any divine mission on earth.

128:4. The Damascus Episode

Jesus spent the last four months of this year in Damascus as the guest of the merchant whom he had first met at Philadelphia on his way to Jerusalem. A representative of this man proposed to devote an extraordinary sum of money to the establishment of a school of religious philosophy at Damascus and he proposed that Jesus should immediately begin a long tour of the world's educational centers preparatory to becoming the head of this new project.

This was one of the greatest temptations that Jesus ever faced in the course of his purely human career. But he would not consent. His mission on earth was not to be supported by institutions of learning; he knew that he must not obligate himself in the least to be directed by the "councils of men," no matter how well-intentioned.

These men of Damascus never associated the later citizen of Capernaum who turned all Jewry upside down with the former carpenter of Nazareth who had dared to refuse the honor which their combined wealth might have procured. Jesus most cleverly and intentionally contrived to detach various episodes of his life so that they never became associated together as the doings of a single individual. He did not want to build up such a human record of achievement as would attract attention from his teaching. As the years passed, it became more difficult to realize that this man was a Son of God on earth.

128:5. The Twenty-Fourth Year (A.D. 18)

This was Jesus' first year of comparative freedom from family responsibility, with James successfully managing the home with Jesus' help in counsel and finances.

In the middle of June Jesus went over to Caesarea to meet with five prominent Jews of Alexandria, who besought him to establish himself in their city as a religious teacher, offering as an inducement to begin with, the position of assistant to the chazan in their chief synagogue. Jesus listened to all they had to say, thanked them for their confidence, and, in declining to go to Alexandria, said, "My hour has not yet come." In subsequent years, when they heard rumors of the Capernaum boatbuilder who was creating such a commotion in Palestine, few of them surmised that he was the same strange-acting Galilean who had so unceremoniously declined the invitation to become a great teacher in Alexandria.

The remainder of this year was the most uneventful of Jesus' whole career, but he made tremendous progress in the mastery of his human mind. He gave his approval for James to marry Esta and Miriam to marry Jacob. When at home, he continued to teach the evening school three times a week, to read the Scriptures often in the synagogue on the Sabbath and to visit with his mother.

128:6. The Twenty-Fifth Year (A.D. 19)

Jesus was one of the most robust and refined specimens of manhood to appear on earth since the days of Adam. His physical development was superb, is mind was active, keen, and penetrating, and his spirit was indeed humanly divine.

The family finances were in the best condition since the disappearance of Joseph's estate, and since he had taken his other brothers to Jerusalem for their first Passover ceremonies, this year Jesus decided to accompany Jude on his first visit to the temple. Jesus feared trouble if he took his young brother through Samaria. Already at Nazareth Jude had got into slight trouble several times because of his hasty disposition, coupled with his strong patriotic sentiments. Arriving in Jerusalem they chanced to meet Lazarus, and while Jesus sought to arrange for their joint celebration of the Passover, Jude started up real trouble for them all. A Roman guard standing nearby had made some improper remarks regarding a Jewish girl and Jude expressed his resentment, whereupon the guard promptly placed Jude under arrest. This was too much for Jude, who expressed his pent-up anti-Roman feelings and, with Jesus by his side, was taken at once to the military prison.

Jesus failed to obtain an immediate hearing for Jude, and the morning following their second day in prison he appeared before the military magistrate in Jude's behalf. By making apologies for his brother's youth and further explaining the provocative nature of the episode, Jesus so handled the case that the magistrate dismissed them with a warning to Jude. Jesus did not tell the family about his young brother's arrest at Jerusalem, but some three weeks after their return Jude himself told them. Jude never forgot the patience and forbearance which his brother-father manifested.

This year Jesus' seasons of deep meditation were often broken into by Ruth and her playmates. The children loved Jesus, and Jesus loved the children.

128:7. The Twenty-Sixth Year (A.D. 20)

As this year began, Jesus became strongly conscious that he possessed a wide range of potential power. He thought much but said little about the relation of himself to his Father in heaven.

All this year the family affairs ran smoothly except for Jude. James and Joseph were in favor of casting him out, but Jesus would not consent. When their patience would be severely tried, Jesus would only counsel, "Be patient. Be wise in your counsel and eloquent in your lives, that your young brother may first know the better way and then be constrained to follow you in it." Jesus' counsel prevented a break in the family, but Jude never was brought to his sober senses until after his marriage.

Jesus had about completed the difficult task of weaning his family from dependence on him and was rapidly preparing for the day when he could consistently leave this Nazareth home to begin the more active prelude to his real ministry for men. He spent a great deal of time this year with the individual members of his family, taking them for long and frequent strolls up the hill and through the countryside..

At last the day had come when all Jesus' brothers were established in their lifework. Jesus presented full title to the repair shop to James, formally and solemnly abdicated as head of Joseph's house, and most touchingly established his brother James as "head and protector of my father's house."

Paper 129: The Later Adult Life of Jesus

THE Son of Man had now made every preparation for detaching himself permanently from the Nazareth home; and this was not easy for him to do. All the family had slowly awakened to the realization that Jesus was making ready to leave them.

129:1. The Twenty-Seventh Year (A.D. 21)

In January of this year Jesus took unceremonious leave of his family, only explaining that he was going over to Tiberias and then on a visit to other cities about the Sea of Galilee. In Capernaum he stopped to pay a visit to his father's friend Zebedee. Zebedee's sons were fishermen; he himself was a boatbuilder. Jesus was an expert in both designing and building, a master at working with wood, and Zebedee had long known of the skill of the Nazareth craftsman. For a long time Zebedee had contemplated making improved boats; he now laid his plans before Jesus and invited him to join him in the enterprise, and Jesus readily consented. He worked with Zebedee only a little more than a year, but during that time he created a new style of boat and established entirely new methods of boatmaking. Jesus became well known to the Galilean fisherfolk as the designer of the new boats, and when it came to the payment of taxes, he registered himself as a "skilled craftsman of Capernaum."

At the Capernaum synagogue he found many new books in the library chests, and spent at least five evenings a week at intense study. The Zebedee family almost worshiped Jesus, and they never failed to attend the conferences of questions and answers which he conducted each evening after supper. Jesus spent one evening with the older folks, one evening with the younger people, and one evening with the Zebedee family and employees. It was among these workers that Jesus was first called "the Master." Frequently Jude came over on the Sabbath to hear Jesus talk in the synagogue, and the more Jude saw of his eldest brother, the more he became convinced that Jesus was a truly great man.

129:2. The Twenty-Eighth Year (A.D. 22)

Before taking leave of Capernaum in March, Jesus had a long talk with John Zebedee. He asked him for a small sum of money to defray his expenses to Jerusalem, that he contemplated traveling extensively until "my hour shall come," and to act in his stead in the matter of sending some money to the family at Nazareth each month until the funds due him should be exhausted. John consulted with his father and they agreed that it would be the better plan to invest these funds in a house and use the income for assisting the family.

Jesus had carried with him to Jerusalem a letter of introduction to the former high priest, Annas, who spent much time showing him the various schools of the rabbis. Although Annas looked upon Jesus as a great man, he was puzzled as to how to advise him, recognizing the foolishness of suggesting that he enter any of the schools of Jerusalem as a student, and yet knowing Jesus would never be accorded the status of a regular teacher inasmuch as he had never been trained in these schools.

Before the end of this week, by apparent chance, Jesus met a wealthy traveler and his son, a young man about seventeen years of age, who hailed from India, being on their way to visit Rome and various other points on the Mediterranean. They were in Jerusalem hoping to find someone whom they could engage as interpreter and tutor for the son. The father proposed to advance to Jesus the wages of one year so that Jesus could entrust such funds to his friends for the safeguarding of his family against want. And Jesus agreed to make the trip. He took Zebedee fully into his confidence regarding this Mediterranean journey, but enjoined him to tell no man.

129:3. The Twenty-Ninth Year (A.D. 23)

The whole of Jesus' twenty-ninth year was spent finishing up the tour of the Mediterranean world. He was known as the *Damascus scribe* and on the return trip as the *Jewish tutor*. The real purpose of his trip was to *know men*. He came very close to hundreds of humankind on this journey—rich and poor, high and low, black and white, educated and uneducated, cultured and uncultured, animalistic and spiritual, religious and irreligious, moral and immoral. He was consistently careful not to build up an overattractive and attention-consuming personal career. He was dedicated to the work of revealing the heavenly Father to his fellow mortals and at the same time was consecrated to the sublime task of living his mortal earth life all the while subject to the will of the same Paradise Father.

By the end of this tour Jesus virtually knew—with all human certainty—that he was a Son of God, a Creator Son of the Universal Father. The last episode of his prehuman experience to be brought forth by the Adjuster was his farewell conference with Immanuel of Salvington just before his surrender of conscious personality to embark upon the Urantia incarnation.

129:4. The Human Jesus

This Mediterranean trip was the fascinating period of his *personal ministry* in contrast with the soon-following epoch of public ministry. Jesus had not yet achieved the complete mastery of his human mind. He was still a man among men. The purely human religious experience of the Son of Man well-nigh reached the apex of attainment during this, the twenty-ninth year. He knows about the thoughts and feelings, the urges and impulses, of the evolutionary and ascendant mortals of the realms, from birth to death.

Jesus did not live his life on earth in order to set an example for all other human beings to copy, but he is everlastingly the inspiration and guide of all Paradise pilgrims from the worlds of initial ascension up through a universe of universes and on through Havona to Paradise. Jesus is the *new and living way* from man to God, from the partial to the perfect, from the earthly to the heavenly, from time to eternity. He came on earth the fullness of God to be manifest to man; he had now become well-nigh the perfection of man awaiting the occasion to become manifest to God. And he did all of this before he was thirty years of age.

Paper 130: On the Way to Rome

THE tour of the Roman world consumed most of the twenty-eighth and the entire twenty-ninth year of Jesus' life on earth. Jesus and the two natives from India, Gonod and his son Ganid, left Jerusalem on a Sunday morning, April 26, A.D. 22. They made their journey according to schedule and said goodbye to each other in the city of Charax on the Persian Gulf on the tenth of December the following year, A.D. 23. On this Mediterranean tour Jesus spent about half of each day teaching Ganid and acting as interpreter during Gonod's business conferences and social contacts. The remainder of each day was at his disposal.

130:1. At Joppa—Discourse on Jonah

During their stay in Joppa, Jesus became warm friends with Gadiah, a Philistine interpreter who worked for one Simon a tanner. Gadiah asked Jesus, "But do you suppose the big fish really did swallow Jonah?" Perceiving that this young man's life had been tremendously influenced by the tradition of Jonah and the whale, Jesus therefore said nothing that would suddenly destroy the foundations of Gadiah's motivation for practical living, and answered in part, "My friend, we are all Jonahs with lives to live in accordance with the will of God, along with other words of spiritual inspiration. Gadiah was mightily moved by Jesus' teaching, and they talked long into the night.

Jesus' last visit with Gadiah had to do with a discussion of good and evil. Gadiah said, "How can God, if he is infinitely good, permit us to suffer the sorrows of evil?" Jesus answered, "My brother, God is love." Evil is the immature choosing and the unthinking misstep of those who are resistant to goodness, beauty, and truth." Jesus further told Gadiah that God in giving us the power to choose between truth and error makes possible the choice of evil and sin.

This was the same Gadiah who listened to the later preaching of Peter and became a profound believer in Jesus of Nazareth.

130:2. At Caesarea

Jesus and his friends tarried in Caesarea while the boat on which they were to travel was being repaired. There was a shortage of skilled woodworkers and Jesus volunteered to assist. A merchant from Mongolia who was a Taoist was so impressed with Jesus' conversation he became a believer in a universal Deity. His son and grandson became Taoist priests teaching the doctrine of One God—the Supreme Ruler of Heaven. One of the young men, Anaxand, who worked with Jesus on the boat, wondered why the Gods did not remove the cruel foreman of this workshop. He was surprised when Jesus told him that since he knew the ways of kindness, perhaps the Gods have brought this erring man near him that he could led the foreman into a better way. "I predict that the good in you," said Jesus, "could overcome the evil in him if you gave it a fair and living chance." Anaxand was mightily moved by Jesus' words. Presently he told his superior what Jesus had said, and that night they both sought Jesus' advice as to the welfare of their souls.

Later on both of these men believed Philip's preaching and became prominent members of the church which Philip founded. The teachings of Jesus would have made an immediate and effective appeal to the minds of the spiritually hungry Asiatic peoples. It is regrettable that one like Peter or Paul could not have gone into China and India whose people were ready for the planting of the seed of the new gospel of the kingdom.

130:3. At Alexandria

This city of a million people had two magnificent harbors, a famous lighthouse, and the greatest library in the world. They went to this library every day. Under Jesus' direction Ganid made a collection of the teachings of all the religions of the world which recognized a Universal Deity. He was much surprised to discover that the best of the authors of the world's sacred literature all more or less clearly recognized the existence of an eternal God and were much in agreement with regard to his character and his relationship with mortal man. At the museum professors gave daily lectures. After days of listening to these lectures, Ganid said, "Teacher Joshua, you know more than these professors; you should stand up and tell them the great things you told me." They intended to attend Philo's lectures but throughout their stay at Alexandria this famous Jew lay sick abed.

130:4. Discourse on Reality

Ganid and Jesus had a long visit with one of the government professors at the university who lectured on the teachings of Plato. While Jesus gave qualified approval of some of the Greek teachings, he began a long dissertation concerning the nature of reality in the universe. In substance, Jesus said to Ganid, "The source of universe reality is the Infinite. The material things of finite creation are the time-space repercussions of the Paradise Pattern and the Universal Mind of the eternal God. Only in the perfection, harmony, and unanimity of will can the creature become as one with the Creator. Personality is that cosmic endowment, that phase of universal reality, which can coexist with unlimited change and at the same time retain its identity in the very presence of all such changes. The value of life is its progressability, even to the heights of God-consciousness. Knowledge is a possession of the mind; truth an experience of the soul. These two views, synchronized and harmonized, reveal the world of reality. The qualities of imperfection (evil) are disclosed by critical observation and by scientific analysis; on the moral level, by human experience. The possibility of making mistakes is inherent in the acquisition of wisdom. All static, dead, concepts are potentially evil; they are deficient in wisdom and devoid of truth."

130:5. On the Island of Crete

On the mountainside in Crete Jesus had his first long talk with Gonod regarding religion, and the father was much impressed. It was during the island sojourn that Gonod first proposed to Jesus that Jesus go back to India with them.

One day when Ganid asked Jesus why he had not devoted himself to the work of a public teacher, Jesus said, "My son, everything must await the coming of its time."

One thing happened on a visit to Fair Havens which Ganid never forgot. A drunken degenerate was attacking a slave girl on the public highway. When Jesus saw the plight of the girl, he rushed forward and drew the maiden away from the assault of the madman. While the frightened child clung to him, Jesus held the infuriated man at a safe distance by his powerful extended right arm until the poor fellow had exhausted himself beating the air with his angry blows. This was probably as near a personal encounter with his fellows as Jesus ever had. But he had a difficult task that evening trying to explain to Ganid why he did not smite the drunken man. Ganid thought this man should have been struck at least as many times as he had struck the girl.

130:6. The Young Man Who was Afraid

Jesus had a long talk with a young man who was fearful and downcast. At first the young man did not wish to talk, so Jesus asked him for the best route to Phenix. As Jesus started to leave, he turned saying that it would be neither kind nor fair for him to leave without making the least effort to answer the young man's longing looks for help. The man then opened up asking for help. Jesus called attention to his strong body and capable mind and told him that he could not run away from his unhappy self, but could use his spirit inspired mind to vanquish fear and solve his problems. Jesus said, in part, "This day, my son, you are to be reborn, re-established as a man of faith, courage, and devoted service to man, for God's sake. Trouble will invigorate you; disappointment will spur you on; difficulties will challenge you; and obstacles will stimulate you. Arise, young man!"

And this youth, Fortune, subsequently became the leader of the Christians in Crete and the close associate of Titus in his labors for the uplift of the Cretan believers.

The travelers stopped at Cyrene, and it was here that Jesus and Ganid carried an injured lad, Rufus, home. The boy's father, Simon, little dreamed that the man whose cross he subsequently bore by orders of a Roman soldier was the stranger who had once befriended his son.

130:7. At Carthage—Discourse on Time and Space

At Carthage Jesus had a long and memorable talk with a Mithraic priest about immortality, about time and eternity. In essence he said, "Time is the stream of flowing temporal events perceived by creature consciousness. The universe of space is a time-related phenomenon. In the universe of universes Paradise and its Deities transcend both time and space. On the inhabited worlds, human personality is the only physically related reality which can transcend the material sequence of temporal events. As man ascends the enlarging view of reality, it is discerned more and more in its wholeness. In this way will circular simultaneity increasingly displace the onetime consciousness of the linear sequence of events. There are seven different conceptions of space as it is conditioned by time. Mind can function independently of the concept of the space-relatedness of material objects. When man attains the mind intervening between the material and the spiritual planes of existence, his ideas of time-space will be enormously expanded both as to quality of perception and quantity of experience. And as personality passes on, upward and inward, to the transcendental levels of Deity-likeness, the time-space concept will increasingly approximate the timeless and spaceless concepts of the Absolutes. The concepts of the absolute level are to be envisioned by the children of ultimate destiny."

130:8. On the Way to Naples and Rome

At Malta Jesus had a long talk with a downhearted and discouraged young man named Claudus. Shortly he became an enthusiastic preacher of the Cynics, and still later on he joined hands with Peter in proclaiming Christianity in Rome and Naples. But Claudus never knew that the man who inspired him in Malta was the Jesus whom he subsequently proclaimed the world's Deliverer.

At Syracuse Jesus effected the rehabilitation of Ezra, the backslidden Jew. And Ezra found God and to the satisfaction of his soul. Later, this Jew, in association with a well-to-do Greek proselyte, built the first Christian church in Syracuse. At Messina Jesus changed the life of a small boy, a fruit vendor, who became a devotee of the Mithraic religion and later on turned to the Christian faith.

From Naples they went by way of Capua to Rome, all three being anxious to see the greatest city in all the world.

Paper 131: The World's Religions

DURING the Alexandrian sojourn of Jesus, Gonod, and Ganid, the young man spent much of his time and no small sum of his father's money making a collection of the teachings of the world's religions about God and his relations with mortal man. There is presented herewith an abstract of Ganid's manuscript which was preserved in India for hundreds of years after his death. He collected this material under ten heads.

131:1. Cynicism

God is supreme; he rules the universe of universes. God is compassionate and merciful. The Most High is the first and the last, the beginning and the end of everything. Our God is omnipotent and bounteous. He is a peace giver and a faithful protector of all who fear and trust him. His divine love springs forth from the holiness of his power. The Most High has endowed man with his own spirit. God gives us the abundant harvest of the good things of this life and eternal salvation in the world to come. God is full of goodness toward all men; we have no friend like the Most High. The Most

High is changeless; and he is our helper in every time of need. We search for the Most High and then find him in our hearts. The man who knows God looks upon all men as equal; they are his brethren. Those who love their fellows and who have pure hearts shall see God. He will guide the honest of heart into the truth, for God is truth. In all your relations with men do good for evil. When you stand before God with a clean heart, you become fearless of all creation. The Most High is like a loving father and mother; he really loves us, his children on earth. The noble man seeks for that high estate wherein the soul of the mortal blends with the spirit of the Supreme.

131:2. Judaism

In the beginning God created the heavens and the earth and all things therein. You shall love the Lord your God with all your heart and with all your soul and with all your might. The heavens declare the glory of God, and the firmament shows his handiwork. The greatness of the Lord is unsearchable. God is our refuge and strength, a very present help in trouble. God has made man a little less than divine and has crowned him with love and mercy. Forget not that pride goes before destruction and a haughty spirit before a fall. He who rules his own spirit is mightier than he who takes a city. They who wait upon the Lord shall renew their strength; they shall mount up with wings like eagles. They shall run and not be weary; they shall walk and not be faint. The Lord is my shepherd; I shall not want. Yes, even though I walk through the valley of the shadow of death, I will fear no evil, for God is with me. Surely goodness and mercy shall follow me all the days of my life, and I shall dwell in the house of the Lord forever. Love your neighbor as yourself; bear a grudge against no man. You shall love God with all your heart; honor your father and mother; you shall not kill; you shall not commit adultery; you shall not steal; you shall not bear false witness; you shall not covet. You are the sons of the living God and are called to become like God and to dwell forever with him in Paradise.

131:3. Buddhism

Out of a pure heart shall gladness spring forth to the Infinite; all my being shall be at peace with this supermortal rejoicing. I have no fear; I am free from anxiety. By faith let us lay hold upon true righteousness. Happiness and peace of mind follow pure thinking and virtuous living. Evil is the fruit of wrongly directed thinking. No man can rob you of the liberty of your own mind. While faith is the energy of the better life, nevertheless, must you work out your own salvation with perseverance. Whoso is thoughtful, prudent, reflective, fervent, and earnest—even while he yet lives on earth—may attain the supreme enlightenment of the peace and liberty of divine wisdom. He is the greatest of warriors who overcomes and subdues himself. Let not anger and hate master you. Speak harshly of no one. Overcome evil with the good. Every mortal who thinks righteously, speaks nobly, and acts unselfishly shall not only enjoy virtue here during this brief life but shall also, after the dissolution of the body, continue to enjoy the delights of heaven.

131:4. Hinduism

God is the creator and controller of the universe of universes. And this one God is our Maker and the last destiny of the soul. God is loving, glorious, and adorable. Make prayer your inmost friend and worship your soul's support. God is our sure leader and unfailing guide, the changeless guardian of everlasting law. God is truth. And it is the desire of God that his creatures should understand him—come fully to know the truth. Truth is eternal; it sustains the universe. Our supreme desire shall be union with the Supreme. Conquer anger with mercy, and vanquish hate by benevolence. By meditation on God, by union with him, there comes ultimate salvation from all material fetters. O God, save us from the threefold ruin of hell—lust, wrath, and avarice! O soul, gird yourself for the spirit struggle of immortality! And they who know that God is enthroned in the human heart are destined to become like him—immortal. Virtue alone walks by man's side as he journeys ever onward toward the gladsome and sunlit fields of Paradise.

131:5. Zoroastrianism

All things come from, and belong to, the One God—all-wise, good, righteous, holy, resplendent, and glorious. The wise course in life is to act in consonance with the spirit of truth. The all-wise God has promised immortality to the pious souls who think purely and act righteously. God is farthest from us and at the same time nearest to us in that he dwells within our souls. God is our most adorable and righteous friend; he is our wisdom, life, and vigor of soul and body. Lord, teach us how to live this life in the flesh while preparing for the next life of the spirit. Grant us that we may attain union with you.

131:6. Suduanism (Jainism)

The Lord of Heaven is supreme. The soul of man may ascend to the highest heaven, there to develop its true spiritual nature, to attain perfection. Self is man's invincible foe, and self is manifested as man's four greatest passions: anger, pride, deceit, and greed. Man's greatest victory is the conquest of himself. When man looks to God for forgiveness, and when he makes bold to enjoy such liberty, he is thereby delivered from fear. Man should journey through life treating his fellow creatures as he would like to be treated.

131:7. Shinto

In both the beauties of nature and the virtues of men does the Prince of Heaven seek to reveal himself and to show forth his righteous nature. I manifested myself by being born into the world as a visible existence. Although I am great and supreme, still I have regard for the prayer of the poorest man. Every time man yields to anxiety, he takes one step away from the leading of the spirit of his heart. Pride obscures God. If you would obtain heavenly help, put away your pride. If you are not right on the inside, it is useless to pray for that which is on the outside. If I hear your prayers, it is because you come before me with a clean heart, with a soul which reflects truth like a mirror.

131:8. Taoism

How pure and tranquil is the Supreme One and yet how powerful and mighty, how deep and unfathomable! This God of heaven is the honored ancestor of all things. If you know the Eternal, you are enlightened and wise. This wondrous Being existed before the heavens and the earth were. He is truly spiritual; he stands alone and changes not. He is indeed the world's mother, and all creation moves around him. All good works of true service come from the Supreme. How great and mighty are his overflowing influence and drawing power! True goodness is like water in that it seeks the lowest places, even those levels which others avoid, and that is because it is akin to the Supreme. And it is a mystery how the Supreme fosters, protects, and perfects the creature without compelling him. He ministers progression, but without domination. Those who aspire to greatness must learn to humble themselves. He is a wise man who regards all parts from the point of view of the whole. Relate yourself to every man as if you were in his place. If you love people, they will draw near you. Do good without thought of benefit to the self. If you know the Eternal, even though your body perish, your soul shall survive in spirit service. When man dies, the spirit begins to wing its long flight on the great home journey.

131:9. Confucianism

What Heaven appoints is without error. Truth is real and divine. Heaven has appointed many subordinates to assist in the instruction and uplifting of the inferior creatures. Benevolence is Heaven's choicest gift to men. Heaven has bestowed its nobility upon the soul of man. We do well when we call the Great Heaven our Father and our Mother. God is with us; therefore we have no fear in our hearts. But this Heaven within me often makes hard demands on my faith. When you find yourself in the wrong, do not hesitate to confess your error and be quick to make amends. A wise man is occupied with the search for truth. To attain the perfection of Heaven is the goal of man. The superior man murmurs not against Heaven nor holds a grudge against men. What you do not like when done to yourself, do not to others. Let compassion be a part of all punishment. While all creatures must die and return to the earth, the spirit of the noble man goes forth to be displayed on high and to ascend to the glorious light of final brightness.

131:10. Our Religion

The Lord our God is one Lord, and you should love him with all your mind and heart while you do your very best to love all his children as you love yourself. Though we cannot see God, we can know him by personal experience. God is not only all-powerful but also all-wise. He intends that all men should be brothers. We live in God and God dwells in us. Always will I try to worship God with the help of the Spirit of Truth. I am going to do my best to treat each of my fellow mortals just as I think God would like to have him treated. And all of this loving service of the children of God enlarges our capacity to receive and experience the joys of heaven. I will every day thank God for his unspeakable gifts. This new religion of ours is very full of joy, and it generates an enduring happiness. I am learning to prove all things and adhere to that which is good. Henceforth will I do my good deeds in secret. I will judge not that I may not be unfair to my fellows. Though I see God in these other religions, I find him in 'our religion' as being more beautiful, loving, merciful, personal, and positive. But most of all, this great and glorious Being is my spiritual Father; I am his child. And by no other means than my honest desire to be like him, I am eventually to find him and eternally to serve him. At last I have a religion with a marvelous God, and he is a God of eternal salvation.

Paper 132: The Sojourn at Rome

SINCE Gonod carried greetings from the princes of India to Tiberius, the Roman ruler, on the third day after their arrival in Rome the two Indians and Jesus appeared before him. The morose emperor was unusually cheerful on this day and chatted long with the trio. And when they had gone from his presence, the emperor, referring to Jesus, remarked to the aide, "If I had that fellow's kingly bearing and gracious manner, I would be a real emperor, eh?"

There were many citizens of India in Rome, and often one of Gonod's own employees would accompany him as interpreter so that Jesus would have whole days to himself. The inhabitants of Rome embraced the citizens of every country of the Eastern Hemisphere. Jesus' desire to study and mingle with this cosmopolitan aggregation of Urantia mortals was the chief reason why he consented to make this journey. Jesus selected five of the leading Stoics, eleven of the Cynics, and sixteen of the mystery-cult leaders and spent much of his spare time for almost six months in intimate association with these religious teachers. Never once did he attack their errors. He would select the truth in what they taught and then proceed so to embellish and illuminate this truth. Out of this group of thirty-two Jesus-taught religious leaders in Rome, only two were unfruitful; the thirty became pivotal individuals in the establishment of Christianity in Rome.

Just three factors were of paramount value in the early setting of the stage for the rapid spread of Christianity throughout Europe: 1. the choosing of Simon Peter as an apostle; 2. the talk in Jerusalem with Stephen, whose death led to the winning of Saul of Tarsus; 3. the preliminary preparation of these thirty Romans for the subsequent leadership of the new religion in Rome and throughout the empire; none of these thirty or Stephen ever realized they had once talked with this man whose name became the subject of their religious teaching.

132:1. True Values

It was with Angamon, the leader of the Stoics, that Jesus had an all-night talk early during his sojourn in Rome. This man subsequently became a great friend of Paul and proved to be one of the strong supporters of the Christian church at Rome. In substance, Jesus taught Angamon: "The standard of true values must be looked for in the spiritual world. The scientist is limited to the discovery of the relatedness of material facts. A purely materialistic science harbors within itself the potential seed of the destruction of all scientific striving. The materialistic scientist and the extreme idealist are destined always to be at loggerheads. In every age scientists and religionists must recognize that they are on trial before the bar of human need. They must eschew all warfare between themselves while they strive valiantly to justify their continued survival by enhanced devotion to the service of human progress."

132:2. Good and Evil

Mardus was the acknowledged leader of the Cynics of Rome. In part, Jesus taught him: "The soul that survives time and emerges into eternity must make a living and personal choice between good and evil as they are determined by the true values of the spiritual standards established by the divine spirit which the Father in heaven has sent to dwell within the heart of man. The spiritually blind individual is destined to become an intellectual parrot, a social automaton, and a slave to religious authority. An experience is good when it heightens the appreciation of beauty, augments the moral will, enhances the discernment of truth, and enlarges the capacity to love and serve one's fellows. The ability to entertain error or experience evil will not be fully lost until the ascending human soul achieves final spirit levels. Goodness is living, relative, always progressing, invariably a personal experience, and everlastingly correlated with the discernment of truth and beauty. Until you attain Paradise levels, goodness will always be more of a quest than a possession. At Paradise levels goodness is no longer partial, contrastive, and comparative; it has become divinely complete and spiritually replete; it approaches the purity and perfection of the Supreme."

132:3. Truth and Faith

Nabon was a Greek Jew and foremost among the leaders of the Mithraic cult in Rome. Nabon had thought to make a convert of Jesus; he little realized that Jesus was preparing him to become one of the early converts to the gospel of the kingdom. The substance of Jesus' teaching was: "The truth cannot be defined with words, only by living. Knowledge originates in science; wisdom, in true philosophy; truth, in the religious experience of spiritual living. Knowledge deals with facts; wisdom, with relationships; truth, with reality values. Natural man is slow to initiate changes in his habits of thinking and in his techniques of living. There is never conflict between true knowledge and truth. But truth can never become man's possession without the exercise of faith. And all such true faith is predicated on profound reflection, sincere self-criticism, and uncompromising moral consciousness. Faith is the inspiration of the spiritized creative imagination. The human soul (personality) of man survives mortal death by identity association with this indwelling spark of divinity, which is immortal. Universe progress is characterized by increasing personality freedom because it is associated with the progressive attainment of higher and higher levels of self-understanding and consequent voluntary self-restraint. Prayer becomes the great unifier of the various inspirations of the creative imagination and the faith urges of a soul trying to identify itself with the spirit ideals of the indwelling and associated divine presence."

132:4. Personal Ministry

Jesus spent much time gaining an intimate knowledge of all races and classes of men. His usual technique of social contact was to draw people out and into talking with him by asking them questions and end by their asking him questions. As a rule, to those he taught the most, he said the least. In this manner Jesus personally came into affectionate and uplifting contact with upward of five hundred mortals of the realm. He always regarded this six months as one of the richest and most informative of any like period of his earth life.

He talked with a Roman senator on politics and statesmanship who spent the rest of his life vainly trying to induce his colleagues to the idea of the people supporting the government. Jesus spent one evening with a wealthy slaveholder and the next day this man, Claudius, gave freedom to one hundred and seventeen slaves. To the speaker at the forum Jesus said, "If you could only enjoy the inspiring satisfaction of knowing God as your spiritual Father, then you might employ your powers of speech to liberate your fellows from the bondage of darkness and from the slavery of ignorance." This was the Marcus who heard Peter preach in Rome and became his successor. When they crucified Simon Peter; it was this man who defied the Roman persecutors and boldly continued to preach the new gospel. Meeting a poor man who had been falsely accused, Jesus went with him before the magistrate and the judge reopened the case, and when the evidence had been sifted, the judge discharged the prisoner. Of all Jesus' activities during these days of personal ministry, this came the nearest to being a public appearance.

132:5. Counseling the Rich Man

A certain rich man, a Roman citizen and a Stoic, asked Jesus what he would do with wealth if he had it, and Jesus answered him, "I would bestow material wealth for the enhancement of material life, even as I would minister knowledge, wisdom, and spiritual service for the enrichment of the intellectual life, the ennoblement of the social life, and the advancement of the spiritual life. I would administer material wealth as a wise and effective trustee of the resources of one generation for the benefit and ennoblement of the next and succeeding generations."

But the rich man was not fully satisfied with Jesus' answer and asked for more detailed advice. Jesus suggested the man analyze the origin of his wealth as well as fair and honest ways of its use. When Jesus had finished counseling him, this wealthy Roman said, "My good friend, I perceive you are a man of great wisdom and goodness, and tomorrow I will begin the administration of all my wealth in accordance with your counsel."

132:6. Social Ministry

Here in Rome also occurred that touching incident in which the Creator of a universe spent several hours restoring a lost child to his anxious mother. Jesus commented to Ganid, "You know, Ganid, most human beings are like the lost child. They spend much of their time crying in fear and suffering in sorrow when, in very truth, they are but a short distance from safety and security.... Did we not supremely enjoy this ministry of restoring the child to his mother? So do those who lead men to God experience the supreme satisfaction of human service."

There was the widow with five children whose husband had been accidentally killed, and Jesus and Ganid did not cease their efforts to help this family until they had found a position for the eldest boy so that he could help in the care of the family.

That night, Gonod said to Jesus, good-naturedly, "I propose to make a scholar or a businessman of my son, and now you start out to make a philosopher or philanthropist of him." And Jesus smilingly replied, "Perhaps we will make him all four; then can he enjoy a fourfold satisfaction in life as his ear for the recognition of human melody will be able to recognize four tones instead of one." Then said Gonod, "I perceive that you really are a philosopher. You must write a book for future generations." And Jesus replied, "Not a book—my mission is to live a life in this generation and for all generations. I—" but he stopped, saying to Ganid, "My son, it is time to retire."

132:7. Trips About Rome

Jesus, Gonod, and Ganid made five trips away from Rome to points of interest. On their visit to the northern Italian lakes Jesus had the long talk with Ganid concerning the impossibility of teaching a man about God if that man does not desire to know God.

In Switzerland, up in the mountains, Jesus had an all-day talk with both father and son about Buddhism. Said Gonod, "I would really like to know what you think of Buddha." And Jesus answered in part, "Your Buddha was much better than Buddhism. Buddha was a great man, even a prophet to his people, but he early lost sight of his spiritual Father. He tried to live and teach as a messenger of God, but without God. Buddha guided his ship of salvation right up to the safe harbor but there the good ship ran aground. Buddha knew God in spirit but failed clearly to discover him in mind; the Jews discovered God in mind but largely failed to know him in spirit."

Then exclaimed Ganid, "Teacher, let's you and I make a new religion, one good enough for India and big enough for Rome, and maybe we can trade it to the Jews for Yahweh." And Jesus replied, "Ganid, religions are not made. The religions of men grow up over long periods of time." What a scene for the celestial intelligences to behold, this spectacle of the Indian lad proposing to the Creator of a universe that they make a new religion! When man goes in partnership with God, great things may, and do, happen.

Paper 133: The Return from Rome

WHEN preparing to leave Rome, Jesus said goodbye to none of his friends. Before the end of the second year small groups of those who had known him found themselves drawn together by their common interest in his teachings and through mutual memory of their good times with him.

And these small groups of Stoics, Cynics, and mystery cultists continued to hold these irregular and informal meetings right up to the time of the appearance in Rome of the first preachers of the Christian religion.

Having sent their belongings ahead to Tarentum, the three travelers walked leisurely across Italy over the great Appian Way, encountering all sorts of human beings on their journey—noble Roman citizens, Greek colonists and the progeny of great numbers of inferior slaves. One day Ganid asked Jesus a direct question as to what he thought of India's caste system. Said Jesus in part, "Though human beings differ in many ways, the one from another, before God and in the spiritual world all mortals stand on an equal footing."

133:1. Mercy and Justice

One afternoon, as they neared Tarentum, they observed a rough and bullying youth brutally attacking a smaller lad. Jesus hastened to the assistance of the assaulted youth, and when he had rescued him, he tightly held on to the offender until the smaller lad had made his escape. The moment Jesus released the little bully, Ganid pounced upon the boy and began soundly to thrash him, and to Ganid's astonishment Jesus promptly interfered. After he had restrained Ganid and permitted the frightened boy to escape, the young man excitedly exclaimed, "I cannot understand you, Teacher. If mercy requires that you rescue the smaller lad, does not justice demand the punishment of the larger and offending youth?" In answering, Jesus said, "Ganid, it is true, you do not understand. Mercy ministry is always the work of the individual, but justice punishment is the function of the social, governmental, or universe administrative groups." But Ganid was not fully satisfied. On another occasion he did draw from Jesus the opinion that organized society had every right to employ force in the execution of its just mandates.

133:2. Embarking at Tarentum

While tarrying at the ship landing, waiting for the boat to unload cargo, the travelers observed a man mistreating his wife. As was his custom, Jesus intervened in behalf of the person subjected to attack. He gently tapped the irate husband on the shoulder and asked to speak to him in private. Jesus said that something terrible must have happened to the man as he looked like a man of compassion. The husband admitted that he had lost his temper and promised to use better control in the future. And then, in bidding him farewell, Jesus said, "My brother, always remember that man has no rightful authority over woman unless the woman has willingly and voluntarily given him such authority.... It is Godlike to share your life and all that relates thereto on equal terms with the mother partner who so fully shares with you that divine experience of reproducing yourselves in the lives of your children."

As they went on board the boat, they looked back upon the scene of the teary-eyed couple standing in silent embrace. Having heard the latter half of Jesus' message to the man, Gonod resolved to reorganize his home when he returned to India.

133:3. At Corinth

By the time they reached Corinth, Ganid was becoming very much interested in the Jewish religion, and he requested Jesus to take him to the synagogue service. That day they met one Crispus, the chief ruler of this synagogue. Many times they went back to the synagogue services. While Ganid studied family life, Jesus was teaching Crispus the better ways of religious living. Later, when Paul was preaching in this very synagogue, and when the Jews had rejected Jesus' message, Crispus with his entire family embraced the new religion, and became one of the chief supports of the Christian church which Paul subsequently organized at Corinth.

Jesus and Ganid were often guests in another Jewish home, that of Justus, who lived alongside the synagogue. And many times, subsequently, when the Apostle Paul sojourned in this home, did he listen to the recounting of these visits with the Indian lad and his Jewish tutor, while both Paul and Justus wondered whatever became of such a wise and brilliant Hebrew teacher.

One evening as they strolled about Corinth, they were accosted by two public women. Ganid spoke sharply to them and rudely motioned them away. When Jesus saw this, he said to Ganid, "You mean well, but you should not presume thus to speak to the children of God, even though they chance to be his erring children. Do you happen to know all of the circumstances which led them to resort to such methods of obtaining a livelihood?" The courtesans were astonished at what he said even more than was Ganid. Jesus observed that these women had not intentionally chosen this sort of life and took them to the home of Justus. Leaving the two women in the care of Martha, Justis's wife, Jesus said, "I will pray for your spiritual guidance while you make plans for a new and better life on earth and eternal life in the great beyond." The elder of these two women died a short time thereafter, with bright hopes of eternal survival, and the younger woman worked at Justus' place of business and later became a lifelong member of the first Christian church in Corinth.

When Paul first went to Corinth, he had not intended to make a prolonged visit. But he did not know how well the Jewish tutor had prepared the way for his labors.

133:4. Personal Work in Corinth

Jesus and Ganid had many more interesting experiences in Corinth. They had close converse with a great number of persons who greatly profited by the instruction received from Jesus. To the Roman centurion he said, "Render unto Caesar the things which are Caesar's and unto God the things which are God's." To the earnest leader of the Mithraic cult he said, "Know you not that the mystery of eternal salvation dwells within your own soul?" To the Epicurean teacher he said, "The great thing in all human experience is the realization of knowing the God whose spirit lives within you." To the Greek contractor and builder he said, "My friend, as you build the material structures of men, grow a spiritual character in the similitude of the divine spirit within your soul." To the Roman judge he said, "As you judge men, remember that you yourself will also some day come to judgment before the bar of the Rulers of a universe." Jesus admonished a Chinese merchant, "Worship only God, who is your true spirit ancestor." To the runaway lad Jesus said, "Remember, there are two things you cannot run away from—God and yourself."

Finally Gonod's business was finished, and they prepared to sail for Athens.

133:5. At Athens—Discourse on Science

They shortly arrived at Athens, the cultural center of the onetime Alexandrian empire. A great university still thrived here, and the trio made frequent visits to its halls of learning.

Both father and son greatly enjoyed the discussion on science which Jesus had one evening with a Greek philosopher. After this pedant had finished his discourse, Jesus said in part, "Scientists may some day measure the energy of gravitation, light, and electricity, but these same scientists can never (scientifically) tell you what these universe phenomena are. Science deals with physical-energy activities; religion deals with eternal values. True philosophy grows out of the wisdom which does its best to correlate these quantitative and qualitative observations. Logic is valid in the material world, and mathematics is reliable when limited in its application to physical things; but neither is to be regarded as wholly dependable or infallible when applied to life problems. A social group of human beings in co-ordinated working harmony stands for a force far greater than the simple sum of its parts. When both science and religion become less dogmatic and more tolerant of criticism, philosophy will then begin to achieve unity in the intelligent comprehension of the universe. Regardless of how divergent the universe phenomena of fact and value may appear to be, they are, after all, unified in the Supreme."

They were all more than astounded at the words of Jesus, and when the Greek took leave of them, he said, "At last my eyes have beheld a Jew who thinks something besides racial superiority and talks something besides religion."

133:6. At Ephesus—Discourse on the Soul

On leaving Athens, the travelers went by way of Troas to Ephesus, the capital of the Roman province of Asia. Christianity secured its start in Ephesus largely through the efforts of Paul, who resided here more than two years, making tents for a living and conducting lectures on religion and philosophy each night in the school of Tyrannus. A progressive thinker connected with this school of philosophy had repeatedly heard Jesus use the word "soul," and finally asked him what he meant by "soul." Jesus replied in part, "The soul is the self-reflective, truth-discerning, and spirit-perceiving part of man which forever elevates the human being above the level of the animal world. Moral self-consciousness is true human self-realization and constitutes the foundation of the human soul, and the soul is that part of man which represents the potential survival value of human experience. The ability to know God and the urge to be like him, are the characteristics of the soul. The divine spirit arrives simultaneously with the first moral activity of the human mind, and that is the occasion of the birth of the soul. It comes near to being an entity intervening between the material and the spiritual. Material science cannot demonstrate the existence of a soul, neither can pure spirit-testing."

133:7. The Sojourn at Cyprus—Discourse on Mind

Shortly the travelers set sail for Cyprus, stopping at Rhodes. It was their plan to enjoy a period of real rest and play on this visit to Cyprus as their tour of the Mediterranean was drawing to a close. For two weeks the trio greatly enjoyed themselves, and then, without warning, young Ganid was suddenly taken grievously ill. Jesus skillfully and tenderly cared for the lad for several weeks, and during Ganid's convalescence of three weeks.

The last week of their sojourn in the mountains Jesus and Ganid had a long talk on the functions of the human mind. Jesus told him that when any animal becomes self-conscious, it becomes a primitive man. Such an attainment results from a co-ordination of function between impersonal energy and spirit-conceiving mind, and it is this phenomenon which warrants the bestowal of the spirit of the Father in heaven. The fact of self-conscious existence, associated with the reality of his subsequent spiritual experience, constitutes man a potential son of the universe and foreshadows his eventual attainment of the Supreme Unity of the universe. The human mind does not well stand the conflict of double allegiance. The supremely happy and efficiently unified mind is the one wholly dedicated to the doing of the will of the Father in heaven.

The next day they departed for Salamis, where they embarked for Antioch on the Syrian coast.

133:8. At Antioch

Jesus became sober and reflective as he drew nearer Palestine and the end of their journey. He visited with few people in Antioch; he seldom went about in the city. In answer to Ganid's question as to why his teacher manifested so little interest in Antioch, Jesus said, "This city is not far from Palestine; maybe I shall come back here sometime."

Ganid already had begun to make practical use of some of Jesus' teachings. A certain Indian connected with his father's business in Antioch felt he had been put in the wrong job. Ganid counseled with the man, but of all that he said, the quotation of a Hebrew proverb did the most good: "Whatsoever your hand finds to do, do that with all your might."

After preparing their luggage for the camel caravan, they passed on down to Sidon and thence over to Damascus, and after three days they made ready for the long trek across the desert sands.

133:9. In Mesopotamia

The caravan trip across the desert was not a new experience for these much-traveled men. After Ganid had watched Jesus help with the loading of their twenty camels and observed him volunteer to drive their own animal, he exclaimed, "Teacher, is there anything that you cannot do?" Jesus only smiled, saying, "The teacher surely is not without honor in the eyes of a diligent pupil." And so they set forth for the ancient city of Ur.

At last the day came for the separation. They were tearful of eye but courageous of heart. Ganid said, "Farewell, Teacher, but not forever. When I come again to Damascus, I will look for you. I love you, for I think the Father in heaven must be something like you. I will remember your teaching, but most of all, I will never forget you." Said the father, "Farewell to a great teacher, one who has made us better and helped us to know God." And Jesus replied, "Peace be upon you, and may the blessing of the Father in heaven ever abide with you." And Jesus stood on the shore and watched as the small boat carried them out to their anchored ship.

Later on in life, when Ganid heard of the strange teacher in Palestine who terminated his career on a cross, though he recognized the similarity between the gospel of this Son of Man and the teachings of his Jewish tutor, it never occurred to him that these two were actually the same person.

Paper 134: The Transition Years

DURING the Mediterranean journey Jesus had carefully studied the people he met and the countries through which he passed, and at about this time he reached his final decision as to the remainder of his life on earth. He now deliberately returned to Galilee to await the beginning of his life-work as a public teacher of truth and began to lay plans for a public career. He had found out through personal and human experience that Palestine was the best place in all the Roman world wherein to set forth the closing chapters, and to enact the final scenes, of his life on earth.

134:1 The Thirtieth Year (A.D. 24)

After taking leave of Gonod and Ganid at Charax, Jesus went to Nazareth, stopping only a few hours at Capernaum where he talked to James and turned over to him the little house which John Zebedee had managed to buy. In Nazareth, Jesus visited with his family and friends, spent some time at the repair shop with his brother Joseph, but devoted most of his attention to Mary and Ruth. All the children except Ruth were now married.

During this time, the conductor of a large caravan which was passing through the city was taken violently ill, and Jesus, being a linguist, volunteered to take his place. Since this trip would necessitate his absence for a year, Jesus called a family conference at which he proposed that his mother and Ruth go to Capernaum to live in the home which he had so recently given to James.

This was one of the more unusual years in the inner experience of the Son of Man. The personality of Jesus was preparing for his great change in attitude toward the world.

134:2. The Caravan Trip to the Caspian

It was the first of April when Jesus left Nazareth on the caravan trip to the Caspian Sea region, going from Jerusalem by way of Damascus and Lake Urmia through Assyria, Media, and Parthia to the southeastern Caspian Sea region. It was a full year before he returned from this journey. Of all his world travels this Caspian Sea trip carried Jesus nearest to the Orient and enabled him to gain a better understanding of the Far-Eastern peoples. He made intimate and personal contact with every one of the surviving races of Urantia excepting the red. He equally enjoyed his personal ministry to each of these varied races and blended peoples, and all of them were receptive to the living truth which he brought them.

The caravan trip was successful in every way. Jesus functioned during this year in an executive capacity, being responsible for the material entrusted to his charge and for the safe conduct of the travelers making up the caravan party. And he most faithfully, efficiently, and wisely discharged his multiple duties.

On the return from the Caspian region, Jesus gave up the direction of the caravan at Lake Urmia, where he tarried for slightly over two weeks.

134:3. The Urmia Lectures

On the way to the Caspian Sea, Jesus had stopped several days for rest at the old Persian city of Urmia on the western shores of Lake Urmia. On a nearby offshore island was a temple of religion built by a wealthy merchant citizen, Cymboyton, and his three sons. Lectures and discussions in this school of religion were conducted daily. Cymboyton arranged with Jesus to sojourn with them for two weeks on his return trip and give twenty-four lectures on "The Brotherhood of Men." This was the most systematic and formal of all the Master's teaching on Urantia. More than thirty religions and religious cults were represented on the faculty of this temple of religious philosophy. There was but one doctrine which had to be accepted in order to gain a seat on this faculty: every teacher must represent a religion which recognized God—some sort of supreme Deity.

[The midwayers prepared the summary of Jesus' teachings at Urmia but there arose a disagreement between the seraphim of the churches and the seraphim of progress as to the wisdom of including these teachings in the Urantia Revelation. Finally, the Melchizedek chairman of the revelatory commission appointed a commission of three midwayers to prepare the Master's Urmia teachings as adapted to twentieth-century religious and political conditions on Urantia which were edited by the Melchizedek chairman. The following excerpts are included here:]

134:4. Sovereignty—Divine and Human

The brotherhood of men is founded on the fatherhood of God. The kingdom of heaven is a spiritual relationship between God and man. Religious peace—brotherhood—can never exist unless all religions are willing to completely divest themselves of all ecclesiastical authority and fully surrender all concept of spiritual sovereignty. God alone is spirit sovereign. The kingdom of heaven in the hearts of men will create religious unity (not necessarily uniformity). Spiritually, all men are equal. The concept of equality never brings peace except in the mutual recognition of some overcontrolling influence of supersovereignty. There can be no lasting religious peace on Urantia until all religious groups freely surrender all their notions of divine favor, chosen people, and religious sovereignty.

134:5. Political Sovereignty

War on Urantia will never end so long as nations cling to the illusive notions of unlimited national sovereignty. There are only two levels of relative sovereignty on an inhabited world: the spiritual free will of the individual mortal and the collective sovereignty of mankind as a whole. The difficulty in the evolution of political sovereignty from the family to all mankind, lies in the inertia-resistance exhibited on all intervening levels. Internationalism is a step in the right direction. But peace will not come to Urantia until every so-called sovereign nation surrenders its power to make war into the hands of a representative government of all mankind. When a world government controls the world's land, air, and naval forces, peace on earth and good will among men can prevail—but not until then. How many world wars must be fought and how many leagues of nations must fail before men will be willing to establish the government of mankind and begin to enjoy the blessings of permanent peace?

134:6. Law, Liberty, and Sovereignty

Freedom is the gift of civilization made possible by the enforcement of LAW. There shall be wars and rumors of wars just as long as the world's political sovereignty is divided up and unjustly held by a group of nation-states. Global sovereignty will prevent global wars—nothing else can. In the creation of the global government of mankind, the nations are not giving up sovereignty so much as they are actually creating a real, bona fide, and lasting world sovereignty which will henceforth be fully able to protect them from all war. Local affairs will be handled by local governments; national affairs, by national governments; international affairs will be administered by global government. The individual will enjoy far more liberty under world government. Soon may a global language evolve, and there will be at least some hope of sometime having a global religion—or religions with a global viewpoint.

134:7. The Thirty-First Year

When Jesus returned from the journey to the Caspian Sea, he knew that his world travels were about finished. He made only one more trip outside of Palestine, into Syria. At Antioch the Son of Man lived for over two months, and for three weeks of this period he worked as a tentmaker. Ten years later, when the Apostle Paul was preaching in Antioch and heard his followers speak of the doctrines of the Damascus scribe, he little knew that his pupils had heard the voice, and listened to the teachings, of the Master himself.

From Antioch Jesus went south along the coast to Caesarea and Joppa, then traveled inland to Jamnia, Ashdod, Gaza, to Beersheba. From here he then started on his final tour, stopping at Hebron, Bethlehem, Jerusalem, Beeroth, Lebonah, Sychar, Shechem, Samaria, Geba, En-Gannim, Endor, Madon, then journeyed north through Magdala and Capernaum to Caesarea Philippi.

The indwelling Thought Adjuster now led Jesus to forsake the dwelling places of men and betake himself up to Mount Hermon that he might finish his work of mastering his human mind and complete the task of effecting his full consecration to the remainder of his lifework on earth. This period of isolation on Mount Hermon marked the termination of his purely human career. And Jesus lived alone with God for six weeks on the slopes of Mount Hermon.

134:8. The Sojourn on Mount Hermon

After spending some time in the vicinity of Caesarea Philippi, Jesus made his way to Mount Hermon where he procured supplies and a lad, Tiglath, who was to leave food in a stone container in a designated spot twice a week. Jesus had ascended the mountain only a short way when he paused to pray, among other things asking his Father to send back the guardian seraphim to "be with Tiglath."

After more than five weeks of unbroken communion with his Paradise Father, Jesus became absolutely assured of his nature and of the certainty of his triumph over the material levels of time-space personality manifestation. He asked his Father if he might be permitted to hold conference with his Satania enemies as the Son of Man. Satan (representing Lucifer) and the rebellious Planetary Prince, Caligastia, were present with Jesus and were made fully visible to him. To the many proposals and counterproposals of the emissaries of Lucifer, Jesus only made reply, "May the will of my Paradise Father prevail, and you, my rebellious son, may the Ancients of Days judge you divinely. I am your Creator-father; I can hardly judge you justly, and my mercy you have already spurned. I commit you to the adjudication of the Judges of a greater universe." To all the Lucifer-suggested compromises and makeshifts, to all such specious proposals about the incarnation bestowal, Jesus only made reply, "The will of my Father in Paradise be done." And when the trying ordeal was finished, the detached guardian seraphim returned to Jesus' side and ministered to him.

On an afternoon in late summer, amid the trees and in the silence of nature, Michael of Nebadon won the unquestioned sovereignty of his universe.

134:9. The Time of Waiting

At end of the summer, Jesus had a family meeting in Capernaum and the next day started for Jerusalem with John Zebedee for the feast of the tabernacles. John noted a great change in Jesus. They spent almost three weeks in and around the city. Both of them were present at the solemn services of the day of atonement. To the Son of Man this performance was pitiful and pathetic. He burned to give vent to the declaration of the real truth about his Father's loving character, but his faithful Monitor admonished him that his hour had not yet come. In the midst of the week of the feast of tabernacles Jesus took leave of John, saying that he desired to retire to the hills where he might the better commune with his Paradise Father.

When he arrived back at Capernaum, Jesus presented himself for work, saying, "It behooves me to keep busy while I wait for my hour to come." He worked several months, until January of the following year, in the boatshop, by the side of his brother James. As time passed, rumors came to Capernaum of one John who was baptizing penitents in the Jordan, preaching, "The kingdom of heaven is at hand; repent and be baptized." Jesus listened to these reports but worked on, making boats, until John had journeyed up the river to a point near Pella in the month of January of the next year, A.D. 26. Jesus then laid down his tools, declaring, "My hour has come," and presently presented himself to John for baptism.

A great change had been coming over Jesus. Few of the people recognized in the public teacher the same person they had known and loved as a private individual in former years.

Paper 135: John the Baptist

JOHN the Baptist was born March 25, 7 B.C. For five months Elizabeth had kept secret Gabriel's visitation; and when she told her husband, Zacharias, he was greatly troubled and fully believed her narrative only after he had an unusual dream about six weeks before the birth of John. Excepting the visit of Gabriel and the dream of Zacharias, there was nothing unusual or supernatural connected with the birth of John the Baptist. John grew up as an ordinary child, in the City of Judah, a small village near Jerusalem. Zacharias and Elizabeth had a small farm on which they raised sheep and Zacharias received a regular allowance from the temple funds dedicated to the priesthood. The most eventful occurrence in John's early childhood was the visit, in company with his parents, to Jesus and the Nazareth family, when he was six years old. There was no synagogue school in this little village but both Zacharias and Elizabeth spent a great deal of time on John's mental and spiritual training. Zacharias had only short periods of service at the temple in Jerusalem so that he devoted much of his time to teaching his son.

135:1. John Becomes a Nazarite

John had no school from which to graduate at the age of fourteen, but his parents had selected this as the appropriate year for him to take the formal Nazarite vow. Accordingly, they took their son to Engedi, down by the Dead Sea, the southern headquarters of the Nazarite brotherhood , and there the lad was duly and solemnly inducted into this order for life. From there the family proceeded to Jerusalem, where John completed taking his Nazarite vows.

John returned home from Jerusalem to tend his father's sheep and grew up to be a strong man with a noble character. At sixteen, as a result of reading about Elijah, John became greatly impressed and decided to adopt Elijah's style of dress. From that day on he always wore a hairy garment with a leather girdle. At sixteen he was more than six feet tall and almost full grown. With his flowing hair and peculiar mode of dress he was indeed a picturesque youth.

135:2. The Death of Zacharias

After an illness of several months Zacharias died in July, A.D. 12, when John was just past eighteen years of age. In September of this year Elizabeth and John made a journey to Nazareth to visit Mary and Jesus. John had just about made up his mind to launch out in his lifework, but he was admonished, not only by Jesus' words but also by his example, to return home, take care of his mother, and await the "coming of the Father's hour." After bidding Jesus and Mary good-bye at the end of this enjoyable visit, John did not again see Jesus until the event of his baptism in the Jordan.

John and Elizabeth returned to their home and began to lay plans for the future. By the end of two years they had all but lost their home, so they decided to go south with the sheep herd. John was twenty when they moved to Hebron, near Engedi, where he tended his sheep in the so-called "wilderness of Judea." John made frequent visits to Engedi but was entirely different from the majority of the Nazarites and found it very difficult fully to fraternize with the brotherhood. But he was very fond of Abner, the acknowledged leader and head of the Engedi colony.

135:3. The Life of a Shepherd

John's life as a shepherd afforded him a great deal of time for thought. He talked much with Ezda, an orphan lad whom he had in a way adopted, and who cared for the herds when John made trips to Hebron to see his mother and to sell sheep, as well as when he went down to Engedi for Sabbath services.

Elizabeth kept John posted about Palestinian and world affairs, and his conviction grew deeper and deeper that the time was fast approaching when the old order was to end; that he was to become the herald of the approach of a new age, "the kingdom of heaven." And he fairly vibrated with the mounting impulse to go forth and proclaim to all men, "Repent! Get right with God! Get ready for the end; prepare yourselves for the appearance of the new and eternal order of earth affairs, the kingdom of heaven."

135:4. The Death of Elizabeth

On August 17, A.D. 22, when John was twenty-eight years of age, his mother suddenly passed away. On returning to Engedi from her funeral, he presented his flocks to the brotherhood and for a season detached himself from the outside world while he fasted and prayed. For two and a half years he lived at Engedi, reading much in the sacred writings which he found at the home of the Nazarites. In Malachi he read, "Behold, I will send you Elijah the prophet before the coming of the great and dreadful day of the Lord." John was ripe for the proclamation of the message of the coming kingdom, but this expectation of the coming of Elijah held him back for more than two years. He finally dared to think that, since the first of the prophets was called Elijah, so the last should be known, eventually, by the same name. It was the influence of Elijah that caused John to adopt his methods of direct and blunt assault upon the sins and vices of his contemporaries. He was a clear thinker, a powerful speaker, and a fiery denunciator.

At last he thought out the method of proclaiming the new age, the kingdom of God. He swept aside all doubts and departed from Engedi one day in March of A.D. 25 to begin his short but brilliant career as a public preacher.

135:5. The Kingdom of God

About one hundred years before the days of Jesus and John a new school of religious teachers arose in Palestine, the apocalyptists. These new teachers taught that creation was about to pass into its final stage; the kingdoms of this world were about to become the kingdom of God. There was a general feeling that the end of the rule of the gentile nations was drawing near. All were agreed that some drastic purging or purifying discipline would of necessity precede the establishment of the new kingdom on earth. The Messiah was to bring in the establishment of the new kingdom, the kingdom of God. Who would this Messiah be? The older teachers clung to the doctrine of the son of David; the newer taught that, since the new kingdom was a heavenly kingdom, the new ruler might also be a divine personality, a Son of God, a heavenly Prince, long held in waiting thus to assume the rulership of the earth made new. Such was the religious background of the Jewish world when John went forth proclaiming, "Repent, for the kingdom of heaven is at hand!"

135:6. John Begins to Preach

Early in the month of March, A.D. 25, John journeyed around the western coast of the Dead Sea and up the river Jordan to opposite Jericho. He established himself near the entrance to the ford and began to preach to the people who passed by on their way back and forth across the river. It was apparent to all who heard John that he was more than a preacher; the great majority went away believing that they had heard the voice of a prophet. There was still another and a *new* feature about the work of this Nazarite preacher: He baptized every one of his believers in the Jordan "for the remission of sins."

Only fifteen months intervened between the time John began to preach and baptize and his arrest and imprisonment at the instigation of Herod Antipas, but in this short time he baptized considerably over one hundred thousand penitents. John was a heroic but tactless preacher. He counseled all, "Make ready for the end of the age—the kingdom of heaven is at hand."

135:7. John Journeys North

John still had confused ideas about the coming kingdom and its king. In mind John might be confused, but in spirit never. He was sorely in doubt as to the part Jesus would play in such events. As John journeyed north, he thought much about Jesus. It was at Adam that he first made reference to Jesus. In answer to the direct question which his disciples asked him, "Are you the Messiah?" John answered, "There will come after me one who is greater than I, whose sandal straps I am not worthy to stoop down and unloose. I baptize you with water, but he will baptize you with the Holy Spirit. "

135:8. Meeting of Jesus and John

By December of A.D. 25, when John reached the neighborhood of Pella in his journey up the Jordan, his fame had extended throughout all Palestine. Jesus had spoken favorably of John's message, and this had caused many from Capernaum to join John's cult of repentance and baptism, including James and John Zebedee. They went to see John once a week and brought back to Jesus fresh, first-hand reports of the evangelist's work.

Sunday morning, January 13, A.D. 26 Jesus laid down his tools and announced to the three workmen in the room with him, "My hour has come." He went out to his brothers James and Jude, repeating, "My hour has come—let us go to John." They arrived on the scene of John's baptizing about noon of the next day. John did not look up to see Jesus until the Son of Man stood in his immediate presence. When John recognized Jesus, he greeted his cousin in the flesh and asked, "But why do you come down into the water to greet me?" And Jesus answered, "To be subject to your baptism." John replied, "But I have need to be baptized by you. Why do you come to me?" And Jesus whispered to John, "Bear with me now, for it becomes us to set this example for my brothers standing here with me, and that the people may know that my hour has come."

John trembled with emotion as he made ready to baptize Jesus of Nazareth in the Jordan at noon on Monday, January 14, A.D. 26. Thus did John baptize Jesus and his two brothers James and Jude. John dismissed the crowd, and as they were departing, the four men still standing in the water heard a strange sound, and presently there appeared for a moment an apparition immediately over the head of Jesus, and they heard a voice saying, "This is my beloved Son in whom I am well pleased." A great change came over the countenance of Jesus, and coming up out of the water in silence he took leave of them, going toward the hills to the east. And no man saw Jesus again for forty days.

135:9. Forty Days of Preaching

After the experience of this day the preaching of John took on new and certain notes of proclamation concerning the coming kingdom and the expected Messiah. These forty days were a difficult period for John and his disciples. What was to be the relation of John to Jesus? John rather decided, with the minority, that Jesus had come to establish the spiritual kingdom of heaven.

It was early on the morning of Sabbath, February 23, that the company of John, engaged in eating their morning meal, looked up toward the north and beheld Jesus coming to them. As he approached, John stood upon a large rock and, lifting up his sonorous voice, said, "Behold the Son of God, the deliverer of the world! Jesus bade them return to their food while he sat down to eat with John, his brothers James and Jude having returned to Capernaum. Early in the morning of the next day Jesus took leave of John and his disciples, going back to Galilee. To John's inquiries about his own preaching and mission Jesus only said, "My Father will guide you now and in the future as he has in the past." And these two great men separated that morning on the banks of the Jordan, never again to greet each other in the flesh.

135:10. John Journey's South

Since Jesus had gone north into Galilee, John felt led to retrace his steps southward. Never again did John preach as he had before baptizing Jesus. He somehow felt that the responsibility of the coming kingdom was no longer on his shoulders.

Near the village of Adam John made the memorable attack upon Herod Antipas for unlawfully taking the wife of another man. John's preaching had gradually changed into a proclamation of mercy for the common people, while he denounced with renewed vehemence the corrupt political and religious rulers. Herod Antipas became alarmed lest he and his disciples should start a rebellion. Herod also resented John's public criticisms of his domestic affairs. In view of all this, he decided to put John in prison. Accordingly, very early in the morning of June 12, before the multitude arrived to hear the preaching and witness the baptizing, the agents of Herod placed John under arrest.

135:11. John in Prison

John had a lonely and somewhat bitter experience in prison, where he languished for more than a year and a half. This experience was a great test of his faith in, and loyalty to, Jesus.

After John had been in prison several months, a group of his disciples in visiting him criticized Jesus for not delivering him from prison. John answered in part, "This man can do nothing unless it has been given him by his Father in heaven. You well remember that I said, 'I am not the Messiah, but I am one sent on before to prepare the way for him.' He must increase but I must decrease. I am of this earth and have declared my message. Jesus of Nazareth comes down to the earth from heaven and is above us all. The Son of Man has descended from God, and the words of God he will declare to you." These disciples were amazed and departed in silence. John was also much agitated, for he perceived that he had uttered a prophecy. Never again did he wholly doubt the mission and divinity of Jesus. Jesus knew all about this. He had great love for John and knowing fully the great things in preparation for John when he departed from this world, he constrained himself not to interfere in the natural outworking of the great preacher-prophet's career.

Just a few days before his death John again sent trusted messengers to Jesus, inquiring, "Is my work done? Why do I languish in prison?" Jesus sent back word, saying in part, "Tell him that I have not forgotten but to suffer me also this, for it becomes us to fulfill all righteousness. Tell the beloved herald of my earth mission that he shall be abundantly blessed in the age to come if he finds no occasion to doubt and stumble over me." This message greatly comforted John and did much to stabilize his faith and prepare him for the tragic end of his life in the flesh.

135:12. Death of John the Baptist

Herod feared to release John lest he instigate rebellion; he feared to put him to death lest the multitude riot, for thousands believed that John was a holy man, a prophet. Therefore Herod kept him in prison, not knowing what else to do with him. Besides, John was also a victim of the intense and bitter hatred of Herodias, Herod's unlawful wife.

In celebration of his birthday Herod made a great feast in the palace. Since Herodias had failed to bring about John's death by direct appeal to Herod, she now set herself to the task of having him put to death by cunning planning. In the course of the evening's entertainment Herodias presented her daughter to dance before the banqueters. Herod was very pleased and said, "Ask me on this my birthday for whatever you desire, and I will give it to you, even to the half of my kingdom." Herodias said to her daughter, "Go to Herod and ask for the head of John the Baptist." And the young woman, returning to the banquet table, said to Herod, "I request that you forthwith give me the head of John the Baptist on a platter."

Herod was filled with fear and sorrow, but because of his oath and because of all those who sat at meat with him, he would not deny the request. So was

John that night beheaded in the prison. When John's disciples heard of this, they came to the prison for the body of John, and after laying it in a tomb, they went and told Jesus.

Paper 136: Baptism and the Forty Days

JESUS began his public work at the height of the popular interest in John's preaching and at a time when the Jewish people of Palestine were eagerly looking for the appearance of the Messiah. There was a great contrast between John and Jesus. The burden of John's message was, Repent! flee from the wrath to come. Jesus' message was always followed by the gospel, the good tidings of the joy and liberty of the new kingdom.

136:1. Concepts of the Expected Messiah

The Jews entertained many ideas about the expected deliverer. They devoutly believed that the Messiah would deliver the Jewish people from Roman domination, the majority believing that they continued to languish under Roman rule because of their national sins. John's preaching, "Repent and be baptized, for the kingdom of heaven is at hand," could mean only one thing to any devout Jew: The coming of the Messiah. There was one feature of the bestowal of Michael which was utterly foreign to the Jewish conception of the Messiah, and that was the *union* of the two natures, the human and the divine.

136:2. The Baptism of Jesus

Many devout souls were baptized by John for the good of Israel. They feared lest some sin of ignorance on their part might delay the coming of the Messiah. It is therefore evident that Jesus in no sense received John's baptism as a rite of repentance or for the remission of sins. Ordinarily, when a mortal of the realm attains such high levels of personality perfection, there occur those preliminary phenomena of spiritual elevation which terminate in eventual fusion of the matured soul of the mortal with its associated divine Adjuster. This ceremony was the final act of Jesus' purely human life on Urantia. As John laid his hands upon Jesus to baptize him, the indwelling Adjuster took final leave of the perfected human soul of Joshua ben Joseph. And in a few moments this divine entity returned from Divinington as a Personalized Adjuster and chief of his kind throughout the entire local universe of Nebadon. Only the eyes of Jesus beheld the Personalized Adjuster. Throughout the remainder of Jesus' earth life this Personalized Adjuster was associated with him in all his labors; Jesus was in constant communion with this exalted Adjuster.

136:3. The Forty Days

After his baptism, during his isolation in the Perean hills, Jesus determined upon the policy to be pursued and the methods to be employed in the new and changed phase of earth life which he was about to inaugurate. He now fully recalled the bestowal charge and its instructions administered by his elder brother, Immanuel, ere he entered upon his Urantia incarnation. Jesus was now informed, upon the highest authority of the local universe and the superuniverse, that his bestowal work was finished in so far as it affected his personal status in relation to sovereignty and rebellion.

136:4. Plans for Public Work

Day by day, up in the hills, Jesus formulated the plans for the remainder of his Urantia bestowal. Carefully he thought over the advice given him concerning his methods of labor, and that he was to leave no permanent writing on the planet. On his next visit to Nazareth he destroyed all of his writing in the carpenter shop, and in the old home.

On the third day of this isolation Jesus promised himself he would go back to the world to finish his earth career, and that in a situation involving any two ways he would always choose the Father's will.

The forty days in the mountain wilderness were not a period of great temptation but rather the period of the Master's *great decisions.*

136:5. The First Great Decision

The first great decision had to do with whether or not he would make use of the vast assemblage of celestial hosts sent by their commanders to wait upon his will. Jesus decided that he would *not* utilize a single one of these personalities unless it should become evident that this was his *Father's will.* Notwithstanding this general decision, this vast host remained with him throughout the balance of his earth life, always in readiness to obey the least expression of their Sovereign's will. Jesus assigned the immediate command of this attendant host of universe personalities to his recently Personalized Adjuster. The Adjuster took great pains to point out to Jesus that, while such an assembly of universe creatures could be limited in their space activities by the delegated authority of their Creator, such limitations were not operative in connection with their function in time. In order to prevent the appearance of apparent time miracles, it was necessary for Jesus to remain constantly time conscious.

136:6. The Second Decision

Jesus now turned his thoughts toward himself. As far as his personal necessities were concerned, and in general even in his relations with other personalities, he now deliberately chose to pursue the path of normal earthly existence; he definitely decided against a policy which would transcend, violate, or outrage his own established natural laws. The Master thereby chose a program of living which was the equivalent of deciding against miracles and wonders. He chose to go on pursuing the policy of refusing to defend himself. Jesus revealed to the creatures of his universe the technique of the new and better way, the higher moral values of living and the deeper spiritual satisfactions of evolutionary human existence on the worlds of space.

136:7. The Third Decision

Having made his decisions regarding such matters as food and physical ministration to the needs of his material body, the care of the health of himself and his associates, there remained yet other problems to solve. What would be his attitude when confronted by personal danger? He decided to exercise normal watchcare over his human safety but to refrain from all superhuman intervention when the crisis of his life in the flesh should come. Throughout his entire earth life Jesus was consistently loyal to this decision.

136:8. The Fourth Decision

The next great problem concerned whether or not he should in any manner lend his universe powers for winning the adherence of his fellow men, to the gratification of the Jewish hankering for the spectacular and the marvelous. He decided that he should not. Even when he permitted the manifestation of numerous time-shortening ministrations of mercy, he almost invariably admonished the recipients of his healing ministry to tell no man about the benefits they had received. Jesus very wisely foresaw that the working of miracles and the execution of wonders would not reveal God nor save men. He knew the methods of the world—how people gained their ends in politics and commerce by compromise and diplomacy. Would he utilize this knowledge in the furtherance of his mission on earth? No! And he knew the futility of the Caligastia method of trying to get ahead of the natural, slow, and sure way of accomplishing the divine purpose. Jesus chose to establish the kingdom of heaven in the hearts of mankind by natural, ordinary, difficult, and trying methods, just such procedures as his earth children must subsequently follow in their work of enlarging and extending that heavenly kingdom. The Master triumphantly put loyalty to his Father's will above every other earthly and temporal consideration.

136:9. The Fifth Decision

Jesus now turned his attention to the choice of methods to be employed in the proclamation and establishment of the kingdom of God. How should he organize his followers for effective effort and intelligent co-operation? As the days passed, with ever-increasing clearness Jesus perceived what kind of a truth-revealer he was to become. He discerned that God's way was not going to be the easy way. He began to realize that the cup of the remainder of his human experience might possibly be bitter, but he decided to drink it.

And now he made his final decision regarding the Scriptures which his mother had taught him, reaching the conclusion that such utterances did not refer to him. At last, and finally, the human mind of the Son of Man made a clean sweep of all these Messianic difficulties and contradictions—Hebrew scriptures, parental training, chazan teaching, Jewish expectations, and human ambitious longings; once and for all he decided upon his course. He would return to Galilee and quietly begin the proclamation of the kingdom and trust his Father to work out the details of procedure day by day.

136:10. The Sixth Decision

On the last day of this memorable isolation, before starting down the mountain to join John and his disciples, the Son of Man made his final decision. And this decision he communicated to the Personalized Adjuster in these words, "And in all other matters, as in these now of decision-record, I pledge you I will be subject to the will of my Father." And when he had thus spoken, he journeyed down the mountain. And his face shone with the glory of spiritual victory and moral achievement.

Paper 137: Tarrying Time in Galilee

EARLY on Saturday morning, February 23, A.D. 26, Jesus came down from the hills to rejoin John's company encamped at Pella. All that day Jesus mingled with the multitude. He ministered to a lad who had injured himself in a fall and journeyed to the near-by village of Pella to deliver the boy safely into the hands of his parents.

137:1. Choosing the First Four Apostles

During this Sabbath Andrew and Simon spent much time with Jesus. Andrew accompanied Jesus to Pella with the injured boy. On the way back Andrew told Jesus he had made up his mind to follow him. Jesus heartily welcomed him. On returning Andrew informed his brother Simon of his decision and suggested that Simon do likewise. Since they were leading disciples of John the Baptist, they consulted him and John encouraged them to follow Jesus. Then Andrew beckoned to Jesus to draw aside while he announced that his brother desired to join himself to the service of the new kingdom. And in welcoming Simon as his second apostle, Jesus said, "Simon, your enthusiasm is commendable, but it is dangerous to the work of the kingdom. I admonish you to become more thoughtful in your speech. I would change your name to Peter." Later James and John Zebedee arrived on the scene and learning of Jesus' selection of Andrew and Simon rushed to Pella and awakened Jesus who was sleeping and asked why they had not been chosen first. Jesus assured them that they were also his disciples.

137:2. Choosing Philip and Nathaniel

Sunday morning, February 24, A.D. 26, Jesus and his four disciple-apostles departed for Galilee. On their way toward Galilee they saw Philip of Bethsaida and Nathaniel coming toward them. Philip went forward to greet his friends while Nathaniel rested under the shade of a tree by the roadside. Peter took Philip to one side and proceeded to explain that they had all become associates of Jesus in the new kingdom and strongly urged Philip to volunteer for service. Philip was in a quandary. Andrew suggested to Philip, "Why not ask the Teacher?" Philip went straight to Jesus, asking, "Teacher, shall I go down to John or shall I join my friends who follow you?" And Jesus answered, "Follow me." Philip now hurried back to break the news of his decision to his friend Nathaniel. After some discussion, Philip led Nathaniel to Jesus, who, looking benignly into the face of the sincere doubter, said, "Behold a genuine Israelite, in whom there is no deceit. Follow me." And Nathaniel, turning to Philip, said, "You are right. He is indeed a master of men. I will also follow, if I am worthy." And Jesus nodded to Nathaniel, again saying, "Follow me." They all remained overnight with Joseph in Jesus' boyhood home.

137:3. The Visit to Capernaum

Jesus prepared to pay a hurried visit to his mother at Capernaum, stopping at Magdala to see his brother Jude. Jude was present at Jesus' baptism and, with his brother James, had become a firm believer in Jesus' mission on earth. Mary was thrilled with expectation. On the next day, Tuesday, they all journeyed over to Cana for the wedding of Naomi. Mary had not been so joyous in years. She journeyed to Cana in the spirit of the queen mother on the way to witness the coronation of her son.

137:4. The Wedding at Cana

By noon on Wednesday almost a thousand guests had arrived in Cana, more than four times the number bidden to the wedding feast. As the day wore on, Jesus became increasingly conscious that the people were expecting him to perform some wonder. Early in the afternoon Mary and James made bold to ask Jesus when he had planned to manifest himself as the "supernatural one." They saw they had aroused his characteristic indignation. He said only, "If you love me, then be willing to tarry with me while I wait upon the will of my Father who is in heaven." The mother of the bridegroom confided to Mary that the supply of wine was exhausted And Mary confidently said, "Have no worry—I will speak to my son. He will help us." As Jesus was standing alone in a corner of the garden, his mother approached him, saying, "My son, they have no wine." And Jesus answered, "My good woman, what have I to do with that...Why do you trouble me again with these matters?" And then, breaking down in tears, Mary entreated him, "But, my son, I promised them that you would help us; won't you please do something for me?" Jesus laid his hand tenderly upon her head, saying, "Now, now, Mother Mary, grieve not over my apparently hard sayings...Most gladly would I do what you ask of me if it were a part of the Father's will—" He now realized that he had already said—or rather desirefully thought—too much. Of all persons present at the marriage feast of Cana, Jesus was the most surprised. Others had expected him to work a wonder, but that was just what he had purposed not to do. Jesus now fully comprehended that he must constantly be on guard lest his indulgence of sympathy and pity become responsible for repeated episodes of this sort.

137:5. Back in Capernaum

Jesus, with his newly chosen disciple-apostles departed very early the next morning for Capernaum. On this journey Jesus talked over many things of importance to the coming kingdom with his newly chosen associates and especially warned them to make no mention of the turning of the water into wine. After supper that evening, in this home of Zebedee and Salome, there was held one of the most important conferences of all Jesus' earthly career. Jesus set out to make clear to them who he was and what was to be his mission on earth and how it might possibly end, they were stunned. They could not grasp what he was telling them. That night Jesus did not sleep. In the long hours of that night of meditation Jesus came clearly to comprehend that he never would be able to make his followers see him in any other light than as the long-expected Messiah. The next morning Jesus joined his friends at breakfast. He directed his apostles to return to their nets while he made ready to go with Zebedee to the boatshop.

137:6. Events of a Sabbath Day

Jesus' first public appearance following his baptism was in the Capernaum synagogue on Sabbath, March 2, A.D. 26. The synagogue was crowded to overflowing. They expected to behold some extraordinary manifestation of supernatural power. But they were destined to disappointment. When Jesus stood up, the ruler of the synagogue handed him the Scripture roll, and he read from the Prophet Isaiah. When he had finished this reading, he simply said, "Be patient and you shall see the glory of God; even so shall it be with all those who tarry with me and thus learn to do the will of my Father who is in heaven." And the people went to their homes, wondering what was the meaning of all this. That afternoon Jesus and his apostles, with James and Jude, entered a boat and pulled down the shore a little way, where they anchored while he talked to them about the coming kingdom. And they understood more than they had on Thursday night. Jesus told them to make no mistake, for we go forth to labor for a generation of sign seekers.

137:7. Four Months of Training

For four long months Jesus held over one hundred long and earnest, though cheerful and joyous, sessions with these six associates and his own brother James. Nothing, absolutely nothing, miraculous happened. They were held together by his matchless personality and by the gracious words which he spoke to them evening upon evening. In this time of waiting Jesus endeavored to teach his associates what their attitude should be toward the various religious groups and the political parties of Palestine. Jesus' words always were, "We are seeking to win all of them, but we are not of any of them." He unfailingly impressed upon his associates that they must "show forth love, compassion, and sympathy." In later years after seasons of intense public work, the apostles looked back upon these four months as the most precious and profitable of all their association with the Master. Jesus taught these men all they could assimilate. He did not precipitate confusion by the presentation of truth too far beyond their capacity to comprehend.

137:8. Sermon on the Kingdom

On Sabbath, June 22, Jesus occupied the synagogue pulpit. Among his comments Jesus said that, I have come to proclaim the establishment of the Father's kingdom. And this kingdom shall include the worshiping souls of Jew and gentile, rich and poor, free and bond, for my Father is no respecter of persons; his love and his mercy are over all. The Father sends his spirit to indwell the minds of men, and later I shall send the Spirit of Truth to guide you. My kingdom is not of this world. Unless you seek entrance into the kingdom with the faith and trusting dependence of a little child, you shall in no wise gain admission. Where the spirit of God teaches and leads the soul of man, there in reality is the kingdom of heaven. He who would be great in my Father's kingdom must first become server of all. This new kingdom is like a seed growing in the good soil of a field. It does not attain full fruit quickly. The kingdom of heaven is at hand, and all who enter therein shall find abundant liberty and joyous salvation. Those who enter the kingdom shall ascend to my Father. I come proclaiming faith, the gift of God, as the price of entrance into the kingdom of heaven. If you would but believe that my Father loves you with an infinite love, then you are in the kingdom of God.

Paper 138: Training the Kingdom's Messengers

AFTER preaching the sermon on "The Kingdom," Jesus called the six apostles together and began to disclose his plans for visiting the cities around and about the Sea of Galilee. His brothers James and Jude were very much hurt because they were not called to this conference. This was the starting point of an ever-widening gulf between Jesus and his family. They very nearly rejected him. Only Ruth, the youngest, remained unswervingly loyal to her father-brother.

138:1. Final Instructions

The next day, Sunday, June 23, A.D. 26, Jesus imparted his final instructions to the six. He directed them to go forth, two and two, to teach the glad tidings of the kingdom and advised against public preaching. He desired them to acquire practical experience in dealing personally with their fellow men. Before they began this first two weeks of service, Jesus announced to them that he desired to ordain twelve apostles and authorized each of them to choose one man from among his early converts for membership in the projected corps of apostles. This morning, as they separated to go to their work, there was a bit of concealed depression in each heart. Besides their fear and timidity, this was not the way they had pictured the kingdom of heaven being inaugurated. Meantime Jesus went over to Nazareth to visit with members of his family. Jesus did everything humanly possible, consistent with his dedication to the doing of his Father's will, to retain the confidence and affection of his family.

138:2. Choosing the Six

This first missionary tour of the six was eminently successful. They all discovered the great value of direct and personal contact with men. Jesus, after each man had presented his selection for the new apostleships, asked all the others to vote upon the nomination; thus all six of the new apostles were formally accepted by all of the older six. Then Jesus announced that they would all visit these candidates and give them the call to service. The newly selected apostles were: 1. Matthew Levi, the customs collector of Capernaum, selected by Andrew; 2. Thomas Didymus, a fisherman of Tarichea, selected by Philip; 3. James Alpheus, a fisherman and farmer of Kheresa, selected by James Zebedee; 4. Judas Alpheus, the twin brother of James Alpheus, also a fisherman, selected by John Zebedee; 5. Simon Zelotes, a high officer in the patriotic organization of the Zealots, selected by Peter; 6. Judas Iscariot, who had experience with finances and was selected by Nathaniel.

Jesus spent a full day with the six, answering their questions and listening to the details of their reports, for they had many interesting and profitable experiences to relate.

138:3. The Call of Matthew and Simon

The next day Jesus and the six went to call upon Matthew. Andrew stepped forward with Jesus, who, looking into Matthew's face, said, "Follow me." Matthew told Jesus of the banquet he had arranged for that evening. Peter then took Matthew aside and explained that he had invited one Simon to join the apostles and secured his consent that Simon be also bidden to this feast. After a noontide luncheon at Matthew's house they all went with Peter to call upon Simon the Zealot. When Peter led Jesus up to Simon, the Master greeted the fiery patriot and only said, "Follow me." In those days it was the custom for all interested persons to linger about the banquet room to listen to the conversation and speeches of the men of honor. Accordingly, most of the Capernaum Pharisees were present on this occasion. Later in the evening one of the more malignant of the Pharisees went so far as to criticize Jesus' conduct to Peter. When Jesus began to speak, he said that they were glad to welcome Matthew and Simon and observed that those who were criticizing him in their hearts should know that he came to proclaim joy to the socially downtrodden and spiritual liberty to the moral captives. "I have come, not to call the righteous, but sinners."

138:4. The Call of the Twins

On the morrow all nine of them went by boat over to Kheresa to execute the formal calling of the next two apostles, James and Judas Alpheus. James Zebedee presented the Master to the Kheresa fishermen, and Jesus, gazing on them, nodded and said, "Follow me." That afternoon Jesus reminded them, "All men are my brothers. My Father in heaven does not despise any creature of our making. The kingdom of heaven is open to all men and women. . . . The door of the kingdom is wide open for all who desire to know the truth and to find God." Later in the evening Jesus gave his apostles their first lesson dealing with the origin, nature, and destiny of unclean spirits, but they could not comprehend the import of what he told them. After a night of rest the entire party, now numbering eleven, went by boat over to Tarichea.

138:5. The Call of Thomas and Judas

Thomas the fisherman and Judas the wanderer met Jesus and the apostles at the fisher-boat landing at Tarichea, and Thomas led the party to his nearby home. Philip now presented Thomas as his nominee for apostleship and Nathaniel presented Judas Iscariot, the Judean, for similar honors. Jesus looked upon Thomas and said, "Thomas, you lack faith; nevertheless, I receive you. Follow me." To Judas Iscariot the Master said, "Judas, we are all of one flesh, and as I receive you into our midst, I pray that you will always be loyal to your Galilean brethren. Follow me."

Jesus took the twelve apart for a season to pray with them and to instruct them in the nature and work of the Holy Spirit, but again did they largely fail to comprehend the meaning of those wonderful truths. The next day during the after-supper hours he talked to them about the ministry of seraphim, and some of the apostles comprehended his teaching. They rested for a night and the next day departed by boat for Capernaum. Zebedee and Salome had gone to live with their son David so that their large home could be turned over to Jesus and his twelve apostles.

138:6. The Week of Intensive Training

The next week was devoted to a program of intense training. Each day the six new apostles were put in the hands of their respective nominators for a thoroughgoing review of all they had learned and experienced in preparation for the work of the kingdom. Evenings they all assembled in Zebedee's garden to receive Jesus' instruction. It was at this time that Jesus established the mid-week holiday for rest and recreation. Jesus endeavored to make clear to his apostles the difference between his teachings and his *life among them* and the teachings which might subsequently spring up *about* him. Said Jesus, "My kingdom and the gospel related thereto shall be the burden of your message. Be not sidetracked into preaching *about* me and *about* my teachings."

138:7. Another Disappointment

Simon Peter, James Zebedee, and Judas Iscariot came to ask Jesus what positions they were to occupy in the establishment of the kingdom. Beckoning the other apostles to join them, Jesus said in part, "My little children, how long shall I bear with you! Have I not made it plain to you that my kingdom is not of this world? I have told you many times that I have not come to sit on David's throne. Banish from your minds this idea that my kingdom is a rule of power or a reign of glory." Once more were his associates shocked, stunned.

When Jesus found they had very little money, he recommended that they spend two weeks fishing, adding, "And then will you go forth to become fishers of men." This plan of fishing two weeks and going out to do personal work in behalf of the kingdom for two weeks was followed for more than five months.

138:8. First Work of the Twelve

Near the middle of August, in the year A.D. 26, they went forth two and two to the fields of work assigned by Andrew. Jesus alternated in going out with the various couples. Jesus taught them to preach the forgiveness of sin through faith in God without penance or sacrifice. He enjoined his apostles to refrain from discussing John the Baptist, the voice at his baptism, and the turning of water into wine at Cana. The common people marveled at the teaching and ministry of Jesus and his apostles. Jesus taught his apostles that faith was the only requisite to entering the Father's kingdom. The disciples early learned that the Master had a profound respect and sympathetic regard for every human being he met. Though Jesus' public teaching mainly consisted in parables and short discourses, he invariably taught his apostles by questions and answers. The apostles were at first shocked by, but early became accustomed to, Jesus' treatment of women; he made it very clear to them that women were to be accorded equal rights with men in the kingdom.

138:9. Five Months of Testing

This somewhat monotonous period of alternate fishing and personal work proved to be a grueling experience for the twelve apostles, but they endured the test. These five months of work with Jesus led these apostles, each one of them, to regard him as the best friend he had in all the world. This season of public inactivity was a great trial to Jesus' family. By the time Jesus was prepared to launch forth on his public work, his entire family (except Ruth) had practically deserted him. By the end of this period the twelve had worked out fairly satisfactory plans for the care of their respective families.

138:10. Organization of the Twelve

The apostles early organized themselves in the following manner: 1. Andrew was designated chairman and director general of the twelve; 2. Peter, James, and John were appointed personal companions of Jesus; 3. Philip was made steward of the group; 4. Nathaniel watched over the needs of the families of the twelve; 5. Matthew was the fiscal agent of the apostolic corps; 6. Thomas was manager of the itinerary; 7. James and Judas the twin sons of Alpheus were assigned to the management of the multitudes; 8. Simon Zelotes was given charge of recreation and play; 9. Judas Iscariot was appointed treasurer.

The Master and his disciple-apostles went on in this simple manner until Sunday, January 12, A.D. 21, when he called them together and formally ordained them as ambassadors of the kingdom and preachers of its glad tidings.

Paper 139: The Twelve Apostles

THESE twelve men represented many different types of human temperament, and they had not been made alike by schooling. Do not make the mistake of regarding the apostles as being altogether ignorant and unlearned. All of them, except the Alpheus twins, were graduates of the synagogue schools. They were lacking in so-called higher education.

139:1. Andrew, The First Chosen

Andrew, chairman of the apostolic corps of the kingdom, was born in Capernaum. He was the oldest child in a family of five: himself, his brother Simon, and three sisters. Andrew and Simon Peter were fishermen and partners of James and John the sons of Zebedee. Andrew was 33, a full year older than Jesus and the oldest of the apostles. Andrew was the ablest man of the twelve, a good organizer but a better administrator. Although Andrew was never an effective preacher, he was an efficient personal worker. Andrew and Peter were very unlike in character and temperament yet they got along together splendidly. Of all the apostles, Andrew was the best judge of men. His great service to the kingdom was in advising Peter, James, and John concerning the choice of the first missionaries. Andrew admired Jesus because of his consistent sincerity, his unaffected dignity.

Very soon after Jesus' ascension on high, Andrew began the writing of a personal record of many of the sayings and doings of his departed Master. Later Andrew journeyed through Armenia, Asia Minor, and Macedonia and, after bringing many thousands into the kingdom, he was apprehended and crucified. It was two full days before this robust man expired on the cross, and throughout these tragic hours he continued effectively to proclaim the glad tidings of the salvation of the kingdom of heaven.

139:2. Simon Peter

When Simon joined the apostles, he was thirty years of age. He was married, had three children, and lived at Bethsaida. When Jesus gave Simon the name Peter, he did it with a smile; it was to be a sort of nickname. Simon was well known to all his friends as an erratic and impulsive fellow. Peter was a fluent speaker, eloquent and dramatic. He was also a natural and inspirational leader of men. The one trait which Peter most admired in Jesus was his supernal tenderness. Peter was one of the most inexplicable combinations of courage and cowardice that ever lived on earth. His great strength of character was loyalty, friendship. He was the first one of the apostles to make wholehearted confession of Jesus' combined humanity and divinity.

Peter was the outstanding preacher of the twelve; he did more than any other one man, aside from Paul, to establish the kingdom and send its messengers to the four corners of the earth in one generation. But Peter persisted in making the mistake of trying to convince the Jews that Jesus was, after all, really and truly the Jewish Messiah. Peter's wife was a very able woman; for years she labored acceptably as a member of the women's corps, and the day her illustrious husband yielded up his life, she was thrown to the wild beasts in the arena at Rome. Peter regarded himself as the recipient of high honors when his captors informed him that he must die as his Master had died—on the cross.

139:3. James Zebedee

James, the older of the two apostle sons of Zebedee, whom Jesus nicknamed "sons of thunder," was thirty years old when he became an apostle. He was married, had four children, and lived near his parents in the outskirts of Capernaum. This able apostle was a temperamental contradiction; he seemed really to possess two natures, both of which were actuated by strong feelings. Next to Peter, unless it was Matthew, James was the best public orator among the twelve. His one great weakness was spells of unaccountable silence. The outstanding feature of James's personality was his ability to see all sides of a proposition. He was a well-balanced thinker and planner. Along with Andrew, he was one of the more level-headed of the apostolic group. He was an excellent balance wheel for Peter. That characteristic of Jesus which James most admired was the Master's sympathetic affection. Of all the twelve, James came the nearest to grasping the real import and significance of Jesus' teaching.

Herod Agrippa feared James above all the other apostles and he was the first apostle to be put to death with the sword by Herod. James lived his life to the full, and when the end came, he bore himself with such grace and fortitude that even his accuser was so touched that he rushed away from the scene of James's death to join himself to the disciples of Jesus.

139:4. John Zebedee

When he became an apostle, John was twenty-four years old and was the youngest of the twelve. He was unmarried and lived with his parents at Bethsaida. Both before and after becoming an apostle, John functioned as the personal agent of Jesus in dealing with the Master's family, and he continued to bear this responsibility as long as Mary the mother of Jesus lived. Peter, James, and John were assigned as personal aides to Jesus soon after they became apostles. John Zebedee had many lovely traits of character, but one which was not so lovely was his inordinate but usually well-concealed conceit. The strongest trait in John's character was his dependability; he was prompt and courageous, faithful and devoted. John was a man of few words except when his temper was aroused. But he was gifted with a remarkable and creative imagination. Those characteristics of Jesus which John most appreciated were the Master's love and unselfishness. Jesus' ever deferring his slightest wish to the will of the Father in heaven and his daily life of implicit trust made such a profound impression on John that it produced marked and permanent changes in his character. John had a cool and daring courage which few of the other apostles possessed.

Several years after the martyrdom of James, John married his brother's widow. The last twenty years of his life he was cared for by a loving granddaughter. John was in prison several times and was banished to the Isle of Patmos for a period of four years. While in prison John wrote the Book of Revelation, which you now have in greatly abridged and distorted form. As the years passed, John, together with James the Lord's brother, learned to practice wise conciliation when they appeared before the civil magistrates. John traveled much, labored incessantly, and after becoming bishop of the Asia churches, settled down at Ephesus. He directed his associate, Nathan, in the writing of the so-called "Gospel according to John," at Ephesus, when he was ninety-nine years old. Of all the twelve apostles, John Zebedee eventually became the outstanding theologian. He died a natural death at Ephesus in A.D. 103 when he was one hundred and one years of age.

139:5. Philip The Curious

Philip was twenty-seven years of age when he joined the apostles; he had recently been married, but he had no children at this time. Philip was always wanting to be shown; the lack of imagination was the great weakness of his character. It was Philip's duty to see that they were at all times supplied with provisions, and he was a good steward. His strongest characteristic was his methodical thoroughness. He was the typical everyday and commonplace average man. Philip was greatly lacking in spiritual insight and asked many foolish questions. He was a very persuasive and successful personal worker. He was not easily discouraged. The one quality about Jesus which Philip so continuously admired was the Master's unfailing generosity.

Philip was the first to go forth to win souls for the kingdom outside of the immediate Jewish ranks. His wife was an efficient member of the women's corps, a fearless woman. She stood at the foot of Philip's cross encouraging him to proclaim the glad tidings even to his murderers, and when his strength failed, she began the recital of the story of salvation by faith in Jesus and was silenced only when the irate Jews rushed upon her and stoned her to death. Their eldest daughter, Leah, continued their work, later on becoming the renowned prophetess of Hierapolis. Philip was a mighty man in the kingdom and he was finally crucified for his faith and buried at Hierapolis.

139:6. Honest Nathaniel

When Nathaniel joined the apostles, he was twenty-five years old and was the next to the youngest of the group. He was the youngest of a family of seven, unmarried, and the only support of aged and infirm parents with whom he lived at Cana. Nathaniel and Judas Iscariot were the two best educated men among the apostles. Nathaniel's duty was to look after the families of the twelve.

Nathaniel was both honest and sincere. The weakness of his character was his pride. He was disposed to prejudge individuals in accordance with his personal opinions. In many respects Nathaniel was the odd genius of the twelve. He was the apostolic philosopher and dreamer, but he was a very practical sort of dreamer. He was probably the best storyteller among the twelve. Judas did not think Nathaniel took his apostleship sufficiently seriously. Many times when things were becoming tense and tangled among the apostles Nathaniel would relieve the tension by a bit of philosophy or a flash of humor; good humor, too. What Nathanial most revered about Jesus was his tolerance and broadmindedness.

Nathaniel went into Mesopotamia and India proclaiming the glad tidings of the kingdom and baptizing believers. He was a great man in the kingdom and died in India.

139:7. Matthew Levi

Matthew was a publican, a customs collector in Capernaum, where he lived. He was thirty-one years old and married and had four children. He was a man of moderate wealth, the only one of any means belonging to the apostolic corps. He was a good business man and was gifted with the ability to make friends and to get along smoothly with a great variety of people. Andrew appointed Matthew the financial representative of the apostles. He did all his financial work in a quiet and personal way and raised most of the money among the more substantial class of interested believers. He gave practically the whole of his modest fortune to the work of the Master and his apostles, but they never knew of this generosity, save Jesus, who knew all about it. Matthew was a keen judge of human nature and a very efficient propagandist. His strong point was his wholehearted devotion to the cause; his weakness was his shortsighted and materialistic viewpoint of life. It was the Master's forgiving disposition which Matthew most appreciated.

He was one of the apostles who made extensive notes on the sayings of Jesus, and these notes were used as the basis of Isador's narrative which has become known as the Gospel according to Matthew. Matthew journeyed north, preaching the gospel of the kingdom and baptizing believers. It was in Thrace, at Lysimachia, that certain unbelieving Jews conspired with the Roman soldiers to encompass his death.

139:8. Thomas Didymus

When Thomas joined the apostles, he was twenty-nine years old, was married, had four children, and resided at Tarichea. He grew up having a very disagreeable and quarrelsome disposition. Even his wife was glad to see him join the apostles. But the better his associates knew Thomas, the more they liked him. They found he was superbly honest and unflinchingly loyal. Thomas was the real scientist of the apostolic group. He had a logical, skeptical type of mind, but he had a form of courageous loyalty which forbade those who knew him intimately to regard him as a trifling skeptic. Thomas's great strength was his superb analytical mind coupled with his unflinching courage—when he had once made up his mind. His great weakness was his suspicious doubting. In the organization of the twelve Thomas was assigned to arrange and manage the itinerary. He was a good executive, an excellent businessman, but he was handicapped by his many moods. Thomas revered his Master because of his superbly balanced character. He probably enjoyed the highest intellectual understanding and personality appreciation of Jesus of any of the twelve. Again and again would he stand out against some project as being foolhardy and presumptuous, but after the twelve would elect to do that which he had so strenuously opposed, Thomas was the first to say, "Let's go! "He was a good loser." As far as personal physical courage was concerned, he was one of the bravest among the twelve. Thomas is the great example of a human being who has doubts, faces them, and wins.

Thomas had a trying time during the days of the trial and crucifixion. For a while he succumbed to his doubting depression but eventually rallied his faith and courage. He gave wise counsel to the apostles after Pentecost and went to Cyprus, Crete, the North African coast, and Sicily, preaching the glad tidings of the kingdom and baptizing believers until he was apprehended by the agents of the Roman government and was put to death in Malta. Just a few weeks before his death he had begun the writing of the life and teachings of Jesus.

139:9 and 139:10. James and Judas Alpheus

James and Judas were the sons of Alpheus, the twin fishermen living near Kheresa. They were twenty-six years old and married, James having three children, Judas two. There is not much to be said about these two commonplace fisherfolk. They loved their Master and Jesus loved them. Andrew assigned them to the work of policing the multitudes. They were always ready to lend a helping hand to any one of the apostles. James and Judas had neither strong points nor weak points. James especially loved Jesus because of the Master's simplicity. Judas was drawn toward Jesus because of the Master's unostentatious humility. They were simple and ignorant, but they were also big-hearted, kind, and generous.

The twins served faithfully until the end and (save John) they were the first to believe in his resurrection. Soon after their Master was crucified, they returned to their families and nets; their work was done.

139:11. Simon the Zealot

Simon Zelotes was an able man of good ancestry and lived with his family at Capernaum. He was twenty-eight years old when he became attached to the apostles. He was a fiery agitator and was also a man who spoke much without thinking. Simon Zelotes was given charge of the diversions and relaxation of the apostolic group. Simon's strength was his inspirational loyalty; his great weakness was his material-mindedness. The one thing about Jesus which Simon so admired was the Master's calmness, his assurance, poise, and inexplicable composure. Simon was a great debater; he did like to argue. He was a rebel by nature and an iconoclast by training. After the dispersion because of the Jerusalem persecutions, Simon went into temporary retirement. He was in despair, but in a few years he rallied his hopes and went forth to proclaim the gospel of the kingdom. He went to Alexandria and, after working up the Nile, penetrated into the heart of Africa. Thus he labored until he was an old man and feeble. and he died and was buried in the heart of Africa.

139:12. Judas Iscariot

Judas Iscariot was thirty years of age and unmarried when he joined the apostles. He was probably the best-educated man among the twelve and the only Judean in the Master's apostolic family. Judas was an only son of unwise parents. As he grew up, he had exaggerated ideas about his self-importance. His parents were Sadducees, and when their son joined John's disciples, they disowned him. Andrew appointed Judas treasurer of the twelve, a position which he was eminently fitted to hold. Judas really was a great executive, a farseeing and able financier. He was a stickler for organization. He was always financially loyal to his Master and his fellow apostles. Money could never have been the motive for his betrayal of the Master. Judas had no outstanding trait of personal strength, though he had many outwardly appearing traits of culture and habits of training. He was a good thinker but not always a truly honest thinker. He was a poor loser. His sense of values and loyalties was defective. There was no special trait about Jesus which Judas admired above the generally attractive and exquisitely charming personality of the Master. He really entertained the notion that Jesus was timid and somewhat afraid to assert his own power and authority. Judas grew intellectually regarding Jesus' teachings about the kingdom, but he did not make progress in the acquirement of spiritual character as did the other apostles. The Master many times, both privately and publicly, had warned Judas that he was slipping, but divine warnings are usually useless in dealing with embittered human nature. Judas entered into the base and shameful intrigue to betray his Lord and Master and quickly carried the nefarious scheme into effect.

When the sordid and sinful business was all over, this renegade mortal rushed out and committed the final act in the drama of fleeing from the realities of mortal existence—suicide. The worlds have found it difficult to forgive Judas, and his name has become eschewed throughout a far-flung universe.

Paper 140: The Ordination of the Twelve

JUST before noon on Sunday, January 12, A.D. 27, Jesus called the apostles together for their ordination as public preachers of the gospel of the kingdom. When he had assembled all twelve, he journeyed with them to the highlands north of Capernaum where he proceeded to instruct them in preparation for their formal ordination.

140:1. Preliminary Instruction

Jesus told them in part, "The new kingdom which my Father is about to set up in the hearts of his earth children is to be an everlasting dominion. The power of this kingdom shall consist in the glory of the divine spirit that shall come to teach the minds and rule the hearts of the reborn citizens of this heavenly kingdom. Faith alone will pass you through its portals, but you must bring forth the fruits of my Father's spirit if you would continue to ascend in the progressive life of the divine fellowship. Your message to the world shall be: Seek first the kingdom of God and his righteousness, and in finding these, all other things essential to eternal survival shall be secured therewith. Whosoever would become great in the Father's kingdom shall become a minister to all. And it will not be so much by the words you speak as by the lives you live that men will know you have learned of the realities of the kingdom. "And while I would lay no grievous burdens upon your minds, I am about to put upon your souls the solemn responsibility of representing me in the world when I shall presently leave you as I now represent my Father in this life which I am living in the flesh."

140:2. The Ordination

Jesus now instructed the twelve mortals to kneel in a circle about him. He then placed his hands upon the head of each apostle. When he had blessed them, he extended his hands and prayed, "My Father, I now bring to you these men, my messengers. From among our children on earth I have chosen these twelve to go forth to represent me as I came forth to represent you. Love them and be with them as you have loved and been with me. And now, my Father, give these men wisdom as I place all the affairs of the coming kingdom in their hands. And I would, if it is your will, tarry on earth a time to help them in their labors for the kingdom. And again, my Father, I thank you for these men, and I commit them to your keeping while I go on to finish the work you have given me to do." Thus the Creator of the universe placing the affairs of the divine brotherhood of man under the direction of human minds.

140:3. The Ordination Sermon

Then Jesus spoke, saying, "Now that you are ambassadors of my Father's kingdom, you have thereby become a class of men separate and distinct from all other men on earth. You are not now as men among men but as the enlightened citizens of another and heavenly country among the ignorant creatures of this dark world. When you find my children in distress, speak encouragingly to them, saying, 'Happy are the poor in spirit, the humble, for theirs are the treasures of the kingdom of heaven; happy are they who hunger and thirst for righteousness, for they shall be filled; happy are the meek, for they shall inherit the earth; happy are the pure in heart, for they shall see God; happy are they who mourn, for they shall be comforted; happy are they who weep, for they shall receive the spirit of rejoicing; happy are the merciful, for they shall obtain mercy; happy are the peacemakers, for they shall be called the sons of God; happy are they who are persecuted for righteousness' sake, for theirs is the kingdom of heaven; happy are you when men shall revile you and persecute you and shall say all manner of evil against you falsely; rejoice and be exceedingly glad, for great is your reward in heaven.'"

140:4. You are the Salt of the Earth

The so-called "Sermon on the Mount" was Jesus' ordination charge to the twelve apostles. In part, he told them, "You are the salt of the earth," "You are the light of the world," "Let your light so shine before men that they may see your good works and be led to glorify your Father who is in heaven," "By their fruits you shall know them." While light dispels darkness, it can also be so "blinding" as to confuse and frustrate. Unselfishness is the badge of human greatness. The highest levels of self-realization are attained by worship and service. Personality is basically changeless; that which changes—grows—is the moral character. While inherited urges cannot be fundamentally modified, emotional responses to such urges can be changed. Without a worthy goal, life becomes aimless and unprofitable, and much unhappiness results. Education should be a technique of learning (discovering) the better methods of gratifying our natural and inherited urges. Happiness is little dependent on environment, though pleasing surroundings may greatly contribute thereto.

140:5. Fatherly and Brotherly Love

Jesus taught his followers to manifest *fatherly* love rather than *brotherly* love. Fatherly affection would require that you should love your fellow mortals as Jesus loves you. The Master introduced this momentous discourse by calling attention to four faith attitudes as the prelude to the subsequent portrayal of his four transcendent and supreme reactions of fatherly love. He first talked about those who were poor in spirit, hungered after righteousness, endured meekness, and who were pure in heart. Such spirit-discerning mortals could be expected to attain such levels of divine selflessness as to be able to attempt the amazing exercise of fatherly affection; that even as mourners they would be empowered to show mercy, promote peace, and endure persecutions, and throughout all of these trying situations to love even unlovely mankind with a fatherly love. To see God—by faith—means to acquire true spiritual insight. And spiritual insight enhances Adjuster guidance, and these in the end augment God-consciousness. Fatherly love delights in returning good for evil.

140:6. The Evening of the Ordination

Andrew told Jesus the apostles had trouble understanding the teachings regarding the kingdom. To the twelve gathered in the Zebedee garden Jesus said in part, "You find it difficult to receive my message because you would build the new teaching directly upon the old, but I declare that you must be reborn. If you would enter the kingdom, you must have a righteousness that consists in love, mercy, and truth—the sincere desire to do the will of my Father in heaven." Jesus explained that the Father evaluates people by the inner motivation of their thoughts, their intents and real desires. He said that he had come not to teach them rules of government, trade, or social behavior but to comfort the minds, liberate the spirits, and save the souls of man. They were not to interpret his message literally, but to discern the spirit of his teachings. At the request of Peter for a private conference, Jesus met with each of the twelve, except the twins who were asleep, for a private meeting.

140:7. The Week Following the Ordination

Jesus suggested that they prepare to go to Jerusalem to preach and teach, but when Thomas said he felt the need for more training Jesus agreed to continue his instruction. During the week of further training the apostles also met with the many people who came asking about the coming kingdom. Andrew would select one of the apostles and assign him to a group of visitors, and sometimes all twelve of them were so engaged. Jesus many times repeated to his apostles the two great motives of his postbaptismal mission on earth: 1. to reveal the Father to man; 2. to lead men to become son-conscious—to faith-realize that they are the children of the Most High.

At the last conference, Peter and James came to Jesus, saying, "We are ready—let us now go forth to take the kingdom." To which Jesus replied, "May your wisdom equal your zeal and your courage atone for your ignorance." Though the apostles failed to comprehend much of Jesus' teaching, they did not fail to grasp the significance of the charmingly beautiful life he lived with them.

140:8. Thursday Afternoon on the Lake

Jesus well knew that his apostles were not fully assimilating his teachings. He decided to give some special instruction in a boat to Peter, James, and John, hoping they would be able to clarify the ideas of their associates. He taught the active and alert submission to God's will. And he made it plain on this afternoon that he approved of the social punishment of evildoers and criminals. We should have faith—confidence in the eventual triumph of divine justice and eternal goodness. Never make the mistake of identifying Jesus' teachings with any political or economic theory, with any social or industrial system. He made it clear that indiscriminate kindness may be blamed for many social evils. It seemed to be his purpose in all social situations to teach patience, tolerance, and forgiveness. The family occupied the very center of Jesus' philosophy of life here and hereafter, but he repeatedly refused to lay down laws regarding marriage and divorce. He made no direct attack on the possession of property, but he did insist that it is eternally essential that spiritual values come first. What he aimed at in his life appears to have been a superb self-respect. Fidelity was a cardinal virtue in his estimate of character, while courage was the very heart of his teachings. The three apostles were shocked this afternoon when they realized that their Master's religion made no provision for spiritual self-examination. But Jesus said nothing which would proscribe self-analysis as a prevention of conceited egotism. Jesus' teaching stands apart from all religions, as such, albeit it is the living hope of every one of them. He exalted love—truth, beauty, and goodness—as the divine ideal and the eternal reality.

140:9. The Day of Consecration

This Sabbath afternoon Jesus assembled the apostles around him on the hillside and reviewed many features of the ordination sermon. Then, calling them before him one by one, he commissioned them to go forth in the world as his representatives. The Master's consecration charge was: "Go into all the world and preach the glad tidings of the kingdom. Liberate spiritual captives, comfort the oppressed, and minister to the afflicted. Freely you have received, freely give." Jesus advised them to take neither money nor extra clothing. And finally he said, "Behold I send you forth as sheep in the midst of wolves; be you therefore as wise as serpents and as harmless as doves."

140:10. The Evening After the Consecration

That evening while teaching in the house, Jesus talked at great length, trying to show the twelve what they must *be*, not what they must *do*. He reiterated, "In the kingdom you must *be* righteous in order to do the work." Many times did he repeat, "*Be* you therefore perfect, even as your Father in heaven is perfect." It was a difficult task to persuade these Galilean fishermen that, in the kingdom, *being* righteous, by faith, must precede *doing* righteousness in the daily life of the mortals of earth.

Another great handicap in this work of teaching the twelve was their tendency to take highly idealistic and spiritual principles of religious truth and remake them into concrete rules of personal conduct. Jesus lived his earth life on Urantia, not to set a personal example of mortal living for the men and women of this world, but rather to create *a high spiritual and inspirational ideal* for all mortal beings on all worlds.

That same evening, while eating supper, Jesus explained that the morality of any act is determined by the individual's motive. John asked Jesus, "Master, what is the kingdom of heaven?" Jesus answered, "The kingdom of heaven consists in these three essentials: first, recognition of the fact of the sovereignty of God; second, belief in the truth of sonship with God; and third, faith in the effectiveness of the supreme human desire to do the will of God—to be like God. And this is the good news of the gospel: that by faith every mortal may have all these essentials of salvation."

Paper 141: Beginning the Public Work

ON January 19, A.D. 27, Jesus and the twelve apostles made ready to depart for Jerusalem. Just before leaving, the apostles missed the Master, and Andrew went out to find him. After a brief search he found Jesus sitting in a boat down the beach, and he was weeping. And Jesus, going back with

Andrew to join the twelve, said to him, "No one of you has grieved me. I am saddened only because none of my father Joseph's family have remembered to come over to bid us Godspeed."

141:1. Leaving Galilee

They tarried near Pella for more than two weeks, teaching and preaching. By the end of the first week several hundred people had assembled. Jesus did no public preaching. Andrew divided the multitude and assigned the preachers for the forenoon and afternoon assemblies; after the evening meal Jesus talked with the twelve. On one of these evenings he told them something about the forty days which he spent in the hills near this place. From night to night Andrew carefully instructed his fellow apostles in the delicate and difficult task of getting along smoothly with the followers of John the Baptist.

During this first year of Jesus' public ministry more than three fourths of his followers had previously followed John and had received his baptism. This entire year of A.D. 27 was spent in quietly taking over John's work in Perea and Judea.

141:2. God's Law and the Father's Will

The night before they left Pella, Jesus gave the apostles some further instruction with regard to the new kingdom. He told them that the kingdom of heaven is the realization and acknowledgement of God's rule within the hearts of man. When the Father's will is your law, you are hardly in the kingdom. But when the Father's will becomes truly *your* will, then are you in very truth in the kingdom. Some of the apostles grasped something of this teaching, but none of them comprehended the full significance of this tremendous announcement, unless it was James Zebedee.

141:3. The Sojourn at Amathus

The Master and his apostles remained near Amathus for almost three weeks. Peter, James, and John did most of the public preaching. Philip, Nathaniel, Thomas, and Simon did much of the personal work. Jesus was truly a master of men. There was a subtle commanding influence in his rugged, nomadic, and homeless life. There was intellectual attractiveness and spiritual drawing power in his authoritative manner of teaching, in his lucid logic, his strength of reasoning, his sagacious insight, his alertness of mind, his matchless poise, and his sublime tolerance. With all of this physical and intellectual influence manifest in the Master's presence, there were also all those spiritual charms of being which have become associated with his personality—patience, tenderness, meekness, gentleness, and humility. Jesus of

Nazareth was indeed a strong and forceful personality; he was an intellectual power and a spiritual stronghold. His personality not only appealed to the spiritually minded women among his followers, but also to the educated and intellectual Nicodemus and to the hardy Roman soldier, and red-blooded, rugged Galilean fishermen called him Master.

141:4. Teaching about the Father

Jesus spent much time with the apostles instructing them in the new concept of God; again and again did he impress upon them that *God is a Father*, not a great and supreme bookkeeper to subsequently sit in judgment upon them. In answer to Thomas's question, "Who is this God of the kingdom?" Jesus replied, "God is your Father, and religion—my gospel—is nothing more nor less than the believing recognition of the truth that you are his son." He told them about diseases of the body, mind difficulties, and the possession of evil spirits, but told them that evil spirits would not trouble people after he sends the Spirit of Truth.

141:5. Spiritual Unity

One of the most eventful of all the evening conferences at Amathus was the session having to do with the discussion of spiritual unity. James Zebedee had asked, "Master, how shall we learn to see alike and thereby enjoy more harmony among ourselves?" Jesus replied in part, "James, James, when did I teach you that you should all see alike? You do not have to see alike or feel alike or even think alike in order spiritually to be alike. Your apostolic harmony must grow out of the fact that the spirit hope of each of you is identical in origin, nature, and destiny."

Repeatedly he told them it was not his desire that those who believed in him should become dogmatized and standardized. Again and again he warned his apostles against the formulation of creeds and the establishment of traditions as a means of guiding and controlling believers in the gospel of the kingdom.

141:6. Last Week at Amathus

Near the end of the last week at Amathus, Simon Zelotes brought to Jesus one Teherma, a Persian doing business at Damascus. When Simon Zelotes and Jesus were alone, Simon asked the Master, "Why is it that I could not persuade him? Why did he so resist me and so readily lend an ear to you?" Jesus answered, "Simon, Simon, how many times have I instructed you to refrain from all efforts to take something out of the hearts of those who seek salvation? How often have I told you to labor only to put something into these hungry souls? Lead men into the kingdom, and the great and living truths of the kingdom will presently drive out all serious error." That night

Jesus discoursed to the apostles on the new life in the kingdom. He said in part, "When you enter the kingdom, you are reborn. You cannot teach the deep things of the spirit to those who have been born only of the flesh; first see that men are born of the spirit before you seek to instruct them in the advanced ways of the spirit."

141:7. At Bethany Beyond Jordan

The second week of the sojourn at Bethany beyond Jordan, Jesus took Peter, James, and John into the hills for a three days' rest. The Master taught these three many new and advanced truths about the kingdom of heaven. He sought to impress upon all teachers of the gospel of the kingdom that their only business was to reveal God to the individual man as his Father. Jesus made it plain that he had come to establish personal and eternal relations with men which should forever take precedence over all other human relationships. The only reward which he held out for his children was: in this world—spiritual joy and divine communion; in the next world—eternal life in the progress of the divine spirit realities of the Paradise Father. Jesus laid great emphasis upon what he called the two truths of first import in the teachings of the kingdom: the attainment of salvation by faith, and faith alone, associated with the revolutionary teaching of the attainment of human liberty through the sincere recognition of truth—"You shall know the truth, and the truth shall make you free."

141:8. Working in Jericho

Throughout the four weeks' sojourn at Bethany, several times each week Andrew would assign apostolic couples to go up to Jericho for a day or two. On these Jericho visits the apostles began more specifically to carry out Jesus' instructions to minister to the sick; they visited every house in the city and sought to comfort every afflicted person. In Jericho they were overtaken by a delegation from Mesopotamia that had come to confer with Jesus. The apostles had planned to spend but a day here, but when these truth seekers from the East arrived, Jesus spent three days with them, and they returned to their various homes along the Euphrates happy in the knowledge of the new truths of the kingdom of heaven.

141:9. Departing for Jerusalem

On Monday, the last day of March, Jesus and the apostles began their journey up the hills toward Jerusalem. Lazarus of Bethany had been down to the Jordan twice to see Jesus, and every arrangement had been made for the Master and his apostles to make their headquarters with Lazarus and his sisters at Bethany as long as they might desire to stay in Jerusalem. Here Jesus and the apostles tarried for five days, resting and refreshing themselves. On Sunday morning, April 6, Jesus and the apostles went down to Jerusalem; and this was the first time the Master and all of the twelve had been there together.

Paper 142: The Passover at Jerusalem

THE first day in Jerusalem Jesus called upon his friend of former years, Annas, the onetime high priest and relative of Salome, Zebedee's wife. When Jesus perceived Annas's coldness, he took immediate leave, saying as he departed, "Fear is man's chief enslaver and pride his great weakness; will you betray yourself into bondage to both of these destroyers of joy and liberty?" But Annas made no reply. The Master did not again see Annas until the time when Annas sat with his son-in-law in judgment on the Son of Man.

142:1. Teaching in the Temple

Throughout this month Jesus or one of the apostles taught daily in the temple. The multitudes who came to celebrate the Passover heard this teaching of Jesus, and hundreds of them rejoiced in the good news. The chief priests and rulers of the Jews became much concerned about Jesus and his apostles and debated among themselves as to what should be done with them. These interested men and women carried the news of Jesus' message from this Passover celebration to the uttermost parts of the Roman Empire and also to the East. This was the beginning of the spread of the gospel of the kingdom to the outside world. No longer was the work of Jesus to be confined to Palestine.

142:2. God's Wrath

There was in Jerusalem in attendance upon the Passover festivities one Jacob, a wealthy Jewish trader from Crete, and he came to Andrew making request to see Jesus privately. Andrew arranged this secret meeting with Jesus at Flavius's home the evening of the next day. Said Jacob to Jesus, "But, Rabbi, Moses and the olden prophets tell us that Yahweh is a jealous God, a God of great wrath and fierce anger." Jesus explained that immature children may see their father as angry when they need to be chastised but as they grow up they discern their father's love in these early disciplines. So also with immature cultures but now Jesus said he has come to reveal the loving nature of the Father in heaven. You, Jacob, should now rejoice to enter the kingdom and have his will of love dominate your life. And Jacob answered, "Rabbi, I believe; I desire that you lead me into the Father's kingdom."

142:3. The Concept of God

The twelve apostles that night asked Jesus many questions about the Father in heaven. The Master proceed to instruct them about the evolution of the concept of Deity: 1. Yahweh—the god of the Sinai clans; 2. the Most High—the concept of the Father, El Elyon, proclaimed by Melchizedek; 3. El Shaddai—the Egyptian concept of the God of heaven; 4. Elohim—the teaching of the Paradise Trinity; 5. The Supreme Yahweh—the concept of a Universal Creator who was simultaneously all-powerful and all-merciful; 6. the Father in heaven—our teaching provides a religion wherein the believer is a son of God.

Never before had the apostles been so shocked as they were upon hearing this recounting of the growth of the concept of God.

142:4. Flavius and Greek Culture

Flavius, the Greek Jew, was a great lover of the beautiful in art and sculpture, the house which he occupied when sojourning in Jerusalem was a beautiful edifice. Flavius was agreeably surprised when Jesus entered the home that, instead of rebuking him for having these supposedly idolatrous objects scattered about the house, he manifested great interest in the entire collection. Said Jesus in part, "In an age when my Father was not well understood, Moses was justified in his attempts to withstand idolatry. Henceforth, intelligent men may enjoy the treasures of art without confusing such material appreciation of beauty with the worship and service of the Father in Paradise, the God of all things and all beings."

Flavius believed all that Jesus taught him. The next day he went to Bethany beyond the Jordan and was baptized by the disciples of John.

142:5. The Discourse on Assurance

One of the great sermons which Jesus preached in the temple this Passover week was in answer to a question asked by a man from Damascus: "But, Rabbi, how shall we know of a certainty that you are sent by God, and that we may truly enter into this kingdom which you and your disciples declare is near at hand?" Jesus told him that they should judge their message by their fruits. If we proclaim to you the truths of the spirit, the spirit will witness in your hearts that our message is genuine. If you do the will of the Father in heaven, you shall never fail in the attainment of the eternal life of progress in the divine kingdom. The evidence to all the world that you have been born of the spirit is that you sincerely love one another.

142:6. The Visit with Nicodemus

One evening at the home of Flavius there came to see Jesus one Nicodemus, a wealthy and elderly member of the Jewish Sanhedrin. Nicodemus informed Jesus that he wanted to know more about Jesus' teaching of the coming kingdom. Jesus told Nicodemus that one must be born again from above to see the kingdom of God. "How can this be?" countered Nicodemus.

Jesus explained that just as one cannot see the wind but can observe its effect, so it is with everyone born of the spirit.

Nicodemus was thoroughly sincere and did summon faith enough to lay hold of the kingdom. He faintly protested when his colleagues of the Sanhedrin sought to condemn Jesus without a hearing; and with Joseph of Arimathea, he later boldly acknowledged his faith and claimed the body of Jesus, even when most of the disciples had fled in fear from the scenes of their Master's final suffering and death.

142:7. The Lesson on the Family

After the busy period of teaching and personal work of Passover week in Jerusalem, Jesus spent the next Wednesday at Bethany with his apostles, resting. Thomas wanted to know how they should teach people to live after the kingdom more fully comes. Very plainly Jesus explained that the kingdom of heaven was an evolutionary experience, beginning here on earth and progressing up through successive life stations to Paradise. People in another age will understand the gospel of the kingdom when it is presented in terms expressive of the family relationship. And then he explained that such a quality of brotherly affection would invariably manifest itself in unselfish and loving social service. In the family we must recognize: 1. the fact of existence—parenthood is inherent in nature; 2. security and pleasure; 3. education and training; 4. discipline and restraint; 5. companionship and loyalty; 6. love and mercy—real families are built upon tolerance, patience, and forgiveness; and 7. provision for the future. Jesus emphasized that his teaching should be understood in their spiritual meaning, not translated into the language of the flesh.

142:8. In Southern Judea

By the end of April the opposition to Jesus among the Pharisees and Sadducees had become so pronounced that the Master and his apostles decided to leave Jerusalem for a while, going south to work in Bethlehem and Hebron. While the apostles taught the gospel and ministered to the sick, Jesus and Abner spent at Engedi, visiting the Nazarite colony. This sojourn in the south of Judea was a restful and fruitful season of labor; many souls were added to the kingdom. By the first days of June the agitation against Jesus had so quieted down in Jerusalem that the Master and the apostles returned to instruct and comfort believers. And thus affairs moved along quietly until the last days of June, when one Simon, a member of the Sanhedrin, publicly espoused the teachings of Jesus, after so declaring himself before the rulers of the Jews. Immediately a new agitation for Jesus' apprehension sprang up and grew so strong that the Master decided to retire into the cities of Samaria and the Decapolis.

Paper 143: Going Through Samaria

AT the end of June, A.D. 27, because of the increasing opposition of the Jewish religious rulers, Jesus and the twelve departed from Jerusalem. The people of southern Samaria heard Jesus gladly, and the apostles, with the exception of Judas Iscariot, succeeded in overcoming much of their prejudice against the Samaritans. The last week of July, Jesus and his associates made ready to depart for the new Greek cities of Phasaelis and Archelais near the Jordan.

143:1. Preaching at Archelais

The apostolic party had their first experience preaching to well-nigh exclusive gatherings of gentiles—Greeks, Romans, and Syrians. The apostles told Jesus the Romans and Greeks make light of their message, claiming that it is fit for only weaklings and slaves who would soon perish from the face of the earth. The Master responded by telling them that the Father in Paradise does rule the universe of universes by the compelling power of his love. "Love is the greatest of all spirit realities. Truth is a liberating revelation, but love is the supreme relationship." He asked them if John looked like a weakling or did they see him enslaved by fear? Jesus assured them that the service of the kingdom on earth would call for all the courageous manhood that they and their coworkers could muster. Many of them would be put to death for their loyalty to the gospel of the kingdom. This was one of the most impassioned addresses which Jesus ever delivered to the twelve. The result upon the public preaching and personal ministry of the apostles was immediate; from that very day their message took on a new note of courageous dominance.

143:2. Lesson on Self-Mastery

Andrew asked Jesus if they were to practice self-denial as John taught or were they to strive for the self-control of Jesus' teaching? The Master replied that he had come with a new message of self-forgetfulness and self-control. The new law of the spirit endows you with the liberty of self-mastery in place of the old law of the fear of self-bondage and the slavery of self-denial. The Father's children who have been born of the spirit are ever and always masters of the self and all that pertains to the desires of the flesh. Your secret of the mastery of self is bound up with your faith in the indwelling spirit, which ever works by love. If you are born of the spirit, you are forever delivered from the self-conscious bondage of a life of self-denial and watchcare over the desires of the flesh, and you are translated into the joyous kingdom of the spirit, and the fruits of the spirit are the essence of the highest type of enjoyable and ennobling self-control—true self-mastery.

143:3. Diversion and Relaxation

About this time a state of great nervous and emotional tension developed among the apostles and their immediate disciple associates. Andrew consulted with Jesus who suggested they take a three day period for rest and relaxation on Mount Sartaba. Jesus told Andrew to privately advise each person not to mention any of their problems while on this rest period. Upon reaching the top of the mountain, Jesus seated them about him while he said, "My brethren, you must all learn the value of rest and the efficacy of relaxation. You must realize that the best method of solving some entangled problems is to forsake them for a time. Then when you go back fresh from your rest or worship, you are able to attack your troubles with a clearer head and a steadier hand, not to mention a more resolute heart." The third day when they started down the mountain and back to their camp, a great change had come over them. Their return from this holiday marked the beginning of a period of greatly improved relations with the followers of John.

143:4. The Jews and the Samaritans

For more than six hundred years the Jews had been at enmity with the Samaritans. This religious enmity dated from the return of the former from the Babylonian captivity, when the Samaritans worked to prevent the rebuilding of Jerusalem. It was a severe test of their loyalty to the Master when he said, "Let us go into Samaria." But in the year and more they had been with Jesus, they had developed a form of personal loyalty which transcended even their faith in his teachings and their prejudices against the Samaritans.

143:5. The Woman of Sychar

When the Master and the twelve arrived at Jacob's well, Jesus, being weary from the journey, tarried by the well while Philip took the apostles with him to assist in bringing food and tents from Sychar. When a woman of Sychar came up with her water pitcher and prepared to draw from the well, Jesus said to her, "Give me a drink." Her name was Nalda and she was minded openly to become flirtatious. Jesus commanded her to bring her husband, and when she said she had no husband, Jesus told her that the man she was living with was not her husband. He further told her that if she could only understand, she would ask him for a draught of the living water. Nalda apologized and asked for this living water. She then avoided seeking help for her soul by asking a theological question, and then said that the Deliverer that John told about would declare all things. And Jesus, interrupting Nalda, said with startling assurance, "I who speak to you am he."

This was the first direct, positive, and undisguised pronouncement of his divine nature and sonship which Jesus had made on earth; and it was made to a woman, a Samaritan woman, and a woman of questionable character in the eyes of men up to this moment, but a woman whom the divine eye beheld as having been sinned against more than as sinning of her own desire and as now being a human soul who desired salvation, desired it sincerely and wholeheartedly, and that was enough. Nalda returned to the city, and ere the sun went down, a great crowd had assembled at Jacob's well to hear Jesus.

143:6. The Samaritan Revival

The twelve had just returned with food, and they besought Jesus to eat with them. But Jesus knew that darkness would soon be upon them; so he persisted in his determination to talk to the people before he sent them away. Jesus and the apostles went into Sychar and preached two days before they established their camp on Mount Gerizim. And many of the dwellers in Sychar believed the gospel.

Jesus spoke to the apostles about the realities which are central in the kingdom of God. In any religion it is easy to allow values to become disproportionate and to permit facts to occupy the place of truth in one's theology. The fact of the cross became the center of Christianity but it not the central truth of the life and teachings of Jesus of Nazareth. And again and again he impressed upon them that love is the greatest relationship in the universe.

143:7. Teachings about Prayer and Worship

True religion is the act of an individual soul in its self-conscious relations with the Creator; organized religion is man's attempt to socialize the worship of individual religionists. Worship—contemplation of the spiritual—must alternate with service, contact with material reality. Work should alternate with play; religion should be balanced by humor. Prayer is designed to make man less thinking but more realizing; it is not designed to increase knowledge but rather to expand insight. Worship is intended to anticipate the better life ahead and then to reflect these new spiritual significances back onto the life which now is. Worship is the technique of looking to the One for the inspiration of service to the many. Prayer is self-reminding—sublime thinking; worship is self-forgetting—superthinking. Worship is the act of a part identifying itself with the Whole; the finite with the Infinite; the son with the Father; time in the act of striking step with eternity.

Paper 144: At Gilboa and the Decapolis

THE month of September Jesus spent here alone with his apostles, teaching and instructing them in the truths of the kingdom. He knew that the days of the preliminary work of teaching and preaching were about over.

Jesus had therefore decided to spend some time in retirement rehearsing his apostles and then to do some quiet work in the cities of the Decapolis until John should be either executed or released to join them in a united effort.

144:1. The Gilboa Encampment

As time passed, the twelve became more devoted to Jesus and increasingly committed to the work of the kingdom. Their devotion was in large part a matter of personal loyalty. Jesus told the twelve much about his early life and his experiences on Mount Hermon; he also revealed something of what happened in the hills during the forty days immediately after his baptism. And he directly charged them that they should tell no man about these experiences until after he had returned to the Father. Much of this time Jesus was alone on the mountain near the camp in personal communion with his Father. The central theme of the discussions throughout the entire month of September was prayer and worship. The twelve longed to know what form of petition Jesus would approve. And it was chiefly because of this need for some simple petition for the common people that Jesus at this time consented to teach them a suggestive form of prayer.

144:2. The Discourse on Prayer

The ideal prayer is a form of spiritual communion which leads to intelligent worship. True praying is the sincere attitude of reaching heavenward for the attainment of your ideals. Prayer is the breath of the soul and should lead you to be persistent in your attempt to ascertain the Father's will. Ask and it shall be given you; seek and you shall find; knock and it shall be opened to you. Men ought always to pray and not become discouraged. Your persistence, however, is not to win favor with God but to change your earth attitude and to enlarge your soul's capacity for spirit receptivity. Genuine faith will remove mountains of material difficulty which may chance to lie in the path of soul expansion and spiritual progress.

144:3. The Believer's Prayer

But the apostles were not yet satisfied; they desired Jesus to give them a model prayer which they could teach the new disciples. Jesus said, "If, then, you still desire such a prayer, I would present the one which I taught my brothers and sisters in Nazareth: "Our Father who is in heaven, hallowed be your name. Your kingdom come; your will be done on earth as it is in heaven. Give us this day our bread for tomorrow; refresh our souls with the water of life. And forgive us every one our debts, as we also have forgiven our debtors. Save us in temptation, deliver us from evil, and increasingly make us perfect like yourself.

Jesus taught the twelve always to pray in secret. Jesus taught that effective prayer must be unselfish, believing, sincere, intelligent, and trustful—in submission to the Father's all-wise will. When Jesus spent whole nights in prayer, it was mainly for his disciples, particularly for the twelve. The Master prayed very little for himself.

144:4. More about Prayer

The earnest and longing repetition of any petition never fails to expand the soul's capacity for spiritual receptivity. The soul's spiritual capacity for receptivity determines the quantity of heavenly blessings which can be personally appropriated and consciously realized as an answer to prayer. Prayer is an antidote for harmful introspection. As prayer may be likened to recharging the spiritual batteries of the soul, so worship may be compared to the act of tuning in the soul to catch the universe broadcasts of the infinite spirit of the Universal Father. Prayer is a psychologic process of exchanging the human will for the divine will. Prayer is a part of the divine plan for making over that which is into that which ought to be.

144:5. Other Forms of Prayer

From time to time, during the remainder of Jesus' sojourn on earth, he brought to the notice of the apostles several additional forms of prayer. Many of them were from other inhabited planets, illustrated by this one: Our perfect and righteous heavenly Father, this day guide and direct our journey. Sanctify our steps and co-ordinate our thoughts. Ever lead us in the ways of eternal progress. Fill us with wisdom to the fullness of power, and vitalize us with your infinite energy. Inspire us with the divine consciousness of the presence and guidance of the seraphic hosts. Guide us ever upward in the pathway of light; justify us fully in the day of the great judgment. Make us like yourself in eternal glory, and receive us into your endless service on high.

144:6. Conference with John's Apostles

John had recently appointed twelve of his leaders to be apostles, following the precedent of Jesus. For three weeks these twenty-four men were in session three times a day and for six days each week. Jesus refused to advise them and left them for two weeks. Andrew and Abner alternated in presiding over these joint meetings of the two apostolic groups.

The first item the group agreed upon was the adoption of the prayer which Jesus had so recently taught them. They next decided that, as long as John lived, both groups of twelve apostles would go on with their work, and that joint meetings for one week would be held every three months at places to be agreed upon from time to time. They finally agreed that, as long as

John lived, or until they might jointly modify this decision, only the apostles of John would baptize believers and only the apostles of Jesus would finally instruct the new disciples. And then was it voted that, in case of John's death, the apostles of Jesus would begin to baptize with water as the emblem of the baptism of the divine Spirit. John's apostles preached, "Repent and be baptized." Jesus' apostles proclaimed, "Believe and be baptized."

144:7. In the Decapolis Cities

Throughout the months of November and December, Jesus and the twenty-four worked quietly in the Greek cities of the Decapolis. Always does the socialized religion of a new revelation pay the price of compromise with the established forms and usages of the preceding religion. John's followers, in joining Jesus' followers, gave up just about everything except water baptism. For these two months the group worked most of the time in pairs, one of Jesus' apostles going out with one of John's. And they won many souls among these gentiles and apostate Jews. Abner became a devout believer in Jesus and was later on made the head of a group of seventy teachers whom the Master commissioned to preach the gospel.

144:8. In Camp Near Pella

The latter part of December they all went over near the Jordan, close by Pella, where they again began to teach and preach. It was while Jesus was teaching the multitude one afternoon that some of John's special friends brought the Master the last message which he ever had from the Baptist. Jesus paused to say to John's friends, "Go back and tell John that he is not forgotten. Tell him what you have seen and heard, that the poor have good tidings preached to them. Verily, verily, I say to you, among those born of women there has not arisen a greater than John the Baptist; yet he who is but small in the kingdom of heaven is greater because he has been born of the spirit and knows that he has become a son of God." And the apostles of John were firmly knit to Jesus from that day forward. John was greatly comforted, and his faith was strengthened by the words of Jesus and the message of Abner. Jesus, among other things, said, "Come, therefore, all you who labor and are heavy laden, and you shall find rest for your souls. Take upon you the divine yoke, and you will experience the peace of God, which passes all understanding."

144:9. Death of John the Baptist

John the Baptist was executed by order of Herod Antipas on the evening of January 10, A.D. 28. When Jesus heard the report of John's death, he called the twenty-four together and said, "John is dead. Herod has beheaded him. Tonight go into joint council and arrange your affairs accordingly. There shall be delay no longer. The hour has come to proclaim the kingdom openly and with power. Tomorrow we go into Galilee." Accordingly, early on the morning of January 13, A.D. 28, Jesus and the apostles, accompanied by some twenty-five disciples, made their way to Capernaum and lodged that night in Zebedee's house.

Paper 145: Four Eventful Days at Capernaum

JESUS and the apostles arrived in Capernaum the evening of Tuesday, January 13. The news that Jesus had returned rapidly spread throughout the city, and early the next day, Mary the mother of Jesus hastened away, going over to Nazareth to visit her son Joseph. Through Andrew, Jesus arranged to speak in the synagogue on the coming Sabbath day. Late on Friday evening Jesus' baby sister, Ruth, secretly paid him a visit. No human being, save John Zebedee, ever knew of this visit, and John was admonished to tell no man. Ruth was the only member of Jesus' family who consistently and unwaveringly believed in the divinity of his earth mission from the times of her earliest spiritual consciousness right on down through his eventful ministry, death, resurrection, and ascension. Baby Ruth was the chief comfort of Jesus, as regards his earth family, throughout the trying ordeal of his trial, rejection, and crucifixion.

145:1. The Draught of Fishes

On Friday morning of this same week, when Jesus was teaching by the seaside, the people crowded him so near the water's edge that he signaled to David Zebedee and two associates, who had just come in near shore from a fruitless night of fishing on the lake, to come and rescue him. After Jesus had finished teaching the people, he said to David, "As you were delayed by coming to my help, now let me work with you. Let us go fishing." But Simon, one of David's assistants, answered, "Master, it is useless. We toiled all night and took nothing; however, at your bidding we will put out and let down the nets." When they had proceeded to the place designated by Jesus, they let down their nets and enclosed such a multitude of fish that they feared the nets would break, so much so that they signaled to their associates on the shore to come to their assistance. They filled three boats with fish, almost to sinking.

From that day David Zebedee, this Simon, and their associates forsook their nets and followed Jesus. But this was in no sense a miraculous draught of fishes. Jesus knew the habits of the fish in the Sea of Galilee. On this occasion he merely directed these men to the place where the fish were usually to be found at this time of day.

145:2. Afternoon at the Synagogue

The next Sabbath, at the afternoon service in the synagogue, Jesus preached his sermon on "The Will of the Father in Heaven." This sermon was an effort on Jesus' part to make clear the fact that religion is a personal experience. No longer must you approach the Father in heaven as a child of Israel but as a child of God. God loves you—every one of you—as individuals. The Father in heaven wills that his children on earth should begin that eternal ascent of the Paradise career to find the Creator, to know God and to seek to become like him.

Just as Jesus finished speaking, a young man in the congregation was seized with a violent epileptic attack. Jesus bade the people be quiet and, taking the young man by the hand, said, "Come out of it"—and he was immediately awakened. This young man was not possessed of an unclean spirit or demon; he was a victim of ordinary epilepsy. As a result of this commonplace incident the report was rapidly spread through Capernaum that Jesus had cast a demon out of a man and miraculously healed him in the synagogue at the conclusion of his afternoon sermon.

145:3. The Healing at Sundown

Soon after the setting of the sun Peter's wife heard voices in the front yard and, on going to the door, saw a large company of sick folks assembling. When the Master stepped out of the front entrance of Zebedee's house, his eyes met an array of stricken and afflicted humanity. A voice from the front yard exclaimed, "Master, speak the word, restore our health, heal our diseases, and save our souls." Among other things, Jesus said, "If it should be the will of Him who sent me and not inconsistent with my dedication to the proclamation of the gospel of the kingdom of heaven, I would desire to see my children made whole—and—" And, in a moment of time, 683 men, women, and children were made whole, were perfectly healed of all their physical diseases and other material disorders. Such a scene was never witnessed on earth before that day, nor since. But of all the beings who were astonished at this sudden and unexpected outbreak of supernatural healing, Jesus was the most surprised.

145:4. The Evening After

From a human standpoint, this was probably the greatest day of all the great days of the apostles' association with Jesus. Their lingering doubts of Jesus' divinity were banished. They were literally intoxicated with the ecstasy of their bewildered enchantment. But when they sought for Jesus, they could not find him. When Jesus did return to their midst, the hour was late. Jesus refused the congratulations and adoration of the twelve and the others who had lingered to greet him, only saying, "Rejoice not that my Father is powerful to heal the body, but rather that he is mighty to save the soul. Let us go to our rest, for tomorrow we must be about the Father's business." And again did twelve disappointed, perplexed, and heart-sorrowing men go to their rest; few of them, except the twins, slept much that night.

145:5. Early Sunday Morning

Neither did Jesus sleep much that Saturday night. He arose that Sunday morning long before daybreak and went all alone to one of his favorite places for communion with the Father. The theme of Jesus' prayer on this early morning was for wisdom and judgment that he might not allow his human sympathy, joined with his divine mercy, to make such an appeal to him in the presence of mortal suffering that all of his time would be occupied with physical ministry to the neglect of the spiritual.

Peter aroused James and John, and the three went to find their Master. For more than four hours Jesus endeavored to explain to these three apostles what had happened. He sought to make plain to his personal associates the real reasons why the kingdom of the Father could not be built upon wonder-working and physical healing. But they could not comprehend his teaching. Andrew sought Jesus to come to minister to the large crowd of people. Among other things, Jesus said, "It is not the will of my Father that I should return with you to cater to these curious ones and to become occupied with the ministry of things physical to the exclusion of the spiritual. Go, then, and prepare for our immediate departure while I here await your return." James and Jude came to see Jesus but he had departed. And so, on that Sunday afternoon, Jesus and the apostles started out upon their first really public and open preaching tour of the cities of Galilee, but they did not visit Nazareth.

Paper 146: First Preaching Tour of Galilee

THE first public preaching tour of Galilee began on Sunday, January 18, A.D. 28. This was the first time Jesus permitted his associates to preach without restraint. On this tour he cautioned them on only three occasions; he admonished them to remain away from Nazareth and to be discreet when passing through Capernaum and Tiberias.

146:1. Preaching at Rimmon

The small city of Rimmon had once been dedicated to the worship of a Babylonian god of the air, Ramman. Jesus and the twenty-four devoted much of their time to the task of making plain the difference between these older beliefs and the new gospel of the kingdom. Many of the better of the Babylonian and Persian ideas of light and darkness, good and evil, time and eternity, were later incorporated in the doctrines of so-called Christianity and their inclusion rendered the Christian teachings more immediately acceptable to the peoples of the Near East. In like manner, the inclusion of many of Plato's theories of the ideal spirit or invisible patterns of all things visible and material made Paul's Christian teachings more easy of acceptance by the western Greeks.

146:2. At Jotapata

Nathaniel was confused in his mind about the Master's teachings concerning prayer, thanksgiving, and worship, and in response to his question Jesus spoke at great length in further explanation of his teaching. The conscious and persistent regard for iniquity in the heart of man gradually destroys the prayer connection of the human soul with the spirit circuits. That prayer which is inconsistent with the known and established laws of God is an abomination to the Paradise Deities. By opening the human end of the channel of the God-man communication, mortals make immediately available the ever-flowing stream of divine ministry. They who would receive mercy must show mercy.

What the true son desires and the infinite Father wills IS. Prayer does not change the divine attitude toward man, but it does change man's attitude toward the changeless Father. Prayer may not be employed to avoid the delays of time or to transcend the handicaps of space. If you are ever in doubt as to what you would ask of the Father, ask in my name, and I will present your petition in accordance with your real needs and desires and in accordance with my Father's will. Jesus taught that after praying we should remain for a time in silent receptivity to afford the indwelling spirit the better opportunity to speak to the listening soul.

146:3. The Stop at Ramah

At Ramah Jesus had the memorable discussion with the aged Greek philosopher who taught that science and philosophy were sufficient to satisfy the needs of human experience. Jesus told him, "Where you leave off, we begin. Religion is a revelation to man's soul dealing with spiritual realities which the mind alone could never discover or fully fathom. Intellectual strivings may reveal the facts of life, but the gospel of the kingdom unfolds the truths of being." The old philosopher was susceptible to the Master's mode of approach, and being sincerely honest of heart, he quickly believed this gospel of salvation. Sincere men are unafraid of the critical examination of their true convictions and noble ideals. Said Jesus, "While you cannot observe the divine spirit at work in your minds, there is a practical method of discovering the degree to which you have yielded the control of your soul powers to the teaching and guidance of this indwelling spirit of the heavenly Father, and that is the degree of your love for your fellow men." Throughout his entire earth life Jesus gave his followers very little instruction regarding the socialization of religion.

146:4. The Gospel at Iron

At this time all the synagogues of Galilee and Judea were open to Jesus. Iron was the site of extensive mineral mines for those days, and since Jesus had never shared the life of the miner, he spent most of his time, while sojourning at Iron, in the mines. Late on the afternoon of the third day at Iron, as Jesus was returning from the mines, he chanced to pass the squalid hovel of a certain leprous man who knelt before him saying, "Lord, if only you would, you could make me clean. I have heard the message of your teachers, and I would enter the kingdom if I could be made clean." As Jesus looked upon him, the man fell upon his face and worshiped. Then the Master stretched forth his hand and, touching him, said, "I will—be clean." And immediately he was healed. Jesus charged him to tell no man but go to the priest and offer the sacrifices for his cleansing. But this man began to publish his cleansing throughout the town. As a result of his spreading abroad the news that Jesus had healed him, the Master was so thronged by the sick that Jesus was forced to rise early the next day and leave the village. This cleansing of the leper was the first so-called miracle which Jesus had intentionally and deliberately performed up to this time.

146:5. Back in Cana

They were doing well with their work of bringing people into the kingdom when, on the third day, there arrived in Cana a certain prominent citizen of Capernaum, Titus, whose son was critically ill and asked Jesus to heal him. Jesus complained that people believe only when they see wonders. But the nobleman pleaded with Jesus, saying, "My Lord, I do believe, but come ere my child perishes, for when I left him he was even then at the point of death." And when Jesus had bowed his head a moment in silent meditation, he suddenly spoke, "Return to your home; your son will live." Titus hastened back to Capernaum and discovered that his son's fever left him at the time Jesus said that his son would live. This was not a miracle of curing physical disease. It was merely a case of preknowledge concerning the course of natural law, just such knowledge as Jesus frequently resorted to subsequent to his baptism. And when Jesus saw that the whole countryside was aroused, he said, "Let us go to Nain."

146:6. Nain and the Widow's Son

As Jesus and his apostles drew near the gate of the city, they met a funeral procession on its way to the nearby cemetery, carrying the only son of a widowed mother of Nain. Jesus discovered the young man was not dead, so, turning to the mother, he said, "Weep not. Your son is not dead; he sleeps." And then, taking the young man by the hand, Jesus said, "Awake and arise." And the youth who was supposed to be dead presently sat up and began to speak, and Jesus sent them back to their homes. Jesus endeavored to calm the multitude and vainly tried to explain that the lad was not really dead, but it was useless. And again was Jesus so besieged as a physician that he departed early the next day for Endor.

146:7. At Endor

At Endor Jesus escaped for a few days from the clamoring multitudes in quest of physical healing. During their sojourn at this place the Master recounted for the instruction of the apostles the story of King Saul and the witch of Endor. Jesus plainly told his apostles that the stray and rebellious midwayers who had oftentimes impersonated the supposed spirits of the dead would soon be brought under control. He told his followers that, after he returned to the Father, and after they had poured out their spirit upon all flesh, no more could such semispirit beings possess the feeble-and evil-minded among mortals. Jesus further explained to his apostles that the spirits of departed human beings do not come back to the world of their origin to communicate with their living fellows.

Paper 147: The Interlude Visit to Jerusalem

JESUS and the apostles arrived in Capernaum on Wednesday, March 17, and spent two weeks at the Bethsaida headquarters before they departed for Jerusalem.

147:1. The Centurion's Servant

On the day before they made ready to go to Jerusalem for the feast of the Passover, Mangus, captain of the Roman guard stationed at Capernaum, asked through the synagogue rulers for Jesus to cure his sick servant. Jesus agreed to go with them. The Roman captain sent his friends to stop Jesus from coming into his house, saying that he was not worthy of such honor. The captain said that he could send soldiers to do his bidding, so he believed Jesus could cure his servant without coming into his house. When Jesus heard this, he said, "I marvel at the belief of the gentile. Verily, verily, I say to you, I have not found so great faith, no, not in Israel." Then, turning from the house, he said, "Let us go hence." And from that hour the servant began to mend and was eventually restored to his normal health and usefulness.

But we never knew just what happened on this occasion. We only know of the fact of the servant's complete recovery.

147:2. The Journey to Jerusalem

Early on the morning of Tuesday, March 30, Jesus and the apostolic party started on their journey to Jerusalem for the Passover. They arrived on the afternoon of Friday, April 2, and established their headquarters, as usual, at Bethany. They had hardly got themselves settled at Bethany when from near and far those seeking healing for their bodies, comfort for troubled minds, and salvation for their souls, began to congregate. Therefore they pitched tents at Gethsemane, and the Master would go back and forth from Bethany to Gethsemane to avoid the crowds which so constantly thronged him. The apostolic party spent almost three weeks at Jerusalem, but Jesus enjoined them to do no public preaching, only private teaching and personal work. At Bethany they quietly celebrated the Passover. And this was the first time that Jesus and all of the twelve partook of the bloodless Passover feast.

147:3. The Pool of Bethesda

The afternoon of the second Sabbath in Jerusalem, John said to Jesus, "Come with me, I would show you something." John conducted Jesus out through one of the Jerusalem gates to a pool of water called Bethesda. He brought Jesus to the pool thinking that the sight of the assembled sufferers would make such an appeal to the Master's compassion that he would be moved to perform a miracle of healing. Jesus replied, "John, why would you tempt me to turn aside from the way I have chosen?" But then Jesus said to those assembled, "Many of you are here, sick and afflicted, because of your many years of wrong living. . . . Verily, verily, I say to you, He who hears the gospel of the kingdom and believes in this teaching of sonship with God, has eternal life." One man, who had been many years downcast and grievously afflicted by the infirmities of his troubled mind, rejoiced at Jesus' words and, picking up his bed, went forth to his home, even though it was the Sabbath day. Then said Jesus to John, "Let us depart ere the chief priests and the scribes come upon us and take offense that we spoke words of life to these afflicted ones."

147:4. The Rule of Living

On the evening of this same Sabbath day, at Bethany, Nathaniel asked Jesus a question about doing to others as we wish them to do to us, citing the example of a lustful man who thus wickedly looks upon his intended consort in sin. When Jesus heard Nathaniel's question, he immediately stood upon his feet and, pointing his finger at the apostle, said, "Nathaniel, Nathaniel! What manner of thinking is going on in your heart? Do you not receive my teachings as one who has been born of the spirit? . . . Let me now teach you concerning the differing levels of meaning attached to the interpretation of this rule of living." Jesus told them of the levels of the flesh, feelings, mind, brotherly love, morals, and the spiritual level. The level of spirit insight and spiritual interpretation impels us to recognize in this rule of life the divine command to treat all men as we conceive God would treat them. Nothing Jesus had said to the apostles up to this time had ever more astonished them. They continued to discuss the Master's words long after he had retired

147:5. Visiting Simon the Pharisee

Though Simon was not a member of the Jewish Sanhedrin, he was an influential Pharisee of Jerusalem. He was a half-hearted believer, and notwithstanding that he might be severely criticized therefor, he dared to invite Jesus and his personal associates, Peter, James, and John, to his home for a social meal. A woman came in who had been a keeper of a brothel but had become a believer and changed her life began anointing Jesus' feet with perfume and wetting his feet with her tears. Simon thought this was inappropriate and Jesus knowing his thoughts pointed out that this woman had been forgiven much and she was very thankful. Turning around, Jesus said to the woman, "You have indeed repented of your sins, and they are forgiven. Be not discouraged by the thoughtless and unkind attitude of your fellows; go on in the joy and liberty of the kingdom of heaven." That evening Jesus told the apostles that what you are becoming is of infinitely more important than what you are today. He said the woman was farther away from God than Simon but her soul was in progressive motion and had tremendous spiritual possibilities for the future.

Many other semiprivate meetings and banquets did Jesus attend with the high and the low, the rich and the poor, of Jerusalem before he and his apostles finally departed for Capernaum.

147:6. Returning to Capernaum

The chief priests and the religious leaders of the Jews decided that Jesus would have to be apprehended on a religious charge and be tried by the Sanhedrin. Therefore a commission of six secret spies was appointed to follow Jesus, to observe his words and acts. But the spies did not have long to wait for their opportunity to accuse Jesus and his associates of Sabbath breaking. When they saw Andrew rub the grain in his hand, they went up to him and said, "Do you not know that it is unlawful to pluck and rub the grain on the Sabbath day?" When Andrew intimated that they were quibblers, they were indignant, and rushed back to protest to Jesus. Jesus told them that it was good that they were interested in keeping the Sabbath holy and said that the Sabbath was made for man not man for the Sabbath. He said, "And if you are here present with us to watch my words, then will I openly proclaim that the Son of Man is lord even of the Sabbath." Jesus' antagonism to the Jewish traditions and slavish ceremonials was always positive.

147:7. Back in Capernaum

When Jesus was conducting one of his customary classes of questions and answers the leader of the six spies asked him why his disciples did not fast. Jesus said that it is natural for the children of light to pray but fasting is not a part of the gospel of the kingdom of heaven. He further observed that men do not put new wine in old wine skins, lest the new wine burst the skins. He said, "Therefore do my disciples show wisdom in that they do not bring too much of the old order over into the new teaching of the gospel of the kingdom. That which is old and also true must abide. Likewise, that which is new but false must be rejected. But that which is new and also true, have the faith and courage to accept."

147:8. The Feast of Spiritual Goodness

That night, long after the usual listeners had retired, Jesus continued to teach his apostles. He began this special instruction by quoting from the Prophet Isaiah regarding fasting and serving others. And then long into the night Jesus propounded to his apostles the truth that it was their faith that made them secure in the kingdom of the present and the future, and not their affliction of soul nor fasting of body. He exhorted the apostles at least to live up to the ideas of the prophet of old and expressed the hope that they would progress far beyond even the ideals of Isaiah and the older prophets. His last words that night were, "Grow in grace by means of that living faith which grasps the fact that you are the sons of God while at the same time it recognizes every man as a brother."

Paper 148: Training Evangelists at Bethsaida

FROM May 3 to October 3, A.D. 28, Jesus and the apostolic party were in residence at the Zebedee home at Bethsaida. Throughout this five months' period of the dry season an enormous camp was maintained by the seaside near the Zebedee residence. This tented city was under the general supervision of David Zebedee, assisted by the Alpheus twins. Throughout this period the apostles would go fishing at least one day a week. The twelve were permitted to spend one week out of each month with their families or friends. While Andrew continued in general charge of the apostolic activities, Peter was in full charge of the school of the evangelists.

148:1. A New School of the Prophets

Peter, James, and Andrew were the committee designated by Jesus to pass upon applicants for admission to the school of evangelists. This school was conducted on the plan of learning and doing. What the students learned during the forenoon they taught to the assembly by the seaside during the afternoon. After supper they informally discussed both the learning of the forenoon and the teaching of the afternoon. The one hundred and more evangelists trained during this five months by the seaside represented the material from which (excepting Abner and John's apostles) the later seventy gospel teachers and preachers were drawn. These evangelists, though they taught and preached the gospel, did not baptize believers until after they were later ordained and commissioned by Jesus as the seventy messengers of the kingdom.

148:2. The Bethsaida Hospital

In connection with the seaside encampment, Elman, the Syrian physician, with the assistance of a corps of twenty-five young women and twelve men, organized and conducted what should be regarded as the kingdom's first hospital. As far as we know, no so-called miracles of supernatural healing occurred among the one thousand afflicted and ailing persons who went away from this infirmary improved or cured. However, the vast majority of these benefited individuals ceased not to proclaim that Jesus had healed them. The camp disbanded a short time before the season for the increase in chills and fever drew on.

148:3. The Father's Business

Not since his baptism had the Master been so much alone as during this period of the evangelists' training encampment at Bethsaida. Whenever any one of the apostles ventured to ask Jesus why he was absent so much from their midst, he would invariably answer that he was "about the Father's business." When the Master desired to go to the hills about the Father's business, he would summon to accompany him any two of the apostles who might be at liberty. We have been led to infer that the Master, during many of these solitary seasons in the hills, was in direct and executive association with many of his chief directors of universe affairs.

148:4. Evil, Sin, and Iniquity

It was the habit of Jesus two evenings each week to hold special converse with individuals who desired to talk with him, in a certain secluded and sheltered corner of the Zebedee garden. At one of these evening conversations in private Thomas asked the Master why it is necessary to be born of the spirit in order to enter the kingdom and what is evil. Among other things, Jesus said, "Evil is the unconscious or unintended transgression of the divine law, the Father's will. Evil is likewise the measure of the imperfectness of obedience to the Father's will. Sin is the conscious, knowing, and deliberate transgression of the divine law, the Father's will. Sin is the measure of unwillingness to be divinely led and spiritually directed. Iniquity is the willful, determined, and persistent transgression of the divine law, the Father's will. Iniquity is the measure of the continued rejection of the Father's loving plan of personality survival and the Sons' merciful ministry of salvation."

148:5. The Purpose of Affliction

At another of these private interviews in the garden Nathaniel asked Jesus why the loving Father in heaven permits so many of his children on earth to suffer so many afflictions. The Master told him that the natural order of this world has been so many times upset by the sinful adventures of certain rebellious traitors to the Father's will. And that he has come to make a beginning of setting these things in order. The Father does not purposely afflict his children. Man brings down upon himself unnecessary affliction as a result of his persistent refusal to walk in the better ways of the divine will. It is the Father's will that mortal man should work persistently and consistently toward the betterment of his estate on earth. Do not doubt the love of the Father just because some just and wise law of his ordaining chances to afflict you because you have innocently or deliberately transgressed such a divine ordinance.

148:6. The Misunderstanding of Suffering—Discourse on Job

It was this same evening at Bethsaida that John also asked Jesus why so many apparently innocent people suffered from so many diseases and experienced so many afflictions. Jesus referred to the afflictions of Job to illustrate how good men can have the wrong idea of God. He assured John that God loves the poor just as much as the rich; he is no respecter of persons. The Father speaks within the human heart as a still, small voice, saying, "This is the way; walk therein. Do you not comprehend that God dwells within you, that he has become what you are that he may make you what he is!" The Father in heaven does not willingly afflict the children of men. Man suffers from the accidents of time, the transgression of the laws of life and light, and his own iniquitous persistence in rebellion against the righteous rule of heaven on earth. Job found the God of comfort and salvation in spite of erroneous teachings. John's entire afterlife was markedly changed as a result of this conversation with the Master in the garden.

148:7. The Man with the Withered Hand

The second Sabbath before the departure of the apostles and the new corps of evangelists on the second preaching tour of Galilee, Jesus spoke in the Capernaum synagogue on the "Joys of Righteous Living." The Pharisaic spies induced a man with a withered hand to approach him and ask if it would be lawful to be healed on the Sabbath day. Jesus told them that he knew why they had sent this man to him, and declared that it is lawful to do good to men on the Sabbath day. When Jesus healed the man, the people were minded to turn upon the Pharisees, but Jesus forbid them to do so. The angered Pharisees then went to Herod to influence him against Jesus, but Herod advised them to take their complaints to Jerusalem. This is the first case of a miracle to be wrought by Jesus in response to the challenge of his enemies.

148:8. Last Week at Bethsaida

The last week of the sojourn at Bethsaida the Jerusalem spies became much divided in their attitude toward Jesus and his teachings. Three of these Pharisees were tremendously impressed by what they had seen and heard.

Meanwhile, at Jerusalem, Abraham, a young and influential member of the Sanhedrin, publicly espoused the teachings of Jesus and was baptized in the pool of Siloam by Abner. Certain wealthy Jews of Alexandria invited Jesus to come to their city for the purpose of establishing a joint school of philosophy and religion as well as an infirmary for the sick. But Jesus courteously declined the invitation. About this time there arrived at the Bethsaida encampment a trance prophet from Bagdad, one Kirmeth. Before Jesus interceded for the Bagdad prophet, David Zebedee, with the assistance of a self-appointed committee, had taken Kirmeth out into the lake and, after repeatedly plunging him into the water, had advised him to depart hence—to organize and build a camp of his own. The new Jerusalem convert, Abraham the Pharisee, gave all of his worldly goods to the apostolic treasury, and this contribution did much to make possible the immediate sending forth of the one hundred newly trained evangelists.

148:9. Healing the Paralytic

On Friday afternoon, October 1, when Jesus was holding his last meeting with the apostles, evangelists, and other leaders of the disbanding encampment there occurred one of the strangest and most unique episodes of all Jesus' earth life. While the house was thronged with people and entirely surrounded by eager listeners, a man long afflicted with paralysis was carried down from Capernaum on a small couch by his friends. They were unable to get him to Jesus so they ascended to the roof and after loosening the tiles, they lowered the sick man on his couch by ropes immediately in front of the Master. The paralytic apologized for interrupting his teaching but asked to be healed that he might serve in the kingdom of heaven. Jesus, seeing his faith, said to the paralytic, "Son, fear not; your sins are forgiven. Your faith shall save you." The Pharisees began to say to themselves that this is blasphemy, only God can forgive sin. Jesus perceiving their thoughts told them that the Son of Man has the power to forgive sins. The paralytic arose and walked out before them all. And it was about this time that the messengers of the Sanhedrin arrived to bid the six spies return to Jerusalem. The leader and two of his associates returned with the messengers to Jerusalem, while three of the spying Pharisees confessed faith in Jesus and, going immediately to the lake, were baptized by Peter and fellowshipped by the apostles as children of the kingdom.

Paper 149: The Second Preaching Tour

THE second public preaching tour of Galilee began on Sunday, October 3, A.D. 28, and continued for almost three months, ending on December 30. James Zebedee administered the charge to the evangelists. At the conclusion of James's remarks Jesus said to the 117 evangelists, "Go now forth to do the work as you have been charged, and later on, when you have shown yourselves competent and faithful, I will ordain you to preach the gospel of the kingdom."

David Zebedee maintained a permanent headquarters for the work of the kingdom in his father's house at Bethsaida. David employed forty to fifty messengers in this intelligence division. While thus employed, he partially supported himself by spending some of his time at his old work of fishing.

149:1. The Widespread Fame of Jesus

By the time the camp at Bethsaida had been broken up, the fame of Jesus, particularly as a healer, had spread to all parts of Palestine and through all of Syria and the surrounding countries. There began to appear about the time of this mission—and continued throughout the remainder of Jesus' life on earth—a peculiar and unexplained series of healing phenomena. It was never revealed to us just what occurred in these cases of spontaneous or unconscious healing. The Master never explained to his apostles how these healings were effected, other than that on several occasions he merely said, "I perceive that power has gone forth from me." It is our opinion that, in the personal presence of Jesus, certain forms of profound human faith were literally and truly compelling in the manifestation of healing—Jesus did frequently suffer men to heal themselves in his presence by their powerful, personal faith.

149:2. Attitude of the People

Jesus understood the minds of men. He knew what was in the heart of man, and had his teachings been left as he presented them, the only commentary being the inspired interpretation afforded by his earth life, all nations and all religions of the world would speedily have embraced the gospel of the kingdom. The two great mistakes of his followers were to connect the gospel teaching directly onto the Jewish theology, and to organize the Christian teaching so completely about the person of Jesus which tended to eclipse his saving message: the fatherhood of God and the brotherhood of man. The most astonishing and the most revolutionary feature of Michael's mission on earth was his attitude toward women. In one generation Jesus lifted women out of the disrespectful oblivion and the slavish drudgery of the ages. People found him entirely free from the superstitions of that day. He was not a militant revolutionist; he was a progressive evolutionist. On both friends and foes he exercised a strong and peculiarly fascinating influence. And all this is still true; even today and in all future ages, the more man comes to know this God-man, the more he will love and follow after him.

149:3. Hostility of the Religious Leaders

The religious leaders at Jerusalem were becoming well-nigh frantic as a result of the recent conversion of young Abraham and by the desertion of the three spies who had been baptized by Peter, and who were now out with the evangelists on this second preaching tour of Galilee. Many of the leaders of the Jews had closed the doors of their hearts to the spiritual appeal of the gospel. From this day on they ceased not to plan and plot for the Master's destruction.

149:4. Progress of the Preaching Tour

At one of these evening sessions one of the younger evangelists asked Jesus a question about anger, and the Master among other things said that anger indicates your lack of tolerant brotherly love plus your lack of self-respect and self-control. Anger depletes the health, debases the mind, and handicaps the spirit teacher of man's soul.

On this same occasion the Master talked to the group about the desirability of possessing well-balanced characters. He deplored all tendency toward overspecialization, toward becoming narrow-minded and circumscribed in life's activities. He called attention to the fact that any virtue, if carried to extremes, may become a vice; that courage and faith can sometimes lead unthinking souls on to recklessness and presumption, and how prudence and discretion, when carried too far, lead to cowardice and failure. Truly educated persons are not satisfied with remaining in ignorance of the lives and doings of their fellows.

149:5. Lessons Regarding Contentment

When Jesus was visiting the group of evangelists working under the supervision of Simon Zelotes, Simon asked the Master why some persons are so much more happy and contented than others. Jesus said that some persons are naturally more happy than others. Much, very much, depends upon the willingness of man to be led and directed by the Father's spirit which lives within him. Men should make the best of their lives on earth, having thus sincerely exerted themselves; they should cheerfully accept their lot and exercise ingenuity in making the most of that which has fallen to their hands. Jesus hardly regarded this world as a "vale of tears." He rather looked upon it as the birth sphere of the eternal and immortal spirits of Paradise ascension, the "vale of soul making."

149:6. The "Fear of the Lord"

It was at Gamala, during the evening conference, that Philip said to Jesus, "Master, why is it that the Scriptures instruct us to 'fear the Lord,' while you would have us look to the Father in heaven without fear?" And Jesus replied to Philip, saying that he, Jesus, came to reveal the Father's love so that we will be attracted to the worship of the Eternal by the drawing of a son's affectionate recognition and reciprocation of the Father's profound and perfect love. He said, "Your forebears feared God because he was mighty and mysterious. You shall adore him because he is magnificent in love, plenteous in mercy, and glorious in truth. I have come into the world to put love in the place of fear, joy in the place of sorrow, confidence in the place of dread, loving service and appreciative worship in the place of slavish bondage and meaningless ceremonies."

149:7. Returning to Bethsaida

By Thursday, December 30 all of the apostolic party and the teaching evangelists had arrived at the Zebedee home. The group remained together over the Sabbath day, after which the entire party was granted a two weeks' recess to go home to their families, visit their friends, or go fishing. Of the 117 evangelists who participated in this second preaching tour of Galilee, only about seventy-five survived the test of actual experience and were on hand to be assigned to service at the end of the two weeks' recess.

Paper 150: The Third Preaching Tour

ON Sunday evening, January 16, A.D. 29, Abner, with the apostles of John, reached Bethsaida and went into joint conference with Andrew and the apostles of Jesus the next day. Among the many matters considered by this joint conference was the practice of anointing the sick with certain forms of oil in connection with prayers for healing. The apostles of John had always used the anointing oil, but the apostles of Jesus refused to bind themselves by such a regulation. On Tuesday, January 18, the twenty-four were joined by the tested evangelists in preparation to being sent forth on the third preaching tour of Galilee. This third mission continued for a period of seven weeks. The evangelists were sent out in groups of five, while the apostles went out two and two.

150:1. The Women's Evangelistic Corps

Of all the daring things which Jesus did in connection with his earth career, the most amazing was his sudden announcement on the evening of January 16: "On the morrow we will set apart ten women for the ministering work of the kingdom." These ten women selected and commissioned by Jesus were: Susanna, the daughter of the former chazan of the Nazareth synagogue; Joanna, the wife of Chuza, the steward of Herod Antipas; Elizabeth, the daughter of a wealthy Jew of Tiberias and Sepphoris; Martha, the elder sister of Andrew and Peter; Rachel, the sister-in-law of Jude; Nasanta, the daughter of Elman, the Syrian physician; Milcha, a cousin of the Apostle Thomas; Ruth, the eldest daughter of Matthew Levi; Celta, the daughter of a Roman centurion; and Agaman, a widow of Damascus. Subsequently, Jesus added two other women to this group—Mary Magdalene and Rebecca, the daughter of Joseph of Arimathea. The ten elected Susanna as their chief and Joanna as their treasurer. From this time on they furnished their own funds. The charge which Jesus gave these ten women as he set them apart for gospel teaching and ministry was the emancipation proclamation which set free all women and for all time. And this liberation of women was practiced by the apostles immediately after the Master's departure, albeit they fell back to the olden customs in subsequent generations. Paul, despite the fact that he conceded all this in theory, never really incorporated it into his own attitude and personally found it difficult to carry out in practice.

150:2. The Stop at Magdala

When any of the women believers desired to see the Master or confer with the apostles, they went to Susanna, and in company with one of the twelve women evangelists, they would go at once into the presence of the Master or one of his apostles. It was at Magdala that the women first demonstrated their usefulness and vindicated the wisdom of their choosing. When the party entered Magdala, these ten (later twelve) women evangelists were free to enter the evil resorts and as the result of this ministry Mary Magdalene was won for the kingdom. Mary Magdalene became the most effective teacher of the gospel among this group of twelve women evangelists. They went on through the remainder of Jesus' life on earth, and when the last and tragic episode in the drama of Jesus' life was being enacted, notwithstanding the apostles all fled but one, these women were all present, and not one either denied or betrayed him.

150:3. Sabbath at Tiberias

The Sabbath services of the apostolic party had been put in the hands of the women by Andrew, upon instructions from Jesus. The women selected Joanna to have charge of this occasion, and the meeting was held in the banquet room of Herod's new palace.

Late that evening Jesus gave the united group a memorable talk on "Magic and Superstition." In summary Jesus told them, 1. the courses of the stars in the heavens have nothing whatever to do with the events of human life on earth; 2. the examination of the internal organs of an animal recently killed can reveal nothing about the outcome of human affairs; 3. the spirits of the dead do not come back to communicate with their families; 4. charms and relics are impotent to heal disease or ward off disaster; 5. casting lots is not a method designed to disclose the divine will; 6. divination, sorcery, and witchcraft are superstitions of ignorant minds; 7. the interpretation of dreams is largely a superstitious speculation; 8. the spirits of good or evil cannot dwell within material symbols; 9. the practices of the enchanters, the wizards, the magicians, and the sorcerers, were derived from superstitions; 10. he exposed and denounced their belief in spells, ordeals, bewitching, cursing, signs, mandrakes, knotted cords, and all other forms of ignorant and enslaving superstition.

150:4. Sending the Apostles out Two and Two

The next evening Jesus said, "You see for yourselves that the harvest is plenteous, but the laborers are few. Let us all, therefore, pray the Lord of the harvest that he send forth still more laborers into his fields." Among other things he told them not to be afraid of those who can kill the body, but who are not able to destroy the soul. They should labor earnestly to save the whole family, but they who love father or mother more than this gospel are not worthy of the kingdom. When the twelve had heard these words, they made ready to depart. And they did not again come together until the time of their assembling at Nazareth to meet with Jesus and the other disciples as the Master had arranged.

150:5. What Must I Do to Be Saved?

One evening at Shunem Rachel asked Jesus this question, "Master, what shall we answer when women ask us, What shall I do to be saved?" When

Jesus heard this question, he answered that they should believe the gospel of the kingdom, accept divine forgiveness and by faith recognize the indwelling spirit of God. You cannot buy salvation; you cannot earn righteousness. Salvation is the gift of God, and righteousness is the natural fruit of the spirit-born life of sonship in the kingdom. Realization of sonship is incompatible with the desire to sin. Kingdom believers hunger for righteousness and thirst for divine perfection.

150:6. The Evening Lessons

At the evening discussions Jesus talked upon many subjects, such as: "The Love of God," "Humility and Meekness," "Peace and Perfection," and "Wisdom and Worship."

They were informed as to the whereabouts and movements of all the workers by David's messengers. It had been arranged that they should assemble at Nazareth to meet the Master on Friday, March 4. By midafternoon, Andrew and Peter, the last to arrive, had reached the encampment prepared by the early arrivals and situated on the highlands to the north of the city. And this was the first time Jesus had visited Nazareth since the beginning of his public ministry.

150:7. The Sojourn at Nazareth

This Friday afternoon Jesus walked about Nazareth quite unobserved and wholly unrecognized. He passed by the home of his childhood and the carpenter shop and spent a half hour on the hill which he so much enjoyed when a lad. While the inhabitants of Nazareth had heard much about the doings of their former carpenter, they were offended that he had never included his native village in any of his earlier preaching tours. Thus did the Master find himself in the midst of, not a welcome homecoming, but a decidedly hostile and hypercritical atmosphere. But this was not all. His enemies, knowing that he was to spend this Sabbath day in Nazareth and supposing that he would speak in the synagogue, had hired numerous rough and uncouth men to harass him and in every way possible make trouble. The attitude of Jesus' family toward him had also tended to increase this unkind feeling of the citizenry. The orthodox among the Jews even presumed to criticize Jesus because he walked too fast on the way to the synagogue this Sabbath morning.

150:8. The Sabbath Service

This Sabbath was a beautiful day, and all Nazareth, friends and foes, turned out to hear this former citizen of their town discourse in the synagogue. Many of the apostolic retinue had to remain without the synagogue; there was not room for all who had come to hear him. The regular service began by the recital of prayers, eulogies, and a benediction. The chazan then handed Jesus a scripture roll and Jesus read from Deuteronomy and Isaiah, "The spirit of the Lord is upon me because he has anointed me to preach good tidings to the poor. He has sent me to proclaim release to the captives and the recovering of sight to the blind, to set at liberty those who are bruised and to proclaim the acceptable year of the Lord." And then Jesus said, "Today are these Scriptures fulfilled," and spoke for almost fifteen minutes on "The Sons and Daughters of God." Following his talk, Jesus stepped down into the crowd who pressed forward to ask questions. The disciples and evangelists recognized that trouble was brewing and tried to lead the Master away, but he would not go with them.

150:9. The Nazareth Rejection

Jesus found himself surrounded in the synagogue by a great throng of his enemies and a sprinkling of his own followers. He good-naturedly responded to their critical questions and statements, and would have managed the crowd and effectively disarmed even his violent enemies had it not been for the tactical blunder of one of his own apostles, Simon Zelotes, who, with the help of Nahor, served notice on the enemies of the Master to go hence. And so, under the leadership of hirelings, these ruffians laid hold upon Jesus and rushed him out of the synagogue to the brow of a nearby precipitous hill, where they were minded to shove him over the edge to his death below. But just as they were about to push him over the edge of the cliff, Jesus turned suddenly upon his captors and, facing them, quietly folded his arms. He said nothing as he started to walk forward, the mob parted and permitted him to pass on unmolested.

This turbulent ending of the third public preaching tour had a sobering effect upon all of Jesus' followers. They were beginning to realize the meaning of some of the Master's teachings; they were awaking to the fact that the kingdom would come only through much sorrow and bitter disappointment.

Paper 151: Tarrying and Teaching by the Seaside

BY March 10 all of the preaching and teaching groups had forgathered at Bethsaida. That Saturday night the Master talked for more than an hour to the assembled groups on "The mission of adversity and the spiritual value of disappointment." This was a memorable occasion, and his hearers never forgot the lesson he imparted.

151:1. The Parable of the Sower

About this time Jesus first began to employ the parable method of teaching the multitudes. While Jesus was setting in a boat meditating on the next move in extending the work of the kingdom, a large crowd assembled. Peter asked if he should speak to them and Jesus said that he would tell them a story. Jesus began the recital of the parable of the sower in which a sower distributed seed. Some seed fell on the wayside and was devoured by birds; other seed fell on rocky places and when the sun came out the plants withered; some seed fell among the thorns and the thorns choked the plants; still other seed fell on good ground and, growing, yielded, some thirtyfold, some sixtyfold, and some a hundred fold. When he had finished speaking, Jesus said, "He who has ears to hear, let him hear." The apostles wanted to know why Jesus spoke in parables and Jesus told them that those who are interested will discern the meaning of the teachings and their enemies will be confused.

151:2. Interpretation of the Parable

Both Peter and Nathaniel interpreted the parable as an allegory and argued about which was correct. Finally Thomas said that he recalled Jesus teaching them that they should employ true stories, not fables, and that we should select a story best suited to the illustration of the one central and vital truth which we wished to teach the people. It is wrong to interpret a parable as an allegory. Andrew agreed with Thomas' explanation and asked him to tell them his view of the meaning of the parable. Thomas said he believed the parable teaches one great truth: No matter how faithfully and efficiently we execute our divine commissions, they are going to be attended by varying degrees of success; and that all such differences in results are directly due to conditions inherent in the circumstances of our ministry, conditions over which we have little or no control. Jesus arose and said, "Well done, Thomas; you have discerned the true meaning of parables; but both Peter and Nathaniel have done you all equal good in that they have so fully shown the danger of undertaking to make an allegory out of my parables."

151:3. More About Parables

The whole of the next evening was devoted to the further discussion of parables. Jesus told them that they could not speak different words for each class of hearers, but they could tell a story to convey their teaching; and each group, even each individual, will be able to make his own interpretation of their parable in accordance with his own intellectual and spiritual endowments. Jesus advised against the use of either fables or allegories in teaching the truths of the gospel. The parable provides for a simultaneous appeal to vastly different levels of mind and spirit. The parable stimulates the imagination, challenges the discrimination, and provokes critical thinking; it promotes sympathy without arousing antagonism. The use of the parable form of teaching enables the teacher to present new and even startling truths while at the same time he largely avoids all controversy and outward clashing with tradition and established authority. The parable also possesses the advantage of stimulating the memory of the truth taught.

151:4. More Parables by the Sea

The next day Jesus again taught the people from the boat, saying that the kingdom of heaven is like a man who sowed good seed in his field; but while he slept, his enemy came and sowed weeds among the wheat and hastened away. At the harvest time the weeds are burned and the grain is stored in the barn.

The kingdom of heaven is like a grain of mustard seed which a man sowed in his field. Now a mustard seed is the least of seeds, but when it is full grown, it becomes the greatest of all herbs.

The kingdom of heaven is also like leaven which a woman took and hid in three measures of meal, and in this way it came about that all of the meal was leavened.

The kingdom of heaven is also like a treasure hidden in a field, which a man discovered. In his joy he went forth to sell all he had that he might have the money to buy the field.

The kingdom of heaven is also like a merchant seeking goodly pearls; and having found one pearl of great price, he went out and sold everything he possessed that he might be able to buy the extraordinary pearl.

Again, the kingdom of heaven is like a sweep net which was cast into the sea, and it gathered up every kind of fish. The fishermen then sorted out the fish, gathering the good into vessels while the bad they threw away. Many other parables spoke Jesus to the multitudes.

151:5. The Visit to Kheresa

The multitude continued to increase throughout the week and Jesus suggested that they go to the other side of the lake to rest. On the way across the lake they encountered one of those violent and sudden windstorms which are characteristic of the Sea of Galilee. Jesus lay asleep in the stern of the boat under a small overhead shelter. Peter was at the right-hand oar near the stern. When the boat began to fill with water, he dropped his oar and, rushing over to Jesus, shook him vigorously in order to awaken him, and when he was aroused, Peter said, "Master, don't you know we are in a violent storm? If you do not save us, we will all perish." As Jesus came out in the rain, he looked at Peter and said, "Why are all of you so filled with fear? Where is your faith? Peace, be quiet." Jesus had hardly uttered this rebuke to Peter the angry waves almost immediately subsided. All this was purely coincidental as far as we can judge; but the apostles, particularly Simon Peter, never ceased to regard the episode as a nature miracle.

151:6. The Kheresa Lunatic

The group went up a hillside covered with caverns when a lunatic who lived in these hillside caverns rushed up to them. This man, whose name was Amos, was afflicted with a periodic form of insanity. During one of his lucid intervals he had heard Jesus and became a halfhearted believer in the gospel of the kingdom. He asked Jesus for help and Jesus told him that he was not possessed of a devil and commanded him to come out of his spell. He was immediately restored to his right mind. As the swine herders rushed into the village to spread the news of the taming of the lunatic, the dogs charged upon a small and untended herd of about thirty swine and drove most of them over a precipice into the sea. Amos believed that the evil spirits entered the swine causing them to rush to their destruction in the sea below. The swine-raising gentiles asked Jesus to leave. Amos wanted to go with them but Jesus asked him to return to his people and show them what God had done for him.

Paper 152:
Events Leading up to the Capernaum Crisis

A GREAT crowd was waiting for Jesus when his boat landed that Tuesday forenoon. Jairus, one of the rulers of the synagogue, asked Jesus to heal his daughter who was at the point of death. Jesus agreed to go with him. In the crowded street with people pressing against him, Jesus suddenly stopped and said, "Someone touched me." Looking about his eyes fell on a nearby woman, Veronica, who admitted she touched his garment to be cured of a scourging hemorrhage. When Jesus heard this, he took the woman by the hand and, lifting her up, said, "Daughter, your faith has made you whole; go in peace."

And this case is a good illustration of many apparently miraculous cures which attended upon Jesus' earth career, but which he in no sense consciously willed.

152:1. At Jairus's House

Even before they entered the ruler's yard, one of his servants came out, saying, "Trouble not the Master; your daughter is dead." But Jesus said to the grief-stricken father, "Fear not; only believe." When he had put all of the mourners out of the room Jesus turned to the mother, saying, "Your daughter is not dead; she is only asleep." Jesus, going up to where the child lay, took her by the hand and said, "Daughter, I say to you, awake and arise!" And when the girl heard these words, she immediately rose up and walked across the room. Jesus explained that the maiden had been in a state of coma following a long fever, and that he had merely aroused her, that he had not raised her from the dead. He likewise explained all this to his apostles, but it was futile; they all believed he had raised the little girl from the dead. Never before Jesus was on earth, nor since, has it been possible so directly and graphically to secure the results attendant upon the strong and living faith of mortal men and women.

152:2. Feeding the Five Thousand

The Master had so little rest over the Sabbath that on Sunday morning, March 27, he sought to get away from the people, going to the opposite shore of the lake, where they proposed to obtain much needed rest in a beautiful park south of Bethsaida-Julias. By Wednesday noon about five thousand men, women, and children were assembled here. The people, even though they were hungry, would not go away. It was being quietly whispered about that Jesus had chosen this quiet spot outside the jurisdiction of all his enemies as the proper place to be crowned king. The people had been with them for three days and Jesus said he would like to feed them. Andrew told him that Mark who carried their food had only five barley loaves and two dried fishes. Jesus asked for the loaves and fishes and breaking them he gave the food to the apostles and their associates. When the crowd had finished eating, Jesus said to the disciples, "Gather up the broken pieces that remain over so that nothing will be lost." And when they had finished gathering up the fragments, they had twelve basketfuls. And this is the first and only nature miracle which Jesus performed as a result of his conscious preplanning.

152:3. The King-Making Episode

The reaction of the multitude to this sudden and spectacular supplying of their physical needs was profound and overwhelming. No wonder, then, that the multitude, when it had finished feasting, rose as one man and shouted, "Make him king!" This mighty shout of the multitude had hardly ceased to reverberate from the near-by rocks when Jesus stepped upon a huge stone and, lifting up his right hand to command their attention, said, "My children, you mean well, but you are short-sighted and material-minded." He told them his kingdom is not of this world. "This kingdom of heaven which we proclaim is a spiritual brotherhood, and no man rules over it seated upon a material throne. My Father in heaven is the all-wise and the all-powerful Ruler over this spiritual brotherhood of the sons of God on earth....If you must have a king, let the Father of lights be enthroned in the heart of each of you as the spirit Ruler of all things." These words of Jesus sent the multitude away stunned and disheartened. Jesus, before going off to be alone in the hills, turned to Andrew and said, "Take your brethren back to Zebedee's house and pray with them, especially for your brother, Simon Peter."

152:4. Simon Peter's Night Vision

None of the twelve was so crushed and downcast as Simon Peter. As the hours of darkness and hard rowing passed, Peter grew weary and fell into a deep sleep of exhaustion. In his dream Peter saw Jesus coming walking on the sea. When the Master seemed to walk on by the boat, Peter cried out, "Lord, if it really is you, bid me come and walk with you on the water." In connection with the latter part of his dream Peter arose from the seat whereon he slept and actually stepped overboard and into the water. And he awakened from his dream as Andrew, James, and John reached down and pulled him out of the sea. To Peter this experience was always real. He sincerely believed that Jesus came to them that night.

152:5. Back in Bethsaida

Thursday morning, before daylight, they anchored their boat offshore near Zebedee's house and sought sleep until about noontime. Andrew was first up and, going for a walk by the sea, found Jesus, in company with Mark, sitting on a stone by the water's edge. Jesus asked Andrew to assemble everyone and when assembled he told them he was disappointed with their material mindedness. Now, he reminded them, they saw that the working of miracles and the performance of material wonders will not win souls for the spiritual kingdom. Of the five thousand who were fed only about five hundred persisted in following after him.

Jesus then announced that he wished to withdraw for a few days of rest with his apostles before they made ready to go up to Jerusalem for the Passover. Jesus was preparing for a great crisis of his life on earth, and he therefore spent much time in communion with the Father in heaven.

152:6. At Gennesaret

While resting at the home of a wealthy believer in the Gennesaret region, Jesus held informal conferences with the twelve every afternoon. The ambassadors of the kingdom were a serious, sober, and chastened group of disillusioned men. It requires time for men and women to effect radical and extensive changes in their basic and fundamental concepts of social conduct, philosophic attitudes, and religious convictions. In less than one month's time the enthusiastic and open followers of Jesus, who numbered more than fifty thousand in Galilee alone, shrank to less than five hundred. Jesus taught the appeal to the emotions as the technique of arresting and focusing the intellectual attention; the mind thus aroused and quickened is the gateway to the soul that leads to true character transformations.

These twelve men were slowly awaking to the realization of the real nature of their task as ambassadors of the kingdom, and they began to gird themselves for the trying and testing ordeals of the last year of the Master's ministry on earth.

152:7. At Jerusalem

Sunday, April 3, Jesus, accompanied only by the twelve apostles, started from Bethsaida on the journey to Jerusalem. On arrival, they stayed in different homes. Jesus forbade them to do any public teaching. Jesus entered Jerusalem only once during this Passover. During this sojourn at Jerusalem the twelve learned how bitter the feeling was becoming toward their Master. They departed from Jerusalem all believing that a crisis was impending. They arrived back to Bethsaida, Friday, April 29. Jesus dispatched Andrew to ask the ruler of the synagogue for permission to speak at the Sabbath afternoon service. And Jesus well knew that that would be the last time he would ever be permitted to speak in the Capernaum synagogue.

Paper 153: The Crisis at Capernaum

ON Friday evening and on Sabbath morning, the apostles noticed that Jesus was seriously occupied with some momentous problem. Not in months had they seen the Master so preoccupied and uncommunicative. The apostles speculated on what was about to happen. It was from among such a group of depressed and disconsolate followers that Jesus went forth on this beautiful Sabbath afternoon to preach his epoch-making sermon in the Capernaum synagogue.

153:1. The Setting of the Stage

A distinguished congregation greeted Jesus at three o'clock on this exquisite Sabbath afternoon in the new Capernaum synagogue. The day before, fifty-three Pharisees and Sadducees had arrived from Jerusalem; more than thirty of the leaders and rulers of the neighboring synagogues were also present. Sitting by the side of these Jewish leaders, in the synagogue seats of honor, were the official observers of Herod Antipas. Jesus comprehended that he faced the immediate declaration of avowed and open warfare by his increasing enemies, and he elected boldly to assume the offensive. Both his friends and his foes pondered just one thought, and that was: "Why did he himself so deliberately and effectively turn back the tide of popular enthusiasm?"

It was after this sermon in the synagogue that Judas Iscariot entertained his first conscious thought of deserting. But he did, for the time being, effectively master all such inclinations.

153:2. The Epochal Sermon

Jesus introduced this sermon by reading from Deuteronomy telling Israel they would be smitten by their enemies because they will not hearken to the voice of God, and from Jeremiah saying that since they would not listen to the prophets their city would be made a curse to all the nations of the earth. Jesus asked them what evidence they wanted regarding his mission on earth. He told them that they already had sufficient evidence to enable them to make their decision. "Verily, verily, I say to many who sit before me this day, you are confronted with the necessity of choosing which way you will go; and I say to you, as Joshua said to your forefathers, 'choose you this day whom you will serve.' Today, many of you stand at the parting of the ways. . . . I have come to proclaim spiritual liberty, teach eternal truth, and foster living faith." There followed an extended discussion that lasted more than three hours.

153:3. The After Meeting

One of the questions centered around Jesus saying that he was the bread of life. Jesus responded that his life in the flesh is a bestowal of the bread of heaven, that we can become one in spirit with him even as Jesus is one in spirit with the Father. We can be nourished by the eternal word of God, which is the bread of life. Another question called attention to the fact that Jesus and the apostles did not properly wash their hands before eating. Jesus said that it is not that which enters into the mouth that spiritually defiles the man, but rather that which proceeds out of the mouth and from the heart. "Do you not know it is from the heart that there come forth evil thoughts, wicked projects of murder, theft, and adulteries, together with jealousy, pride, anger, revenge, railings, and false witness? And it is just such things that defile men, and not that they eat bread with ceremonially unclean hands." He observed that they transgress the commandments of God by the laws of their tradition, and avoided helping needy parents by saying this money was given to God. "Altogether willing are you to reject the word of God while you maintain your own traditions." All of this can the better be understood when it is recalled that these Jews looked upon eating with unwashed hands in the same light as commerce with a harlot, and both were equally punishable by excommunication.

153:4. Last Words in the Synagogue

In the midst of the discussions of this after meeting, one of the Pharisees from Jerusalem brought to Jesus a distraught youth who was possessed of an unruly and rebellious spirit. The Master was moved with compassion and cast out the evil spirit. One of the Pharisees said, "Have nothing to do with this man; he is in partnership with Satan." Then said Jesus, "How can

Satan cast out Satan? . . . If you were not blinded by prejudice and misled by fear and pride, you would easily perceive that one who is greater than devils stands in your midst." Jesus warned them that whoever knowingly ascribes the works of God to the doing of devils will never obtain forgiveness since they will never seek nor receive forgiveness. They then asked for a sign to prove his authority to teach, and Jesus said no sign would be given but that which they already had.

153:5. The Saturday Evening

Time and again had Jesus dashed to pieces the hopes of his apostles, but no time of disappointment or season of sorrow had ever equaled that which now overtook them. And there was admixed with their depression a real fear for their safety. But most of all they were bewildered by Jesus' sudden change of tactics. And now, on top of all of these worries, when they reached home, Jesus refused to eat. For hours he isolated himself in one of the upper rooms. It was almost midnight when Joab, the leader of the evangelists, returned and reported that about one third of his associates had deserted the cause. It was a little after midnight when Jesus came down from the upper chamber and stood among the twelve and their associates. He told them that he recognized that they were disturbed but that it was unavoidable. Why were they grieving when a new day is dawning? Now as such a time as this, would they also desert? And when Jesus had finished speaking, Simon Peter said, "Yes, Lord, we are sad and perplexed, but we will never forsake you." And as Peter ceased speaking, they all with one accord nodded their approval of his pledge of loyalty. Then said Jesus, "Go to your rest, for busy times are upon us; active days are just ahead."

Paper 154: Last Days at Capernaum

ON the eventful Saturday night of April 30 a council was being held between Herod Antipas and a group of special commissioners representing the Jerusalem Sanhedrin. These scribes and Pharisees urged Herod to arrest Jesus. But Herod refused to take action against him as a political offender. One of Herod's official family, Chuza, had informed him that Jesus did not propose to meddle with the affairs of earthly rule; that he was only concerned with the establishment of the spiritual brotherhood of his believers, which brotherhood he called the kingdom of heaven.

154:1. A Week of Counsel

From May 1 to May 7 Jesus held intimate counsel with his followers at the Zebedee house. At this time there were only about one hundred disciples who had the moral courage to brave the opposition of the Pharisees and openly declare their adherence to Jesus. On Friday of this week official action was taken by the rulers of the Capernaum synagogue closing the house of God to Jesus and all his followers. Jairus resigned as chief ruler and openly aligned himself with Jesus. This Saturday night marked the time of the lowest ebb in the tide of popular regard for Jesus and his teachings. From then on there was a steady, slow, but more healthful and dependable growth in favorable sentiment and in its far-flung spiritual implications.

154:2. A Week of Rest

Sunday, May 8, A.D. 29, at Jerusalem, the Sanhedrin passed a decree closing all the synagogues of Palestine to Jesus and his followers. This summary action of the Sanhedrin was followed by the resignation of five of its members. The rulers of the Hebron synagogue refused to acknowledge the right of the Sanhedrin to exercise such jurisdiction over their assembly. Shortly thereafter the Hebron synagogue was destroyed by fire. This same Sunday morning, Jesus declared a week's holiday. Wherever Jesus went there always lurked nearby two or three of David's most trusted messengers, who had no uncertain orders from their chief respecting the safeguarding of Jesus.

Nathaniel and James Zebedee suffered from more than a slight illness and one night Jesus ministered to them. He never used his power to heal members of his earth family or his immediate followers. The spiritualization of the human soul requires intimate experience with the educational solving of a wide range of real universe problems.

154:3. The Second Tiberias Conference

On May 16 the second conference at Tiberias between the authorities at Jerusalem and Herod Antipas was convened. A new effort was made to have Herod place Jesus under arrest, but he refused to do their bidding. However, Herod did agree to the plan of permitting the Sanhedrin authorities to seize Jesus and carry him to Jerusalem to be tried on religious charges. Strong pressure from many sides was brought to bear upon Herod before he consented to grant this permission, and he well knew that Jesus could not expect a fair trial before his bitter enemies at Jerusalem.

154:4. Saturday Night in Capernaum

On this same Saturday night, in Capernaum a group of fifty leading citizens met at the synagogue to discuss the momentous question: "What shall we do with Jesus?" They talked and debated until after midnight, but they could not find any common ground for agreement. His enemies maintained that his teachings were impractical, and the men of many subsequent generations have said the same things—and they are partially right. But all such doubters forget that a much better civilization could have been built upon his teachings, and sometime will be. This world has never seriously tried to carry out the teachings of Jesus on a large scale.

154:5. The Eventful Sunday Morning

On this Sunday morning, May 22, before daybreak, one of David's messengers arrived in great haste from Tiberias, bringing the word that Herod had authorized, or was about to authorize, the arrest of Jesus by the officers of the Sanhedrin. Jude's sister-in-law informed Jesus' family and Mary, James, Joseph, Jude, and Ruth planned to assemble at Zebedee's house. Jesus selected twelve of the evangelists and the twelve apostles to accompany him. About 7:30 this morning Jesus began his parting address to almost one hundred believers who had crowded indoors to hear him. This was a solemn occasion for all present, but Jesus seemed unusually cheerful and he inspired all of them with his words of faith, hope, and courage.

154:6. Jesus' Family Arrives

It was about eight o'clock on this Sunday morning when five members of Jesus' earth family arrived. They had decided to urge Jesus to come home with them. The Pharisees had met with them the evening before and Mary was convinced that she could influence Jesus. When they reached the Zebedee house, Jesus was in the very midst of delivering his parting address to the disciples. The house was crowded, so they established themselves on the back porch and had word passed to Jesus. Simon Peter interrupted his talking and said, "Behold, your mother and your brothers are outside, and they are very anxious to speak with you." They heard his musical voice say that they should have no fear for him, that he had no mother, brothers, or sisters but that whoever does the will of his Father in heaven is his mother, brother, and sister. Mary fainted when she heard this. Jesus intended to visit with his family but was forced to flee before he had this opportunity.

154:7. The Hasty Flight

It was almost half past eight this beautiful morning when this company of twenty-five manned the oars and pulled for the eastern shore of the Sea of Galilee. Jesus was never again to make his home at the house of Zebedee. For a time they remained in the domains of Philip, going from Kheresa up to Caesarea-Philippi, thence making their way over to the coast of Phoenicia. The Jerusalem officers refused to believe he had escaped them; the Pharisees and their assistants spent almost a full week vainly searching for him in the neighborhood of Capernaum. Jesus' family were filled with confusion and consternation. They enjoyed no peace of mind until Thursday afternoon, when Ruth returned from a visit to the Zebedee house, where she learned from David that her father-brother was safe and in good health and making his way toward the Phoenician coast.

Paper 155: Fleeing Through Northern Galilee

SOON after landing near Kheresa on this eventful Sunday, Jesus and the twenty-four went a little way to the north, where they spent the night in a beautiful park familiar to them south of Bethsaida-Julias. Before retiring for the night, the Master called his followers around him and discussed with them the plans for their projected tour through Batanea and northern Galilee to the Phoenician coast.

155:1. Why Do the Heathen Rage?

Jesus called attention to the Psalmist statement, "Why do the heathen rage and the peoples plot in vain?" He told them that his kingdom is founded on love, proclaimed in mercy, and established by unselfish service. You who have professed entrance into the kingdom of heaven are altogether too vacillating and indefinite in your teaching conduct. You are hardly worthy of the kingdom when your service consists so largely in an attitude of regretting the past, whining over the present, and vainly hoping for the future. If you, by truth co-ordination, learn to exemplify in your lives this beautiful wholeness of righteousness, your fellow men will then seek after you that they may gain what you have so acquired. The extent to which you have to go with your message to the people is, in a way, the measure of your failure to live the whole or righteous life, the truth-co-ordinated life."

155:2. The Evangelists in Chorazin

On Monday morning, May 23, Jesus directed Peter to go over to Chorazin with the twelve evangelists while he, with the eleven, departed for Caesarea-Philippi. Peter and the evangelists sojourned in Chorazin for two weeks, preaching the gospel of the kingdom to a small but earnest company of believers. But they were not able to win many new converts. This was a veritable baptism of adversity for the twelve evangelists. On June 7 they departed for Caesarea-Philippi to join Jesus and the apostles.

155:3. At Caesarea-Philippi

The sojourn at Caesarea-Philippi was a real test to the eleven apostles. Though they made few converts during these two weeks, they did learn much that was highly profitable from their daily conferences with the Master. The apostles learned that the Jews were spiritually stagnant and dying because they had crystallized truth into a creed. Truth should serve as a signpost of spiritual guidance and progress to give creative and life-giving power. There is grave danger in allowing a sense of sacredness to become attached to nonsacred things. When religion is wholly spiritual in motive, it makes all life more worth while. Jesus never grew weary of pointing out to the twelve the great danger of accepting religious symbols and ceremonies in the place of religious experience. His whole earth life was consistently devoted to the mission of thawing out the frozen forms of religion into the liquid liberties of enlightened sonship.

155:4. On the Way to Phoenicia

On Thursday morning, June 9, this group of twenty-five teachers of truth left Caesarea-Philippi to begin their journey to the Phoenician coast. While pausing for lunch under the shadow of an overhanging ledge of rock, near Luz, Jesus delivered one of the most remarkable addresses which his apostles ever listened to throughout all their years of association with him. Simon Peter wanted to know why they were fleeing from their enemies and Thomas asked what was wrong with the religion of their enemies in Jerusalem. Jesus said he would first answer the question of Thomas as it would prove to be more helpful.

155:5. The Discourse on True Religion

While the religions of the world have a double origin—natural and revelatory—there are three distinct forms of religious devotion: primitive religion—the religion of fear; the religion of civilization—the religion of the mind; and true religion—the religion of revelation. Until the races become highly intelligent and more fully civilized, there will persist many of those childlike and superstitious ceremonies which are so characteristic of the evolutionary religious practices of primitive and backward peoples. Until the human race progresses to the level of a higher and more general recognition of the realities of spiritual experience, large numbers of men and women will continue to show a personal preference for those religions of authority which require only intellectual assent. The religion of the spirit means effort, struggle, conflict, faith, determination, love, loyalty, and progress. Jesus asked which of them would now prefer to take the easy path of conformity to an established and fossilized religion or discovering for themselves the beauties of the realities of a living and personal experience in the eternal truths and supreme grandeurs of the kingdom of heaven? All twenty-four rose to their feet intending to accept his challenge, but Jesus raised his hand and told them to go apart by themselves in communion with the Father to find the unemotional answer to his question. After traveling some distance, Peter asked Jesus to speak to them further.

155:6. The Second Discourse on Religion

Jesus recognized that they had left the religion of authority for the assurances of the spirit of adventurous and progressive faith. He told them not to commit the folly of calling that divine which is wholly human, and fail not to discern the words of truth which come not through the traditional oracles of supposed inspiration. We need to be born again, born of the spirit. The religion of the mind ties you hopelessly to the past; the religion of the spirit consists in progressive revelation and ever beckons you on toward higher and holier achievements in spiritual ideals and eternal realities. The religion of the spirit leaves you forever free to follow the truth wherever the leadings of the spirit may take you. Human unity and mortal brotherhood can be achieved only by and through the superendowment of the religion of the spirit. Never forget there is only one adventure which is more satisfying and thrilling than the attempt to discover the will of the living God, and that is the supreme experience of honestly trying to do that divine will. And fail not to remember that the will of God can be done in any earthly occupation. There are two positive and powerful demonstrations of the fact that you are God-knowing, and they are: 1. the fruits of the spirit of God showing forth in your daily routine life; 2. the fact that your entire life plan furnishes positive proof that you have unreservedly risked everything you are and have on the adventure of finding the God of eternity, whose presence you have foretasted in time. But, mistake not, the Father will ever respond to the faintest flicker of faith.

Paper 156: The Sojourn at Tyre and Sidon

ON Friday afternoon, June 10, Jesus and his associates arrived in the environs of Sidon where they stopped at the home of a well-to-do woman who had been a patient in the Bethsaida hospital.

156:1. The Syrian Woman

There lived near the home of Karuska, where the Master lodged, a Syrian woman, Norana, who had heard much of Jesus as a great healer and teacher and brought her daughter who was afflicted with a grievous nervous disorder. When Norana arrived with her daughter, the Alpheus twins explained through an interpreter that the Master was resting and could not be disturbed; whereupon Norana replied that she and the child would remain right there until the Master had finished his rest. Peter and Thomas could not convince her to leave, so Simon Zelotes told her she should not expect the Master to "take the bread intended for the children of the favored household and cast it to the dogs." Her daughter was seized with a violent convulsion and she told them that she heard that their Master loved all people and they were not worthy to be his disciples. Jesus had heard all this through an open window and came out and said, "O woman, great is your faith, so great that I cannot withhold that which you desire; go your way in peace. Your daughter already has been made whole." Although they were told to tell no one, they broadcast it throughout the countryside and Jesus found it advisable to change his lodging.

156:2. Teaching in Sidon

As the twenty-four began their labors in Sidon, Jesus went to stay in the home of Justa and her mother, Bernice. The apostles and the evangelists were greatly cheered by the manner in which the gentiles of Sidon received their message; during their short sojourn many were added to the kingdom. In many ways these gentile believers appreciated Jesus' teachings more fully than the Jews. The theme of Jesus' instructions during the sojourn at Sidon was spiritual progression. He told them they could not stand still; they must go forward in righteousness or retrogress into evil and sin. Jesus greatly enjoyed the keen sense of humor which these gentiles exhibited. Jesus greatly regretted that his people, the Jews, were so lacking in humor. "They also lack consistency; they strain at gnats and swallow camels."

156:3. The Journey up the Coast

On Tuesday, June 28, the Master and his associates left Sidon, going up the coast to Porphyreon and Heldua. They were well received by the gentiles, and many were added to the kingdom during this week of teaching and preaching. By this time the apostles and the evangelists were becoming accustomed to working among these so-called gentiles. It was a great surprise to the apostles and evangelists to observe the eagerness of these gentiles to hear the gospel and to note the readiness with which many of them believed.

156:4. At Tyre

From July 11 to July 24 they taught in Tyre. Each of the apostles took with him one of the evangelists, and thus two and two they taught and preached in all parts of Tyre and its environs. The polyglot population of this busy seaport heard them gladly, and many were baptized into the outward fellowship of the kingdom. Every day believers came out from the city to talk with Jesus at his resting place. The Master spoke in Tyre only once, on the afternoon of July 20, when he taught the believers concerning the Father's love for all mankind and about the mission of the Son to reveal the Father to all races of men. There was such an interest in the gospel of the kingdom among these gentiles that, on this occasion, the doors of the Melkarth temple were opened to him, and it is interesting to record that in subsequent years a Christian church was built on the very site of this ancient temple.

156:5. Jesus' Teaching at Tyre

On this Wednesday afternoon, in the course of his address, Jesus first told his followers the story of the white lily which rears its pure and snowy head high into the sunshine while its roots are grounded in the slime and muck of the darkened soil beneath. "Likewise," said he, "mortal man, while he has his roots of origin and being in the animal soil of human nature, can by faith raise his spiritual nature up into the sunlight of heavenly truth and actually bear the noble fruits of the spirit." In discussing temptation Jesus told them that the best way to surmount temptation was not to supplant one desire for another superior desire by the force of human will, but to truly developed an actual interest in, and love for, those higher and more idealistic forms of conduct. You will in this way be delivered through spiritual transformation. Do not become discouraged by the discovery that you are human. The mistakes which you fail to forget in time will be forgotten in eternity. Lighten your burdens of soul by speedily acquiring a long-distance view of your destiny, a universe expansion of your career. Divine love cannot be self-contained; it must be unselfishly bestowed. God-knowing individuals are not discouraged by misfortune or downcast by disappointment. Believers are immune to the depression consequent upon purely material upheavals. It is not possible to respect yourself more than you love your neighbor. Tact is the fulcrum of social leverage, and tolerance is the earmark of a great soul.

156:6. The Return from Phoenicia

Jesus and his apostles eventually made their way to Gennesaret on the western shores of the lake of Galilee, south of Capernaum, where they had appointed to meet with David Zebedee, and where they intended to take counsel as to the next move to be made in the work of preaching the gospel of the kingdom. The enemies of Jesus thought he would not likely ever return to bother them. Philip, the brother of Herod, had become a halfhearted believer in Jesus and sent word that the Master was free to live and work in his domains. Even Herod Antipas experienced a change of heart and sent word to him that he had not authorized his apprehension in Perea, thus indicating that Jesus would not be molested if he remained outside of Galilee; and he communicated this same ruling to the Jews at Jerusalem. And that was the situation about the first of August, A.D. 29, when the Master returned from the Phoenician mission and began the reorganization of his scattered, tested, and depleted forces for this last and eventful year of his mission on earth. The issues of battle are clearly drawn as the Master and his associates prepare to begin the proclamation of a new religion, the religion of the spirit of the living God who dwells in the minds of men.

Paper 157: At Caesarea-Philippi

BEFORE Jesus took the twelve for a short sojourn in the vicinity of Caesarea-Philippi, he arranged through the messengers of David to go over to Capernaum on Sunday, August 1, for the purpose of meeting his family. A group of Pharisees called upon Mary and sensing that Jesus might come remained all day. And so again, through no fault of either, Jesus and his earth family failed to make contact.

157:1. The Temple-Tax Collector

As Jesus, with Andrew and Peter, tarried by the lake near the boatshop, a temple-tax collector came upon them and, recognizing Jesus, called Peter to one side and asked if Jesus paid the temple tax. Sensing that the tax collector was trying to entrap them in the act of refusing to pay the customary half shekel temple tax, Peter assured him that they would pay the tax. But none of them had any money. When Peter told Jesus of their problem, Jesus suggested that Peter go fishing, sell the fish and pay the tax for all three of them. This was overheard by a secret messenger of David who signaled to an associate fishing near the shore. As Peter was going toward the boat Jesus said, half-humorously, "Go hence! maybe you will catch the fish with the shekel in its mouth." This fisherman friend presented Peter with several large baskets of fish which were sold and the tax was paid. It is not strange that there is a record of Peter's catching a fish with a shekel in its mouth that was expanded into a miracle as recorded by the writer of Matthew's Gospel.

157:2. At Bethsaida-Julias

On Monday, August 8, while Jesus and the twelve apostles were encamped in Magadan Park, near Bethsaida-Julias, more than one hundred believers, the evangelists, the women's corps, and others interested in the establishment of the kingdom, came over from Capernaum for a conference. And many of the Pharisees came also. The Pharisees asked for a sign of Jesus' authority to teach. Jesus told them that it was strange that they could tell the signs of the weather but were utterly unable to discern the signs of the times. "To those who would know the truth, already has a sign been given; but to an evil-minded and hypocritical generation no sign shall be given." At the conference this evening it was decided to undertake a united mission throughout all the cities and villages of the Decapolis as soon as Jesus and the twelve should return from their proposed visit to Caesarea-Philippi. Jesus warned them not to be deceived by learning of the Pharisees and Sadducees and their profound loyalty to the forms of religion. He urged them to lovingly serve their fellows with intelligent ministry.

157:3. Peter's Confession

Early Tuesday morning Jesus and the twelve apostles left Magadan Park for Caesarea-Philippi, the capital of the Tetrarch Philip's domain. Caesarea-Philippi was situated in a region of wondrous beauty. The heights of Mount Hermon were in full view to the north, while from the hills just to the south a magnificent view was had of the upper Jordan and the Sea of Galilee. As they paused for lunch, Jesus suddenly confronted the twelve with the first question he had ever addressed to them concerning himself. He asked this surprising question, "Who do men say that I am?" They told him that he was regarded as a prophet or as an extraordinary man by all who knew him. When Jesus had listened to this report, he drew himself upon his feet, and looking down upon the twelve sitting about him in a semi-circle, with startling emphasis he pointed to them with a sweeping gesture of his hand and asked, "But who say you that I am?" There was a moment of tense silence. Then Simon Peter, springing to his feet, exclaimed, "You are the Deliverer, the Son of the living God." And the eleven sitting apostles arose to their feet with one accord, thereby indicating that Peter had spoken for all of them. When Jesus had beckoned them again to be seated he said, "This has been revealed to you by my Father. The hour has come when you should know the truth about me. But for the time being I charge you that you tell this to no man."

157:4. The Talk About the Kingdom

During most of the night and since they had arisen that morning, Simon Peter and Simon Zelotes had been earnestly laboring with their brethren to bring them all to the point of the wholehearted acceptance of the Master, not merely as the Messiah, but also as the divine Son of the living God. While Andrew continued as the director-general of the apostolic corps, his brother, Simon Peter, was becoming, increasingly and by common consent, the spokesman for the twelve. They were all seated in the garden at just about noon when the Master appeared. They all arose to their feet as he approached them. With a commanding gesture he indicated that they should be seated. Never again did the twelve greet their Master by arising when he came into their presence. After they had partaken of their meal, Jesus suddenly looked up into their faces and asked if they still held Peter's identity of the Son of Man. He was assured that they did. Jesus told them that this was a revelation of the spirit of the Father to their inmost souls and on this foundation he would build the brotherhood of the kingdom of heaven. "To you and your successors I now deliver the keys of the outward kingdom—the authority over things temporal."

157:5. The New Concept

The new and vital feature of Peter's confession was the clear-cut recognition that Jesus was the Son of God, of his unquestioned divinity. Jesus had sought to live his life on earth and complete his bestowal mission as the Son of Man. But he now recognized that such a plan could hardly be carried through successfully. He therefore elected boldly to announce his divinity, acknowledge the truthfulness of Peter's confession, and directly proclaim to the twelve that he was a Son of God.

157:6. The Next Afternoon

Neither Peter nor the other apostles had a very adequate conception of Jesus' divinity. He came that we all might have life and have it more abundantly. Jesus now entered upon the fourth and last stage of his human life in the flesh. The first stage was that of his childhood. The second stage was the years of youth and advancing manhood, ending with his baptism. The third period embraced the times when his apostles knew him as the Son of Man. During the fourth period he became known to the apostles as the Son of God. A new significance attaches to all of Jesus' teachings from this point on, such as the following: "No man in this world now sees the Father except the Son who came forth from the Father. But if the Son be lifted up, he will draw all men to himself, and whosoever believes this truth of the combined nature of the Son shall be endowed with life that is more than age-abiding." "Nevertheless, I tell you that the Father and I are one. He who has seen me has seen the Father. My Father is working with me in all these things, and he will never leave me alone in my mission, even as I will never forsake you when you presently go forth to proclaim this gospel throughout the world."

157:7. Andrew's Conference

That evening Andrew took it upon himself to hold a personal and searching conference with each of his brethren, except Judas Iscariot. Andrew was now so worried by Judas's attitude that, later on that night, after all the apostles were fast asleep, he sought out Jesus and presented his cause for anxiety to the Master. Said Jesus, "It is not amiss, Andrew, that you have come to me with this matter, but there is nothing more that we can do; only go on placing the utmost confidence in this apostle. And say nothing to his brethren concerning this talk with me." When Jesus would send the apostles off to pray, Judas indulged in thoughts of fear, subtle doubts about the mission of Jesus, and feelings of revenge. Now Jesus planned to take his apostles along with him to Mount Hermon, that they may be strengthened for the trying times ahead.

Paper 158: The Mount of Transfiguration

IT was near sundown on Friday afternoon, August 12, A.D. 29, when Jesus and his associates reached the foot of Mount Hermon, near the very place where the lad Tiglath once waited while the Master ascended the mountain alone to settle the spiritual destinies of Urantia and technically to terminate the Lucifer rebellion. Since the apostles could not attain the spiritual level appropriate for the transfiguration experience, Jesus took Peter, James, and John who usually accompanied him.

158:1. The Transfiguration

Early on the morning of Monday, August 15, Jesus and the three apostles began the ascent of Mount Hermon. They reached their destination, about halfway up the mountain, shortly before noon. The Master could have relinquished the struggle this day on Mount Hermon and returned to his rule of the universe domains, but he elected to meet the last and full measure of the present will of his Paradise Father. It was about three o'clock on this beautiful afternoon that Jesus took leave of the three apostles for a long conference with Gabriel and the Father Melchizedek, not returning until about six o'clock. As they partook of their meager evening meal, they talked over the affairs of the Lucifer rebellion while seated about the glowing embers of their fire until the apostles' eyes grew heavy. When the three had been fast asleep for about half an hour, they were suddenly awakened by a near-by crackling sound, and much to their amazement they beheld Jesus in intimate converse with two brilliant beings. These three conversed in a strange language, and Peter erroneously conjectured that the beings with Jesus were Moses and Elijah. Presently, a silvery cloud drew near and overshadowed the four of them. The apostles now became greatly frightened, and as they fell down on their faces to worship, they heard a voice say, "This is my beloved Son; give heed to him." And when the cloud vanished, Jesus touching them said, "Arise and be not afraid; you shall see greater things than this." But the apostles were truly afraid; they were a silent and thoughtful trio as they made ready to descend the mountain shortly before midnight.

158:2. Coming Down the Mountain

For about half the distance down the mountain not a word was spoken. Jesus then began the conversation by remarking, "Make certain that you tell no man, not even your brethren, what you have seen and heard on this mountain until the Son of Man has risen from the dead." The three apostles were shocked and bewildered by the Master's words, "until the Son of Man has risen from the dead." Although Peter, James, and John pondered all this in their minds, they spoke not of it to any man until after the Master's resurrection. As they continued to descend the mountain, Jesus told them that the will of the Father must prevail, and if they choose to follow their own wills, they must be prepared to suffer many disappointments and experience many trials.

158:3. Meaning of the Transfiguration

The transfiguration was the occasion of the acceptance of the fullness of the bestowal mission of Michael by the Eternal Son of Paradise brought by Gabriel. It was also the testimony of the satisfaction of the Infinite Spirit as to the fullness of the Urantia bestowal given through the Universe Mother Spirit spoken through the Father Melchizedek. Jesus welcomed this testimony regarding the success of his earth mission presented by the messengers of the Eternal Son and the Infinite Spirit, but he noted that his Father did not indicate that the Urantia bestowal was finished. After this celestial visitation Jesus sought to know his Father's will and decided to pursue the mortal bestowal to its natural end. After the formal visitation of Gabriel and the Father Melchizedek, Jesus held informal converse with these, his Sons of ministry, and communed with them concerning the affairs of the universe.

158:4. The Epileptic Boy

It was shortly before breakfast time on this Tuesday morning when Jesus and his companions arrived at the apostolic camp. The nine apostles had been arguing about their possible places in the coming kingdom. As they drew near, they discerned a considerable crowd gathered around the apostles and soon began to hear the loud words of argument and disputation of this group of about fifty persons. James of Safed brought his son about fourteen years old who was both an epileptic and demon-possessed. Simon Zelotes and Judas Iscariot tired to cure him but failed, then Andrew tried to heal him without success. They were a dejected and chastened group. But James of Safed would not give up. Although they could give him no idea as to when Jesus might return, he decided to stay on until the Master came back.

158:5. Jesus Heals the Boy

As Jesus drew near, the nine apostles were more than relieved to welcome him. The anxious father of the afflicted lad stepped forward and, kneeling at Jesus' feet, told Jesus about his afflicted son and asked Jesus to heal him. And as they talked, the youth was seized with a violent attack and fell in their midst, gnashing his teeth and foaming at the mouth. Jesus said, "Question not my Father's power of love, only the sincerity and reach of your faith. All things are possible to him who really believes." And then James of Safed replied, "Lord, I believe. I pray you help my unbelief." When Jesus heard these words, he stepped forward and, taking the lad by the hand, said, "I will do this in accordance with my Father's will and in honor of living faith. My son, arise! Come out of him, disobedient spirit, and go not back into him." And placing the hand of the lad in the hand of the father, Jesus said, "Go your way. The Father has granted the desire of your soul."

158:6. In Celsus' Garden

They remained overnight with Celsus, and that evening in the garden, after they had eaten and rested, Thomas commented that although they could not be told what happened on the mountain, would Jesus talk to them about their defeat with the epileptic boy. Jesus told them that in due time they would be told about what took place on the mountain. He regretted that they were still concerned about their seeking preferred places in the kingdom of heaven and reminded them that those who would be greatest in the Father's spiritual brotherhood must become little in their own eyes and become the servers of their brethren. In their failure, Jesus told them their purpose was not pure; their motive was not divine; their ideal was not spiritual or altruistic, and their procedure was not based on love nor the will of the Father in heaven. The Master reminded them that they could not time-shorten the course of established natural phenomena except when such things are in accordance with the Father's will and in the presence of living faith. Jesus told them that he was now entering the last phase of his bestowal. "And remember what I am saying to you, The Son of Man will be put to death, but he shall rise again."

158:7. Peter's Protest

Early this Wednesday morning Jesus and the twelve departed from Caesarea-Philippi for Magadan Park near Bethsaida-Julias. After their lunch, Andrew asked Jesus to explain why he had talked about dying. Jesus assured them that he was not talking in parables, that he was not their concept of the Messiah, that he would be rejected by the Jerusalem leaders, be killed and raised from the dead. Simon Peter rushed to Jesus, laid his hand on the Master's shoulder and declared that this would not happen to him. Jesus sternly rebuked him as a stumbling block to doing the Father's will, saying, "If any man would come after me, let him disregard himself, take up his responsibilities daily, and follow me. For whosoever would save his life selfishly, shall lose it, but whosoever loses his life for my sake and the gospel's, shall save it. What does it profit a man to gain the whole world and lose his own soul?" What a shock these words were to these Galilean fishermen who persisted in dreaming of an earthly kingdom with positions of honor for themselves!

158:8. At Peter's House

Entering Capernaum at twilight, they went by unfrequented thoroughfares directly to the home of Simon Peter for their evening meal. Jesus asked them what they had been talking about in the afternoon. He knew they had been discussing what positions they were to have in the coming kingdom; who should be the greatest, and so on. Jesus beckoned to one of Peter's little ones and, setting the child down among them, said, "Verily, verily, I say to you, except you turn about and become more like this child, you will make little progress in the kingdom of heaven. Whosoever shall humble himself and become as this little one, the same shall become greatest in the kingdom of heaven.... But most of all, see that you despise not one of these little ones, for their angels do always behold the faces of the heavenly hosts." When Jesus had finished speaking, they entered the boat and sailed across to Magadan.

Paper 159: The Decapolis Tour

WHEN Jesus and the twelve arrived at Magadan Park, they found awaiting them a group of almost one hundred evangelists and disciples, including the women's corps. On this Thursday morning, August 18, the Master called his followers together and directed that each of the apostles should associate himself with one of the twelve evangelists, and that with others of the evangelists they should go out in twelve groups to labor in the cities and villages of the Decapolis. The women's corps and others of the disciples he directed to remain with him. Jesus allotted four weeks to this tour, instructing his followers to return to Magadan not later than Friday, September 16.

159:1. The Sermon on Forgiveness

One evening at Hippos, in answer to a disciple's question, Jesus taught the lesson on forgiveness. He told the parable of the shepherd who goes in search of one sheep who has gone astray. It is not the will of the Father that one person go astray. There is more joy in heaven over one sinner who repents than in the ninety and nine who need no repentance. If your brother sins against you, go to him with tact and patience to show him his fault. If your brother will not hear you, take one or two mutual friends with you, if he still refuses to hear your brethren, tell the whole story to the congregation and let them take such action as they deem wise. While we may not sit in judgment on the souls of our fellows, we should maintain the temporal order. Where two or three of people agree concerning any of these things, it shall be done for you if your petition is not inconsistent with the will of the Father in heaven.

"Where two or three believers are gathered together, there am I in the midst of them." Simon Peter asked how many times we should forgive our brother, seven times? And Jesus answered Peter, "Not only seven times but even to seventy times and seven." He then told the parable of the steward who owed the king a large debt and when threatened with prison, the steward pleaded with the king who took compassion on him and forgave the debt. This steward then placed one of his fellows in prison showing no mercy. When the king heard of this he placed the steward in prison until he paid all that was owed. "Freely you have received the good things of the kingdom; therefore freely give to your fellows on earth." Jesus invested legislative and judicial authority in the group, not in the individual.

159:2. The Strange Preacher

Jesus went over to Gamala to visit John and those who worked with him at that place. That evening John told Jesus that a man in Ashtaroth was teaching in Jesus' name but had never been with them, so he forbid this man to do this. Then said Jesus, "Forbid him not. Do you not perceive that this gospel of the kingdom shall presently be proclaimed in all the world? . . . My son, in matters of this sort it would be better for you to reckon that he who is not against us is for us." Nevertheless, many times did the apostles take offense at those who made bold to teach in the Master's name who had not been taught by Jesus. This man whom John forbade to teach and work in Jesus' name did not heed the apostle's injunction. He raised up a considerable company of believers at Kanata. This man, Aden, had been led to believe in Jesus through the testimony of the demented man whom Jesus healed near Kheresa.

159:3. Instruction for Teachers and Believers

At Edrei, where Thomas and his associates labored, Jesus gave expression to the principles which should guide those who preach truth. Always respect the personality of man. Never should a righteous cause be promoted by force, overpowering arguments, or appealing to fear. Make your appeals directly to the divine spirit that dwells within the minds of men. Idleness is destructive of self-respect; therefore, admonish your brethren ever to keep busy at their chosen tasks. Forewarn all believers regarding the fringe of conflict which must be traversed by all who pass from the life as it is lived in the flesh to the higher life as it is lived in the spirit. In preaching the gospel of the kingdom, you are simply teaching friendship with God. When my children once become self-conscious of the assurance of the divine presence, such a faith will expand the mind, ennoble the soul, reinforce the personality, augment the happiness, deepen the spirit perception, and enhance the power to love and be loved. Teach all believers that those who enter the kingdom are not thereby rendered immune to the accidents of time or to the ordinary catastrophes of nature. I do not promise to deliver you from the waters of adversity, but I do promise to go with you through all of them.

159:4. The Talk with Nathaniel

And then went Jesus over to Abila, where Nathaniel and his associates labored. Nathaniel questioned the authority of the Hebrew scriptures. Jesus told him that the scriptures contain much that does not reflect the character and teachings of the Father in heaven. They represent the views of the times of their origin. It is deplorable that there is belief in their infallibility. Never forget, the Father does not limit the revelation of truth to any one generation or to any one people. "Mark you well my words, Nathaniel, nothing which human nature has touched can be regarded as infallible." Sadly some of the teachers of this traditionalism know this truth but are moral cowards, intellectually dishonest. Nathaniel was enlightened, and shocked, by the Master's pronouncement. He long pondered this talk in the depths of his soul, but he told no man concerning this conference until after Jesus' ascension; and even then he feared to impart the full story of the Master's instruction.

159:5. The Positive Nature of Jesus' Religion

At Philadelphia, where James was working, Jesus taught the disciples about the positive nature of the gospel of the kingdom. Jesus made the care of God for man like the solicitude of a loving father for the welfare of his dependent children and then made this teaching the cornerstone of his religion. Jesus required his followers to react positively and aggressively to every life situation. Jesus abhorred the idea either of retaliation or of becoming just a passive sufferer or victim of injustice. He taught them to return good for evil, to assert the will so as to become master of the situation, to overcome evil with good. One of the apostles once asked what he should do if a stranger forced him to carry his pack for a mile? Jesus answered, "If you can think of nothing more effectively positive to do, you can at least carry the pack a second mile. That will of a certainty challenge the unrighteous and ungodly stranger." Jesus portrayed the elemental needs of the soul with a new insight and a new bestowal of affection.

159:6. The Return to Magadan

The mission of four weeks in the Decapolis was moderately successful. On Friday, September 16, the entire corps of workers assembled by prearrangement at Magadan Park. The messengers of David were present and made reports concerning the welfare of the believers everywhere. About this time Abner moved his base of operations from Hebron to Bethlehem, and this latter place was also the headquarters in Judea for David's messengers.

David maintained an overnight relay messenger service between Jerusalem and Bethsaida. The Perean mission developed into a campaign of preaching and teaching which extended right on down to the time of their arrival at Jerusalem and of the enactment of the closing episodes of Jesus' earth career.

Paper 160: Rodan of Alexandria

ON Sunday morning, September 18, Andrew announced that no work would be planned for the coming week. All of the apostles, except Nathaniel and Thomas, went home to visit their families or to sojourn with friends. Nathaniel and Thomas were very busy with their discussions with a certain Greek philosopher from Alexandria named Rodan. This Greek had recently become a disciple of Jesus through the teaching of one of Abner's associates.

160:1. Rodan's Greek Philosophy

Early Monday morning, Rodan began a series of ten addresses to Nathaniel, Thomas, and a group of some two dozen believers. The more complex civilization becomes, the more difficult will become the art of living. The more rapid the changes in social usage, the more complicated will become the task of character development. Social maturity is equivalent to the degree to which man is willing to surrender the gratification of mere transient and present desires for the entertainment of those superior longings of progressive advancement toward permanent goals of idealistic spiritual realities. The mature human being soon begins to look upon all other mortals with feelings of tenderness and with emotions of tolerance. Only a brave person is willing honestly to admit, and fearlessly to face, what a sincere and logical mind discovers. But the greatest of all methods of problem solving I have learned from Jesus, the isolation of worshipful meditation—by actually subjecting the total personality to the consciousness of contacting with divinity, and to do all of this with an eye single to the glory of God. And this is true because our ideal is final, infallible, eternal, universal, absolute, and infinite.

160:2. The Art of Living

It is the ability to communicate and share meanings that constitutes human culture and enables man, through social associations, to build civilizations. The most effective of all social groups is the family. Many noble human impulses die because there is no one to hear their expression. Truly, it is not good for man to be alone. Of all social relations calculated to develop character, the most effective and ideal is the affectionate and understanding friendship of man and woman in the mutual embrace of intelligent wedlock.

It is worth any price, any sacrifice, requisite for its possession. Men enrich the soul by pooling their respective spiritual possessions. Likewise, in this same way, man is enabled to avoid that ever-present tendency to fall victim to distortion of vision, prejudice of viewpoint, and narrowness of judgment. Isolation tends to exhaust the energy charge of the soul. Loving and intimate human associations tend to rob suffering of its sorrow and hardship of much of its bitterness. There is positive strength in the knowledge that you live for the welfare of others, and that these others likewise live for your welfare and advancement.

160:3. The Lures of Maturity

The effort toward maturity necessitates work, and work requires energy. Whence then comes the energy to do these great things? The secret of all this problem is wrapped up in spiritual communion, in worship. Meditation makes the contact of mind with spirit; relaxation determines the capacity for spiritual receptivity. And this interchange of strength for weakness, courage for fear, the will of God for the mind of self, constitutes worship. When these experiences are frequently repeated, they crystallize into habits, and such habits eventually formulate themselves into a spiritual character. The mature man wins the hearty co-operation of his associates, thereby many times multiplying the fruits of his life efforts. This new gospel of the kingdom renders a great service to the art of living in that it supplies a new and richer incentive for higher living. On every mountaintop of intellectual thought are to be found relaxation for the mind, strength for the soul, and communion for the spirit.

160:4. The Balance of Maturity

The essentials of the temporal life are good health, clear thinking, material needs, the ability to withstand defeat, and education and wisdom. The mind of man becomes the mediator between material things and spiritual realities.

Ability is that which you inherit, while skill is what you acquire. Skill is one of the real sources of the satisfaction of living. The wise man is able to distinguish between means and ends. The noblest of all memories are the treasured recollections of the great moments of a superb friendship. Life will become a burden of existence unless you learn how to fail gracefully and lose cheerfully. You must be fearless of disappointment. Success may generate courage and promote confidence, but wisdom comes only from the experiences of adjustment to the results of one's failures.

Failure is simply an educational episode—a cultural experiment in the acquirement of wisdom. Wisdom ever dominates knowledge and always glorifies culture.

160:5. The Religion of the Ideal

You have told me that your Master regards genuine human religion as the individual's experience with spiritual realities. I have regarded religion as man's experience of reacting to something which he regards as being worthy of the homage and devotion of all mankind. If you are not a positive and missionary evangel of your religion, you are self-deceived in that what you call a religion is only a traditional belief or a mere system of intellectual philosophy. Regardless of the name applied to this ideal of spirit reality, it is God. Religion reaches out for undiscovered ideals, unexplored realities, superhuman values, divine wisdom, and true spirit attainment. The religion of Jesus transcends all our former concepts of the idea of worship in that he not only portrays his Father as the ideal of infinite reality but is personally attainable. That, I submit, is the highest concept of religion the world has ever known, and I pronounce that there can never be a higher since this gospel embraces the infinity of realities, the divinity of values, and the eternity of universal attainments. I am finally convinced that there are no attainable ideals of reality or values of perfection apart from the eternal and Universal Father. The religion of Jesus demands living and spiritual experience. And all of this must be made personal to us by the revelation of the Spirit of Truth.

Paper 161: Further Discussions with Rodan

ON Sunday, September 25, A.D. 29, the apostles and the evangelists assembled at Magadan. Jesus surprised all by announcing that early the next day he and the twelve apostles would start for Jerusalem to attend the feast of tabernacles. He directed that the evangelists visit the believers in Galilee, and that the women's corps return for a while to Bethsaida. Nathaniel and Thomas secured the Master's permission to remain at Magadan for a few days to engaged in earnest debate with Rodan.

161:1. The Personality of God

There was one matter on which Rodan and the two apostles did not see alike, and that was the personality of God. While the apostles found themselves in difficulty trying to prove that God is a person, Rodan found it still more difficult to prove he is not a person. Rodan contended that personalities must have full and mutual communication with beings of equality and since God has no equal, he cannot be a personality, even though he may be the source of personality. By Monday night Thomas gave up. But by Tuesday night Nathaniel had won Rodan to believe in the personality of the Father, and he effected this change in the Greek's views by observing that the Eternal

Son and the Infinite Spirit were fully equal with the Father and demonstrated the possibility that all members of the Trinity were personalities. The personality of Jesus demonstrated the personality of God. Since personality represents man's highest concept of human reality and divine values, God must be a divine and infinite personality. While God must be infinitely more than a personality, he cannot be anything less.

161:2. The Divine Nature of Jesus

Nathaniel and Thomas jointly presented their views of the divine nature of the Master in that Jesus has admitted his divinity. The life of Jesus demonstrates a person who transcends human potentials. He is the friend even of sinners; he dares to love his enemies. The better you know him, the more you will love him. We do not believe that a mere human could live such a blameless life under such trying circumstances. His wisdom is extraordinary. He lives day by day in perfect accord with the Father's will. He prays for us and with us, but he never asks us to pray for him. He even professes to forgive sins and does heal diseases. No mere man would sanely profess to forgive sin; that is a divine prerogative. The uniqueness of his character and the perfection of his emotional control convince us that he is a combination of humanity and divinity. He seems to know the thoughts of men's minds and to understand the longings of their hearts. We are constantly impressed by the phenomenon of his superhuman knowledge. He speaks with the authority of a divine teacher. He even dares to assert that he and the Father are one. When Nathaniel and Thomas had concluded their conferences with Rodan, they hurried on toward Jerusalem to join their fellow apostles.

Rodan became a mighty man, yielding up his life in Greece with others when the persecutions were at their height.

161:3. Jesus' Human and Divine Minds

Consciousness of divinity was a gradual growth in the mind of Jesus up to the occasion of his baptism. After he became fully self-conscious of his divine nature, prehuman existence, and universe prerogatives, he seems to have possessed the power of variously limiting his human consciousness of his divinity. At times he appeared to avail himself of only that information which was resident in the human intellect. On other occasions he appeared to act with such fullness of knowledge and wisdom as could be afforded only by the utilization of the superhuman content of his divine consciousness. And then on almost numberless occasions did we witness the working of this combined personality of man and God as it was activated by the apparent perfect union of the human and the divine minds. This is the limit of our knowledge of such phenomena; we really do not actually know the full truth about this mystery.

Paper 162: At the Feast of Tabernacles

ON the way to Jerusalem Jesus and the apostles sought to secure lodging at a Samaritan village but were rejected. James and John wanted to "bid fire to come down from heaven" and devour these Samaritans. Jesus severely rebuked them. Thus because of sectarian prejudice these Samaritans denied themselves the honor of showing hospitality to the Creator Son of a universe. Jesus and the twelve remained in the vicinity of Jerusalem about four and one-half weeks. Jesus himself went into the city only a few times. He spent a considerable portion of October with Abner and his associates at Bethlehem.

162:1. The Dangers of the Visit to Jerusalem

Knowing that the Sanhedrin had sought to bring Jesus to Jerusalem for trial the apostles had been literally stunned by his sudden decision to attend the feast of tabernacles. During the feast of tabernacles Jesus went boldly into Jerusalem on several occasions and publicly taught in the temple. This he did in spite of the efforts of his apostles to dissuade him. His presence in Jerusalem at the feast of tabernacles sufficed forever to put an end to all whisperings about fear and cowardice. Many of the members of the Sanhedrin either secretly believed in Jesus or else were decidedly averse to arresting him during the feast. The efforts of Abner and his associates throughout Judea had also done much to consolidate sentiment favorable to the kingdom. But the audacious boldness of Jesus in publicly appearing in Jerusalem overawed his enemies; they were not prepared for such a daring challenge. These teachings were really the official or formal announcement of the divinity of Jesus to the Jewish people and to the whole world.

162:2. The First Temple Talk

The first afternoon that Jesus taught in the temple he was asked how he could teach so effectively having been untaught by the rabbis and why the rulers sought to kill him. Jesus told them that his teachings come from the Father. "The rulers seek to kill me because they resent my teaching about the good news of the kingdom, a gospel that sets men free from the burdensome traditions of a formal religion of ceremonies. . . . they well know that, if you honestly believe and dare to accept my teaching, their system of traditional religion will be overthrown, forever destroyed." The Pharisees with their leaders decided that something should be done to put a stop to these public appearances of Jesus in the temple courts. Accordingly, Eber, the proper officer of the Sanhedrin, with two assistants was dispatched to arrest Jesus. They were so impressed by Jesus that they returned to their leaders telling them that they should go and hear him. The Sanhedrin disbanded in confusion, and Jesus withdrew to Bethany for the night.

162:3. The Woman Taken in Adultery

A group of the hired agents of the Sanhedrin brought a woman taken in adultery to Jesus asking what they should do with her. If he said stone her according to the law of Moses, they would involve him with the Roman law which denied the Jews the right to execute people. If he forbade stoning the woman, they would accuse him before the Sanhedrin of setting himself above Moses and the Jewish law. If he remained silent, they would accuse him of cowardice. But the Master so managed the situation that the whole plot fell to pieces of its own sordid weight. This woman was forced by her husband to prostitute her physical charms for financial gain and entered into a bargain with the hirelings of the Jewish rulers to confront Jesus. Jesus, looking over the crowd, saw her husband, and walked around to near where this degenerate husband stood and wrote upon the sand a few words which caused him to depart in haste. Then he came back before the woman and wrote again upon the ground for the benefit of her would-be accusers; and when they read his words, they, too, went away. And when the Master had written in the sand the third time, the woman's companion in evil took his departure. Jesus told her, "I know about you; neither do I condemn you. Go your way in peace." And this woman, Hildana, forsook her wicked husband and joined herself to the disciples of the kingdom.

162:4. The Feast of Tabernacles

This was the feast of the harvest ingathering. It was a combination of vacation pleasures with the solemn rites of religious worship. It was an elaborate ceremony in which seventy bullocks were sacrificed involving four hundred and fifty priests with a corresponding number of Levites officiating.

162:5. Sermon on the Light of the World

On the evening of the next to the last day of the feast, when the scene was brilliantly illuminated by the lights of the candelabras and the torches, Jesus stood up in the midst of the assembled throng and said, "I am the light of the world. He who follows me shall not walk in darkness but shall have the light of life." "You who would kill the Son of Man know not whence I came, who I am, or whither I go." "Truly, you know neither me nor my Father, for if you had known me, you would also have known the Father." "I am not of this world, and I live in the eternal light of the Father of lights. You all have had abundant opportunity to learn who I am, but you shall have still other evidence confirming the identity of the Son of Man." "I am the light of life, and every one who deliberately and with understanding rejects this saving light shall die in his sins." "When the Son of Man is lifted up, then shall you all know that I am he, and that I have done nothing of myself but only as the Father has taught me."

162:6. Discourse on the Water of Life

On the last day, just after the water and the wine had been poured down upon the altar by the priests, Jesus, standing among the pilgrims, said, "If any man thirst, let him come to me and drink. From the Father above I bring to this world the water of life." "When the Son of Man has finished his work on earth, there shall be poured out upon all flesh the living Spirit of Truth. Those who receive this spirit shall never know spiritual thirst.... To every one who has faith shall this bestowal of the spirit become the true teacher of the way which leads to life everlasting." And Jesus continued to answer the questions of both the multitude and the Pharisees.

162:7. The Discourse on Spiritual Freedom

On the afternoon of the last day of the feast and after the apostles had failed in their efforts to persuade him to flee from Jerusalem, Jesus again went into the temple to teach. Finding a large company of believers assembled in Solomon's Porch, he spoke to them, saying, "If my words abide in you and you are minded to do the will of my Father, then are you truly my disciples. You shall know the truth, and the truth shall make you free.... I know that you are Abraham's seed, yet your leaders seek to kill me because my word has not been allowed to have its transforming influence in their hearts. Their souls are sealed by prejudice and blinded by the pride of revenge." Jesus observed that their teachers say he has a devil but those who deal honestly with their souls know full well that he is not a devil. "Verily, verily, I say to you who believe the gospel that, if a man will keep this word of truth alive in his heart, he shall never taste death.... Though you know not the Father, I truly know him. Even Abraham rejoiced to see my day, and by faith he saw it and was glad." The unbelieving Jews sought to stone him but the Master quickly escaped to a secret meeting place near Bethany where Martha, Mary, and Lazarus awaited him.

162:8. The Visit with Martha and Mary

It had been arranged that Jesus should lodge with Lazarus and his sisters at a friend's house. For years it had been the custom for these three to drop everything and listen to Jesus' teaching whenever he chanced to visit them. On this occasion Martha was busy preparing the evening meal and went to Jesus asking that Mary come and help her. Jesus asked her why she was anxious about so many things, that Mary had chosen the more important thing. Both of them should learn to serve in co-operation and both should refresh their souls in unison. The lesser matters of life should give way before the greater things of the heavenly kingdom.

162:9. At Bethlehem with Abner

At this time, Abner was making his headquarters at Bethlehem, and from that center many workers had been sent to the cities of Judea and southern Samaria and even to Alexandria. Throughout his visit to the feast of tabernacles, Jesus had divided his time about equally between Bethany and Bethlehem. Jesus and Abner completed the arrangements for the consolidation of the work of the two groups of apostles. Before leaving Bethlehem for the last time, the Master made arrangements for them all to join him in the united effort which was to precede the ending of his earth career in the flesh. The apostles and Jesus arrived at the Magadan Park on November 2. The apostles were greatly relieved to have the Master back on friendly soil; no more did they urge him to go up to Jerusalem to proclaim the gospel of the kingdom.

Paper 163: Ordination of the Seventy at Magadan

A FEW days after the return of Jesus and the twelve to Magadan from Jerusalem, Abner and a group of some fifty disciples arrived from Bethlehem. At this time there were also assembled at Magadan Camp the evangelistic corps, the women's corps, and about one hundred and fifty other true and tried disciples from all parts of Palestine. From this group the Master subsequently chose the seventy teachers and sent them forth to proclaim the gospel of the kingdom. Regular instruction began on Friday, November 4, and continued until Sabbath, November 19. Jesus gave a talk to this company each morning. Peter taught methods of public preaching; Nathaniel instructed them in the art of teaching; Thomas explained how to answer questions; while Matthew directed the organization of their group finances.

163:1. Ordination of the Seventy

The seventy were ordained by Jesus on Sabbath afternoon, November 19, at the Magadan Camp, and Abner was placed at the head of these gospel preachers and teachers. David and the majority of his messenger corps and a company of believers numbering over four hundred assembled on the shore of the lake of Galilee to witness the ordination of the seventy. Before the ordination Jesus said, "The harvest is indeed plenteous, but the laborers are few; therefore I exhort all of you to pray that the Lord of the harvest will send still other laborers into his harvest." He told them they were going as lambs among wolves. They were to take no purse and were to stay as guests in homes and not move to another home that might have better lodging. They were to be as wise as serpents and harmless as doves. Early the next morning Abner sent the seventy messengers into all the cities of Galilee, Samaria, and Judea. After six weeks they returned to the new camp near Pella.

163:2. The Rich Young Man and Others

One earnest disciple came to Jesus asking to go home to bury his father; another disciple wanted to go home to comfort his family. Jesus told them his gospel messengers have forsaken all to follow him. Andrew brought a rich young man, Matadormus, a member of the Jerusalem Sanhedrin and a devout believer who wished to be ordained. After much discussion, Jesus, kissing the kneeling young man on the forehead, said, "If you would be my messenger, go and sell all that you have and, when you have bestowed the proceeds upon the poor or upon your brethren, come and follow me, and you shall have treasure in the kingdom of heaven." He arose and went away sorrowful, for he had great possessions. Almost every human being has some one thing which is held on to as a pet evil. Later on he did obey the Master's injunction and became treasurer of the Jerusalem church. Man may not share his supreme loyalty to a spiritual ideal with a material devotion.

163:3. The Discussion About Wealth

When Matadormus left, Jesus said, "You see how difficult it is for those who have riches to enter fully into the kingdom of God! Spiritual worship cannot be shared with material devotions; no man can serve two masters." Peter asked if all who followed Jesus should give up all their worldly goods and Jesus said only those who would be apostles. Jesus spoke to all of the twelve: "Verily, verily, I say to you, there is no man who has left wealth, home, wife, brethren, parents, or children for my sake and for the sake of the kingdom of heaven who shall not receive manifold more in this world, perhaps with some persecutions, and in the world to come eternal life. But many who are first shall be last, while the last shall often be first."

163:4. Farewell to the Seventy

As the seventy went forth on their first mission, Jesus emphasized that the gospel should be proclaimed to all the world, not to expect miracles when ministering to the sick, to not lose time with overmuch visiting, and to accept the hospitality of the first house of their stay without seeking better quarters. Teach that man's whole duty is summed up in this one commandment: Love the Lord your God with all your mind and soul and your neighbor as yourself. Peter than preached their ordination sermon, telling them not to neglect their daily worship, to exercise courage, faith, zeal, and initiative. They were enjoined to have kindness and courtesy.

163:5. Moving the Camp to Pella

Jesus and the twelve now prepared to establish their last headquarters in Perea, near Pella. The kingdom was taking on a new phase. Daily, pilgrims arrived from all parts of Palestine and even from remote regions of the Roman Empire. On December 18 David Zebedee, with the help of his messenger corps, loaded on to the pack animals the camp equipage and proceeded down the lake shore and along the Jordan to a point about one-half mile north of the apostolic camp where in less than a week he was prepared to offer hospitality to almost fifteen hundred pilgrim visitors. The apostolic camp could accommodate about five hundred. Near the end of December and before the return of the seventy, almost eight hundred visitors were gathered about the Master, and they found lodging in David's camp.

163:6. The Return of the Seventy

On Friday, December 30, the seventy messengers were arriving by couples, accompanied by numerous believers, at the Pella headquarters. The evening meal was delayed for more than an hour while these enthusiasts for the gospel of the kingdom related their experiences. At last Jesus was able to see men going out to spread the good news without his personal presence. The Master now knew that he could leave this world without seriously hindering the progress of the kingdom. And it was at this time that Jesus experienced one of those rare moments of emotional ecstasy which his followers had occasionally witnessed. He said, "I thank you, my Father, Lord of heaven and earth, that, while this wonderful gospel was hidden from the wise and self-righteous, the spirit has revealed these spiritual glories to these children of the kingdom. . . . and I rejoice to know that the good news will spread to all the world. . . . I am mightily moved as I realize you are about to deliver all authority into my hands. . . . To you and to all who shall follow in your steps down through the ages, let me say, I always stand near, and my invitation-call is, and ever shall be, Come to me all you who labor and are heavy laden, and I will give you rest. Take my yoke upon you and learn of me, for I am true and loyal, and you shall find spiritual rest for your souls."

163:7. Preparation for the Last Mission

The next few days were busy times in the Pella camp; preparations for the Perean mission were being completed. People came to Jesus throughout the whole Roman world. Throughout this three months' period at least ten of the apostles remained with Jesus. The women's corps had recently trained a larger corps of fifty women. Perpetua, Simon Peter's wife, became a member of this new division of the women's corps and was intrusted with the leadership of the enlarged women's work under Abner. After Pentecost she remained with her illustrious husband, accompanying him on all of his missionary tours; and on the day Peter was crucified in Rome, she was fed to the wild beasts in the arena. This new women's corps also had as members the wives of Philip and Matthew and the mother of James and John. The kingdom of heaven is the spiritual brotherhood of man founded on the eternal fact of the universal fatherhood of God.

Paper 164: At the Feast of Dedication

AS the camp at Pella was being established, Jesus, taking with him Nathaniel and Thomas, secretly went up to Jerusalem to attend the feast of the dedication. Not until they passed over the Jordan at the Bethany ford, did the two apostles become aware that their Master was going on to Jerusalem. They remonstrated with him most earnestly, and using every sort of argument, they sought to dissuade him. He replied only, "I would give these teachers in Israel another opportunity to see the light, before my hour comes."

164:1. Story of the Good Samaritan

In the course of the evening a certain lawyer, seeking to entangle Jesus in a compromising disputation, said, "Teacher, I would like to ask you just what I should do to inherit eternal life?" Jesus answered, "What is written in the law and the prophets; how do you read the Scriptures?" The lawyer, knowing the teachings of both Jesus and the Pharisees, answered, "To love the Lord God with all your heart, soul, mind, and strength, and your neighbor as yourself." Then said Jesus, "You have answered right; this, if you really do, will lead to life everlasting." But the lawyer desiring to justify himself while also hoping to embarrass Jesus said, "But, Teacher, I should like you to tell me just who is my neighbor?" Jesus than told the parable of the Good Samaritan and asked the lawyer which of the three was the neighbor of him who fell among the robbers. And when the lawyer perceived that he had fallen into his own snare, he answered, "He who showed mercy on him." And Jesus said, "Go and do likewise."

164:2. At Jerusalem

Jesus went up to the feast of the dedication for just one purpose: to give the Sanhedrin and the Jewish leaders another chance to see the light. The principal event of these few days in Jerusalem occurred on Friday night at the home of Nicodemus. Here were gathered together some twenty-five Jewish leaders who believed Jesus' teaching. On this occasion Jesus' hearers were all learned men, and both they and his two apostles were amazed at the breadth and depth of the remarks which the Master made to this distinguished group. When this little meeting broke up, all went away mystified by the Master's personality, charmed by his gracious manner, and in love with the man. They sought to advise Jesus concerning his desire to win the remaining members of the Sanhedrin. They offered to go with him before the Sanhedrin but the Master told them it would do no good and multiply the wrath visited on them.

"Go, each of you, about the Father's business as the spirit leads you while I once more bring the kingdom to their notice in the manner which my Father may direct."

164:3. Healing the Blind Beggar

This Sabbath morning, as Jesus and his two apostles drew near the temple, they encountered a well-known beggar, a man who had been born blind, sitting at his usual place. Jesus assured the apostles that neither the sin of this man or his parents caused his blindness as the Jewish leaders taught. Some even believed that this was the result of sins of a former life. The Master found it difficult to make men believe that their souls had not had previous existences. Jesus decided to use this beggar, Josiah, in his plans for that day's work. He made spittle of clay and placed on Josiah's eyes and told him to wash it off in the pool of Siloam. Both the spittle and the pool were regarded as efficacious. When his sight was restored people who knew him were amazed. This is one of the strangest of all the Master's miracles. This man did not ask for healing, but was done as an open challenge to the Sanhedrin.

164:4. Josiah Before the Sanhedrin

Although it violated a rule of meeting on the Sabbath, the Sanhedrin convened the council. But they did not call Jesus before them; they feared to. Instead, they sent forthwith for Josiah. They told him that this man could not be from God because he did not observe the Sabbath. A serious division arose among them. When Josiah's parents was brought before them they were afraid to speak freely and told them to ask Josiah about his healing. But Josiah was neither dumb nor lacking in humor; so he replied to the officer of the court, "Whether this man is a sinner, I know not; but one thing I do know—that, whereas I was blind, now I see. . . . I have told you exactly how it all happened, and if you did not believe my testimony, why would you hear it again? Would you by any chance also become his disciples?" When Josiah had thus spoken, the Sanhedrin broke up in confusion.

164:5. Teaching in Solomon's Porch

While the Sanhedrin was examining Josiah, Jesus taught the people in Solomon's Porch for over two hours. He hoped the Sanhedrin would summon him but they were afraid to do so. Some of the Jewish teachers asked him if he was the Messiah. Jesus told them that he had repeatedly told them who he was and that his good works was further testimony that he was from God. "The teacher of truth attracts only those who hunger for the truth and who thirst for righteousness. My sheep hear my voice and I know them and they follow me. And to all who follow my teaching I give eternal life; they shall never perish, and no one shall snatch them out of my hand." Some of the unbelieving Jews rushed over to where they were still building the temple to pick up stones to cast at Jesus, but the believers restrained them. Jesus meet Nathaniel and Thomas and after Josiah was thrown out of the synagogue they went to Josiah's home. Josiah expressed belief in Jesus and his teaching and was taken with them to the camp at Pella. Josiah became a life-long preacher of the gospel of the kingdom.

Paper 165: The Perean Mission Begins

ON Tuesday, January 3, A.D. 30, Abner, the former chief of the twelve apostles of John the Baptist, a Nazarite and onetime head of the Nazarite school at Engedi, now chief of the seventy messengers of the kingdom, called his associates together and gave them final instructions before sending them on a mission to all of the cities and villages of Perea. This Perean mission continued for almost three months and was the last ministry of the Master. Throughout this tour of Perea the women's corps, now numbering sixty-two, took over most of the work of ministration to the sick.

165:1. At the Pella Camp

By the middle of January more than twelve hundred persons were gathered together at Pella, and Jesus taught this multitude at least once each day when he was in residence at the camp. The evenings Jesus reserved for the usual sessions of questions and answers with the twelve and other advanced disciples. The evening groups averaged about fifty. By the middle of March, the time when Jesus began his journey toward Jerusalem, over four thousand persons composed the large audience which heard Jesus or Peter preach each morning. The Master chose to terminate his work on earth when the interest in his message had reached a high point. The twelve paid little or no attention to the field work, only going out with Jesus to visit Abner's associates from time to time.

165:2. Sermon on the Good Shepherd

A company of over three hundred Jerusalemites, Pharisees and others, had gathered at Pella; and it was in the presence of these Jewish teachers and leaders, as well as in the hearing of the twelve apostles, that Jesus preached the sermon on the "Good Shepherd." "The true shepherd gathers his flock into the fold for the night in times of danger. And when the morning has come, he enters into the fold by the door, and when he calls, the sheep know his voice. Every shepherd who gains entrance to the sheepfold by any other means than by the door is a thief and a robber. . . . Some of you are not of my fold; you know not my voice, and you do not follow me. And because you are false shepherds, the sheep know not your voice and will not follow you. . . . And now, lest some of you too easily comprehend this parable, I will declare that I am both the door to the Father's sheepfold and at the same time the true shepherd of my Father's flocks. . . . I have come that you all may have life and have it more abundantly. . . . I have many other sheep not of this fold, and these words are true not only of this world. . . . But, mind you, if I lay down my life, I will take it up again." On the morrow about half of these Jewish teachers professed belief in Jesus, and the other half in dismay returned to Jerusalem and their homes.

165:3. Sabbath Sermon at Pella

By the end of January the Sabbath-afternoon multitudes numbered almost three thousand. On Saturday, January 28, Jesus preached the memorable sermon on "Trust and Spiritual Preparedness." "Beware of the leaven of the Pharisees which is hypocrisy, born of prejudice and nurtured in traditional bondage, albeit many of these Pharisees are honest of heart and some of them abide here as my disciples. . . . But I say to you, my friends, when they seek to destroy the Son of Man, be not afraid of them. Fear not those who, although they may be able to kill the body, after that have no more power over you. . . . Say what you will about the Son of Man, and it shall be forgiven you; but he who presumes to blaspheme against God shall hardly find forgiveness. When men go so far as knowingly to ascribe the doings of God to the forces of evil, such deliberate rebels will hardly seek forgiveness for their sins. . . . And when our enemies bring you before the rulers of the synagogues and before other high authorities, be not concerned about what you should say and be not anxious as to how you should answer their questions, for the spirit that dwells within you shall certainly teach you in that very hour what you should say in honor of the gospel of the kingdom. . . . The invitation ever has been and always will be, Whosoever will, let him come and freely partake of the water of life."

When Jesus had finished speaking, many went forth to be baptized by the apostles in the Jordan while he listened to the questions of those who remained.

165:4. Dividing the Inheritance

A certain young man came to Jesus asking him to tell his brother to divide their father's inheritance with him. The Master told him that he did not give attention to material things. "Take heed and keep yourselves free from covetousness; a man's life consists not in the abundance of the things which he may possess. Happiness comes not from the power of wealth, and joy springs not from riches." Jesus went on to tell the parable of the rich man who built new barns to store his goods and that night robbers broke into his house and killed him and plundered his barns. Jesus sent the young man away, saying to him, "My son, what shall it profit you if you gain the whole world and lose your own soul?" Jesus explained that it is not a sin to have honest wealth provided that your treasure is in heaven, for where your treasure is there will your heart be also. "The love of riches all too often obscures and even destroys the spiritual vision. Fail not to recognize the danger of wealth's becoming, not your servant, but your master."

165:5. Talks to the Apostles on Wealth

That evening after supper, when Jesus and the twelve gathered together for their daily conference, Andrew asked the Master if he would repeat his teaching about wealth for their benefit. Jesus told them they should not be concerned about materials things. "If you give your lives truly to the gospel, you shall live by the gospel. If you are only believing disciples, you must earn your own bread and contribute to the sustenance of all who teach and preach and heal. If you are anxious about your bread and water, wherein are you different from the nations of the world who so diligently seek such necessities? Devote yourselves to your work, believing that both the Father and I know that you have need of all these things. Let me assure you, once and for all, that, if you dedicate your lives to the work of the kingdom, all your real needs shall be supplied. Seek the greater thing, and the lesser will be found therein; ask for the heavenly, and the earthly shall be included. The shadow is certain to follow the substance."

165:6. Answer to Peter's Question

As they sat thinking, Simon Peter asked if Jesus was speaking for the guidance of apostles or for the disciples. And Jesus replied that this was a time of testing where a man's soul is revealed. Remember that much has been given to you; therefore much will be required of you. There may be divisions in families and members will be set against each other. "True, each of these believers shall have great and lasting peace in his own heart, but peace on earth will not come until all are willing to believe and enter into their glorious inheritance of sonship with God. Nevertheless, go into all the world proclaiming this gospel to all nations, to every man, woman, and child."

Paper 166: Last Visit to Perea

FROM February 11 to 20, Jesus and the twelve made a tour of all the cities and villages of northern Perea where the associates of Abner and the members of the women's corps were working. They found these messengers of the gospel meeting with success, and Jesus repeatedly called the attention of his apostles to the fact that the gospel of the kingdom could spread without the accompaniment of miracles and wonders. The gospel from this time on reflected not so much Jesus' personality as his teachings. But his followers did not long follow his instructions, for soon after Jesus' death and resurrection they departed from his teachings and began to build the early church around the miraculous concepts and the glorified memories of his divine-human personality.

166:1. The Pharisees at Ragaba

On Sabbath, February 18, Jesus was at Ragaba, where there lived a wealthy Pharisee named Nathaniel who made breakfast for twenty Pharisees and invited Jesus as the guest of honor. The Master immediately took his seat at the left of Nathaniel without going to the water basins to wash his hands. Nathaniel was shocked by this failure of the Master to comply with the strict requirements of Pharisaic practice. After considerable whispering between Nathaniel and an unfriendly Pharisee Jesus finally said that they might have inquired about the new gospel but were devoted to their own self-righteousness. "How carefully you cleanse the outside of the cups and the platters while the spiritual-food vessels are filthy and polluted! You make sure to present a pious and holy appearance to the people, but your inner souls are filled with self-righteousness, covetousness, extortion, and all manner of spiritual wickedness. Your leaders even dare to plot and plan the murder of the Son of Man." He also pointed out the extensive wrong-doing of the lawyers. And when Jesus had finished speaking at Nathaniel's table, he went out of the house without partaking of food. And of the Pharisees who heard these words, some became believers in his teaching and entered into the kingdom, but most continued to oppose him.

166:2. The Ten Lepers

The next day Jesus went with the twelve over to Amathus and as they approached the city, they encountered a group of ten lepers who sojourned nearby. Nine were Jews and one a Samaritan. When the lepers saw Jesus drawing near them, not daring to approach him, they stood afar off and cried to him, "Master, have mercy on us; cleanse us from our affliction. Heal us as you have healed others." When Simon Zelotes observed the Samaritan among the lepers, he sought to induce the Master to pass on into the city without even hesitating to exchange greetings with them. Jesus told them if they would be made whole to go show themselves to the priests. When the Samaritan saw he was healed, he turned back glorifying God and kneeled at Jesus' feet giving thanks for his healing. Jesus looked at the twelve, especially Simon Zelotes, and asked where were the Jews that were healed.

166:3. The Sermon at Gerasa

As Jesus and the twelve visited with the messengers of the kingdom at Gerasa, one of the Pharisees who believed in him asked him, "Lord, will there be few or many really saved?" And Jesus answered in part, "I declare that salvation is first a matter of your personal choosing. Even if the door to the way of life is narrow, it is wide enough to admit all who sincerely seek to enter, for I am that door. And the Son will never refuse entrance to any child of the universe who, by faith, seeks to find the Father through the Son. . . . Many who are first will be last, and those who are last will many times be first. . . . Unless you are born again, born of the spirit, you cannot enter the kingdom of God. . . . And so, whether few or many are to be saved altogether depends on whether few or many will heed the invitation. I am the door, I am the new and living way, and whosoever wills may enter to embark upon the endless truth-search for eternal life."

166:4. Teaching About Accidents

Thomas asked Jesus if spiritual beings produced events in the material world and if angels are able to prevent accidents. Jesus explained that natural events have natural causes. "All too long have your fathers believed that prosperity was the token of divine approval; that adversity was the proof of God's displeasure. I declare that such beliefs are superstitions. . . . In the matter of sickness and health, you should know that these bodily states are the result of material causes; health is not the smile of heaven, neither is affliction the frown of God. The Father's human children have equal capacity for the reception of material blessings; therefore does he bestow things physical upon the children of men without discrimination. When it comes to the bestowal of spiritual gifts, the Father is limited by man's capacity for receiving these divine endowments. Although the Father is no respecter of persons, in the bestowal of spiritual gifts he is limited by man's faith and by his willingness always to abide by the Father's will."

166:5. The Congregation at Philadelphia

The synagogue of Philadelphia had never been subject to the supervision of the Sanhedrin at Jerusalem and therefore had never been closed to the teachings of Jesus and his associates. At this time, Abner was teaching three times a day in the Philadelphia synagogue. This very synagogue later on became a Christian church and was the missionary headquarters for the promulgation of the gospel through the regions to the east. It was long a stronghold of the Master's teachings and stood alone in this region as a center of Christian learning for centuries.

After the death and resurrection of Jesus, the Jerusalem church, of which James (Jesus' brother) was head, began to have serious difficulties with the Philadelphia congregation of believers. And this estrangement with Jerusalem explains why nothing is heard of Abner and his work in the Gospel records of the New Testament. Philadelphia was really the headquarters of the early church in the south and east as Antioch was in the north and west. Abner fell out with Peter and James over questions of administration and the jurisdiction of the Jerusalem church; he parted company with Paul over differences of philosophy and theology. In his last years Abner denounced Paul as the "clever corrupter of the life teachings of Jesus of Nazareth, the Son of the living God."

During the later years of Abner and for some time thereafter, the believers at Philadelphia held more strictly to the religion of Jesus, as he lived and taught, than any other group on earth. Abner lived to be 89 years old, dying at Philadelphia on November 21, A.D. 74.

Paper 167: The Visit to Philadelphia

WHEN Jesus arrived at Philadelphia, he was accompanied by over six hundred followers. This was a period when the gospel was proclaimed with power, without miracles, and most of the time without the personal presence of Jesus or even of his apostles. They were much rejoiced over the progress of the gospel at Philadelphia and among the nearby villages. The messengers of David also brought word of the further advancement of the kingdom throughout Palestine, as well as good news from Alexandria and Damascus.

167:1. Breakfast with the Pharisees

There lived in Philadelphia a very wealthy and influential Pharisee who had accepted the teachings of Abner, and who invited Jesus to his house Sabbath morning for breakfast. About forty Pharisees and leading men attended. One of the leading Pharisees of Jerusalem went to the seat of honor but was asked to sit lower as this was reserved for Jesus.

Near the end of the meal there came in from the street a man long afflicted with a chronic disease and now in a dropsical condition. This man was a believer, having recently been baptized by Abner's associates. He made no request of Jesus for healing, but had reasoned in his heart that his sorry plight might possibly appeal to the Master's compassion. The self-righteous Pharisee voiced his resentment that this man was permitted to enter the room. Jesus asked if it was lawful to heal the sick on the Sabbath. No one responded. Jesus then went over to the sick man and said, "Arise and go your way. You have not asked to be healed, but I know the desire of your heart and the faith of your soul." The Master speaking to the group suggested that one should not seek the highest seats. "Forget not, every one who exalts himself shall be humbled, while he who truly humbles himself shall be exalted."

167:2. Parable of the Great Supper

At the close of the breakfast Jesus told the parable of the Great Supper: A ruler gave a great supper and when those invited gave many different excuses why they could not come, he sent his servants to the highways and byways and invited the poor and outcast to the supper and the house was filled.

One of the Pharisees comprehended the meaning of the parable and confessed his faith in the gospel of the kingdom and was baptized. Abner preached on this parable that night at the general council of believers. The next day all of the apostles endeavored to interpret the meaning of the parable. Jesus listened to the differing interpretations but refused to offer help in understanding the parable. He would only say, "Let every man find out the meaning for himself and in his own soul."

167:3. The Woman with the Spirit of Infirmity

Abner had arranged for the Master to teach in the synagogue on this Sabbath day. At the conclusion of the service Jesus looked down before him upon an elderly woman who wore a downcast expression, and who was much bent in form. As Jesus touching her bowed-over form on the shoulder, he said, "Woman, if you would only believe, you could be wholly loosed from your spirit of infirmity." And this woman, who had been bowed down and bound up by the depressions of fear for more than eighteen years, believed the words of the Master and by faith straightened up immediately. When she saw that she had been made straight, she lifted up her voice and glorified God. Jesus frequently delivered such victims of fear from their spirit of infirmity.

The chief ruler of the synagogue was an unfriendly Pharisee who complained that Jesus had violated the Sabbath. As a result a follower of Jesus was put in his place. One of David's messengers brought an urgent message to Jesus from his friends at Bethany.

167:4. The Message from Bethany

Very late on Sunday night, February 26, a runner from Bethany arrived at Philadelphia, bringing a message from Martha and Mary which said, "Lord, he whom you love is very sick." At first Jesus made no reply. There occurred one of those strange interludes, a time when he appeared to be in communication with something outside of, and beyond, himself. And then, looking up, he addressed the messenger in the hearing of the apostles, saying, "This sickness is really not to the death. Doubt not that it may be used to glorify God and exalt the Son." Early Wednesday morning Jesus decided to return to Bethany. The apostles tried to prevent him from doing so. Finally Thomas said, "Let us go and die with him."

167:5. On the Way to Bethany

At their noon lunchtime, on Wednesday, Jesus talked to his apostles and this group of followers on the "Terms of Salvation," and at the end of this lesson told the parable of the Pharisee and the publican: The Pharisee thanked God that he was better than others; the publican said, "God be merciful to me a sinner." The publican had God's approval.

That night the unfriendly Pharisees sought to entrap the Master by inducing him to discuss marriage and divorce. Jesus exalted marriage as the most ideal and highest of all human relationships. Likewise, he intimated strong disapproval of the lax and unfair divorce practices of the Jerusalem Jews. He did much to augment the apostles respect for women and children and for the home.

167:6. Blessing the Little Children

That evening Jesus' message regarding marriage and the blessedness of children spread all over Jericho, so that the next morning, long before Jesus and the apostles prepared to leave, scores of mothers came to where Jesus lodged, bringing their children and desired that he bless the little ones. The apostles endeavored to send the women away, but they refused to depart until the Master laid his hands on their children and blessed them. When the apostles loudly rebuked these mothers, Jesus, hearing the tumult, came out and indignantly reproved them, saying, "Suffer little children to come to me; forbid them not, for of such is the kingdom of heaven." And when the Master had spoken to his apostles, he received all of the children, laying his hands on them, while he spoke words of courage and hope to their mothers.

Jesus impressed upon his apostles the great value of beauty as an influence leading to the urge to worship, especially with children; that beauty is most religious when it is most simple and naturelike; that the child should be introduced to worship in nature's outdoors and later accompany his parents to public houses of religious assembly which have artistic beauty.

167:7. The Talk about Angels

As they were journeying, Nathaniel asked Jesus about angels. Jesus told him that angels were a separate order of created beings who are the spirit servants in heaven; that it is by the ministry of the angels that one world may be kept in touch with other worlds; that some are assigned to the service of the human races; that as man progresses toward Paradise he does traverse a state analogous to the state of angels; that angels are very much concerned with the means whereby man's spirit is released from the tabernacles of the flesh and his soul escorted to the mansions in heaven.

And he would have spoken further with Nathaniel regarding the ministry of angels, but he was interrupted by the approach of Martha, who hastened to greet him.

Paper 168: The Resurrection of Lazarus

IT was shortly after noon when Martha started out to meet Jesus. Her brother, Lazarus, had been dead four days and had been laid away in their private tomb at the far end of the garden late on Sunday afternoon. They had been greatly puzzled by the messenger's statement that Jesus said, "... this sickness is really not to the death."

When Martha met Jesus, she fell at his feet, exclaiming, "Master, if you had been here, my brother would not have died!" Jesus reached down and, lifting her upon her feet, said, "Only have faith, Martha, and your brother shall rise again." Martha acknowledged his ultimate resurrection of the last day. Then said Jesus, "I am the resurrection and the life; he who believes in me, though he dies, yet shall he live. In truth, whosoever lives and believes in me shall never really die. Martha, do you believe this?" And Martha acknowledged her belief. Jesus asked for Mary, and when she arrived she also said that Lazarus would not have died if Jesus had been there.

168:1. At the Tomb of Lazarus

As the Master was led to the tomb with the two sorrowing sisters, he wept. Jesus felt sorry for Martha and Mary; he hesitated to raise Lazarus knowing Lazarus would be subject to bitter persecution. Universe records show that Jesus' Personalized Adjuster issued orders for the detention of Lazarus's Thought Adjuster fifteen minutes before Lazarus died.

And so, on this Thursday afternoon at about half past two o'clock, was the stage all set in this little hamlet of Bethany for the enactment of the greatest of all works connected with the earth ministry of Michael of Nebadon. When Jesus spoke those words of command, "Take away the stone," Martha and Mary had conflicting emotions. Jesus reminded them that he had said that this sickness was not to the death. The apostles, with the assistance of willing neighbors, laid hold upon the stone and rolled it away from the entrance to the tomb. The Jews firmly believed that a soul had gone on to the abode of departed spirits ere the fourth day had dawned.

168:2. The Resurrection of Lazarus

As this company of some forty-five mortals stood before the tomb, Jesus lifted up his eyes and said, "Father, I am thankful that you heard and granted my request. I know that you always hear me, but because of those who stand here with me, I thus speak with you, that they may believe that you have sent me into the world, and that they may know that you are working with me in that which we are about to do." And when he had prayed, he cried with a loud voice, "Lazarus, come forth!"

In just twelve seconds of earth time the hitherto lifeless form of Lazarus began to move and presently sat up on the edge of the stone shelf whereon it had rested. His body was bound about with grave cloths, and his face was covered with a napkin. And as he stood up before them—alive—Jesus said, "Loose him and let him go." Lazarus greeted Jesus and the apostles and asked the meaning of the grave cloths and why he had awakened in the garden. Martha told Lazarus of his death, burial, and resurrection. Then went Lazarus over to Jesus and, with his sisters, knelt at the Master's feet to give thanks and offer praise to God. Jesus, taking Lazarus by the hand, lifted him up, saying, "My son, what has happened to you will also be experienced by all who believe this gospel except that they shall be resurrected in a more glorious form." Lazarus could hardly comprehend what had occurred.

168:3. Meeting of the Sanhedrin

At one o'clock the next day, Friday, the Sanhedrin met to deliberate further on the question, "What shall we do with Jesus of Nazareth?" After more than two hours of discussion and acrimonious debate, a certain Pharisee presented a resolution calling for Jesus' immediate death without trial and in defiance of all precedent. But this resolution did not come to a vote since fourteen members of the Sanhedrin resigned in a body when such an unheard-of action was proposed. When these resignations were subsequently acted upon, five other members were thrown out because their associates believed they entertained friendly feelings toward Jesus. The following week Lazarus and his sisters were summoned to appear before the Sanhedrin. When their testimony had been heard, no doubt could be entertained that Lazarus had been raised from the dead. These Jewish leaders were persuaded that, if he were not immediately stopped, very soon all the common people would believe in him. Caiaphas the high priest said, "It is better that one man die, than that the community perish." Early Sunday morning Jesus and the apostles started on their journey back to the Pella encampment.

168:4. The Answer to Prayer

On the way from Bethany to Pella the apostles asked Jesus many questions, especially about the answer to prayer.

His answers, briefly summarized, are as follows: 1. prayer is an expression of the finite mind in an effort to approach the Infinite; there never can be an unbroken continuity between the making of a prayer and the reception of the full spiritual answer thereto; 2. when a prayer is apparently unanswered, the delay often betokens a better answer; 3. the prayers of time, when indited by the spirit and expressed in faith, are often so vast and all-encompassing that they can be answered only in eternity; 4. the prayer of the material being can many times be answered only when such an individual has progressed to the spirit level; 5. the prayer of a God-knowing person may be so distorted by ignorance the petitioner wholly fails to recognize it as the answer to his prayer; 6. all true prayers are addressed to spiritual beings, and all such petitions must be answered in spiritual terms; 7. no prayer can hope for an answer unless it is born of the spirit and nurtured by faith in accordance with that supreme wisdom and that divine love actuating those beings to whom you pray; 8. superior wisdom sometimes dictates that the answer to prayer be delayed, modified, segregated, transcended, or postponed to another stage of spiritual ascension; 9. do not hesitate to pray the prayers of spirit longing, but the answers will be on deposit when it will become possible for you to recognize and appropriate the long-waiting answers to your earlier but ill-timed petitions; 10. all genuine spirit-born petitions are certain of an answer, but you should remember that you are progressive creatures of time and space in your personal reception of the full answers to your manifold prayers and petitions.

168:5. What Became of Lazarus

Lazarus remained at the Bethany home until the week of the crucifixion of Jesus, when he received warning that the Sanhedrin had decreed Jesus' death. And so Lazarus took hasty leave of his sisters at Bethany, never permitting himself to rest long until he had reached Philadelphia. Soon after this, Martha and Mary disposed of their lands at Bethany and joined their brother in Perea. Meantime, Lazarus had become the treasurer of the church at Philadelphia. He became a strong supporter of Abner in his controversy with Paul and the Jerusalem church and ultimately died, when 67 years old, of the same sickness that carried him off when he was a younger man at Bethany.

Paper 169: Last Teaching at Pella

LATE on Monday evening, March 6, Jesus and the apostles arrived at the Pella camp. This was the last week of Jesus' sojourn there, and he was very active in teaching the multitude and instructing the apostles. Word regarding the resurrection of Lazarus had reached the encampment two days before the Master's arrival, and the entire assembly was agog. The Pharisees and the chief priests had begun to formulate their charges and to crystallize their accusations. They objected to the Master's teachings because he was a friend of publicans and sinners, a blasphemer, a lawbreaker, and in league with devils.

169:1. Parable of the Lost Son

On Thursday afternoon Jesus talked to the multitude about the "Grace of Salvation." In the course of this sermon he retold the story of the lost sheep and the lost coin and then added his favorite parable of the prodigal son. This was one of the most touching and effective of all the parables which Jesus ever presented to impress upon his hearers the Father's willingness to receive all who seek entrance into the kingdom of heaven.

Jesus was very partial to telling these three stories at the same time. He presented the story of the lost sheep to show that, when men unintentionally stray away from the path of life, the Father is mindful of such lost ones and goes out, with his Sons, the true shepherds of the flock, to seek the lost sheep. He then would recite the story of the coin lost in the house to illustrate how thorough is the divine searching for all who are confused, confounded, or otherwise spiritually blinded by the material cares and accumulations of life. And then he would launch forth into the telling of this parable of the lost son, the reception of the returning prodigal, to show how complete is the restoration of the lost son into his Father's house and heart.

169:2. Parable of the Shrewd Steward

One evening in an answer to a question by Simon Zelotes, Jesus told the parable of the Shrewd Steward: This shrewd but unjust steward wasted and squandered his master's funds and when the master learned of this, he called the steward in for an accounting. The steward, knowing he would be dismissed, called in his lord's debtors and reduced what was owed so that after he was dismissed, he would have friends of these debtors. "And it is in this way that the sons of this world sometimes show more wisdom in their preparation for the future than do the children of light. . . . I affirm that he who is faithful in little will also be faithful in much, while he who is unrighteous in little will also be unrighteous in much. . . . And again I assert that no man can serve two masters; either he will hate the one and love the other, or else he will hold to one while he despises the other. You cannot serve God and mammon."

169:3. The Rich Man and the Beggar

Simon Peter told the Nazarite allegory of the rich man, Dives, who lived splendidly, and the beggar, Lazarus, who lay at the rich man's gate and desired to be fed. When the beggar died he was carried to Abraham's bosom. Later the rich man departed from this world and awakened in Hades. He pleaded for Lazarus to come and cool his lips with water. He was informed that this was impossible. Then Dives asked for Lazarus to go back and warn his brothers. Abraham told him that if they did not heed Moses and the prophets they would not be persuaded if one were to rise from the dead.

Although both the apostles and his disciples frequently asked Jesus questions about the parable of Dives and Lazarus, he never consented to make comment thereon.

169:4. The Father and His Kingdom

Jesus always had trouble trying to explain to the apostles that, while they proclaimed the establishment of the kingdom of God, the Father in heaven was not a king. Jesus never gave his apostles a systematic lesson concerning the personality and attributes of the Father in heaven. His teaching regarding the Father all centered in the declaration that he and the Father are one; that he who has seen the Son has seen the Father. He never made other pronouncements about his Father except to the woman of Samaria at Jacob's well, when he declared, "God is spirit." Jesus well knew that God can be known only by the realities of experience.

You can know God, not by understanding what Jesus said, but by knowing what Jesus was. And when the Master made reference to his Father as God, he usually employed the Hebrew word signifying the plural God (the Trinity) Elohim and not the word Yahweh. Jesus never claimed to be the manifestation of Elohim (God) in the flesh. Never did Jesus say, "Whoso has heard me has heard God." But he did say, "He who has *seen* me has seen the Father." You can know the Eternal as a Father; you can worship him as the God of universes, the infinite Creator of all existences.

Paper 170: The Kingdom of Heaven

SATURDAY afternoon, March 11, Jesus preached his last sermon at Pella. This was among the notable addresses of his public ministry, embracing a full and complete discussion of the kingdom of heaven. In this narrative we will amplify the address by adding numerous statements made by Jesus on previous occasions and by including some remarks made only to the apostles during the evening discussions of this same day. We will also make certain comments dealing with the subsequent outworking of the kingdom idea as it is related to the later Christian church.

170:1. Concepts of the Kingdom of Heaven

The prophets presented the kingdom of God as a present reality and a future hope. The later Jewish concept was a worldwide and transcendental kingdom of supernatural origin and miraculous inauguration. The Persian teachings portrayed the establishment of a divine kingdom as the achievement of the triumph of good over evil at the end of the world. Jesus elected to appropriate the most vital and culminating heritage of both the Jewish and Persian religions. Concerning the kingdom, his last word always was, "The kingdom is within you." The kingdom of heaven, as it has been understood and misunderstood down through the centuries of the Christian era, embraced four distinct groups of ideas: 1. the concept of the Jews; 2. the concept of the Persians; 3. the personal-experience concept of Jesus—"the kingdom of heaven within you"; 4. the composite and confused concepts which the founders and promulgators of Christianity have sought to impress upon the world.

170:2. Jesus' Concept of the Kingdom

The Master made it clear that the kingdom of heaven must begin with, and be centered in, the dual concept of the truth of the fatherhood of God and the correlated fact of the brotherhood of man. It resulted in the possession of new courage and augmented spiritual power. It was in itself a new standard of moral values, a new ethical yardstick wherewith to measure human conduct. It portrayed the ideal of a resultant new order of human society. It taught the pre-eminence of the spiritual compared with the material. The new gospel affirmed that human salvation is the revelation of a far-reaching divine purpose to be fulfilled and realized in the future destiny of the endless service of the salvaged sons of God. Jesus taught that two things are essential to faith-entrance into the kingdom: 1. faith, sincerity; to be open-minded and teachable like an unspoiled child; 2. truth hunger; Jesus sought to substitute many terms for the kingdom such as the family of God, the Father's will, the fellowship of believers, and the liberated sons of God.

170:3. In Relation to Righteousness

Though Jesus taught that faith, simple childlike belief, is the key to the door of the kingdom; he also taught that, having entered the door, there are the progressive steps of righteousness which every believing child must ascend in order to grow up to the full stature of the robust sons of God. It is in the consideration of the technique of receiving God's forgiveness that the attainment of the righteousness of the kingdom is revealed. God's forgiveness is made actually available and is personally experienced by man just in so far as he forgives his fellows. It therefore is evident that the true and inner religion of the kingdom unfailingly and increasingly tends to manifest itself in practical avenues of social service. The righteousness of any act must be measured by the motive. The religion of the kingdom is personal, individual; the fruits, the results, are familial, social. Jesus never failed to exalt the sacredness of the individual as contrasted with the community. But he also recognized that man develops his character by unselfish service; that he unfolds his moral nature in loving relations with his fellows.

170:4. Jesus' Teaching About the Kingdom

Jesus never gave a precise definition of the kingdom. In the course of this Sabbath afternoon's sermon, Jesus noted no less than five phases of the kingdom, and they were: 1. the personal and inward experience of the spiritual life; 2. the enlarging brotherhood of gospel believers; 3. the supermortal brotherhood of invisible spiritual beings; 4. the prospect of the more perfect fulfillment of the will of God; 5. the kingdom in its fullness, the future spiritual age of light and life on earth.

The Master on this occasion placed emphasis on the following five points as representing the cardinal features of the gospel of the kingdom: 1. the preeminence of the individual; 2. the will as the determining factor in man's experience; 3. spiritual fellowship with God the Father; 4. the supreme satisfactions of the loving service of man; 5. the transcendency of the spiritual over the material in human personality.

Jesus promised a new revelation of the kingdom on earth and at some future time; he also promised sometime to come back to this world in person.

170:5. Later Ideas of the Kingdom

Having summarized the teachings of Jesus about the kingdom of heaven, we are permitted to narrate certain later ideas which became attached to the concept of the kingdom and to engage in a prophetic forecast of the kingdom as it may evolve in the age to come. The church, as a social outgrowth of the kingdom, would have been wholly natural and even desirable. The evil of the church was not its existence, but rather that it almost completely supplanted the Jesus concept of the kingdom. It is just because the gospel of Jesus was so many-sided that within a few centuries students of the records of his teachings became divided up into so many cults and sects.

Mistake not! there is in the teachings of Jesus an eternal nature which will not permit them forever to remain unfruitful in the hearts of thinking men. The kingdom as Jesus conceived it has to a large extent failed on earth; for the time being, an outward church has taken its place; but you should comprehend that this church is only the larval stage of the thwarted spiritual kingdom. Thus does the so-called Christian church become the cocoon in which the kingdom of Jesus' concept now slumbers. The kingdom of the divine brotherhood is still alive and will eventually and certainly come forth from this long submergence.

Paper 171: On the Way to Jerusalem

THE day after the memorable sermon on "The Kingdom of Heaven," Jesus announced that on the following day he and the apostles would depart for the Passover at Jerusalem.

No matter what Jesus said about the nonmaterial character of the kingdom, he could not wholly remove from the minds of his Jewish hearers the idea that the Messiah was to establish some kind of nationalistic government with headquarters at Jerusalem. Salome the mother of James and John Zebedee came to Jesus and asked that her sons sit on his right hand and left hand when he established his kingdom. Jesus asked James and John, "Are you able to drink the cup I am about to drink?" And without a moment of thought, they answered that they were able to do so. Jesus was saddened that they did not know what they were asking. Later James and John apologized to the other apostles and were restored in the good graces of their brethren. Jesus told them that whosoever would be great among them, let him first become their servant. Less than one month later when Salome saw their teacher hanging on a Roman cross, she remembered the foolish request she had made for her sons.

171:1. The Departure from Pella

On the forenoon of Monday, March 13, Jesus and his twelve apostles took final leave of the Pella encampment. Acting on the instructions of Andrew, David Zebedee closed the visitors' camp at Pella on Wednesday, March 15. At this time almost four thousand visitors were in residence, not including the one thousand and more persons who sojourned with the apostles at what was known as the teachers' camp. Much as David disliked to do it, he sold the entire equipment to numerous buyers and proceeded with the funds to Jerusalem, subsequently turning the money over to Judas Iscariot. Andrew had directed David to discontinue the messenger service.

Sometime after the resurrection and also after the death of his mother, David betook himself to Philadelphia, having first assisted Martha and Mary in disposing of their real estate; and there, in association with Abner and Lazarus, he spent the remainder of his life, becoming the financial overseer of all those large interests of the kingdom which had their center at Philadelphia during the lifetime of Abner.

171:2. Counting the Cost

When Jesus and the company of almost one thousand followers arrived at the Bethany ford Jesus climbed upon a huge stone and delivered that discourse which has become known as "Counting the Cost." The Master said in part, "You who would follow after me from this time on, must be willing to pay the price of wholehearted dedication to the doing of my Father's will. If you would be my disciples, you must be willing to forsake father, mother, wife, children, brothers, and sisters. If any one of you would now be my disciple, you must be willing to give up even your life just as the Son of Man is about to offer up his life for the completion of the mission of doing the Father's will on earth and in the flesh. If you are unwilling to renounce all that you are and to dedicate all that you have, then are you unworthy to be my disciple. Again and again have I told you that my kingdom is not of this world, but you will not believe me. He who has ears to hear let him hear what I say."

His apostles, together with the leading disciples, thought much about these words, but still they clung to the belief that, after this brief period of adversity and trial, the kingdom would certainly be set up somewhat in accordance with their long-cherished hopes.

171:3. The Perean Tour

For more than two weeks Jesus and the twelve, followed by a crowd of several hundred disciples, journeyed about in southern Perea, Jesus met Abner at Heshbon, and Andrew directed that the labors of the seventy should not be interrupted by the Passover feast. And this was the last time Abner ever saw Jesus in the flesh. Jesus' farewell to Abner was: "My son, I know you will be true to the kingdom, and I pray the Father to grant you wisdom that you may love and understand your brethren."

The apostles had reached the conclusion that Jesus might, in an emergency, assert his divine power and put to shame his enemies. The majority of them and many of his inner disciples did not believe it possible for Jesus to die; believing that he was "the resurrection and the life," they regarded him as immortal and already triumphant over death.

171:4. Teaching at Livias

It was during this night at Livias that Simon Zelotes and Simon Peter, having conspired to have delivered into their hands at this place more than one hundred swords, received and distributed these arms to all who would accept them and wear them concealed beneath their cloaks. (Jesus knew about this.) Early on Thursday morning, before the others were awake, Jesus called Andrew and asked him to assemble the apostles. When gathered together he told them not to put their trust in the uncertainties of the flesh. He again said that he would be delivered into the hands of the religious rulers, concluding with, "And when they kill the Son of Man, be not dismayed, for I declare that on the third day he shall rise. Take heed to yourselves and remember that I have forewarned you." Again were the apostles amazed, stunned; but they could not bring themselves to regard his words as literal.

Friendly Pharisees warned Jesus that Herod also now decided to kill him. To his apostles, Jesus said, among other things, "O Jerusalem, Jerusalem, which kills the prophets and stones the teachers of truth! How often would I have gathered your children together even as a hen gathers her own brood under her wings, but you would not let me do it! Behold, your house is about to be left to you desolate!"

171:5. The Blind Man at Jericho

Late on the afternoon of Thursday, March 30, Jesus and his apostles approached the walls of Jericho. As they came near the gate of the city, they encountered a throng of beggars, among them one Bartimeus, an elderly man who had been blind from his youth. Hearing the crowd approaching, Bartimeus cried repeatedly for Jesus to have mercy upon him. When Jesus heard this, he asked for Bartimeus to be brought to him. Addressing the blind man, Jesus said, "What do you want me to do for you?" Then answered Bartimeus, "I would have my sight restored." And when Jesus heard this request and saw his faith, he said, "You shall receive your sight; go your way; your faith has made you whole." Immediately Bartimeus received his sight, and he remained near Jesus, glorifying God, until the Master started on the next day for Jerusalem, and then he went before the multitude declaring to all how his sight had been restored in Jericho.

171:6. The Visit to Zaccheus

When the Master's procession entered Jericho, it was nearing sundown, and he was minded to abide there for the night. As Jesus passed by the customs house, Zaccheus the chief publican, or tax collector, happened to be present, and he much desired to see Jesus. Zaccheus was very rich and had heard much about this prophet of Galilee. Not being able to penetrate the crowd, Zaccheus ran ahead and climbed up into a sycamore tree whose spreading branches overhung the roadway. As Jesus passed by, he stopped and, looking up at Zaccheus, said, "Make haste, Zaccheus, and come down, for tonight I must abide at your house." They went at once to the home of Zaccheus, and a Jericho Pharisees criticized Jesus for staying with a publican and a sinner. When Jesus heard this criticism, he looked down and smiled at Zaccheus. Whereupon Zaccheus promised to bestow one half of all of his goods upon the poor and if he wrongfully exacted aught from any man, he would restore fourfold. When Zaccheus had ceased speaking, Jesus said, "Today has salvation come to this home, and you have become indeed a son of Abraham."

171:7. "As Jesus Passed By"

Jesus spread good cheer everywhere he went. He was full of grace and truth. His associates never ceased to wonder at the gracious words that proceeded out of his mouth. Jesus really understood men; therefore could he manifest genuine sympathy and show sincere compassion. Jesus could help men so much because he loved them so sincerely. He truly loved each man, each woman, and each child. He could be such a true friend because of his remarkable insight—he knew so fully what was in the heart and in the mind of man. He was an expert in the comprehension of human need, clever in detecting human longings. Jesus was never in a hurry. He had time to comfort his fellow men "as he passed by." Great things happened not only because people had faith in Jesus, but also because Jesus had so much faith in them. Most of the really important things which Jesus said or did seemed to happen casually, "as he passed by." There was so little of the professional, the well-planned, or the premeditated in the Master's earthly ministry It was literally true, "He went about doing good." And it behooves the Master's followers in all ages to learn to minister as "they pass by"—to do unselfish good as they go about their daily duties.

171:8. Parable of the Pounds

The parable of the pounds, unlike the parable of the talents, which was intended for all the disciples, was spoken more exclusively to the apostles and was largely based on the experience of Archelaus and his futile attempt to gain the rule of the kingdom of Judea. This is one of the few parables of the Master to be founded on an actual historic character. In the parable the nobleman gave his twelve servants the sum of one pound to trade diligently. When the stewards were called for a reckoning one had ten pounds, another five pounds, and the last had the original pound wrapped in a napkin. The ruler said to take this pound from the slothful servant and give it to him who has ten pounds. "To every one who has shall be given more, but from him who has not, even that which he has shall be taken away from him."

Nathaniel observed that ability is the practical measure of life's opportunities. You will never be held responsible for the accomplishment of that which is beyond your abilities. The Master grants the lesser reward for lesser faithfulness when there is like opportunity.

Paper 172: Going into Jerusalem

JESUS and the apostles arrived at Bethany shortly after four o'clock on Friday afternoon, March 31, A.D. 30. Lazarus, his sisters, and their friends were expecting them. Arrangements had been made for Jesus to stay with a neighboring believer, one Simon, the leading citizen of the little village. That evening Jesus received many visitors, and the common folks of Bethany and Bethphage did their best to make him feel welcome. The chief priests were informed that Jesus lodged at Bethany, but they thought best not to attempt to seize him among his friends. Jesus knew all about this; but he was majestically calm. While the Master slept that night, the apostles watched over him, by twos, and many of them were girded with swords.

172:1. Sabbath at Bethany

Six days before the Passover, on the evening after the Sabbath, all Bethany and Bethphage joined in celebrating the arrival of Jesus by a public banquet at the home of Simon. This supper was in honor of both Jesus and Lazarus; it was tendered in defiance of the Sanhedrin. Nothing out of the ordinary happened until near the close of the feasting when Mary the sister of Lazarus stepped forward from among the group of women onlookers and, going up to where Jesus reclined as the guest of honor, proceeded to open a large alabaster cruse of very rare and costly ointment; and after anointing the Master's head, she began to pour it upon his feet as she took down her hair and wiped them with it. Judas Iscariot stepped over to where Andrew reclined and said that the Master should rebuke such waste. Jesus, knowing what they thought and hearing what they said, put his hand upon Mary's head as she knelt by his side and, with a kindly expression upon his face, said that Mary should be left alone seeing that she had done a good thing in her heart. "Rather do I say to you that in the ages to come, wherever this gospel shall be preached throughout the whole world, what she has done will be spoken of in memory of her."

It was because of this rebuke, which he took as a personal reproof, that Judas Iscariot finally made up his mind to seek revenge for his hurt feelings. The chief priests now decided that Lazarus must also die.

172:2. Sunday Morning with the Apostles

On this Sunday morning, in Simon's beautiful garden, the Master called his twelve apostles around him and gave them their final instructions preparatory to entering Jerusalem. He advised them to refrain from doing any public work during this Passover sojourn in Jerusalem. Early that morning David Zebedee had turned over to Judas the funds realized from the sale of the equipment of the Pella encampment, and Judas, in turn, had placed the greater part of this money in the hands of Simon, their host, for safekeeping in anticipation of the exigencies of their entry into Jerusalem. Jesus held converse with Lazarus and instructed him to avoid the sacrifice of his life to the vengefulness of the Sanhedrin. In a way, all of Jesus' followers sensed the impending crisis, but they were prevented from fully realizing its seriousness by the unusual cheerfulness and exceptional good humor of the Master.

172:3. The Start for Jerusalem

Jesus decided to make a public entry into Jerusalem as a person of peace riding on a donkey, suggested by a passage in Zechariah. There were several hundred pilgrims gathered around Jesus and David, and David's messengers went into Jerusalem telling people Jesus was making a triumphal entry into the city.

As they came to the brow of Olivet, the pilgrims beheld Jesus weeping. The Master said that they were about to reject the Son of Peace, which would result in their enemies destroying them. When he had finished speaking, the procession began the descent of Olivet and presently were joined by the multitude of visitors who had come from Jerusalem waving palm branches, shouting hosannas, and otherwise expressing gleefulness and good fellowship. The Pharisees hastened on ahead of the procession to rejoin the Sanhedrin, remarking that "if we do not stop these ignorant ones, all the world will go after him."

172:4. Visiting About the Temple

While the Alpheus twins returned the donkey to its owner, Jesus and the apostles detached themselves from their immediate associates and strolled about the temple. No attempt was made to molest Jesus, as the Sanhedrin greatly feared the people. The apostles little understood that this triumphal entry was the only human procedure which could have been effective in preventing Jesus' immediate arrest upon entering the city. The Master desired to give the inhabitants of Jerusalem this one last chance to hear the gospel and receive, if they would, the Son of Peace.

Sitting by the treasury they saw a poor widow cast in two mites; Jesus commented that she had given more than all the rest for that was all she had, even her living. As the evening drew on, they returned to Bethany.

172:5. The Apostles' Attitude

This Sunday evening, after the triumphal entry into Jerusalem, as they returned to Bethany, no twelve human beings ever experienced such diverse and inexplicable emotions. Andrew was thoroughly bewildered, well-nigh confused; he was concerned about the attitude of some of the twelve who he knew were armed with swords. Simon Peter could not understand why Jesus did not speak to the multitude when they arrived at the temple. James Zebedee could not comprehend the Master's purpose in permitting this wild acclaim and then in refusing to say a word to the people when they arrived at the temple; John Zebedee came somewhere near understanding why Jesus did this. Philip was entirely unsettled by the suddenness and spontaneity of the outburst. He was relieved that he did not have to feed the multitude. Nathaniel, aside from the symbolic and prophetic aspects, came the nearest to understanding the Master's reason for enlisting the popular support of the Passover pilgrims. Matthew was the most depressed of the twelve on the way back to Bethany that evening, but by morning he was much cheered; he was, after all, a cheerful loser. Thomas was the most bewildered and puzzled man of all the twelve. By bedtime the Master's cleverness in staging the tumultuous entry into Jerusalem had begun to make a somewhat humorous appeal. This Sunday started off as a great day for Simon Zelotes. By five o'clock that afternoon he was a silent, crushed, and disillusioned apostle. To the Alpheus twins this was a perfect day. Of all the apostles, Judas Iscariot was the most adversely affected by this processional entry into Jerusalem. Judas was tremendously influenced by the ridicule of his Saducean friends. At heart, this ordained ambassador of the kingdom was already a deserter; it only remained for him to find some plausible excuse for an open break with the Master.

Paper 173: Monday at Jerusalem

EARLY on this Monday morning, by prearrangement, Jesus and the apostles assembled at the home of Simon in Bethany, and after a brief conference they set out for Jerusalem. It was about nine o'clock on this beautiful morning when these men arrived at the temple. Jesus mounted one of the teaching platforms and began to address the gathering crowd.

173:1. Cleansing the Temple

A huge commercial traffic had grown up in association with the services and ceremonies of the temple worship. This sale of animals in the temple prospered because, when the worshiper purchased such an animal he could be sure the intended sacrifice would not be rejected on the ground of possessing real or technical blemishes. The temple dues and animal purchases were to be paid with Jewish coin which required money-changers who charged high prices for the exchange. As Jesus was about to begin his address, a violent and heated argument had arisen over the alleged overcharging of a Jew from Alexandria, while at the same moment the air was rent by the bellowing of a drove of some one hundred bullocks which was being driven from one section of the animal pens to another. Jesus stepped down from the teaching platform and, going over to the lad who was driving the cattle through the court, took from him his whip of cords and swiftly drove the animals from the temple. By this time the assembled pilgrims were electrified, and with uproarious shouting they moved toward the bazaars and began to overturn the tables of the money-changers. In less than five minutes all commerce had been swept from the temple. Jesus, returning to the speaker's stand, spoke to the multitude, "You have this day witnessed that which is written in the Scriptures: 'My house shall be called a house of prayer for all nations, but you have made it a den of robbers.'"

173:2. Challenging the Master's Authority

When Jesus had just begun his discourse on "The Liberty of Sonship," a group of elders of Israel made their way up near him and, interrupting him in the customary manner, asked, "By what authority do you do these things?" Jesus countered with the question, "Did John get his authority from heaven or from men?" They said they did not know because if they said from men the multitude would turn on them and if they said from heaven they knew Jesus would ask why they did not believe him. Looking down upon them, Jesus said, "Neither will I tell you by what authority I do these things." They attempted no more questions that day; they retired to take further counsel among themselves. But the people were not slow to discern the dishonesty and insincerity in these questions asked by the Jewish rulers.

173:3. Parable of the Two Sons

As the caviling Pharisees stood there, Jesus told a parable about a landowner with two sons. The landowner asked the younger son to work in the vineyard. At first the son refused, then changed his mind and went to work. The father asked the older son to work who agreed and when his father left did not do so. Jesus asked which son really did his father's will. The people said, "The first son." Jesus responded, "Even so; and now do I declare that the publicans and harlots, even though they appear to refuse the call to repentance, shall see the error of their way and go on into the kingdom of God before you, who make great pretensions of serving the Father in heaven while you refuse to do the works of the Father."

Jesus did not despise the Pharisees and Sadducees personally. It was their systems of ceremony, tradition, and authority which he sought to discredit.

173:4. Parable of the Absent Landlord

The Master, turning his attention to the listening multitude, told another parable: A good man planted a vineyard and rented it to tenants while he went on a long journey. Later he repeatedly sent servants to receive his rental.

Some of the tenants beat or stoned the servants and others they sent away empty-handed. He then sent his steward and him they killed. Finally he sent his beloved son whom they also killed. Jesus asked what the lord would do those wicked tenants. The people said that he would destroy those miserable men and let out his vineyard to honest farmers.

When some perceived that this parable referred to the Jewish nation, they said, "God forbid that we should go on doing these things." Jesus, turning to a group of the Sadducees and Pharisees, said, "And so once more do I warn you that, if you continue to reject this gospel, presently will the kingdom of God be taken away from you and be given to a people willing to receive the good news and to bring forth the fruits of the spirit."

173:5. Parable of the Marriage Feast

Jesus addressed himself again to the assembled crowd and spoke the parable of the wedding feast: The kingdom of heaven may be likened to a king who made a marriage feast for his son and dispatched messengers who had been invited. Many of those who had once promised to attend at this time refused to come. Again he sent out messengers but the invited guests in open rebellion mistreated the messengers, even killing some of them. Then this insulted king ordered out his armies and the armies of his allies and instructed them to destroy these rebellious murderers and to burn down their city. When he had punished those who spurned his invitation, he appointed yet another day for the wedding feast and sent messengers out in the highways inviting good and bad, rich and poor, so that at last the wedding chamber was filled with willing guests. When all was ready, the king came in to view his guests, and much to his surprise he saw there a man without a wedding garment since he had freely provided wedding garments for all his guests. Then the king told his servants to cast out this thoughtless guest. He would have none here except those who delight to accept his invitation, and who do him the honor to wear those guest garments so freely provided for all.

After speaking this parable, Jesus was about to dismiss the multitude when a sympathetic believer asked what sign he would give them whereby they should know that he was the Son of God. And when the Master heard this, he said, "Only one sign shall be given you." And then, pointing to his own body, he continued, "Destroy this temple, and in three days I will raise it up." Even his own apostles did not comprehend the significance of this utterance, but subsequently, after his resurrection, they recalled what he had said.

On the way up Olivet Jesus instructed Andrew, Philip, and Thomas that, on the morrow, they should establish a camp nearer the city which they could occupy during the remainder of the Passover week. The apostles all felt that something tremendous was about to happen.

Paper 174: Tuesday Morning in the Temple

THIS Tuesday morning Jesus met the apostles, the women's corps, and some two dozen other prominent disciples at the home of Simon. At this meeting he said farewell to Lazarus, giving him that instruction which led him so soon to flee to Philadelphia in Perea. Jesus also said good-bye to the aged Simon, and gave his parting advice to the women's corps, as he never again formally addressed them. This morning Jesus greeted each of the twelve with a personal salutation. To Andrew he said, "Be not dismayed by the events just ahead. Keep a firm hold on your brethren and see that they do not find you downcast of ridicule." And when he had concluded these greetings, he departed for Jerusalem with Andrew, Peter, James, and John as the other apostles set about the establishment of the Gethsemane camp.

174:1. Divine Forgiveness

For several days Peter and James had been engaged in discussing their differences of opinion about the Master's teaching regarding the forgiveness of sin. Peter told Jesus that James believed that the Father forgives us even before we ask him while Peter maintained that repentance must precede forgiveness. Jesus said that they differed because they did not understand the intimate and loving relations between the creature and the Creator. Divine forgiveness is inevitable; it is inherent and inalienable in God's infinite understanding. When you love your brother, you have already forgiven him. If you are wise parents, you will love and understand your children, even forgive them when transient misunderstanding has apparently separated you. The child may feel a separation but the true father is never conscious of any such separation. Sin is an experience of creature consciousness; it is not a part of God's consciousness.

174:2. Questions by the Jewish Rulers

Tuesday morning, when Jesus arrived in the temple court and began to teach, he had uttered but few words when a group of the younger students from the academies asked him if it was lawful to give tribute to Caesar. Jesus asked to be shown the tribute money and asked them whose image was on the coin. And when they answered him, "Caesar's," Jesus said, "Render to Caesar the things that are Caesar's and render to God the things that are God's." When he had thus answered these young scribes and their Herodian accomplices, they withdrew from his presence, and the people, even the Sadducees, enjoyed their discomfiture. Even the youths who had endeavored to entrap him marveled greatly at the unexpected sagacity of the Master's answer.

174:3. The Sadducees and the Resurrection

Before Jesus could get started with his teaching, another group came forward to question him, this time a company of the learned and crafty Sadducees. Their spokesman said that according to Moses if a married man died his brother should take the wife and raise up seed for the deceased brother. A certain man having six brothers died and all six brothers took his wife and died childless. In the resurrection whose wife will she be, since all seven of these brothers had her? Jesus knew, and so did the people, that these Sadducees were not sincere in asking this question. Nevertheless, he condescended to reply to their mischievous question. He told them that in the worlds to come they neither marry nor are given in marriage.

When Jesus had finished speaking the Sadducees withdrew, and some of the Pharisees so far forgot themselves as to exclaim, "True, true, Master, you have well answered these unbelieving Sadducees." The common people marveled at the wisdom of his teaching.

174:4. The Great Commandment

It was the prearranged plan of the confederated Pharisees, scribes, Sadducees, and Herodians to fill up the entire day with these entangling questions, hoping thereby to discredit Jesus before the people and at the same time effectively to prevent his having any time for the proclamation of his disturbing teachings. Then came forward one of the groups of the Pharisees to ask harassing questions, and the spokesman, a lawyer, asked Jesus, "What is the greatest commandment?" Jesus answered in part, "There is but one commandment, and that one is the greatest of all, and that commandment is: 'Hear O Israel, the Lord our God, the Lord is one; and you shall love the Lord your God with all your heart and with all your soul, with all your mind and with all your strength'; and the second commandment is, 'You shall love your neighbor as yourself'; in these two commandments hang all the law and the prophets."

The lawyer agreed, and Jesus looked down upon him and said, "My friend, I perceive that you are not far from the kingdom of God." That very night the lawyer went out to the Master's camp, professed faith in the gospel of the kingdom, and was baptized by Josiah, one of the disciples of Abner.

174:5. The Inquiring Greeks

About noontime, as Philip was purchasing supplies for the new camp which was that day being established near Gethsemane, he was approached by a group of believing Greeks who asked to see Jesus. Not knowing what to do Philip contacted Andrew and the two of them led the Greeks to Jesus. Jesus said that the Father had sent him into the world to reveal the Father's loving kindness. The children of Abraham were about to reject him, but he welcomed these Greeks and all people who accepted the gospel of the kingdom. (The Greeks had held a conference at the home of Nicodemus and thirty of them had elected to enter the kingdom.) Said Jesus, "He who believes this gospel, believes not merely in me but in Him who sent me.... And these words which the Father directed me to speak to the world are words of divine truth, everlasting mercy, and eternal life.... He who selfishly loves his life stands in danger of losing it; but he who is willing to lay down his life for my sake and the gospel's shall enjoy a more abundant existence on earth and in heaven, life eternal.... Shall I say, Father save me from this awful hour? No! For this very purpose have I come into the world and even to this hour. Rather will I say, and pray that you will join me: Father, glorify your name; your will be done."

When Jesus had thus spoken, the Personalized Adjuster appeared before him, saying, "I have glorified my name in your bestowals many times, and I will glorify it once more." While the Jews and gentiles here assembled heard no voice, they could not fail to discern that the Master had paused in his speaking while a message came to him from some superhuman source. Then Jesus continued to speak, "Let me assure you that victory shall eventually crown our united efforts to enlighten the world and liberate mankind.... And now I declare to you that I, if I be lifted up on earth and in your lives, will draw all men to myself and into the fellowship of my Father."

Having thus spoken, Jesus led the way over the narrow streets of Jerusalem back to the temple.

Paper 175: The Last Temple Discourse

SHORTLY after two o'clock on this Tuesday afternoon, Jesus, accompanied by eleven apostles, Joseph of Arimathea, the thirty Greeks, and certain other disciples, arrived at the temple and began the delivery of his last address in the courts of the sacred edifice. Before beginning the discourse, Jesus tenderly looked down upon this audience which was so soon to hear his farewell public address of mercy to mankind coupled with his last denunciation of the false teachers and the bigoted rulers of the Jews.

175:1. The Discourse

Jesus reviewed his ministry to his people and observed that they were about to reject his teachings. He and his apostles had done their utmost to live in peace with their brethren and the traditions of Israel. But there cannot be peace between light and darkness, truth and error. He had offered sonship with God to all the Jewish nation. Even then it was not too late for this people to receive the word of heaven and to welcome the Son of Man. "I solemnly warn you that you are about to lose your position in the world as the standard-bearers of eternal truth and the custodians of the divine law." Until the Most Highs overthrow Israel, they should co-operate with their leaders. Jesus pointed out the many egocentric, arrogant, and evil characteristics of their leaders. They were reminded that those who would be greatest should become the servers of all. Jesus said that he had no malice toward the chief priests and rulers. "Woe upon you, scribes and Pharisees, hypocrites! You would shut the doors of the kingdom of heaven against sincere men because they happen to be unlearned in the ways of your teaching. . . . . Woe upon you, chief priests and rulers who lay hold of the property of the poor. . . . Woe upon you, false teachers, blind guides! . . . Woe upon you who dissimulate when you take an oath! . . . Woe upon all of you who reject truth and spurn mercy! Many of you are like whited sepulchres, which outwardly appear beautiful but within are full of dead men's bones and all sorts of uncleanness. . . . O Jerusalem and the children of Abraham, you who have stoned the prophets and killed the teachers that were sent to you, even now would I gather your children together as a hen gathers her chickens under her wings, but you will not! And now I take leave of you . . . and your house is left to you desolate!"

175:2. Status of Individual Jews

The fact that the spiritual leaders and the religious teachers of the Jewish nation onetime rejected the teachings of Jesus and conspired to bring about his cruel death, does not in any manner affect the status of any individual Jew in his standing before God. How cruel and unreasoning to compel innocent Jewish people to suffer for the sins of their progenitors, misdeeds of which they are wholly ignorant, and for which they could in no way be responsible! Those who follow the teachings of Jesus, must cease to mistreat the individual Jew as one who is guilty of the rejection and crucifixion of Jesus. God is no respecter of persons, and salvation is for the Jew as well as for the gentile.

175:3. The Fateful Sanhedrin Meeting

It was just before midnight on this Tuesday, April 4, A.D. 30, that the Sanhedrin, as then constituted, officially and unanimously voted to impose the death sentence upon both Jesus and Lazarus. This was the answer to the Master's last appeal to the rulers of the Jews which he had made in the temple only a few hours before. The passing of death sentence (even before his trial) upon the Son of God was the Sanhedrin's reply to the last offer of heavenly mercy ever to be extended to the Jewish nation, as such.

175:4. The Situation in Jerusalem

At the conclusion of Jesus' last discourse in the temple, the apostles once more were left in confusion and consternation. Unfortunately, Judas only heard the last part of Jesus' last discourse. That night all Jerusalem was given over to the serious and suppressed discussion of just one question: "What will they do with Jesus?" At the home of Nicodemus more than thirty prominent Jews who were secret believers in the kingdom agreed that they would make open acknowledgment of their allegiance to the Master in the very hour they should hear of his arrest. And that is just what they did. The Sadducees wanted Jesus' death because he threatened their wealth and power. The Pharisees held that Jesus was a lawbreaker and charged him with blasphemy because he alluded to God as his Father. And this was the situation in Jerusalem and among men on this eventful day while a vast concourse of celestial beings hovered over this momentous scene on earth, anxious to do something to assist their beloved Sovereign but powerless to act because they were effectively restrained by their commanding superiors.

Paper 176: Tuesday Evening on Mount Olivet

THIS Tuesday afternoon, as Jesus and the apostles passed out of the temple on their way to the Gethsemane camp, Matthew, calling attention to the temple construction, said: "Master, observe what manner of buildings these are. See the massive stones and the beautiful adornment; can it be that these buildings are to be destroyed?" As they went on toward Olivet, Jesus said, "You see these stones and this massive temple; verily, verily, I say to you: In the days soon to come there shall not be left one stone upon another." Nathaniel asked, "Tell us, Master, how shall we know when these events are about to come to pass?"

176:1. The Destruction of Jerusalem

Jesus told the apostles not to be troubled when they hear of wars and rumors of wars. They would be thrown out of the synagogue and put in prison and some would be killed. When they stand before judges the spirit would teach them how to respond. "Be patient! doubt not that this gospel of the kingdom will triumph over all enemies and, eventually, be proclaimed to all nations." When they see Jerusalem being encompassed by the Roman armies, they were told, they must flee to the mountains. Because of this warning practically all of the believers fled from Jerusalem and found safe shelter in Pella. The apostles insisted in believing this was in preparation of the coming of a "new Jerusalem" and the reappearing of the Messiah.

176:2. The Master's Second Coming

On several occasions Jesus had made statements which led his hearers to infer that, while he intended presently to leave this world, he would most certainly return to consummate the work of the heavenly kingdom. The doctrine of the second coming of Christ thus became early incorporated into the teachings of the Christians. "The gospel of the kingdom will go to all the world and this salvation will spread to all peoples. And when the kingdom shall have come to its full fruition, be assured that the Father in heaven will not fail to visit you with an enlarged revelation of truth and an enhanced demonstration of righteousness. . . . So also will I, after my Father has invested me with all power and authority, continue to follow your fortunes and to guide in the affairs of the kingdom by the presence of my spirit, who shall shortly be poured out upon all flesh. . . . I also promise that I will sometime return to this world. . . . But when I return, it shall be with power and in the spirit. . . . But the times of the reappearing of the Son of Man are known only in the councils of Paradise. . . . What the whole world must face as a literal fact at the end of an age, you, as individuals, must each most certainly face as a personal experience when you reach the end of your natural life and thereby pass on to be confronted with the conditions and demands inherent in the next revelation of the eternal progression of the Father's kingdom." Of all the discourses which the Master gave his apostles, none ever became so confused in their minds as this one.

176:3. Later Discussions at the Camp

As they gathered about the campfire, some twenty of them, Thomas asked what should be their attitude when Jesus was away. Jesus told then that their connection to the kingdom was spiritual and individual. What does it matter if nations fall or the end of the world comes? We are not to be disturbed by temporal upheavals or perturbed by terrestrial cataclysms. Each generation should carry on their work in view of the possible return of the Son of Man.

Jesus then told a parable of the talents: A great man, before starting on a long journey, gave one servant five talents, one two talents, and to another one talent. When he returned, the servant with five talents had earned five more. The one with two talents had gained two more. They were rewarded accordingly. The servant with one talent had buried it for safe keeping. The lord said this talent should be taken from him and given to the person with ten talents.

"My Heavenly Father requires that his children grow in grace and a knowledge of the truth. . . . Truth is living; the Spirit of Truth is ever leading the children of light into new realms of spiritual reality and divine service. You are not given truth to crystallize into settled, safe, and honored forms. What a sorry sight for successive generations of the professed followers of Jesus to say, regarding their stewardship of divine truth, 'Here, Master, is the truth you committed to us a hundred or a thousand years ago. We have lost nothing; we have faithfully preserved all you gave us; we have allowed no changes to be made in that which you taught us; here is the truth you gave us.' But such a plea concerning spiritual indolence will not justify the barren steward of truth in the presence of the Master. In accordance with the truth committed to your hands will the Master of truth require a reckoning."

176:4. The Return of Michael

Of all the Master's teachings no one phase has been so misunderstood as his promise sometime to come back in person to this world. Many of us are inclined to believe that Jesus will return to Urantia many times during the ages to come. But we have not the slightest idea as to when or in what manner he may choose to come. If every eye is to behold him, and if only spiritual eyes are to discern his presence, then must his advent be long deferred. The second advent of Michael on earth is an event of tremendous sentimental value to both midwayers and humans; but it is of no serious concern whether we go to him or whether he should chance first to come to us. Be you therefore ever ready to welcome him on earth as he stands ready to welcome you in heaven.

Paper 177: Wednesday, the Rest Day

AFTER breakfast the Master informed Andrew that he intended to be absent for the day. David Zebedee had three well-armed and stalwart Galileans to go with him but Jesus refused this protection. As Jesus started off alone, John Mark came forward with a small basket containing food and water and suggested to Jesus that, if he intended to be away all day, he might find himself hungry. The Master smiled on John and reached down to take the basket.

177:1. One Day Alone with God

As Jesus was about to take the lunch basket from John's hand, the young man ventured to say that Jesus would be more free to worship if he took care of the lunch and he would be silent and ask no questions. Presently the Master let go of the basket and told John that they would have a good visit and that John could ask any questions he wanted to. The Master spent this last day of quiet on earth visiting with this truth-hungry youth and talking with his Paradise Father. This event has become known on high as "the day which a young man spent with God in the hills." Jesus visited much with John, talking freely about the affairs of this world and the next. John Mark was thrilled by the memory of this day with Jesus in the hills, but he never forgot the Master's final admonition, spoken just as they were about to return to the Gethsemane camp, when he said, "Well, John, we have had a good visit, a real day of rest, but see to it that you tell no man the things which I told you." And John Mark never did reveal anything that transpired on this day which he spent with Jesus in the hills.

177:2. Early Home Life

In the course of this day's visiting with John Mark, Jesus spent considerable time comparing their early childhood and later boyhood experiences. Jesus told John that he would become a "mighty messenger of the kingdom" because of his early training in the home which gave him laudable self-confidence and normal feelings of security. He said, "Love, John, is the supreme reality of the universe when bestowed by all-wise beings, but it is a dangerous and oftentimes semiselfish trait as it is manifested in the experience of mortal parents." John possessed a strong and well-knit character because he grew up in a home where love prevailed and wisdom reigned. A human being's entire afterlife is enormously influenced by what happens during the first few years of existence.

177:3. The Day at Camp

The apostles spent most of this day walking about on Mount Olivet and visiting with the disciples who were encamped with them, but early in the afternoon they became very desirous of seeing Jesus return. Nathaniel made a speech on "Supreme Desire," saying that if they had wanted to go along with Jesus as much as John Mark did, Jesus would have taken them with him. David Zebedee knew that Jesus would be killed and sent for his mother and the mother of Jesus and every member of his family to come to Jerusalem. That evening, after returning to the camp, Jesus visited with the Greeks, and had it not been that such a course would have greatly disturbed his apostles and many of his leading disciples, he would have ordained these twenty Greeks, even as he had the seventy.

177:4. Judas and the Chief Priests

Judas Iscariot went to an informal meeting at the home of Caiaphas the high priest. The preceding day Judas told some of his relatives and certain Sadducean friends that he was withdrawing from the movement and was flatteringly assured that his withdrawal would be hailed by the Jewish rulers as a great event. And now, as never before, Judas found himself becoming strangely resentful that Jesus had never assigned him a position of greater honor. He had set out to get honor for himself, and if this could be secured simultaneously with getting even with those who had contributed to the greatest disappointment of his life, all the better. Judas was assured that he would receive his reward for this service. It was arranged to arrest Jesus the next evening (Thursday). Judas returned to his associates at the camp intoxicated with thoughts of grandeur and glory such as he had not had for many a day. Judas did not realize it, but he was a coward.

177:5. The Last Social Hour

Since it was Wednesday, this evening at the camp was a social hour. The Master endeavored to cheer his downcast apostles, but that was well-nigh impossible. Jesus made careful inquiry about all of their families and, looking over toward David Zebedee, asked if anyone had heard recently from his (Jesus') mother, his youngest sister, or other members of his family. David looked down at his feet; he was afraid to answer.

This was the occasion of Jesus' warning his followers to beware of the support of the multitude. Silent messengers came and went, communicating with only David Zebedee. Before the evening had passed, certain ones knew that Lazarus had taken hasty flight from Bethany. John Mark was ominously silent after returning to camp, notwithstanding he had spent the whole day in the Master's company, indicating clearly that Jesus had told him not to talk. Even the Master's good cheer and his unusual sociability frightened them. They vaguely sensed what was coming, and none felt prepared to face the test.

Paper 178: Last Day at the Camp

JESUS planned to spend this Thursday, his last free day on earth as a divine Son incarnated in the flesh, with his apostles and a few loyal and devoted disciples. Soon after the breakfast hour on this beautiful morning, the Master led them to a secluded spot a short distance above their camp and there taught them many new truths. This talk of Thursday forenoon was his farewell address to the combined camp group of apostles and chosen disciples, both Jews and gentiles. Judas did not return to the camp until midafternoon, a short time before Jesus led the twelve into Jerusalem to partake of the Last Supper.

178:1. Discourse on Sonship and Citizenship

Jesus talked to about fifty of his trusted followers for almost two hours and answered a score of questions regarding the relation of the kingdom of heaven to the kingdoms of this world. The kingdoms of this world may often find it necessary to employ physical force in the execution of their laws and for the maintenance of order. In the kingdom of heaven true believers will not resort to physical force. There is nothing incompatible between sonship in the spiritual kingdom and citizenship in the secular or civil government. You shall not render spiritual worship to earthly rulers. The material-minded sons in darkness will never know of your spiritual light of truth unless you draw very near them with unselfish social service. As faith-enlightened and spirit-liberated sons of the kingdom of heaven, you face a double responsibility of duty to man and duty to God while you voluntarily assume a third and sacred obligation: service to the brotherhood of God-knowing believers. Display wisdom and exhibit sagacity in your dealings with unbelieving civil rulers. The persistent preaching of this gospel of the kingdom will some day bring to all nations a new and unbelievable liberation, intellectual freedom, and religious liberty. You are indeed to be gentle in your dealings with erring mortals, but you are also to be valiant in defense of righteousness, mighty in the promulgation of truth, and aggressive in the preaching of this gospel of the kingdom, even to the ends of the earth. And my spirit shall be upon you, now and even to the end of the world.

178:2. After the Noontime Meal

David Zebedee, through the work of his secret agents in Jerusalem, was fully advised concerning the progress of the plan to arrest and kill Jesus. He was about to tell Jesus but Jesus stopped him, telling David that he knew all about it. In conversation with John Mark the day before, it was arranged that the apostles would observe the Passover in the Mark upper room. Judas was prevented from hearing about these arrangements. In a discussion with David Zebedee, Judas gave him all of the apostolic money and receipts for all money on deposit. It was about half past four o'clock when the Master prepared to lead the twelve apostles into Jerusalem.

178:3. On the Way to the Supper

As they drew near the place where Jesus had tarried the previous evening to discourse on the destruction of Jerusalem, they stopped and Jesus reminded the apostles that he would soon be leaving them. They could do nothing to defend him as he followed the Father's plan for the ending of his life. They should take heed lest they be killed also. They would ascend to the worlds on high and sit with him in the spirit kingdom of the Father. "You must first pass through much tribulation and endure many sorrows—and these trials are even now upon us—and when you have finished your work on earth, you shall come to my joy, even as I have finished my Father's work on earth and am about to return to his embrace."

When the Master had spoken, he arose, and they all followed him down Olivet and into the city. John Mark had followed them all the way into the city, and after they had entered the gate, he hurried on by another street so that he was waiting to welcome them to his father's home when they arrived.

Paper 179: The Last Supper

THE apostles were entirely at a loss to understand the Master's announcement that they would celebrate the Passover one day early. They thought, at least some of them did, that he knew he would be placed under arrest before the time of the Passover supper on Friday night and was therefore calling them together for a special supper on this Thursday evening. Others thought that this was merely a special occasion which was to precede the regular Passover celebration. After receiving the greetings of welcome extended by the father and mother of John Mark, the apostles went immediately to the upper chamber while Jesus lingered behind to talk with the Mark family.

179:1. The Desire for Preference

When the apostles had been shown upstairs by John Mark, they beheld a large and commodious chamber, which was completely furnished for the supper. They expected the Master to arrive any moment, but they were in a quandary as to whether they should seat themselves or await his coming and depend on him to assign them their places. While they hesitated, Judas stepped over to the seat of honor, at the left of the host, and signified that he intended there to recline as the preferred guest. John Zebedee laid claim to the next preferred seat. Simon Peter was so enraged at this assumption of choice positions by Judas and John that he marched clear around the table and took his place on the lowest couch. With the highest and the lowest positions thus occupied, the rest of the apostles chose places in the following order: on the right of the Master, John; on the left, Judas, Simon Zelotes, Matthew, James Zebedee, Andrew, the Alpheus twins, Philip, Nathaniel, Thomas, and Simon Peter. They were still engaged in voicing angry recriminations when the Master appeared in the doorway. Without comment he went to his place, and he did not disturb their seating arrangement.

179:2. Beginning the Supper

For a few moments after the Master had gone to his place, not a word was spoken. Jesus looked them all over and, relieving the tension with a smile, said in part, "I have greatly desired to eat this Passover with you. I shall not again eat with you until you sit down with me in the kingdom which my

Father will give me when I have finished that for which he sent me into this world." Jesus began thus to talk to his apostles because he knew that his hour had come. The Master knew he had revealed the Father's love on earth and had shown forth his mercy to mankind. Likewise, he knew Judas Iscariot had fully made up his mind to deliver him that night into the hands of his enemies. And so, with the full knowledge that the Father had put all things under his authority, the Master now prepared to enact the parable of brotherly love.

179:3. Washing the Apostles' Feet

After drinking the first cup of the Passover, Jesus arose from the table and silently made his way over to near the door, where the water pitchers, basins, and towels had been placed. The Master removed his outer garment, gird himself with a towel, and begin to pour water into one of the foot basins. Imagine the amazement of these twelve men when they saw him make his way to the lowest seat of the feast, where Simon Peter reclined, and, kneeling down in the attitude of a servant, make ready to wash Simon's feet. As the Master knelt, all twelve arose as one man to their feet and Peter said that he would not allow Jesus to wash is feet. The Master said then Peter would have no part in that which he was about to perform; whereupon, Peter asked Jesus then to wash his hand and head. The Master went around the table, in silence, washing the feet of his twelve apostles, not even passing by Judas.

When Jesus had finished washing the feet of the twelve, he donned his cloak, returned to his place as host, and after looking over his bewildered apostles, said in part, "Do you really understand what I have done to you? You call me Master, and you say well, for so I am. If, then, the Master has washed your feet, why was it that you were unwilling to wash one another's feet? He who would be great among you, let him become as the younger; while he who would be chief, let him become as one who serves. If you are willing to become fellow servants with me in doing the Father's will, in the kingdom to come you shall sit with me in power, still doing the Father's will in future glory."

179:4. Last Words to the Betrayer

For some minutes the apostles ate in silence, but under the influence of the Master's cheerful demeanor they were soon drawn into conversation. Jesus told them that he would not be with them by tomorrow night but it was not necessary that one of them should betray him. Each asked, "Is it I?" When Judas asked this question, Jesus handed him bread dipped in the dish of herbs, saying, "You have said." After an exchange with John telling him who the betrayer was, Jesus said to Judas, "What you have decided to do, do quickly." And when Judas heard these words, he arose from the table and hastily left the room. This supper, with its tender episodes and softening touches, was Jesus' last appeal to the deserting Judas, but it was of no avail.

179:5. Establishing the Remembrance Supper

As they brought Jesus the third cup of wine, he arose from the couch and, taking the cup in his hands, blessed it, saying, "Take this cup, all of you, and drink of it. This shall be the cup of my remembrance. This is the cup of the blessing of a new dispensation of grace and truth. This shall be to you the emblem of the bestowal and ministry of the divine Spirit of Truth." When they had finished drinking this new cup of remembrance, the Master took up the bread and, after giving thanks, broke it in pieces and, directing them to pass it around, said, "Take this bread of remembrance and eat it. I have told you that I am the bread of life. And this bread of life is the united life of the Father and the Son in one gift. The word of the Father, as revealed in the Son, is indeed the bread of life."

In instituting this remembrance supper, the Master resorted to parables and symbols. In this way he sought to prevent successive generations from crystallizing his teaching and binding down his spiritual meanings by the dead chains of tradition and dogma. Notwithstanding the Master's effort thus to establish this new sacrament of the remembrance, those who followed after him in the intervening centuries saw to it that his express desire was effectively thwarted in that his simple spiritual symbolism of that last night in the flesh has been reduced to precise interpretations and subjected to the almost mathematical precision of a set formula. Of all Jesus' teachings none have become more tradition-standardized.

After they had engaged in meditation for a few moments, Jesus continued speaking, "When you do these things, recall the life I have lived on earth among you and rejoice that I am to continue to live on earth with you and to serve through you."

Paper 180: The Farewell Discourse

AFTER the conclusion of the Last Supper, the Master said that in the future they would have to make provisions for themselves in their ministry. He would soon leave them, but in the age to come they would see him when they ascend to the kingdom which the Father has given him.

180:1. The New Commandment

Jesus told the apostles that he was giving them a new commandment: "That you love one another even as I have loved you. And by this will all men know that you are my disciples if you thus love one another.... Greater love can no man have than this: that he will lay down his life for his friends. . . . The Father and I will both work with you, and you shall experience the divine fullness of joy if you will only obey my command to love one another, even as I have loved you." It is loyalty, not sacrifice, that Jesus demands. Sacrifice implies servant-mindedness; love and loyalty to Jesus makes service a supreme joy.

180:2. The Vine and the Branches

Then Jesus stood up again and continued teaching his apostles: "I am the true vine, and my Father is the husbandman. I am the vine, and you are the branches. And the Father requires of me only that you shall bear much fruit. The vine is pruned only to increase the fruitfulness of its branches. . . . He who lives in me, and I in him, will bear much fruit of the spirit and experience the supreme joy of yielding this spiritual harvest. . . . As the Father has loved me, so have I loved you. Live in my love even as I live in the Father's love. If you do as I have taught you, you shall abide in my love even as I have kept the Father's word and evermore abide in his love."

How long will it take the world of believers to understand that prayer is not a process of getting your way but rather a program of taking God's way, an experience of learning how to recognize and execute the Father's will?

180:3. Enmity of the World

The Master continued, saying in part, "When I have left you, be not discouraged by the enmity of the world. I have chosen you out of the world to represent the spirit of another world. If they dare to persecute me, they will also persecute you. If my words offend the unbelievers, so also will your words offend the ungodly. But I will not leave you alone in the world. Very soon, after I have gone, I will send you a spirit helper. You shall have with you one who will take my place among you, one who will continue to teach you the way of truth, who will even comfort you. Let not your hearts be troubled. You believe in God; continue to believe also in me. Even though I must leave you, I will not be far from you. I have already told you that in my Father's universe there are many tarrying-places."

180:4. The Promised Helper

Jesus continued to teach, saying in part, "When I have gone to the Father, and after he has fully accepted the work I have done for you on earth, and after I have received the final sovereignty of my own domain, I shall say to my Father: Having left my children alone on earth, it is in accordance with my promise to send them another teacher. And when the Father shall approve, I will pour out the Spirit of Truth upon all flesh. Today I can be with you only in person. In the times to come I will be with you and all other men who desire my presence, wherever you may be, and with each of you at the same time. Do you not discern that it is better for me to go away; that I leave you in the flesh so that I may the better and the more fully be with you in the spirit?"

180:5. The Spirit of Truth

The new helper which Jesus promised to send into the hearts of believers, to pour out upon all flesh, is the Spirit of Truth. The new teacher is the conviction of truth, the consciousness and assurance of true meanings on real spirit levels. You can know the truth, and you can live the truth; you can experience the growth of truth in the soul and enjoy the liberty of its enlightenment in the mind, but you cannot imprison truth in formulas, codes, creeds, or intellectual patterns of human conduct. Static truth is dead truth, and only dead truth can be held as a theory. Wisdom comprises the consciousness of knowledge elevated to new levels of meaning and activated by the presence of the universe endowment of the adjutant of wisdom. The God-knowing individual is constantly elevating wisdom to the living-truth levels of divine attainment. Love, unselfishness, must undergo a constant and living readaptive interpretation of relationships in accordance with the leading of the Spirit of Truth. The old religion taught self-sacrifice; the new religion teaches only self-forgetfulness, enhanced self-realization in conjoined social service and universe comprehension. Neither tradition nor a ceremonial system of formal worship can atone for the lack of genuine compassion for one's fellows.

180:6. The Necessity for Leaving

After Peter, James, John, and Matthew had asked the Master numerous questions, he continued his farewell discourse by saying in part, "It is really profitable for you that I go away. If I go not away, the new teacher cannot come into your hearts. The Spirit of Truth shall eventually guide you into all truth as you pass through the many abodes in my Father's universe. This spirit comes forth from me, and he will reveal my truth to you. Everything which the Father has in this domain is now mine; wherefore did I say that this new teacher would take of that which is mine and reveal it to you. And all the worlds will be blessed in this same revelation of life in effecting the overthrow of death. Hitherto have you made all your requests in my Father's name. After you see me again, you may also ask in my name, and I will hear you. Mortal man cannot see the spirit Father; therefore have I come into the world to show the Father to your creature eyes. But when you have become perfected in spirit growth, you shall then see the Father himself."

Paper 181: Final Admonitions and Warnings

AFTER the farewell discourse had been discussed and had begun to settle down in their minds, Jesus again called the apostles to order and began the impartation of his final admonitions and warnings.

181:1. Last Words of Comfort

Jesus told them that when he was delivered from his material body, he would send his Spirit of Truth which would indwell and lead each of them and all other believers of the gospel of the kingdom. "The Spirit of Truth will become in them a well of living water springing up into eternal life." He would thus be able to lead them through the many, many stations in the Father's eternal creation. Each spiritual station is designed to prepare them for the next one ahead, until they attain the divine estate wherein they are spiritually perfected even as the Father is perfect. We are to strive to do the Father's will rather than trying to imitate the earth life of Jesus. "Peace I leave with you; my peace I give to you. I make these gifts not as the world gives—by measure—I give each of you all you will receive. Let not your heart be troubled, neither let it be fearful." A certain amount of both stoicism and optimism are serviceable in living a life on earth, but neither has aught to do with that superb peace which the Son of God bestows upon his brethren in the flesh. The peace of Jesus is, then, the peace and assurance of a son who fully believes that his career for time and eternity is safely and wholly in the care and keeping of an all-wise, all-loving, and all-powerful spirit Father.

181:2. Farewell Personal Admonitions

The Master then addressed himself to saying good-bye individually and to giving each a word of personal advice, together with his parting blessing.

He asked John to look after his earth family and welcome them when they see the light and enter the kingdom; and to dedicate his life to teaching his brethren to love one another as Jesus had loved them.

Jesus warned Simon Zelotes that he did not understand the spiritual nature of the kingdom and that after his disappointment and discouragement, he would go forth proclaiming this gospel in great power.

Matthew Levi was urged to dedicate his whole future life service to showing all men that God is no respecter of persons.

Jesus informed James Zebedee that people even in their death would witness to the gospel, and that true wisdom embraces discretion as well as courage.

Andrew was relieved of his administrative responsibilities and was asked to dedicate the remainder of his life to promoting the practical aspects of brotherly love among his brethren.

The Alpheus twins were instructed to return to their former work, realizing that to him who is God-knowing, there is no such thing as common labor or secular toil.

When Philip's material mindedness was blessed with spiritual vision he was to go forth preaching of the gospel of the kingdom. "And always remember, Philip, he who has seen me has seen the Father."

Jesus told Nathaniel that sincerity is most serviceable in the work of the kingdom when it is wedded to discretion; and that the Spirit of Truth would teach them much which they were unable to understand.

Thomas was told that he sometimes lacked faith but never lacked courage. He was to dedicate his life to the great work of showing how the critical material mind of man can triumph over the inertia of intellectual doubting.

The Master recognized that Simon Peter would dedicate his life to the public proclamation of the gospel but was concerned that he should learn to think before speaking. When Peter professed his loyalty, Jesus told him that this very night he would deny him three or four times.

"But remember my promise: When I am raised up, I will tarry with you for a season before I go to the Father. And even this night will I make supplication to the Father that he strengthen each of you for that which you must now so soon pass through. I love you all with the love wherewith the Father loves me, and therefore should you henceforth love one another, even as I have loved you."

Paper 182: In Gethsemane

IT was about ten o'clock this Thursday night when Jesus led the eleven apostles from the home of Elijah and Mary Mark on their way back to the Gethsemane camp. John Mark hearing them coming downstairs, he arose and, quickly throwing a linen coat about himself, followed them through the city. And John Mark remained so near the Master throughout this night and the next day that he witnessed everything and overheard much of what the Master said from this time on to the hour of the crucifixion. When the apostles arrived at the camp, they asked Andrew what had become of Judas. Andrew remarked, "I do not know where Judas is, but I fear he has deserted us."

182:1. The Last Group Prayer

A few moments after arriving at camp, Jesus said to them, "My friends and brethren, my time with you is now very short, and I desire that we draw apart by ourselves while we pray to our Father in heaven for strength to sustain us in this hour and henceforth in all the work we must do in his name." Jesus acknowledged that his hour had now come and that he was about to reassume his duties as Universe Sovereign. He asked the Father to be with the apostles as they go forth representing him in the world. Those who served with him in humiliation, he looked forward to being with him in universe power and glory.

When Jesus had finished his earth life, this name of the Father had been so revealed that the Master, who was the Father incarnate, could truly say: I am the bread of life. I am the living water. I am the light of the world. I am the desire of all ages. I am the open door to eternal salvation. I am the reality of endless life. I am the good shepherd. I am the pathway of infinite perfection. I am the resurrection and the life. I am the secret of eternal survival. I am the way, the truth, and the life. I am the infinite Father of my finite children. I am the true vine; you are the branches. I am the hope of all who know the living truth. I am the living bridge from one world to another. I am the living link between time and eternity. Thus did Jesus enlarge the living revelation of the name of God to all generations.

182:2. Last Hour Before the Betrayal

David Zebedee and John Mark took Jesus to one side and revealed that they knew that Judas intended to betray him into the hands of his enemies. Jesus told them that all things would work together for the glory of God and the salvation of men. He then sent the apostles to their rest but asked Peter, James, and John to remain with him.

All of the apostles except Nathaniel and Andrew were armed with swords. Jesus asked David's most fleet and trustworthy messenger, Jacob, to go to Abner at Philadelphia telling him what was about to happen and told Jacob that an unseen messenger would run by his side. Then he informed the chief of the Greeks of the events of the next couple of days. None of the apostles expected anything out of the ordinary to happen that night. David Zebedee told Jesus how much he appreciated working with him and informed him that Jesus' family was now in Jericho. David and John Mark had arranged to watch the two approaches to the camp, but John was so overcome with combined devotion and curiosity that he forsook his sentinel post and followed after Jesus, hiding himself in the bushes, from which place he saw and overheard all that transpired during those last moments in the garden and just before Judas and the armed guards appeared to arrest Jesus.

182:3. Alone in Gethsemane

When they arrived at the place of his devotions, he bade the three sit down and watch with him while he went off about a stone's throw to pray. And when he had fallen down on his face, he prayed, "My Father, I came into this world to do your will, and so have I. I know that the hour has come to lay down this life in the flesh, and I do not shrink therefrom, but I would know that it is your will that I drink this cup. Send me the assurance that I will please you in my death even as I have in my life." Three times after praying Jesus found his three apostles asleep.

While no mortal can presume to understand the thoughts and feelings of the incarnate Son of God at such a time as this, we know that he endured great anguish and suffered untold sorrow, for the perspiration rolled off his face in great drops. A mighty angel came down by his side to comfort him. He was at last convinced that the Father intended to allow natural events to take their course. Before Judas and the soldiers arrived, the Master had fully regained his customary poise; the spirit had triumphed over the flesh. Once more the Son of Man was prepared to face his enemies with equanimity and in the full assurance of his invincibility as a mortal man unreservedly dedicated to the doing of his Father's will.

Paper 183: The Betrayal and Arrest of Jesus

WHEN two excited messengers arrived seeking David Zebedee, the Greek sentinel aroused the Greeks. The Master mildly admonished them all to return to their tents but they were reluctant to do so. Jesus left them and walked to the olive press near the entrance to Gethsemane Park. He feared that if the eight apostles were awake they might be arrested along with him. Jesus sat down, alone, on the olive press, where he awaited the coming of the betrayer, and he was seen at this time only by John Mark and an innumerable host of celestial observers.

183:1. The Father's Will

It was, indeed and in truth, the will of the Father that his Son should drink to the full the cup of mortal experience, from birth to death, but the Father in heaven had nothing whatever to do with instigating the barbarous behavior of those supposedly civilized human beings who so brutally tortured the Master and so horribly heaped successive indignities upon his nonresisting person. The Father in heaven desired the bestowal Son to finish his earth career naturally. Accordingly, Jesus elected to lay down his life in the flesh in the manner which was in keeping with the outworking of natural events.

183:2. Judas in the City

After Judas so abruptly left the table while eating the Last Supper, he went directly to the home of his cousin, and then did the two go straight to the captain of the temple guards. Judas requested the captain to assemble the guards and informed him that he was ready to lead them to Jesus. The Master and the eleven left the home of Elijah Mark fully fifteen minutes before the betrayer and the guards arrived. Judas knew that many at the Olivet camp were armed and asked for a company of forty armed soldiers. He was not only disloyal, but he was a real coward at heart.

It was necessary to go to Pilot himself in order to obtain permission to employ the armed Roman guards. Accordingly, when Judas Iscariot started out from the temple, about half after eleven o'clock, he was accompanied by more than sixty persons—temple guards, Roman soldiers, and curious servants of the chief priests and rulers.

183:3. The Master's Arrest

Judas planned to appear to be warning the apostles but Jesus prevented this by greeting him as a betrayer and identified himself to the Roman captain. Judas stepped up to Jesus and, placed a kiss upon his brow. When Malchus, the Syrian bodyguard of the high priest, stepped up to Jesus and made ready to bind his hands, Peter drew his sword and with the others rushed forward to smite Malchus. Jesus raised a forbidding hand and commanded Peter to put up his sword. The Roman captain fearing that the followers of the Master might try to rescue him ordered that they be seized. Jesus' followers quickly fled back into the ravine. John Mark was nearly captured, losing his linen coat. John and David Zebedee awakened the eight apostles and told them of the arrest of Jesus. Simon Peter and John Zebedee followed after Jesus. John Mark suspected they were taking Jesus to the home of Annas and arrived ahead of the mob, hiding near the entrance gate.

183:4. Discussion at the Olive Press

After a short informal discussion, Simon Zelotes stood up on the stone wall of the olive press and exhorted his fellow apostles and the other disciples to hasten on after the mob and effect the rescue of Jesus. The majority of the company would have been disposed to follow his aggressive leadership had it not been for the advice of Nathaniel, who called their attention to Jesus' oft-repeated teachings regarding nonresistance. Thomas observed that Jesus refused to allow his friends to defend him, and persuaded them to scatter, every man for himself, with the understanding that David Zebedee would maintain a clearinghouse. Shortly after daybreak Jude arrived and David Zebedee sent word to Jesus' family, by Jude, to forgather at the house of Martha and Mary in Bethany and there await news which his messengers would regularly bring them.

183:5. On the Way to the High Priest's Palace

The captain of the temple guards wanted to take Jesus to Caiaphas but the Roman captain decided to take him to Annas for his preliminary examination. Neither captain would speak to Judas—they held him in such contempt. The commander of the temple guards, seeing John, told his assistant to bind John. But the Roman captain said that John was neither a traitor nor a coward and that Roman law allows that a prisoner may have at least one friend to stand with him before the judgment bar. And this explains why John Zebedee was permitted to remain near Jesus all the way through his trying experiences this night and the next day. Jesus said nothing all the way to his appearance before Annas.

Paper 184: Before the Sanhedrin Court

ANNAS wanted to maintain his prestige as the chief ecclesiastical authority of the Jews and detain Jesus until the first morning sacrifice in the temple, around three o'clock, when it was lawful to call together the court of the Sanhedrin. Jesus spent about three hours at the palace of Annas on Mount Olivet. John Zebedee was free and safe in the palace of Annas not only because of the word of the Roman captain, but also because he and his brother James were well known to the older servants, having many times been guests at the palace as the former high priest was a distant relative of their mother, Salome.

184:1. Examination by Annas

Annas, enriched by the temple revenues, his son-in-law the acting high priest, and with his relations to the Roman authorities, was indeed the most powerful single individual in all Jewry. Annas had not seen Jesus for several years, and Jesus was even more majestic and well poised than Annas remembered him. Annas was reluctant to participate in the murder of a good man. Driving the money-changers out of the temple aroused his enmity far more than had Jesus' teachings.

Annas asked Jesus several questions but Jesus did not answer. Then Annas asked Jesus if he did not care if he, Annas, was friendly before his trial. When Jesus heard this, he said, "Annas, you know that you could have no power over me unless it were permitted by my Father. Some would destroy the Son of Man because they are ignorant; they know no better, but you, friend, know what you are doing. How can you, therefore, reject the light of God?" Annas was bewildered but continued asking questions about his teachings. When Jesus told him all Jerusalem knew about his teachings, the chief steward struck Jesus in the face. Annas in his confusion left the room leaving Jesus alone with the household attendants and the temple guards for almost an hour. When Annas returned, he asked Jesus if he was the Messiah and Jesus replied, "So you have said."

184:2. Peter in the Courtyard

When John saw Simon Peter arrive at the gate, he asked the portress to let Peter in and she gladly assented. Peter went over to the charcoal fire to warm himself. His mind was in a whirl of confusion. The portress came over and asked him if he was one of Jesus' disciples, which Peter denied. Soon another servant came over saying he saw Peter in the garden when Jesus was arrested. Peter was thoroughly alarmed and said, "I know not this man, neither am I one of his followers." About this time the portress asked why he is denying that he is a disciple and Peter again denied all knowledge of Jesus with much cursing and swearing. Later a man standing nearby told Peter his speech reveals that he is a Galilean and again Peter denied all connection with his Master. An hour later the gate-keeper and her sister teasingly charged him with being a follower of Jesus. As he again denied the accusation, he heard the cock crow and he remembered the warning of the Master and he was crushed with a sense of guilt.

When the palace doors opened, the guards led Jesus past on the way to Caiaphas. As the Master passed Peter, he saw, by the light of the torches, the look of despair on the face of his former self-confident and superficially brave apostle, and he turned and looked upon Peter. Peter never forgot that look as long as he lived. It was such a glance of commingled pity and love as mortal man had never beheld in the face of the Master. He sat down by the side of the road and wept bitterly.

184:3. Before the Court of Sanhedrists

It was about half past three o'clock this Friday morning when the chief priest, Caiaphas, called the Sanhedrist court of inquiry to order. This was a special trial court of some thirty Sanhedrists and was convened in the palace of the high priest. John Zebedee was present with Jesus throughout this so-called trial. The entire court was startled and somewhat confused by his majestic appearance. More than a score of false witnesses were on hand to testify against Jesus, but their testimony was so contradictory and so evidently trumped up that the Sanhedrists themselves were very much ashamed of the performance. Throughout all this false testimony the Master made no reply to their many false accusations. But Caiaphas could not longer endure the sight of the Master standing there in perfect composure and unbroken silence. He, shaking his accusing finger in the Master's face, said, "I adjure you, in the name of the living God, that you tell us whether you are the Deliverer, the Son of God." Jesus answered, "I am. Soon I go to the Father, and presently shall the Son of Man be clothed with power and once more reign over the hosts of heaven." After Jesus had so unexpectedly answered Caiaphas, the high priest stepped forward and smote him in the face with his hand; other members of the court, in passing out of the room, spit in Jesus' face, and many of them mockingly slapped him with the palms of their hands. And thus in disorder and with such unheard-of confusion this first session of the Sanhedrist trial of Jesus ended at half past four o'clock. Thirty prejudiced and tradition-blinded false judges, with their false witnesses, are presuming to sit in judgment on the righteous Creator of a universe.

184:4. The Hour of Humiliation

The Jewish law required that, in the matter of passing the death sentence, there should be two sessions of the court. This second session was to be held on the day following the first, but these men waited only one hour. The temple guards and servants of the high priest mocked Jesus, spit upon him, and cruelly buffeted him. When this started Jesus sent John out of the room. Throughout this awful hour Jesus uttered no word.

The human heart cannot possibly conceive of the shudder of indignation that swept out over a vast universe as the celestial intelligences witnessed this sight of their beloved Sovereign submitting himself to the will of his ignorant and misguided creatures on the sin-darkened sphere of unfortunate Urantia. These are the moments of the Master's greatest victories in all his long and eventful career as maker, upholder, and savior of a vast and far-flung universe. Having lived to the full a life of revealing God to man, Jesus is now engaged in making a new and unprecedented revelation of man to God. Jesus is now revealing to the worlds the final triumph over all fears of creature personality isolation.

184:5. The Second Meeting of the Court

At five-thirty o'clock the court reassembled, and Jesus was led into the adjoining room, where John was waiting. This session of the court lasted only a half hour, and they had drawn up the indictment of Jesus, as being worthy of death, under three heads: 1. that he was a perverter of the Jewish nation; he deceived the people and incited them to rebellion; 2. that he taught the people to refuse to pay tribute to Caesar; 3. that, by claiming to be a king and the founder of a new sort of kingdom, he incited treason against the emperor.

This entire procedure was irregular and wholly contrary to the Jewish laws. When it was done, three of the Pharisees took their leave; they wanted to see Jesus destroyed but they would not formulate charges against him without witnesses and in his absence. At six o'clock that morning Jesus was led forth from the home of Caiaphas to appear before Pilate for confirmation of the sentence of death which this Sanhedrist court had so unjustly and irregularly decreed.

Paper 185: The Trial Before Pilate

SHORTLY after six o'clock on this Friday morning, April 7, A.D. 30, Jesus was brought before Pilate. Though Pilate conducted much of Jesus' examination within the praetorium halls, the public trial was held outside on the steps leading up to the main entrance.

185:1. Pontius Pilate

If Pontius Pilate had not been a reasonably good governor of the minor provinces, Tiberius would hardly have suffered him to remain as procurator of Judea for ten years. Although he was a fairly good administrator, he was a moral coward. He failed to grasp the fact that these Hebrews had a real religion, a faith for which they were willing to die. Of all the Roman provinces, none was more difficult to govern than Judea. Pilate never really understood the problems involved in the management of the Jews and, therefore, very early in his experience as governor, made a series of almost fatal and well-nigh suicidal blunders. And it was these blunders that gave the Jews such power over him. As a result of one of these mistakes, Pilate was ordered to Rome. Tiberius died while Pilate was on his way to Rome and he was not reappointed as procurator of Judea. He never fully recovered from the regretful condemnation of having consented to the crucifixion of Jesus. Finding no favor in the eyes of the new emperor, he retired to the province of Lausanne, where he subsequently committed suicide.

Claudia Procula, Pilate's wife, had heard much of Jesus through the word of her maid-in-waiting. After the death of Pilate, Claudia became prominently identified with the spread of the good news.

185:2. Jesus Appears Before Pilate

When Jesus and his accusers had gathered in front of Pilate's judgment hall, the Roman governor came out and asked what accusations they had. The spokesman for the Sanhedrist court attempted to get Pilate to approve the death sentence without giving any charges. When Pilate refused to do so, they said Jesus was guilty of: 1. perverting our nation and stirring up our people to rebellion; 2. forbidding the people to pay tribute to Caesar; 3. calling himself the king of the Jews and teaching the founding of a new kingdom.

When Jesus did not respond to the charges, Pilate took him into the hall to examine him privately. Pilate was confused in mind, fearful of the Jews in his heart, and mightily stirred in his spirit by the spectacle of Jesus' standing there in majesty not in silent contempt, but with an expression of genuine pity and sorrowful affection.

185:3. The Private Examination by Pilate

Pilate took Jesus and John Zebedee into a private chamber and asked him about the charges against Jesus. After some discussion with Jesus and John, Pilate was now certain that the prisoner had done nothing worthy of death. He had trouble understanding that Jesus proclaimed a spiritual kingdom. Among other things, Jesus said, "My presence here before you in these bonds is sufficient to show all men that my kingdom is a spiritual dominion, even the brotherhood of men who, through faith and by love, have become the sons of God. And this salvation is for the gentile as well as for the Jew. And even now do I declare to you that every one who loves the truth hears my voice." Then said Pilate, half in ridicule and half in sincerity, "Truth, what is truth—who knows?" After questioning the Master, Pilate went back to the chief priests and the accusers of Jesus and said, "I have examined this man, and I find no fault in him." The Sanhedrists threatened Pilate if he let Jesus go free. Since Jesus was from Galilee, Pilate sent him to Herod to gain time for thought.

185:4. Jesus Before Herod

Herod had long heard of Jesus, and he was very curious about him. When they brought Jesus before Herod, the tetrarch was startled by Jesus' stately appearance and the calm composure of his countenance. Herod did not remember that Jesus had appeared before him in Sepphoris pleading for a just decision regarding the money due his father, Joseph. For some fifteen minutes Herod asked Jesus questions, but the Master would not answer. Finally, being convinced that Jesus would neither talk nor perform a wonder for him, Herod, after making fun of him for a time, arrayed him in an old purple royal robe and sent him back to Pilate.

185:5. Jesus Returns to Pilate

Pilate, when the guards had brought Jesus back to him, went out on the front steps of the praetorium and told the chief priests and Sanhedrists that he found no fault in Jesus. Presently a vast crowd appeared to ask for the release of a prisoner in honor of the Passover feast. Thinking that he might escape his predicament, Pilate asked if they wished him to release Barabbas, a murderous robber, or Jesus. The chief priests and the Sanhedrin councilors all shouted at the top of their voices, "Barabbas, Barabbas!"

Just then a messenger arrived and gave Pilate a letter from his wife saying, "I pray you have nothing to do with this innocent and just man whom they call Jesus. I have suffered many things in a dream this night because of him." Again Pilate tried to persuade the crowd to save Jesus but they only shouted, "Crucify him! Crucify him!" Pilate was terrorized by the insistent clamor of the mob, acting under the direct leadership of the chief priests and the councilors of the Sanhedrin; nevertheless, he decided upon at least one more attempt to appease the crowd and save Jesus.

185:6. Pilates Last Appeal

Pilate would make one last appeal to their pity. He ordered the Jewish guards and the Roman soldiers to take Jesus and scourge him. As Jesus was bound to the whipping post, they again put upon him the purple robe, and plaiting a crown of thorns, they placed it upon his brow then spit upon him and struck him in the face with their hands. Then Pilate led forth the bleeding and lacerated prisoner and, presenting him before the mixed multitude, said, "Behold the man! Again I declare to you that I find no crime in him, and having scourged him, I would release him."

There stood Jesus of Nazareth, his face bloodstained and his form bowed down with suffering and grief. This sight sent a mighty shudder through the realms of a vast universe, but it did not touch the hearts of those who had set their minds to effect the destruction of Jesus. Then the high priest himself stepped forward and, going up to Pilate, angrily declared that Jesus ought to die because he made himself out to be the Son of God. Pilate was all the more afraid and led Jesus inside the building that he might further examine him.

185:7. Pilate's Last Interview

As Pilate, trembling with fearful emotion, sat down by the side of Jesus he asked him who he really was. At first Jesus did not reply but after further comments by Pilate, Jesus told him that he, Pilate, could have no authority over the Son of Man unless the Father in heaven allowed it; but that Pilate was not so guilty as his betrayer and Annas who delivered him, since Pilate was ignorant of the gospel. Again Pilate told the crowd that he found no reason to consent to the death of Jesus and was about to release him when Caiaphas, shaking an avenging finger in Pilate's face, declared that if he released Jesus he, Pilate, was no friend of Caesar and that he would tell Caesar so. Then did Pilate realize that there was no hope of saving Jesus since he was unwilling to defy the Jews.

185:8. Pilate's Tragic Surrender

Here stood the Son of God incarnate as the Son of Man. He was arrested without indictment; accused without evidence; adjudged without witnesses; punished without a verdict; and now was soon to be condemned to die by an unjust judge who confessed that he could find no fault in him.

The mob cheered when Pilate ordered the release of Barabbas. Then Pilate ordered a basin and some water, and there before the multitude he washed his hands, saying, "I am innocent of the blood of this man. You are determined that he shall die, but I have found no guilt in him. See you to it. The soldiers will lead him forth." And then the mob cheered and replied, "His blood be on us and on our children."

Paper 186: Just Before the Crucifixion

AS Jesus and his accusers started off to see Herod, the Master turned to the Apostle John and said, "John, you can do no more for me. Go to my mother and bring her to see me ere I die." After John Zebedee had told them all that had happened since the midnight arrest of Jesus, Mary his mother went at once in the company of John to see her eldest son. When Mary started out with John to go to her son, his sister Ruth refused to remain behind with the rest of the family. Since she was determined to accompany her mother, her brother Jude went with her.

186:1. The End of Judas Iscariot

As Caiaphas was engaged in making his report to the Sanhedrin regarding the trial and condemnation of Jesus, Judas appeared before them to claim his reward for the part he had played in his Master's arrest and sentence of death. All of these Jews loathed Judas; they looked upon the betrayer with only feelings of utter contempt. Judas anticipated being called before the full meeting of the Sanhedrin and there hearing himself eulogized. Imagine the great surprise of this egotistic traitor when a servant of the high priest handed him a bag containing thirty pieces of silver—the current price of a good, healthy slave.

Judas was humiliated, disillusioned, and utterly crushed. From a distance Judas saw them raise the cross piece with Jesus nailed thereon and he rushed back, forced his way in before the Sanhedrin saying he had betrayed innocent blood, and threw the thirty pieces of silver over the temple floor. His despair was desperate and well-nigh absolute. On he journeyed through the city and outside the walls, on down into the terrible solitude of the valley of Hinnom, where he climbed up the steep rocks and, taking the girdle of his cloak, fastened one end to a small tree, tied the other about his neck, and cast himself over the precipice. Ere he was dead, the knot which his nervous hands had tied gave way, and the betrayer's body was dashed to pieces as it fell on the jagged rocks below.

186:2. The Master's Attitude

When Jesus was arrested, he knew that his work on earth, in the likeness of mortal flesh, was finished. He fully understood the sort of death he would die, and he was little concerned with the details of his so-called trials.

There was but one question which would always elicit an answer; when asked if he were the Son of God, Jesus unfailingly made reply. He had acquired that type of human character which could preserve its composure and assert its dignity in the face of continued and gratuitous insult. The onlooking celestial hosts could not refrain from broadcasting to the universe the depiction of the scene of "Pilate on trial before Jesus." Jesus said little during these trials, but he said enough to show all mortals the kind of human character man can perfect in partnership with God. Pilate spoke more truly than he knew when, after Jesus had been scourged, he presented him before the multitude, exclaiming, "Behold the man!" As Pilate spoke, there echoed throughout all Nebadon, "Behold God and man!" In his matchless life Jesus never failed to reveal God to man. Now, in these final episodes of his mortal career and in his subsequent death, he made a new and touching revelation of man to God.

186:3. The Dependable David Zebedee

David Zebedee believed that Jesus' enemies would return; so he early removed some five or six tents up the ravine. Here he proposed to hide and at the same time maintain a center, or co-ordinating station, for his messenger service. David had hardly left the camp when the temple guards arrived. Finding no one there, they contented themselves with burning the camp and then hastened back to the temple. David sent messengers about every half hour with reports to the apostles, the Greeks, and Jesus' earthly family. David proposed to assemble his messengers early Sunday morning at the home of Nicodemus so that they would be on hand to spread the news in case Jesus rose from the dead.

186:4. Preparation for the Crucifixion

It was a little after eight o'clock when Pilate turned Jesus over to the soldiers and a little before nine o'clock when they started for the scene of the crucifixion. Much of the delay in starting off with Jesus for the site of the crucifixion was due to the last-minute decision of the captain to take along two thieves who had been condemned to die. As soon as the thieves could be made ready, they were led into the courtyard, where they gazed upon Jesus, one of them for the first time, but the other had often heard him speak, both in the temple and many months before at the Pella camp.

186:5. Jesus' Death in Relation to the Passover

There is no direct relation between the death of Jesus and the Jewish Passover. It was man and not God who planned and executed the death of Jesus on the cross. The gospel of the good news that mortal man may, by faith, become spirit-conscious that he is a son of God, is not dependent on the death of Jesus. True, indeed, all this gospel of the kingdom has been tremendously illuminated by the Master's death, but even more so by his life. The Father in heaven loved mortal man on earth just as much before the life and death of Jesus on Urantia as he did after this transcendent exhibition of the copartnership of man and God. While the Father in heaven loves us no more because of this bestowal of Michael, all other celestial intelligences do. Jesus is not about to die as a sacrifice for sin. The salvation of God for the mortals of Urantia would have been just as effective and unerringly certain if Jesus had not been put to death by the cruel hands of ignorant mortals. You mortals are the sons of God, and only one thing is required to make such a truth factual in your personal experience, and that is your spirit-born faith.

Paper 187: The Crucifixion

THE centurion in charge of these twelve soldiers was the same captain who had led forth the Roman soldiers the previous night to arrest Jesus in Gethsemane. What Jesus is now about to do, submit to death on the cross, he does of his own free will.

187:1. On the Way to Golgotha

Before leaving the courtyard of the praetorium, the soldiers placed the crossbeam on Jesus' shoulders. The legend which the centurion carried to put on the cross of Jesus had been written by Pilate himself in Latin, Greek, and Aramaic, and it read: "Jesus of Nazareth—the King of the Jews." The Jewish authorities tried to get him to change it but he refused.

During the siege of Jerusalem, just forty years after the crucifixion of Jesus, all of Golgotha was covered by thousands upon thousands of crosses upon which, from day to day, there perished the flower of the Jewish race. A terrible harvest, indeed, of the seed-sowing of this day.

Some women weeping dared to follow by Jesus' side and he told them not to weep for him but for themselves because of the terrible time coming to Jerusalem. As the Master trudged along on the way to the crucifixion, he was very weary; he was nearly exhausted. He had had neither food nor water since the Last Supper at the home of Elijah Mark, not to mention the abusive scourgings with their accompanying physical suffering and loss of blood.

Shortly after passing through the gate on the way out of the city, as Jesus staggered on bearing the crossbeam, his physical strength momentarily gave way, and he fell beneath the weight of his heavy burden. When the captain saw this, knowing what Jesus had already endured he ordered a passerby, one Simon from Cyrene, to take the crossbeam from Jesus' shoulders and compelled him to carry it the rest of the way to Golgotha. After the resurrection and before leaving Jerusalem, Simon became a valiant believer in the gospel of the kingdom, and when he returned home he led his family into the heavenly kingdom. His two sons, Alexander and Rufus, became very effective teachers of the new gospel in Africa. But Simon never knew that Jesus, whose burden he bore, and the Jewish tutor who once befriended his injured son, were the same person.

187:2. The Crucifixion

The cross was not high, the Master's feet being only about three feet from the ground. Crucifixion was resorted to in order to provide a cruel and lingering punishment, the victim sometimes not dying for several days. There existed a society of Jewish women who always sent a representative to crucifixions for the purpose of offering drugged wine to the victim in order to lessen his suffering. But when Jesus tasted this narcotized wine, as thirsty as he was, he refused to drink it. Jesus' only words as they nailed him to the crossbeam, were, "Father, forgive them, for they know not what they do."

The Apostle John, with Mary the mother of Jesus, Ruth, and Jude, arrived on the scene just after Jesus had been hoisted to his position on the cross, and just as the captain was nailing the title above the Master's head. As Jesus saw his mother, with John and his brother and sister, he smiled but said nothing. Meanwhile the four soldiers had divided his clothes among them, casting lots for the tunic. This prevented his followers from having garments of superstitious relic worship.

187:3. Those Who Saw the Crucifixion

At about half past nine o'clock this Friday morning, Jesus was hung upon the cross. Before eleven o'clock, upward of one thousand persons had assembled to witness this spectacle of the crucifixion of the Son of Man. Standing near the cross at one time or another during the crucifixion were Mary, Ruth, Jude, John, Salome (John's mother), and a group of earnest women believers including Mary's sister the wife of Clopas, Mary Magdalene, and Rebecca.

By half past eleven o'clock most of the jesting and jeering crowd had gone its way; less than fifty persons remained on the scene. The soldiers now prepared to eat lunch. When Jesus saw them eat and drink, he looked down upon them and said, "I thirst." When the captain of the guard heard Jesus say, "I thirst," he took some of the wine from his bottle and, putting the saturated sponge stopper upon the end of a javelin, raised it to Jesus so that he could moisten his parched lips.

Jesus had purposed to live without resort to his supernatural power, and he likewise elected to die as an ordinary mortal upon the cross.

187:4. The Thief on the Cross

One of the brigands railed at Jesus saying that if he were the Son of God, why did he not save himself and them? The other thief, who had many times heard Jesus teach, reproached him saying that they were suffering justly but Jesus was suffering unjustly, and that they should be seeking forgiveness and salvation. When Jesus heard this, he turned his face toward him and smiled approvingly. When the malefactor saw the face of Jesus turned toward him, he mustered up his courage, fanned the flickering flame of his faith, and said, "Lord, remember me when you come into your kingdom." And then Jesus said, "Verily, verily, I say to you today, you shall sometime be with me in Paradise."

Just after the repentant thief heard the Master's promise that they should sometime meet in Paradise, John returned from the city, bringing with him his mother and a company of almost a dozen women believers. John took up his position near Mary the mother of Jesus, supporting her. Her son Jude stood on the other side. As Jesus looked down upon this scene, it was noontide, and he said to his mother, "Woman, behold your son!" And speaking to John, he said, "My son, behold your mother!" And then he addressed them both, saying, "I desire that you depart from this place." And so John and Jude led Mary away from Golgotha then hastened back to the scene of the crucifixion. After Mary left, the other women withdrew for a short distance and remained in attendance upon Jesus until he expired on the cross.

After the Passover Mary returned to Bethsaida, where she lived at John's home for the rest of her natural life. Mary did not live quite one year after the death of Jesus.

187:5. Last Hour on the Cross

Although it was early in the season for such a phenomenon, shortly after twelve o'clock the sky darkened by reason of the fine sand in the air. When the Master gave up his life shortly after this hour, less than thirty people were present. The believers present were all women except two, Jude, Jesus' brother, and John Zebedee.

The last conscious thought of the human Jesus was concerned with the repetition in his mind of a portion of the Book of Psalms, such as "My God, my God, why have you forsaken me?" Jesus did not for one moment doubt that he had lived in accordance with the Father's will. He was merely reciting in his vanishing consciousness many scriptures, such as this twenty-second Psalm. His last request was a second time he said, "I thirst," and the captain again moistened his lips with the sponge wet with the sour wine. When the Master finally breathed his last, there were present at the foot of his cross John Zebedee, Jude, Ruth, Mary Magdalene, and Rebecca.

It was just before three o'clock when Jesus, with a loud voice, cried out, "It is finished! Father, into your hands I commend my spirit." And when he had thus spoken, he bowed his head and gave up the life struggle.

When the Roman centurion saw how Jesus died, he smote his breast and said, "This was indeed a righteous man; truly he must have been a Son of God." And from that hour he began to believe in Jesus.

Because of the Passover and the Sabbath, the Jews did not want the bodies to be exposed on Golgotha and received Pilate's permission for soldiers to break the legs and dispatch Jesus and the two brigands. The soldiers were surprised to find Jesus already dead. In order to make sure of his death, one of the soldiers pierced Jesus' left side with his spear. The overwhelming emotional agony and the acute spiritual anguish of Jesus brought an end to his mortal life in the flesh in a little less than five and one-half hours. After such a life—and at such a death—the Master could truly say, "It is finished."

187:6. After the Crucifixion

In the midst of the darkness of the sandstorm, about half past three o'clock, David Zebedee sent out the last of the messengers carrying the news of the Master's death. After the death of the Master, John sent the women, in charge of Jude, to the home of Elijah Mark. John himself, being well known by this time to the Roman centurion, remained at Golgotha until Joseph and Nicodemus arrived on the scene with an order from Pilate authorizing them to take possession of the body of Jesus.

Thus ended a day of tragedy and sorrow for a vast universe whose myriads of intelligences had shuddered at the shocking spectacle of the crucifixion of the human incarnation of their beloved Sovereign; they were stunned by this exhibition of mortal callousness and human perversity.

Paper 188: The Time of the Tomb

THE day and a half that Jesus' mortal body lay in the tomb of Joseph is a chapter in the earth career of Michael which is little known to us. The rulers of the Jews had planned to have Jesus' body thrown in the open burial pits of Gehenna. Joseph of Arimathea and Nicodemus received permission from Pilate to receive the body of Jesus for proper burial.

188:1. The Burial of Jesus

When Joseph presented Pilate's order for the Master's body to the centurion, the Jews raised a tumult and clamored for its possession. In their raving they sought violently to take possession of the body, and when they did this, the centurion and his soldiers drove back the angry mob. When order had been restored, the centurion read the permit from Pilate to the Jews and assured Joseph and Nicodemus that no one would interfere with the burial. They decided to place Jesus in Joseph's new family tomb, hewn out of solid rock. Those who bore the material body of Jesus to the tomb were Joseph, Nicodemus, John, and the Roman centurion.

When properly embalmed the body was reverently placed on a shelf in the tomb, after which the centurion signaled for his soldiers to help roll the doorstone up before the entrance to the tomb.

The women who lingered near the tomb did not think Jesus was properly prepared for burial and decided to return Sunday morning to properly prepare the body.

Aside from David Zebedee and Joseph of Arimathea, very few of Jesus' disciples really believed that he was due to arise from the tomb on the third day.

188:2. Safeguarding the Tomb

To make sure the followers of Jesus did not remove his body from the tomb, the Jewish leaders went to Pilate and ask for a Roman guard to be stationed at Jesus' tomb for at least three days. Pilate gave them ten soldiers and with ten Jewish guards a watch was placed at the tomb. These men rolled yet another stone before the tomb and set the seal of Pilate on and around these stones, lest they be disturbed without their knowledge. And these twenty men remained on watch up to the hour of the resurrection, the Jews carrying them their food and drink.

188:3. During the Sabbath Day

Throughout this Sabbath day the disciples and the apostles remained in hiding, while all Jerusalem discussed the death of Jesus on the cross.

We are not able fully to explain just what happened to Jesus of Nazareth during this period of a day and a half when he was supposed to be resting in Joseph's new tomb. We have sometimes dared to explain these things to ourselves somewhat as follows: The Creator consciousness of Michael must have been at large. The acquired spirit identity of the man of Nazareth must have been consigned to the custody of the Paradise Father. We think the human or mortal consciousness of Jesus slept during these thirty-six hours. There are records extant which show that during this period the supreme council of Salvington, numbering one hundred, held an executive meeting on Urantia under the presidency of Gabriel. There are also records showing that the Ancients of Days of Uversa communicated with Michael regarding the status of the universe of Nebadon during this time. We know that at least one message passed between Michael and Immanuel on Salvington while the Master's body lay in the tomb. The records of Edentia indicate that the Constellation Father of Norlatiadek was on Urantia, and that he received instructions from Michael during this time of the tomb. And there is much other evidence which suggests that not all of the personality of Jesus was asleep and unconscious during this time of apparent physical death.

188:4. Meaning of the Death on the Cross

Although Jesus did not die this death on the cross to atone for the racial guilt of mortals, there are significances attached to this death of Jesus on the cross which should not be overlooked. While the mortals of the realms had salvation even before Jesus lived and died on Urantia, it is nevertheless a fact that his bestowal on this world greatly illuminated the way of salvation; his death did much to make forever plain the certainty of mortal survival after death in the flesh. Though it is hardly proper to speak of Jesus as a sacrificer, a ransomer, or a redeemer, it is wholly correct to refer to him as a savior. The infinite love of God is not secondary to anything in the divine nature. Salvation should be taken for granted by those who believe in the fatherhood of God. The great thing about the death of Jesus is the superb manner and the matchless spirit in which he met death.

188:5. Lessons from the Cross

The cross of Jesus portrays the full measure of the supreme devotion of the true shepherd for even the unworthy members of his flock. The cross forever shows that the attitude of Jesus toward sinners was neither condemnation nor condonation, but rather eternal and loving salvation. Love is truly contagious and eternally creative. Divine love does not merely forgive wrongs; it absorbs and actually destroys them. The sufferings of Jesus were not confined to the crucifixion. In reality, Jesus of Nazareth spent upward of twenty-five years on the cross of a real and intense mortal existence. On millions of inhabited worlds, tens of trillions of evolving creatures who may have been tempted to give up the moral struggle and abandon the good fight of faith, have taken one more look at Jesus on the cross and then have forged on ahead, inspired by the sight of God's laying down his incarnate life in devotion to the unselfish service of man. Greater love no man can have than this: that he would be willing to lay down his life for his friends—and Jesus had such a love that he was willing to lay down his life for his enemies, a love greater than any which had hitherto been known on earth. When thinking men and women look upon Jesus as he offers up his life on the cross, they will hardly again permit themselves to complain at even the severest hardships of life. The death on the cross was not to effect man's reconciliation to

God but to stimulate man's realization of the Father's eternal love and his Son's unending mercy, and to broadcast these universal truths to a whole universe.

Paper 189: The Resurrection

SOON after the burial of Jesus on Friday afternoon, the chief of the archangels of Nebadon, then present on Urantia, summoned his council of the resurrection of sleeping will creatures. They concluded they could do nothing to facilitate the resurrection of the Creator. The Personalized Adjuster of Jesus told the assembled celestial hosts that their Creator-father had the power to lay down his life and to take it up again.

189:1. The Morontia Transit

At two forty-five Sunday morning, the Paradise incarnation commission, consisting of seven unidentified Paradise personalities, arrived on the scene and immediately deployed themselves about the tomb. At ten minutes before three, intense vibrations of commingled material and morontia activities began to issue from Joseph's new tomb, and at two minutes past three o'clock, this Sunday morning, April 9, A.D. 30, the resurrected morontia form and personality of Jesus of Nazareth came forth from the tomb. The material body was still in the tomb.

There is much about the resurrection of Jesus which we do not understand. He came forth from this tomb of Joseph in the very likeness of the morontia personalities who emerge from the resurrection halls of the first mansion world of the local system of Satania.

After talking to Gabriel, the chief of the Melchizedeks, and the Most High of Edentia, he addressed the assembled morontia groups: "Having finished my life in the flesh, I would tarry here for a short time in transition form that I may more fully know the life of my ascendant creatures and further reveal the will of my Father in Paradise." The transitory experience of the Master as a personality midway between the material and the spiritual has begun.

189:2. The Material Body of Jesus

At ten minutes past three o'clock the chief of archangels approached Gabriel and asked for the mortal body of Jesus for immediate dissolution. When given permission by Gabriel, they made ready to remove the body of Jesus from the tomb preparatory to according it the dignified and reverent disposal of near-instantaneous dissolution. It was assigned the secondary Urantia midwayers to roll away the stones from the entrance of the tomb.

When the watching Jewish guards and the Roman soldiers, in the dim light of the morning, saw this huge stone begin to roll away from the entrance of the tomb, apparently of its own accord, they were seized with fear and panic and they fled in haste from the scene. The Jewish leaders bribed the guards to say that while they slept his disciples came and took away the body.

The Christian belief in the resurrection of Jesus has been based on the fact of the "empty tomb." The tomb of Joseph was empty, not because the body of Jesus had been rehabilitated or resurrected, but because the celestial hosts had been granted their request to afford it a special and unique dissolution.

189:3. The Dispensational Resurrection

A little after half past four o'clock this Sunday morning, Gabriel summoned the archangels to his side and made ready to inaugurate the general resurrection of the termination of the Adamic dispensation on Urantia. The morontia Michael appeared before Gabriel telling him to let the roll call of the planetary resurrection begin. The circuit of the archangels then operated for the first time from Urantia. When Gabriel gave the signal, there flashed to the first of the system mansion worlds the voice of Gabriel, saying, "By the mandate of Michael, let the dead of a Urantia dispensation rise!" Then all the survivors of the human races of Urantia who had fallen asleep since the days of Adam, and who had not already gone on to judgment, appeared in the resurrection halls of mansonia in readiness for morontia investiture.

This was the third of the planetary roll calls, or complete dispensational resurrections. The first occurred at the time of the arrival of the Planetary Prince, the second during the time of Adam, and this, the third, signalized the morontia resurrection, the mortal transit, of Jesus of Nazareth.

189:4. Discovery of the Empty Tomb

A little before three o'clock this Sunday morning, when the first signs of day began to appear in the east, five of the women started out for the tomb of Jesus with the mission of anointing Jesus' body. They were Mary Magdalene, Mary the mother of the Alpheus twins, Salome the mother of the Zebedee brothers, Joanna the wife of Chuza, and Susanna the daughter of Ezra of Alexandria. They had prepared an abundance of special embalming lotions, and they carried many linen bandages with them. Arriving at the tomb, they were greatly surprised to see the stone rolled away from the entrance. While they stood there, atremble with fear, Mary Magdalene ventured around the smaller stone and dared to enter the open sepulchre. She saw that the Master's body was gone and uttered a cry of alarm and anguish. The other women fled but then started back to the tomb and saw that it was empty.

Presently they observed a silent and motionless stranger. Mary Magdalene, assuming he might be the garden caretaker, rushed toward him and asked where he had taken the Master. When the stranger did not answer, Mary began to weep. Then spoke Jesus to them, asking who they were seeking, and after some conversation, he addressed the Magdalene with a familiar voice, saying, "Mary." And when she heard that word of well-known sympathy and affectionate greeting, she knew it was the voice of the Master, and she rushed to kneel at his feet while she exclaimed, "My Lord, and my Master!"

Jesus asked them to inform his apostles—and Peter—that they had talked to him. But the apostles did not believe the women, thinking they had seen a vision. But when Mary Magdalene repeated the words and Peter heard his name, he rushed out of the upper chamber, followed closely by John, in great haste to reach the tomb and see these things for himself.

189:5. Peter and John at the Tomb

When John and Peter arrived at the tomb, they saw it was just as the women had described. They could not clearly perceive what had happened. Peter at first suggested that the grave had been rifled, but John reasoned that the grave would hardly have been left so orderly if the body had been stolen. As they came out of the tomb the second time, they found Mary Magdalene returned and weeping before the entrance.

As Mary lingered after Peter and John had gone, the Master again appeared to her, saying, "Be not doubting; have the courage to believe what you have seen and heard. Go back to my apostles and again tell them that I have risen, that I will appear to them, and that presently I will go before them into Galilee as I promised." Mary hurried back to the Mark home and told the apostles she had again talked with Jesus, but they would not believe her. But when Peter and John returned, they ceased to ridicule and became filled with fear and apprehension.

Paper 190: Morontia Appearances of Jesus

THE resurrected Jesus now prepares to spend a short period on Urantia for the purpose of experiencing the ascending morontia career of a mortal of the realms. The mortals of the realms will arise in the morning of the resurrection with the same type of transition or morontia body that Jesus had when he arose from the tomb on this Sunday morning. These bodies do not have circulating blood, and such beings do not partake of ordinary material food.

190:1. Heralds of the Resurrection

When the apostles refused to believe the report of the five women, Mary Magdalene returned to the tomb and the others went back to Joseph's house, where they related their experiences to his daughter and the other women. And the women believed their report.

Shortly after six o'clock the daughter of Joseph of Arimathea and the four women who had seen Jesus went over to the home of Nicodemus, where they related all these happenings to Joseph, Nicodemus, David Zebedee, and the other men there assembled. Joseph and David were disposed to believe the report, so much so that they hurried out to inspect the tomb, and they found everything just as the women had described. From the tomb David and Joseph went immediately to the home of Elijah Mark, where they held a conference with the ten apostles in the upper chamber. They refused to believe; however around 9:30 David sent his 26 messengers with word that Jesus has risen.

David helped Martha and Mary disposed of their earthly possessions, and he accompanied them on their journey to join their brother, Lazarus, at Philadelphia the day after his marriage to Ruth, Jesus' youngest sister.

190:2. Jesus' Appearance at Bethany

From the time of the morontia resurrection until the hour of his spirit ascension on high, Jesus made nineteen separate appearances in visible form to his believers on earth.

Mary Magdalene and David Zebedee with his mother had arrived at Bethany to discuss the report of Jesus' resurrection. About noon of this Sunday at Bethany Jesus appeared to his brother, James, saying, "James, I come to call you to the service of the kingdom. Join earnest hands with your brethren and follow after me." They talked for almost three minutes. James rushed into the house and told them that he had seen and talked with Jesus.

While they were talking around two o'clock Jesus appeared before his earth family and their friends, twenty in all. He greeted them and asked why they waited so long before choosing to follow the light of truth with a whole heart. When they moved toward him, he vanished from their sight. They all wanted to rush off to the city to tell the doubting apostles about what had happened, but James restrained them because of certain things Jesus had said to him. Mary Magdalene, only, was permitted to return to Joseph's house.

190:3. At the Home of Joseph

The fifth morontia manifestation of Jesus to the recognition of mortal eyes occurred in the presence of some twenty-five women believers assembled at the home of Joseph of Arimathea, at about fifteen minutes past four o'clock.

Mary Magdalene was telling the women what had happened at Bethany when a sudden and solemn hush fell over them; they beheld in their very midst the fully visible form of the risen Jesus. He greeted them, saying, "Peace be upon you. In the fellowship of the kingdom there shall be neither Jew nor gentile, rich nor poor, free nor bond, man nor woman. You also are called to publish the good news of the liberty of mankind through the gospel of sonship with God in the kingdom of heaven. Go to all the world proclaiming this gospel and confirming believers in the faith thereof. And while you do this, forget not to minister to the sick and strengthen those who are fainthearted and fear-ridden. And I will be with you always, even to the ends of the earth." And when he had thus spoken, he vanished from their sight.

190:4. Appearance to the Greeks

About half past four o'clock, at the home of one Flavius, the Master made his sixth morontia appearance to some forty Greek believers there assembled. While they were engaged in discussing the reports of the Master's resurrection, he manifested himself in their midst and told them to go to all the world proclaiming this gospel. The Greeks did not sleep that night hoping that Jesus might again visit them.

Rumors of Jesus' resurrection and reports concerning the many appearances to his followers were spreading rapidly, and the whole city was being wrought up to a high pitch of excitement. The Sanhedrin was soon to begin the consideration of these new problems which had been so suddenly thrust upon the Jewish rulers.

190:5. The Walk with Two Brothers

At Emmaus, about seven miles west of Jerusalem, there lived two brothers, shepherds, who had spent the Passover week in Jerusalem attending upon the sacrifices, ceremonials, and feasts. Cleopas, the elder, was a partial believer in Jesus; at least he had been cast out of the synagogue. His brother, Jacob, was not a believer, although he was much intrigued by what he had heard about the Master's teachings and works.

As these two brothers trudged along the road to Emmaus, they talked in great earnestness about Jesus, his teachings, work, and rumors that his tomb was empty. As they made their way toward home, the morontia manifestation of Jesus, his seventh appearance, came alongside them as they journeyed on. Jesus asked them what they were talking about and when told, Jesus said that he was more than acquainted with these teachings and proceeded to enlighten them.

By this time they had come near to the village where these brothers dwelt, and as Jesus was about to leave them, they invited him into their home. They sat down to eat, and as Jesus began to break bread and hand it to them, their eyes were opened. Cleopas recognized that their guest was the Master himself, and then Jesus vanished from their sight. They would not stop to eat. About nine o'clock that evening and just before the Master appeared to the ten, these two excited brothers broke in upon the apostles in the upper chamber, declaring that they had seen Jesus and talked with him.

Paper 191:
Appearances to the Apostles and Other Leaders

RESURRECTION Sunday was a terrible day in the lives of the apostles; ten of them spent the larger part of the day in the upper chamber behind barred doors. Thomas was brooding over his troubles alone at Bethphage.

All day long John upheld the idea that Jesus had risen from the dead. John Mark kept them in touch with developments. For the first time in all these years the apostles realized how much they had been dependent on David's messengers.

The Master put off the first morontia appearance to the apostles for a number of reasons. First, he wanted them to have time, after they heard of his resurrection, to think well over what he had told them about his death and resurrection when he was still with them in the flesh; he wanted Peter to wrestle through with some of his peculiar difficulties before he manifested himself to them all. In the second place, he desired that Thomas should be with them at the time of his first appearance. Thomas remained away from his associates until the next Saturday evening, when, after darkness had come on, Peter and John went over to Bethphage and brought him back with them.

191:1. The Appearance to Peter

It was near half past eight o'clock this Sunday evening when Jesus appeared to Simon Peter in the garden of the Mark home. As Peter was strolling in the garden, he thought of the message, "Go tell my apostles—and Peter," and clenching his fists he spoke aloud, "I believe he has risen from the dead; I will go and tell my brethren." And as he said this, there suddenly appeared in front of him the form of a man, who spoke to him in familiar tones, saying, "Peter, the enemy desired to have you, but I would not give you up. I knew it was not from the heart that you disowned me; therefore I forgave you even before you asked. Gird yourself, Simon, for the battle of a new day, the struggle with spiritual darkness and the evil doubtings of the natural minds of men." Peter and the morontia Jesus talked of things past, present, and future for almost five minutes; then the Master vanished from his gaze, saying, "Farewell, Peter, until I see you with your brethren."

Peter rushed to the upper chamber and into the presence of his fellow apostles, exclaiming in breathless excitement, "I have seen the Master; he was in the garden. I talked with him, and he has forgiven me." Andrew then intimated that Peter had seen things which were not real before. Simon Peter was very much hurt by his brother's insinuations and immediately lapsed into crestfallen silence. The twins felt very sorry for Peter, and they both went over to express their sympathy and to say that they believed him and to reassert that their own mother had also seen the Master.

191:2. First Appearance to the Apostles

Shortly after nine o'clock that evening, the Master, in morontia form, suddenly appeared in the midst of them, saying, "Peace be upon you. Why are you so frightened when I appear, as though you had seen a spirit? Did I not tell you about these things when I was present with you in the flesh? Did I not say to you that the chief priests and the rulers would deliver me up to be killed, that one of your own number would betray me, and that on the third day I would rise? Wherefore all your doubtings and all this discussion about the reports of the women, Cleopas and Jacob, and even Peter? How long will you doubt my words and refuse to believe my promises? And now that you actually see me, will you believe? Even now one of you is absent. When you are gathered together once more, and after all of you know of a certainty that the Son of Man has risen from the grave, go hence into Galilee. Have faith in God; have faith in one another; and so shall you enter into the new service of the kingdom of heaven. I will tarry in Jerusalem with you until you are ready to go into Galilee. My peace I leave with you."

When the morontia Jesus had spoken to them, he vanished in an instant from their sight. This was the Master's ninth morontia appearance.

191:3. With the Morontia Creatures

The next day, Monday, was spent wholly with the morontia creatures then present on Urantia. The morontia Jesus sojourned with these splendid intelligences for forty days.

The Master's morontia form was adjusted for transition through all seven morontia stages, and he entered the embrace of the Most Highs of Edentia on Sunday, the 14th. As the Master progressed in the morontia career, it became, technically, more and more difficult for the morontia intelligences and their transforming associates to visualize the Master to mortal and material eyes.

And it was by these very morontia experiences that the Creator Son of Nebadon really finished and acceptably terminated his seventh and final universe bestowal.

191:4. The Tenth Appearance (At Philadelphia)

The tenth morontia manifestation of Jesus to mortal recognition occurred a short time after eight o'clock on Tuesday, April 11, at Philadelphia, where he showed himself to Abner and Lazarus and some one hundred and fifty of their associates, including more than fifty of the evangelistic corps of the seventy. This appearance occurred just after the opening of a special meeting in the synagogue which had been called by Abner to discuss the crucifixion of Jesus and the more recent report of the resurrection.

The meeting was just being opened by Abner and Lazarus when the entire audience of believers saw the form of the Master appear suddenly and saluting the company, saying among other things, "Peace be upon you. You all know that we have one Father in heaven, and that there is but one gospel of the kingdom. You are to love all men as I have loved you; you are to serve all men as I have served you. Go, then, into all the world proclaiming this gospel of the fatherhood of God and the brotherhood of men to all nations and races and ever be wise in your choice of methods for presenting the good news to the different races and tribes of mankind. Freely you have received this gospel of the kingdom, and you will freely give the good news to all nations. Fear not the resistance of evil, for I am with you always, even to the end of the ages. And my peace I leave with you." And he vanished from their sight.

191:5. Second Appearance to the Apostles

When Thomas was brought back to the Mark home he listened to the telling of the stories of the Master's various appearances, but he steadfastly refused to believe.

They were having their evening meal at a little after six o'clock, with Peter sitting on one side of Thomas and Nathaniel on the other, when the doubting apostle said he would not believe unless he saw the Master with his own eyes. The morontia Master suddenly appeared and, standing directly in front of Thomas, said, "Peace be upon you. For a full week have I tarried that I might appear again when you were all present to hear once more the commission to go into all the world and preach this gospel of the kingdom." When the Master had spoken for some time, he looked down into the face of Thomas and said, "And you, Thomas, who said you would not believe unless you could see me and put your finger in the nail marks of my hands, have now beheld me and heard my words; and though you see no nail marks on my hands, since I am raised in the form that you also shall have when you depart from this world, what will you say to your brethren? You will acknowledge the truth, for already in your heart you had begun to believe even when you so stoutly asserted your unbelief. Your doubts, Thomas, always most stubbornly assert themselves just as they are about to crumble. Thomas, I bid you be not faithless but believing—and I know you will believe, even with a whole heart." When Thomas heard these words, he fell on his knees before the morontia Master and exclaimed, "I believe! My Lord and my Master!" Then said Jesus to Thomas, "You have believed, Thomas, because you have really seen and heard me. Blessed are those in the ages to come who will believe even though they have not seen with the eye of flesh nor heard with the mortal ear.... And now go all of you to Galilee, where I will presently appear to you." After he said this, he vanished from their sight.

191:6. The Alexandrian Appearance

On Tuesday evening, April 18, at about half past eight o'clock, Jesus appeared to Rodan and some eighty other believers, in Alexandria. This appearance occurred just after David's messenger brought news of Jesus' crucifixion and said the David believed Jesus would rise again. Even as Nathan spoke, the morontia Master appeared there in full view of all. Jesus said, "Peace be upon you. That which my Father sent me into the world to establish belongs not to a race, a nation, nor to a special group of teachers or preachers. This gospel of the kingdom belongs to both Jew and gentile, to rich and poor, to free and bond, to male and female, even to the little children.... As the Father sent me into this world, even so now send I you. You are all called to carry the good news to those who sit in darkness. This gospel of the kingdom belongs to all who believe it; it shall not be committed to the custody of mere priests. Soon will the Spirit of Truth come upon you, and he shall lead you into all truth. Go you, therefore, into all the world preaching this gospel, and lo, I am with you always, even to the end of the ages." When the Master had so spoken, he vanished from their sight.

Imagine the surprise of David's herald of the resurrection, who arrived the second day after this, when they replied to his announcement, saying, "Yes, we know, for we have seen him. He appeared to us day before yesterday."

Paper 192: Appearances in Galilee

BY the time the apostles left Jerusalem for Galilee, the Jewish leaders had quieted down considerably. From this time on, Peter was the generally recognized head of the apostolic corps. Matthias, whom they chose to take the place of Judas, became their treasurer. Early this Monday morning when the apostles departed for Galilee, John Mark went along.

192:1. Appearance by the Lake

About six o'clock Friday morning, April 21, the morontia Master made his thirteenth appearance—the first in Galilee—to the ten apostles as their boat drew near the shore close to the usual landing place at Bethsaida. As they neared the shore, they saw someone on the beach, near the boat landing, standing by a fire. It had occurred to none of them that the person on the shore was the Master. As they dropped anchor and prepared to enter the small boat for going ashore, Jesus asked them if they had caught anything; when they said they had not, he told them to cast the net on the right side of the boat and it was immediately filled with fish. John then whispered to Peter, "It is the Master," and Peter cast himself in the water to come to shore.

By this time John Mark was up and, seeing the apostles coming ashore with the heavy-laden net, ran down the beach to greet them. Seeing Jesus, he rushed up and, kneeling, said, "My Lord and my Master." Jesus asked them to bring the fish (there were 153) and prepare for some breakfast; there was already a fire and much bread. John Mark prepared seven good-sized fish and served the hungry apostles, after which Jesus served John Mark.

Catching the fish was no miracle; Jesus knew where the fish were. Jesus visited with the ten apostles and John Mark for more than an hour, and then he walked up and down the beach, talking with them two and two.

192:2. Visiting With the Apostles Two and Two.

Jesus beckoned to Peter and to John that they should come with him for a stroll on the beach. Jesus asked John to give up his intolerance and devote his life to proving that love is the greatest thing in the world. The Master asked Peter three times if he loved him, then said, "Feed my sheep. Do not forsake the flock. Be an example and an inspiration to all your fellow shepherds. Love the flock as I have loved you and devote yourself to their welfare even as I have devoted my life to your welfare. And follow after me even to the end." Jesus then went for a walk with Andrew and James, telling Andrew to trust his brethren more, even Peter, and to counsel his brother James later. He told James to be less impatient with his brethren and cultivate patience. Jesus next talked with Thomas and Nathaniel, telling Thomas to serve his brethren and cease doubting. He told Nathaniel to add love to his philosophy and be less critical. Walking with Philip and Matthew, he told both of them to teach and proclaim the gospel to all peoples. Then he walked and talked with the Alpheus twins, James and Judas, and told them that all upright work is sacred, to do their work as for God. As he left the apostles, he said, "Farewell, until I meet you all on the mount of your ordination tomorrow at noontime."

192:3. On the Mount of Ordination

At noon on Saturday, April 22, the eleven apostles assembled by appointment on the hill near Capernaum, and Jesus appeared among them. At this time the eleven apostles knelt in a circle about the Master and heard him repeat the charges and saw him re-enact the ordination scene. All was the same except the Master's prayer. He now spoke with the authority of the ruler of his universe. The Master spent just one hour on this mount with his ambassadors, and when he had taken an affectionate farewell of them, he vanished from their sight.

During this entire week Jesus was occupied with the morontia creatures on earth and with the affairs of the morontia transition which he was experiencing on this world.

192:4. The Lakeside Gathering

Peter, early in the week, sent out word that a public meeting would be held by the seaside the next Sabbath at three o'clock in the afternoon. Accordingly, on Saturday, April 29, at three o'clock, more than five hundred believers from the environs of Capernaum assembled at Bethsaida to hear Peter preach his first public sermon since the resurrection. The apostle was at his best, and after he had finished his appealing discourse, few of his hearers doubted that the Master had risen from the dead. As he finished speaking, the Master appeared in morontia form and, speaking to them in familiar accents, said, "Peace be upon you, and my peace I leave with you." When he had thus appeared and had so spoken to them, he vanished from their sight.

Because of certain things said to the eleven while they were in conference with the Master on the mount of ordination, they were to return to Jerusalem. Accordingly, early the next day, Sunday, April 30, the eleven left Bethsaida for Jerusalem.

This was a sad homecoming for John Mark. Just a few hours before he reached home, his father, Elijah Mark, suddenly died from a hemorrhage in the brain. John Mark did all he could to comfort his mother and, speaking for her, invited the apostles to continue to make their home at her house. And the eleven made this upper chamber their headquarters until after the day of Pentecost.

Already had begun the first steps of changing the gospel of the kingdom—sonship with God and brotherhood with man—into the proclamation of the resurrection of Jesus. And so, under the vigorous leadership of Peter and ere the Master ascended to the Father, his well-meaning representatives began that subtle process of gradually and certainly changing the religion *of* Jesus into a new and modified form of religion *about* Jesus.

Paper 193: Final Appearances and Ascension

THE sixteenth morontia manifestation of Jesus occurred on Friday, May 5, in the courtyard of Nicodemus, about nine o'clock at night. Assembled here at this time were the eleven apostles, the women's corps and their associates, and about fifty other leading disciples of the Master, including a number of the Greeks.

This company of believers had been visiting informally for more than half an hour when, suddenly, the morontia Master appeared in full view and immediately began to instruct them. Said Jesus in part, "Peace be upon you. This is the most representative group of believers—apostles and disciples, both men and women—to which I have appeared since the time of my deliverance from the flesh. I admonish you ever to remember that your mission among men is to proclaim the gospel of the kingdom—the reality of the fatherhood of God and the truth of the sonship of man. That which the world needs most to know is: Men are the sons of God, and through faith they can actually realize, and daily experience, this ennobling truth. Therefore, go you now into all the world preaching this gospel of the kingdom of heaven to all men. Love all men as I have loved you; serve your fellow mortals as I have served you. Only tarry here in Jerusalem while I go to the Father, and until I send you the Spirit of Truth. He shall lead you into the enlarged truth, and I will go with you into all the world. I am with you always, and my peace I leave with you."

193:1 The Appearance at Sychar

About four o'clock on Sabbath afternoon, May 13, the Master appeared to Nalda and about seventy-five Samaritan believers near Jacob's well, at Sychar. On this day, just as they had finished their discussions of the reported resurrection, Jesus suddenly appeared before them, saying, "Peace be upon you. You rejoice to know that I am the resurrection and the life, but this will avail you nothing unless you are first born of the eternal spirit, thereby coming to possess, by faith, the gift of eternal life. . . . Go, then, into all the world telling this good news to all creatures of every race, tribe, and nation. My spirit shall go before you, and I will be with you always."

193:2. The Phoenician Appearance

The Master's eighteenth morontia appearance was at Tyre, on Tuesday, May 16, when he appeared at the close of a meeting of believers, saying, "Peace be upon you. You rejoice to know that the Son of Man has risen from the dead because you thereby know that you and your brethren shall also survive mortal death. . . . Those who are born of the spirit will immediately begin to show forth the fruits of the spirit in loving service to their fellow creatures. And the fruits of the divine spirit which are yielded in the lives of spirit-born and God-knowing mortals are: loving service, unselfish devotion, courageous loyalty, sincere fairness, enlightened honesty, undying hope, confiding trust, merciful ministry, unfailing goodness, forgiving tolerance, and enduring peace. . . . You may enter the kingdom as a child, but the Father requires that you grow up, by grace, to the full stature of spiritual adulthood. And when you go abroad to tell all nations the good news of this gospel, I will go before you, and my Spirit of Truth shall abide in your hearts. My peace I leave with you."

193:3. Last Appearance in Jerusalem

Early Thursday morning, May 18, Jesus made his last appearance on earth as a morontia personality. As the eleven apostles were about to sit down to breakfast in the upper chamber of Mary Mark's home, Jesus appeared to them and said, "Peace be upon you. I have asked you to tarry here in Jerusalem until I ascend to the Father, even until I send you the Spirit of Truth. . . . From the very beginning of our associations I always had two or three of you constantly by my side or else very near at hand, even when I communed with the Father. Trust, therefore, and confide in one another. And this is all the more needful since I am this day going to leave you alone in the world. The hour has come; I am about to go to the Father."

When he had spoken, he beckoned for them to come with him, and he led them out on the Mount of Olives, where he bade them farewell preparatory to departing from Urantia.

193:4. Causes of Judas's Downfall

As we look back upon this tragedy, we conceive that Judas went wrong, primarily, because he was very markedly an isolated personality; he also failed to increase in love and grow in spiritual grace. He persistently harbored grudges and fostered such psychologic enemies as revenge and the generalized craving to "get even" with somebody for all his disappointments. He never acquired a philosophic technique for meeting disappointment. He did not like to face facts frankly; he was dishonest in his attitude toward life situations. This unfortunate combination of individual peculiarities and mental tendencies conspired to destroy a well-intentioned man who failed to subdue these evils by love, faith, and trust.

193:5. The Master's Ascension

It was almost half past seven o'clock this Thursday morning, May 18, when Jesus arrived on the western slope of Mount Olivet with his eleven silent and somewhat bewildered apostles. As he stood there before them, without being directed they knelt about him in a circle, and the Master said, "I bade you tarry in Jerusalem until you were endowed with power from on high. I am now about to take leave of you; I am about to ascend to my Father, and soon, very soon, will we send into this world of my sojourn the Spirit of Truth; and when he has come, you shall begin the new proclamation of the gospel of the kingdom, first in Jerusalem and then to the uttermost parts of the world. Love men with the love wherewith I have loved you and serve your fellow mortals even as I have served you. By the spirit fruits of your lives impel souls to believe the truth that man is a son of God, and that all men are brethren. Remember all I have taught you and the life I have lived among you. My love overshadows you, my spirit will dwell with you, and my peace shall abide upon you. Farewell." When the morontia Master had thus spoken, he vanished from their sight.

The Master went to Edentia by way of Jerusem, where the Most Highs returned him to the status of Paradise sonship and supreme sovereignty on Salvington.

193:6. Peter Calls a Meeting

Acting upon the instruction of Peter, John Mark and others went forth to call the leading disciples together at the home of Mary Mark. By ten thirty, one hundred and twenty of the foremost disciples of Jesus living in Jerusalem had forgathered to hear the report of the farewell message of the Master and to learn of his ascension.

Among this company was Mary the mother of Jesus. She had returned to Jerusalem with John Zebedee when the apostles came back from their recent sojourn in Galilee. Soon after Pentecost she returned to the home of Salome at Bethsaida. James the brother of Jesus was also present at this meeting.

Simon Peter made a thrilling report of the last meeting of the eleven with their Master and most touchingly portrayed the Master's final farewell and his ascension disappearance. The apostles then went downstairs and elected Matthias as the new apostle and treasurer.

Soon after Pentecost the twins returned to their homes in Galilee. Simon Zelotes was in retirement for some time before he went forth preaching the gospel. Thomas worried for a shorter period and then resumed his teaching. Nathaniel differed increasingly with Peter regarding preaching *about* Jesus in the place of proclaiming the former gospel of the kingdom; he spent more than a year in Philadelphia and then went on into the lands beyond the Mesopotamian preaching the gospel as he understood it. This left but six of the original twelve apostles to become actors on the stage of the early proclamation of the gospel in Jerusalem: Peter, Andrew, James, John, Philip,and Matthew.

Paper 194: Bestowal of the Spirit of Truth

ABOUT one o'clock, as the one hundred and twenty believers were engaged in prayer, they all became aware of a strange presence in the room. At the same time these disciples all became conscious of a new and profound sense of spiritual joy, security, and confidence. This new consciousness of spiritual strength was immediately followed by a strong urge to go out and publicly proclaim the gospel of the kingdom and the good news that Jesus had risen from the dead. Peter stood up and declared that this must be the coming of the Spirit of Truth which the Master had promised them and proposed that they go to the temple and begin the proclamation of the good news committed to their hands. And they did just what Peter suggested. They unintentionally stumbled into the error of substituting some of the facts associated with the gospel for the gospel message itself.

194:1. The Pentecost Sermon

This day happened to be the Jewish festival of Pentecost, and thousands of visitors from all parts of the world were in Jerusalem. It was about two o'clock when Peter stood up in that very place where his Master had last taught in this temple and delivered that impassioned appeal which resulted in the winning of more than two thousand souls.

The leaders of the Jews were astounded at the boldness of the apostles, but they feared to molest them because of the large numbers who believed their story. Pentecost was the great festival of baptism and therefore they were in no way disconnecting themselves from the Jewish faith. Even for some time after this the believers in Jesus were a sect within Judaism.

194:2. The Significance of Pentecost

The Spirit of Truth enables each new generation to have a new and up-to-date version of the gospel. The spirit never creates a consciousness of himself, only a consciousness of Michael, the Son. Sooner or later, the concealed truths of the fatherhood of God and the brotherhood of men will emerge to effectually transform the civilization of all mankind. In less than a month after the bestowal of the Spirit of Truth, the apostles made more individual spiritual progress than during their almost four years of personal and loving association with the Master.

Human beings are subject to the following spirit influences: 1. the seven adjutant mind-spirits of the local universe Mother Spirit; 2. the spirit of the Infinite Spirit and the Universe Mother Spirit—the Holy Spirit; 3. the Spirit of Truth; 4. the spirit presence of the Eternal Son—the spirit gravity of the universe of universes and the certain channel of all spirit communion; 5. the bestowed spirit of the Universal Father—the Thought Adjusters. After the fusion of the mortal spirit-born soul with the Paradise Thought Adjuster, mortals subsequently attain the divinity and glorification of the Paradise Corps of the Finality.

194:3. What Happened at Pentecost

The Spirit of Truth is concerned primarily with the revelation of the Father's spirit nature and the Son's moral character. As the indwelling spirit of the "new teacher," the Master has, since Pentecost, been able to live his life anew in the experience of every truth-taught believer. The religion of Jesus is a new gospel of faith to be proclaimed to struggling humanity. This new religion is founded on faith, hope, and love. The spiritual forward urge is the most powerful driving force present in this world; the truth-learning believer is the one progressive and aggressive soul on earth. At last, true religion is delivered from the custody of priests and all sacred classes and finds its real manifestation in the individual souls of men. The religion of Jesus fosters the highest type of human civilization in that it creates the highest type of spiritual personality and proclaims the sacredness of that person. Truth provides for the everlasting expansion and endless growth of the religion which Jesus lived and the gospel which he proclaimed. The bestowal of the Spirit of Truth was independent of all forms, ceremonies, sacred places, and special behavior. Pentecost endowed mortal man with the power to forgive personal injuries, to keep sweet in the midst of the gravest injustice, to remain unmoved in the face of appalling danger, and to challenge the evils of hate and anger by the fearless acts of love and forbearance.

The secret of a better civilization is bound up in the Master's teachings of the brotherhood of man, the good will of love and mutual trust. After Pentecost, in the brotherhood of the kingdom woman stood before God on an equality with man. No longer can man presume to monopolize the ministry of religious service. The religion of Jesus is the most powerful unifying influence the world has ever known. The joy of this outpoured spirit, when it is consciously experienced in human life, is a tonic for health, a stimulus for mind, and an unfailing energy for the soul.

194:4. Beginnings of the Christian Church

The gospel of the kingdom, the message of Jesus, had been suddenly changed into the gospel of the Lord Jesus Christ. Christ was about to become the creed of the rapidly forming church. It was a fellowship of believers in Jesus, not a fellowship of brothers in the family kingdom of the Father in heaven. They called each other brother and sister; they greeted one another with a holy kiss. They confidently expected that Jesus would return to complete the establishment of the Father's kingdom during their generation. Thousands of earnest believers sold their property and disposed of all their capital goods and other productive assets. Very soon the believers at Antioch were taking up a collection to keep their fellow believers at Jerusalem from starving. At first they baptized in the name of Jesus; it was almost twenty years before they began to baptize in "the name of the Father, the Son, and the Holy Spirit."

The Sadducees began to put the leaders of the Jesus sect in jail until they were prevailed upon to accept the counsel of one of the leading rabbis, Gamaliel, who advised them to let these people alone, that if this work is of men it will be overthrown and if of God you will not be able to overthrow them.

Two Greeks, Stephen and Barnabas, made many converts in Jerusalem. These able Greeks did not so much have the Jewish viewpoint. They began to preach more as Jesus taught, and this brought them into immediate conflict with the Jewish rulers. In one of Stephen's public sermons, they proceeded to stone him to death on the spot. This was the specific cause for the formal organization of the early Christian church. The church at Jerusalem was organized under the leadership of Peter, and James the brother of Jesus was installed as its titular head. The church at Antioch was first called Christianity and before the time of Paul was under Greek leadership.

Paper 195: After Pentecost

PETER was the real founder of the Christian church; Paul carried the Christian message to the gentiles, and the Greek believers carried it to the whole Roman Empire. A new order of living was presented to the hungry hearts of these Western peoples. It was not a simple spiritual appeal, such as Jesus had presented to the souls of men, but was a new order of human society. And as such a pretension it quickly precipitated the social-moral clash of the ages.

At first, Christianity won as converts only the lower social and economic strata. But by the beginning of the second century the very best of Greco-Roman culture was increasingly turning to this new order of Christian belief. The triumph of Christianity was due to Paul's organization ability. It contained the best of Greek philosophy and Hebrew theology. Christian leaders made wise compromises with other religions. But mistake not! these compromised ideals of the Master are still latent in his gospel, and they will eventually assert their full power upon the world.

Christianity owes very much, to the Greeks. At Nicaea, Athanasius preserved the true nature of Jesus.

195:1. Influence of the Greeks

There was something strangely alike in Greek philosophy and many of the teachings of Jesus. They had a common goal—both aimed at the emergence of the individual. The Greeks were hungry for spiritual truth and were willing to borrow good ideas from the Jews. It was the Greeks who literally forced the Romans subsequently to accept this new religion, as then modified, as a part of Greek culture. As illuminated by the content of Jesus' message, the united product of the centuries of the thought of these two peoples now became the driving power of a new order of human society and, to a certain extent, of a new order of human religious belief and practice. Paul assaulted the West with the Christian version of the gospel of Jesus. And wherever the Greek culture prevailed throughout the West, there Hellenized Christianity took root. The Eastern version of the message of Jesus, notwithstanding that it remained more true to his teachings, continued to follow the uncompromising attitude of Abner. It never progressed as did the Hellenized version and was eventually lost in the Islamic movement.

195:2. The Roman Influence

Much of the early persecution of Christians in Rome was due solely to their unfortunate use of the term "kingdom" in their preaching. The Romans were a great people. They could govern the Occident because they did govern themselves. Such unparalleled honesty, devotion, and stalwart self-control was ideal soil for the reception and growth of Christianity. The Roman was by nature and training a lawyer. And so did these Romanized Greeks force both Jews and Christians to philosophize their religion, to co-ordinate its ideas and systematize its ideals, to adapt religious practices to the existing current of life. A succession of Greek-cultural and Roman-political victories had consolidated the Mediterranean lands into one empire, with one language and one culture, and had made the Western world ready for one God.

195:3. Under the Roman Empire

Rome overcame the tradition of nationalism by imperial universalism and for the first time in history made it possible for different races and nations at least nominally to accept one religion. That which gave greatest power to Christianity was the way its believers lived lives of service and even the way they died for their faith during the earlier times of drastic persecution. The teaching regarding Christ's love for children soon put an end to the widespread practice of exposing children to death when they were not wanted, particularly girl babies. The second century after Christ was the best time in all the world's history for a good religion to make progress in the Western world. Even a good religion could not save a great empire from the sure results of lack of individual participation in the affairs of government, overtaxation, amusement madness, Roman standardization, the degradation of woman, and a state church which became institutionalized nearly to the point of spiritual barrenness. While some of the ideals of Jesus were sacrificed in the building of Christianity, it should in all fairness be recorded that, by the end of the second century, practically all the great minds of the Greco-Roman world had become Christian.

195:4. The European Dark Ages

The church, being an adjunct to society and the ally of politics, was doomed to share in the intellectual and spiritual decline of the so-called European "dark ages." During this time, religion became more and more monasticized, asceticized, and legalized. In a spiritual sense, Christianity was hibernating. When the renaissance dawned Christianity brought into existence numerous sects suited to special intellectual, emotional, and spiritual types of human personality. Christianity exhibits a history of having originated out of the unintended transformation of the religion of Jesus into a religion about Jesus. It further presents the history of having experienced Hellenization, paganization, secularization, institutionalization, intellectual deterioration, spiritual decadence, moral hibernation, threatened extinction, later rejuvenation, fragmentation, and more recent relative rehabilitation.

Religion is now confronted by the challenge of a new age of scientific minds and materialistic tendencies. In this gigantic struggle between the secular and the spiritual, the religion of Jesus will eventually triumph.

195:5. The Modern Problem

The twentieth century has brought new problems for Christianity and all other religions to solve. Truth often becomes confusing and even misleading when it is dismembered, segregated, isolated, and too much analyzed. Religion is the revelation to man of his divine and eternal destiny.

Religion is a purely personal and spiritual experience and must forever be distinguished from man's other high forms of thought. Do not try to satisfy the curiosity or gratify all the latent adventure surging within the soul in one short life in the flesh. Be patient! Harness your energies and bridle your passions; be calm while you await the majestic unfolding of an endless career of progressive adventure and thrilling discovery. As you view the world, remember that the black patches of evil which you see are shown against a white background of ultimate good. When there is so much good truth to publish and proclaim, why should men dwell so much upon the evil in the world? We find God through the leadings of spiritual insight—the love of the beautiful, the pursuit of truth, loyalty to duty, and the worship of divine goodness. But of all these values, love is the true guide to real insight.

195:6. Materialism

Scientists have unintentionally precipitated mankind into a materialistic panic. When the materialistic-secular panic is over, the religion of Jesus will not be found bankrupt. In reality, true religion cannot become involved in any controversy with science. At the time of this writing the worst of the materialistic age is over; the day of a better understanding is already beginning to dawn. The higher minds of the scientific world are no longer wholly materialistic in their philosophy. Modern science has left true religion—the teachings of Jesus as translated in the lives of his believers—untouched. All science has done is to destroy the childlike illusions of the misinterpretations of life. Materialism is there, but it is not exclusive; mechanism is there, but it is not unqualified; determinism is there, but it is not alone. Moral convictions based on spiritual enlightenment and rooted in human experience are just as real and certain as mathematical deductions based on physical observations, but on another and higher level. The influence of the cosmic mind constantly injects spontaneity into even the material worlds. Religious leaders are making a great mistake when they try to call modern man to spiritual battle with the trumpet blasts of the Middle Ages. Religion must provide itself with new and up-to-date slogans.

195:7. The Vulnerability of Materialism

Science should do for man materially what religion does for him spiritually: extend the horizon of life and enlarge his personality. True science can have no lasting quarrel with true religion. The inconsistency of the modern mechanist is: If this were merely a material universe and man only a machine, such a man would be wholly unable to recognize himself as such a machine. Man is a material fact of nature, but his life is a phenomenon which transcends the material levels of nature in that it exhibits the control attributes of mind and the creative qualities of spirit. Art is mortal morontia, the intervening field between man, the material, and man, the spiritual. The universe is not like the laws, mechanisms, and the uniformities which the scientist discovers, and which he comes to regard as science, but rather like the curious, thinking, choosing, creative, combining, and discriminating scientist who thus observes universe phenomena and classifies the mathematical facts inherent in the mechanistic phases of the material side of creation.

195:8. Secular Totalitarianism

But even after materialism and mechanism have been more or less vanquished, the devastating influence of twentieth-century secularism will still blight the spiritual experience of millions of unsuspecting souls. Modern secularism has been fostered by two world-wide influences. The father of secularism was the narrow-minded and godless attitude of nineteenth and twentieth-century so-called science—atheistic science. The mother of modern secularism was the totalitarian medieval Christian church. Secularism had its inception as a rising protest against the almost complete domination of Western civilization by the institutionalized Christian church. The majority of professed Christians of Western civilization are unwittingly actual secularists. The tyrannical and dictatorial political state is the direct offspring of scientific materialism and philosophic secularism. Twentieth-century secularism tends to affirm that man does not need God. But beware! this godless philosophy of human society will lead only to unrest, animosity, unhappiness, war, and world-wide disaster. The complete secularization of science, education, industry, and society can lead only to disaster. During the first third of the twentieth century Urantians killed more human beings than were killed during the whole of the Christian dispensation up to that time. And this is only the beginning of the dire harvest of materialism and secularism; still more terrible destruction is yet to come.

195:9. Christianity's Problem

Paganized and socialized Christianity stands in need of new contact with the uncompromised teachings of Jesus; it languishes for lack of a new vision of the Master's life on earth. A new and fuller revelation of the religion of Jesus is destined to conquer an empire of materialistic secularism and to overthrow a world sway of mechanistic, naturalism. Urantia is now quivering on the very brink of one of its most amazing and enthralling epochs of social readjustment, moral quickening, and spiritual enlightenment. Religion does need new leaders, spiritual men and women who will dare to depend solely on Jesus and his incomparable teachings. The modern age will refuse to accept a religion which is inconsistent with facts and out of harmony with its highest conceptions of truth, beauty, and goodness. The hour is striking for a rediscovery of the true and original foundations of present-day distorted and compromised Christianity—the real life and teachings of Jesus. The world needs more firsthand religion. Christianity is threatened by slow death from formalism, overorganization, intellectualism, and other nonspiritual trends. The modern Christian church is not such a brotherhood of dynamic believers as Jesus commissioned continuously to effect the spiritual transformation of successive generations of mankind.

195:10. The Future

Christianity has indeed done a great service for this world, but what is now most needed is Jesus. It is futile to talk about a revival of primitive Christianity; you must go forward from where you find yourselves. Modern culture must become spiritually baptized with a new revelation of Jesus' life and illuminated with a new understanding of his gospel of eternal salvation.

"The kingdom of God is within you" was probably the greatest pronouncement Jesus ever made, next to the declaration that his Father is a living and loving spirit. The call to the adventure of building a new and transformed human society by means of the spiritual rebirth of Jesus' brotherhood of the kingdom should thrill all who believe in him as men have not been stirred since the days when they walked about on earth as his companions in the flesh. But Christianity, as it is subdivided and secularized today, presents the greatest single obstacle to its further advancement; especially is this true concerning the Orient.

The Christian churches of the twentieth century stand as great, but wholly unconscious, obstacles to the immediate advance of the real gospel—the teachings of Jesus of Nazareth. The non-Christian world will hardly capitulate to a sect-divided Christendom. The living Jesus is the only hope of a possible unification of Christianity. The true church—the Jesus brotherhood—is invisible, spiritual, and is characterized by unity, not necessarily by uniformity. And this brotherhood is destined to become a living organism in contrast to an institutionalized social organization. It may well utilize such social organizations, but it must not be supplanted by them.

There is no excuse for the involvement of the church in commerce and politics; such unholy alliances are a flagrant betrayal of the Master. But in this brotherhood of Jesus there is no place for sectarian rivalry, group bitterness, nor assertions of moral superiority and spiritual infallibility. The hope of modern Christianity is that it should cease to sponsor the social systems and industrial policies of Western civilization while it humbly bows itself before the cross it so valiantly extols, there to learn anew from Jesus of Nazareth the greatest truths mortal man can ever hear—the living gospel of the fatherhood of God and the brotherhood of man.

Paper 196: The Faith of Jesus

JESUS enjoyed a sublime and wholehearted faith in God. His faith was neither traditional nor merely intellectual; it was wholly personal and purely spiritual. Never on all the worlds of this universe, in the life of any one mortal, did God ever become such a *living reality* as in the human experience of Jesus of Nazareth. In the human life of Jesus faith was personal, living, original, spontaneous, and purely spiritual. Even in the face of apparent defeat or in the throes of disappointment and threatening despair, he calmly stood in the divine presence free from fear and fully conscious of spiritual invincibility. The all-consuming and indomitable spiritual faith of Jesus never became fanatical, for it never attempted to run away with his well-balanced intellectual judgments concerning the proportional values of practical and commonplace social, economic, and moral life situations. The Son of Man was a splendidly unified human personality. Always did the Master co-ordinate the faith of the soul with the wisdom-appraisals of seasoned experience.

Jesus never prayed as a religious duty. To him prayer was a sincere expression of spiritual attitude, a declaration of soul loyalty, a recital of personal devotion, an expression of thanksgiving, an avoidance of emotional tension, a prevention of conflict, an exaltation of intellection, an ennoblement of desire, a vindication of moral decision, an enrichment of thought, an invigoration of higher inclinations, a consecration of impulse, a clarification of viewpoint, a declaration of faith, a transcendental surrender of will, a sublime assertion of confidence, a revelation of courage, the proclamation of discovery, a confession of supreme devotion, the validation of consecration, a technique for the adjustment of difficulties, and the mighty mobilization of the combined soul powers to withstand all human tendencies toward selfishness, evil, and sin.

The secret of his unparalleled religious life was this consciousness of the presence of God; and he attained it by intelligent prayer and sincere worship—unbroken communion with God—and not by leadings, voices, visions, or extraordinary religious practices. His sense of dependence on the divine was so complete and so confident that it yielded the joy and the assurance of absolute personal security. He made robust and manly decisions, courageously faced manifold disappointments, resolutely surmounted extraordinary difficulties, and unflinchingly confronted the stern requirements of duty. It required a strong will and an unfailing confidence to believe what Jesus believed and as he believed.

196:1. Jesus—The Man

No matter how great the fact of the sovereignty of Michael, you must not take the human Jesus away from men. The Master has ascended on high as a man, as well as God; he belongs to men; men belong to him. He was the most truly religious man who has ever lived on Urantia. The time is ripe to witness the figurative resurrection of the human Jesus from his burial tomb amidst the theological traditions and the religious dogmas of nineteen centuries. What a transcendent service if, through this revelation, the Son of Man should be recovered from the tomb of traditional theology and be presented as the living Jesus to the church that bears his name, and to all other religions! One of the most important things in human living is to find out what Jesus believed, to discover his ideals, and to strive for the achievement of his exalted life purpose. Of all human knowledge, that which is of greatest value is to know the religious life of Jesus and how he lived it.

196:2. The Religion of Jesus

Some day a reformation in the Christian church may strike deep enough to get back to the unadulterated religious teachings of Jesus, the author and finisher of our faith. The gospel of the kingdom is founded on the personal religious experience of the Jesus of Galilee; Christianity is founded almost exclusively on the personal religious experience of the Apostle Paul. The New Testament is a superb Christian document, but it is only meagerly Jesusonian.

The great mistake that has been made by those who have studied the Master's life is that some have conceived of him as entirely human, while others have thought of him as only divine. Throughout his entire experience he was truly both human and divine, even as he yet is. The whole Christian movement tended away from the human picture of Jesus of Nazareth toward the exaltation of the risen Christ, the glorified and soon-returning Lord Jesus Christ. Jesus founded the religion of personal experience in doing the will of God and serving the human brotherhood. Many of his apparently hard sayings were more of a personal confession of faith and a pledge of devotion than commands to his followers.

Jesus did not share Paul's pessimistic view of humankind. The Master looked upon men as the sons of God and foresaw a magnificent and eternal future for those who chose survival. He saw most men as weak rather than wicked, more distraught than depraved. But no matter what their status, they were all God's children and his brethren. He taught men to place a high value upon themselves in time and in eternity.

196:3. The Supremacy of Religion

Personal, spiritual religious experience is an efficient solvent for most mortal difficulties; it is an effective sorter, evaluator, and adjuster of all human problems. Religion does not remove or destroy human troubles, but it does dissolve, absorb, illuminate, and transcend them. True religion unifies the personality for effective adjustment to all mortal requirements. There are just three elements in universal reality: fact, idea, and relation. The religious consciousness identifies these realities as science, philosophy, and truth. Philosophy would be inclined to view these activities as reason, ·dom, and faith—physical reality, intellectual reality, and spiritual rea' are in the habit of designating these realities as thing, meaning. The progressive comprehension of reality is the equivalent c' God. The full summation of human life is the knowledge cated by fact, ennobled by wisdom, and saved—justifie'

It appears that all human progress is effected bv revelational evolution. Man's contact with the hi is only through the purely subjective exper' shiping him, of realizing sonship with hi. art, philosophy, ethics, and morals, but not ، all indissolubly interrelated in human experience. Religious insight possesses the power of turning defeat into higher desires and new determinations. Love is the highest motivation which man may utilize in his universe ascent. But love must always be redefined on successive levels of morontia and spirit progression. Some men's lives are too great and noble to descend to the low level of being merely successful. Be not discouraged; human evolution is still in progress, and the revelation of God to the world, in and through Jesus, shall not fail. The great challenge to modern man is to achieve better communication with the divine Monitor that dwells within the human mind. Man's greatest adventure in the flesh consists in the well-balanced and sane effort to advance the borders of self-consciousness out through the dim realms of embryonic soul-consciousness in a wholehearted effort to reach the borderland of spirit-consciousness—contact with the divine presence. And God-consciousness is equivalent to the integration of the self with the universe, and on its highest levels of spiritual reality. When all is said and done, the Father idea is still the highest human concept of God.

www.ingramcontent.com/pod-product-compliance
Lightning Source LLC
Chambersburg PA
CBHW071107160426
43196CB00013B/2493